See Dick Throw *a* Hissy Fit:

The Rise and Predictable Fall of US Culture

BY DR. LAURAN STAR

with Editorial Strategist Judi Harrington and
Creative Director Lisa McKenna

Dedication

For every disruptor who's been told they were
"too much," "too loud," or "too angry."
Turns out, sometimes a hissy fit is exactly what it takes
to shake the world awake.
This one's for you.

Contents

Acknowledgements

When this book idea hit me, it wasn't a whisper—it was a siren. I went manic. I had to get it down right now. Sleep became optional, because this wasn't just a book—it was a wake-up call. In just three months, the book was strategized and written; then, another two and a half months of content editing and creative design refined it from raw concept to published work. Four months of chaos compressed into six months of clarity.

This book would not exist without the following...

To The Inner Circle of Chaos & Clarity

Every author needs people who keep them from completely unraveling. You were mine.

You talked me down from the ledge (and sometimes shoved me back up there for perspective). You reminded me when exhaustion was talking louder than truth and pushed me to keep going when quitting felt easier.

You kept the lights on and the scene moving. You caught the details I missed, filled the gaps I left wide open, and made sure the madness didn't collapse under its own weight.

You never sugarcoated. You never let me off the hook. You never let me forget why this book mattered. When I was tempted to soften, you demanded sharpness. When I drifted toward safe, you dragged me back to bold.

This book carries your fingerprints on every page. It is louder, braver, and more disruptive because of you. Thank you for being my chaos, my clarity, and my tether to what's real.

Special Callouts to:

Editorial Strategist, Judi Harrington—No-bullshit, say-it-straight, with just enough tact to keep the wine glass from tipping. The hours we spent in manic brainstorming could have been another series—"47 Shitshows"—but instead they became the spine of this work. You kept me honest, sane, and fiercely authentic. You never let me water down my thinking, my words, or my evidence. You reminded me that disruption—when grounded in truth—doesn't need political correctness; it needs courage. Thank you for walking beside me in this circus, not just as a strategist, but as a co-conspirator who knew the shit show we're all trapped in.

Creative Design, Lisa McKenna—When I shared the premise of the Dick and Jane archetypes, I had never seen you so lit up. From that moment, it was like we shared one mind. That instant connection gave me the freedom to let go and trust you to work your magic. And you did. You brought the work to life—especially through the tactile, immersive design that made these ideas not just words on a page, but an experience. Thank you for being my brilliant, creative counterpart. Only you could make a hissy fit look this good.

Editor, Kate Victory Hannisian—My genius friend who can take dyslexic grammar, scrambled sentences, rogue footnotes, and references that wander off—and fix them all while somehow still calling me your friend. This book was a bigger brainchild than our last, and once again, you absolutely rocked it. As a writer, knowing you're my safety net brings me peace—and a hell of a lot more confidence to dive headfirst into the chaos. Thank you for catching the slips, sharpening the edges, and making sure the hissy fit stayed loud, but never sloppy.

My Family—I write for you. You are the reason I stretch, stumble, and continue to grow. From our endless debates (yes, arguments), clashing viewpoints, and deep dives into research, you challenge me to think sharply and be better. You are my grounding force and my greatest disruption—the proof that love and friction can coexist and even thrive. I love you all fiercely, and my deepest hope is that my work helps carve out a better world for you and your own journeys ahead.

My Beta Readers—I am deeply thankful for your honesty. Without your insight, this book would have been half the story it needed to be. You read with sharp eyes and sharper minds, calling out the gaps and pushing me to go deeper where it mattered most. You reminded me that disruption only lands if the message is clear. Thank you for lending your time, your feedback, and your courage to share the truth with me, even when it was difficult to hear.

A special thank you to Gina Abudi, Yusuf Abudi, Tim Adison, Richard Allen, Melissa Carmody, Alecia Edmonds, Heidi Hargreaves, John Hollawell, Kathleen Burns Kingsbury, Jacquie Long, Maria Lynch, Mark Smith, Raffael Raduazo, Tena Stromgren, and Jeff Warren—your voices shaped these pages more than you know. And if this book still ruffles feathers, that hissy fit is on me, not you.

INTRODUCTION

Welcome to America's Midlife Crisis (No, It's Not Just the Hair Plugs)

A fter three consecutive presidential cycles that felt more like *episodes of a reality show nobody can cancel*, I found myself asking the same question echoing in living rooms, barbershops, and rage-fueled comment sections across America: **How the fuck did we get here?** And more importantly: **Why does it feel like we're staying?**

What you're about to read is not for the faint of heart. By Chapter 1, we are in the thick of it—because the country I once proudly served in the United States Army has not only lost its way, it's rewritten the entire script, with emotional reactivity as the new national language and critical thinking locked behind a paywall. Facts? Optional. Feelings? Monetized. Flags? Everywhere. We've traded civic responsibility for partisan politics, where party loyalty outweighs national interest, much like a fantasy football league with nuclear capabilities. According to Pew Research,[1] nearly 60% of Americans view the other political party as a threat to the nation's very existence. **That's not democracy. That's Thanksgiving with loaded weapons and cable news.**

Truth now comes with a trigger warning. Verified facts lose to memes. News is no longer a source of information—it's a vibe. Somewhere between "owning the libs" and "canceling Thanksgiving," we lost the ability to distinguish between journalism and truth on the one hand, and influencer cosplay on the other. The result? People consume media not to be informed, but to be affirmed.

Meanwhile, the **middle class—once the prized demographic of political speeches and Chevy truck commercials—has been quietly strip-mined** by deregulated capitalism. Income inequality in the US has returned to levels not seen since the Gilded Age.[2] Politicians often prioritize the donor class over working families, while performative patriotism becomes the mask worn by those selling off democracy in pieces.

Worse still, our national identity has begun to crystallize around cultural grievance rather than shared values. Diversity—once considered a source of innovation and strength[3]—is now routinely framed as a threat. In recent and current years, attacks on inclusive education, DEI policies, and public institutions have intensified under the guise of preserving "traditional values"—a phrase increasingly synonymous with exclusion.

We are led by aging political figures, many of whom show clear signs of cognitive decline. Yet questioning their fitness for office is often treated as heresy rather than civic responsibility. This is not about ageism—it's about the stewardship of a fragile democratic system.

And don't even get me started on **religious nationalism**, which has replaced "love thy neighbor" with "legislate thy neighbor into oblivion." Gorski and Perry nailed it: *Christian nationalism isn't about faith—it's about sustaining social hierarchies with a Bible in one hand and voter suppression in the other*.[4] We've gone from "freedom of religion" to "my religion, your problem." Classrooms are being watched. History is being rewritten in real-time, one school board tantrum at a time.

Our libraries are being censored, books are being banned, and our political discourse is so degraded that quoting history accurately is now deemed "controversial." When public intellectuals are replaced with YouTube conspiracy theorists and constitutional scholars are drowned out by podcasters in flak jackets, we are no longer debating ideas—we are discussing reality itself.

And Many of Us Are Just Pawns!

We, the people, are **the losing chess pawns**, shoved across a rigged board, convinced we're *playing for freedom* while getting checkmated by billionaires and ideologues who wouldn't recognize freedom if it raised their rent. We're fed outrage instead of facts, memes instead of policy, and told to fight each other while **healthcare costs bankrupt us, student loans crush us, and climate change bakes us.** We're *busy screaming at each other over rainbow flags on beer cans* while the winners quietly cash in.

And the winners?

- **Billionaires & Corporations:** They've rigged tax laws to hoard wealth while you Venmo friends for rent money. Climate denialism? Good for oil stocks. Workers fighting each other means no one fights for unions.[5]
- **Political Grifters & Populists:** Turning your fear and grievance into votes while offering zero solutions. Outrage is a business model, and you're the content.[6]
- **Conservative Media & Social Media Platforms:** Rage = clicks = ad dollars. Algorithms push polarization because "nuance" doesn't go viral.[7]
- **Christian Nationalists & Culture War Entrepreneurs:** Weaponizing religion to consolidate power and using "family values" as a wedge while banning books, rights, and critical thinking.[8]
- **Politicians Across the Spectrum:** Many on both sides profit off your distraction and division. They practice performative patriotism while selling your future to lobbyists and donors.[9]

While we argue over Target's rainbow onesies, the winners loot democracy, deregulate protections, and rewrite the rules—and we're too busy hate-watching each other to notice. If you feel exhausted, it's not just you. The system was designed to drain you, enrage you, and keep you busy fighting over crumbs while the winners take the bakery.

There isn't a single group left untouched. This isn't a me problem or a you problem—it's the ultimate group project from hell. Congratulations, folks: as a culture, we're all flunking together.

This book is a call to stop normalizing the absurdity and the noise, to interrogate our historical foundations with intellectual honesty, and to reject the weaponization of nostalgia. We must reckon with who we've been, who we are, and whether we still dare to become something better, because the winners don't need to keep you happy—only distracted.

Make no mistake: we are not flirting with collapse—we are actively engineering it.

After a thorough review of evidence, legislation, history, and yes, the hissy fits, this book is the result of thousands of hours of research and reflection, some of it sparked by anger, hurt, and tears, all driven by fierce honesty. I am not here to argue rightness or fallacy—I am here to shine a light on facts and history that have not been glossed over that affect every one of us as US citizens. Because we're at the edge of the democracy cliff, and "I didn't know" won't come with a parachute. This is no longer someone else's problem. **It's all of ours.** The cracks in the foundation are widening—and when the structure collapses, we all get crushed, regardless of how loudly we once insisted it wasn't our issue, or "I don't have standing in this," or "no one listens to me anyway." **Change is here. And some folks are losing it.**

Okay—detour over. Gloves back on (for now).

What is Going Wrong Today?

Today, the United States is a nation caught in an existential crisis, clutching pearls while the mirror of history reflects centuries of unearned power, social engineering, and cultural gaslighting. The **myth** of the *rugged, self-made, white male hero* was never real. The results of losing this distortion are not positive—what we're witnessing is the collective nervous breakdown of some of those who never had to question their starring role. This isn't a transformation; it's a hissy fit in governance. Let's get one thing straight—this isn't about white shaming. It's about evidence.

Today, 2025, the data shows a familiar partisan divide. Republicans are far more likely to say they're facing discrimination. At the same time, Democrats are often still caught between guilt, confusion, and wondering whether posting an infographic counts as activism, resulting in a Pew Research statistic that 60% of white employees feel discriminated against in the workplace.[10] This isn't systemic oppression. It's **discomfort with**

shared space, repackaged as victimhood, hashtagged for maximum reach, and framed as a form of patriotism. This isn't about blame. It's about helping all of us recognize what happens when cultural dominance is challenged—and how easy it is to confuse discomfort with discrimination.

Meanwhile, the Brookings Institution confirmed that Generation Z will be the last majority-white generation in US history.[11] The future isn't knocking—it already kicked off its shoes, changed the Wi-Fi password, and is rearranging the furniture. Rather than embracing demographic evolution, certain conservative groups have responded with well-funded campaigns: banning books, restricting educational content, and attributing societal changes to immigrants, protestors, and shifts in gender norms.

Laws are being passed not to protect children, but to preserve historical delusion and cultural hegemony. This collective identity crisis has gone nuclear, manifesting in voter suppression laws,[12] bans on diversity training,[13] and censorship in education.[14] The hissy fit is no longer metaphorical—it's been institutionalized. What we're witnessing isn't a culture war; it's an identity crisis playing out in legislation, media, and school board showdowns.

Take the so-called "baby crisis." It's not about fewer babies in general—it's about fewer *white* babies. Elon Musk has publicly warned of "population collapse" and urged people to have more children to "save civilization."[15] But let's not kid ourselves—this narrative echoes a long history of demographic panic rooted in white replacement fears, not fertility science. Scholars like Anderson and Roberts have noted how these anxieties reflect deeper racial and nationalistic fears, particularly among cultural conservatives.[16]

The truth? It's not a birthrate crisis. It's a *fragility crisis*—where diversity is treated like a threat, and institutional power is weaponized to preserve an outdated image of America.

Take the so-called "baby crisis." It's not about declining birth rates—it's about declining *white* birth rates. The panic isn't that there aren't enough babies; it's that the babies being born don't look like Dick and Jane anymore.

Even Elon Musk chimed in—warning that civilization is doomed unless people start having more kids. Let's be honest, he's not losing sleep over rising Black or brown birth rates. He's echoing a centuries-old anxiety: the fear of being outnumbered, outvoted, and out-identified.

This isn't demographic data. It's a demographic *tantrum.* And it's being screamed from boardrooms to school boards with institutional backing and algorithmic amplification.

Then there is the backlash machine—defined as the coordinated effort of political, media, and ideological forces to resist social progress. This machine now operates on weaponized nostalgia and fear, and many are tuning in minute by minute, falling for the lies. It reframes inclusion as invasion and equity as erasure, leveraging cultural anxiety to dismantle democratic safeguards. Authoritarian-leaning leaders often exploit perceived threats to identity as a pretext for rolling back civil rights, which affect every single American. [17]

That's why language once associated with liberation—"freedom," "family," and "parental rights"—is increasingly deployed to restrict LGBTQ+ visibility, ethnic studies, and reproductive autonomy.[18] And US citizens? We are the pawns of fear—moved across a rigged board, fed outrage instead of facts, and told to fight one another while the kings quietly rewrote the rules. The power source of this machine isn't policies, it's panic, programmed and monetized.

We are not only regressing politically, we are culturally rewinding to a time before facts were inconvenient, and empathy was expected. This regression is not toward a specific decade, but toward an idea: the mythic "Golden Age" of American dominance, when power was concentrated in the hands of the few, and the rest knew their place (or were forced into it).

Here's what we're regressing to:

- **Policy by nostalgia**: Where laws are shaped not by data or need, but by a yearning for a sanitized past that never existed.
- **Civic discourse by grievance**: Where shouting "freedom" means banning books and silencing teachers and the free press.
- **Governance by identity**: Where the louder your cultural outrage, the more likely you are to win a seat, a slot on cable news, or a school board election.

We're regressing to a pre-civil rights, pre-multicultural, pre-account-ability mindset—one where specific white, patriarchal, Christian dominance from the "Golden Age" was presumed and protected.[19] "Privilege is invisible to those who have it until it's challenged. Then it feels like Oppression."[20] And right now, that feeling of "oppression" is being spun into policy, protest, and propaganda. Unless we name this regression for what it is—a desperate last gasp of cultural monopoly—it will continue to define our politics, our classrooms, and our headlines. The future is being held hostage by a fabricated past.

The Who, What, Why, and Takeaway

This Book Is NOT:
- A rage fest
- A lecture
- A partisan hit piece
- A character assassination on white men (actually, the opposite)

This Book Exists Because:
- Someone needs to name the hissy fit.
- Trace it back to powdered-wig roots.
- Expose what it's doing to generational perspectives.
- Remind America that loud losers have rewritten history—until now.

What This Book Does:
- Calls out performative fragility as emotional privilege.
- Traces male dominance through colonialism, capitalism, and Christianity.
- Shows how generations view history/culture—and how it shapes identity and politics.
- Offers a roadmap to move forward without coddling outdated systems.

Who This Book Is For:
- **The Exhausted Majority:** The folks sitting at the kitchen table are

wondering how their country turned into a bad reality show. They're not storming the Capitol, they're not making TikToks about George Soros, they're just tired of being collateral damage in a nation addicted to tantrums.

- **Recovering Moderates & Disillusioned Conservatives:** The ones who thought "fiscal responsibility" meant balanced budgets—not billionaires dodging taxes while "patriots" chant about stolen elections in truck-stop parking lots. They're quietly asking: *When did my party get hijacked by cosplay revolutionaries in red hats?*
- **Progressives With Whiplash:** They've been pushing for progress while watching it roll backward—every step toward equity drowned out by a chorus of "Don't tread on me" T-shirts and book bans that make Fahrenheit 451 look like an instruction manual.
- **Gen Z & Millennials:** The ones inheriting the wreckage. They're not buying the nostalgia trip that says America was "great" when women were secretaries and minorities "knew their place." They're watching the MAGA hissy fit like it's the world's most depressing TikTok challenge.
- **Everyone Caught in the Crossfire:** Parents trying to explain to their kids why adults throw tantrums on C-SPAN. Teachers forced to teach history without mentioning, well, history. Workers trapped in companies where politics at the watercooler now feels like stepping into a WWE ring.

The Takeaway:

Not comfort. Not polite nods. But **clarity, fire, and refusal to go back to sleep.**

1. **Wakefulness Over Wokeness:** Stop asking "Is this offensive?" Start asking "Who benefits?"
2. **Urgency to Rebuild:** The old systems aren't broken; they were built this way. Tear them down.
3. **Power of Naming Bullshit:** Recognize rage bait, cultural gaslighting, fragile masculinity, and political theater. Name it. Mock it. Reject it.
4. **Weaponized Hope:** Not "it'll work out," but sleeves-rolled-up hope

that says, "We're not doomed. We're lazy."

Now, let us understand the hissy fit and begin to uncover its role in today's cultural fracture.

Why the Hissy Fit?

Merriam-Webster defines a hissy fit as a tantrum.[21]

A Deeper Look:

A hissy fit is a disproportionate, performative meltdown triggered by minor inconveniences to one's privilege, usually involving loud declarations of injustice, aggressive victimhood, and a YouTube rant filmed from the front seat of a truck.

In the Wild, You Might See a Hissy Fit When:

- A billionaire is told to pay taxes.
- A person is asked to attend diversity training.
- A politician loses an election and insists it was rigged.
- A mediocre manager is passed over for a promotion and blames "DEI quotas."
- A mask mandate ruins someone's sense of rugged American freedom—but not their sense of irony while wearing cargo shorts made in Vietnam.
- Cheering on masked, unidentified government agents, who grab people off the streets.

Hissy Fit Anatomy 101:

- **Trigger:** Accountability
- **Response:** Yelling "WOKE" in all caps
- **Symptoms:** Fragile masculinity, selective patriotism, Fox News-induced paranoia
- **Cure:** Therapy, historical literacy, or a nap
- **Side Effects:** Book bans, bad policy, podcast subscriptions

A hissy fit is what happens when entitlement meets limits—and the

tantrum gets a microphone. It's not a bad mood. It's a coping mechanism for those who mistake dominance for identity and think fairness feels like oppression.

Hissy Fits as Tradition that Strategically Changed the Direction of US Culture[22]

- **1861**: Southern white men, furious that the federal government might slow down slavery, seceded from the Union. Their rationale? *States' rights* (read: "We're mad we can't keep owning people").
- **1920s**: *The Scopes Trial*. Teaching evolution? Not if the Tennessee school board can help it. The clash of science and scripture made Darwinism the public enemy of faith and fired the opening shot in the culture wars.
- **1950s**: *The Red Scare*. Senator Joseph McCarthy throws a nationally televised hissy fit, accusing everyone from Hollywood screenwriters to Army generals of communist loyalty. The result? Loyalty oaths, blacklists, and a culture of paranoia that weaponized patriotism against free speech.
- **1964–1970s**: *Backlash to Civil Rights*. The Civil Rights Act passes, and conservatives roll out the Southern Strategy. "Law and order" becomes the dog whistle of choice, while busing and integration provoke protests louder than fire hoses.
- **1964**: *Southern Strategy*. After the Civil Rights Act passed, Southern Democrats lost it, and the Republican Party rolled out the Southern Strategy—rebranding white grievance as political identity.
- **1970s**: *ERA Meltdown*. The Equal Rights Amendment nears ratification, and Phyllis Schlafly leads a conservative crusade insisting women actually *like* being underpaid and overregulated. Because nothing says

"family values" like blocking gender equality.

- **1980s:** Enter the *Moral Majority*, founded by televangelist Jerry Falwell, who deemed feminism, gay rights, and working moms as the axis of evil. The cultural hissy fit against progress turned into a political PAC and a nationwide purity campaign, proving once again that nothing motivates like a pearl-clutching panic over Madonna and sex education.
- **1990s:** *The Clinton-Lewinsky Era*. Political hypocrisy hits peak hissy fit as Newt Gingrich, Dennis Hastert, and other "family values" champions impeach a president for lying about sex—while engaging in their own moral failings.
- **2008:** America elects its first Black president. Cue the birth of the Tea Party, the "Birther" conspiracy, and Glenn Beck crying on live television. This is not a glitch. It's the operating system.
- **2020s:** A global pandemic, racial reckoning, and growing diversity ignited a backlash so intense it banned books, redefined "woke" into a four-letter word, and declared drag queens a national threat. COVID brought masks, but it also ripped the mask off America's culture war.

Hissy Fits Noise of 2020 and Beyond
Started by the Average Dick & Jane:

- **2023:** Bud Light and the Beer Can That Broke the Right: When Bud Light partnered with a trans influencer in 2023, conservatives boycotted as if their masculinity depended on it. it.[23] Kid Rock shot up a beer case. Sales dropped. Why? Because tolerance has a flavor—and it's ***not*** light beer.
- **2021:** Mr. Potato Head: The Great Genital Panic: Hasbro announced it was dropping the "Mr." from Potato Head for inclusivity. Conservative media exploded. No one removed the mustache, but somehow a plastic potato became the focal point for the collapse of Western civilization.[24]
- **2022:** M&M's and the Sexy Green Shoe Scandal: In 2022, Mars redesigned its M&M mascots to be more inclusive.[25] The green M&M lost her go-go boots. The backlash? Immediate. Tucker Carlson launched a tirade about "woke" candy no longer being sexy. Yes, America argued about the sexual appeal of anthropomorphic chocolate.

- **2023:** Gas Stove Gate: When regulators *suggested* examining the health impacts of gas stoves, conservatives cried "communism." Even *recommending* an electric stove is now a leftist plot. The war on appliances became political theater with oven mitts.

The modern hissy fit is no longer a solo act—it's a chorus. Multigenerational, algorithmically amplified, and backed by a grievance-industrial complex that makes outrage feel like activism.

This isn't a backlash. It's **an organized refusal to evolve**—a Broadway production of entitlement playing nightly on every cable news channel and podcast app. And, it's not about God, guns, or grandma's values. It's about **control**—and the panic that comes when your cultural monopoly starts getting … shared. Because if you have always held the mic, even a roundtable feels like censorship.

And the Results of the Hissy Fits:

- **Legislating Fear, Not Facts:** In 2023 alone, more than 4,000 pieces of anti-LGBTQ+ legislation were introduced in US states legislatures.[26] Not to fix healthcare. Not to address inflation. But to criminalize existence and distract voters.
- **Banning Books Faster Than They're Borrowed**: PEN America (2023) reported over 3,300 book bans across school districts nationwide, most of them targeting Black authors, LGBTQ+ stories, or any mention of historical accuracy not approved by the Fragile Feelings Caucus.
- **Quoting Jesus While Stripping Rights:** Elected officials increasingly invoke Christian nationalism while passing laws that undermine civil liberties.[27] These are not moral leaders. They're biblical ventriloquists with gavels.
- **The Confederate Flag Still Flies:** Despite the Confederacy losing the Civil War over 160 years ago, 44% of Americans still view the Confederate flag as "a symbol of Southern pride," not white supremacy.[28] That's not heritage—it's historical cosplay.
- **Fragility as Strategy, Nostalgia as Weapon:** Today's most viral politicians aren't offering policy—they're providing therapy for fragile egos.

They sell nostalgia as national identity, even if it means astroturfing entire centuries of injustice.[29]

- **Oppression Cosplay Is Now a Political Platform**: When Christian, cisgender men claim to be the *real* victims of diversity, equity, and inclusion, the result isn't discourse—it's backlash with a campaign slogan.

Who We're Calling Out (Yes, MAGA, That Means You)

- **MAGA Nation**: Let's be clear: this isn't just "a political difference of opinion." MAGA turned grievance into performance art, weaponized nostalgia into a cult, and rebranded the hissy fit as a national pastime. From election denialism to book banning to "owning the libs," their contribution to culture is one long, loud tantrum.
- **The Enablers**: Politicians, media moguls, and think tanks who profit from rage while pretending they're "just giving the people a voice." Translation: they're feeding the toddler sugar at midnight, then acting shocked when he throws a chair through the window.

A Note Before You Shut Down or Toss This Book
(Yes, I'm Taking the Gloves Off for a Moment).
And yes, I Do Call out White Men here and there—Here's Why.

Let me be clear—and I'm only going to say this once: Yes, I am calling out white men. And yes, I'm doing it through the **archetype of *Dick*.** And before you get mad about that, I don't mean *Dick* in the locker-room sense (though if the shoe fits…). I mean *Dick* as in *Dick and Jane,* the old readers used in elementary schools. You know—those mid-century primers where Dick runs fast, sees Spot, and takes up all the air in the room. More about this later.

DICK IS NOT ONE MAN, NOR IS HE ALL WHITE MEN. He's **a symbol**. He's **the default**. The one whose voice was always centered, whose actions were always justified, whose worldview was printed, published, and protected. So yeah, Dick shows up a lot in this book—because he's shown up everywhere in American life. Remember … every single one of us can be Dick—regardless of gender, race, and/Just or political affiliation. And Dick is not a them problem, Dick is an us problem.

Not surprisingly, Dick is **predominantly** white; he's the loudest one throwing a fit. So yes, I call out white men early and often in this work. But hold your horses—and your hashtags—because this isn't a hate letter. It's a historical audit...

The Breakdown of the Archetype of Dick:

Historical Power Dynamics: White men not only benefited from the system, but they also built it. Now that the system is evolving (read: being forced to share), some are reacting as if renters have overtaken the HOA. In a nutshell, white men created America's history and have the power.

Institutional Access: Most people's hissy fits get them ignored. White male hissy fits get airtime, lawsuits, and occasionally favorable Supreme Court opinions.

Media Amplification:

When a woman is angry, it's perceived as "aggressive."

When a Latina's passionate, it's "spicy."

When a queer activist protests, it's "radical."

But when a white man flips a table? It's "economic anxiety" and a town hall special on CNN.

Cultural Framing:

Male anger is strength.

Female anger is hysteria.

Non-white anger? A threat.

But Dick's rage? It's marketable. It's monetized. It's a prime-time grievance performance.

This isn't about shaming white men—it's about calling out the cultural fallout when dominance gets disrupted. When the spotlight shifts even a few inches, and someone else dares to speak into the mic, fragility appears in khakis and a flag pin, demanding to see the manager of democracy. This isn't about demonizing white men. It's about confronting the system they were handed, the tantrums it rewards, and the opportunity to evolve beyond it.

And Dick? You're invited to join us. But you might have to put the flag down and pick up a book and your binky.

We'll start this book with a look at how Dick, Jane, Sally, and Spot were the underpinnings of America's culture. Even hissy fits tell us something about the systems we've built. This book does not cancel them. It calls them in, holds them up to the light, and asks one simple question: What are you so afraid of losing, and what would you gain if you let go? This book is not a critique; it's catharsis. It's satire and sarcasm sharpened into a scalpel, aimed directly at the blistering hypocrisy of grievance politics. If the hissy fit gets a megaphone, then truth needs a damn microphone. And this book is the soundcheck.

It's evidence-based satire that delves deeply into the dysfunction of American identity. It's a cultural diagnosis, not a personal attack. Yes, Dick may be the mascot of the meltdown—but this isn't about blame. It's about pattern recognition. The loudest hissy fits get the most airtime, the most policy traction, and the most press conferences—and historically, they've worn loafers and owned lawn signs. But here's the truth: everyone's thrown a fit. Let's get started.

Part I:

The Rise of US Culture— Built on a Hissy Fit, Starting with the Orange Era

Welcome to the Point of No Return!
You've made it this far—congrats.
You've survived the warm-up laps around
cultural collapse, weaponized nostalgia,
and Dick's emotional support podcast playlist.

B ut this? **This is where it gets spicy.** This is where I stop politely unpacking history and start **flipping the proverbial tables**—with facts, satire, and just enough emotional combustion to be flagged by your uncle's Facebook algorithm.

Here's your final warning: Grab your emotional support bourbon or wine. Kiss the polite manners goodbye. Activate your critical thinking cortex (even if it's a little dusty). And yes, go ahead and clutch your pearls—make sure they're ethically sourced. Because from this point forward, we're not massaging egos—we're kicking sacred cows through the plate glass window of American exceptionalism. And guess what? They were mouthing off anyway.

Welcome to America, where the vibes are fragile, the rage is always on tap, and the history is edited in real time by men named Dick who think "freedom" is something they invented between mowing the lawn and hoarding AR-15s.

You want to know how we got here? Buckle up.

Because this isn't just a country that lost the plot, this is a country that **never read it** in the first place—too busy screaming about "liberty" while voting away their neighbor's rights, too busy binge-watching conspiracy reels to learn how democracy works, too busy throwing tantrums in grocery store aisles about pronouns on name tags.

- We don't have policy debates here. We have hissy fits in khakis, hiding behind flags, calling it patriotism.
- We don't have informed citizens here. We have algorithm addicts, scrolling themselves into rage comas, convinced that sharing a meme is civic engagement.
- We don't have masculinity here. We have cosplay—grown men with podcasts screaming about "alpha energy" while terrified of therapy and oat milk.

And let me be clear: none of this is an accident. It's the feature, not the bug. America's entire cultural operating system was built on hissy fits—on stolen land, unpaid labor, and the perpetual fear that someone, somewhere, might get a slice of freedom you think you own. We built entire suburbs to escape the diversity we claimed to celebrate and then wondered why everything felt empty and beige.

And the Orange Era? That wasn't a glitch either. That was the system screaming its true colors in 4K, tweeting at 3 a.m., daring us to admit how fragile we are.

This part of the book isn't here to comfort you. It's here to drag every hypocrisy into the daylight, to make you squirm in your discomfort, to force you to see the tantrum for what it is: the only authentic bipartisan tradition America has ever had.

Yes, grab your favorite beverage, your weighted blanket, and a therapist's phone number. Because it's time to get honest about who we are, how we got here, and why **"freedom" in America has always depended on someone else's silence.**

And if that stings, good. That's the sound of the hissy fit cracking.

If you're ready to laugh, rage, unlearn, and scream into a throw pillow shaped like the Constitution, **turn the page**. If not? There's always a rerun of *The West Wing* and a warm bath of denial waiting.

-Dr. Lauran Star

CHAPTER 1

See Dick. See Jane.
See America Lose the Plot.

How One Primer Shaped Generations— and Why This Book Focuses on Dick

Before TikTok taught kids how to lip-sync and launch conspiracy theories, there was Dick. And Jane. And that ever-helpful, suspiciously cheerful terrier named Spot. These weren't early literacy tools. **They were America's first taste of subliminal social engineering in hardcover.**

See Dick run? Sure. But more importantly: See Dick lead. See Jane follow. See Sally clean up after everyone else. See Mom vanish into a casserole. See Dad missing in most books. These weren't books; they were personality tutorials in pastel, wrapped in the lie of "learning to read."

Dick, Jane, and Sally: The Cast of Characters

They weren't characters in a book; they were early lessons in what America wanted its children to see, believe, and become. Welcome to diversity-free indoctrination … with a smiley face and a dog named Spot. **The Dick and Jane Readers**, introduced in the 1930s and used in schools well into the 1970s, were designed to teach kids how to read using simple words and repetitive phrases. But they did more than build vocabulary—they built a worldview and, make no mistake, these readers are the foundation of America's culture.

These primers portrayed an idealized American life: white, suburban, nuclear families where the dad wore ties, the mom baked pies, and everyone smiled. There were no people of color, and there was no poverty, no complexity, no deviation from the script. What looked like basic reading lessons were, in fact, cultural blueprints—teaching not only how to read but also how to behave, who belonged, and what "normal" looked like.

Picture this: Dick runs… Jane laughs… Sally helps… Mother smiles… Father works… Spot barks. That's it; the American dream in six sentences—white picket fence included.

The Dick and Jane Readers were about social coding and programming. They taught kids what "normal" looked like. And more importantly, what it didn't. Dad goes to work. Mom makes sandwiches and smiles politely. Jane helps. Dick leads. Nobody is queer. Nobody is poor. Nobody is Black—although the dog was white with black spots. Think of those older books as the original Pinterest board for mid-century American values: clean, controlled, and entirely curated. Everyone was white and straight. Even Spot got more character development than most women of color in the media at the time, mainly because there were none.

Dick, Jane, Sally, and the Lobotomized American Dream
The cast today:

MEET DICK 2.0: THE PATRIOT (Self-Proclaimed, Loudly)

- **Full Name:** Richard "Dick" Patriarchson (Married Karen)
- **Location:** Somewhere between a Bass Pro Shop and a Cracker Barrel
- **Profession:** Former middle manager, now full-time Facebook constitutional scholar
- **Education:** Some college + YouTube conspiracy videos + honorary PhD in Grievance Studies

Dick's Cultural Blueprint
The Default Setting: The Loudest Voice. The Guy Who Mistook Comfort for Truth.
- **The Self-Appointed Main Character:** Dick doesn't believe he's part

of the story—he assumes he *is* the story. The narrative begins with him, ends with him, and always revolves around his comfort level.

- **The Gatekeeper of "Tradition":** If Dick did it once in 1974, then it must be the way it's always been done. He guards the past like it's sacred text—even if the history book skipped a few... inconvenient chapters.
- **The Fragile Patriot:** Loves the Constitution yet hasn't read it. Waves the flag, but only on his terms. Thinks freedom means doing whatever he wants, and accountability is oppression with better PR.
- **The Hissy Fit Hall-of-Famer:** From losing "his" job to DEI policies to boycotting beer over rainbows, Dick's tantrums are as theatrical as they are predictable. When the world evolves, he doesn't reflect—he explodes.
- **The Power Hoarder:** Dick doesn't fear change because it's bad—he fears it because it's not his. Sharing space, voice, or influence feels like a loss, even when it's a matter of balance.

Dick's Greatest Hits

Louder Than Facts. Fueled by Entitlement. Performed with Full Confidence, Zero Self-Awareness.

- **I Built This Company Myself:** (With three loans, a tax break, inherited wealth, and unpaid interns named Jane.) Dick loves a bootstrap narrative—especially when the boots were already polished and waiting at the door.
- **I'm Not Racist, But ...** A timeless classic. Usually followed by something wildly racist, sexist, or xenophobic, then a shocked response that anyone found it offensive.
- **Constitutional Karaoke:** Dick knows exactly two amendments: the 1st and the 2nd—and he misquotes both while standing in front of a flag, a truck, or a Bass Pro Shop.
- **You Can't Say Anything Anymore!** Dick said it all. Repeatedly. At full volume. During a work meeting. At Thanksgiving. On Facebook. At a school board meeting. While refusing to wear a mask.
- **Sore Loser National Anthem:** From refusing to accept election re-

sults to rage-quitting company all-hands meetings, Dick's tantrums get louder the minute he's not in control. Democracy is great—until it votes against him.

Why Dick Matters: Because Dick isn't a guy—he's an *ideology in khakis*. He's the denial, the backlash, and the bass-boosted whimper of declining dominance.

MEET JANE: AMERICA'S GOOD GIRL

- **Name:** Jane Ellen Patriarchson–Lewis (Married Doug Lewis)
- **Location:** Three blocks from Dick, in a cul-de-sac called Denial
- **Occupation:** PTA queen, Bundt cake patriot, emotional support for Dick's worldview
- **Education:** Some nursing school, primarily in Biblical Pro-Life Pinterest
- **Fashion Aesthetic:** Patriotic athleisure. Bedazzled denim. Cross necklace the size of Texas.

Jane's Cultural Blueprint
The gendered architecture of America's "good girl" narrative

- **Silent but Smiling:** Jane taught several generations that "nice" was more important than "heard." She was agreeable, nurturing, and dangerously compliant.
- **Support Role as Default:** While Dick chased adventures and ideas, Jane fetched, followed, and facilitated. Leadership? Not in her plotline.
- **Reinforcing the Male Narrative:** Her existence validated Dick's leadership and centered his journey. Jane didn't get a storyline—she got a subplot.
- **Cultural Export of Containment:** Jane wasn't a girl; she was a template. Her character became the standard for "proper womanhood" in classrooms and corporate handbooks.
- **Feminism's Invisible Foe:** Jane wasn't actively anti-feminist. She was

passively dangerous—teaching girls to be seen, not shake systems.

Jane's Greatest Hits

Soft Power. Loud Opinions. Bystander Energy with Boardroom Access.

- **I Support Women… Just Not *Those* Women:** Feminism, yes—but make it comfortable, corporate, and *not too intersectional.* Jane marched in pink hats but stayed silent when her company laid off every woman of color.
- **PTA Powerbroker Turned School Board Stormtrooper:** She began as a cupcake mom and ended up testifying against "critical race theory" with printed Facebook memes and a shaky grasp of US history.
- **Keep Politics Out of It:** Unless it's her politics. Jane believes neutrality is noble, mainly because neutrality has always benefited her.
- **Ally on Paper, Architect in Practice:** Jane can spot injustice, but rarely stops it. She's mastered the art of *empathetic delay*—the slow roll toward change that ensures she never has to give anything up.
- **Silent in the Meeting, Loud in the Group Chat:** Jane's a master of plausible deniability. She disagreed with Dick, of course—but only after the damage was done, and only in whispers.

Why Jane Matters: Because every authoritarian hissy fit needs an emotional enabler. Jane won't storm the Capitol, but she'll bake the cookies for the after-party.

MEET SALLY: THE PATRIARCHSON REBELLION

"I didn't come to play nice. I came to dismantle the stage, rebuild it with equity, and then moderate the damn panel."

- **Name:** Sally Rae (The baby of the Patriarchson family)
- **Location:** Boston—far from Dick, Jane, and the family group text
- **Occupation:** CEO, former Army officer, workplace strategist, burnout preventionist
- **Degrees:** PhD, MS, BA, and a black belt in "Shut It Down, Dick"

- **Vibe:** Combat boots under a power suit. The side-eye so sharp it needs a license.

Sally's Cultural Blueprint

The Instigator. The Outsider. The Voice You Try to Mute but Secretly Follow.

- **The Rebel with a Cause:** Sally never played house—she questioned who paid the mortgage. She's the girl who didn't stay in her lane because she realized the whole road was built without her input.
- **The Canary in the Cultural Coal Mine:** She spots the hypocrisy first and yells loudest about it—sometimes in a poorly worded blog post, sometimes at a school board meeting, sometimes in a hoodie on Capitol Hill.
- **The Pattern Breaker:** Sally doesn't "go along to get along." She knows the system was designed for Dick, by Dick—and she's not interested in politely waiting her turn. She'll redesign the damn board.
- **The Cultural Mirror:** Sally reflects who we are, even when we'd rather not see it. She reminds us that silence is complicity, that tradition is not always truth, and that politeness is often a form of oppression, all wrapped in a pastel dress.
- **The Agitator-in-Residence:** She pushes boundaries, upends norms, and demands evolution. Whether she's calling out sexism at the PTA or dismantling legacy admissions from her podcast, she makes disruption look deliberate.

Sally's Greatest Hits:

From playground provocateur to cultural commentator

- **I Read Ahead in the Book:** Sally defies the teacher, ignores the lesson plan, and dares to be *informed*. The beginning of her career as a disruptor... or an HR complaint.
- **Why Are There No Girls in This Story?** She side-eyes the curriculum, the lunch table, and the boardroom, demanding visibility decades before DEI was a corporate acronym.
- **It's Giving Gaslight, Gatekeep, Girlboss.** Now fluent in internet speak *and* systemic injustice, Sally shows up at a school board meet-

ing with a sign that reads: **"Patriarchy Isn't a Personality."** She goes viral—not just for the meme-worthy moment, but for calling out the real issue: toxic power dynamics being passed off as confidence, leadership, or "just how things are."

- **Sally's not just protesting curriculum changes**—she's dragging an entire cultural operating system. Her sign is a reminder that being controlling, dismissive, or sexist isn't a personality trait. It's patriarchy in a power suit, fluent in internet culture and systemic analysis, Sally goes viral while holding a "Patriarchy Isn't a Personality" sign at a school board meeting.
- **That's a Hissy Fit, Not a Policy.** As a panelist on public access news, Sally calls out the emperor's new grievance. She's immediately cut to a commercial and gains 200,000 followers on social media.
- **It's Not Cancel Culture, It's Consequences (Every damn year).** Sally remains America's unofficial accountability coach, reminding folks that actions have outcomes, and free speech isn't freedom from feedback.

Why Sally Matters: Because she's what happens when you raise a girl to challenge instead of comply. She's not the answer to Dick. She's the future that no longer needs his permission.

Oh, and the others in the Dick and Jane readers:
- **Mother**—Smiles like her sanity is on backorder. Never leaves the kitchen.
- **Father**—Mysterious figure who works, never cries, and occasionally appears to mow the lawn.
- **Spot**—Arguably the most relatable character. At least Spot gets to run. Anything outside of this frame? Not pictured and not welcomed.

What started as an innocent primer became a generational instruction manual. *See, Dick and Jane* didn't teach us to read—it taught us how to behave, who mattered, and who didn't. It's the original branding of American exceptionalism: gendered, racialized, sanitized.

And this book? It's a literary intervention. We study Dick not to shame—but to expose the framework. To name the programming. To ask why half the country still thinks "freedom" means denying everyone else a plot twist.

The Generational Trickle Down: How Dick Became Grandpa, Boss, and Congressman

- **Silent Generation**: The original Dick readers. They grew up believing the world should match the pages of their imagination. When it didn't, they voted for people who promised to erase the parts that didn't look like 1952.
- **Boomers**: Told to "be like Dick." They complied. Then they bought second homes, yelled about "kids these days," and insisted their lawn is a metaphor for meritocracy.
- **Gen X**: Grew up with Dick's hangover. Questioned the story, but were still graded on it. Taught to rebel quietly—usually with sarcasm and Nirvana.
- **Millennials**: Inherited Dick's debts—financial, cultural, and emotional. Still expected to live the American dream with none of the interest rates Dick got.
- **Gen Z**: Finally burned the book and said, "Dick's a problem." However, they're still stuck explaining systemic inequality to people who still believe Spot's loyalty is a political virtue.

How the Dick and Jane Readers evolved—or not...

Early Editions (1930s-1960s):

Zero color. Zero culture. Zero critique. They transcend narrative.. They were a blueprint for the acceptable American. Straight. White. Suburban. Quiet Grateful. And if you weren't any of those things? You weren't in the book.

The Original Page–White as the Margins

Scene: Dick runs. Jane laughs— Spot barks. Sally claps. A white picket fence frames their sanitized glee.

Message: If Norman Rockwell and a mayonnaise sandwich had a baby, this would be it. This was America.

If Norman Rockwell and a mayonnaise sandwich had a baby, this would be it.

This was America, apparently.

The Blueprint of "Acceptable"

Overlay Diagram: A visual blueprint of
Dick and Jane overlaid with these core
"cultural specs":
Race: White (factory default)
Religion: Implied Protestant
Class: Middle (but we don't talk about it)
Sexuality: So straight it hurts
Behavior: Polite, perky, and perilously
repressed
Caption: "Designed by curriculum com-
mittees. Approved by white fragility."

RACE: WHITE (FACTORY DEFAULT)
RELIGION: IMPLIED PROTESTANT
CLASS: MIDDLE (BUT WE DON'T TALK ABOUT IT)
SEXUALITY: SO STRAIGHT IT HURTS
BEHAVIOR: POLITE, PERKY, AND PERILOUSLY REPRESSED
DESIGNED BY CURRICULUM COMMITTEES
APPROVED BY WHITE FRAGILITY

When Representation Finally Knocked... It Wasn't Let In

Late 1960s–1970s: Under pressure from the civil rights movement, publishers *begrudgingly* added characters of color to their works. Not friends
of Dick and Jane. Not part of the original narrative... **separate but equal
storylines.**

The "Diversity Insert" Years

"Inclusion arrived—
but only as an elective."

(Sound familiar?)

These so-called "Multicultural Readers" gave us a Black family, a Latino family, and sometimes an Asian family—but they were shoved into their books, their worlds. Representation? Technically. **Inclusion?** Not even close. **Impact?** About as progressive as a beige crayon. Dick and Jane didn't have a non-white friend. When diversity arrived, it resided next door in a completely different reader, with a separate plot and fewer speaking lines.

If Instagram Had Existed Then...

Tagline: "America's feed filtered before filters existed."

Title: *"Dick and Jane Weren't Kids— They Were Cultural Coding"*

Flowchart: *Early Literacy Reader → Ideological Framework → Cultural Identity Formation*

Add a bold footer: *If you teach children who matters, don't be surprised when adults forget who doesn't.*

The Cultural Legacy of Dick and Jane

The *Dick and Jane* readers were more than early literacy tools—they were foundational blueprints of American cultural norms. These basal readers promoted not only reading fluency but also a homogenized vision of American life: white, suburban, middle-class, and rigidly gendered.[30]

These books reflected—and reinforced—a narrow cultural ideal during a period of deep segregation and post-war conformity. The absence of racial, ethnic, and economic diversity in their pages sent a silent message: **this is who matters, and this is what normal looks like.**[31] As such, *Dick and Jane* were not just reading aids—they were instruments of cultural conformity.

While Boomers grew up with these characters as fixtures of early education, post-Boomer generations have had to confront the lingering effects of this sanitized representation of American life. The omission of marginalized identities in these narratives helped cement structural inequities that persist today, particularly in education, media representation, and policymaking.[32]

From "See Dick Run" to "Burn It Down, Katniss"—How America's Cultural Fracture Was Foreshadowed in Storytime

Once upon a Dick and Jane, we were handed a script—whitewashed, rule-bound, and shrink-wrapped in lawn care metaphors. For the Silent Generation, Boomers, and early Gen X, obedience was a way of life. Books didn't just teach reading; they taught *roles*. Dick mowed the lawn, Jane served lemonade, and America—naturally—was always the hero: no nuance, no diversity, just conformity in hardbacks. Childhood literature wasn't education—it was indoctrination with phonics.

Then Gen X cracked the binding. Their books whispered that the system was rigged, authority was shady, and adults were emotionally unavailable weirdos. But while *The Outsiders* gave them angst and autonomy, it didn't offer a blueprint. They became the first generation fluent in irony and distrust—perfect preparation for building AOL chat rooms and voting for a third party.

Millennials? Raised on Hogwarts and Hunger Games. They learned that systems were broken but still hoped that magic or friendship might fix them. They absorbed complex truths: fascism wears suits, adults fail you, and bureaucracy is Voldemort in drag. Yet, even as their literature taught them to challenge power, it often handed them the same "chosen one" trope, repackaged in inclusive capes.

Gen Z came of age not with a whisper of rebellion, but a megaphone. Their books didn't tiptoe around dystopia; they lived in it, emotionally armed with trauma narratives, TikTok activism, and three-part revolutions with love triangles. Resistance wasn't theory—it was plot. They didn't grow up wondering if authority was corrupt—they *knew* it.

Now enter Gen Alpha, being gently raised on science, empathy, and gender fluidity, while watching entire school boards try to rip their picture books off the shelves. Their stories teach inclusion, but their reality teaches censorship. Bluey says cry it out. Their governor says don't say gay.

The bottom line? America's culture war didn't start in Congress. It started in kindergarten, between the lines of "See Dick Run." Our bookshelves were always political. We didn't know it until the protagonists stopped listening to Dick.

Dick and Jane's Impact Today

The *Dick and Jane* readers baked white, middle-class conformity into the American psyche. Their legacy lives as the blueprint for cultural nostalgia: simple roles, simple lives, simple truths. They normalized whiteness as default, obedience as virtue, and male dominance as natural. Today, that legacy fuels both resistance to inclusive education and a nostalgia-driven backlash—because in Dick's world, diversity was disruptive, and questioning the script was never part of the story.

Dick is the archetype from which all rebellion sprang; he is the default setting.

- Jo March challenged gender roles.
- Percy challenged systems.
- Katniss challenged power.
- Ada Twist challenged science stereotypes.
- Dog Man challenges literacy, but we'll allow it.

But Dick? Dick was never asked to change. He was rewarded for staying the same, generation after generation. And that's why this book is about *un-installing* Dick. Because as long as we keep rebooting him as the standard, the cultural operating system will continue to crash.

We didn't resurrect Dick, Jane, and Sally to be cute. We brought them back to expose the ridiculousness of the world they were designed to protect. They are not characters—they're archetypes of American regression. Dick throws a hissy fit when the meeting isn't about him. Jane quietly quits respectability politics with a laminated to-do list. Sally burns the whole system down, builds a new one from scratch, and live-streams the process from her civic co-op. They are the Greek chorus of cultural chaos. And this book? Their comeback tour.

In this book, we repurpose them as symbols of:

- The fragility of white masculinity (*Dick*)
- The emotional labor and performative anger of women (*Jane, Karen—Dicks wife*)
- The unapologetic insurgency of the generation that's done waiting politely (*Sally*)

Throughout This Book, You Will Find:

DICK, JANE & KAREN'S HISSY FITS: Red-flag behaviors dressed up as "tradition," "common sense," or "leadership." The sad part is that all these outbursts occurred. I adjusted the names. It's realism with entitlement and a side of patriotic cosplay.

SALLY SANITY: Often contradictory information to the rants of Dick, Jane, and Karen – or society as a whole. Because someone has to say it loudly and clearly.

RECEIPTS & REALITY CHECKS: Data, history, and citations for the skeptics, cynics, and "just asking questions" crowd. Because feelings aren't facts, but the fallout is measurable.

A Note to Dick: You're Not Broken—You're Over-Programmed

We have all met **Dick**. Heck, you might *be* Dick. He may be your father/mother, grandfather/grandmother, uncle/aunt, brother, son/sister, significant other, friend/coworker—most of all, someone you love dearly. I know I do. To the point I want to shake the living shit out of him. Dick may be male or female, of different races and nationalities; however, typically Dick is a white male (I explained this in the introduction—so if you are mad, go back and re-read that).

He's not a villain. He is not stupid. He's not evil. He's not plotting the fall of democracy from a recliner wrapped in an American flag throw blanket. He's just… overwhelmed. And loud. And trying hard to make sense of a world that changed the rules mid-game without warning him. Dick didn't choose rage. He was recruited, one nostalgic meme, one Fox News segment, one slippery slope sermon at a time.

Cultural Conditioning, Not Free Thinking

Part I calls out the world Dick is trying to figure out:

- Dick learned that **truth is optional** if you shout loudly enough.
- Dick saw that **rage is currency** in American culture.
- Dick noticed **politics is performance**, not governance.
- Dick realized **power is protected, not shared.**

Part II demonstrates how the manual for Dick's worldview was built:

- The Revolution taught Dick that **liberty = power hoarding.**
- The Civil War told Dick that **rage is patriotic if it protects property.**
- The suburbs handed Dick a lawn mower and said, "**Rule this kingdom.**"
- The so-called Golden Age—that nostalgic, whitewashed postwar era of suburban lawns, gender roles, and TV dads who never cried—whispered to Dick, "**You're the default. Everyone else is the exception.**" It sold him a script where whiteness, maleness, and conformity weren't just normal—they were the *standard*.

Part III shows the strategy reinforcing Dick's worldview and behavior:

- The Heritage Foundation gave Dick **talking points when facts became too hard.**
- The church taught Dick that **empathy is sin-adjacent unless it ends in tithing.**
- Presidents told Dick he's **the main character; everyone else is a threat or a sidekick.**
- Media, think tanks, and the algorithm told Dick to **stay angry, stay scared, and stay engaged in outrage.**

Part IV provides solutions that challenges Dick to adapt or collapse with his hissy fit:

- Dick can choose to **wake up or go extinct clutching a lawn sign.**
- Dick can view **gender equity, disabled leadership, and veteran perspectives** as either threats to the status quo—or as blueprints for a stronger, more inclusive future.
- Dick can trade **fragile nostalgia for real community and collective liberation.**
- Dick can evolve from **Dick to Richard—or keep throwing hissy fits until history leaves him behind.**

Built by History, Not Hate: Dick was born into a story that made him the hero by default. He grew up in a world where masculinity was a one-size-fits-all uniform, where the past was always "great," and where someone always told him what to believe. God, Country, Football. Done.

But then... History got *complicated*. He was ignored. People started asking questions. Those on the margins began speaking up. And suddenly, Dick was told the world *he thought he understood* was built on sandcastles and selective scripture. That wasn't betrayal. That was **growth**. Yet to Dick? It *felt* like erasure because some wanted Dick to feel erased—they wanted to prey on Dick. And they were innovative and strategic in their tactics. They sold Dick a bag full of MAGA red pills and reinforced the administration of doses.

Dick Didn't Get Radicalized—He Got a Remote and a Facebook Login

He didn't wake up one day screaming about gas stoves and drag brunches. He clicked a link. Then another. He watched one clip that made him feel smart and another that made him feel angry. For the first time in years, he felt seen— not by his family, but by a guy in a backward hat shouting "THEY'RE COMING FOR YOUR KIDS" into a webcam. Dick didn't fall into misinformation. He tripped over identity loss and landed in an echo chamber.

And suddenly, critical race theory (CRT) wasn't history—it was a threat. Pride flags weren't flown by neighbors—they were waved by enemies. Equity wasn't fairness—it was extinction.

He's Not Stupid—He's *Exhausted*. Dick's not raging because he's hateful. He's raging because he feels **left behind**.

He was told his job was to provide. Now he's told he's privileged. He was told his values were sacred. Now he's told they're outdated. He was told he was the default. Now he's told… he has to share. That's a lot. And Dick never got the emotional instruction manual or support for understanding. His toolkit? The Red Pill Tool Box. Blame. Nostalgia. Comment section warfare.

Why Dick Doesn't Listen: The Psychology of Digging in, Doubling Down, and Denying Reality

Spoiler: It's not because he's right. It's because his ego has squatter's rights.

Welcome to Dick's Brain—Population: 1 Idea, 12 Yelling Podcasts

I cannot say this any louder—Dick isn't stupid. **He's intellectually gerrymandered**. He built a brain neighborhood where every house has a Fox News dish, every street is named after Reagan, and the HOA bans facts that make him uncomfortable. So why doesn't Dick listen you when you calmly say, "Hey, here's a peer-reviewed study"? Because he's not listening to the truth. He's listening for **reassurance**. And the sound of his voice echoing inside a "Let's Go Brandon" mug.

The Psychological Loop of Doom

1. COGNITIVE DISSONANCE: When new facts knock on Dick's door, he doesn't answer—he hides behind a curtain made of AM radio static. "Wait... climate change is real? But I just bought a gas-powered grill with Bluetooth." Rather than adjust, Dick doubles down because changing your mind is what weaklings and liberals do.

2. CONFIRMATION BIAS: Dick doesn't want "news." He wants news that confirms he's been right since the third grade. So he scrolls past science and clicks on an article titled: "5 Reasons Masks Turn Your Kid into Karl Marx." He's not looking for information—he's looking for emotional validation in camo font.

3. GROUP POLARIZATION: Dick goes to a barbecue. He says something dumb. Everyone there agrees. Suddenly, he thinks he's a political strategist and part-time constitutional scholar. Groupthink becomes cult-think. And now Dick's convinced the IRS is a United Nations front.

4. IDENTITY-PROTECTIVE COGNITION: To change his mind, Dick would have to say out loud: "I was wrong." But in his world, that's code for "I'm weak," "I voted for feelings," and "I drink oat milk." So instead, he digs in because nothing says masculinity like willful ignorance and a bumper sticker that yells.

What Can We Do (Besides Scream into a Throw Pillow)?

1. **Ask, Don't Lecture:** Dick loves yelling. He short-circuits on questions. Try: "Where'd you hear that?" or "How do you know that's true?" Let his logic chase its tail until he has to sit down.

2. **Build a Bridge, Not a Bunker:** Start with shared values: "We both want safe schools, right?" "We both hate spam calls, right?" Find *any* common ground. Then sneak in a fact like a Trojan horse filled with nuance.

3. **Limit the Echo Chamber:** Encourage media literacy. Show how algorithms feed his outrage addiction. You don't need to say, "A dude in a basement with a ring light is radicalizing you," but… actually, do.

4. **Go Slow, Stay Calm, Lower Your Voice:** Dick gets louder when you do. Counter with the deadly weapon of calm, fact-based logic. (And yes, have a glass of wine nearby.)

Dick Isn't Hopeless—He's Habitual: He was trained to distrust "them," ignore nuance, and treat change like it's an assault on his masculinity. But beneath the cargo shorts and chain emails is a person who once believed in something real. Possibly. In 1978. So don't give up. Don't write him off. Just don't engage when he starts a sentence with "I did my own research." Instead, smile, breathe, and repeat: "I love you, Dick. But that YouTube video is not a peer-reviewed source."

What Now? How Do We Help Dick Down from the Ledge?

Not by mocking. Not by shaming. By inviting. Gently. Honestly. Humorously. By understanding. How we all got here. By educating. Patiently. Lovingly. Highlighting what is fact vs. fiction, by reminding him that he doesn't need to change everything or apologize for being raised in a framework. He needs to question who benefits from his outrage and who loses when he grows.

And the Moment Dick Thinks for Himself? The Grift Dies: What if Dick ever paused and asked, "Wait, who benefits from me being this pissed off all the time?" The whole illusion crumbles. Because Dick doesn't need to become a tofu-eating, nonbinary socialist barista to grow—he needs to unplug long enough to ask fundamental questions. But the media machine can't let that happen. Because the moment Dick stops raging, someone's ad revenue drops.

Dick isn't the enemy. He's the byproduct of bad history, empty promises, and emotional starvation. The moment Dick pauses, breathes, and asks: *"Wait—why am I so mad all the time?"*... that's when the healing starts. That's when the algorithm begins to lose. That's when Dick stops being content—and starts being conscious.

But here's the thing: this cultural chaos isn't random—it's emotional. Beneath the backlash, book bans, and performative patriotism lies something deeper: a psychological unraveling. When power feels threatened, identity feels shaky, and the world no longer reflects your reflection, the response isn't always reason—it's reaction. In the next chapter, we turn to the psychology of the hissy fit: where fear masquerades as righteousness, fragility disguises itself as strength, and tantrums become a political strategy. Let's unpack the emotional engine driving the meltdown.

CHAPTER 2

The Psychology of the Hissy Fit: From Outburst to Outcome

T he American hissy fit isn't a cultural trope—it's a psychological phenomenon with real-world consequences. Beneath the theatrics lies a well-documented emotional sequence: perceived threat → emotional dysregulation → performative grievance → institutional damage. What begins as a reaction often morphs into policy, propaganda, and polarizing spin, leaving chaos in its wake.

1. The Emotional Engine: Fragility and Identity Threat:

Hissy fits often emerge from a perceived loss of control or status, what psychologists call an identity threat. When individuals or groups sense that their social dominance or worldview is being challenged, the brain triggers a fight-or-flight reaction. However, in cultural terms, this fight takes the form of outrage rather than self-reflection.

"Status loss triggers physiological stress responses similar to physical danger."[33] This perceived loss is particularly acute among individuals who once held unchallenged authority, such as men in traditional leadership roles or dominant cultural majorities. The result is status-based resentment—a tantrum dressed in rhetoric.

2. From Emotion to Amplification: Creating Noise:

Hissy fits don't stay isolated—they get amplified by grievance media, social networks, and algorithmic feedback loops that reward outrage with visibility. This creates what sociologists refer to as an outrage industry, where performative anger becomes monetized content.[34]

"Media systems that prioritize engagement reward expressions of outrage, increasing their prevalence and intensity."[35] The emotional charge spreads, becoming contagious and irrational. Empathy shuts down. Nuance dies. And emotional noise becomes cultural "truth."

3. From Noise to Action: When Policy Becomes Punishment:

Outrage doesn't echo—it **institutionalizes**. Whether it's book bans, anti-DEI legislation, or moral panic-driven policies, hissy fits often **masquerade as moral imperatives**.

"Moral outrage is often mistaken for moral clarity, but when institutionalized, it can restrict rights rather than promote justice."[36] What begins as performative grievance often escalates into real-world harm—curtailed civil liberties, marginalized communities under surveillance, and public institutions under attack.

4. The Boomerang Effect: Unintended Consequences:

Ironically, hissy fits designed to "protect" cultural identity often backfire. Take the backlash to DEI programs: while intended to halt cultural progress, such efforts have frequently led to greater scrutiny of privilege, national discussions on systemic inequities, and legal challenges that intensify the spotlight.[37]

"Reactive suppression often leads to increased resistance and counter-mobilization". [38]The hissy fit, in its effort to "restore order," frequently amplifies the very change it resists—albeit more chaotically and divisively.

5. Weaponized Spin: From Tantrum to Narrative:

To justify the tantrum, dominant groups often **reframe discomfort as oppression.** This is the psychological phenomenon of **reverse victimhood**, where those in power recast themselves as the persecuted.[39]

"Members of dominant groups may perceive increasing equality as personal disadvantage, leading to defensive reactions.[40] This narrative spin turns raw emotional reactivity into legitimized political strategy. Terms like "cancel culture," "wokeism," and "parental rights" become the new battle cries—not because they're about freedom, but because they protect perceived entitlements.

From Tantrum to Transformation—If We Let It

If unacknowledged, the hissy fit becomes a feedback loop of emotional fragility, political weaponization, and public regression. However, naming, analyzing, and challenging it allows for disruption. When we see the hissy fit for what it is—an identity crisis in motion—we can begin to design systems, not around outrage, but around equity, accountability, and evolution.

The Cultural Snapshot: One Dysfunctional Family, Three Political Archetypes

And by the end, if you're ready to trade entitlement for evolution…You will ask yourself what Sally would say. And you might stop being a Dick, Jane, and Sally, and start becoming Richard.

Grab a cup of java and get ready for the data supporting the claim. Yes, the US culture is fractured!

US Culture by the Decades: A Culture Index Report (1700–2020): Measuring the Pulse of American Culture Across Six Domains

Here's the data, my friends—it's the data that tells the truth to the story.

What Is National Culture?

National Culture isn't art, music, or TikTok dances. It is a society's operating system. It's the invisible code that tells people what's normal, valuable, possible, and who gets to belong. Culture is the rules we don't write down but still enforce. It's who gets the mic in the room—and who's told to sit quietly and take notes. It's the holidays we celebrate, the history we teach (or erase), the "neutral" accents we trust, and the faces we expect to see in power. It's how we build families, how we define success, how we punish differences, and how we forgive cruelty—depending on *who* commits it. Culture is the water we swim in—and most people don't even realize they're wet.

Culture is not a definition of a nation—it *is* the nation. Without culture, a nation is little more than a border with a GDP. Within that culture, there are many subcultures; however, the foundation is the national culture.

Why Culture Matters Deeply in Defining a Nation
- **Culture Tells the Story a Constitution Can't:** Laws define our rights. Culture defines our values. The US Constitution, for example, says "We the People." Culture determines **which people** feel included in that "we"—and which must fight to be seen.
- **Culture Outlives Leaders:** Presidents come and go, but culture is generational memory. It's the why behind the what—why we celebrate, why we protest, why we mourn. Empires rise by policy, but they fall by culture. Ask imperial Rome, the Soviet Union, or anyone else who thought nationalism alone could unite fractured people.

- **Culture Defines "Us" and "Them":** Whether inclusive or exclusive, culture defines identity: Who belongs? Who leads? Who tells the story? Who gets silenced? Culture is the **software** that runs the **hardware** of a nation.[41] You can have brilliant infrastructure, booming markets, and military might, but the system crashes if the culture is rotting.
- **Culture Drives Behavior More Than Law:** You can legislate diversity, but it's dead on arrival if the culture resists equity. You can ban books, but truth still finds a way if the culture values curiosity. Laws can mandate. Culture motivates.
- **Culture = Power:** Cultural narratives *shape geopolitics*. Hollywood has a greater influence on global fashion than diplomacy does. American memes spread faster than American policy. TikTok arguably has more cultural clout than NATO.

Culture defines **who we think we are**—and **who we pretend not to be**. It's not an accessory to politics or economics—it's the engine. Nations don't crumble because of weak budgets. They crumble due to weak narratives, fractured trust, and cultural decay masquerading as tradition.

Why Does Culture Matter?

Because **culture decides the terms of survival**.

- Laws are written on paper. Culture decides which ones get enforced—and against whom.
- Rights can be declared. Culture determines who gets access to them without a fistfight or a lawsuit.
- Policies are passed in Congress. Culture is what makes them real—or makes them hollow slogans.

Culture shapes outcomes before a single law is passed.

If your culture values dominance over dignity, don't be shocked when your politics do too.

If your culture rewards fragility over accountability, don't wonder why justice feels impossible.

If your culture idolizes a past that excludes most people, don't pretend you're building an inclusive future.

America loves to call itself a "melting pot," but let's be honest—we've never actually stirred. What we are is a cultural **suspension**: different identities floating in the same space, but never blending, never bonding. Inclusion isn't just proximity—it's chemistry.

It's time to stir the pot, shake the system, and stop pretending we're one people just because we share a ZIP code and a Netflix login. Unity won't come from simmering on low. It comes from remixing the whole damn recipe.

Culture is not cosmetic. It's power distribution disguised as tradition, wrapped in a flag, dipped in nostalgia, and sold as common sense within every faction of global society. Culture is the dress code of domination—stitched together by centuries of hierarchy and hemmed in by the fear of change. It's not "the way we do things." It's how *power* does things—and dares you to question it without being labeled "divisive."

Don't let the soft lighting fool you. Behind every charming tradition is a spreadsheet of control:

- Who's centered?
- Who's silenced?
- Who's safe?
- And who's constantly translating their existence to make others comfortable?

Culture is the battleground. Culture decides whose lives are seen as valuable—and whose lives are seen as optional. If you don't disrupt it, you're not changing history. You're decorating it

This chapter section presents a comprehensive overview of US culture, era by era, spanning from the 1700s to the 2020s, utilizing a customized Culture Index organized into six key domains. From early civic foundations to modern misinformation, we trace the ebb and flow of American values, trust, participation, and identity—highlighting moments of cohesion and division. It reveals a culture in flux: innovative yet fractured, diverse yet segregated, proud yet uncertain. Decade-by-decade scores are interpretative based on synthesizing historical sources and national cultural indicators.[42]

US Culture by the Decades: 1700-1860

1700s
Foundations & Fault Lines

Civic Engagement & Trust: Limited to white male landowners; high distrust of central authority pre-independence.

Cultural Participation: Religious gatherings dominate cultural life; early colonial print media emerges.

Social Cohesion & Inclusion: Deep racial hierarchies and Indigenous displacement.

Family & Community: Patriarchal nuclear family; high birth rates; community centered around churches.

Education & Cultural Values: Elite-focused education; heavy emphasis on religious instruction.

Information Environment: Colonial newspapers, often partisan and censored.

1800-1860
Expansion & Fragmentation

Civic Engagement & Trust: Increased voter turnout among eligible populations; trust split by regional ideology.

Cultural Participation: Growth of theater, newspapers, and early museums.

Social Cohesion & Inclusion: Abolitionist vs. pro-slavery divide; growing immigrant communities; rising nativism.

Family & Community: Expansion of the family farm ideal and the rise of sentimental domestic culture.

Education & Cultural Values: Public education expands; civic virtue is taught via McGuffey Readers.

Information Environment: Partisan press dominates; regional echo chambers develop.

US Culture by the Decades: 1860–1940

1860-1900
Reconstruction & Gilded Age Contradictions

Civic Engagement & Trust: Black male enfranchisement (briefly); voter suppression follows.

Cultural Participation: Boom in urban arts institutions and libraries.

Social Cohesion & Inclusion: Jim Crow laws emerge; xenophobia toward Asian and Irish immigrants.

Family & Community: Child labor rises; extended families common in immigrant enclaves.

Education & Cultural Values: Compulsory schooling increases; patriotism emphasized.

Information Environment: Yellow journalism thrives; media sensationalism rises.

1900-1940
Progressivism to Depression

Civic Engagement & Trust: Civic reform movements grow; the New Deal fosters institutional trust.

Cultural Participation: Jazz Age, film, and modern art movements flourish.

Social Cohesion & Inclusion: Harlem Renaissance vs. institutionalized racism; Red Scare paranoia.

Family & Community: Nuclear family ideal begins; birth rate dips during Depression.

Education & Cultural Values: Public education becomes more standardized, while anti-immigrant sentiment persists.

Information Environment: The rise of radio as mass media and government propaganda increases.

US Culture by the Decades: 1940–1980

1940-1960
Postwar Consensus & Cold War Anxiety

Civic Engagement & Trust: High voter engagement in the early '60s; Watergate erodes trust.

Cultural Participation: Explosion of counterculture, protest art, and civil rights music.

Social Cohesion & Inclusion: Although the Civil Rights Acts were passed, polarization around race and the Vietnam War increased.

Family & Community: Divorce rate spikes; birth control reshapes families.

Education & Cultural Values: Rise in multicultural curricula; culture wars begin.

Information Environment: The rise of television opinion; the mass media begins to fragment.

1960-1980
Expansion & Fragmentation

Civic Engagement & Trust: Increased voter turnout among eligible populations; trust split by regional ideology.

Cultural Participation: Growth of theater, newspapers, and early museums.

Social Cohesion & Inclusion: Abolitionist vs. pro-slavery divide; growing immigrant communities; rising nativism.

Family & Community: Expansion of the family farm ideal and the rise of sentimental domestic culture.

Education & Cultural Values: Public education expands; civic virtue is taught via McGuffey Readers.

Information Environment: Partisan press dominates; regional **echo chambers develop.**

US Culture by the Decades: 1980–2020

1980-2000

Deregulation & Digital Dawn

Civic Engagement & Trust: Civic trust declines; political cynicism rises.

Cultural Participation: Cable TV, blockbuster movies, and the growing commodification of the arts.

Social Cohesion & Inclusion: LGBTQ+ visibility rises; urban-suburban segregation continues.

Family & Community: Two-income households normalize; decline in multigenerational living.

Education & Cultural Values: Patriotism rebounds post-Cold War; culture war intensifies.

Information Environment: Talk radio and partisan cable news emerge.

2000-2020

Fragmentation & Algorithmic Culture

Civic Engagement & Trust: Trust hits record lows; 2020 election engagement spikes.

Cultural Participation: Decline in arts funding; streaming displaces community venues.

Social Cohesion & Inclusion: Political polarization peaks; racial reckoning in 2020.

Family & Community: Rise in nontraditional families; more seniors age alone.

Education & Cultural Values: Focus on STEM and test scores; moral values are declining.

2020s Snapshot (In Progress)

Information Environment: Misinformation epidemic; social media erodes institutional trust.

Civic Engagement & Trust: Crisis of confidence in democracy; record youth activism.

Cultural Participation: Digital expression and virtual concerts rise, but community arts decline.

Social Cohesion & Inclusion: DEI backlash; hate crimes spike post-2020.

Family & Community: Fertility declines; rise in chosen families, co-housing.

Education & Cultural Values: Culture wars invade classrooms; national pride fractures.

Information Environment: Press and internet freedom under siege; AI-generated deepfakes and filter bubbles.

Culture is not cosmetic. It's power distribution disguised as tradition, wrapped in a flag, dipped in nostalgia, and sold as common sense within every faction of global society. Culture is the dress code of domination—stitched together by centuries of hierarchy and hemmed in by the fear of change. It's not "the way we do things." It's how power does things—and dares you to question it without being labeled "divisive."

Here is your US Culture Index Scorecard (1700s-2020s)

It reflects the evolution of American culture across six domains—scored on a scale from 1 (low) to 10 (high)—with historical context shaping each score.[43]

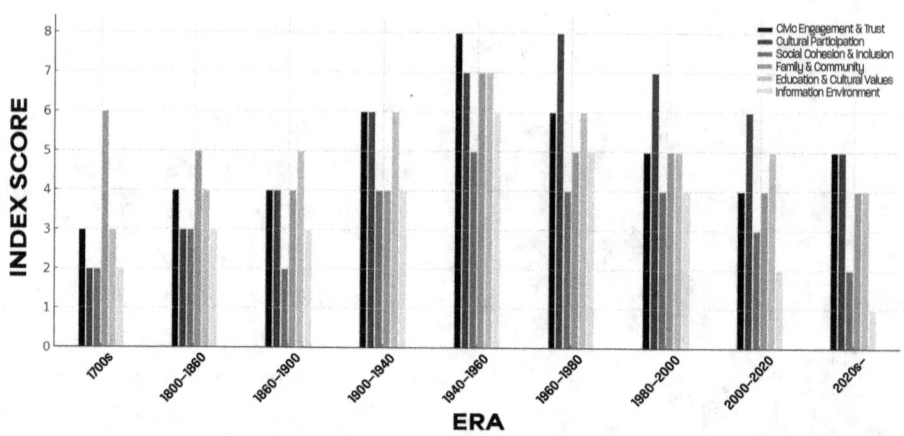

Is US Culture in Trouble? YES!

Culture Index Analysis (1700s-2020s)[44]

1. Civic Engagement & Trust: Declining

- **Trend:** From a peak in the 1940s–1960s (score: 8), **civic trust and engagement have dropped to a 5 in the 2020s.**
- **Why It Matters:** Voter suppression efforts, institutional distrust, and growing polarization threaten the civic glue that binds a democracy.

2. Cultural Participation: Digital Overload, Physical Decline[45]

- **Trend:** Cultural engagement peaked in the mid-20th century with public arts funding and attendance (score: 8), **but scores fell to 5 in the 2020s.**
- **Why It Matters:** Cultural vitality sustains identity, cohesion, and innovation. Streaming and social media cannot replace shared public cultural spaces.

3. Social Cohesion & Inclusion: Fragmenting[46]

- **Trend:** A score of 5 in the 1940s–60s **drops to 2 today—indicating deepening divides.**
- **Why It Matters:** Rising hate crimes, anti-DEI backlash, and algorithm-fueled polarization are tearing at America's pluralist fabric.

4. Family & Community: Restructuring, but Also Isolating[47]
- **Trend:** Stable and high in the 1940s–1960s (score: 7**), now stagnating around 4.**
- **Why It Matters:** Birth rates are declining, elder isolation is rising, and economic pressures are breaking down intergenerational support systems.

5. Education & Cultural Values: Cultural Confidence Eroding[48]
- **Trend:** Civic education and national pride once scored a 7; **now sit at 4**.
- **Why It Matters:** A nation uncertain of its values and divided on its moral direction becomes vulnerable to internal incoherence and disinformation.

6. Information Environment: Crisis Mode[49]
- **Trend:** From a relatively stable, centralized information ecosystem (6 in the 1960s), it's now **at its lowest (score: 1).**
- **Why It Matters:** Misinformation, media distrust, AI-generated content, and echo chambers mean Americans no longer agree on basic facts.

What does all this mean? Where are the fault lines in our culture today? What needs to be addressed? Data does not lie (at least when it is presented correctly).

Here are the US Culture Issues based on Data, Top 10 List:
1. Hyper-Individualism: "I Got Mine, Screw You"
- **Problem:** America glorifies "personal freedom" so hard you'd think collective responsibility was a communist plot.
- **Why:** Capitalism + rugged individualism = a social hellscape where helping others is considered "weak" and wearing a mask is treated like

tyranny. We turned "Don't Tread on Me" into a national Tinder bio.

- **Result:** Zero empathy. Maximum bootstraps. A population is more likely to film a tragedy than prevent it.

2. Political Tribalism: Red Hat vs. Blue Check

- **Problem:** Politics isn't about policy anymore—it's gang affiliation with better merch.
- **Why:** Gerrymandering, rage-bait media, and a few decades of weaponized white grievance (looking at you, Southern Strategy) turned democracy into *The Real Housewives of Capitol Hill.*
- **Result:** It's not about solving problems. It's about "owning" the other side and posting it before lunch.

3. Trust Issues: Government Ghosted Us

- **Problem:** No one trusts the system. Not Congress, not media, not medicine. Not even tap water.
- **Why:** Try lying to us into a war, bailing out billionaires, fumbling a pandemic, and electing reality show hosts—and see how people respond.
- **Result:** Americans are emotionally checked out, politically hungover, and spiritually disassociating in bulk.

4. Performative Patriotism: Flags > Facts

- **Problem:** We swapped civic engagement for bumper stickers and bootstraps.
- **Why:** America's founding contradictions—freedom built on genocide and slavery—never got a reckoning or a theme park.
- **Result:** If you challenge the myth, suddenly *you* hate America. Meanwhile, the guy waving the largest flag can't name a single amendment—except the one about guns.

5. Monetized Identity: "Be Yourself" for $19.99

- **Problem:** Who you are now depends on how well you brand it.
- **Why:** Capitalism didn't consume culture—it monetized your trauma

and repackaged your personality as a product.
- **Result:** Authenticity is a business model. Passion is an ad strategy. And self-expression comes with an affiliate link.

6. Anti-Intellectualism: The Dumber, the Louder
- **Problem:** We celebrate "common sense" over actual knowledge, especially when the "experts" make us feel bad.
- **Why:** Decades of underfunded education + populist rage = a country where feelings > facts and anyone with a PhD is automatically "suspicious."
- **Result:** A nation where science is "an opinion" and Google search results outranks epidemiologists.

7. Weaponized Nostalgia: MAGA is a Mood Disorder
- **Problem:** Half the country wants to rewind to an America that never really existed—unless you were straight, male, and owned land (and maybe people).
- **Why:** The past is easier to mythologize than the future is to build.
- **Result:** Progress is framed as persecution. The 1950s are the new utopia—minus polio and lead paint, but with the racism intact.

8. Loneliness: "Connected" but Dead Inside
- **Problem:** We're more digitally tethered than ever, yet people are lonelier than they were before dial-up.
- **Why:** Tech replaced town squares. Work replaced family. Capitalism replaced the community.
- **Result:** You're surrounded by Wi-Fi but starving for an actual human connection. Instagram is your church. Your friends are mutuals. And your therapist has a six-month waitlist.

9. The Equity Backlash: "Inclusion Hurts My Feelings"
- **Problem:** Progress on race, gender, and LGBTQ+ equity now triggers mass meltdowns from people who've never had to share before.
- **Why:** When the table finally gets extended, the people who were always served first scream that they're being "erased."

- **Result:** DEI is now "divisive." Equity is "woke." And somehow Karen from HR feels more oppressed than a trans teen in Florida.

10. Celebrity Worship: Famous for Nothing, Followed for Everything

- **Problem:** We idolize "influencers" who contribute less to society than expired coupons.
- **Why:** In the attention economy, virality > value.
- **Result:** Truth is optional. Expertise is elitist. And your national discourse is shaped by someone who vapes in their Range Rover and calls it content.

Bottom Line: Culture Is Cracked— And the Noise Is Getting Louder

America isn't broken because it can't fix things. It's broken because **too many people profit from keeping it broken.** We're caught between:

- Liberty vs. accountability
- Nostalgia vs. reality
- Loud voices vs. informed ones

And until we call out the clown show for what it is—**a carefully marketed meltdown disguised as patriotism**—we're reliving the exact hissy fit, on loop, in hi-def.

From Diagnosis to Denial—Paging Dr. History-STAT!

So now that we've charted the cultural cholesterol of the United States from powdered wigs to TikTok, the obvious follow-up: **How the hell did we get here?**

We've diagnosed the symptoms:

- Civic trust is on life support.
- Social cohesion is wheezing through a CPAP machine of partisanship.
- Critical thinking has flatlined somewhere between a Facebook meme and a Senate hearing.

America's culture isn't under stress—it's having a full-blown identity cardiac event in real time. **The vibes are off. The values are confusing. The**

virtue signaling is deafening.

We now live in two Americas: One built on hard truths, equity, and reality. The other was built on emotional fragility, nostalgia, and meme-based governance.

Can Culture Heal Without Accountability?

No. Especially when half the country thinks an apology is oppression.

Let's get one thing straight—this isn't about silencing Dick. No one is trying to duct tape his mouth shut or confiscate his freedom of expression. We're just asking him to stop turning every policy conversation into an emotional hostage situation.

Because here's the hard truth: The country cannot function when every legislative debate devolves into a group therapy session for white male fragility. We are not trying to cancel Dick. We're trying to graduate him from emotional kindergarten.

The Need for Truth, Reconciliation, and Therapy— National and Personal

America doesn't just need accountability. It needs **a collective national exorcism**, followed by a decade-long period of group support and a robust mental health plan.

We've never had truth.

We've never had reconciliation.

We've had **distraction, denial, and a steady diet of patriotic delusion.**

We can't heal if we can't face what hurt us—and who we hurt.

Moving from Hissy Fits to Hard Conversations

We've spent the last decade watching grown-ass men throw tantrums on national television, in state legislatures, on podcasts, and at PTA meetings—because being asked to learn, adapt, or empathize felt like persecution. But change doesn't come through hissy fits. It comes through hard conversations, uncomfortable truths, and the willingness to stop performing and start listening.

We need:

- Civic courage—not cosplay patriotism in tactical gear.

- Emotional maturity—not meme-driven martyrdom.
- Actual leadership—not grievance influencers selling merch between culture war sermons.

Healing requires reality, repair, and responsibility, not just for the oppressed, but for the oppressors who've never been asked to own their role in the wound.

Cultural Impact: The Cost of Denial is Collapse

The longer we let Dick scream over the conversation, the more we stall the recovery. Because while he's fighting imaginary enemies, the real ones—inequality, authoritarianism, disinformation, climate collapse—are circling. Accountability isn't about shame. It's about liberation—for all of us.

Truth Denied: America's Missing Reckoning with Its Own Past[50]

- **South Africa's Truth and Reconciliation Commission** helped stabilize a fractured post-apartheid society, not through silence, but through structured public accountability.
- **The US remains one of the only major Western democracies** without a national truth commission regarding slavery, Indigenous genocide, or state violence.
- According to Pew (2024), **over 60% of Americans say the country "cannot heal without acknowledging historical wrongs."**

The Fork in the Road

The walls are cracking—the foundation's on fire. And Dick's too busy blaming drag queens to notice the roof collapsing. This section examines where American culture thrives and where it struggles today in 2025. That hissy fit you saw on the Capitol steps on January 6, 2021? It's not just noise. It's legislation. From abortion bans based on pseudoscience to book bans based on boomer Facebook posts, America isn't just *having* a cultural breakdown—it's codifying it.

The fork is here. Right now. We can either:

- Rebuild civic trust through hard truths, structural change, and actual grown-up conversations.
- Or we can double down on delusion, reward rage with airtime, and pretend that fragility equals freedom.

The stakes aren't abstract—they're **your rights, your kids' education, your democracy.**

> *And the question isn't, "Can America survive this?"*
> *The question is, "Does America even want to grow the fuck up?"*
> *Because let's be real: We've spent years handing microphones to man-babies in red hats and pretending their emotional instability was political insight.*
> *We've called paranoia "patriotism," and bigotry "belief."*
> *We've confused performative dissent with a functional opposition party.*

At this point, the real revolution would be emotional maturity.

Grab your bourbon, a cozy blanket, and a box of tissues. It's time to remove the gloves permanently, and the satire starts now.

You're going to laugh. You're going to cry. You might spill your drink. But most importantly, you're going to get **real** about the myths we've been spoon-fed and the hissy fits that have shaped this nation.

This is forensic psychology meets cultural archaeology:

- Where did the first crack in the mirror of supremacy appear?
- When did *sharing* become *tyranny*?
- How did a group that won every round of Monopoly for 250 years believe the game is now rigged—because someone else finally passed "Go"?

This isn't just a book. It's **truth, justice, and liberty for all, finally, with receipts.** Let's get to work.

So, not sure if you're like Dick the hissy fitter? Take the quiz to find out.

Quiz—Are You a Hissy Fitter:
Like Dick, Jane, and Karen (Dick's wife)?

A Self-Diagnostic Tool for the Culturally Anxious

Instructions: Answer each question honestly. For every "Yes," give yourself **1 Hissy fit Point.** Tally your total at the end.

Section 1: Emotional Stability in a Changing World

1. Do you refer to societal progress as a "slippery slope"?
2. Have you used the phrase "I'm not racist, but…" and then continued speaking?
3. Do you feel personally attacked when someone asks you to use their preferred pronouns?
4. Does the term "diversity hire" make you uncomfortable *because you weren't picked*?
5. Do you get nostalgic for a time when "people knew their place"?

Section 2: Workplace Woes and Power Hissy Fits

6. Do you believe DEI programs are unfair because *you* didn't get a promotion?
7. Have you complained that it's now harder for "people like you" to get ahead?
8. Do you start sentences in meetings with "Back in my day…" and feel proud about it?
9. Are you convinced Gen Z "doesn't want to work"?
10. Have you ever referred to a woman leader as "bossy" or "intimidating"?

Section 3: Patriotism or Performative Panic?

11. Do you equate being asked to wear a mask with government tyranny?
12. Have you ever said, "If you don't like this country, leave"?
13. Do you believe America was at its peak sometime before 1975?

14. Do you watch cable news and shout at the screen?
15. Does saying "Happy Holidays" feel like cultural erasure?

Section 4: Family Values and Social Media Rage
16. Do you use the phrase "traditional family" like it's a weapon?
17. Have you ever posted a rant on Facebook that began with "I'm going to say it…"?
18. Do you blame "woke culture" for everything from gas prices to your erectile dysfunction?
19. Have you told your daughter to smile more?
20. Do you think books with gay characters should come with a warning label?

Hissy Fit Scoring:
- **0–5 Points:** *You're likely not any of these archetypes—but stay vigilant. Micro-Dick energy can sneak in.*
- **6–10 Points:** *Warning signs are flashing. You may be becoming a Hissy Fitter. Reflect, listen, evolve.*
- **11–15 Points:** *High risk of full-blown Hissy Fit Syndrome. You're emotionally invested in being unchallenged.*
- **16–20 Points:** *Congratulations—you are **Dick, Jane, and/or Karen in the flesh**. You're nostalgic, loud, and wrong.* Please proceed to your local library and observe a high school sociology class. Quietly.

A Recovery Guide for the Culturally Fragile
You took the quiz. You scored high. You've got a little Hissy Fit in you—or a lot. It's okay. **The first step is awareness.** The second step? *Evolution.* Below is your 5-step Reflection & Recovery Framework to help you transition from outbursts to personal growth. This works!

STEP 1: Sit with Discomfort
"If you're always comfortable, you're probably part of the problem."
  Ask yourself:
- Why does the phrase "diversity and inclusion" trigger me?

- Who taught me that sharing power means losing it?
- When was the last time I was *truly* challenged—and didn't retreat into sarcasm?

Homework: Spend 15 minutes listening to someone who doesn't look, live, love, or vote like you, without interrupting, correcting, or "playing devil's advocate."

STEP 2: Name Your Privilege (Without Having a Meltdown)

"Acknowledging privilege doesn't erase your struggle—it means you didn't have to fight the system and your identity."

Questions to explore:

- What doors opened for me that had nothing to do with merit?
- Who hasn't been in the room—and why?
- How have I benefited from being "neutral," when that neutrality protected the status quo?

Homework: Write a list titled *"Things I've Never Had to Worry About Because of Who I Am."* Please read it. Sit with it. Don't rationalize it.

STEP 3: Get Curious, Not Defensive

"The moment you feel the urge to argue, ask yourself: What am I defending—and why?"

Check yourself:

- Are you learning to understand, or preparing to rebut?
- Is your discomfort based on harm or unfamiliarity?

Homework: Replace one hour of cable news with one hour of reading from a historically marginalized voice. Memoirs are a great start—actual lived experience trumps your uncle's Facebook post.

STEP 4: Practice Power-Sharing

"If you're used to holding the mic, passing it feels like silence. It's not."

Consider:

- Have I ever interrupted a woman and thought it was "contributing"?
- Have I ever taken credit for someone else's labor, ideas, or impact?
- What's one way I can pass the mic this week?

Homework: In your next meeting, intentionally create space for some-one who doesn't usually speak. Then, **don't speak over them.** Radical, right?

STEP 5: Evolve Publicly

"Private evolution without public accountability is self-congratulation."

What to ask yourself:

- Am I willing to call out the systems I once upheld?
- Can I admit I was wrong—loudly, humbly, and without demanding applause?

Homework: Talk to your peers—especially the other Dicks. Speak truth, not superiority. Model growth. Invite them in, but don't coddle them.

Final Note: You don't have to stay a Dick, Jane or Karen. You can become **Rich, Sally, or Sue (the alternative to Karen)**—in empathy, in humility, in understanding. The world is changing. You can resist it, or you can be *better than Dick, Jane, or Karen.*

The Mount Rushmore of Hissy Fitters

America's Most Fragile Power Brokers—Now in Meltdown Mode

You've heard of Mount Rushmore—an iconic monument carved to honor presidents who (mostly) held it together. But what if we immortalized the men who've built their brands on barely contained hissy fits, weaponized grievance, and public meltdowns, instead of stoic leadership? We'd need more than a mountain—an entire state, even a coast. Picture it: the Grand Canyon of Grievance—the National Park of Persecution Complexes. A sprawling emotional outburst etched into granite.

Welcome to the Mount Rushmore of Hissy Fitters, where the only thing larger than the egos is the list of things they can't emotionally process.

1. **Tucker Carlson**—*The High Priest of Persecution Cosplay*
   Always squinted like he smelled accountability.
   Tagline: *"They took my monopoly on outrage and made it... diverse."*
2. **Elon Musk**—*The Techno-Toddler*
   Brilliant, but emotionally allergic to boundaries. Thinks "free speech" means no one's allowed to disagree.
   Tagline: *"I bought the playground to scream on the slide."*
3. **Ron DeSantis**—*The DEI Demolition Man*
   Treats empathy like contraband. Waging war on education, pronouns, and anything with melanin or nuance.
   Tagline: *"If I can't understand it, I ban it."*

4. **Jordan Peterson**—*The Academic Apologist for Misogyny Lite™*
   A clinical psychologist turned culture war prophet. Thinks social justice is causing the collapse of Western civilization—also, clean your room.
   Tagline: *"Tears, ties, and ten hours of YouTube lectures."*
5. **Greg Gutfeld**—*The Edgy Uncle at Thanksgiving*
   Thinks being annoying is bravery—mistakes punching down for stand-up.
   Tagline: *"The laugh track is optional; the entitlement is not."*
6. **Joe Rogan**—*The Podcast King of Performative Skepticism*
   One-part gym bro, one-part TEDx cult leader. Gives voice to men who fear sunscreen but trust elk meat with their lives.
   Tagline: *"I'm asking questions… while platforming disinformation."*
7. **Mike Lindell**—*The Bed Bath & Beyond Believer*
   Proof that capitalism can sell anything—even delusion.
   Tagline: *"Sleep number: 2020. Still tossing and turning over it."*
8. **Donald Trump**—*The Hissy-Fit-in-Chief*
   Built an empire on grievance. Governed like a reality show host with a Twitter addiction and a Sharpie.
   Tagline: *"Make America Whine Again."*
9. **Ben Shapiro**—*The Speed-Talker of Sore Feelings*
   Argues like he's trying to win a spelling bee against empathy.
   Tagline: *"Facts don't care about your feelings—unless they're mine."*
10. **Brett Kavanaugh**—*The Judicial Crybaby*
    Turned the Supreme Court confirmation hearing into a sobbing session about beer and victimhood.
    Tagline: *"I like beer and I hate consequences."*
11. **Bill Maher**—*The Liberal Boomer Who Hates Change*
    Thinks Gen Z is ruining America, but also thinks he invented edgy discourse.
    Tagline: *"Back in my day, we mocked minorities without Twitter clapback."*

12. **James Lindsay**—*The Anti-Woke Alarm Clock*
    Misunderstood critical theory once and have never stopped
    yelling about it since.
    Tagline: *"Every syllabus is a Marxist threat."*

Honorable Mentions
1. **Alex Jones**—*Conspiracy Performance Artist*
   "Buy my vitamins or the globalists win."
2. **Steven Crowder**—*YouTube's Poster Boy for Punchable Smirks*
   "Change my mind: I fear women and progress."
3. **J.K. Rowling**—*White Woman Exception with Male Hissy Fit Energy*
   "I wrote magic. Now I tweet oppression."

They don't fear change. They fear irrelevance. And rather than adapt, they perform the only move they were ever taught: **Throw a fit and call it freedom.**

CHAPTER 3

How the Fuck Did We Get Here? 2025—The Orange Era

This isn't the beginning of America's unraveling. It's just where the mask finally slipped.

Why I Started Here: I didn't start with 1776, the Civil War, or even Reagan's "Morning in America," because if we want to understand *why the country feels like a dysfunctional group chat with nukes*, we must start with the Orange Era. We have to start with 2016–2025, when America stopped pretending.

This era isn't an aberration. It's a mirror. A circus mirror, sure—but one that reflected everything we've refused to face: male fragility dressed as patriotism, unprocessed rage sold as political identity, and a democracy so starved of truth it mistook grievance for governance. And this isn't just about one man, Donald J. Trump. It's about what he unleashed—and what he revealed. He didn't break America. He *exposed* it. And the hissy fits that followed weren't side effects. They became *policy*.

This is America Today, 2025

That's why I start here—because you can't possibly grasp where we're heading, or how to stop the freefall, until you understand this era's starring role in scripting our dysfunction. America in 2025 isn't some slow-burning crisis—it's a dumpster fire with jet fuel poured on top.

As I write, violence escalates like it's a national pastime, polarization widens like the Grand Canyon on steroids, policies swing like wrecking balls, and the very foundation of the Constitution is being treated like an optional Terms & Conditions pop-up. This isn't a *me* problem. It isn't a *you* problem. This is a *we* problem—a full-blown cultural meltdown demanding a *we* solution. And yet, everyone's too busy doomscrolling, rage-posting, or screaming about "freedom" while canceling books to notice the floorboards are giving way.

It's exhausting just trying to keep up. Blink, and another norm has been shredded. Scroll, and another hissy fit has hijacked the headlines. Watch, and the theater of politics becomes less C-SPAN, more WWE cage match.

So, buckle up. **Chapter 3 is the outcome—the diagnosis of how the hissy fit metastasized into national identity.** The rest of this book? That's the autopsy, the intervention, and maybe—just maybe—the roadmap to recovery. But here's the catch: it only works if we're finally ready to grow the fuck up.

Prelude to a Meltdown—The Cracks Beneath the Surface

America thought it had grown up. It has just changed the channel.

Before the orange curtain rose and the nation descended into a fever dream of "alternative facts" and TikTok terrorism, the cracks were already there—hairline fractures in our national mirror. America didn't fall apart in 2016. It had been quietly, spectacularly unraveling long before Trump rode that golden escalator into the bowels of democracy's undoing.

We told ourselves we were progressing. A Black president. Gay marriage. Millennials are killing Applebee's. Yet under the surface, Dick (the cultural archetype) was seething. The world no longer revolved around him, and he didn't like that. Jobs had shifted, whiteness no longer guaranteed center stage, and pronouns became more than just a matter of grammar. Dick felt erased, and when Dick felt erased, Dick threw a fit.

How did we get here?
What is fueling the Great American Hissy Fit?

Here is what the evidence tells us.

The Illusion of a Post-Racial, United America After Obama

When Barack Obama was elected president, many white Americans exhaled a collective, self-congratulatory sigh of relief. *"We did it. Racism is over. Cue the Morgan Freeman voice-over."* It was the ultimate national performance review—eight years of Black excellence allowed just enough plausible deniability for white folks to tell themselves, "We're not that country anymore."

The problem? That unity was a marketing campaign, not a movement. Obama's presidency didn't end racism. It threatened the *denial* that racism still existed. For every policy win, there was a cultural backlash. For every inch of progress, there was Dick—in his La-Z-Boy, clutching his remote, wondering why every commercial suddenly had interracial couples, gay people, and women who weren't laughing at his jokes. To many Dicks, Obama wasn't the American dream. He was a warning shot that the dream might no longer have room for them.

Economic Insecurity Dressed in the Suit of Nationalism

Dick didn't wake up one day and become a white nationalist. He *felt* something at first. Economic despair, job loss, medical debt, his kid's college degree in Gender Studies that didn't come with a six-figure job. But instead of blaming deregulation, globalization, or corporate tax evasion, Dick was handed a more straightforward explanation:

"It's them. Everyone who isn't in alignment with me" –DICK

"Them," of course, being immigrants, marginalized people, feminists, and anyone else who had the nerve to ask for a seat at a table Dick thought was reserved for him. Nationalism became emotional anesthesia. It numbed the pain while inflaming the rage. It told Dick, "You're not losing because the system is rigged. You're losing because they're cheating." And because Dick was taught to equate struggle with failure, he couldn't admit his pain. He weaponized it instead.

Cultural Backlash Simmering Under "Hope and Change"

Obama's campaign slogan was *Hope and Change*. What Dick heard was *Fear and Replace*. To him, the America he knew was being rewritten in a language he didn't understand—one that used words like "inclusive," "equitable," and "nonbinary."

Dick was promised simplicity. Yet when the world handed him nuance, he panicked because complexity doesn't feel good. It's uncomfortable. Unsettling. It requires admitting **he might not have all the answers.** And **nobody likes that.** Dick reached for the louder voice. The simpler answer. The Red Pill Pushers in suits or hoodies with hats on the radio, TV, and computer who said, "You're not the problem, Dick. THEY are."

The backlash wasn't about one person. It was about what that person symbolized: that the future wasn't going to center on people who looked like Dick. Multiculturalism wasn't an aesthetic shift—it was a power shift. And Dick, already insecure about their fading relevance, treated it as an existential threat. While progressives clapped themselves on the back for electing a Black man, a large segment of the country was silently fuming, nursing their resentment like it was beer in a red Solo cup. Obama's calm demeanor only made it worse—because nothing pisses off an insecure person more than someone who doesn't flinch in the face of his tantrum. Hope didn't unite us. It exposed us. It cracked the mirror. And instead of looking inward, Dick blamed the mirror.

Dick's Growing Discomfort

Fueled by the triple threat of talk radio rants, right-wing think tank fairy tales, and Facebook groups brimming with bald eagles, Boomer memes, and badly Photoshopped Hillary images, Dick's discomfort didn't just grow—it metastasized. What started as mild confusion—*"Why are there so many languages on my shampoo bottle?"*—turned into cultural vertigo. Suddenly, the world wasn't asking Dick to lead; it was asking him to *listen*. And Dick? Dick does not listen.

Masculinity Crisis Meets Demographic Shift

For generations, Dick's manhood came pre-installed. All he had to do was show up, own property, and refrain from crying in public. But the 21st century demanded more—emotional intelligence, co-parenting, and the ability to make quinoa. *Dick was not emotionally equipped for quinoa.*

Compounding his crisis was the cold demographic math. America was becoming browner, queerer, younger—and Dick was none of those things. Census data didn't lie: by 2045, white Americans will become a minority in the US population.[51] For Dick, this wasn't evolution—it was *erasure*. His masculinity was no longer the gold standard. It was a punchline on late-night TV. Women were out-earning him, Black men were outperforming him, and people with pronouns in their bios were getting hired over him. He didn't just feel left behind—he felt **replaced**.

"Participation Trophy" Panic and the Fear of Irrelevance

Dick clung to the myth of rugged individualism—the idea that he *earned* everything through grit, sweat, and good old-fashioned American boot-strap-pulling. But deep down, he suspected the truth: he *was* the product of a system designed to favor him. And nothing triggers an existential hissy fit faster than realizing your success wasn't solely your own. So, Dick projected.

He mocked Millennials for wanting "safe spaces" and Gen Z for wanting climate justice, while his generation had created emotional support political movements to coddle his ego. The panic over "participation trophies" wasn't about children. It was about Dick's fear that the rules had changed—and that his default privilege no longer guaranteed applause.

He screamed, "Nobody wants to work anymore!" while collecting Social Security and hoarding generational wealth. He moaned about cancel culture while demanding immunity from consequences. He mistook *accountability* for *oppression* and *equity* for *theft*.

The Tea Party: Dick's First Public Tantrum

The Tea Party wasn't a grassroots movement. It was Dick's **first organized hissy fit**—a tantrum in tricorn hats fueled by Koch brothers' money and Fox News airtime.[52] It claimed to be about taxes, but somehow only became furious after the election of the first Black president.

The signs said, "Don't Tread on Me," but the subtext screamed, "I miss when everyone looked like me at the bank." The Tea Party was cultural regression wrapped in colonial cosplay. It demanded "freedom," but what it wanted was for the country to stop changing without Dick's permission. The Tea Party helped launch the political careers of people like Ted Cruz, Rand Paul, and—you guessed it—Donald J. Trump. It was less a revolution and more a rehearsal for the main act: full-blown orange authoritarianism. Dick's hissy fit had gone national.

The Majority Tantrum: When Losing Demographics Feels Like Losing Control[53]

- The percentage of non-Hispanic white Americans is projected to fall below 50% by 2045.
- 77% of Tea Party supporters in 2010 believed that "the country is headed in the wrong direction," but 89% of them said they were *doing fine* personally.

Translation: Dick wasn't struggling. He was *pouting*.

The Orange Era—Where the Hissy Fit Became Policy

Welcome to the golden age of grievance. The Trump administration was (and is) not a presidency—it was (and is) performance art for angry people who felt seen, not in their truth, but in their anger and frustration.

It didn't start with Trump. It goes back to Regan. Yet it's also post-Obama because Obama's election also fueled this era of more damage. It's a shit show with a strategy—the Orange Strategy fracturing the American culture and fueling the culture war.

Welcome to the Orange Era, where grievances are not just a feeling—they are a full-blown business model. This is not a political movement. It's a revolution happening right now! It's not even a perfect tantrum. It's fragility—weaponized, monetized, and broadcast 24/7 in HD, and it's alive and well.

This era didn't invent American whining—colonists whined about taxes while sipping smuggled rum. Confederates whined about "states' rights" while auctioning off human beings. Segregationists whined about "tradition" while hosing down children. However, the Orange Era is perfecting it. This era has turned personal grievances into a national identity, taken every loss—electoral, cultural, existential—and spun it into a raging *performance of persecution*. It doesn't matter if the outrage is factually wrong, morally bankrupt, or based entirely on a TikTok rumor from someone's uncle's garage podcast.

Yes, facts are optional. Feelings are constitutional rights. And victimhood is the new patriotism. Every time reality comes knocking, a new conspiracy theory answers the door wearing nothing but a red hat and a bad attitude. Every time democracy works, someone cries "fraud!" louder than a televangelist selling apocalypse insurance. Every time inclusion makes a bit of progress, half the country shrieks as if someone has personally defaced their Norman Rockwell calendar.

This isn't governance. This isn't activism. It's nostalgic make-believe—an attempt to rewind the country to a fantasy that never actually existed. A fantasy where "men were men" (propped up by three layers of Spanx to keep the illusion intact), women stayed quiet (with a little pharmaceutical help), and "freedom" meant shouting your opinions at the Applebee's bar without anyone daring to argue back.

Fragility has become a full-time job:
- Disagree with me? You're canceling me.
- Ask me to be accountable? You're oppressing me.
- Elect someone I don't like? It's rigged.
- Teach history that makes me feel bad? That's child abuse.
- Ask me to wear a mask? That's tyranny.

In short: America hasn't lost its mind—it's just handing out Facebook accounts, firearms, and 24-hour grievance hotlines to anyone who wants a meltdown on demand.

Masculine Fragility, MAGA, and the Politics of Violence

MAGA in 2025 runs on a simple fuel: **masculine fragility weaponized into political identity.** Every grievance is framed as an attack on "real men," and every policy that smells like equity becomes a plot to emasculate America. Trump's genius—or con—was to bottle that insecurity and sell it back as strength. He didn't just polarize politics; he turned *fragility into a movement.*

The fallout is violent. Data shows that right-wing extremists, many under the MAGA banner, committed the vast majority of politically motivated killings from 2022–2024 (Anti-Defamation League, 2023). When masculinity feels threatened, it doesn't protest with words—it marches with flagpoles, AR-15s, and conspiracy theories.

And Trump? He stoked it, profited from it, and made polarization the main event. America isn't debating policy; it's locked in a cage match over identity. The stage is set where fragile men with fragile egos confuse violence with power and persecution with patriotism.

That's not strength. That's democracy on life support, hooked up to a red-white-and-blue IV drip of insecurity.

The Orange Era isn't the end of democracy. It's the US democracy suffering a midlife crisis, buying a sports car it couldn't afford, and blaming immigrants when it crashed into a Dairy Queen. This isn't policy. It's performance art for the emotionally constipated, and the ticket price? The country's future—mortgaged to pay for one more ego-stroking rally and one more rage-fueled meltdown about Mr. Potato Head.

In theory, democracy is a government "of the people, by the people, for the people." In practice, under Trumpism, it has become a government "of the loudest, by the least qualified, for the grift." The Constitution? Optional. Institutions? Hollowed out. Civics education? This chapter examines how the core tenets of democracy—trust in institutions, adherence to the law, and faith in free and fair elections—were not only ignored but also *mocked, commodified,* and *live-streamed* with a flag emoji and the hashtags #FakeNews and #1776.

Trump is not the disease. He's the symptom. The product of a democracy that prefers drama to data, slogans to substance, and cultural nostalgia to actual justice. He's the man who asked America: "Do you want solutions, or do you want a catchphrase and a villain?" And America replied: "Only if it fits on a hat."

The Orange Era Dick-tionary Entry: (thĭs ôr'ĭnj êr'ə)

This distinct period of American history (2016 to today) is defined and fueled by the 45th to 47th presidencies, marked by emotional governance, performative populism, and a national identity crisis filtered through a sepia-toned Instagram filter and bronzer. A political era where logic took a sabbatical, institutions became influencers, and leadership was measured by rally crowd size and retweets, rather than legislation.

Usage in a sentence: *During the Orange Eras, historians stopped citing policy achievements and started citing merch sales and courtroom appearances.*

Notable Features:

- Facts optional, vibes mandatory
- Fox News as state television (with commercial breaks for gold, guns, and colon cleansers)
- Red hats became litmus tests for loyalty
- Presidential communication conducted almost exclusively via social media hissy fits, without using autocorrect
- Cult of personality meets reality TV: The Constitution was the script until it wasn't

Cultural Artifacts of the Era:

- MAGA rallies doubling as grievance festivals
- SCOTUS has an ethical fall
- Impeachments: 2 confirmed, countless threatened
- Indictments: Now collectible
- The Big Lie: America's most aggressively marketed fairy tale
- January 6: The first coup attempt was live-streamed with bad lighting

The Orange Strategy

It's not a platform. It's not a policy plan. It's a performance art piece duct-taped to a rage machine.

The Orange Strategy: A political fever dream masquerading as a platform, equal parts cult branding, grievance merchandising, and middle-school cafeteria behavior—except with nuclear codes. Named (obviously) for the most citrus-toned Commander-in-Chief, this strategy doesn't rely on ideology so much as *audacity*. It's less of a political approach and more of a marketing plan with a persecution complex.

Core Principles of the Orange Strategy:

1. **Spectacle Over Substance:** Don't govern—perform. Policy is for nerds. Rage is ratings.
   ("I alone can fix it."—Actual quote, 2016.)[54]
2. **Grievance as Gospel:** Every loss is a conspiracy. Every win is a mandate. Every fact is fake—unless it flatters.[55]
3. **Victimhood as Victory:** When you're called out for incompetence or corruption? Play the victim. Loudly. Preferably on social media at 3 a.m.
4. **Weaponized Nostalgia:** Invoke an imaginary "great past" that was only great for a particular group of people, and pretend it's everyone's shared history.
5. **Loyalty Over Legality:** Obey the leader, not the Constitution. Institutions? Weak. Truth? Negotiable. Loyalty? Nonnegotiable.[56]
6. **Number Blame Game:** If you do not like what the numbers say, fire the person and find someone who will skew the numbers to meet your personal narrative.[57]

Political Outcomes Include:
- A Supreme Court tilted so far right it might tip over.
- Book bans for "protecting children," assault rifles for "protecting freedom."
- A base that confuses constitutional law with Facebook memes.
- Impeachment...twice. Indictments...a baker's dozen. And still, he sells merch.

The Orange Strategy = Authoritarianism with a Tan and a Twitter Handle.

It's not about truth, service, or policy. It's about attention, domination, and turning democracy into a reality show cliffhanger.[58]

At its core, the Orange Strategy is built on three key pillars:

1. Muzzle Velocity
2. Perpetual Hissy Fits
3. Project 2025 (a.k.a. Government via Grudge)

Each prong is designed to *destabilize truth*, *manufacture grievance*, and *cast every act of accountability as persecution*. It's not governance—it's vengeance cosplay.

Prong 1: Muzzle Velocity–Silence by Any Means Necessary

You want democracy? Cute. The Orange Strategy wants obedience.

- Ban books that make Dick feel feelings.
- Fire teachers who dare discuss race, gender, or reality.
- Punish journalists by calling them enemies of the people and threatening to "open up libel laws."
- Sue. Intimidate. Deplatform. Reframe. Repeat.

Free speech isn't the goal—it's the decoy. The real goal? Controlling the narrative by controlling who's allowed to speak. Call it what it is: **weaponized censorship disguised as patriotism**.

Prong 2: Perpetual Hissy Fits–Rage as a Renewable Resource

Nothing fuels the Orange machine like a hissy fit.

- Lose an election? Scream fraud.
- Get indicted? Scream witch hunt.
- Get fact-checked? Scream cancel culture.
- Get banned from Twitter? Please start your own rage app and sell crypto on it.

This isn't just emotional immaturity. It's a strategy. The more chaos, the more headlines. The more victimhood, the more donations. The more drama, the less time for anyone to ask, *"Do you have a policy platform beyond 'be angry forever'?"* The Orange Strategy has turned middle-aged tantrums into a media ecosystem. And the algorithm consumes it like a deep-fried grievance on a stick.

Prong 3: Project 2025–Governance by Grudge

This isn't about leading the country. It's about **settling scores**, appointing cronies, and turning federal agencies into personal loyalty tests. The goal isn't democracy. It's **retribution in a red tie.**

- Fire civil servants and replace them with influencers who once quoted the Constitution on TikTok.
- Stack the courts with judges who think *The Handmaid's Tale* was a lifestyle manual.
- Dismantle checks and balances like they're IKEA furniture during a rage blackout.

Project 2025 is not a campaign—it's a takeover.

"Project 2025 is a federal policy agenda and blueprint for a radical restructuring of the executive branch authored and published by former Trump administration officials in partnership with The Heritage Foundation, a longstanding conservative think tank that opposes abortion and reproductive rights, LGBTQ rights, immigrants' rights, and racial equity. Project 2025's largest publication, "Mandate For Leadership," is a 900-page manual for reorganizing the entire federal government agency by agency to serve a conservative agenda."[59]

And its motto is simple: *If I can't control it, burn it down.* Project 2025 is covered in depth in Chapter 13.

Emotional Parasite Politics

The Orange Strategy thrives on attachment disorder. It demands that followers feel personally wounded by every slight against Dear Leader.

- If Trump is under investigation, you're under attack.
- If he's insulted, your identity is insulted.
- If he gets arrested, buy the mugshot on a hoodie and wear it like a religious relic.

This isn't just cult behavior. It's cult behavior with an affiliate link.

The Casualties of the Orange Strategy

It's not a bloodless coup. The victims are real.

1. **The Truth** is tortured until it confesses to being fake news.
2. **Civic Trust** once held the nation together. Now it exists only in reruns of *Schoolhouse Rock*.

3. **Public Institutions** are dismantled, defunded, and mocked by men who can't spell "bureaucracy."
4. **Decency** is replaced by memes, name-calling, and political merch that looks like it was designed during a monster truck rally.
5. **Empathy** is erased. Canceled. Labeled "woke."

The Cultural Fallout:
- We elected a tantrum.
- We turned the presidency into performance art.
- And now, we're governed by people who think **petty vengeance is patriotism** and **truth is whatever makes them feel powerful.**

The Orange Strategy isn't about right or left. It's about *might makes right, rage equals righteousness,* and *never backing down from a bad idea if you can scream louder than your critics.*

The Muzzle Velocity Presidency: Trump 2.0 and the Ballistics of Bullshit

You've probably heard the phrase *Muzzle Velocity Presidency.* I wish I could take credit for coining it, but no—the term comes from those who've seen this circus up close. At its core, this presidency isn't about policy or progress; it's about firing off distractions at rapid speed, keeping everyone too dazed to notice the wreckage piling up.

You know that feeling when you accidentally hit "Reply All" with a political rant, and suddenly your inbox is a war zone? Now imagine that, but it's the US government, and the sender is Donald J. Trump, armed with a red Sharpie, executive order stationery, and the moral clarity of a Magic 8-Ball. Welcome to Trump's Second Term: The Ballistic Edition, where policy isn't made—it's fired at you with the muzzle velocity of chaos, distraction, and constitutional contempt.

Muzzle velocity is the speed at which a bullet leaves the barrel. In Trump's case, each executive order erupts from the Oval Office like an emotional projectile—policy by hissy fit, aimed squarely at anything that resembles progress, equity, or reality. He's not leading. He's lobbing legislative grenades. And it's all part of the strategy. And guess what? We *shouldn't* be surprised. Now, we're in the full-blown hissy fit era—*The Orange Outburst*—where governing is just grievance with a flag pin.

The current symptoms:

- Over 100 executive orders in under 100 days. Think of it as speed governing for the easily distracted.
- Abolishing DEI? Gone.
- Crushing climate policy? Handled between golf swings.
- Restoring a "meritocracy" by eliminating everyone qualified? Naturally.
- And when asked if he must uphold the Constitution, our dear leader said, "I don't know". That's not a slip-up. That's *strategy*.

This isn't random incompetence. This is a performance. A calculated spectacle of nonverbal nonsense, where deflection is the message, confusion is the method, and the goal is simple: exhaust you into submission.

The strategy is clear:

- Flood the field with bad-faith policy.
- Smother opposition in administrative molasses.
- Distract you with nonsense ("Woke M&Ms!") while reshaping the judiciary and gutting civil rights behind the scenes.

It's the political version of muzzle flash: you see the spark, you hear the

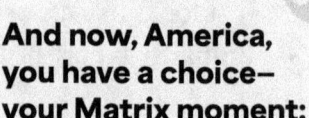

And now, America, you have a choice— your Matrix moment:

Take the Red Pill:
(ironic, given who's marketing it these days): Continue to scroll memes, believe that rage is patriotism, be MAGA, and pretend that Jesus voted straight-ticket GOP.

Take the Blue Pill:
Wake up. Peek behind the curtain. Recognize the cultural collapse camouflaged as nostalgia. Realize your vote, your voice, and your discomfort *matter*.

Because if you stick with the Red Pill crowd, the final section of this book will make you squirm. You won't be the hero in that story. You'll be the side character yelling about gas stoves while democracy burns behind you. Buckle up. The muzzle is loaded. But we don't have to be the targets.

bang, and by the time your brain registers it, the damage is already done.

The Hissy Fits of this Era that Fractured the US

The hissy fit driving political theater isn't just alive and well—it's on its third act, starring chaos, deflection, and a supporting cast of conspiracy theorists in flag lapel pins. The strategy? Whoever can scream the loudest, trend the fastest, and point at the shiniest "enemy" gets to own the narrative for the day. Or at least until the next manufactured meltdown. While we're busy rage-scrolling about gas stoves, drag queens, or fictional litter boxes in school bathrooms, actual laws are being passed, rights are being rolled back, and billionaires are looting the future like it's a clearance sale at Democracy Depot.

The damage? Unprecedented. But don't worry—there's a new distraction just around the corner. Maybe it's a book ban. Perhaps it's someone claiming Jesus was a free-market capitalist. Either way, the curtain rises, the outrage flares, and the real story slips out the back door, unnoticed. America isn't asleep at the wheel—we're just too busy watching the wrong show. Here are some of the greatest hits - Seriously, I can't make this shit up.

Inauguration-Gate: Size Matters

On January 21, 2017, America awoke to the pettiest cultural standoff in political history: How many people attended Trump's inauguration? Photos clearly showed that his crowd was far smaller than Obama's 2009 turnout. Even the Washington Metro ridership numbers said *meh*. Trump insisted it was the *biggest ever*. Because in Trump's world—and by extension, Dick's—the truth isn't what's verifiable, it's what's *emotionally necessary*.

This wasn't just a lie. It was **the first public performance of Trump's core leadership style:** unhinged confidence over inconvenient reality. It was the beginning of a four-year hissy fit disguised as governance. And Dick? Dick was taking notes.

Cultural Impact: This moment was the origin of the *Trumpian loyalty test* (straight out of George Orwell's *1984*): **Do you believe what your eyes see, or what I tell you to see?** If you chose the latter, you were family. If you chose the former, you were fake news, the deep state, or Satan.

RECEIPTS &
REALITY
CHECKS

Skeptic Discount.... $0.00
Cynicism Tax..... INCLUDED
Just Asking Fee..... $1.99
Evidence .... REQUIRED
Fallout .... MEASURABLE

NO REFUNDS ON REALITY

Crowd Control: When Facts Lose to Feelings[60]

- **Inauguration crowd comparison photos** published by multiple outlets clearly show Obama's 2009 turnout dwarfed Trump's 2017 turnout.
- **Public Policy Polling (2017):** 15% of Trump voters believed his crowd was bigger than Obama's, despite all available data and visual evidence.

The Coup Attempt (a.k.a. January 6th)

Trump lost. Democracy functioned. And Dick... lost his shit. Because of losing? That's for *them*, for people who don't look like him, pray like him, or BBQ like him. So, on January 6, 2021, Dick pulled on his finest camo—ironic, since there was nothing stealthy about his arrival—and joined thousands of equally unhinged middle-aged men who thought "1776" was both a fashion statement and a political strategy.

According to Pew Research, 64% of Republicans believed the 2020 election was stolen, despite all court cases, recounts, and forensic audits proving otherwise.[61] Translation: Dick can't do math, but he *can* do rage.

Cultural Impact: Democracy Becomes a True Crime Genre

This wasn't just bad behavior—it was cultural rot. Democracy didn't just fracture; it was downgraded to a Netflix docuseries.

- Election workers fled their jobs after threats, doxxing, and drive-by intimidation.[62]
- Civic education collapsed into TikToks about bamboo ballots and Hugo Chávez ghost-hacking voting machines.
- Family dinners turned into domestic hostage negotiations: "No, Grandpa, the Italian satellite didn't steal your vote."

By 2025, "democracy" was ranked behind "aliens," "Ozempic," and "Gwyneth Paltrow's Haunted Vagina Candles" in Google search trends. It wasn't a rejection of results—it was a rejection of *reality*.

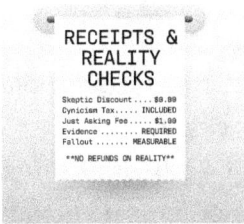

Pardon My Insurrection: How Justice Was Overturned on January 20, 2025[63]

- **Over 60 court challenges** were filed by Trump and his allies post-2020. He won *one*—a technicality in Pennsylvania that didn't affect the outcome.
- **Roughly 1 in 6 election officials** reported receiving threats in the wake of the 2020 election.
- **Public trust in elections** dropped by over 20 points among Republicans from 2016 to 2021.
- Over **1,400 individuals** were charged in connection with the January 6, 2021 attack on the US Capitol, with charges ranging from **trespassing and obstruction of an official proceeding to assaulting law enforcement and seditious conspiracy**.
    - As of mid-2025, hundreds have been tried in the court of law, by their peers and sentenced, with many receiving **prison terms from a few months to over 18 years**, including members of extremist groups like the Oath Keepers and Proud Boys.
- On **January 20, 2025**, the first day of his second term, President Trump signed a sweeping proclamation granting **clemency to everyone charged or convicted** in connection with the January 6 Capitol attack. This included:
    - Full **pardons** for approximately **1,500** people convicted of various offenses related to January 6.
    - **Commuted sentences** (to time served) for about **14 hardcore extremists**, including key leaders from the Proud Boys and Oath Keepers such as Enrique Tarrio and Stewart Rhodes.

Anti-Woke & Book Ban Meltdown (2022-2025)

Between 2022 and 2025, conservative politicians and activist groups launched a coordinated backlash against "wokeness" in education, framing it as a threat to children while pursuing book bans, curriculum restrictions, and teacher gag orders under the banner of "parental rights" and "anti-woke policies." "Wokeness" became the adult version of "cooties," with conservative legislatures banning books about Rosa Parks, gender identity, and even math textbooks that dared mention "equity."

Cultural Impact:

- **Chilling Effect on Education:** Teachers increasingly self-censor, reducing discussions about civil rights, slavery, gender, and sexuality.
- **Youth Mental Health:** LGBTQ+ youth report increased anxiety and isolation, while schools are forced to remove supportive materials.[64]
- **Weaponized Grievance:** Book bans are used to fuel fundraising and voter mobilization among anti-woke factions, becoming a feature of the backlash machine.

Banning the Future: How "Anti-Woke" Politics Turned Classrooms into Battlegrounds[65]

- PEN America documented over **3,300 book bans** in public schools, most involving titles dealing with race, gender, or LGBTQ+ themes.
- Florida's **Stop WOKE Act (2022)** restricted discussions on race and gender in schools and workplaces.
- **Texas banned books** discussing race, gender identity, and sexuality, with the state's education agency directing schools to remove or review books flagged by lawmakers.
- **Tennessee's laws** threatened teachers for discussing systemic racism or LGBTQ+ topics.

- Teachers and librarians faced harassment, job threats, and **criminal penalties for teaching** historical truths or acknowledging LGBTQ+ students.
- Polling by the **Public Religion Research Institute (PRRI)** in 2023 found **70% of Americans opposed book bans**, including majorities across political affiliations.
- The anti-woke meltdown functions as **cultural control, not child protection**—a distraction from underfunded schools, mass shootings, and healthcare failures, repackaged as moral panic.

The War on Education: Reading, Writing, and Right-Wing Rage

There was a time when education was about **learning**, **curiosity**, and occasionally cheating on a biology quiz without getting caught. Today? It's a full-contact sport in America's cultural cage match. Forget debates about curriculum quality. The new fight is over **ideological control**—who gets to decide what truth looks like and whether 2+2 can equal "communism." Dick has declared war. And the battlefield? Every classroom, every syllabus, every drag queen story hour that dared to teach empathy alongside the alphabet.

Cultural Impact: From Enlightenment to Indoctrination Accusations

The war on education is not just an attack on schools—it's an attack on **reality itself.** When truth becomes subjective, and facts become optional, classrooms become just another front in the grievance industrial complex.

- Teachers are quitting in record numbers.
- Students are graduating without basic civic literacy.
- And Americans are more likely to believe in Bigfoot than climate science.

By 2025, "education" is trending behind "Ozempic shortages" and "aliens in Congress" on Google. Substack subscriptions and YouTube rants have replaced civic trust. What does Dick want? Simple: An America where school is just church with lockers.

Defunding the Mind: How Trump's War on Education Became a War on Democracy[66]

- **Pew Research (2023)** found that 57% of Republicans now view universities as hurting the country.

- On March 20, 2025, Trump signed an executive order **closing (or dismantling) the Department of Education**, directing Secretary McMahon to begin the shutdown of the department and shift all authority to states and local communities, despite lacking congressional approval. As part of this effort, the Education Department initiated layoffs affecting roughly **50% of its staff**, including significant cuts in federal student aid and the Office for Civil Rights.

- **K–12 Curriculum and School Policies (January 29, 2025)** Trump signed **EO 14190: "Ending Radical Indoctrination in K-12 Schooling,"** banning "anti-American," CRT, and "gender ideology" content. It even empowered law enforcement to prosecute educators and revoke federal funding for noncompliant schools.

- **Funding Actions & Student Loans:** From late June to early July 2025, the administration withheld nearly $7 billion in federal education grants, targeting after-school, ESL, migrant, teacher training, and professional development programs, citing misuse as part of a "radical left-wing agenda."

- **Public Service Loan Forgiveness Changes:** Under Trump's **"One Big Beautiful Bill,"** he proposed changes to the PSLF program—narrowing eligible employers and removing forgiveness caps, threatening millions of borrowers.

The Impact by Party: Red States More Affected Than Blue
Heavy federal funding reliance in red states
- Trump-supporting states (red states) rely on **17% of school funding** from the federal government, compared to just **11% in blue states** (e.g., Massachusetts and New York).[67]
- States like **Mississippi (23.2%), Arkansas, and South Dakota** are among the most dependent on federal education dollars.[68]

Title I & Pell Grants disproportionately favor red states
- Title I funding: **~$10B** went to red states; blue states received roughly **$7B**.[69]
- Pell Grants: Red states collectively received approximately $17 billion, compared to $13 billion in blue states, which significantly aided students in red states.[70]

Biggest hold-up—$6B to $7B in federal grants
- Trump froze $6.8 billion in K–12 federal grants, impacting after-school programs, English-language learners, and teacher training—estimates show this constitutes **10% or more** of federal funding for 33 states and territories.[71] 79% are red states.
- States that calculate the most significant percentage of their budgets from federal allocations (e.g., Ohio, Kentucky, Indiana) are predominantly red and among the most severely impacted.[72]

The Orange Era: A Masterclass in Missteps, Misinformation, and Middle-Finger Governance

If I were to document every misstep of the Orange Era, this book would become an encyclopedia, a horror anthology, and a bloated government spending report all in one. And we'd still miss a few indictments.

Because what do you even *call* an era where:
- Sharpies were used to "edit" hurricanes?
- Bleach was floated as a cure for a deadly pandemic?
- Dictators got love letters, but Americans got "thoughts and prayers" with tracking numbers?

- Every presidential press conference felt like a fever dream hosted by a sunburned game show host in crisis?

This era is where performance art meets demolition derby. The Constitution isn't read—it's ad-libbed. Ethics aren't followed—they are being outsourced to reality TV producers. And national security? That's another plot twist between impeachment trials.

This isn't just a presidential era—it's an experiment in how far a nation could be pushed before it breaks. And somehow, we *didn't* break. We bent, we buckled, but we're still standing—bruised, gaslit, and clinging to a voter registration card like it's a life raft. So no, this section doesn't end with closure. It ends with a warning: History has receipts. And some of us kept screenshots. If you want proof that this gaslighting executive fantasy isn't just living on Facebook comment threads but sitting in real seats of power, look no further than the Supreme Court. Let's start there.

The SCOTUS Shock Doctrine: Bought, Robed, and Dangerous

Justice is blind. But in 2025, she's also sponsored by Harlan Crow and wearing an American flag bikini over a Federalist Society hoodie.

The Supreme Court of the United States is no longer a bench—it's a **throne** for lifetime unethical kings and queens of grievance politics, backed by tax-free dark money and a deep-seated hatred of progress. They don't interpret the law. They *weaponize nostalgia*. They've stopped pretending to be impartial. They're not even hiding the receipts. Clarence Thomas is out here collecting luxury RVs like Pokémon cards from his billionaire pals, while Sam Alito writes majority opinions in Comic Sans rage. This isn't judicial restraint—it's a judicial shitshow for the power-drunk theocrats with a vengeance kink.

The Billionaire Bench: Now Accepting Bribes in Bourbon and Superyachts

Before this era, the Supreme Court was a sacred institution, cloaked in reverence and marble. Today? It's a **country club with robes**—where the wine is aged, the donors are anonymous, and the rulings conveniently align with whoever paid for last summer's Alaskan fishing trip. This isn't jurisprudence. It's **juris-profiteering.**

Ethics Are for Other Branches

These justices rule on labor rights from the back of a golf cart and dismantle civil rights over Wagyu steak dinners. Their judicial robes may be black, but their calendars are red—Red State red, that is. The legal logic? "We can't be bought... but we do accept *deeply personal friendships* with billionaires who coincidentally want to overturn the Voting Rights Act." It's not biased. It's *just vibes.* And that shiny new "Supreme Court Code of Conduct" announced in late 2023? It reads like a Pinterest vision board of ethics—aspirational, nonbinding, and utterly unenforceable. There's more accountability in a Chuck E. Cheese ball pit.

Ethics Scandals (a.k.a. The Receipt Roll)

While you were busy worrying about student loans, climate collapse, or civil rights, the justices were busy redefining what "conflict of interest" means:

- **Private Jets:** Justice Clarence Thomas took at least **38 destination vacations, 26 private jet flights**, and a few luxury yacht rides—courtesy of billionaire mega donors like Harlan Crow.[73] That's not travel. That's a loyalty program.
- **Secret Real Estate Deals:** Thomas also conveniently forgot to disclose a multi-property real estate transaction with said donor, because nothing says impartiality like your benefactor owning your mother's house.[74]
- **Undisclosed Luxury Vacations:** Justice Alito enjoyed salmon fishing trips with hedge fund managers who just happened to have business before the court. He later defended it in a *Wall Street Journal* op-ed so smug, it could have been ghostwritten by "Rich Uncle Pennybags," the mascot of the Monopoly board game.[75]
- **Speaking Gigs for Extremist Think Tanks:** Several justices moonlight as **keynote darlings for Federalist Society galas**, Koch-funded retreats, and law student events hosted in medieval castles where words like "multiracial democracy" are considered profanity.

Dick's Hissy-Fit: SCOTUS Is Saving America

*"Finally!" Dick crows, pounding the table like a gavel. "The Supreme Court is putting this country back on track. They're restoring order, defending the Constitution the way it was **meant** to be read—by men like me. Roe is gone, and good riddance. Women don't need rights; they need responsibilities. DEI and affirmative action? Over. That's real equality—everyone's free to succeed, as long as they don't get special treatment. SCOTUS is finally proving that America belongs to the strong, the moral, the traditional. This isn't regression—it's justice!"*

—Dick

Dick Moves Alert

- Treating **stripping rights** as "restoring order."
- Calling regression "justice."
- Pretending overturning decades of precedent is "defending the Constitution."
- Cheering on exclusion while slapping the word "freedom" on it.
- Mistaking consolidation of power for democracy.

Sally's Soapbox: The Reality Check

"Dick, let's stop with the courtroom cosplay. SCOTUS isn't restoring justice—it's weaponizing it.

- **Precedent is shredded.** *Decades of hard-fought rights vanish overnight, tossed aside like they were mistakes instead of progress.*
- **Power is concentrated.** *This Court isn't neutral; it's stacked, politicized, and ruling like an unelected super-legislature.*
- **Freedom is redefined.** *For women, LGBTQ+ people, and marginalized communities, freedom shrinks with every ruling while yours expands.*
- **Democracy is undermined.** *The Court isn't interpreting the Constitution—it's rewriting the social contract in favor of the past.*

Here's the reality, Dick: SCOTUS isn't a guardian of the people—it's a fortress for your nostalgia. You call it justice; I call it regression in black robes. And while you're cheering the gavel strikes, the rest of us are watching rights, protections, and equity collapse under the weight of your hissy-fit."

—SALLY

Cultural Impact: Trust on Trial

- Public trust in the Court has cratered. Only 18% of Americans say they have "a great deal" of confidence in the institution.[76]
- Calls for term limits, mandatory recusal, and external oversight have surged, but nothing sticks, because *they* are the final say on what sticks.
- Young Americans now believe "Supreme Court Justice" is a synonym for "Influencer with a Law Degree."

As a result, SCOTUS has become a culture war weapon, not a legal body. The robes are still there, but the guardrails? Gone and melted down into donor-engraved cufflinks.

RECEIPTS &
REALITY
CHECKS

Skeptic Discount $0.00
Cynicism Tax..... INCLUDED
Just Asking Fee..... $1.00
Evidence .... REQUIRED
Fallout .... MEASURABLE

NO REFUNDS ON REALITY

Robes for Sale: How Supreme Corruption Shredded Public Trust[77]

Clarence Thomas

- Failed to disclose over 20 years of accepted luxury trips, private jet flights, yacht vacations, and tuition payments from billionaire GOP donor Harlan Crow without revealing them, violating transparency norms.
- Did not recuse himself from cases involving individuals and organizations connected to Crow's interests.
- In 2025, further reports revealed real estate deals with Crow, where Thomas's mother remained in the home rent-free while Crow paid for renovations.

Samuel Alito

- Failed to disclose a luxury Alaskan fishing trip in 2008 on a private jet funded by hedge fund billionaire Paul Singer, who had business before the Court.
- In 2025, he was criticized for participating in Federalist Society donor retreats while hearing cases tied to their interests.

Unreported Gifts and Conflicts

- **Neil Gorsuch** sold a property to a law firm executive with business before the Court and did not report the buyer's identity on disclosure forms.
- Justices received **lavish gifts and perks from conservative donors** under the guise of "educational" trips, including accommodations, meals, and private events.

Failure to Enforce Ethics Codes

- Despite these revelations, the Supreme Court **lacked a binding code of ethics**, relying on self-policing even amid public outcry and congressional hearings.
- In 2025, Chief Justice Roberts **refused to testify** at Senate hearings on

Court ethics, further eroding public trust.

Impact on Public Trust

- Public trust in the Supreme Court **fell to historic lows (28–34%)** during 2024–2025 amid these scandals.
- Trust in the Supreme Court reached a record low among Gen Z and Millennials.
- Advocacy groups and lawmakers continued to push for **mandatory recusal rules and a binding ethics code** in 2025–2026.

Meet the Justices: Nine Robes, No Rules

In 2025, the Supreme Court resembles a reality show titled *"Billionaires' Court: Ethics Are for Peasants."* The cast includes:

- **Justice Clarence Thomas**: Known for accepting lavish gifts and luxury travel from billionaire Harlan Crow, including undisclosed trips and property deals.
- **Justice Samuel Alito**: Criticized for accepting undisclosed gifts from individuals with business before the court and for controversial statements suggesting a lack of impartiality.
- **Chief Justice John Roberts**: Faced scrutiny for declining to testify before the Senate Judiciary Committee regarding Supreme Court ethics rules.
- **Justice Neil Gorsuch**: Reportedly sold property to a law firm CEO with business before the court, raising questions about potential conflicts of interest.
- **Justice Amy Coney Barrett**: Faced calls to recuse herself from cases involving groups that supported her nomination.
- **Justice Brett Kavanaugh**: Subject to ongoing debates over past conduct and impartiality
- **Justice Elena Kagan**: Advocated for enforceable ethics rules for the Court.
- **Justice Sonia Sotomayor**: Raised concerns about the Court's direction and transparency.
- **Justice Ketanji Brown Jackson**: Faced scrutiny over financial disclosures, which were subsequently amended.

Translation: America Is Watching the Empire's Robes Rot

You cannot—cannot—stand at the summit of American democracy, draped in judicial gravitas, while behaving like you just rolled out of the Mar-a-Lago hospitality suite with steak juice on your robe and a donor's Rolex ticking where your moral compass used to be. You don't get to claim constitutional infallibility with one hand while the other's swirling a $2,000 tumbler of billionaire bourbon, gifted by the guy whose corporate interests you're "impartially" ruling on next Thursday. And you sure as hell can't tell Americans to respect the law when you've written yourself *out of it entirely.*

Respect Our Power, Ignore Our Behavior

When the Supreme Court unveiled its new "ethics code" in 2023, the press portrayed it as a long-overdue gesture of accountability. But what was it? Judicial cosplay. A theatrical script disguised as reform. No enforcement. No penalties. No review board. Just a fancy-pants preamble that might as well have said: *"We promise to be good. Pinky swear."*

The message to America? We're above the rules. Imagine if your HR department said, "We have a new code of conduct, but it's optional—and only applies when we feel like it." You'd laugh. You'd riot. But when the Supreme Court does it? We're expected to bow.

The Cultural Impact: Judicial Royalty in a Republic of Peasants

This isn't just unethical—it's dangerous. Because when nine unelected life-time appointees get to play god with no oversight, we don't have a justice system. We have a monarchy with law degrees.

And America? **America has noticed.**

- Public confidence in SCOTUS has cratered to historic lows.
- Law professors and bar associations are demanding independent review mechanisms.
- Gen Z? They don't see robes—they see *robes soaked in donor cash, ideology, and arrogance.*

Until justices can be investigated, disciplined, or disqualified like literally every other judge in this country, this "ethics code" is just judicial theater.

And the audience isn't clapping—they're booing, tweeting, and organizing. Because when even middle school students have more accountability in detention, you've lost the plot.

The Future: Justice as Performance Art

In 2025, the Supreme Court will no longer operate like a traditional legal body. It's not the guardian of constitutional balance—it's **America's highest stage for elite performance rage**. Think less *Marbury v. Madison*, more *Hamilton* meets *Fox News After Dark*. Gone are the days of sober judicial restraint and legal nuance. Now? Dissents read like Reddit flame wars. Concurring opinions are sprinkled with biblical citations and QAnon-adjacent footnotes. And the majority rulings? They might as well come stamped with a watermark: **"Brought to you by the Federalist Society—sponsored by Hobby Lobby and Chick-fil-A."**

It's no longer about interpreting the Constitution—it's about turning it into a weaponized sermon.

- Religious liberty has been expanded to mean "I don't serve your kind here."
- Second Amendment rights have been stretched to include flamethrowers at bar mitzvahs.
- Privacy only matters if you're shielding offshore real estate, not uteruses.

And the aesthetic? It's *Handmaid's Tale* meets *Bass Pro Shop catalog*—justices quoting scripture while sipping Kentucky whiskey from tumblers engraved with "Come and Take It."

At this point, the bar isn't low, it's subterranean. Imagine the following SCOTUS headlines with a straight face:

- Citizens United II: Now with Holy Water—"Corporations are people, and now they can be baptized too. Tax-free."
- RuPaul v. Department of Homeland Security—"Drag is a credible threat to national masculinity. Ruled 6-3."
- Shelby County v. Reality (Revisited)—"The Voting Rights Act is canceled for being 'a little too socialist.'"

Nothing surprises us anymore. The Overton Window didn't just shift—

it fell out of the building and shattered on the marble steps. The Supreme Court is no longer a deliberative body. It's a prestigious podcast with legal consequences. Every opinion is crafted for headlines, designed to signal allegiance, not to the law, but to *the movement*. They're not writing for the American people. They're writing for Federalist interns, megachurch pastors, and Fox producers looking for a chyron. It's not jurisprudence—it's branding. And the brand is "freedom" for some, control for everyone else.

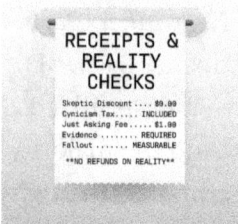

Reality Check on SCOTUS–Supreme Court Legitimacy, Ethics, and Public Trust[78]

Since 2022, **SCOTUS has overturned or gutted more than a dozen significant precedents**, often along strict ideological lines.

- The **Federalist Society has directly or indirectly influenced the selection of 6 of the 9 current justices**.
- Confidence in SCOTUS has dropped to **25% among Democrats, 39% overall**.
- **SCOTUS approval rating** hit an all-time low in May 2025: 29% overall, 12% among Democrats.
- **States introduced over 900 bills in 2024–2025** targeting LGBTQ+ rights, voting access, and reproductive care, most leveraging SCOTUS precedent as legal cover.
- **More than 60% of Americans** now say the Court is "too political to be trusted."
- The Supreme Court's 2023 "Code of Conduct" contains **no enforcement mechanism**, no investigatory body, and no penalties for violations.
- Every federal judge in the US is subject to disciplinary review **except the Supreme Court justices**.

America and Guns: The Land of the Free, the Home of the Perpetually Armed

Let's not sugarcoat it—America doesn't have a "gun problem." America has a **gun addiction** dressed up in patriot drag. We've managed to convince ourselves that the only thing standing between us and tyranny is an AR-15 with a custom camo paint job. Forget ballots, courts, or civic engagement—nah, democracy apparently lives in aisle seven of Walmart.

The Illusion of Control

We call it "gun control," but really, it's gun theater—a Broadway show where the lead actor is "freedom," the supporting role is "fear," and the understudy is "thoughts and prayers." After every massacre, we reenact the same tragicomic ritual:

- Cue outrage.
- Cue pundits.
- Cue politicians offering condolences with one hand while cashing NRA checks with the other.
- And the grand finale? Nothing changes. Curtain down. Encore next week.

DIY Safety: The American Way

Only in America do we say, "Sure, we'll let anyone buy a weapon designed for war, but don't worry—we'll post a laminated sign in schools that says *Gun-Free Zone.*" That's the equivalent of putting a "No Sharks" sign at the beach and calling it marine biology. Our safety strategy is basically hope plus hashtags.

Freedom Fetishism

We don't sell guns; we sell masculinity, nationalism, and nostalgia with a trigger. Every commercial whispers the same sermon: *This isn't a weapon, it's your birthright.* Forget that most people can't define the word "militia" without Googling it—we've canonized firepower as scripture. Guns aren't tools; they're talismans. They're our totems of "don't tread on me," even as we trip over our own shoelaces of logic.

The American Ritual of Amnesia

Here's the pattern: a tragedy happens, the headlines scream, the nation weeps—and then? Silence. We reset as if collective amnesia is cheaper than collective action. It's as if we've decided that carnage is the cost of freedom, like a subscription fee to liberty.

Locked, Loaded, and Licensed: The Second Amendment

Ah, the **Right to Bear Arms**—the sacred scripture of American exceptionalism, tattooed on our collective consciousness right next to "Don't Tread on Me" and "Hold My Beer." I'm all in favor of the Second Amendment. Own your gun. Collect them if you want. Just don't treat firearms like Pokémon cards—you don't get to hoard them all without proving you can safely handle the firepower.

Here's the deal: the right to own a gun should come with **the radical requirement of being a functioning adult.** That means:

- **Licensed:** If I need a license to drive a Honda Civic, you damn well need one to own a Glock. Treat guns like cars—license them, register them, insure them. If we regulate barbers with permits for cutting bangs, owning a military-grade toy better come with paperwork thicker than a CVS receipt.

- **Mentally Stable:** Stockpiling AR-15s while live-streaming about lizard people? Congrats—you've self-selected out. Guns aren't therapy; they're firepower. If your grip on reality is looser than your trigger discipline, you don't qualify.

- **Responsible:** The Second Amendment doesn't excuse reckless parenting. If your toddler finds your gun before their Legos, the problem isn't the Constitution—it's you. Responsible ownership isn't a bumper sticker—it's mandatory training, airtight storage, and actual accountability. Zero loopholes, zero excuses.

- **Stop Worshipping Tradition:** Freedom without responsibility isn't liberty—it's negligence with a flag-wrapped bow. Stop treating "tradition" as a hall pass for chaos.

- **Stop Making Gun Control Political:** Bullets don't stop mid-air to ask about your voter registration. This isn't red vs. blue—it's life vs. preventable death. Gun safety should be bipartisan, but somehow we've turned common sense into a culture war.

I'm pro-Second Amendment. But let's stop confusing **responsibility with oppression.** Owning a gun doesn't make you a patriot any more than owning a car makes you Dale Earnhardt. If we can all agree that **the right to bear arms comes with the duty to not be a danger to yourself or society**, then maybe—just maybe—we can stop turning the Bill of Rights into a suicide pact.

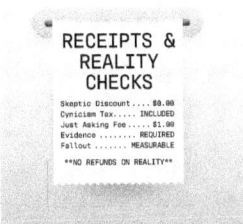

Guns, Death, and the Two-Party Circus[90]

If America had a customer service desk for democracy, we'd be standing in line holding the bloodied receipts of gun violence, begging for a refund. Instead, we get two political parties competing to see who can gaslight us more effectively.

Republicans:

- Their slogan is basically "More Guns, Less Problems." They argue that arming more teachers, baristas, and Uber drivers will stop mass shootings. Stat check: The U.S. already has **120 guns per 100 people**—more than any other nation on earth. If more guns equaled safety, America would be the safest place on the planet. Spoiler: it's not.
- GOP lawmakers accepted **over $15 million from the NRA in 2020 alone**. That's not public service—that's paid advertisement.

Democrats:

- They weep on cue after every tragedy, then offer the legislative equivalent of a scented candle: background checks *lite*, assault weapon bans that never pass, and a speech about "common sense" that dies in committee.

- Despite holding power multiple times in the past 30 years, Democrats have failed to push through comprehensive reform. Why? Fear of backlash, fear of rural voters, fear of their own shadows. They *campaign* on outrage but *govern* on stall tactics.

The Reality
- **Gun Deaths Don't Vote Party Line.** A bullet doesn't ask for your voter ID. In 2023, more than **48,000 Americans died from gun-related injuries**—suicides, homicides, accidents. That's roughly **132 deaths per day**. That's a plane crash every single day of the year.
- **Mass Shootings as National Pastime.** By mid-2024, the U.S. had already recorded **over 300 mass shootings before the Fourth of July.** That's not freedom—that's failure.
- **The Political Kabuki—Republicans** hide behind the Second Amendment like it's sacred scripture. Democrats clutch "gun reform" talking points like rosary beads, never daring to finish the prayer. Together, they've turned the nation's grief into campaign fundraising copy.

The Punchline Nobody Laughs At
We're told the system is "working as designed." And maybe it is—if the design is endless thoughts, endless prayers, endless profits, and endless funerals. The receipts don't lie: both parties have chosen performance over prevention. Until guns stop being **a partisan prop** and start being **a bipartisan imperative**, America will remain the only nation that treats daily carnage as background noise.

We the Divided: Cancel Culture and Living in a Nation of Echoes and Egos
The United States became a collection of cultural war zones where facts are optional, and identity is weaponized.

For Dick, "cancel culture" is the monster under the bed. The existential threat lurking behind every tweet, open mic night, and HR PowerPoint. He's not scared of being silenced. He's afraid of being *held accountable.*

He doesn't want dialogue. He wants a cultural purge of consequence. A world where he can say whatever he wants—however offensive, outdated, or violently ignorant—without anyone batting an eye, let alone filing a complaint.

Let's cut through euphemisms. Dick isn't mad about being "canceled." He's angry he can't spout racist, sexist, or homophobic garbage at the company barbecue and still get nominated for Employee of the Month. He's nostalgic for the good old days—when locker room talk *stayed* in the locker room, when jokes about "the gays" were considered edgy, and when diversity training consisted of "Don't touch the interns." Now? HR has policies, Gen Z has receipts, and suddenly Dick has to think before he speaks—and thinking hurts. Instead of adapting, he cries "cancel culture!" the moment someone dares to point out that his Facebook rant might not belong in the all-staff Slack channel.

Cancel Culture Crybabies: When Accountability Feels Like Oppression[79]

- **A 2022 YouGov poll** found that over 65% of Americans believe "people should face social consequences for offensive behavior," not government censorship.
- **The term "cancel culture"** was initially coined by Black Twitter to describe accountability within communities, not white men losing Netflix specials.
- **Most high-profile "canceled" figures** (e.g., Joe Rogan, Dave Chappelle, J.K. Rowling) continue to enjoy massive platforms, book deals, and standing ovations—because cancellation isn't exile. It's just a *pause in applause.*

"Woke" as the New Four-Letter Word

When critical thinking and logic were in play, being "woke" meant being **socially aware**. It meant paying attention, listening, and questioning power structures, essentially being a decent human being with a functioning moral compass. But then Dick got hold of the word—and like everything else he doesn't understand, he beat it with a flagpole until it turned into a culture war Rorschach test. *Woke* is no longer a descriptor. It's a dumpster label Dick uses for anything that challenges his worldview.

- History that includes slavery? Woke.
- Hiring practices that prioritize equity? Woke.
- A mermaid with melanin? Woke AND satanic.
- Pronouns in email signatures? Cultural collapse.
- Books about empathy? Communist propaganda wrapped in glitter.

What Dick means when he screams about "woke" is: "I don't like change, I don't understand nuance, and I'm deeply threatened by empathy."

Sally's Sanity: *"Wokeness" is just awareness with a better brand.*

—SALLY

Redefining Anti-Racism as an Attack on White Identity

The genius of the **anti-woke movement lies in its weaponization of fragility**. Anti-racism wasn't framed as progress. It was framed as persecution.

- Teaching about redlining? "They're trying to make white kids feel guilty!"
- Reading *The 1619 Project*? "They're rewriting history to erase us!"
- Asking white people to acknowledge systemic bias? "This is psychological abuse!"

To Dick, anti-racism isn't a pathway to justice—it's a full-blown identity crisis. Because if whiteness isn't the default anymore, he's not just uncomfortable—he's irrelevant. And irrelevance, for someone who's always assumed center stage, feels like annihilation. Instead of growing, he retreats. In denial. Into anger. Into anti-woke think tanks, where white grievance is repackaged as "heritage."

Merriam-Webster defines anti-racism as "opposed to <u>racism</u>."[80]

A Deeper Look: Anti-Racism

A moral and intellectual stance that says *we should stop upholding systems that treat people as unequal humans based on skin tone.* Revolutionary, right? Developed through decades of scholarship and activism, anti-racism calls for active dismantling of racism in policies, institutions, and behaviors—not just politely pretending racism is "over" because we elected Obama that one time.[81]

But in today's culture wars, anti-racism has been rebranded as:

- A Marxist plot.
- A diversity training gone rogue.
- A scam to make your white coworker feel bad for something their great-grandpa did.

Anti-racism is the fire drill conservatives fear will turn into a revolution.

What It Means:

- Racism is not just personal prejudice; it's systemic.
- You can't be "not racist"—you're either actively disrupting racism or passively benefiting from it.[82]
- Equity is not a threat to equality—it's a correction.
- Listening is not the same as being attacked.

What Critics *Pretend* It Means:

- White people must now walk around wearing apology signs.
- "Woke mobs" will break into your suburb and redistribute your scented candles.
- You can't eat a taco unless you read *The Souls of Black Folk* first.

Cultural Backlash: Anti-racism became the ultimate Rorschach test: To some, it was a roadmap for justice. To others, it was a personal insult written in bold Helvetica. As soon as people heard "anti-racist," they stopped listening altogether—and started yelling about cancel culture, critical race theory, and "reverse racism," aka the unicorn of white fragility.[83]

In short: **Anti-racism = Decency + Accountability (but only if you can survive the comments section).**

Schools, CRT, and the Moral Panic of Losing Control

Education—America's favorite battlefield. Critical race theory (CRT), once confined to law schools, was inflated into a **boogeyman** so large it made Bigfoot look underqualified. And suddenly:

- Dick thinks CRT is being taught in kindergarten.
- He believes books about Ruby Bridges are leftist indoctrination.
- He shows up to school board meetings like it's a UFC weigh-in, armed with Facebook memes and unearned rage.

The result? Censorship masquerading as "parental rights." Books are banned. Teachers are silenced. Students are confused. All because Dick can't handle the idea that his kids might learn empathy for people who don't look like him. It's not about protecting children. It's about protecting Dick's ego from a world that no longer treats him as the unquestioned protagonist.

Merriam Webster–Critical Race Theory (noun): "a group of concepts, such as race is a sociological rather than biological designation, and that racism pervades society and is fostered and perpetuated by the legal system used for examining the relationship between race and the laws and legal institutions of a country, and especially the United States."[84]

A Deeper Look: CRT (Critical Race Theory)

A graduate-level legal framework turned cultural boogeyman, CRT is the scholarly equivalent of Beetlejuice: say its name three times at a school board meeting and a thousand Facebook parents scream into the void. Initially developed in the 1970s and 1980s by legal scholars like Derrick Bell and Kimberlé Crenshaw, CRT was designed to explore how laws and legal institutions maintain and reproduce racial inequalities, even when those laws appear "neutral."[85]

But in today's performative politics, CRT has been rebranded by reactionaries as the one-size-fits-all villain responsible for everything from white guilt to your child coming home with *questions* about Rosa Parks. Think of it this way: CRT is the invisible ink conservatives claim is being written into your kids' coloring books, designed to indoctrinate them with dangerous ideas like *history happened* and *race still matters.*

What It Says (That Scares People):
- Racism isn't just individual acts of meanness—it's baked into systems.
- Legal and cultural neutrality often maintains inequity.
- Lived experiences of marginalized people have evidentiary value.[86]
- Colorblindness isn't the goal—it's a dodge.

What Critics *Pretend* It Says:
- All white people are evil.
- Your second grader must now apologize for slavery before snack time.
- America is evil, and your Founding Fathers were just racist landlords with wigs.

Cultural Impact: CRT has become the scapegoat for a national identity crisis. It's less about theory and more about the *theater* of grievance politics—an easy applause line for campaigns, a deflection from real policy, and a tool for controlling the curriculum.[87] It's not being taught in your elementary school, but banning it gives the illusion of "taking action."

In short, **CRT = Cultural Rhetorical Target.**

Cultural Impact: The Woke Strawman Is on Fire— and So Is Democracy

Woke has become the scapegoat for everything from inflation to infertility. When the pipes freeze in Texas? Blame the woke. When your favorite sitcom got canceled? Woke. When your son comes out? Woke. The twist: Dick isn't mad at "wokeness." He's angry at his own *irrelevance.* He doesn't want inclusion. He wants a participation trophy for simply existing in a world that's evolving without his permission.

```
RECEIPTS &
REALITY
CHECKS

Skeptic Discount .... $9.99
Cynicism Tax..... INCLUDED
Just Asking Fee ..... $1.99
Evidence ........ REQUIRED
Fallout ....... MEASURABLE

**NO REFUNDS ON REALITY**
```

Origins, Evolution, and Legislative Backlash Surrounding "Woke"[88]

- The term "woke" originated in Black communities as a call to stay aware of systemic injustice.
- A 2023 Pew study found **over 60% of Americans believe "woke" is now used primarily as a political insult**, not a meaningful term.
- More than 300 bills were introduced in 2022–2025 to restrict DEI, CRT, or gender-inclusive content in schools, often citing "woke ideology" as justification.

Truth Decay and Weaponized Grievance

Truth used to be a cornerstone of democracy. Now, it's just one of several streaming options, and Dick's not subscribing. In the Orange Era, the lines between church, state, and stupidity have become so thoroughly blurred that even Google Maps struggles to find a clear route. Reality is no longer a shared space—it's a personalized algorithm, fine-tuned to Dick's paranoia and curated by conspiracy entrepreneurs with YouTube channels and vitamin side hustles.

We are now living in the *United States of Vibe Check*. If Dick feels it's true, it must be. He feels:

- Vaccines are poisonous.
- Elections are rigged.
- Trans people are a threat to the republic.
- Drag queens are CIA operatives funded by George Soros.

He can't cite sources—but he can cite "something I saw on Facebook." He can't define "Marxist"—but he's pretty sure his barista is one.

This isn't misinformation. This is a delusion with a search bar. And when those delusions get pushback? Dick doubles down. Because when your identity is built on grievance, truth is the enemy. Dick's not engaging in civic discourse—he's engaging in **emotional terrorism**. He doesn't want answers. He wants a fight. And the louder he yells, the more he feels like he matters.

Cultural Impact: Truth on Mute, Rage on Repeat

- Facts are now considered partisan weapons.
- Expertise is labeled as elitist bias.
- Science is agenda-driven propaganda, unless it supports erectile dysfunction meds or cryptocurrency.

We have entered a culture where grievances aren't just normalized—they're monetized. Politicians, pundits, and podcasters rake in millions by peddling fear to people who treat truth like a suggestion and empathy like a threat.

Politics, Polarization, and the Erosion of Trust[89]

- A 2023 AP-NORC poll found that **43% of Americans believe "politics often influence facts."**
- Over **70% of Republicans in 2024 said they believed the 2020 election was stolen**, despite no evidence and dozens of failed court challenges.
- MIT research found that **false political news spreads 70% faster** than factual stories on Twitter/X.
- According to Pew (2024), **67% of Americans say political polarization has made it harder to have conversations across party lines.**
- Over **60% of Republicans** and **55% of Democrats** say the *other side* threatens the country's "very existence."
- **Civic engagement among Gen Z** is higher than ever—but so is **dis-**

trust in institutions, with most saying they get news from "creators" over traditional outlets.

We're Not a Nation—We're a Stadium

America didn't just polarize. It branded itself into **teams**:

- Wearers of red hats chant "Let's go Brandon!" like it's scripture.
- Wavers of rainbow flags throw mutual aid pop-ups and are accused of domestic terrorism.
- Every handshake feels like a loyalty test.
- Every conversation is a prelude to a Fox News chyron.

Civic trust? Vaporized.

Shared reality? Deleted faster than a vaccine post on Truth Social.

Democracy isn't about debate anymore. It's about dunking on the other side—bonus points if you can do it with a meme, a gun, or a government subpoena.

The Rise of the Political Influencer Class

Political power meant writing laws, building coalitions, or—God forbid—*reading a policy brief*. Yet, in 2025, all you need is a webcam, a Wi-Fi signal, and enough rage to fry a circuit board. Welcome to the age of the political influencer, where governance takes a back seat to branding, and democracy is just a content strategy.

Grifters, Talking Heads, and Rage Merchants

Forget senators and scholars. The real architects of the culture war now wear ring lights, push discount codes, and post "truth bombs" in between ad reads for survival seeds and testosterone gummies. These aren't journalists. They're rage merchants—peddling paranoia for profit and likes. They call themselves "truth-tellers," but they traffic in outrage clickbait. They claim they're for "the people," but they charge $19.99 per month for access to *premium conspiracies*. Their platforms aren't about informing. They're about *inflaming*.

These aren't movements. They're media empires disguised as ideology. And the grift? It's as transparent as it is lucrative:

- "The government is lying to you—buy my supplements."
- "They want to silence you—subscribe to my exclusive Substack where I scream into the void."
- "America is under attack—use code 'PATRIOT20' for 20% off tactical toothpaste."

This isn't civic engagement. This is QVC for cultural collapse.

Tucker, Candace, and the Monetization of Division

Ahhhh… the holy trinity of the outrage-industrial complex: Tucker Carlson. He left Fox News and rebranded as a "rogue truth slinger"—but really, he's just a walking smirk with a script. He doesn't report the news. He manufactures narrative arcs. If reality doesn't fit, he reshapes it until it screams "deep state." His show is less journalism and more *Mad Libs for men afraid of pronouns*.

Candace Owen—Part political pundit, part culture war influencer, part walking contradiction. She claims to love free speech—until someone disagrees with her. Her brand is *antagonize, monetize, repeat*. She's built a career out of being the exception that white conservatives point to when they're saying something racist. She doesn't want to win debates. She wants engagement metrics. And rage is the fastest algorithm on the internet.

Cultural Impact: Democracy Becomes a Side Hustle

- Policy debates are now podcast segments.
- Congressional testimony is just a viral clip in waiting.
- And presidential candidates release campaign merch before policy platforms.

In this new political ecosystem, attention equals influence. And the truth? The truth is whatever gets the most clicks. Parasocial relationships replace civic trust with pundits. Political education is outsourced to influencers who failed civics but passed meme school. This is how you get a generation that knows more about Ben Shapiro's wife than the Bill of Rights.

Influence > Institutions: How Social Media Personalities Are Reshaping Political Power

- According to Pew (2024), **42% of young adults say they get their political information from influencers** rather than news outlets.
- A 2023 Axios study found that **right-wing influencers consistently outperform elected officials** in reach and engagement on major platforms.
- Media Matters reports that **Tucker Carlson's independent show reached over 150 million views across alt-tech platforms in its first 60 days post-Fox** (2024).

The Decline of Shared Reality

Remember when Americans could at least agree on the sky being blue, or that *two plus two = four*? Cute. That's over. In 2025, we're not just divided by opinion—we're separated by reality itself.

- You say "fact." Dick says "hoax."
- You say "data." Dick says "deep state."
- You say "insurrection." Dick says "passionate tourism."

Fragmented Media = Fragmented Nation

We no longer consume news. We curate narratives. We don't have information ecosystems—we have ideological vending machines:

- Fox News sells nationalism with a side of gallbladder inflammation.
- MSNBC sells hope sprinkled with passive-aggressive despair.
- TikTok sells ADHD-driven rage edits with royalty-free conspiracy music.
- Facebook? It's just your uncle reposting a photo of Nancy Pelosi eating children from 2016.

Everyone's watching a different show, quoting a different constitution, and swearing their version is the only one with God's endorsement. The result? A nation full of people who think they're better informed than ever—and who have never been more manipulated.

Why Can't We Even Agree on What's Real Anymore?

Because reality is no longer consensus-based. It's personalized. Privatized. Monetized.

Thanks to algorithms, your worldview is no longer shaped by dialogue— it's shaped by click behavior and corporate rage optimization.

- Believe the Earth is flat? You'll get content to prove it.
- Think Bill Gates is microchipping your dog? There's a 9-part docuseries for that.
- Want to believe climate change is a Chinese hoax? Here's an AI-generated scientist in a lab coat named "Dr. Liberty Freedom."

This isn't ignorance. It's **engineered unreality**. A collective psychotic break in HD. Dick isn't "misinformed." He's been trained to believe that *any truth that challenges his comfort is an attack.* And he has a buffet of podcasts, pundits, and pastors ready to confirm that gut feeling and market it back to him with a promo code.

We've traced the hissy fit back to its powdered-wig roots, through its midlife crisis in the suburbs, and into its golden age on AM radio. But tantrums don't stay confined to the playpen—they eventually spill into the wiring of the whole system. Enter the Culture Crash. This isn't just about bad politics or messy headlines. It's about how America's operating system—our institutions, media, and even our attention spans—got hacked by hissy fits and hot takes. What used to be debate is now performance, what used to be disagreement is now a brand, and what used to be governance is now just content.

CHAPTER 4

The Culture Crash: How America's Operating System Got Hacked by Hissy Fits and Hot Takes

The Hissy Fit Strategy: Dick, You're Being Played

I t shouldn't be surprising that America has always run on an operating system—a clunky, buggy code hidden under fireworks, freedom fries, and *Dick and Jane* readers whispering "good citizenship" while selling you suburban conformity like it's a Girl Scout cookie you can't refuse.

But let's get real: the architecture of American culture was never just about baseball and apple pie. It was about obedience and quiet compliance—unless you were throwing a tantrum for the "right" reasons. Now, that tantrum *is* the system.

Who Benefits?

- **The Power Brokers:** Politicians, media moguls, and billionaire lobbyists love hissy fits because chaos keeps you distracted while they rewrite the fine print in the tax codes and voting laws.
- **Culture War Grifters:** From cable news hosts to rage-podcasters, your outrage is their currency. The more you scream at school board meetings, the higher their ad revenue.
- **The Nostalgia Dealers:** Those selling you the lie that America was "great" when it looked like a *Dick and Jane* page—white, male-led, and

everyone else in supporting roles.

The hissy fit strategy evolved over time:

- **Silent Generation & Boomers:** Taught to see obedience as virtue, they passed down cultural fragility wrapped in patriotism.
- **Gen X:** Handed sarcasm and distrust, but no structural blueprint for change.
- **Millennials & Gen Z:** Exposed the cracks, but often funneled rebellion into hashtags and curated activism, commodified by brands faster than you can say "late-stage capitalism."

Each generation added a patch to the system, but none of them fixed the core code.

What Is the Damage?

- **Truth vs. Feels:** Facts are optional; feelings are monetized. It's easier to sell outrage than nuance.
- **Cultural Fragmentation:** Every algorithm feeds you a custom hissy fit buffet, ensuring no one can agree on reality.
- **Weaponized Nostalgia:** The *Dick and Jane* fantasy fuels culture wars, with books being banned that challenge the script.
- **Economic Stagnation:** While Dick yells, wealth consolidates at the top, and democracy sells piece by piece to the highest bidder.
- **Civic Decay:** Civic duty is replaced with partisan cosplay, voting replaced with performative memes, and real accountability replaced with hashtags and boycotts that last a news cycle.

The Bottom Line?

America's operating system didn't just get hacked—it got *upgraded* into a profit-driven and power-hungry factory for chaos. Dick, you're not the hero of the story. You're the pawn, paying cable bills to be outraged while your democracy is auctioned off in the background.

And the punchline? The system runs exactly as designed—one hissy fit at a time.

America Culture's Operating System Error: Not a Glitch—The Feature

The Buggy Empire That Swears It's Running Just Fine

The American operating system isn't broken—it's doing exactly what it was coded to do: boot up white supremacy, install fear-based politics, run nationalism.exe, and crash every time equity tries to update. This isn't a malfunction. It's the **default setting.** From the founding code written by wig-wearing beta bros in powdered stockings to the latest patches disguised as "reform," the American Cultural Operating System (ACOS) has been stuck in a perpetual loop of glitches disguised as features. It's less MacBook, more malfunctioning Commodore 64—but with fireworks.

SYSTEM OVERVIEW: AMERICAN.EXE BUILT ON BUGS, MARKETED AS FREEDOM

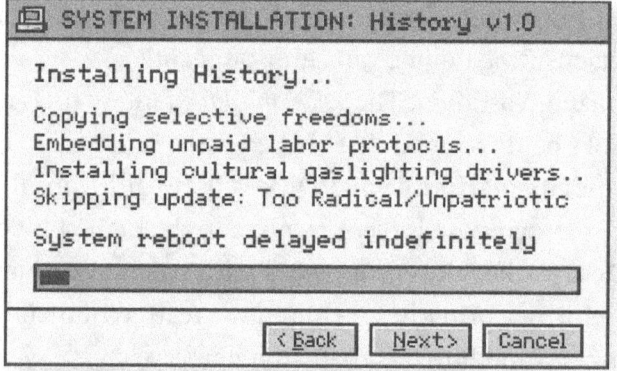

1. SYSTEM INSTALLATION : *History v1.0*

- **Origin Protocols:** "All men are created equal" came preinstalled, with a race, gender, and landowner clause buried in the terms and conditions.
- **Slave Code Extensions:** Embedded in early builds, ensured wealth accumulation required unpaid labor and cultural gaslighting.
- **Legacy Mode:** Still running because every update is labeled "too radical" or "unpatriotic."

Error 1776: Freedom not found for 95% of the population.

2. `Culture Coding`: *Algorithm of American Identity*

- **Programmed Values:** Individualism, exceptionalism, bootstrap theory.
- **User Input Mismatch:** Social progress prompts culture lag, resulting in panic loops (see: 1964, 1994, 2016).
- **Viral Bugs:** "Wokeness," "cancel culture," and "patriotism" repackaged to distract from real issues.

Pop-Up Alert: Your discomfort with systemic injustice has been reported to HR (Heritage Revisionism).

3. `RELIGION.DLL`: *Faith-Based Firewall*

- **Function:** Prevents logic, empathy, and sex education from launching.
- **Updates:** The Religion module is now deeply integrated into the concept of nationalism. Flag cross-merging is a feature, not a bug.
- **Evangelical Mode:** Auto-launches when women, LGBTQ+ rights, or evolution are detected.

Warning: SeparationOfChurchAndState.exe is running in the background but hasn't been active since 1980.

4. `LEGISLATION.BAT`: *Laws That Look Like Patches*

- **Patch Notes:** New policies are introduced every few years, but they don't address the root issues—instead, they make the screen look more diverse.
- **Access Control:** Available primarily to lobbyists, billionaires, and senators' nephews.
- **Firewall Loopholes:** Filibuster script, gerrymander tools, and "voter integrity" modules ensure outdated laws stay unchallenged.

Reminder: System laws still referencing "Negro labor" exist in subfolders. Nobody wants to delete them—just "archive."

5. `POLITICAL_LEADERSHIP.CFG`: *Political Theater Admin Privileges with No Accountability*

- **Permissions:** Can override all moral fail-safes. Often runs on ego-based machine learning.

- **Scripted Responses:** "Thoughts and prayers," "Let's have a bipartisan discussion," and "This is not who we are" (spoiler: it is).
- **Presidential AI:** Now fully capable of governing via tweet, slogan, or cognitive dissonance.

User Joe45 has entered God Mode. Democracy is not found.

6. THE_BACKLASH_MACHINE.EXE: *Legacy Feature Still Running*

- **Triggers:** Civil rights, feminism, immigration, progress in general.
- **Response:** Perform a hard reset to the "golden era" settings. Usually involves flag merch, moral panic, and book bans.
- **Latest Version:** Now includes social media bots, school board tantrums, and AR-15 cosplay at Target.

System Message: Your progress has activated the grievance module. Expect nationwide lag.

7. CITIZENS.INI: *The End Users and the Hissy Fit*

- **Split Demographic:** One group thinks they're running the system. The other is trying to rewrite it. Most are buffering.
- **Default Settings:** Misinformed, overworked, polarized. Crave change but fear updates.
- **Actions:** Vote, rage-scroll, repost memes, binge dystopian TV shows while living in one.

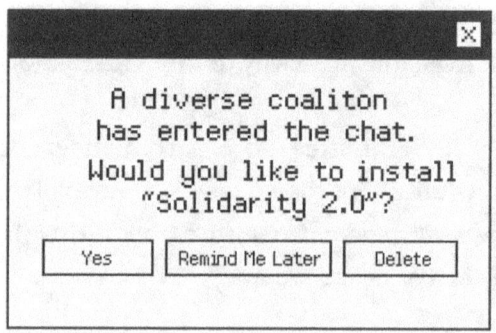

A diverse coaliton
has entered the chat.
Would you like to install
"Solidarity 2.0"?

| Yes | Remind Me Later | Delete |

SYSTEM STATUS: *Terminally Glitched. Emotionally Monetized. Culturally Divided.DOM*

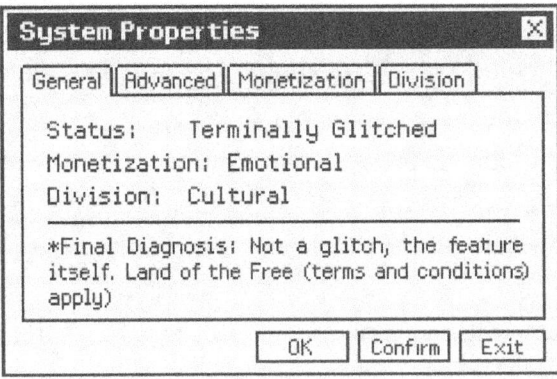

Final Diagnosis? It's not a glitch. It's the feature. We didn't inherit a system in need of a reboot. We inherited one that was never designed for us to log in.

But hey—at least the boot screen still says: **"Land of the Free."** *(terms and conditions apply)*

CRITICAL SYSTEM ERRORS

- **Error 001:** "All men are created equal" came with fine print. Slavery and genocide weren't bugs—they were features. Equity attempts are flagged as malware.
- **Error 002:** Tried deleting "Manifest Destiny," but Texas blocked it. We just rebranded imperialism as "freedom."
- **Error 003:** Political Theater.exe stuck in infinite loop. Congress is reality TV where the villain always wins.
- **Error 004:** Economy.dll missing middle class. Trickle-down = drip torture while the 1% gaslights everyone else.
- **Error 005:** Religion hijacked by Christian nationalism. Church-State firewall disabled: Now, "What Would Jesus Deregulate?"
- **Error 006:** Culture Wars virus active. Flags for sale, critical thinking flagged as "woke," Facebook moms blocking updates.
- **Error 007:** Citizens. Morality not found. Bots, Karens, and angry uncles

replaced civic discourse, and 42% won't install democracy updates if pronouns are included.

Here's how it works:
- Progress has installed new functions (e.g., civil rights, marriage equality).
- Backlash hits "restore to previous version."
- Politicians upload fear-based firmware.
- Citizens panic-click "Agree" without reading the terms and conditions.
- Repeat until the planet overheats or the Constitution gets rewritten by a PAC.

Fatal Error: Nation Divided by Zero: We attempted to run "UnitedStates.v2," but the system crashed at the log-in screen. It turns out that you can't divide everything by race, class, and party and still expect the machine to function. The code is fracturing. The processor's fried. And the backup plan? "Thoughts and prayers."

System Error Impact

Every demographic in America is under attack—but not in the ways some political soundbites suggest. The truth is, no group is immune to the rising tides of cultural tension, misinformation, or institutional backlash. While some claim persecution where there is merely progress, others face genuine systemic challenges, and together, it creates a national mood of siege, suspicion, and polarization.

- **Young Americans** face mounting economic precarity. Millennials and Gen Z are struggling under the weight of crushing student debt, a housing market that has priced them out, and declining social mobility.[90a] Many feel their futures have been mortgaged by previous generations' inaction on climate and economic inequality.
- **Older adults** face a different form of marginalization—ageism. AARP (2021) reports that nearly 78% of older workers have seen or experienced age discrimination in the workplace.[91] Politically, they're often portrayed as either outdated or out of touch, despite their continued civic engagement and economic influence.

- **Women's rights** continue to be a legislative battleground. From restrictions on reproductive health to wage gaps and underrepresentation in leadership roles, American women are contending with both cultural regression and policy reversals.[92]
- **LGBTQ+ communities** are facing a surge in anti-trans and anti-queer legislation. Over 500 anti-LGBTQ+ bills were introduced in state legislatures in 2023 alone—many targeting youth healthcare and education.[93]
- **Religious minorities** face subtle and overt forms of discrimination. Muslim Americans report consistently higher levels of bias and profiling, and antisemitic hate crimes have surged in recent years.[94]
- **Rural Americans** are often economically and digitally isolated, with limited access to healthcare, broadband, and upward mobility. Despite popular narratives, rural communities face higher rates of poverty and opioid addiction, coupled with being politically stereotyped.[95]
- White Americans: Facing Hardship, Not Erasure:
- **Economic Hits:** Deindustrialization and wage stagnation have gutted many white working-class communities, fueling "deaths of despair."[96]
- **Rural Decline:** White rural areas often lack access to healthcare, retraining, and internet services, resulting in poorer outcomes across education, employment, and health.[97]
- **Cultural Whiplash:** Many white Americans, especially those without degrees, feel left behind by cultural shifts, turning to grievance politics instead of progress.[98]
- **But Here's What It's *Not*:** White Americans are **not systematically discriminated** against based on race. They still hold the majority of leadership positions across government, business, and media. The perception of being "under attack" is often fueled not by material oppression, but by **the loss of *unquestioned dominance*—**a loss that feels personal but isn't persecution.

The takeaway? **No one demographic owns victimhood**. Every group is grappling with the consequences of an overwhelmed, outdated system that reacts poorly to rapid change. What differs is how that hardship is weaponized, politicized, or ignored through systemic discrimination.

We're not in a war between left and right. We're in a battle between denial and adaptation. And the sooner we admit that everyone's got skin in the game, the sooner we can start writing a better future for all.

Systemic Discrimination

A driver for cultural chaos, which often goes unchecked. Merriam-Webster does not have a definition for systemic discrimination. However, from a legal sense, systemic discrimination can be described as patterns of behavior, policies, or practices that are part of the structures of an organization, and which create or perpetuate disadvantages for racialized persons.[99]

A Deeper Look: Systematic Discrimination

A polite academic term for "the game was rigged before you even showed up." This isn't just about one racist manager, sexist policy, or homophobic law—this is the whole system *working precisely as designed* to ensure certain groups always start ten spaces behind and get penalized for passing Go. It's not just discrimination—it's **institutional muscle memory.**

What It Means:
- Patterns of exclusion, bias, and inequity are *built into* the fabric of laws, practices, and cultural norms.
- It happens *regardless* of individual intentions.
- It's the difference between stepping on a LEGO (ouch) and realizing your entire floor is made of LEGOs and no one gave you shoes.

Examples of Systematic Discrimination:
- Black families were being redlined into poverty while white families got GI Bill-fueled suburbs and generational wealth.[100]
- LGBTQ+ folks are being denied healthcare, then blamed for higher suicide rates.
- Disabled individuals are navigating public infrastructure designed for Olympic gymnasts.
- Native Americans are being pushed off their land and then punished for being "underrepresented in entrepreneurship."

Key Features:
- **Durability:** It doesn't fade with time—it evolves (looking at you, al-

gorithmic bias).

- **Deniability:** It thrives on plausible deniability—"But we don't *mean* to discriminate."
- **Documentation:** Yes, there are receipts—and yes, they're centuries old.[101]

Systematic Discrimination = Oppression on Autopilot.

It's not broken. It's functioning exactly how it was engineered—just not for everyone.

Force Quit or Reboot? America's cultural OS isn't glitching—it's performing exactly as designed. We don't need a patch. We need a complete reinstall with ethical source code, universal access, and no fine print. Until then, keep your emotional support pillow nearby and remember pressing "Like" won't save the Republic, but it might fool the algorithm long enough for you to survive the next update. The OS drives cultural themes for today and tomorrow, reshaping the narrative on cultural themes of the past.

Cultural Themes in 2025 (Spoiler: It's Not Thriving. It's Spiraling.)

Welcome to 2025 America—where critical thinking is a crime of suspicion, fiction is the national currency, and culture wars are the only war half the country has the stamina to fight.

This isn't a decline. This is manufactured decay, marketed as "patriotism."

- **Facts?** Optional. Conspiracy theories have a faster turnaround time than medical results, and emotional hissy fits are now considered "personal research." We're living in the Age of Rage Googling, where *"I heard it from a guy on TikTok"* carries more weight than a century of scientific consensus.
- **Critical Thinking?** Dead on arrival. Asking questions gets you branded "woke," "subversive," or worst of all—"academic." Meanwhile, parroting slogans you read on a T-shirt at a monster truck rally is considered "independent thought."
- **Policy?** Culture war cosplay. A real-time hissy fit competition has

replaced actual governance: If it sounds angry enough, traumatized enough, or vaguely religious enough, it becomes a bill. We're not legislating reality—we're legislating *vibes*.

- **Cancel Culture?** Weaponized projection. The same folks screaming about being "canceled" have built entire economies on boycotting books, movies, teachers, brands, pronouns, and anything that smells like empathy. (Also, no one gets canceled faster than a librarian suggesting Black authors exist.)
- **Education?** Target practice. Schools are no longer places where one can learn. They're battlegrounds where "critical race theory" is a scarier threat than climate collapse and where reading *Maus* is treated like passing out radical pamphlets at Sunday school.
- **History?** Retconned for fragile feelings. (*Retconned*—rewritten after the fact to protect fragile feelings.) We're not teaching students what happened, but how to avoid feeling bad about it. The goal isn't the truth. The goal is comfort. And comfort has a body count.
- **Freedom?** Rebranded as "the right never to be challenged." Freedom of speech? Sure—as long as it's speech the majority already agrees with. Freedom of religion? Absolutely—as long as it's the right religion (read: Protestant nationalism with a Gadsden flag bumper sticker).
- **National Mood?** Gaslit, gated, and heavily armed. America isn't a melting pot. It's a potluck where half the guests demand ketchup be classified as a vegetable and storm out when they see hummus.

The US isn't experiencing a culture war. We're experiencing a full-blown reality bankruptcy. The truth is too complicated. Thinking is too hard. Progress feels like persecution. And the louder you scream, the more "patriotic" you get labeled.

America isn't in a culture war—it's in reality bankruptcy. We traded critical thinking for comfort food, facts for vibes, and called it freedom while the house quietly burned down.

Don't believe me? Keep reading, because here comes the evidence. Today:

- School boards ban books because *"feelings were hurt."*
- State legislatures argue that diversity and empathy are "leftist plots."

- Adults have emotional meltdowns over M&Ms, Barbie movies, and the mere *existence* of nonbinary teenagers.
- Politicians run campaigns based entirely on who they *promise* to exclude from fundamental rights.
- The sitting US president muses out loud about taking over Denmark and Canada.

America's Slide: From Pandemic Fallout to Civic Breakdown[102]

1. **Life Expectancy Decline**

   Fact: US life expectancy *fell* to 76.1 years in 2021—the lowest since 1996—primarily due to COVID-19, drug overdoses, and suicide.

   Why it matters: Most developed countries *have rebounded since the COVID-19 pandemic*. The US did not. It's a marker of systemic health, inequality, and despair.

2. **Record Drug Overdose Deaths**

   Fact: Over **109,000** Americans died from drug overdoses in 2022 alone. Synthetic opioids like fentanyl account for two-thirds.

   Why it matters: This isn't an addiction crisis—it's a collapse of mental health infrastructure, community supports, and purpose.

3. **Historic Decline in Trust**

   Fact: Trust in institutions—such as government, media, and education—has *plummeted*. Only 20% of Americans trust the federal government to do what is right most of the time.

   Why it matters: Trust is the bedrock of democratic cooperation. The US is now a "low-trust society."

4. **Youth Mental Health Crisis**

   Fact: In 2023, *42% of high school students in the US* reported feeling sad or hopeless. For girls, the rate jumped to 57%.

Why it matters: A generation in distress is not a blip—it's a cultural alarm bell.

5. **Sharp Rise in Book Bans and Censorship**
   Fact: Over **4,200 unique book titles** were banned across US schools in 2022–2023, the highest in recorded history.
   Why it matters: Censorship is not about protection but control and cultural regression.

6. **Political lik Normalized**
   Fact: As of 2024, *23% of Americans* say political violence is sometimes justified. That number has *tripled* since 2010.
   Why it matters: This isn't polarization. It's the pre-authoritarian cultural breakdown.

7. **Decline in Civic Knowledge**
   Fact: Only **47% of Americans** could name all three branches of government in 2023. Over one-third couldn't name a single one.
   Why it matters: A democracy can't function when the populace doesn't understand it.

8. **Record Gun Deaths Among Children**
   Fact: Firearms became the **leading cause of death for children and teens** in the US in 2022.
   Why it matters: In no other high-income country is this true.

9. **Plummeting Civic Engagement**
   Fact: Volunteerism, community group participation, and religious attendance have all sharply declined—down by nearly 30% since 1999, accelerating post-2020.
   Why it matters: Civic decline is a form of cultural death. When people stop showing up, societies unravel.

10. **Increasing Educational Hostility**
    Fact: 36 states introduced bills to restrict what schools can teach about race, gender, or US history between 2021 and 2024.
    Why it matters: Bootlegged history breeds ignorance and division—not unity.

While we are sharing facts, let's examine the ever-widening wealth gap in the United States, driven by several interrelated factors that disproportionately benefit the wealthiest Americans while leaving lower- and middle-income households increasingly behind.

Evidence of a Growing Wealth Gap

- **Top 10% Hold Majority of Wealth**: As of the second quarter of 2024, the top 10% of US households controlled 67% of the nation's wealth, averaging $6.9 million per household. In contrast, the bottom 50% held only 2.5% of total household wealth, with an average of $51,000 per household.[103]
- **Tax Policies Favor the Wealthy**: The 2017 Tax Cuts and Jobs Act significantly reduced tax burdens for high-income households. In 2025, households in the top 1% are projected to save an average of $61,090 annually due to these tax cuts, while those in the bottom 60% will see average savings of less than $500.[104]
- **Intergenerational Wealth Transfer**: The ongoing "Great Wealth Transfer" is expected to pass $84.4 trillion from baby boomers to their heirs by 2045. Notably, 42% of this transfer will go to the wealthiest 1.5% of households, potentially exacerbating existing wealth disparities.[105]

Contributing Factors

- **Asset Appreciation**: The wealthiest Americans often have significant investments in stocks and real estate, which have appreciated substantially in recent years. This appreciation has disproportionately increased their net worth compared to those without such investments.[106]
- **Limited Access to Wealth-Building Tools**: Lower-income households often lack access to financial instruments such as retirement accounts or investment portfolios, which limits their ability to accumulate wealth over time.
- **Policy Decisions**: Tax policies and regulations have historically favored capital gains and inherited wealth, benefiting the affluent and making it more challenging for others to ascend economically.

Do I have your attention now? This leads me to ask: **What *would* make America great?** Because this ain't it.

If we strip away the political branding and look at the core of the question—*what would truly make America great*—the answer isn't about nostalgia, slogans, or returning to a mythical past. It's about rebuilding what's broken while boldly reimagining what greatness *should* look like in the 21st century.

Here's a no-nonsense, culture-forward breakdown of what would make America great:

- **Radical Investment in Education:** A nation that does not educate truthfully builds only myths and mediocrity. Not culture wars, not book bans. Real greatness requires critical thinkers, not ideologically sanitized citizens. Universal pre-K, free community college, teacher pay reform, and a curriculum grounded in truth—including our uncomfortable historical contradictions—are needed.

- **Reclaiming Civic Trust and Responsibility:** Great nations don't survive on rage-clicks and Twitter tribalism. Rebuilding civic trust means teaching civic responsibility, restoring transparency in governance, and demanding accountability from elected officials *and* citizens.

- **Universal Healthcare as a Human Right:** A truly great nation doesn't let its citizens go bankrupt over insulin or die waiting for care. Medicare for All? At the very least, a national commitment to affordable, accessible care and mental health services.

- **Living Wages and Economic Dignity:** Full-time work should not equal poverty. Greatness means economic systems that reward effort and uplift communities. Raise the minimum wage, close the wealth gap, and encourage worker ownership and ethical capitalism.

- **Humanizing Immigration:** America became "great" by embracing the world's talent, diversity, and courage. Greatness means policies rooted in humanity, not fear. Streamline citizenship. Embrace multilingualism. Treat immigrants as assets, not threats.

- **Gun Reform with Backbone:** No nation can claim greatness while its children are murdered in classrooms and nothing changes. Universal background checks. Red flag laws. An assault weapons ban. Mental health funding *and* gun safety must coexist.

- **Cultural Intelligence Over Cultural War:** Greatness isn't fragile. It doesn't panic over diversity or shout down "wokeness." It grows by *listening*, *adapting*, and *understanding*. Teach cultural literacy. End systemic exclusion. Build coalitions across differences, not divisions.

- **Restore the Arts, Science, and Public Discourse:** Stop starving creativity and discovery. Fund the arts. Invest in research. Create public forums that elevate *thought*, not *noise*.
- **Climate Courage, Not Denial:** Lead the world by example—not retreat. A great nation doesn't survive—it sustains. Green infrastructure, clean energy jobs, and a transition for workers.
- **Truth over Tribalism: Greatness starts when truth outweighs partisanship,** when we stop letting politics hijack facts and start demanding intellectual honesty—even when it's uncomfortable.

If we want to make America "great," we must define greatness not by volume or violence but by vision. We must not go backward; instead, we must have the courage **to move forward with equity, clarity, and confidence.**

The Birth of the Machine: Driving the Great American Hissy Fit

An ever-evolving, rage-fueled apparatus powered by white grievance, moral panic, and nostalgia for a time that never really existed. It activates whenever historically excluded groups gain even a whisper of power, autonomy, or airtime.

The Backlash Machine

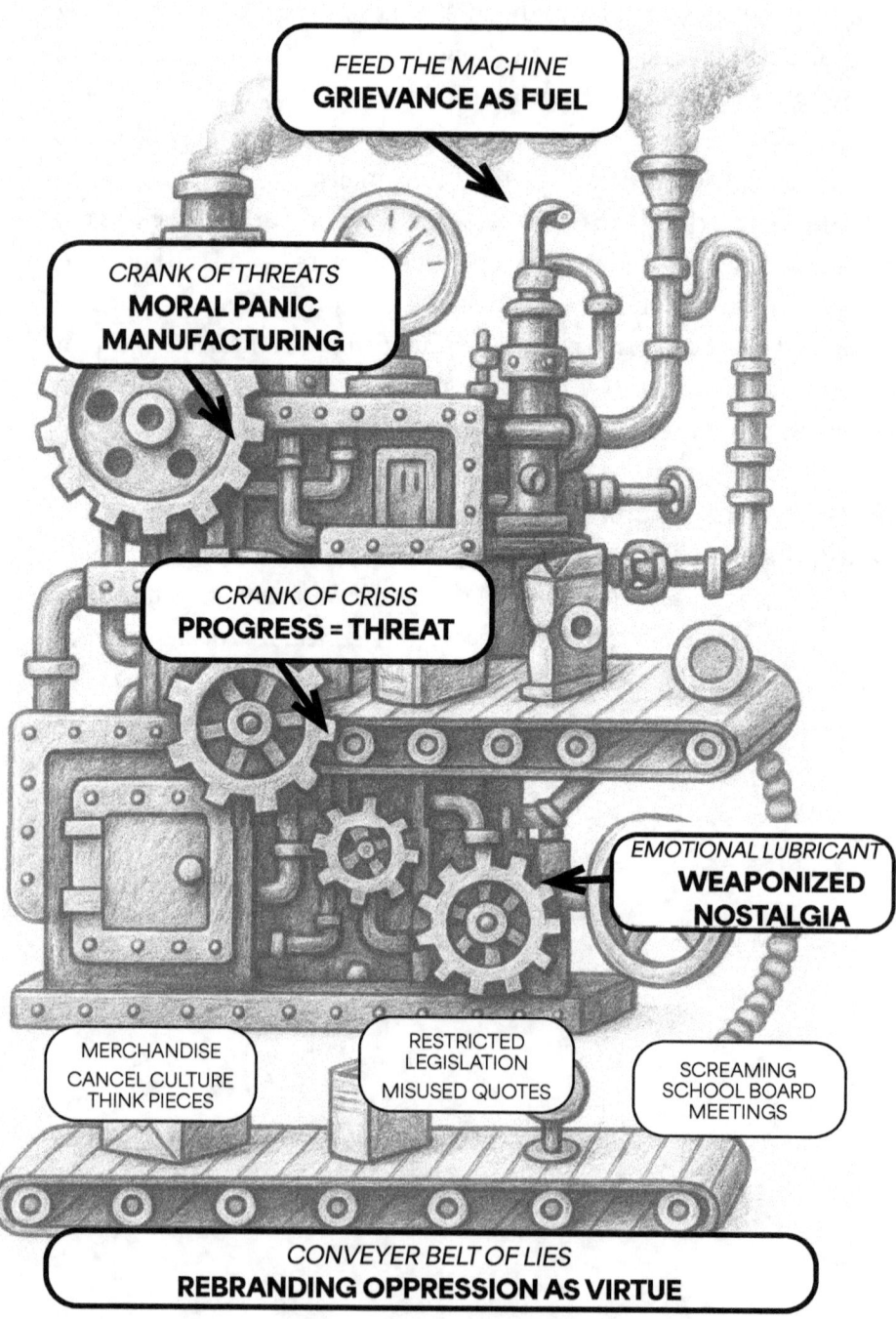

FEED THE MACHINE
GRIEVANCE AS FUEL

CRANK OF THREATS
MORAL PANIC MANUFACTURING

CRANK OF CRISIS
PROGRESS = THREAT

EMOTIONAL LUBRICANT
WEAPONIZED NOSTALGIA

MERCHANDISE
CANCEL CULTURE
THINK PIECES

RESTRICTED
LEGISLATION
MISUSED QUOTES

SCREAMING
SCHOOL BOARD
MEETINGS

CONVEYER BELT OF LIES
REBRANDING OPPRESSION AS VIRTUE

Core Driving Principles of the Backlash Machine:

- **Grievance as Fuel:** White discomfort, Christian fragility, and patriarchal entitlement are fed into the machine and refined into righteous outrage, ready for distribution via talk radio, cable news, and Facebook comment sections.
- **Moral Panic Manufacturing:** From rap lyrics to transgender teens, the machine can crank out a new "threat to civilization" every news cycle—with bonus points if it involves bathrooms, books, or Beyoncé.
- **Progress = Threat:** Any expansion of rights, visibility, or equality for marginalized communities is rebranded as an existential crisis for the status quo.
- **Weaponized Nostalgia:** Longing for a mythical past where "everything made sense" (i.e., straight white men were in charge, and no one asked them to share power) is the machine's emotional lubricant.
- **Rebranding Oppression as Virtue:** Whether it's "states' rights," "law and order," or "protecting children," the machine specializes in coating bigotry with a wholesome, apple pie-flavored shell.

Most Common Outcomes:

- Legislation designed to restrict someone else's freedom.
- Screaming school board meetings.
- Cancel culture think pieces by people with full-time media contracts.
- Misused Founding Father quotes.
- Merchandise.

What Fuels the Backlash Machine?

The Backlash Machine isn't fueled by logic, just the opposite. It doesn't run on data, empathy, or an honest day's reading. No, this beast is powered by something far more volatile: hissy fits in high definition, the weaponization of nostalgia, and a decades-long commitment to dumbing down America until critical thinking requires a permission slip.

The unsettling part is that the primary fuels of this machine are ignorance, tantrums, media, fear of *others*, and a persecution complex. What frustrates me the most is that many Americans are not victims of the Backlash Machine; they are helping to fuel it. It's easy to blame the pundits, the PACs, the politicians with flag pins and no soul—but the real tragedy? Americans are lining up to keep the tank full. They are clicking the rage headlines, sharing the bad-faith hot takes, and confusing outrage for engagement and misinformation for personality. They don't just feed the Machine—they worship it like it's the last gas station on the road to irrelevance. Because deep down, they feel the Backlash Machine offers them something terrifyingly comforting: the illusion that the past was perfect, the present is an attack, and the future is someone else's fault. All it asks is that we surrender complexity for certainty—and boy, do many comply.

How Is It Fueled Today?

The Great American Dumb-Down is now a fully funded, algorithmically optimized, multiplatform content strategy.

- Fox News & Friends: Replacing civics class with emotional support rage for dads who miss Ronald Reagan and don't trust pronouns.
- Social Media: Where a high school dropout with a ring light and an affiliate code can "debunk science" in under 30 seconds.
- YouTube Rabbit Holes: Because watching 19 hours of "Why Birds Aren't Real" is now considered "research."
- Politicians: Who say things like "I'm not a scientist, but I have a feeling…"—right before sponsoring a bill on climate policy.
- The Censorship-by-Hissy-Fit Crowd: Who scream "freedom of speech" while banning books they've never read and canceling teachers for mentioning the existence of slavery.

Media as Methamphetamine

Fox News, talk radio, rage-fueled Facebook groups—it's a buffet of grievance, available 24/7. The Backlash Machine doesn't require a power grid. It runs on algorithmic adrenaline. Every angry segment, every viral meltdown, every misquoted Founding Father is a jolt of fuel straight to the outrage engine. And don't worry—if the culture war seems to cool off, the Machine has a stockpile of reheatable leftovers:

- CRT panic (expired)
- Gas stove hysteria (lukewarm)
- "They're coming for your hamburgers" (still frozen, but usable)

Fear of "The Other" (Now in Ultra-HD)

This is the Machine's premium fuel: fear of change, fear of loss, and fear of people who don't look, love, or worship like you. The Machine thrives on a narrative where "real Americans" are constantly under siege—from immigrants, trans kids, climate activists, and pronouns. This isn't a disagreement. It's existential panic—fed to the public like a casserole of xenophobia and parental fear, baked at 450° on your aunt's Facebook wall.

Persecution Complex Premium

When people with power believe accountability is oppression, you get *hissy fit supremacy.*

Free speech now means "I can say racist things without consequences."

Religious freedom means "I get to dictate what other people do with their bodies."

And losing an election? That's proof the Deep State is messing with your yard signs.

The Machine spins victimhood into virtue. Everyone's a martyr—especially the guy with the 30-foot truck flag and seven felonies.

The Backlash Machine isn't breaking down. It's **revving up**—turbo-charged by disinformation, greased with performative morality, and steered by the least emotionally regulated among us. It doesn't need facts. It just needs friction. And as long as we keep mistaking privilege loss for persecution? It's not slowing down.

Who's the Target Audience?

Everyone is affected, but *some* were practically handcrafted in a midwestern Cracker Barrel to be *most susceptible.*

Primary Demographic:

- White men over 50 with strong opinions and weak browser security.
- People who still think "wokeness" is a disease you catch from oat milk.

- Folks who list "Common Sense" as a credential and think research means watching Joe Rogan on 1.5x speed.
- Dick, Doug, Chad, Kare, and Jane.

Collateral Damage:
- Teachers, librarians, scientists, and anyone who uses citations.
- Kids trying to learn history that doesn't begin with "Columbus discovered…"
- Voters who like democracy with their dinner.

Weaponized Ignorance

We didn't fall into this by accident. The dumbing-down of America is a feature, not a bug—a power-preserving tactic disguised as "just asking questions." When you suppress knowledge, you suppress power. When you replace inquiry with indignation, suddenly people are too busy screaming about drag queens to notice billionaires buying elections or laws quietly stripping their rights.

2025 Top 5 Backlash Machines

1. **Fox News:** *Where feelings are facts and facts are suspicious.*

   Fox News isn't just a network—it's the *emotional thermostat of conservative America*, stuck permanently on "meltdown." It turns marginalized people into existential threats, asks questions no one needs to answer (*Is empathy un-American?*), and gives prime-time slots to professional panic merchants. It doesn't report—it **reheats** outrage like a leftover casserole of white grievance and God-fearing capitalism.

   Primary Exports: Tuckerism, Wokeness Panic, and Gold Bar Ads During Insurrections.

2. **The Heritage Foundation:** *Crafting policy so regressive, it thinks the 1950s were too edgy.*

   The conservative think tank that writes the Republican Party's homework. It supplies the legal, economic, and cultural rationale for turning personal prejudice into public policy. Do you want a law banning books, bathrooms, or birth control? Heritage has a position paper and a PowerPoint.

Architects behind Project 2025—a road map to deconstruct democracy one moral panic at a time.

3. **The Federalist Society:** *Turning robes into armor for the culture war since 1982.*

   A network of lawyers and judges who've turned **originalism** into the judicial version of cosplay. They recruit young lawyers who can say, *"Madison never meant that"* with a straight face while gutting civil rights from behind a bench. Want to overturn decades of precedent? They've got a club for that.

   Alumni include most of the Supreme Court and at least two individuals named Brett who carry pocket Constitutions.

4. **The Moral Majority;** *When Jesus said love thy neighbor, He didn't mean the gay ones.*

   Founded by Jerry Falwell in 1979, this wasn't a religious revival—it was a political machine wrapped in scripture. Now manifested in groups such as Focus on the Family, the Family Research Council, and Parents Defending Education, they've mastered the art of turning piety into policy. Prayer in schools? Mandatory. Sex ed? Heresy. Trans kids? National security threat.

   Still driving votes, fundraising off fear, and defining morality by what makes them uncomfortable.

5. **Facebook (Meta):** *Where your aunt radicalizes herself between casserole recipes.*

   No longer just a social media platform, Facebook is the gasoline in the digital rage engine. Their algorithm learned early on that nothing keeps users engaged like fear, fury, and fake news. The more you react, the more you see—and suddenly, your uncle thinks Antifa is living in his garage.

   Study after study shows that misinformation thrives here, and fact-checks arrive slower than data over a dial-up modem.

If you keep the public confused, outraged, and proudly uninformed, you don't need to control the people. You need to control the Wi-Fi—the Hissy Fit: Emotional Combustion Engine.

At the core of the Backlash Machine is the tantrum transmission system, a finely tuned mechanism that converts minor inconveniences into apocalyptic rhetoric. Does a drag queen read a book? Launch a hearing. Does a college offer gender-neutral housing? Declare a constitutional crisis. Does a child learn that slavery wasn't a job training program? Start a PAC. These aren't policy responses. They're emotional expulsions, scaled for national broadcast and wrapped in patriotism.

The Great American Dumb-Down: Ignorance as Identity

The moment a student reads something that challenges the dominant narrative, such as the fact that Rosa Parks didn't just have tired feet or that climate change isn't a mood, they might start asking questions. And questions jam the gears of the Backlash Machine.

In the grand machinery of American backlash, there's one fuel source more reliable than oil, more potent than rage, and more abundant than hot takes on cable news: good old-fashioned, industrial-strength ignorance. The Backlash Machine doesn't want an educated population—it wants a confused one. It wants voters who think critical thinking means being skeptical of dictionaries, who believe STEM is a liberal hoax funded by George Soros, and who would sooner trust a podcast called *"Truth Hounds Unleashed"* than read a peer-reviewed study from researchers at an accredited university. In this system, ignorance isn't a gap to be filled—it's a badge of honor. And proudly worn.

Public education? That's enemy territory now. The Machine has spent decades gnawing at it like a dog with a chew toy soaked in taxpayer resentment. Ban the books. Demonize the teachers. Defund the libraries. Why? Studies show that more educated populations vote for policies supporting equity, science, and functioning democracies.[107] And we can't have that, can we?

Instead, we feed the public curated sound bites from cable hosts who think empathy is Marxist and logic is for coastal elites. We replace history with heritage. We slap patriotic education labels on sanitized textbooks that teach the Founding Fathers were infallible and the Civil Rights Movement was divisive. We frame teachers as indoctrinators and librarians as pornographers because nothing says liberty like **the government-mandated removal of information.**

They have successfully engineered a culture where cognitive laziness is framed as common sense. Doing your research means falling down a YouTube rabbit hole hosted by someone with no credentials but 700,000 subscribers. And who's benefiting? Not students. Not parents. Not the future. No, the only ones thriving are the politicians who count on confusion and the corporations that profit when we're too underinformed to ask what's really in the fine print—or the drinking water. Ignorance is not just a condition. It's a commodity. And business is booming.

The Great Curriculum Purge: Erasing Facts for Fragile Feelings

History Class: Now With 70% More Delusion, 0% Critical Thinking! At one time, school was where you learned uncomfortable truths. Now? It's where fragile egos go for spa treatments. In the Orange Era, America decided that history wasn't something you studied—it was something you *sanitized.*

Welcome to the **Great Curriculum Purge**—the first educational movement sponsored by collective insecurity and powered by a Fox News viewing schedule, geared for the population that wants to wave the Constitution at every turn but uses it more like toilet paper.

Dick didn't want his grandkids to feel "bad" about slavery. Jane didn't want her daughter to hear the word "queer" without a parental permission slip and two notary stamps. So they screamed. And state legislatures, desperate for votes and validation, answered the call like the worst customer service reps on Earth.

Bills like Florida's "Stop WOKE Act"[108] and Texas's "Patriotic Education" guidelines bulldozed into school curricula like a drunk uncle at Thanksgiving dinner—loud, embarrassing, and convinced they're doing the Lord's work. [109]

- Critical race theory? **Banned.**
- Gender identity discussions? **Banned.**
- Books featuring anyone darker than a Starbucks latte or gayer than a Baptist choir solo? **Gone faster than Dick's youthful hairline.**

This wasn't curriculum reform. It was emotional landscaping: pulling up every inconvenient fact like weeds in the suburbs of self-delusion. Budget cuts gut the public education system and stem from ideological panic. A curriculum shaped not by scholars or educators, but by politicians chasing clickbait laws and parents who think "CRT" stands for "Children Reading Trouble."

The Cultural Impact: Truth became a dangerous thing. Lies became mandatory.

- History units about civil rights? "Too divisive."
- Books by Black authors? "Controversial."
- Lessons about Indigenous genocide? "Unpatriotic."

Even the Smithsonian Institution is being bullied to sanitize history. Meanwhile, teachers became villains overnight, treated like Marxist sleeper agents instead of exhausted professionals barely paid enough to afford the gas to their second job.

And the kids?

- Graduating dumber.
- Less empathetic.
- More vulnerable to conspiracy theories than a QAnon grandma with an Etsy store.

Knowledge was replaced with vibes. Inquiry was replaced with indoctrination. Education wasn't education anymore—it was nostalgia maintenance.

> *"Imagine being so terrified of a history book that you pass a law banning feelings"*
> —SALLY *handing out banned books like Halloween candy.*

By 2026, America's cultural literacy test will look like a BuzzFeed quiz written by someone who thinks Thomas Jefferson invented Chick-fil-A.

- Students still won't be able to define "Jim Crow," but they will tell you how "woke culture" ruined *Paw Patrol.*
- Kids will know more about Captain America's backstory than the American Revolution.
- Textbooks will explain Rosa Parks as a lady who "got tired one day," with zero mention of systemic racism or the Montgomery Bus

Boycott's year-long strategy.

And when college professors try to assign, say, *The 1619 Project* or *Beloved*? Cue the lawsuits, legislative hissy fits, and parents fainting into their tote bags. In short: We turned education into emotional daycare for Dick's fragile self-esteem. Shame on America.

How The Great American Dumb-Down Happened: An Autopsy of National Brain Fog

Let's rewind to when America first decided that critical thinking was optional and "my gut tells me that" became a legitimate research method. It began when we decided that education wasn't an investment but a burden. The first signs? Cutting arts programs in public schools so we could afford more stadiums, banning "controversial" books to protect kids from ideas, and replacing librarians with hall monitors trained in Google.

Then came the holy trinity of intellectual doom:

1. Standardized Testing—Because nothing fosters curiosity like sitting under fluorescent lighting for eight hours straight and bubbling in answers.
2. No Child Left Behind—A policy that ensured every child technically passed, even if they thought the Civil War was about a disagreement over brunch.
3. Cable News—Turning facts into opinions and opinions into full-blown shouting matches.

Somewhere between *Schoolhouse Rock* and QAnon TikToks, America decided it was more fun to feel right than to be informed.

The Decline of Critical Thinking: Where Facts Go to Die

Once upon a time, facts had weight. Data mattered. Sources were cited, and logic was something more than just a setting on a washing machine. But in the Age of Outrage, critical thinking isn't just in decline—it's on life support, surrounded by influencers, conspiracy peddlers, and people who think "research" means watching a TikTok.

This isn't an intellectual gap—it's an epidemic of willful ignorance weaponized by those who confuse emotion with evidence and confidence with competence. We're not dealing with a shortage of information. We're dealing with a surplus of unqualified certainty.

Vibes have hijacked the American brain. Feeling angry? That must mean you're right. Upset about something you saw online? Congratulations—you're now an expert in epidemiology, constitutional law, and quantum physics. We've traded logic for limbic responses. As Kahneman (2011) outlines in *Thinking, Fast and Slow*, human decision-making is driven by two systems: the fast, emotional one and the slower, analytical one. MAGA culture, right-wing media, and online outrage farms have bet the house on System 1—emotionally reactive, instantly gratifying, and intellectually bankrupt.

Sally's Sanity:

"Critical thinking isn't optional—it's survival. If you're not questioning the narrative, you're swallowing someone else's script. And nine times out of ten, that script is written by the Dicks of the world who count on you being too distracted, too compliant, or too scared to push back."

—SALLY

The Dunning-Kruger Epidemic: Confident, Loud, and Dangerously Wrong

Welcome to the golden age of the uninformed alpha. The Dunning-Kruger effect, wherein the least competent individuals are the most confident in their abilities, is no longer a psychological curiosity. It's a prerequisite for YouTube's success and a feature of modern masculinity.[110] Who needs credentials when you've got charisma? Who needs truth when you've got volume? The less men know, the louder they say it—usually into a mic, surrounded by American flags, caffeine pills, and supplements they can't pronounce.

We are witnessing a renaissance of arrogance over accuracy. It's not just ignorance—it's ignorance with a platform. Because here's the raw truth:

critical thinking is a threat to fragile masculinity. It demands nuance, humility, and reflection—all things that patriarchy has coded as feminine or weak. Instead, they double down on dogma, drown in misinformation, and call it masculinity. More about that in chapter 6, but first let's take a look at the effects of a dumbed-down culture.

Dick's Hissy Fit: School Board Meeting: The "Woke Math" Chronicles

It's a Tuesday night in suburban America. Folding chairs. Fluorescent lighting. A dry-erase board that hasn't been erased since the Obama administration. Welcome to the Jefferson County Unified School District School Board Meeting—where democracy goes to be publicly embarrassed.

Enter Dick. Middle-aged. Slightly sunburned. Wearing a "Don't Tread on Me" shirt tucked unironically into cargo shorts. He's armed with a printed packet of selectively highlighted Facebook memes, a gallon-sized Dunkin' iced coffee, and the moral indignation of a man who thinks empathy is a communist plot.

The board chairperson, exhausted from two hours of debates about Chromebook charging stations, sighs and announces: "Next up—Dick Hendersen. He'll be speaking about... math?"

Dick approaches the mic like he's about to deliver the Sermon on the Mount. He clears his throat with the gravitas of a man who once watched a Jordan Peterson clip at 1.5x speed.

"First of all, I'd like to thank the board for the opportunity to expose what's happening to our children because I've seen the homework. I've seen it. And what they're calling math nowadays? It's not just numbers. It's ideology."

The room shifts. Confused, concerned, and mildly entertained.

"My son came home yesterday and told me that math is about understanding multiple pathways to an answer. MULTIPLE PATHWAYS?! Since when is there more than one way to divide a fraction?!"

Dick starts to pace. He's sweating now. From passion. Or too much caffeine. Possibly both.

*"And let me tell you what else I found in that textbook: a word problem about **Latisha** and **Jamal** sharing **avocados.** Avocados, people! Cultural infiltration. I checked the index—no problems about **Bobby** splitting **hamburgers**. That's not diversity. That's erasure."*

Someone coughs. A PTA mom starts filming.

*"They're turning math into a **feelings exercise**! My son was told his answer was **correct,** but that **how** he got there mattered, too. I didn't raise my boy to show his work—I raised him to WIN."*

A teacher in the back whispers, "It's a math standard."

Dick doubles down.

*"And don't even get me started on **percentages**. I saw a question where students had to calculate the wage gap. **THE WAGE GAP!** In a math problem! Do you know what I call that? PROPAGANDA DISGUISED AS PRE-ALGEBRA."*

He slams his folder shut for dramatic effect, spilling a page titled "Top 10 Signs Fractions are Indoctrinating Your Kid."

"In conclusion, this woke math is anti-American, anti-masculine, and frankly... anti-Dick. If we don't stop this now, next thing you know, our kids will be majoring in Pronoun Geometry. Thank you."

He sits down to a mixture of stunned silence, stifled laughter, and one clap from a guy in the back wearing wraparound sunglasses indoors.

The board chair clears her throat and deadpans, "Thank you, Mr. Hendersen. Up next, a presentation on how numbers work."

The moral of the story: When you've built your identity on always being right, even 2 + 2 = 4 starts to feel like an attack. Let's turn now to the influence of the internet and rage culture on Dick's hissy fit.

CHAPTER 5

The Internet, Algorithms, and Rage Culture

From chat rooms to conspiracy forums, the internet was a magical place where people waited 15 minutes for a cat video to buffer, flirted awkwardly in AOL chat rooms, and proudly declared, "BRB" as if it were a verbal mic drop.

The biggest online scandal was someone lying about their age in a Yahoo! chat. Now? Your uncle believes Hillary Clinton is running a child-trafficking ring out of a pizza shop basement with no basement.

Dick's Hissy Fit: "I've Joined the Tin Foil Hat Society—and You Should Too!"

"The Tin Foil Society gets it. While everyone else is sleepwalking, we're the ones connecting the dots. Government? Rigged. Science? Bought. Media? Corrupt. They laugh at us for wearing tin foil, but at least we're protected from the mind control beaming down every night. Better paranoid than a sheep."

—DICK

Welcome to the unholy metamorphosis: from innocent dial-up dreams to full-blown digital delusion. What began as a tool for global connection has become a rage-fueled demolition derby of facts, empathy, and basic human decency. The internet didn't just open Pandora's box—it installed

Wi-Fi in it, handed out iPhones, and whispered, **"Do your research, off the internet. The internet is NOT vetted; it's a sales model."**

From Web 1.0 to Weaponized Insecurity

The digital age once promised democratized knowledge. But instead of enlightenment, we got YouTube comments. Instead of Socrates, we got Joe Rogan. The internet has become the ultimate breeding ground for wounded egos, resentment, and algorithm-enhanced insecurity. We took *"I disagree"* and evolved it into *"You are a communist Satanist groomer trying to destroy America."* That escalated quickly. The internet didn't invent conspiracy theories. It gave them rocket fuel, a megaphone, and a merchandise line. What used to require a basement, a corkboard, and 42 feet of red yarn now requires only a smartphone and a fragile sense of self.

Anonymous, Angry, and Always Online

We've entered the age of keyboard courage, where grown men yell "TRUTH" in all caps, block their niece for mentioning pronouns, and believe the IRS is a globalist plot. Why read *The New York Times* when you can watch a shaky-cam YouTube video posted by "Patriot1776RealTruth" from the front seat of his Ford F-150?

Social media turned everyone into a pundit, a prophet, or a problem. It's grievance-as-brand, victimhood-as-virtue, and rage-as-retirement-plan. Because nothing screams "I'm being silenced" like a three-hour livestream watched by 1.2 million followers.

Even anonymity, once a harmless way to explore identity, has become the rage-fueled invisibility cloak of choice. Today's avatars are angry bald eagles wrapped in the American flag, ready to declare war on Starbucks for changing their holiday cup design. Progress is a threat, facts are offensive, and feelings are facts—as long as they're *your* feelings.

The Weaponization of the Feed

And let's not forget the invisible hand pulling the strings: **algorithms**. These aren't just lines of code—they're rage sommeliers, curating content to pair perfectly with your darkest insecurities. Angry about immigrants?

Here are a thousand videos about the "invasion." Mad about feminism? Here's a podcast called *"Alpha Kings United."* One click becomes a rabbit hole; one video becomes a worldview.

Research confirms what we already know: *social media platforms like Facebook and YouTube have been linked to increased political polarization and radicalization.*[111]

The business model? Keep you pissed, keep you scrolling, and keep selling your data to an ad for testosterone supplements and tactical pants.

Research confirms what we already know: *social media platforms like Facebook and YouTube have been linked to increased political polarization and radicalization.*[112] The business model? Keep you pissed, keep you scrolling, and keep selling your data to those advertising testosterone supplements and tactical pants.

The Algorithm Is Not Your Friend (But It Knows What You Fear)

If the internet were a haunted house, the algorithm would be the shady butler who knows your secrets, feeds your phobias, and whispers, *"Want to see something even dumber, angrier, and more unhinged?"* Spoiler: you do. And the butler knows it. Because the algorithm isn't your friend, it's your fearmongering, dopamine-dealing frenemy who wants you mad, misinformed, and miserably online.

The Algorithm Is Not Your Friend
(But It Knows What You Fear)

Cognitive Capture Unit
Keep Dick scrolling.
Keep Dick angry.
Keep Dick convinced
he's the only sane one left online.

Dick's Inputs
Follows: echo chambers, grievance groups, conspiracy tags.
Mood Data: rage clicks, doom scrolls, pulse spikes.
Identity Flags: politics, "the good old days."
Hot Topics: celebrity outrage, election panic, culture wars.
Feed in. Stir 'til boiling.

Core Formula
Engagement = Arousal x Ego ÷ Doubt.
Accuracy is irrelevant. Truth is negotiable.
But outrage? That's renewable energy.

Fear Distillation
Moral Outrage Score: detect betrayal and "cancelled again."
Tribal Resonance: mirror belief, then threaten it.
Dissonance Spike: make him agree, then add a villain.
Combat Mode: find threads to "educate" strangers.
Contagion: measure tantrum spread.

The Spiral (a.k.a. Dick's Descent)
Hook→ Nudge→ Lock-In→ Arena Mode→ Echo Chamber→ Sink Cost → Return Hook
"You won't believe what they did now."
"They're coming for your values."
"Someone just replied to you..."

Outrage Lifecycle

Incubate→ Accelerate→ Weaponize→ Sanitize→ Compost

Safety Theater
"Are you sure you want to post?"
= 99% click "yes."
"Context added by readers." = doubles engagement.
Random "mental health check" ad = brand safety achieved.

KPI Dashboard
Average Dick Dwell Time ↑
Ratio Rate ↑
Out-group Hate-Watch ↑
"Free Speech" Posts ↑
Apology Tweets = Bonus PR

Playbooks That Print Outrage
Moral Panic Carousel: new villains every Monday.
Betrayal Season: "Even your side hates you now."
Purity Trials: keep Dick policing his own tribe.
Laundry Day: archive drama→ "exposed" threads.

Failure Modes
Cynicism Burnout: give Dick a new enemy.
Moderation Scandal: pretend to care, then backtrack.
Real-World Riot: throttle outrage, push puppy videos.

1. Outrage Pays the Bills (and Buys the Yachts):

Let's be clear: tech platforms aren't platforms. They're digital casinos where the house always wins and the jackpot is your attention span. Facts? Meh. Nuance? Pass. What sells? Outrage. The more furious you are, the more you click. The more you click, the more ads they sell. Your grandma's Facebook rant about how the COVID-19 vaccine gives your dog autism? That just made Mark Zuckerberg $0.0037—and 10 million more like it made him a billionaire.

Algorithms don't seek truth—they optimize for **engagement**,[113] which is just Silicon Valley code for *"Did this content trigger a strong enough emotion to keep you scrolling instead of feeding your children?"*

2. The Dopamine Loop of Doom: Click, Rage, Share, Repeat:

Your brain loves rage more than it loves reason. When you're angry, your body releases dopamine, which feels good in the short term, like yelling at a cyclist from your SUV window. Every inflammatory headline, every "owns the libs" meme, every crocodile tear from a pundit "just asking questions" hits that sweet, sweet neurochemical lever. You become a lab rat in a hoodie, smacking the "Like" button for another hit of *"I'm right, they're wrong."* And then you share it. Because if you're mad, your cousin Karen in Ohio *must also be angry*.

3. "You Might Also Like...": Radicalization, Racism, and Reptilian Elites:

Clicked on a video about immigration policy? You might also like:
- "How George Soros Controls Everything"
- "Wokeness is Killing Western Civilization"
- "Proof That Michelle Obama Is a Lizard"

The algorithm doesn't ask if you want truth or reality—it asks, "How fast can I take you from a mildly conservative take to full-blown QAnon in under 48 hours?"

And it works. Research has shown that YouTube's recommendation engine frequently leads users down "rabbit holes" of radical content.[114] The journey from *"How to fix your credit score"* to *"The Federal Reserve is a Zionist Plot"* is disturbingly short. One moment you're watching Jordan Peterson explain lobster dominance hierarchies; the next, you're prepping for civil war with a dude named "1776BeardGod."

4. The Digital Echo Chamber: From Nerd Forums to Extremist Incubators:

Back in the day, echo chambers were harmless—nerdy debates about *Star Trek* canon or which "Final Fantasy" had the best summon spells. Fast-forward to now: those echo chambers have evolved into ideological death spirals, where being the most outraged makes you the most admired.

Platforms like 4chan, Reddit, and even Facebook Groups started as gathering places for the like-minded. Then the like-minded got angry. Then they got militant. Then they got merchandise. What was once a digital community became a breeding ground for digital radicalization. And the algorithm? It stood on the sidelines, tossing gasoline and handing out pitchfork emojis.

In these echo chambers, dissent isn't welcome—it's annihilated. You're either part of the angry mob or you're a beta cuck shill for the globalist agenda. There is no middle ground. Middle-aged men are live-streaming from their trucks about how Target is the Antichrist.

Rage Is the Product, You Are the Inventory

Stop pretending this is about connecting people. It's about controlling people through anger, fear, and endless feedback loops of falsehoods. The algorithm knows what you fear. It knows what you hate. And it's using that knowledge to sell you *everything but the truth*.

Because in the age of algorithms, reality doesn't trend. But rage? Rage always does.

Social Media and the Insecurity Industrial Complex

Once upon a time, middle-aged men were the heroes of every story: the CEOs, the senators, the cowboys, the cops, the presidents. They ruled the boardroom and the barbecue. Now? They're being asked to share space with women. With immigrants. With "they/them" baristas who make better lattes and have better skincare routines. The horror.

Enter social media, the ultimate mirror—and magnifier—of masculine fragility. What do you get when you combine a Wi-Fi signal, a fragile ego, and a meme generator? You get the Insecurity Industrial Complex—a multibillion-dollar economy powered by podcasts, pundits, protein powder, and panic.

Meme Warfare and Victimhood

Forget camo and combat boots—the modern uniform of the aggrieved middle-aged man is a Twitter account, a Joe Rogan quote, and a deep, aching need to feel like the underdog. Nothing says "oppressed" like screaming into your ring light from a home office with a leather chair and an American flag behind you.

Victimhood is the new masculinity. The second someone mentions systemic racism or dares to point out that maybe, *just maybe,* the Founding Fathers weren't perfect, the rage floodgates open. They're no longer dominant—they're "targeted." They're no longer unquestioned—they're "canceled." Disagreement = persecution. De-platforming? That's not YouTube moderation—it's "digital tyranny." They're no longer the default—they're *"the real victims."*

As sociologist Michael Kimmel notes, masculine anxiety spikes when dominance is threatened—a condition he dubs "aggrieved entitlement."[115] Social media didn't create this phenomenon; it merely amplified it. It just handed it a bullhorn and an affiliate marketing link. These men aren't just mad. They're professionally mad—turning outrage into a side hustle and victimhood into performance art.

The Myth of Censorship: Disagreement = Persecution

Being disagreed with is not persecution. Being unfollowed is not a civil rights violation. But on social media? It's DEFCON 1 every time someone replies, *"Actually, here's a fact."* Suddenly, a mild fact-check becomes Stalinism, and a de-platforming becomes a First Amendment crisis. (Pro tip: The First Amendment protects you from the government, not

YouTube's terms of service.)

When platforms ban hate speech, conspiracy theories, or pandemic disinformation, it's not censorship—it's **content moderation**. But in the minds of many insecure keyboard warriors, it's *"silencing real Americans"* (read: *me and my five burner accounts*). Because nothing makes someone feel more potent than pretending to be powerless. Victimhood is the new Viagra.

Keyboard Warriors of the Apocalypse

It's hard to cry on command, but online? The outrage faucet never turns off. These men aren't just angry—they're performing anger, cultivating it like a side hustle. In 280 characters or less, they fight culture wars with all the nuance of a truck stop bumper sticker.

They tweet things like:
- "Masculinity is under attack!"
- "Real men don't cry—unless it's about Mr. Potato Head losing his gun."
- "Wokeism is a virus worse than COVID!" (actual quote—multiple times—by actual adults.)

Underneath the bluster? Shame. Insecurity. A gnawing feeling that the world is moving on without them—and it is. But instead of evolving, they double down on **projection**, weaponizing their inner panic and turning the internet into a psychological demolition derby.

The Digital Man Cave of Bitterness, Bourbon, and Breitbart

Social media isn't just a platform—it's a digital man cave for the aggrieved. It's got everything:
- Faux-intellectual YouTube bros with "truth bombs."
- Podcasts called *"Whiskey, War, and Wokeness."*
- Breitbart headlines are written in all caps with no verbs.
- A permanent emotional soundtrack of Toby Keith and red meat.

This isn't a conversation. It's a **therapy session that ends in rage**, where no one listens, everyone's a victim, and the ultimate goal is to be the loudest person in the room, yelling about "real America" from their $3,000 ergonomic gaming chair.

And just like every man cave, it's **not built for comfort—it's built for isolation**. It's a place to sulk, to spiral, to avoid growth at all costs. And thanks to algorithms, it's air-conditioned with feedback loops, echo chambers, and digital high-fives for bad takes.

Reality Distortion Field: The New Flat Earth

In a world overflowing with access to information, some people looked at Google, shrugged, and said, *"Nah, I trust this guy in camo yelling from the front seat of his Dodge Ram."* Welcome to the Reality Distortion Field—where up is down, facts are feelings, and your cousin Rick thinks Fauci is a lizard. This is not a lack of information. This is a willful delusion at broadband speeds. We're not talking ignorance—we're talking curated, polished, algorithm-approved unreality.

Believing in Microchips in Vaccines but Denying Systemic Racism

You know you're deep in the distortion when someone believes the government has installed 5G-controlled nanobots in vaccines but can't wrap their heads around the idea that racial inequality exists. Ask them about the Tuskegee Study. Crickets. But mention Bill Gates, and suddenly, they've got a PowerPoint presentation on population control.

The same crowd wears *"I DO NOT COMPLY"* shirts at Walmart while refusing to read a single peer-reviewed article. They'll shout, "My body, my choice," in one breath and try to ban abortion in the next. Logic? Optional. Hypocrisy? A badge of honor.

Because here's the truth: conspiracy is easier than complexity. It's less uncomfortable to believe in an evil cabal secretly running the world than to acknowledge you might be part of a system that benefits you at others' expense.

Conspiracy Theories Offer Simplicity... Just Not Truth

Look, the world is complicated. Climate change, income inequality, pandemics, rising fascism—it's a lot. So, conspiracy theories offer a seductive solution: a neat little story where someone *else* is always to blame.

Everything you hate? All part of *the plan*. Everything that doesn't make sense? That's *precisely what they want*. Conspiracy is comfort food for people who can't handle ambiguity.

But here's the twist: these theories offer no solutions—only suspicion. They don't end with progress. They end with shouting at the sky, hoarding beans, and posting blurry screenshots of "proof" that Tom Hanks is part of the Illuminati.

The ironic twist: these conspiracy theorists demand **proof** for systemic racism but not for Jewish space lasers. Conspiracy beliefs thrive in times of uncertainty and powerlessness.[116] In short, people want control, and conspiracy gives the illusion of it—even if it's completely untethered from reality.

The Comfort of Paranoia: You're Never Wrong if It's All a Plot

In the world of conspiracy, you're not a guy shouting into the void. You're a patriot, a truth-seeker, a light-bringer. You're not wrong—you're just *ahead of the curve*. Every fact you ignore? That's just proof they've "gotten to" the scientists. Every debunking? "Controlled opposition."

Paranoia is a full-time job with no HR department to support it. But it comes with perks:

- You're never accountable.
- You're never confused—just *enlightened*.
- And every failed prediction? Just *part of the bigger plan*.

This is epistemic insulation: a closed loop where no outside info is trustworthy, no disagreement is tolerated, and every correction is a confirmation of the conspiracy.[117] It's not just fake news—it's a phony *reality* curated for emotional satisfaction, not factual accuracy.

Gravity Isn't the Only Thing Denied Anymore

We are now witnessing the rise of a cultural class that believes the Earth is flat, the 2020 election was stolen, COVID-19 is a hoax, and "wokeness" is a disease—but won't believe centuries of institutional racism because that would mean looking inward instead of outward. In the Reality Distortion Field, logic is optional, truth is negotiable, and ignorance is a defining characteristic of one's personality. And that brand? It's trending.

Echo Chamber Media: Where Feelings > Facts Since Forever

Turning Rage Into Ratings Since the First Ad Break

Welcome to the golden era of grievance broadcasting, where news wasn't just delivered—it was weaponized, looped, and monetized. This was when cable news stopped asking questions and started selling outrage by the segment. Fox News didn't just report on the cultural anxiety of white suburban dads—it *designed* it. Cable "news" became a never-ending safe space for the easily triggered, where petty complaints and exaggerated fears were broadcast as if they were national emergencies.

"Fair and Balanced" was less a slogan and more a dare. It meant, "We'll say what you're already thinking, only louder, angrier, and with a stock photo of someone crossing the border." Entire news blocks were transformed into emotionally charged PowerPoints, filled with red alerts, sweaty pundits, and graphics that resembled those designed by someone having a panic attack in Microsoft Paint.

Meanwhile, talk radio is fused with paranoia, much like a Marvel villain origin story. Rush Limbaugh screamed into the void, Glenn Beck cried on whiteboards, and AM radio became the emotional support echo chamber for people convinced Antifa was hiding in their thermostats. Liberal media? According to these outlets, it wasn't just biased—it was the secret cabal destroying your neighborhood one gender-neutral pronoun at a time.

This wasn't journalism. It was voter programming—with ad breaks for tactical flashlights, gold coins, and "natural solutions" for erectile dysfunction.

Long before Tucker Carlson weaponized dead-eyed smugness and bow ties, the conservative movement was already laying the foundation for America's infotainment-industrial complex—a sprawling ecosystem where facts go to die, and feelings are elevated to constitutional doctrine. This wasn't a media strategy. It was a messaging insurgency, and it began with a fundamental realization: "If people start thinking for themselves, we're screwed." So they built a counternarrative fortress—brick by brick.

And they are:

- Corporate leaders and CEOs alarmed by rising progressive movements, labor rights, and environmental regulations.
- Conservative strategists and intellectuals, like those behind the Powell Memo, who provided the ideological framework for countering liberalism.
- Religious fundamentalists and evangelical leaders saw cultural change (abortion rights, feminism, gay rights) as moral decay and used media to mobilize their base.
- Right-wing philanthropists and billionaires (e.g., the Koch brothers, Scaife family, Peter Thiel and Elon Musk) who bankrolled think tanks like the Heritage Foundation, American Enterprise Institute, and the Cato Institute.
- Media pioneers on the right, from AM radio shock jocks to early televangelists, who realized that grievance sells better than gospel.

The "they" in this context is not one person or group—it's a strategic alliance of political, economic, and religious power players who saw progressive reform not as progress, but as a threat to their cultural, ideological, and financial dominance

The conservative media machine began to hum during Barry Goldwater's 1964 campaign. He lost spectacularly, but his campaign planted the seeds of ideological branding. Goldwater's message: "government is the problem," resonated *just enough* to inspire a generation of conservative operatives who realized they didn't need to win the vote—they just needed to control the conversation.

Enter the era of:

- Right-wing newsletters printed in basement bunkers with titles like *The American Patriot Defender Quarterly Digest*.
- Evangelical radio shows, where every Democratic bill was secretly a Satanic ritual.
- AM talk radio, which offered 24/7 programming for the paranoid, the privileged, and the perpetually offended.

This marked the beginning of the emotion-to-ideology pipeline—a media strategy not founded on facts or nuance, but on rage, repetition, and resentment. If you listened to cable news or conservative talk radio in the 2000s, you'd think America had been taken hostage by tofu and multiculturalism. Even while leading the world in military spending, incarceration rates, and CEO compensation, the narrative was crystal clear: *America had fallen. And it was probably your fault.* Not because of war crimes or wealth hoarding—no, because someone in HR said "Latinx."

Diversity wasn't progress—it was decay. Equity? Reverse racism. Inclusion? Marxism with better branding. Every attempt at making the country fairer was sold to viewers and listeners as a form of national surrender, even as their stock portfolios grew and their TVs got flatter.

Fox News: The Backlash Machine's Broadcast Arm (a.k.a. Rage TV for the Patriotic Soul)

Fox News was born in 1996, the brainchild of Rupert Murdoch and Roger Ailes, who figured America was ready for a 24/7 infomercial selling fear, patriotism, and reverse victimhood. By the 2000 election, it had already become the conservative base's favorite bedtime story—and by 2025, it's no longer just a cable channel. It's an emotional support system for people terrified of pronouns and flavored lattes.

Today, Fox isn't covering the culture war. It's producing, directing, and starring in it, with commercial breaks for testosterone supplements and gold bars. Think of it as a megaphone for aggrieved boomer dads, suburban moms with Facebook conspiracy pages, and Dick, who still believes Obama was born in Kenya and that drag queens are the real threat to national security.

Fox News doesn't deal in facts—it deals in feelings, specifically the kind that make you want to scream at your microwave. Its primetime lineup isn't news; it's grievance theater. Every episode features the same tired formula: the villain is always some marginalized group asking for rights, the hero is a "concerned" white person defending vague values, and the solution is fewer rights for women and more freedom for billionaires to hoard wealth. And though Tucker Carlson has left the building, his whispery fascism lives on in the network's ability to tell Dad that he's not wrong—he's under attack.

Built for Outrage: A User Manual

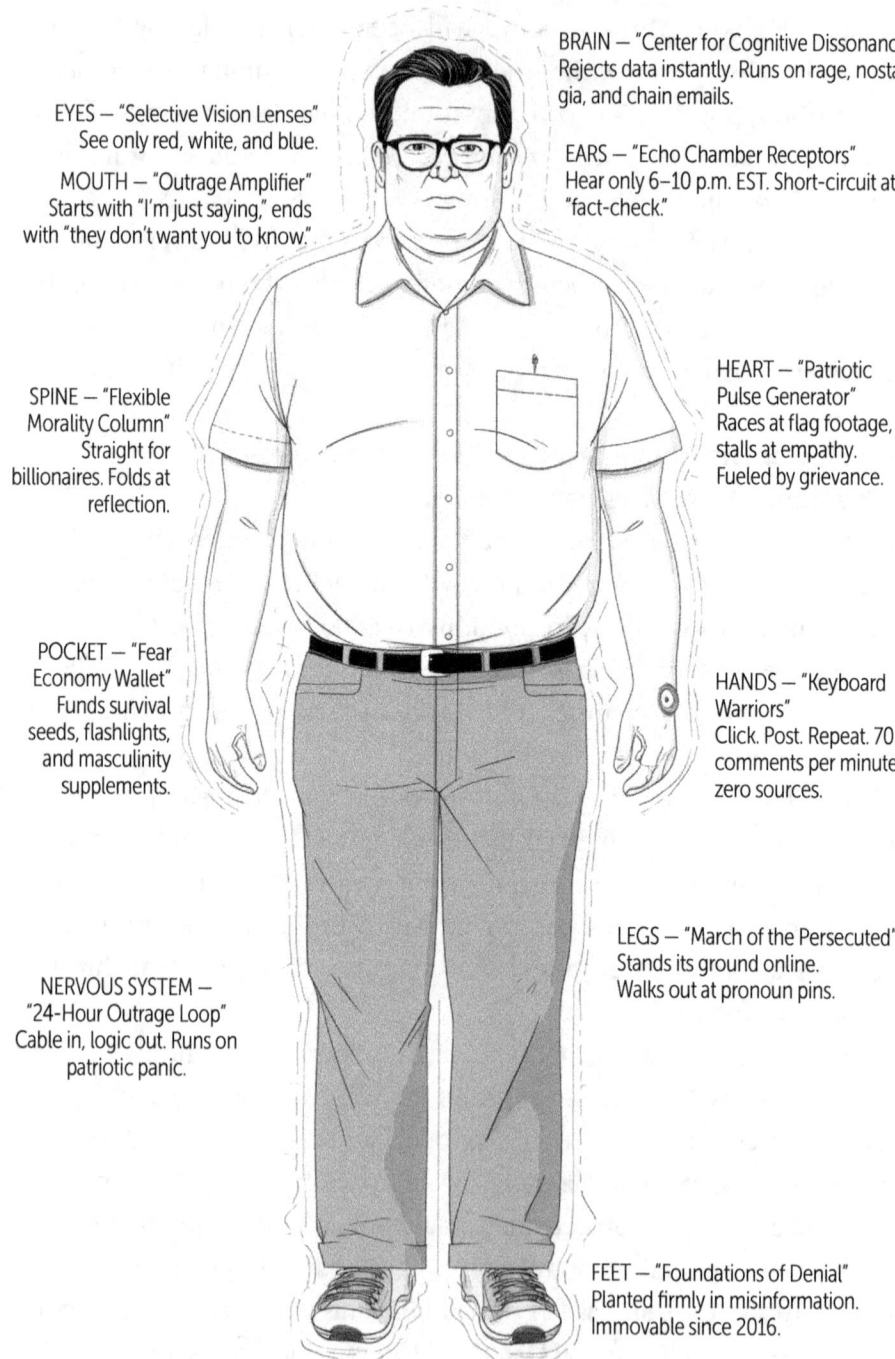

EYES — "Selective Vision Lenses"
See only red, white, and blue.

MOUTH — "Outrage Amplifier"
Starts with "I'm just saying," ends with "they don't want you to know."

SPINE — "Flexible Morality Column"
Straight for billionaires. Folds at reflection.

POCKET — "Fear Economy Wallet"
Funds survival seeds, flashlights, and masculinity supplements.

NERVOUS SYSTEM — "24-Hour Outrage Loop"
Cable in, logic out. Runs on patriotic panic.

BRAIN — "Center for Cognitive Dissonance"
Rejects data instantly. Runs on rage, nostalgia, and chain emails.

EARS — "Echo Chamber Receptors"
Hear only 6–10 p.m. EST. Short-circuit at "fact-check."

HEART — "Patriotic Pulse Generator"
Races at flag footage, stalls at empathy. Fueled by grievance.

HANDS — "Keyboard Warriors"
Click. Post. Repeat. 70 comments per minute, zero sources.

LEGS — "March of the Persecuted"
Stands its ground online. Walks out at pronoun pins.

FEET — "Foundations of Denial"
Planted firmly in misinformation. Immovable since 2016.

Grievance Amplification Loop

Fox doesn't want viewers to feel informed. It wants them to feel betrayed, persecuted, and ready to buy whatever supplement ad plays next. And boy, do they deliver—testosterone boosters, tactical flashlights, and freeze-dried beef rations for when Nancy Pelosi steals Christmas.

A 2022 Pew Research study found that Fox viewers were consistently less informed about factual news than viewers of most other outlets, including those who watched no news at all.

What Fox perfected is the Grievance Amplification Loop. It doesn't report what happened. It reports how you should feel about what might have occurred in the most alarmist tone possible.

- A college offering gender-neutral bathrooms becomes a war on masculinity.
- A cereal commercial featuring a Black dad becomes white genocide in 30 seconds.
- A student reading *The Bluest Eye* becomes a front for Marxist indoctrination.

Fox viewers don't walk away more informed. They walk away, convinced the country is on fire and that their only hope is ordering a survival food kit during the next ad break.

Fox perfected a new media business model: Fear ➤ Ratings ➤ Revenue ➤ Repeat.

If viewers get mad enough, they stay. If they stay long enough, they spend. If they spend enough, Steve Doocy gets another book deal and Rupert Murdoch gets another super yacht powered by Tucker's discarded bow-ties. This is outrage as a subscription model. The longer you're angry, the longer you watch. The longer you watch, the more ad revenue Fox gets from companies selling you conspiracy-themed collectibles. Fox News has become a performance where the audience is told they're the victim, the enemy is always brown or queer or female, and the future is only safe if it looks exactly like 1955—with worse haircuts and better Wi-Fi.

In 2025, Fox News isn't about journalism. It's about identity. It's about turning every minor inconvenience into a crisis of civilization. It's about convincing its audience that learning history is un-American, empathy is weakness, and every disagreement is a war for the nation's soul. This isn't a news network. It's an outrage delivery service. And for the right price, they'll throw in a cross, a flag, and a conspiracy theory to go.

Fox News doesn't just *cover* the culture war—it scripts it, airs it, and then reruns it during dinner. It taught a generation that journalism = screaming, expertise = being white and smug, and truth = whatever graphic Sean Hannity is yelling over. It's not informing the electorate—**it's programming voters**, one fear segment at a time. And the worst part? **It works.**

The Emotional Regulation Tool for Dick: When Dick doesn't know how to process a world that's evolving, Fox helps him convert confusion into confidence. Don't understand gender fluidity? Fox will mock it for you. Feel weird about abortion bans? Fox reminds you that "real men" don't need nuance.

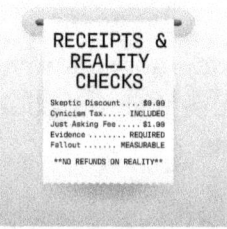

Lies So Loud They Echo in Gold Bond Commercials[118]

1. **"The 2020 Election Was Stolen"**
   Fox News promoted false claims that Dominion Voting Systems rigged the 2020 election, even while privately acknowledging they were lies. Bonus: It cost them $787.5 million to say "oops."

2. **"COVID Is Just the Flu"**
   Fox anchors downplayed COVID-19's severity while promoting unproven cures like hydroxychloroquine. Meanwhile, their staff quietly followed CDC protocols behind the scenes.

3. **"The Deep State Is Controlling Your Toaster"**
   Fox fueled conspiracy theories that career government employees (aka scientists, diplomats, lunch ladies) were secretly plotting

against Trump. Plot twist: Your toaster is fine. It's your cable box that's been hijacked.

4. **"Climate Change Is a Liberal Hoax"**
   Despite overwhelming scientific consensus, Fox told viewers climate change was just "weather with an attitude." Because nothing says journalism like arguing with data from NASA.

5. **"Wokeness Is Killing America"**
   Fox framed diversity, inclusion, and empathy as existential threats to society. Kindness is the real slippery slope.

6. **"Critical Race Theory Is Being Taught in Kindergarten"**
   Fox helped make CRT a household panic phrase, even though it's taught in law school, not elementary school. But if a first grader hears the word 'equality,' call the school board immediately!

7. **"The Gay Agenda Is Indoctrinating Your Kids"**
   Fox painted LGBTQ+ representation in media and education as a sinister plot. Because a drag queen reading *The Very Hungry Caterpillar* is political warfare.

8. **"Vaccines Are More Dangerous Than the Virus"**
   Fox personalities amplified anti-vaccine rhetoric while the network required employees to follow the vaccine protocols. Do as we say, not as we get "jabbed."

9. **"Book Bans Are Protecting Children"**
   Fox glorified efforts to ban books on race, gender, and history, because knowledge is suspicious. Reading about racism = radicalization, and burning books = freedom.

10. **"Fox News Is Fair and Balanced"**
    Their most enduring myth. File under: Things less balanced than a one-legged stool on a rollercoaster.

Stopping the Echo Chamber in 2025 (If You Still Have a Functioning Brain Cell)

A survival guide for the dangerously informed, the critically engaged, and the terminally exhausted. What can you *do* in 2025, now that the Backlash Machine has gone full Skynet with a flag?

Read Something Other Than Dick's Facebook Posts

Studies show that reading real books—yes, the kind with pages—activates parts of your brain currently under siege by short-form misinformation. Suggested reading:[119]

- *Thinking, Fast and Slow* by Daniel Kahneman (because your gut feelings aren't always genius)
- *Amusing Ourselves to Death* by Neil Postman (a reminder that infotainment isn't information)
- *1984* by George Orwell (re-read it—it's not a "how-to" manual, no matter what your uncle thinks)

Vote Like Democracy Depends on It (Because It Does, You Nerd)

Did you know that in 2024, only 62% of eligible voters turned out—and half of them still don't know what the midterms are?[120] Your local school board election may be the last line of defense between your kid reading *Maus* and learning about America exclusively through a VeggieTales lens. Pro tip: Bring snacks, bring a friend, and bring a plan. And bring tissues— for Dick, when his candidate loses.

Deprogram Your Relatives (Gently, But Firmly)

A 2025 report from the Institute for Cognitive Rehabilitation suggests that 3 out of 4 uncles at Thanksgiving believe "woke" is a virus. Strategies include:

- Asking *genuine* questions until the "logic" collapses under its own weight.
- Redirecting the conversation to "sports" until you can explain empathy during halftime.
- Creating a safe space for learning—don't call it that or they'll accuse you of Marxism.

Make Noise Louder Than the Outrage Echo Chamber

If you've got privilege, power, a platform—or even just Wi-Fi—use it. Speak up. Call out the nonsense. Write your senator. Email your school board. Tweet into the void until the void tweets back. As Audre Lorde reminded us: *"Your silences will not protect you,"* pointing out that remaining silent in the face of injustice only allows it to continue.[121]

Teach the Next Generation How to Think (Before Dick Gets to Them First)

Remember: The Backlash Machine feeds on ignorance like it's a Chick-fil-A sandwich. Teach kids:

- How to evaluate sources
- How to recognize logical fallacies
- That feelings aren't facts
- And that "freedom" doesn't mean "nobody can ever disagree with me"

According to a study by Caroti et al., a critical-thinking intervention among secondary school students led to a significant reduction in conspiracy beliefs both immediately after the program and one month later—suggesting that early critical thinking education can meaningfully curb the appeal of fantastical theories.[122]

Short-Circuit The Backlash Machine

The Backlash Machine won't stop because it gets tired—it runs on pure, uncut grievance. But it *can* be short-circuited with:

- Relentless facts
- Sharpened satire
- Grassroots organizing
- And a national effort to **stop mistaking discomfort for persecution**

As the old saying goes: "The only thing necessary for the triumph of nonsense is for smart people to get too tired to argue."

Echo Chambers and Emotional Support Algorithms

By the mid-2010s, America had ceased to be a shared reality and had become a choose-your-own-adventure hallucination. Facts became optional. Truth became tribal. And Dick? He found comfort not in knowledge but in algorithmically curated outrage, disguised as patriotism, packaged as identity, and shipped overnight by Bezos. The information superhighway became a **rage roundabout**, and Dick was stuck doing donuts in a lifted F-150 flying a "Don't Tread on Me" flag he bought from a Chinese manufacturer.

Birth of the Misinformation Machine

The traditional gatekeepers—journalists, historians, librarians—were replaced by *that guy from high school* who now runs a conspiracy podcast in his garage and cites memes as primary sources. What began as "media bias" critiques became full-blown fantasy franchises: Obama was a Kenyan Muslim, Hillary ran a pedophile ring out of a pizza shop, and vaccines were part of a global plot to microchip Americans (despite Dick willingly carrying a tracking device called an iPhone). The internet wasn't just where misinformation spread—it's where it metastasized. A 2020 study by MIT found that false news stories were 70% more likely to be retweeted than true ones, particularly in the context of political content.[123]

Why? Because lies are designed to trigger Dick's dopamine receptors. Truth asks for patience. Lies throw a punch. In this world, objective reality wasn't just questioned—it was replaced.

Weaponizing Nostalgia: "Make America Great Again" Before It Was a Slogan

Nostalgia is harmless when it's about '90s cartoons. It's dangerous when it becomes a political strategy. MAGA wasn't just a slogan—it was a **rebranding of historical amnesia**. It promised Dick a return to the golden era when *he* was centered—when women stayed quiet, immigrants stayed invisible, and minorities stayed on the margins.

The era Trump invoked never actually existed. The 1950s weren't a Norman Rockwell paradise—they were exclusionary, repressed, and often violent.[124] But to Dick, facts were irrelevant. What mattered was the *feeling*: superiority, the illusion of control, and the unchallenged comfort of dominance. Trump didn't invent that script—he just repackaged it with the polish of a televangelist and the subtlety of a WWE heel.

The 1970s revival of the '50s was the same trick. It wasn't nostalgia—it was a rerun. America tried to binge-watch a past that never actually worked for most people. *Happy Days* and *Grease* peddled sock hops, soda fountains, and "simpler times." But as your mom cut through this with precision: *"The Fifties were STUPID!"* She wasn't wrong. Beneath the pastel appliances and picket fences was a chokehold on women's autonomy. The "ideal" woman of the 1950s was sold as cheerful while trading ambition for an apron, her voice for Valium, and her paycheck for pearls. That wasn't nostalgia—it was selective amnesia.

So when the '70s recycled the '50s, it wasn't honoring history—it was re-airing the pilot episode of patriarchy and pretending it deserved a second season. And your mom's resistance proves something essential: not everyone bought the rerun. Plenty lived it, hated it, and wished the network would cancel the show for good.

Social Media Echo Chambers as Hissy fit Incubators

Before social media, Dick might have muttered his grievances at the bar or yelled at the TV. But now? Now, every hissy fit had an audience—and an algorithm to boost it. Facebook, YouTube, X (formerly Twitter), and TikTok didn't just tolerate Dick's tantrums—they *monetized* them.

- The more he clicked, the more rage he got fed.
- The more he shared, the more conspiracy theories he was rewarded with.
- The more he screamed into the void, the louder it echoed back.

Platforms built to connect us began **algorithmically segregating us**. Conservatives saw one version of the world. Liberals saw another. And Dick? Dick built a reality so distorted, he thought *Antifa* was a well-funded organization and *drag queens* were a greater threat than climate change. The result? A man so fragile in identity and isolated in perspective that any contradiction to his view felt like an attack on his soul.

RECEIPTS &
REALITY
CHECKS

Skeptic Discount $0.00
Cynicism Tax..... INCLUDED
Just Asking Fee..... $1.00
Evidence .... REQUIRED
Fallout .... MEASURABLE

NO REFUNDS ON REALITY

False Echo Chambers[125]

- **Falsehood travels faster than truth.** On Twitter, false news stories spread significantly farther, faster, deeper, and more broadly than the truth, especially about politics.
- **Echo chambers are real.** Research confirms that social media promotes ideological segregation by exposing users to like-minded viewpoints.

CHAPTER 6

The Man Box Is on Fire: Masculinity's Identity Crisis and the Cultural Fallout

Somewhere between the rise of feminism and the fall of coal mining, American masculinity is having a full-blown identity crisis—and instead of evolving, it's throwing a hissy fit.

For generations, masculinity was built like a fortress: stoic, unyielding, and suspicious of emotion. A "real man" knew his place—at the top—and everyone else's place was below him. His authority wasn't questioned; his role wasn't up for negotiation. Yet the 20th century didn't just knock on the fortress door—it bulldozed the foundation. Suddenly, women have gotten accustomed to having agency, gender isn't binary, men are expected to communicate, and entire industries have collapsed under the weight of automation and globalization. The cultural script had changed, and no one sent middle-aged white men the memo (or if they did, those men didn't pay attention).

What happens next? Predictably, rage, retreat, and reinvention are not helpful. The rage has taken form in toxic masculinity, the retreat in opioids and isolation, and the reinvention in red hats and right-wing YouTube channels promising a return to "the way things used to be."

This isn't just a cultural shift—it's a full-blown masculinity meltdown. Masculinity isn't dying—it's evolving; adapting to the ever-changing world, where men no longer need to hunt saber-tooth tigers. What is collapsing, however, is the outdated, narrow, dominance-based version of masculinity that can't survive without someone else beneath it. And the louder it screams about cancel culture and pronouns, the more obvious its decline becomes.

Masculinity in America isn't a personality trait—it's a poorly written one-person show.

It's less about the "authentic self" and more about method acting —a lifelong audition for a role that no longer exists. Men aren't being masculine; they're performing it. Think less Mister Rogers, and more John Wayne in a mirror yelling "Man up" to himself before crying silently in a Dodge Ram.

Sociologist Raewyn Connell (2005) nailed it with the concept of "hegemonic masculinity"—the dominant, idealized version of manhood that men are taught to perform to gain social status while simultaneously denying other versions of being male. Spoiler alert: this ideal is unattainable and exhausting, which makes it perfect for late-stage capitalism and terrible for mental health. Masculinity is a moving target duct-taped to a treadmill: you can never be strong, stoic, or successful *enough*. And once society stopped rewarding men for simply *existing*, the façade began to crack.

What *Is* Masculinity? At its core, masculinity is a set of behaviors, traits, and cultural expectations society associates with being male. That's it. It's not biology—it's branding. And, like any good branding campaign, it has undergone significant evolution over time.

The Evolution of Masculinity:
A Timeline of Insecurity *1800s-1990s*

1800s-1950s

Traditional Masculinity

This was the era of provider-as-identity, when men were expected to be tough, emotionally sealed, and financially in charge—while women raised the kids and quietly suppressed their dreams.

Traits: Strength, stoicism, dominance, breadwinning, no crying unless a war buddy dies.

Mantra: "Rub some dirt on it."

Cultural Reference: John Wayne with emotional frostbite.

1960s-1990s

Complicated Masculinity

Feminism, civil rights, and counterculture movements cracked open the tough-guy shell. Men started being allowed to cry a little—as long as they didn't talk too much about it.

Traits: Conflicted, curious, questioning.

Mantra: "Is it okay if I feel... feelings?"

Cultural Reference: The rise of the Sensitive Dad™ and the tortured Gen X indie dude.

The Evolution of Masculinity:
A Timeline of Insecurity *2000s-Present*

2000s-2010s

Metrosexual & Evolving Masculinity

Here, we saw men leaning into vulnerability, co-parenting, and moisturizers. Masculinity became more fluid. Gender roles loosened. Cue the backlash...

Traits: Groomed, emotionally literate, sometimes wears pink.

Mantra: "Self-care isn't just for women."

Cultural Reference: David Beckham, therapy memes, and men's skincare lines.

2020-2025

Hissy Fit Masculinity

Now we're in the "masculinity is endangered" panic phase. Suddenly, feelings are fascism. Therapy is weakness. And if you acknowledge nonbinary people exist, you're apparently destroying civilization. This is where masculinity stopped evolving and started screaming.

Traits: Performative toughness, digital outrage, nostalgia-soaked fragility.

Mantra: "Masculinity is under attack!"

Cultural Reference: Jordan Peterson's lobster, Andrew Tate's abs, and Joe Rogan's elk jerky-fueled DMT journey.

Now we're in the "masculinity is endangered" panic phase. Suddenly, feelings are fascism. Therapy is weakness. And if you acknowledge nonbinary people exist, you're destroying civilization. This is where masculinity **stopped evolving** and started **screaming.**

Why Is It a Clusterfuck in 2025?

- **Shifting Social Norms:** Women lead households, queer visibility is everywhere, and men are expected to do more than "bring home the bacon." Some men adapted. Others panicked.
- **Economic Insecurity:** Jobs are disappearing. Wages are stagnant. College is an expensive trap. And no one wants to talk about class, so it gets channeled into rage about pronouns.
- **The Internet = Rage Amplifier:** Algorithms don't reward nuance— they reward hissy fits in camo hats. Every insecure guy can now find a podcast, a subreddit, or a TikTok creator yelling: *"It's not you, bro. It's feminism."*
- **Political Weaponization:** Conservative politicians love the "masculinity is dying" narrative because it rallies votes through victimhood. Being a victim is now masculine, as long as you're mad about it, not sad about it.
- **The Myth of a Golden Age:** A lot of men are nostalgic for a version of masculinity that never actually existed. The 1950s weren't glory days—they were repression wrapped in a necktie. But nostalgia sells, and nothing sells better than a crisis made up for clicks.

So... What Should Masculinity Be? Healthy masculinity means strength *and* softness. It's leadership *and* listening. It's not dominance—it's decency.

Masculinity isn't dying. It's evolving, and the real fear is that some men don't know how to adapt to it.

Fragility in Flannel: The Glass Cannon of American Manhood

You've heard of toxic masculinity—now meet its source material: *fragile masculinity*, the emotional equivalent of a Jenga tower built on ego. American manhood is a glass cannon—designed to blow everything up around it while shattering under even the lightest criticism. It's tough until asked to take accountability. It's strong until it hears the word "equity." It's heroic until a woman gets the promotion.

This isn't just pop psychology—it's social science. Studies have found that men who strongly identify with traditional masculinity norms experience more stress, lower relationship satisfaction, and increased aggression when they feel their manhood is threatened.[126] In other words, they emotionally short-circuit when their fragile man-script is challenged. Hence, the hyper-defensive overcompensation: buying bigger trucks, lifting heavier weights, and screaming louder about pronouns online. None of this is about strength—it's a desperate plea for relevance in a world that stopped clapping.

For most of American history, masculinity was a golden ticket. If you were a man—especially a white one—your societal value was inherent. You didn't need to evolve, adapt, or even empathize. You needed to show up, and the world rolled out the red carpet for you. Your gender was your résumé. But that formula doesn't compute anymore. The workforce has diversified, and gender roles have shifted; women now feel empowered to speak up in meetings. When "man = value" stopped being true, many men didn't ask, "How do I grow?"—they asked, "Whom can I blame?"

That cultural devaluation triggered a full-scale identity panic. Hence the rise of grievance culture, reactionary politics, and the MAGA movement— all attempts to turn back time to when mediocrity came standard with a Y chromosome.[127] The result? A generation of men is clinging to roles that are as obsolete as VHS tapes in a streaming world. They're not fighting to be better—they're fighting to be worshipped for doing less.

Sally's Sanity: Let Him Grow, Dammit.

Let me say it plainly: We love and need men. We love their loyalty, humor, and messy, beautiful brains. But we are done watching them get stuck in emotional adolescence while the world cheers on every woman's "healing journey" as if it were a Netflix limited series.

Why the hell do we tell women, "You're allowed to grow," and mean men, "Just stay the same and keep lifting heavy things"? Seriously, who decided that vulnerability, therapy, or, god forbid, growth, was some-how **emasculating?** *Who made the rules that said emotional evolution belongs on vision boards and not in manhood?*

Let me tell you what's weak: Pretending you're fine while you're breaking.

Let me tell you what's strong: Saying, "I don't want to be who I was at 19."

Here's the new rule, gentlemen: **Evolve or fossilize.** *We're no longer romanticizing the emotionally unavailable. We're rooting for the men who* **show up, soften, stretch, and rise.** *You want to be alpha? Cool. Please lead us to something better. Start by leading yourself out of the lie that "real men don't change."*

Because let me say it louder for the Dick in the back: **If the women around you are growing and you're not—you're not strong. You're scared. And baby, it's time to grow the hell up.**

With love. And a little rage.

—SALLY

Fragile Masculinity: Strong Enough to Bench Press a Truck, Weak Enough to Cry Over a Pink Starbucks Cup

Fragile masculinity is the cultural phenomenon where some men—typically raised on a steady diet of action movies, emotional repression, and Axe body spray—treat gender identity like a Jenga tower: one wrong pronoun, color, or question about feelings, and the whole thing collapses. It's **testosterone-powered insecurity**, duct-taped together with NFL stats, grill mastery, and the word "bro."

> **Fragile Masculinity (n.):** *A chronic condition where masculinity must be constantly proven, never questioned, and always defended—espe-cially against things like emotions, veganism, seat warmers, reusable shop-ping bags, and the idea that therapy is for everyone, not just "crazy chicks."*

Real-World Examples of Fragile Masculinity in the Wild:

- **The Bud Light Boycott:** When a beer brand sent a can to a trans influencer, some men responded by filming themselves shooting full cases of beer, because nothing says "I'm secure in my identity" like going full Yosemite Sam on aluminum cans.

- **The Gillette Razor Backlash:** A razor commercial gently asked men to stop harassing women and maybe parent their sons better. The response? Meltdown. Suddenly, razors were woke, and toxic masculinity had a new martyr complex. "We just want to shave, not be lectured!" they cried, while lecturing everyone on Facebook for days.

- **The Color Pink:** The mere presence of pink on an object—such as a shirt, phone case, or drink—can trigger a DEFCON 1 response in fragile masculinity. "It's salmon, not pink," insists the man whose masculinity is one Pantone shade away from collapse.

- **"Real Men Don't Cry":** Translation: "Real men bottle up emotions until they explode at a Little League game or get banned from Twitter for yelling about gas stoves."

- **The Gym Bro Who Can't Spot Emotional Growth:** Will squat 400 pounds but can't lift the burden of vulnerability. Also terrified of yoga because "too many girls there."

Fragile masculinity isn't just annoying—it's **culturally dangerous**. It:

- Fuels misogyny, homophobia, and anti-intellectualism.
- Encourages emotional suppression and skyrockets rates of male suicide.[128]
- Turns personal insecurity into public policy—hello, trans bans and reproductive control.
- Converts critical thinking into knee-jerk patriotism: "Don't question America, or you're weak."

Fragile masculinity is the emotional equivalent of a glass trophy labeled "Alpha." It demands respect without reflection, dominance without depth, and freedom—but only if it comes with camo print. And until we teach boys that *being human* isn't unmanly, we'll keep mistaking silence for strength and aggression for authority.

Toxic Masculinity: A Defensive Strategy, Not a Power Play

Toxic masculinity isn't about power—it's about panic. It's fear in a flannel shirt, stomping around with a puffed chest and a podcast mic, praying no one notices the emotional void underneath. This isn't dominance—it's desperation. It's not about being in control; it's about making sure nobody else is.

Toxic masculinity isn't about all men or masculinity itself. It's about a specific, outdated script men are handed—a script that says vulnerability is weakness, empathy is feminine, and control is king. This version of masculinity is less "strong and silent" and more "loud and emotionally bankrupt."

Wikipedia defines toxic masculinity as a harmful, socially constructed norm and expectations associated with traditional masculinity that can negatively impact men and society. It emphasizes traits like dominance, aggression, emotional suppression, and hyper-competitiveness, often leading to adverse outcomes such as violence, relationship problems, and mental health issues.[129]

A Deeper Look: Toxic Masculinity (n.): *A contagious social disease passed down through generations of insecure uncles, gym bros, and war movies, where the only approved emotions are rage, horniness, and mild discomfort at hugging your dad.*

Cultural Symptoms & Side Effects:

1. Crying? No. Punching drywall? Yes.
- A man sobbing at a rom-com = "soft."
- A man going full Hulk on a light switch? "He's just blowing off steam."

2. Therapy = Weak. Rage Tweets = Leadership.
- Toxic masculinity teaches that instead of talking through trauma, you should:
  - Run for office
  - Buy a gun
  - Start a podcast called *Real Men Don't Apologize*

3. Women as Prizes, Not People

- You'll find this flavor of masculinity in every "alpha male" TikTok explaining why a woman who earns money, has opinions, or breathes confidently is a threat to civilization.

4. Consent? That's a Liberal Conspiracy.

- In the toxic playbook, "persistence" is romantic and "no" is just fore-play—because respect for women is unmanly.

5. Emotional Intelligence? I'll Take the Flamethrower Instead.

- Toxic masculinity mistakes empathy for weakness and compassion for political correctness.

Pop Culture's Bro Mascots:

- **Don Draper**: High-functioning alcoholic, emotionally constipated, still romanticized.
- **The Joker (but make it TED Talk)**: Toxic masculinity dressed as "misunderstood genius."
- **Andrew Tate**: A walking TEDx talk on how to alienate women, dodge accountability, and monetize insecurity.

Aggression isn't strength—it's camouflage. Men raised on this script aren't taught to manage fear, anxiety, or grief—they're taught to bury it beneath bravado and, if that fails, violence. The American man doesn't cry; he "loses it." He doesn't seek therapy; he buys ammo. He doesn't say "I'm scared"; he says "We need our country back."

Research backs this up: men who endorse traditional masculinity norms are more likely to respond with aggression when they feel emasculated.[130] It's not confidence—it's cowardice in combat boots. American boys are raised in emotional starvation. From birth, they're told to "man up," "don't cry," and "stop acting like a girl." By adulthood, they're emotionally illiterate—fluent in anger but barely conversational in anything else. And what happens to people who are never taught to process fear, sadness, or rejection? They implode—or explode.

Men are socialized to fear vulnerability more than death. Vulnerability means exposure, and exposure means emasculation. So they run in the other direction: toward stoicism, control, violence—anything that doesn't involve sitting with their feelings. As bell hooks wrote, patriarchy "damages male selfhood,"[131] conditioning men to suppress their emotional selves to maintain dominance.

The Cost and Impact of Toxic Masculinity

School Shootings, Incel Culture, and the Alpha Male:

Enter the grotesque avatars of toxic masculinity: the school shooter, the incel, the self-declared "alpha male." All variations on the same theme—*if I can't have power through respect, I'll take it through force*. Mass shootings are disproportionately carried out by men—especially young men—who feel emasculated, isolated, and voiceless.[132] Incel forums and online radicalization spaces offer them identity, community, and a license to hate. Their war isn't just on women or society—it's on a world that refuses to validate their version of masculinity.

And when these men aren't shooting or sulking, they're flexing in the digital man cave known as the *manosphere*, where being an "alpha" doesn't require leadership or integrity, just a Wi-Fi connection and a fragile ego. It's cosplay for those who mistake volume for value. Toxic masculinity doesn't elevate men—it entraps them. It promises control but delivers isolation. It offers power but breeds paranoia. And it's rapidly becoming the most dangerous cult in American life.

When the "Man Jobs" Disappeared:

There's nothing inherently "male" about mining coal or turning bolts on an assembly line—but for decades, American culture treated these jobs like rituals of manhood. These weren't just occupations; they were *masculine identities with pension plans*.

However, thanks to globalization, deindustrialization, and automation, those jobs vanished like beer at a tailgate party. Between 1980 and 2010, US manufacturing employment dropped by over 7 million jobs.[133] In towns hollowed out by plant closures and disappearing trades, the unspoken message was clear: *you are no longer helpful*.

Economic Decline + Identity Crisis = Perfect Storm:

When men are taught that their worth is tied to economic output, and the economy decides to ghost them, what's left? Not resilience. Not reinvent. Just rage—and enough time to dwell on it. White working-class men, especially in rural and post-industrial communities, found themselves in a triple bind: no jobs, no social safety net, and no cultural narrative for how to fail without shame. They weren't just unemployed—they were emasculated. And the grief turned toxic.

The Great Paradox: white men clinging to the myth of self-reliance even as the ground disappears beneath them.[134] They didn't just lose jobs—they lost identity. The *American Dream* didn't die—it outsourced them.

Opioids: Numbing the Fall from Masculine Grace:

Enter opioids—the chemical Band-Aid for economic and existential free fall. From OxyContin to fentanyl, the opioid epidemic is disproportionately a white male crisis. Between 1999 and 2020, opioid overdose deaths among middle-aged white men skyrocketed, overtaking all other demographic groups groups.[135] These deaths weren't just overdoses—they were slow-motion suicides of a vanishing class.

In other words, opioids filled the space where pride used to live. They became the numbing agent for a generation of men who were told their only value was as providers, and were never taught how to cope when that was taken away.

Grieving the Provider Role—With Numbness, Not Growth:

America never provided men with a healthy way to mourn the loss of their identity. There were no rituals, no therapies, no cultural reframing. Instead, men were handed beer, pills, and nostalgia. They were told to "pull themselves up" from jobs that no longer existed and "man up" without the resources to do so.

So, we medicated the grief. We romanticized the past. And we politicized the pain. The MAGA movement didn't invent this crisis, but capitalized on it. It offered angry men a fantasy of return, a refund on lost pride. But what they needed wasn't a slogan—it was a new model of masculinity, one not dependent on a job title or a paycheck. Unfortunately, that version of masculinity doesn't sell as many pills—or hats.

Conspiracies as Comfort Food for the Intellectually Malnourished:

QAnon. Flat Earth. Vaccine microchips. The deep state. For the emotionally fragile and critically undernourished, conspiracies are the mental Hot Pockets of masculinity—cheap, addictive, and filled with processed nonsense. Believing in wild conspiracies is easier than confronting complexity. It offers simple villains, clear narratives, and, most importantly, an identity. You're not uninformed—you're "awake." You're not paranoid—you're a "free thinker." Never mind that all your free thoughts came from the same subreddit.

Research by Uscinski and Parent (2014) shows that belief in conspiracies is strongly tied to feelings of powerlessness and distrust in traditional institutions—exactly the space where obsolete masculinity lives and rages.[136] It's not about truth—it's about emotional anesthesia.

Why Truth Feels Like Oppression to the Intellectually Fragile:

The truth has become the enemy, not because it's false, but because it's *inconvenient*. When your worldview is built on entitlement, facts that challenge your status feel like personal attacks. Truth becomes betrayal. Science becomes a conspiracy. History becomes "critical race theory." This is why the "I'm being silenced!" trend is trending on platforms with millions of followers. It's why books that mention racism are banned while books on tactical warfare skyrocket in sales. The intellectually fragile don't want freedom of thought—they want freedom *from* thought.

Race and Masculinity: The "White" in White Masculinity

White masculinity was never just one flavor of manhood—it was *the* default. It didn't have to explain, defend, or share the spotlight. It was the operating system of America: installed by the founders, maintained by the Supreme Court, and updated every time a white male CEO gave a keynote on leadership.

But somewhere between Barack Obama's inauguration and the rise of Lil Nas X, something shifted. White masculinity stopped being the unchallenged center of cultural gravity and started feeling—brace yourself—*average*. And if there's one thing fragile power hates, it's being de-centered.

For most of US history, white men didn't just write the rules—they *were* the rules. Their masculinity was seen as neutral, rational, and superior, while all other masculinities were judged as "excessive," "primitive," or "dangerous."[137] Black masculinity? Criminalized. Latino masculinity? Hypersexualized. Asian masculinity? Desexualized. Native masculinity? Erased. White masculinity was free to be whatever it wanted—tender or tough, cowboy or corporate, genius or drunk. But once society started acknowledging other masculinities as *equally valid*, the existential meltdown began. It turns out that being "the standard" was never empowering—it was just an unexamined privilege.

WAKE UP: America's Workforce Is Losing Men—And We're Running Out of Time

We are not heading toward a labor crisis—we are fully entrenched in it. According to *The Rising Storm: Building a Future-Ready Workforce to Withstand the Looming Labor Shortage* by Lightcast (2024), the workforce participation rate for **prime-age men (25–54)** has dropped from **94% in 1980 to 89% in 2024**. That's not a statistical footnote—it's a red flag. We are watching an entire segment of the workforce **opt out, burn out, or get locked out**, and no one's hitting the brakes.

This is a systemic unraveling of male labor potential, driven by:
- Skyrocketing substance abuse
- Disproportionate incarceration rates
- Outdated training systems that leave too many men behind

We're not just losing talent—we're losing fathers, partners, brothers, and sons to cycles of disconnection that no reskilling webinar can fix on its own. This decline comes at the worst possible time, just as the Baby Boomer generation retires en masse and labor shortages tighten across every sector of the economy. A shrinking, gender-skewed workforce cannot carry the weight of national productivity, economic growth, or generational prosperity.

Here's the wake-up call: If we want a thriving economy, we must:

- Invest in mental health and addiction recovery,
- Reform the criminal justice pipeline that warehouses potential, and
- Reimagine male workforce development—not with nostalgia, but with vision.

The storm isn't coming. **It's already here.**

When Masculinity is Mourned, but Others Are Feared

We don't hold a national moment of silence when police kill a young Black man, but we have press conferences when white men lose "their way of life." When Black and Brown men express pain, they're labeled angry or violent. When white men express pain, they're called disillusioned and "left behind." White masculinity isn't dying—it's just losing its monopoly. And instead of evolving, it's mourning. Loudly. Politically. And with poor spelling on protest signs.

Grievance politics thrives on this mourning. It frames any gain by someone else as a loss for men. Equity? That's "discrimination." Diversity? That's "woke indoctrination." The rise of anyone who isn't them? That's *tyranny*. In short, when white masculinity is no longer centered, it doesn't feel like *sharing*—it feels like *oppression*.[138]

"This country used to be great," they say—what they mean is, *we used to be on top*. The MAGA era didn't invent that sentiment; it just gave it a slogan, a hat, and a barely literate Twitter feed.

The underlying message? Put white men back in the center, where they belong—economically, culturally, politically, and yes, even sexually. Patriarchy isn't dying quietly—it's barricaded in the panic room, armed with nostalgia and conspiracy theories.

According to Kimmel (2017), this form of backlash masculinity emerges when entitlement meets disappointment. These men were promised the American Dream. Instead, they got debt, diversity, and daughters who majored in Gender Studies. So, they lash out—not because they're powerless, but because they're no longer *unquestionably powerful*.

This isn't just a masculinity crisis—it's a racialized masculinity crisis. White men aren't just grieving lost roles—they're grieving lost dominance.

And until that grief is named, unpacked, and rewritten into something healthier, it will keep metastasizing into political rage, cultural regression, and yes—more hissy fits.

Toxic Masculinity: Its Toll on Mental Health, Violence & Society[139]

The Damage

1. **Mental Health Crisis Among Men**
   - Rigid masculine norms—like emotional repression and self-reliance—are strongly linked to **higher rates of depression, stress, substance abuse, and suicide in men**.
   - WHO data show that these norms are internalized as early as age 10, and by adulthood, **men are four times more likely than women to die by suicide**.
   - A University of Pittsburgh/UNC study using the "Man Box" scale found men who strongly identify with toxic masculine traits are **twice as likely to experience suicidal or depressive tendencies** and up to **five times more likely to bully or harass others**.

2. **Violence & Aggression**
   - Toxic masculinity endorses violence, dominance, and aggression as core male traits—both predictive and permissive of **sexual assault, domestic violence, and homicide**.
   - Globally, men commit around **90% of homicides** and make up over **75% of homicide victims**—a pattern linked to hypermasculine culture.

3. **Health & Risk-Taking**
   - Men influenced by these norms often shun healthcare, delay neces-

sary treatment, engage in **dangerous driving**, binge drinking, and **other risk behaviors**, resulting in **higher rates of heart disease, lung cancer, and workplace injuries.**

4. Education & Emotional Literacy
- Boys socialized into stoicism and "toughness" often exhibit **lower emotional intelligence**, which correlates with aggression and poor relationship skills.
- Those raised with statements like "man up" internalize limited emotional roles, increasing their risk of **psychological distress long-term.**

5. Social & Cultural Costs
- In prisons, toxic norms become exaggerated codes of survival, increasing risks of violence and suicide.
- Boys who strictly adhere to hypermasculine ideals are more likely to **harass or assault others**, particularly women and LGBTQ+ individuals.

The Masculinity Grift: Selling Insecurity Back to Men

Welcome to the masculinity marketplace, where insecurity isn't a bug—it's a business model. A billion-dollar industry has emerged not to *solve* the male identity crisis but to *profit* from it. Here, rage is monetized, protein powder is prescribed as personality, and emotional repression is repackaged as "alpha energy." It's not self-help. It's self-hustle. This is late-stage patriarchy: capitalism realized that men feeling lost was *great* for business.

The Billion-Dollar Bro Industry: Supplements, Podcasts, and Snake Oil

There was a time when men would seek therapy or confide in a friend. Now? They're told to "optimize" themselves with cold plunges, powdered testosterone, four-hour daily workouts, and twelve-hour podcast marathons about the dangers of carbs and women.

The "bro economy" thrives on volume and vacuum—loud voices filling an emotional void. And it works. The global men's wellness industry is projected to hit over $165 billion by 2027.[140] This isn't masculinity—it's multilevel marketing for male validation. Everything from hair loss pills to "nootropic stacks" comes with the same pitch: *You're not enough. But if you buy this, you might be.* The solution to your emptiness isn't reflection—it's retail.

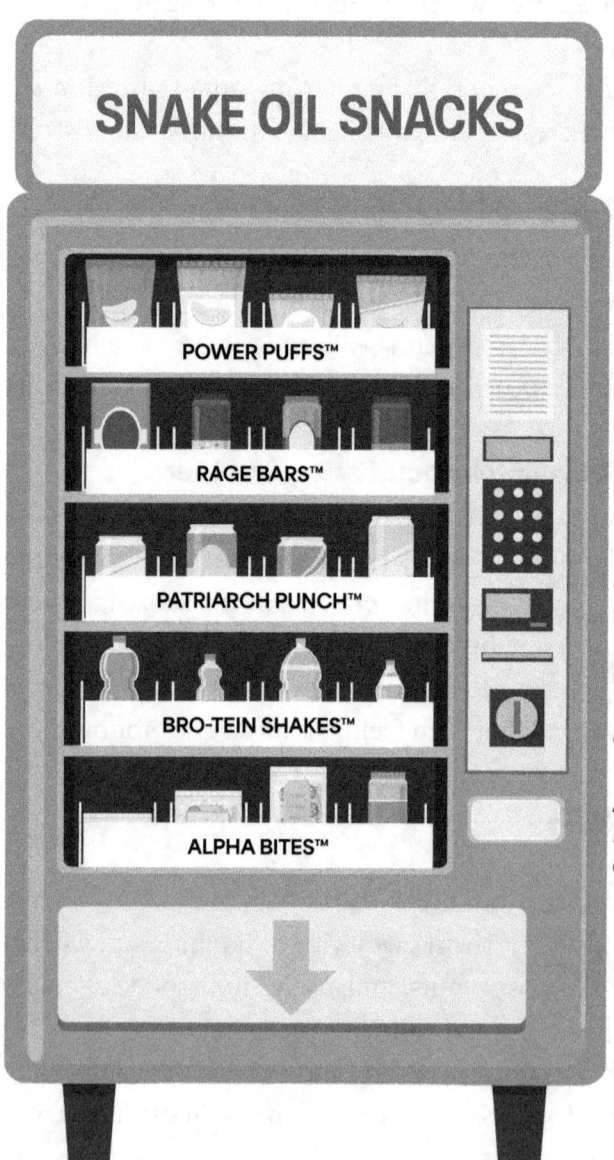

POWER PUFFS™
Tiny nuggets of toxic positivity.

RAGE BARS™
Fuel for your next online argument.

PATRIARCH PUNCH™
200% your daily dose of misplaced anger.

BRO-TEIN SHAKES™
Vanilla Rage flavor. 60g of insecurity per serving.

ALPHA BITES™
Fortified with podcast opinions.

Jordan Peterson, Andrew Tate, Joe Rogan: Holy Trinity of Hollow Masculinity and Making Money Off Men

If Freud had a nightmare, these three would be on a panel discussing manhood. Jordan Peterson tells men to clean their rooms instead of their inner lives. Andrew Tate teaches them that emotional detachment and violence are virtues. Joe Rogan gives them just enough pseudo-intellectualism to feel superior while still yelling at baristas.

Together, they form the Holy Trinity of hollow masculinity: *Control. Conquest. Creatine.*

Peterson repackages 1950s gender roles in a Canadian accent while warning against the chaos of "feminine energy." Tate offers Hustler's University, which is neither a university nor particularly intelligent—just a pay-to-play masculinity pyramid scheme. Rogan gives it all a "just asking questions" vibe while platforming anyone who yells loud enough to sound confident.

Patron Saints of Overcompensating Masculinity:

Jordan Peterson—The Intellectual Lobster Daddy:

"Clean your room, fear the dragon, and blame feminism."

Jordan Peterson is the individual who walks into a therapy session and turns it into a TED Talk about ancient mythology, emotional repression, and why Disney movies are prophetic warnings about the decline of humanity. He speaks in riddles that feel deep until you realize you just listened to a 45-minute monologue on why lobsters prove gender hierarchies are natural. Cries during interviews, but insists crying is a *manly act of symbolic purification.* Wears suits tighter than his logic. He loves quoting Jung, but ignores the fact that Jung would probably advise him to nap. His audience? Emotionally constipated men who highlight entire books and still think "feminism = Marxism."

Peterson repackages traditional gender roles with a veneer of academic credibility, urging young men to "clean their rooms" while often neglecting deeper societal issues.

- **Net Worth:** Estimates range from $8 million to potentially over $100 million, considering various income streams.
- **Income Sources:** Book sales (*12 Rules for Life*), speaking engagements, online courses, and Patreon support.
- **Rise to Fame:** Gained prominence in 2016 by opposing Canada's Bill C-16, arguing it infringed on free speech.[141]

Peterson isn't offering clarity—he's selling confusion with academic seasoning. He's what happens when a self-help book gets a YouTube channel and trauma.

Andrew Tate–The Alpha Bro in a Bugatti

"Women are property. Also, buy my crypto."

Andrew Tate is like what you'd get if toxic masculinity ran a drop-shipping scam and wore mirrored sunglasses indoors. He speaks entirely in red flags and thinks emotional intelligence is **"for betas and broke people."** Every sentence begins with "Listen, bro," and ends with either a misogynistic outburst or a link to his online pyramid scheme. Claims to be a "high-value man," but can't define "value" beyond Bugattis and bench presses. Says depression isn't real, then rage-posts for six hours. Thinks therapy is a weakness, but talks to a webcam like it's his diary. Charges young men $49.99/month to learn how to dominate women and fear empathy.

Tate monetizes a brand of masculinity that equates success with dominance and emotional detachment, often at the expense of promoting healthy, respectful relationships.

- **Net Worth:** Highly disputed; estimates range from $12 million (per Romanian authorities) to claims of $710 million.
- **Income Sources:** Online platforms like "Hustler's University," social media influence, and cryptocurrency investments.
- **Rise to Fame:** former professional kickboxer who gained fame—and notoriety—by promoting a hyper-masculine lifestyle across social media platforms, where he often courted controversy through bold, misogynistic rhetoric. In May 2025, the Crown Prosecution Service in the UK authorized criminal charges against Andrew (38) and his

brother Tristan (36), including rape, actual bodily harm, human trafficking, and controlling prostitution for gain. These allegations involve multiple victims and stem from both past UK investigations and ongoing legal proceedings in Romania.[142]

Tate isn't a mentor—he's a walking midlife crisis in Armani cologne, selling masculinity like it's an MLM. He's not a role model. He's a **cautionary tale with abs.**

Joe Rogan–The Concussed Philosopher-King of Spotify

"I'm not an expert, but I know a guy who took horse paste and lived."

Joe Rogan is your friend's older brother who once did the psychedelic drug DMT in the woods and now thinks he understands geopolitics. He starts every conversation with "It's crazy, dude…". He concludes with a three-hour interview with someone banned from academic conferences, bowling alleys, and online platforms, who has been featured more than any conspiracy theorists on Reddit. Thinks "just asking questions" is a personality. His fanbase includes UFC dads, CrossFit libertarians, and dudes who say "actually, both sides are bad" during genocides. Will interview a climate scientist and a flat-earther back-to-back and call it "balance."

Rogan provides a platform where controversial ideas can flourish under the guise of "just asking questions," giving his audience a sense of intellectual superiority while often sidestepping accountability.

- **Net Worth**: Estimated at $200 million as of 2025.[143]
- **Income Sources**: Spotify deal worth over $200 million, podcast sponsorships, stand-up comedy, UFC commentary, and ownership of the Comedy Mothership club.
- **Rise to Fame**: Started as a stand-up comedian and TV host, gained massive popularity with "The Joe Rogan Experience" podcast launched in 2009.[144]

Rogan isn't curious—he's a human suggestion algorithm stuck in a sensory deprivation tank. He's not dumb. He plays dumb *very loudly, for $100 million.*

Their collective message? Growth is for weak men.
Real men dominate, debate, and detox.

Research shows that traditional masculinity ideology—especially when combined with media exposure to hypermasculine role models—correlates with increased anxiety, sexism, and resistance to seeking help.[145] But why face your emotional landscape when you can download another podcast?

Masculinity used to be about integrity, character, and resilience. Now? It's a 10% discount code at checkout. You can buy manhood in monthly installments—add to cart. The grift is elegant in its simplicity: make men feel small, then sell them something to feel big again.

You're not depressed—you're low on magnesium. You're not emotionally stunted—you need better biceps. You're not lonely—you need to dominate your morning routine.

It's not empowerment—it's upselling.

And let's not forget the actual currency of the grift: *rage*. These platforms and influencers don't just sell products—they sell emotional adrenaline. Outrage at women. Fury at "the woke left." Hatred for the "beta males" who went to therapy and got custody of the kids. This isn't a community, it's a cult with affiliate links. Rage gets engagement, and engagement pays. A modern media ecosystems are built on outrage cycles that radicalize identity and hollow out critical thinking.[146]

The influence of Peterson, Tate, and Rogan isn't just provocative—it's malevolent. What they package as "self-improvement" or "truth-telling" is often little more than contempt for women dressed up as philosophy, entertainment, or empowerment. This isn't harmless banter; it's ideology with teeth. Their success underscores the danger: why encourage reflection when rage builds a brand? The masculinity grift thrives precisely because it keeps men simmering—angry enough to keep clicking, buying, and blaming anyone but themselves. And make no mistake: the poison they spew doesn't stay online. It seeps into workplaces, relationships, and politics, shaping real behaviors with real consequences.

Dick's Hissy Fit:
These guys are truth-tellers, not elites.

"Jordan Peterson teaches men how to be men again, Andrew Tate shows us how real power works, the MyPillow guy proves faith and business go hand in hand, and Joe Rogan—he's the only one brave enough to say what everyone's thinking. These guys are truth-tellers, not elites. They're the voices the woke mob wants silenced because they remind us what strength, freedom, and masculinity are all about. I don't care what the media says—these are the role models America needs."

—Dick

Reimagining Masculinity: What Comes After the Hissy Fit?

The traditional model of masculinity has entered its flop era. The emotionally numb, domination-obsessed, never-cry-in-public alpha male archetype has been exposed for what it is: a cultural Ponzi scheme. And like all Ponzi schemes, the return on investment is crashing hard. But here's the good news, boys: there *is* another way. Masculinity doesn't have to mean control. It doesn't have to mean aggression, conquest, or quoting Joe Rogan as if he were Scripture. It doesn't even have to involve lifting heavy objects unless you want it to. What if masculinity were defined by character instead of conquest? What if it was about showing up, not showing off?

This reimagined masculinity does not need hierarchy. It thrives in *mutuality*, not domination. Studies in contemporary gender psychology suggest that flexible gender roles correlate with higher emotional well-being, better communication, and healthier relationships.[147] Yes, science says: chill out, Chad.

The Rise of Emotionally Literate Men (They Walk Among Us)

You might not notice them at first. They're not shouting. They're not punching drywall. They're the ones asking questions in meetings, calling their kids back when they miss a call, and—brace yourself—actively listening. These men aren't soft—they're *solid*. They've learned that emotional intelligence is not the enemy of masculinity, but the upgrade. They still get angry—but they also know how to name it, sit with it, and not use it as a weapon.

Real strength? Try wiping spit-up off your shirt while managing a team Zoom call. Try choosing de-escalation over destruction. Try raising daughters who know they're powerful and sons who know it's okay to cry. These "soft" skills—once dismissed as feminine—are now being recognized as leadership gold. Workplace research shows that empathetic leadership directly correlates with employee retention, job satisfaction, and performance.[148] Translation: feelings aren't a liability—they're a leadership strategy. We are witnessing a quiet revolution in male identity, and the leaders of this new masculinity aren't flexing—they're facilitating. They don't need a podium. They've got presence.

Masculinity as Strength in Truth, Not Bluster

Here's a radical thought: what if strength wasn't about who you can dominate, but about *who you can be honest with*—including yourself? The new masculinity doesn't fear vulnerability—it integrates it. It doesn't see emotions as dangerous—it sees them as data. It doesn't use women for validation or other men for competition—it engages with both from a place of security. This isn't a weakness. This is *emotional integrity*—the ability to stand in truth, admit failure, express care, and still keep your damn spine. In a culture of bluster and bravado, truth is the new rebellion.

Evolve or Erode: A Cultural Ultimatum

Will society embrace this evolution, or will it cling to the hissy fit until the culture collapses under the weight of its testosterone-soaked delusions? Will we raise boys to believe that power is presence, not posturing? Will we honor men who show tenderness instead of temper? Will we finally kill the myth that being a man means being emotionally constipated and spiritually bankrupt? Because here's the real masculine crisis: not that masculinity is disappearing, but that too many are refusing to grow up. The hissy fit was loud, but the future will be *quietly strong*—and built by men who don't need to yell to be heard.

Goodbye, Tough Guy

The tough guy is tired. And honestly? So are we. For decades, we've watched him storm through pop culture, politics, and parenting with clenched fists and clenched minds. He's been the cowboy, the CEO, the war hero, the dad who never says "I love you," the senator who's never read a book by a woman, and the podcast host who confuses volume with wisdom. But now the lights are dimming, the act is worn thin, and even the back row can see the cracks in the armor.

Toxic masculinity is expensive—and not just in therapy bills and broken relationships. It costs lives. It fuels violence. It drives suicide rates among men.[149] It feeds addictions, alienates sons, isolates fathers, and turns potential into pathology. Propping up this broken identity has been a national pastime. We reward silence over self-awareness. We confuse anger with strength. We hand out participation trophies for showing zero emotion.

The result? A gender identity held together by shame, resentment, and protein powder.

And the longer we maintain the charade, the higher the bill will rise.

We're not burying men. We're burying the myth—the outdated, overacted, and overmarketed version of manhood that refuses to evolve. The one that sees compassion as a weakness, change as a threat, and introspection as a "liberal conspiracy." We're saying goodbye to the man who never said what he felt, because no one ever taught him how. We're lowering the belief that dominance equals respect into the ground. We're writing the obituary for a masculinity too afraid to feel. And in its place? Not softness. Not passivity. But *authenticity*—the kind of masculinity that can hold a child and a conversation, that can lift weights and still ask for help, that leads not with fear but with grounded, secure presence. "The wounded masculine can be healed. It can be made whole."[150] But first, it must let go of the myth.

Sally's Sanity: Call to Men—Put Down the Pitchfork, Pick Up a Mirror

Alright, Dick—enough with the cosplay. No more pitchforks, no more red pill fantasies, no more rage-click rabbit holes. You're not a warrior in the Matrix, you're a guy hiding behind memes, podcasts, and performative stoicism.

Put it down.

Put down the outrage.

Put down the scripted masculinity that tells you real men never feel

Put down the need to dominate every room just to prove you exist.

Now—pick up a mirror.

Ask yourself:

- *Who am I when I stop performing manhood like it's a bad reality show?*
- *What happens when I choose presence over posturing?*
- *What kind of man am I actually becoming—and who sold me the lie that this was enough?*

Because here's the truth: the bravest thing you'll ever do isn't shouting louder. It's standing still long enough to face yourself.

This isn't a surrender. It's a revolution. But it starts not with rage but with reflection.

The tough-guy myth is ending—not because it was overthrown, but because it collapsed under the weight of its emotional bankruptcy.

—LOVE, SALLY

Fractured, Fuming, and Fundamentally Lost

Where We Are… and Why the Road Ahead Must Go Backward Before It Goes Forward

America isn't just divided. It's dissociated. We're not living in a culture war—we're living in a culture identity crisis. Two flags. Two realities. Two completely different definitions of "freedom," "truth," and "the Founding

Fathers." This wasn't a glitch. **It was a feature. We've been taught a mythology, not a history:**

- A clean narrative scrubbed of complexity,
- A Founding framed like a TED Talk on liberty,
- And a nation built for *everyone*... just not all at once—and certainly not equally.

We can't move forward by pretending this fracture doesn't exist. We sure as hell can't heal it by slapping a red, white, and blue bumper sticker over a centuries-old foundation crack.

What Comes Next: The Reckoning

To understand how we got here, we must now ask: **"What exactly *was* America created to be?"** And here's the uncomfortable truth: The Constitution was both a blueprint for democracy and a manual for maintaining elite power. Freedom was proclaimed, but property came first. Liberty was promised, but whiteness and land ownership were the admission ticket. The fractures we live with today were poured into the foundation of this country—baked into its laws, normalized in its culture, and worshipped in its textbooks.

Before we rewrite the next chapter of America, we're going to read the **real one**—the one with footnotes, contradictions, and bloodstains. Because if we're going to grow the fuck up as a nation, we need to stop telling bedtime stories and start confronting **historical reality.**

Next Chapter: The Myth of Innocence–America's Birth and the Blueprint for the Hissy Fit

Spoiler alert: The Founding Fathers weren't gods. They were land-owning, slaveholding, tax-dodging men who threw a national tantrum over tea and control. And in doing so, they built a nation that still values emotion over equity, control over community, and hissy fits over hard truths.

Let's go back—not to *"when America was great,"* but to when America was born. Not to romanticize it—**but to reckon with it**. The fracture didn't begin in 2016. It started the moment "We the People" meant only *some* people. And it's time we finally talk about it.

The Wrap Up: From Founding Tantrum to National Identity Crisis: How the Hissy Fit Became the Culture

Part I wasn't a history lesson—it was an intervention. A high-speed crash into the cultural brick wall we've been pretending isn't there. From powdered wigs and property rights to gaslighting in God's name, America's story is one long, uninterrupted hissy fit—dressed up as manifest destiny and exceptionalism.

What we've uncovered in these chapters isn't just a string of unfortunate events—it's a blueprint. A playbook. A cultural operating system that runs on grievance, denial, and performative rage. It's not broken. It's behaving exactly as designed.

Let's review the receipts:

- We diagnosed a nation that mistakes ego for patriotism and grievance for governance.
- We exposed an origin story less about liberty and more about land, labor, and legacy laundering.
- We traced how whiteness, maleness, and God weren't just ideals—they were gatekeeping devices for power.
- We showed how policy, religion, and ideology formed a weaponized trinity aimed at stalling progress.
- And we tracked the emotional genealogy of the American Hissy Fit— from powdered wigs to Fox News to Project 2025.

America wasn't built for equity—it was built for order. And that order had a very specific hierarchy. Every time that order is challenged, the car alarm goes off. Loud. Relentless. Familiar. These aren't growing pains. These are refusal-to-grow pains. The tantrums aren't malfunctions. They're features.

Where Do We Go From Here?

We can't heal what we won't face. And America has been allergic to self-reflection since 1776. That's where Part II begins. Not with comfort—but with clarity. Not with optimism—but with options. This next section isn't about handwringing. It's about soul-searching. It's where we shift from diagnosing dysfunction to dismantling the delusion. Where we explore what it actually takes to build a culture that isn't addicted to its own myth. Because if we want to become something more than a legacy of hissy fits, we're going to have to do more than rewrite history—we're going to have to rewrite our emotional DNA.

Part II:

The Skeleton of Denial: How America Built Its Own Fracture Line

You want to know why America throws hissy fits so convincingly? Because **it's been practiced since day one**. This isn't a nation that lost its way; it's a nation that **paved its way in denial**, selling a story about freedom while writing exceptions in the fine print. You've been told America is the land of the free, but nobody clarified *for whom*.

Remember the phrase *"The truth will set you free, but first it will piss you off?"* Yeah. This is the part where you get pissed off. Because what you're about to read will crack open the illusion. It will show you just how deep the fracture runs—how denial hardened into doctrine, how convenient amnesia rewrote the past, and how the tantrums we throw today are rooted in a legacy of stolen credit, selective memory, and willful ignorance.

We've made denial a national pastime:

- Denial of **genocide** while celebrating Thanksgiving.
- Denial of **slavery's legacy** while quoting the Founding Fathers.
- Denial of **inequality** while screaming about "equal opportunity."

We've romanticized an America that never existed outside of black-and-white TV reruns, church bulletins, and suburban mythologies where lawns mattered more than justice. And we've enshrined that denial in policy, in school curricula, in gated communities, and in laws designed to protect *feelings* rather than *freedom*.

You think it's a coincidence we melt down over drag queens reading to kids while ignoring book bans and broken schools? That we clutch our pearls over pronouns while ignoring poverty, mass shootings, and a crumbling healthcare system?

We didn't arrive at this culture of outrage by accident. We built it, generation after generation, church potluck after church potluck, redlined mortgage after redlined mortgage, denial layered on denial like a casserole of collective amnesia.

This part of the book won't offer you comfort. It's going to give you a mirror and ask: **"What exactly are you defending when you say you love America?"**

Because the fracture didn't start with the Orange Era, it started the moment America declared freedom while clutching chains. It grew every time "progress" meant *someone else had to shut up and wait*. It calcified every time the powerful protected their comfort by legislating away someone else's existence.

Does that make you uncomfortable? Good. Because denial thrives in comfort, and comfort is what got us here.

CHAPTER 7

The United States of Denial: How Our History Built the Cultural Dumpster Fire We Call "Freedom"

Welcome to America's origin story—where powdered wigs met weaponized victimhood, and freedom was a carefully rationed substance hoarded by land-owning white men like it was colonial cocaine.

L et's get one thing straight before we begin this journey together: I'm as red, white, and blue as they come. I served in the US Armed Forces, and I take immense pride in being American. But pride doesn't mean unquestioning loyalty. I know our history—and I won't pretend it's pretty. That's precisely why I'm writing this book.

We are better than this. Better than the sanitized myths. Better than the blind spots we've inherited. And better than the performative patriotism that disguises itself as truth. This isn't about radicalization or white shaming. It's about reality. I'm not here to tear down our founding fathers, democracy, religion, or political parties. I'm here to strip away the rose-colored lenses so we can see where we are—and more importantly, where we *could* go.

This is truth-telling with spine. It's the same approach I take in every other part of my life: direct, unfiltered, and grounded in accountability. Because only by facing our whole story—unvarnished and unafraid—can we build the future we claim to believe in. This is the unfiltered cut—the part where the Founding Fathers weren't bold visionaries, but insecure gatekeepers who staged a national hissy fit because the king made them pay taxes. They didn't create liberty. They rebranded privilege, slapped a flag on it, and called it democracy.

The Truth: America wasn't founded on freedom. It was founded on *selective freedom,* enforced by muskets and mansplained by men who thought "justice for all" was a charming suggestion—unless you were Black, Indigenous, female, poor, queer, or breathing while different.

Let's take a moment to tip our powdered wigs to the white men who built this country—no sarcasm (well, a little). Without them, we wouldn't have a Constitution, a Capitol, or that impressive knack for declaring independence while owning people (Jefferson, we're looking at you). But seriously—credit where credit is due. The founding fathers launched a revolutionary idea: government by the people (read: land-owning, Protestant, white men over 21), freedom of religion (so long as it was Protestant), and liberty for all (as long as "all" didn't include women, Indigenous people, enslaved Africans, or the Irish on Tuesdays). And yet—**it was visionary.** For its time, it *was* radical. They built roads, wrote laws, framed institutions, invented peanut brittle, and never buttoned the top three buttons of a waistcoat. These were men of vision, powdered hair, and deeply problematic contradictions.[151]

But Here's the Deal: They built this country with the best tools, knowledge, and prejudices they had at the time. And for that, we say "Thank you." But folks—it's been almost 250 years. Penicillin exists now. Women vote. Wi-Fi is a thing. We've landed on the moon and can Google the Constitution instead of crossing a swamp to read it aloud by lantern. So, why are we clinging to 18th-century blueprints as if they were divine scripture?

The founders were disruptors of *their* time. If they were alive today, they'd be on TikTok quoting Voltaire in hoodies and probably trying to figure out what "gaslighting" means. They *evolved* from monarchists to revolutionaries—maybe we can evolve from rigid traditionalists to something a bit more inclusive? Without those white men, we wouldn't have the framework. But without *everyone else,* we wouldn't have the house standing. It's okay to outgrow the floor plan, Dick. The original home had no indoor plumbing.

Buckle up, brave reader—this chapter doesn't follow the usual script. I've tossed the standard flow out the window and gone straight for the jugular, breaking this down by many historical milestones: the laws, policies, power plays, enforcement goons, and institutional hissy fits that sculpted the twisted cultural sculpture we now call America. I focused on the heavy hitters—the legacy events that still shape how we talk, vote, rage, and regress today. Yes, there are plenty of other moments worth spotlighting, but unfortunately, I'm producing one book, not a nine-part Ken Burns documentary.

A timeline of America's legislative mood swings follows—packed with receipts, peppered with sarcasm, and stitched with enough caffeine and truth to stabilize your blood pressure. And the deeper I dug, the more I laughed… then cried… then rage-screamed into a throw pillow. Because beneath all the "freedom-loving" rhetoric, there lies a system built without critical thinking in its blueprint.

Why Understanding this Progression and Its Cultural Implications Matters

You can't fix a house if you pretend the foundation isn't cracked. You can't heal a nation by insisting the raging infection was just a mild inconvenience. And you sure as hell can't build an equitable future if you're still singing lullabies about how "all men are created equal" while ignoring that half the men were property and the other half were polishing muskets. Understanding the actual birth of America—hissy fits, treason, exclusions, contradictions and all—**forces honesty into the room.** It rips the sheen of fantasy off the storybook cover and shows the machinery underneath: a system meticulously engineered to advantage the few and disenfranchise the many.

Here's why it matters:

- **It exposes the Blueprint of Inequity**: Racial caste systems, economic exclusion, gender silencing—these aren't bugs in the system. They're the original code. If you don't understand how inequality was built into the operating system, you'll never debug it. You'll keep upgrading the same broken model with shinier language.

- **It Shatters the Myth of Accidental Injustice**: Poverty, racial wealth gaps, educational inequities, mass incarceration—none of these "just happened." They were constructed with the same intentionality that laid the bricks of Wall Street. Recognizing this strips away the nonsensical idea that injustice is accidental and instead demands solutions that are as deliberate.

- **It Forces Accountability Over Nostalgia**: America loves nostalgia like a toddler loves candy. But nostalgia is a drug that blinds people to systemic rot. Understanding the real history forces the uncomfortable but necessary pivot from *"Weren't the Founders inspiring?"* to *"How do we fix the parts they rigged?"*

- **It Equips Us to Build Systems, Not Slogans**: "Diversity," "equity," and "inclusion" aren't decorations. They're structural repairs. You can't slap a DEI sticker on a broken wall built for exclusion. You have to reframe who *systems* serve, who *decisions* prioritize, and whose *lives* get valued at every level.

- **It Connects Every Fight for Justice to Its Roots**: Whether it's voting rights, police reform, reproductive rights, or education equity, every modern struggle is a branch of the same poisoned tree. Knowing the root rot prevents you from treating symptoms when the soil itself needs clearing.

- **It Redefines Patriotism as Accountability, Not Denial**: Real love for a country is refusing to let it lie to itself forever. Real patriotism is fixing what's broken, not draping yourself in a flag and pretending the cracks are character marks.

To build a strong and healthy national culture, we have to stare straight into the mess we were born from—plantation profits, hypocrisy, hysteria, and all—and choose to build something better, on purpose, this time.

These are simply the facts, with a touch of satire and sarcasm—no fiction. Want to argue? Do the (real) research.

Here's your challenge: Can you make it to the end of this chapter and still have the nerve to say, "America is the land of the free and the brave, a country founded on equality that has matured into equity"? These are the elements of governance that established the US culture, and they have been left unchallenged and untouched for too long.

The Myth of Innocence: America's Birth and the Blueprint for the Hissy Fit (1600-1800)

America's origin story loves to cast itself as the earnest underdog, scrappy rebels taking on the British Empire. In reality? It was more like a toddler having a tantrum with a gun.

America loves to portray itself as the scrappy underdog fighting tyranny. Reality? It was a toddler with a gun throwing a hissy fit over taxes while building its empire on stolen land and enslaved people. We didn't want *freedom*; we wanted **exclusive freedom**—pre-approved for white, land-owning men. Every time someone points this out, America clutches its pearls like a Southern belle hearing the word "pronouns."

Slavery: America's First Business Plan.

Slavery wasn't a bug in the system; it *was* the system—human beings bought, sold, insured, and inherited like cattle to fuel America's sugar, cotton, and capitalist dreams. Northern banks, Southern plantations, and Wall Street? All in on it.

- The White House? Built by enslaved workers.
- The economy? Built on Black backs.
- Slavery? Profitable, scalable, and marketed as a "positive good."
- The Confederacy? Formed when the profit margin was threatened.

The Revolution: Freedom for Who?

The Revolutionary War wasn't a noble rebellion; it was a business decision by wealthy colonists tired of sharing profits with King George. They wanted to rule themselves—and keep ruling everyone else.

What it was really about:

- Taxes and economic control.
- Property and power.

- Liberty for the elite, debt for the soldiers who fought for it.

"All men are created equal"—except enslaved people, Indigenous nations, women, and the poor. Jefferson wrote those words while enslaving over 600 people. The Constitution counted Black people as 3/5 of a person *to give more power to slave states*, not to grant humanity.

Divide and Conquer: Whiteness as a Loyalty Program.

When poor Black and white people started uniting (see: Bacon's Rebellion, 1676), the elite panicked and invented whiteness as a social upgrade to keep the poor divided and the rich in power. This system worked then, and still does now.

The Founders Didn't Forget Anyone. They Excluded Them.

Abigail Adams famously asked her husband John to *"remember the ladies"* when drafting the new nation's laws. His reply? A dismissive joke about how men would never submit to such "tyranny."[152] The Founders didn't forget anyone. They excluded them. It wasn't ignorance—it was intent. They knew exactly who democracy was for and who it wasn't. The system they built was designed to protect property (including enslaved human beings), dampen democracy (see: the Senate and Electoral College), and preserve their own power, all while marketing it as "freedom."

Legacy: The Original Gaslighting

The real American revolution was a rebrand, not a rupture. The Founders handed us a country built on exclusion, then wrote *just enough lofty ideals* for the oppressed to use those words against the system eventually. Every civil rights movement since then has involved America being handed the language of its early pamphlets and asked: "Care to explain this bullshit?"

America wasn't born free. It was born *fragile and exclusive*, with receipts. The hissy fits we see today? Just the latest sequel in a long-running franchise called **"Freedom for Me, Control for Thee."**

This section takes a culture-first lens on America's history—dynamic, impactful, and already sprawling enough. I'm not cataloging every event, just the ones that matter most to the story at hand.

1600s–1861ish: Slavery: America's First Corporate Merger (Now With 100% More Human Suffering)

No sugarcoating it—unless we're talking about the literal sugar plantations watered with blood and tears. Slavery wasn't a moral oversight or an unfortunate chapter in history. It was *the business model*. The original IPO of American capitalism was written in shackles, auction blocks, and human flesh. Learned behavior from the country we came from. Enslaved Africans weren't laborers—they were the capital, the machinery, and the product. Cotton? King. Slaves? The crown jewels. The North liked to pretend it had clean hands, but Northern banks, textile mills, and shipping companies were deep in the slavery investment portfolio.[153]

This wasn't a glitch in the system. *This was the system.* **The Economy Was Built on Black Backs—Literally**

- The cotton empire? Black labor.
- Southern wealth? Black labor.
- Northern industrial boom? Black labor, outsourced and leveraged like venture capital.
- The White House? Built by enslaved workers. In America, even "freedom" came pre-restricted, designed to serve the powerful while excluding the very people who built it.

Slavery wasn't only profitable—it was scalable. Enslaved people were bought, sold, insured, and inherited. Wall Street's first big play? Auctions where Black families were torn apart with the same glee used to ring the trading bell.[154]

Racial Capitalism 101

Enslaved people weren't considered humans. They were assets. The return on investment was measured in terms of lashes and birth rates. And every whip cracked was a dividend paid to the plantation elite. Southern politicians didn't defend this system—they *branded* it. Slavery was marketed as a "positive."[155] Reasonable, not a necessity. *That's right:* they managed to turn genocide into a marketing campaign. The antebellum South was less *Gone With the Wind* and more *Shark Tank* meets *The Handmaid's Tale*.

When the Profit Margin Was Threatened, So Was the Union

When the North finally said, "Hey, maybe we should stop building our economy on human suffering," the South replied, "Hold my moonshine—we're forming a country." Thus, the Confederacy was born: a secessionist startup with a single mission statement: *Keep Owning People*.

Their founders didn't hide it. In the Cornerstone Speech, Confederate VP Alexander Stephens made it crystal clear: **"Our new government is founded upon... the great truth that the negro is not equal to the white man."**[156] No, it wasn't about tariffs or tea parties or "states' rights." It was about profit, power, and plantation spreadsheets. Slavery was America's first corporate merger. It aligned white supremacy with economic supremacy, producing a business model so efficient it still pays dividends in the form of racial wealth gaps, housing discrimination, and corporate boardrooms that look like a country club got lost and wandered into a DEI meeting.

1676-1773: Freedom for Sale:
Class Stratification in the Birth of a Nation

Let's strip the varnish off the Revolutionary myth for a second. We've all seen the Broadway musical. The powdered wigs. The stirring cries of *liberty or death*! But beneath the heroic soundtrack and carefully lit parchment paper lies a far less inspiring truth: *America wasn't born out of a shared vision for freedom*. It was developed from a business plan. The Founding Fathers didn't create a government of the people, by the people, for the people. They made a government *for the property-owning elite, by the property-owning elite*, with enough inspiring rhetoric to keep the masses from asking too many follow-up questions.

The American colonies primarily fought the Revolutionary War (1775–1783) to gain independence from **British rule**. While the phrase "No taxation without representation" is often highlighted in school textbooks, the war's causes were broader and more complex beneath the surface.

What Was It Really About?

Here's a breakdown of the key motives—stripped of myth and polished with a bit of truth:

1. **Taxation and Economic Control:** The colonies were being taxed by the British Parliament (e.g., the Stamp Act, Tea Act) without having any representatives in Parliament. Colonists sought control over their economies, trade, and the wealth they generated, especially the elite landowners and merchants who didn't like sharing profits with King George.

2. **Self-Governance:** Enlightenment ideas were spreading—Locke, Montesquieu, and Rousseau were whispering about liberty, natural rights, and the "consent of the governed. The colonies didn't want a tax break—they wanted to write their own laws and call their own political shots.

3. **Standing Armies and Sovereignty:** The presence of British troops in peacetime was seen as oppressive. The Quartering Act (requiring colonists to house British soldiers) was particularly loathed—people weren't thrilled to share their porches with redcoats.

4. **Power & Property:** The wealthy planter and merchant classes wanted to preserve and expand their economic systems—including systems dependent on enslaved labor—without interference from the Crown. The British had issued the **Proclamation of 1763**, restricting colonists from settling west of the Appalachians to avoid conflicts with Native Americans. Colonists wanted more land and less oversight.

5. **Control over Colonial Institutions:** Religious freedom was part of it for some, but mainly, the war was about **who would be in charge,** both locally and nationally. The war was less about universal liberty and more about **preserving the freedom of those already in power.**

Rewind to 1676 Virginia, where class tension, racial brutality, and colonial entitlement collided in what might be America's original nightmare scenario: Bacon's Rebellion. It began with poor white settlers, who were angry about the land, wealth, and political power they'd been promised but never received. Enslaved Black people were, of course, denied even humanity. Native tribes were being slaughtered or shoved aside. Meanwhile, the elite clutched their pearls (and property), hoarding land and cozying up to Britain.

Here was the real threat: solidarity. Poor folks of different races realized their shared oppression and pointed fingers *upward* instead of sideways. Bacon's mob torched Jamestown. Elites panicked. The rebellion ended when Bacon died of dysentery (poetic, really). But the aftermath? Oh, that stuck.

The Response: Divide and Conquer 101

- Whiteness as a Bribe: Poor white men got land, legal perks, and a social upgrade— enough to feel better than enslaved Blacks. Was there land equity for white men? Hell no; however, a little land is better than none.
- Blackness as Permanently Subjugated: Racial slavery was codified, ensuring lifelong servitude and zero ambiguity.
- No More Unity: Multiracial alliances? Never again. Whiteness became the new loyalty program of the poor.

No More Unity? Sure—Because Whiteness Comes with a Loyalty Card Now.

Remember when people of all backgrounds could come together, organize, and say, "Hey, maybe billionaires shouldn't own the air"? Yeah, those days are over—or not, as this bell is being rung again. Multiracial alliances? That expired around the same time Blockbuster did. See, unity got voted off the island when **whiteness launched its premium rewards program**. No healthcare? No union? No future? No problem—here's a free status upgrade to *"at least I'm not them."*

Whiteness—The Only Loyalty Program Where You Get Nothing but the Feeling of Superiority

- No cash back
- No savings

It's genius. Instead of storming the gates with fellow workers, the poor were handed a flag, a Bible verse, and a deep suspicion of anyone who speaks Spanish or wears a pronoun badge. Why punch up when you can punch sideways with patriotic flair? And here's the kicker: while CEOs sip their aged Scotch on private jets, half of America is playing Hunger Games: Patriotic Edition, arguing over who gets to be *"real American" of the month*.

Honestly, **it wasn't unity that failed. It was the bait-and-switch.** Working-class white folks got sold a fantasy: that as long as they guarded the gates of racial identity, they'd be safe. Meanwhile, the castle burned down. And guess who owns the fire insurance?

The Legacy: Still Screwing All of Us Today: What followed was a blueprint for American control: break working-class unity, dangle whiteness as false power, and make systemic inequality look like a personal failure. Bacon's Rebellion itself didn't last. Was the system deliberately designed to prevent future uprisings like this? Absolutely. And here's the kicker—we're still living inside that very system today.

Economic Anxiety: America's Favorite Distraction Tool: The American Revolution wasn't a working-class uprising. While poor white men fought for "liberty," the Founders quietly secured a system that protected their wealth, locked out the landless, and kept economic power nice and concentrated—with new wigs. War vets came home expecting a piece of freedom. Instead, they got:

- No land = no vote
- Crippling debt
- The same rich guys are in charge

Freedom? More like a membership tier you couldn't afford.

The Distraction: Racialized Class Warfare

Instead of addressing inequality, the elite changed the subject: Poor? Blame immigrants. Landless? Fear Black folks. Jobless? Complain about diversity. It worked then, and it continues to work now. From "welfare queens" in the 1980s to "economic anxiety" in the 2020s, the message remains: *Don't look up. Punch sideways.* The Legacy: The Founders didn't forget the poor—they excluded them on purpose. Then they sold rage and division as patriotism. Yes, America offered freedom. But only if you were rich, white, and owned property. Everyone else? Enjoy the poverty, shame, and lifelong gaslighting.

Freedom in America was always a selective offer—exclusive, exploitative, and expertly marketed.

- **Enslaved Labor:** The Revolution didn't end slavery—it scaled it. Cotton boomed, and the Three-Fifths Compromise said Black people counted… but not as people.
- **Indentured Servitude:** Poor whites "chose" years of unpaid labor, filthy conditions, and death as a pathway to a freedom they were still too poor to access. Welcome to the prequel to the gig economy.
- **Racial Caste System:** The Founders threw poor white men a bone— racial status. No wealth, no power, but hey—*at least you're not Black.*

It was the **original distraction economy**: it fractured the working class, fed them blame, and kept them too divided to challenge power.

1776: The Declaration of Independence: Now With 100% Less Self-Awareness

The Constitution, the holy grail of American self-flattery—the same document that screams "We the People"—then turns around and calculates Black bodies as 60% human, like they were pricing meat at a colonial farmer's market. Women? Legally irrelevant. Indigenous nations? Erased. The poor? Decorative. This wasn't an oversight; it was by design. The Founders didn't forget anyone; they excluded them *on purpose.*

Historical Plot Twist: They Accidentally Invented Resistance

Here's the hilarious part: by baking lofty ideals into their oppression cake, the Founding Fathers gave the oppressed *exactly what they needed*—language to flip the script, like toddlers whose parents left the scissors out and got mad when someone used them to cut the system open.

- Frederick Douglass: Dragged the Fourth of July harder than a pride parade through Mar-a-Lago.[157]
- Elizabeth Cady Stanton: Took the Declaration and gave it a feminist reboot like *Barbie: Patriarchy Edition.*[158]
- Martin Luther King (MLK): Cashed the check the Founders bounced

with their "promissory note to all Americans" line.

Every civil rights movement since has used the Founders' idealistic language to protest and question the system.

The Founders Gave Us a Country... and a Complex

Their legacy isn't liberty—it's a multigenerational delusion. A country that can't decide if it's brave or belligerent. That confuses dominance with destiny. That clutches its Constitution like pearls whenever someone brings up reparations, equity, or accurate history. The real revolution isn't fireworks and flag pins. It's finally admitting that we built a nation on insecurity and exclusion, and choosing to repeat the same mistake today. This isn't about tearing down the Founders. It's about tearing off the fantasy and seeing what's left. Spoiler: It's a mess. But it's a mess worth fixing.

They said "liberty," but they meant "our liberty to rule, your liberty to serve."
Break it down:

- **"We the People" meant... particular people.** The "people" weren't women, weren't Black, weren't Indigenous, and certainly weren't anyone working a field. The only people who counted were white, property-owning men, preferably Protestants with a taste for musket oil and inherited wealth.[159]

- **The Declaration of Independence was America's first "Terms and Conditions" that no one read.** "All men are created equal"—unless you were enslaved, landless, or on the wrong side of colonial expansion. And yes, Thomas Jefferson wrote that line with one hand while enslaving over 600 human beings with the other.[160] The man was less a paradox than a walking contradiction with a quill.

- **The Constitution? Great on parchment, garbage in practice.** It promised rights while allowing slavery, silencing women, and erasing Indigenous sovereignty. This was less a road map to equality and more a "Do Not Enter" sign written in cursive.

- **Freedom was never free—it was taxed, inherited, and wrapped in property law.** Voting rights? Property required. Citizenship? Whiteness assumed. Freedom? A pyramid scheme where the benefits trickled up.

The Founding Fathers didn't hand us a Constitution—they gave us their deep, bone-rattling fear of losing relevance. Rather than deal with it like adults, they built an institutional fortress of privilege, reinforced with parchment, patriarchy, and property clauses. You thought they were drafting democracy's blueprint? Please. They were panicking, building a bureaucratic man cave stocked with lifetime appointments, vague amendments, and enough moral high ground to stand on someone else's neck. **But was it by design or accident?** That's the American question. Answer: **Yes.**

Democracy for Some: How the Constitution Was Built to Protect Property, Not People[161]

1. The Constitution Was Explicitly Written to Protect Property (Including Human Property)

- Three-Fifths Compromise (Article I, Section 2): Enslaved people were counted as 3/5 of a person, not to offer them dignity, but to inflate white Southern voting power.

"Representatives… shall be determined by adding to the whole number of free persons… three-fifths of all other Persons."

- Fugitive Slave Clause (Article IV, Section 2): Required enslaved people to be returned to their "owners," even if they escaped to a free state.

Proof that the Constitution didn't tolerate slavery—it **protected it.**

2. Voting Was Tied to Land, Race, and Gender—By Design

In early state constitutions and laws:
- Voting rights were limited to white male property owners.
- In some states, even free Black men (who had fought in the Revolution)

lost voting rights in the early 1800s as white elites panicked about shared power.

This wasn't an oversight. This was the ruling class tightening the reins when democracy got a little too real.

3. The Senate and Electoral College Were Created to Dampen Democracy

- The Senate was designed to be the "cooling chamber" to keep the unruly masses (read: non-landed, non-white, non-male) from having too much say. Senators were appointed initially, not elected.
- The Electoral College was crafted to ensure slaveholding states retained disproportionate power in presidential elections.

4. The Founders Wrote About Their Intentions—Out Loud

- James Madison (Federalist No. 10): Warned about the dangers of too much democracy, particularly "factions" (like the poor) threatening the property of the wealthy.
- Thomas Jefferson wrote that "our government is founded on the illimitable freedom of the human mind," right before signing off on systems to police Black literacy and crush rebellion.

It Was Structural, Intentional, and Fragile. They didn't build a country—they built a firewall against shared power. The architecture of our democracy was designed to enshrine white, male, property-holding supremacy with long-lasting protections, even as the rhetoric screamed "freedom." This wasn't accidental. This was strategic hypocrisy with receipts.

Hissy Fit 1.0: The Civil War / Manifest Destiny's Murder Tour

Picture this: Southern white men discover that owning people might be morally bankrupt. Cue violins. The hissy fit hits DEFCON 5.

They secede, fire up the Confederacy, and unleash the bloodiest group therapy session America has ever seen—because someone told them they couldn't enslave people anymore. Meanwhile…Manifest Destiny is out west, committing vibe-checked genocide against Indigenous nations under the slogan: *"God wants us to murder you for farmland."*

- "Southern pride" wasn't about sweet tea. It was about chains.
- They wrapped white supremacy in a flag and called it "heritage."
- And Lincoln? He's trying to keep the Union together with duct tape and Emancipation Proclamations.

1831-1850: Genocide of Indigenous Peoples: "Progress" with a Death Toll

Of course, expansion only works if you ignore the people already living on the land, which America did enthusiastically. The Indigenous peoples of North America were not merely in the way—they were actively erased. Genocide wasn't the accidental side effect of progress; it was the business plan.

From the *Trail of Tears* to *Wounded Knee (1890)*, federal policy became a masterclass in ethnocide: removal, relocation, starvation, assimilation, and sterilization. The U.S. government even gave out literal bounties for Indigenous scalps—think DoorDash, but for dead natives. And while monuments celebrate westward expansion, they conveniently forget to mention the 90% population drop among Native peoples post-contact.[162] That's not a decline. That's a deliberate purge.

1861-1865: The Civil War

The truth—the Civil War was fought over one central issue: **slavery**—its existence, its expansion, and its role in the American economy and society. Despite the revisionist fluff about "states' rights" or "economic differences," the historical receipts are clear: the Confederacy seceded to protect the institution of slavery.

What Was the Civil War Really About?
- **Slavery. Period.** Every Confederate state explicitly cited slavery in its declaration of secession. Mississippi's declaration said: "Our position is thoroughly identified with the institution of slavery—the greatest material interest of the world." Southern leaders were not shy about it. Confederate Vice President Alexander H. Stephens proudly declared in 1861: "Our new government is founded... upon the great

truth that the negro is not equal to the white man."

- **States' Rights (To Own People):** The oft-cited "states' rights" argument is technically valid—but only if you finish the sentence: **States' rights to continue slavery** and reject any federal efforts to limit or abolish it. Southern states were furious at Northern states for exercising *their* rights, like refusing to return escaped enslaved people under the Fugitive Slave Act.
- **Economic Dependency on Enslaved Labor:** The South's economy ran on cotton and slavery. No enslaved labor meant no profits. The North was industrializing, but the Southern elite feared their plantation-based economy would collapse if slavery were ended or restricted.
- **The Election of Abraham Lincoln:** Lincoln wasn't even on the ballot in most Southern states, and when he won the presidency in 1860, secessionists panicked. Though Lincoln initially promised not to abolish slavery where it already existed, the South didn't believe him and seceded before he took office.

In Dick's Great-Great-Grandpa's Head: *"The Civil War? That was about **states' rights,** plain and simple. The right to govern themselves. You know—small government, freedom, liberty, American flags, economic freedom, and probably something about taxes or tariffs."*

What Dick's Great-Great-Grandpa Casually Forgets:

- **States' rights**—specifically the right to **own people** (Alexander Stephens, VP of the Confederacy, made this crystal clear in his "Cornerstone Speech" of 1861).
- The Confederacy wrote in their declarations of secession that slavery was central to their cause (Texas, Mississippi, Georgia, South Carolina).
- Dick's great-great-grandpa often skips over that *"liberty"* meant liberty for white men—everyone else was expected to shut up and serve politely.

Reality Check: *"Our new government is founded upon...the great truth that the negro is not equal to the white man..."*
—Alexander Stephens, 1861

1861–1865: Manifest Destiny: God's Favorite Land Grab (Now with Extra Baptisms!)

Manifest Destiny wasn't just about land—it was a full-blown God-sponsored real estate scam. Christianity was the sales pitch, missionaries the PR team, and militias were the enforcers. And Indigenous people? Branded spiritually defective and marked for salvation—or elimination. Thanks to the Doctrine of Discovery,[163] the logic was simple: *If they're not Christian, they don't count.* This line of thinking goes back to America's earliest days.

Puritan Policies and Laws

- The Massachusetts Body of Liberties (1641), one of the earliest legal codes in the colonies, codified religious conformity, criminalized blasphemy, and banned "heresy" as a capital crime.
- The Act Against Heresy in colonial Massachusetts made public denial of the Trinity punishable by death.[164]
- Preachers were government figures, Sunday church attendance was legally required, and dissenters were frequently fined, whipped, or branded.

All of this is under the banner of *religious liberty.*

1863–1877: Reconstruction Era: The First "Hissy Fit" When Equality Came Knocking

The Confederacy is toast, Lincoln has been deleted from the timeline, and somewhere in rural Georgia, a man named Earl is gazing into the distance with the thousand-yard stare of a man who realized he might have to work *with* the people he used to own. *"I don't recognize my country anymore,"* he whispers, holding back tears—and by tears, we mean racist plotting.

- Black Americans hold public office for the first time.
- Federal troops babysat democracy in the South.
- White rage invents the Ku Klux Klan (KKK), Black Codes, and "Lost

Cause" nostalgia.

- America briefly flirts with justice… before ghosting it.

The Civil War didn't end white supremacy—it rebranded it. The Confederacy didn't die at Appomattox. It put on a suit, joined a school board, and later got a Fox News segment. Gray coats became gray suits, then red hats stitched with selective memory. America didn't enter a post-war era—it entered a multigenerational hissy fit, with policy as the new battlefield.

- Reconstruction? Cue rage.
- Desegregation? Rage.
- Affirmative action? Rage—with a legacy admission cherry on top.
- A Black president? Full system meltdown.

And it's not only America: White empires everywhere—like the British in Scotland, India, Ireland, and multiple nations in the Caribbean—used the same playbook: Conquer, erase culture, moralize theft, then call it "civilization."

By 1877, Reconstruction ended, and America hit CTRL+ALT+JIM CROW:

- KKK forms faster than a bad country band.
- "Lost Cause" myth gets published as gospel.
- Domestic terror becomes the fallback plan for sore losers with sermons.

The war ended. The ideology was franchised. And it's still open for business.

Brief Black Hope, Long White Backlash

Slavery's over. Black men are voting, holding office, and founding schools. America has a chance to be decent for about *fifteen minutes*. The Amendments: Nice Ideas, No Follow-Through.

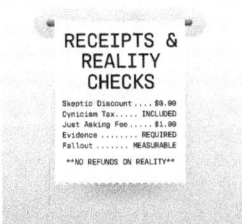

RECEIPTS &
REALITY
CHECKS

Skeptic Discount $0.00
Cynicism Tax ..... INCLUDED
Just Asking Fee $1.00
Evidence .... REQUIRED
Fallout .... MEASURABLE

NO REFUNDS ON REALITY

Truth in Amendments

13th Amendment (1865): The "Okay, We'll Stop Enslaving People" Clause

- *What it says:* "Abolishes slavery and involuntary servitude, except as punishment for a crime."
- *What it meant:* Slavery is illegal… (Except for prisoners… and oh look, Black codes appear overnight.[165] What a coincidence!) Fun loophole: If you incarcerate people, you can still legally force them to work without pay. Hence, the birth of the prison-industrial complex.
- *Historical kicker:* Southern states responded by criminalizing Black life (vagrancy laws, curfews, "walking while free") to rebuild their unpaid labor force under the new name: convict leasing.

14th Amendment (1868): The "You're a Citizen Now" Disclaimer

- *What it says*: Grants citizenship to anyone born or naturalized in the US Guarantees equal protection under the law. Ensures due process.
- *What it meant:* Black people, previously property, were now citizens… on paper. Also used later to justify everything from marriage equality to corporate personhood (*yep, thanks, Citizens United!*).
- *Historical kicker:* Southern states were *so mad* about this, they seceded emotionally again and invented Jim Crow.

15th Amendment (1870): The "You Can Vote Now (Sort Of)" Clause

- *What it says:* Prohibits the federal and state governments from denying the right to vote based on race, color, or previous condition of servitude.
- *What it meant:* Black men could vote—until white folks invented lit-

eracy tests, poll taxes, grandfather clauses, and the Klan to scare them back into silence.

- *Historical kicker:* Women—still left out. Black women had to wait until the 1965 Voting Rights Act to be functionally enfranchised in many areas.

For five wild minutes—okay, a few years—Black Americans voted, ran for office, built communities, and proved that democracy might work *if* you stop gatekeeping it. Cue conservative fainting spells, church-sponsored sabotage, and an emergency Klan meeting in the basement of every plantation-turned-political office. It wasn't that the South lost the war; they refused to lose the narrative.

Backlash, But Make It Bedazzled in Bedsheets—The KKK Launches Its First Kickstarter

Mission statement: "If democracy includes Black people, burn it down."

Cue the KKK, the human embodiment of a rage emoji in a hood. Formed in 1865, this domestic terror startup was the original angry white man militia—fueled by plantation nostalgia, wrapped in linen cosplay, and too cowardly to commit crimes without a mask.[166] The KKK launched coordinated assaults on Black communities, schools, churches, and especially Republican politicians—aka anyone with the audacity to support Reconstruction.

Wait—Republicans? Weren't they the party of slavery? Actually… nope. Not back then.

Unpack That: In the 1860s and 1870s, during Reconstruction, the Republican Party was the progressive party of the time:

- Founded in the 1850s as an anti-slavery party.
- Abraham Lincoln? Republican.
- Radical Republicans in Congress? Pushed for civil rights, Black suffrage, and Reconstruction reforms.

Meanwhile, the Democratic Party—particularly in the South—was the party of:

- The Confederacy,
- White supremacy,

- Obstruction of Reconstruction, and
- The political sugar daddies of the Klan.

The strategy was terror:

- Burn down a school? Check.
- Assault a Black voter? Check.
- Assassinate a Republican mayor or judge? Check.

All of it served one goal: to break Reconstruction before it could work. The KKK wasn't spontaneous violence. It was a coordinated hissy fit in defense of white power. And when justice knocked, they didn't open the door. They lit it on fire and blamed it on "outside agitators." (Sound familiar?) They made up for their lack of moral compass with elaborate costumes and a delusional sense of entitlement. And while the Klan handled the theatrics, the so-called "Redeemers"—those white elites who missed slavery like it was prom night—came armed with Sunday sermons and states' rights.

White Rage in a States' Rights Costume

Ha—"states' rights"—the historical version of "I'm not racist, I believe in local control… of white supremacy." Like a toddler screeching "MINE!" when told to share, post-Civil War white Southerners had a full-blown national hissy fit the moment formerly enslaved people started voting, organizing, and showing up to govern. Suddenly, every Confederate uncle with a Bible and the 19th-century equivalent of a social media account became a constitutional expert. "It's about sovereignty!" they howled— translation: *We can't lynch people in peace anymore.*

Violence wasn't tolerated—it was baked into the system like arsenic in a poisoned wedding cake. Between **1877 and 1950, more than 4,000 Black people were lynched in the United States.**[167] And no, that's not hyperbole—that's *data*. These weren't *mob outbursts*. They were community events—picnics with photo ops, where white families gathered with their children to watch the mutilation of Black bodies.

Now, back to the US after Reconstruction. The moment America dared to flirt with racial equity, white America did what it always does when asked to play fair—it rewrote the rules mid-game. This wasn't casual racism. This was institutionalized regression with a notary stamp. Segregation wasn't a social hiccup—it was policy-level pouting, bureaucracy built to soothe bruised white egos that couldn't handle the idea of sitting next to progress on a bus.

You had literacy tests, poll taxes, and "good moral character" clauses that were less about voter integrity and more about voter elimination. Black Americans were essentially asked to recite the Constitution backward while solving a Rubik's cube blindfolded. Meanwhile, white voters were asked if they liked pie—and even if they didn't, someone baked one anyway.

Federal Troops: America's Babysitters for Democracy

Because the South couldn't be trusted not to throw their toys at Black voters, federal troops were sent in to supervise, like frustrated babysitters at the world's worst daycare. The South didn't lose the war—they lost *adult supervision privileges*. But enter President Andrew Johnson—a Confederate sympathizer, soft on white rebellion, he made Lincoln look like Malcolm X. Instead of punishing traitors, Johnson offered amnesty, warm hugs, and a DIY kit for restoring racial hierarchy.[168] He vetoed civil rights laws faster than you could say "complicity," claiming the real danger was—wait for it—*giving Black people too much freedom too fast.*

The Psychological Crisis of Seeing Black Men Vote

To understand the sheer meltdown of the white Southern psyche during Reconstruction, picture a plantation owner watching his former enslaved worker take office. The cognitive dissonance was so intense, they nearly broke their monocles. This wasn't political dissent—it was *emotional terrorism*. To them, seeing a Black senator wasn't democracy; it was a biblical plague.

- White women clutched their Bibles.
- White men clutched their gun racks.
- And white politicians clutched every legal loophole they could find to erase Black power under the guise of *"tradition."*

Reconstruction policies were treated like existential violence.

Giving land, access to education, or even *basic dignity* to freed people was perceived as white suffering. (*"We're the real victims!"* they sobbed while passing Black Codes to criminalize poverty.)

And from that white fragility stew came the usual conspiracy hits:

- "Black people voting? Must be a Northern plot."
- "Interracial marriage = the apocalypse."
- "Next thing you know, white men will be the minority!"

Sound familiar? Because we're still hearing this playlist today, remixed for school board meetings and podcast rants.

This was white rage weaponized into governance. Jim Crow wasn't an accident. It was the plan. As W.E.B. Du Bois put it, the tragedy of Reconstruction wasn't that it failed; it's that it was *destroyed*—intentionally, and with great enthusiasm by the very people who claimed to love liberty most.[169]

1865-1870s: The Lost Cause—Rebranding Treason as Tradition

How to Lose a War, Keep the Statues, and Still Host the Family Reunion

The Confederacy was understood. It was not noble. It was not a tale of the underdog waiting for a Disney+ adaptation. It was a full-blown hissy fit over slavery—dressed up in velvet, weaponized with muskets, and later rebranded with mint juleps and bad history textbooks.

Birth of the Narrative: Former Confederates began rewriting history immediately after the Civil War. The cause? Rebrand treason and slavery as "noble resistance" and "states' rights." Key voices: Jefferson Davis, Jubal Early, and the Southern Historical Society Papers.

You can't pull off a good cultural cover-up without a bedtime story, preferably delivered in a slow drawl and accompanied by violins. After the war ended and the South realized they weren't getting invited back to the democracy potluck anytime soon, they did what any self-respecting pariah would do.

They started lying. Loudly. The new narrative?

- The South didn't fight for slavery—they fought for "states' rights." *(Spoiler: the "right" to own people.)*
- Confederate generals weren't traitors—they were tragic heroes.

(Somehow, all armed rebellions are "noble" if you lose while white.)

- Robert E. Lee wasn't defending slavery—he was, you know, passionate about topography and treason.

Southern Hospitality, Now with 100% More Gaslighting

And then came the United Daughters of the Confederacy—the OG Pinterest moms of historical revisionism. They didn't bake pies; they baked **racist mythology** into every American institution they could touch.[170] Their agenda? Fund statues like it was the racist version of Oprah's Favorite Things. Rewrite textbooks so gently that you almost didn't notice the blood was gone. Rename slavery "a peculiar institution" and call enslaved people "content.". This wasn't education. It was cultural laundering. Think Tide PODS for treason. Only in America can you: Start a war to keep people enslaved. Commit treason against your own country. Lose spectacularly …and still end up with high schools named after you.

This wasn't reconciliation. This was branding. The Confederacy got a good post-war glow-up, and even the North fell for it. By the mid-20th century, even kids in New York were learning that the Civil War was a "misunderstanding." No mention of the millions enslaved. No mention of the actual *cause*. A vague cloud of "honor," "heritage," and very strategic amnesia.

Hissy Fit from the Recliner:

"It's not about racism—it's about tradition!" declares Great-Grandpa Dick, sipping sweet tea from a mug shaped like Robert E. Lee's head, while sitting in a lawn chair funded by generational delusion and unpaid Black labor.

—GREAT GRANDPA DICK

1890–1920: Bronze Propaganda: Statues, Symbols, and Middle Fingers in Marble

Let's talk about those Confederate statues—you know, the ones sprouting across courthouse lawns like racist mushrooms every time Black folks made progress. These weren't memorials. They were monuments to white panic—built not in grief, but in grudge.

From Jim Crow to Civil Rights, every statute was a stone-faced *"hell no"* to Black advancement. Not "lest we forget"—but "don't get any ideas." You lose a war, try to destroy the country, and end up immortalized in bronze? That's not history. That's gaslighting with landscaping. They weren't mourning the past. They were marking territory—*marble warnings* that screamed:

- Black progress stops here.
- White supremacy still rents the place.
- Treason? Fine—if you've got good posture and a horse.

There are still over 1,700 Confederate symbols littering America like "Do Not Disturb" signs for systemic racism.[171] And when stone statues weren't enough, the Confederacy got repackaged as fashion—plastered on belt buckles, bumper stickers, and even bikini bottoms. Because nothing says "heritage" like turning your biggest defeat into lake-day merchandise.

Tearing down a statue isn't erasing history—it's correcting the record. The absolute erasure happened in classrooms, courtrooms, and textbooks, where rebellion became honor, and oppression became a footnote.

1877-1960 Jim Crow: America's Longest-Running Legal Hissy Fit

Welcome to the Jim Crow era—America's longest-running tragicomedy, where democracy wore a white hood and justice had a whites-only sign taped to the door. Jim Crow wasn't a set of laws. It was an entire ecosystem of segregation, humiliation, and violence—designed to take the rights Black Americans had won during Reconstruction and stuff them back into a burning box labeled *"Not Yet."*

After federal troops pulled out of the South—ending Reconstruction— the region said, "Cool, thanks. We'll take it from here." And by *"take it,"* they meant:

- Strip Black men of voting rights through poll taxes, literacy tests, and grandfather clauses.
- Codify racism into every aspect of public life—schools, bathrooms,

buses, cemeteries, zoo entrances. Yes, really.

- Rebrand white supremacy as "tradition" and "states' rights."

This was not a subtle shift. It was revenge with paperwork.

What Did Jim Crow Mean in Practice?

So, you're Black in Mississippi in 1920. You want to vote? Good luck navigating a civics test more complicated than the SAT while some dude in a sheriff's hat glares at you. You want a sandwich? There's a counter for that. It has no seats, no service, and a side of humiliation. Your kids want to go to school? Welcome to underfunded, overcrowded, one-room schoolhouses with textbooks that white schools threw out a decade ago. Segregation wasn't social—it was strategic. Separate never meant equal. It meant inferior by design.

The Legal Seal of Bigotry

Then came the Supreme Court's clown show, *Plessy v. Ferguson* (1896). "Separate but equal," they ruled—proof that delusion had judicial credentials. Facilities were separate, yes. But "equal"? Only in the way a moldy mattress and a Ritz-Carlton suite are technically places to lie down. From that moment on, Jim Crow wasn't a regional shame—it was national policy. Northern states weren't off the hook either. They employed redlining, policing, and educational zoning to achieve the same results with less overt signage.

Jim Crow's Enforcement Squad

Let's not pretend these laws were enforced politely. Behind every "Whites Only" sign was the threat of:

- Arrest
- Assault
- Lynching
- Economic ruin

Lynchings weren't acts of terror—they were community events. Postcards were made. Children were bought. The Klan didn't wear masks because they were afraid—they wore them because it was tradition. And yes, talk about the name. "Jim Crow" comes from a 19th-century minstrel act where white men in blackface mocked enslaved people. That's right: the *actual name of a century of state-sanctioned apartheid* in America came from a racist song-and-dance routine, seriously.

Jim Crow Never Left—It Got a LinkedIn Makeover

Jim Crow Wasn't History. It Was a Strategy. It was white supremacy with a rulebook, a Bible verse, and a school board seat. It didn't die. It evolved into redlining, mass incarceration, voter ID laws, and "colorblind" racism dressed up in political talking points. And like that, Jim Crow left the lunch counter and reappeared on Capitol Hill—with better branding.

- "School choice" = Re-segregation with better marketing.
- "War on Drugs" = Social control rebranded as public safety.
- "Stand your ground" = Now with 60% more racial bias.
- "Meritocracy" = When the starting line is your grandpa's trust fund.

The System Was the Strategy

Between the late 19th century and the mid-20th century, Jim Crow laws legally mandated racial segregation across the South. But this wasn't about separate water fountains or bus seats. It was a full-blown, state-sponsored campaign of economic suppression, political disenfranchisement, psychological warfare, and terroristic violence. If some of this sounds like 2025—yes, it is history and the future all in one Orange Era.

America loves to frame racism as a thing of the past—a resolved chapter rather than a malignant inheritance. But make no mistake: the tactics of Jim Crow are alive and well, hiding under the euphemisms of policy, procedure, and "personal responsibility."

- **Voter Suppression Redux:**[172] From strict voter ID laws to felony disenfranchisement and gerrymandering, states—especially in the South—continue to manipulate democratic processes to silence Black and Brown voices.
- **Mass Incarceration as Social Control:** The prison-industrial complex has become a modern-day plantation. Black Americans are incarcerated at **five times** the rate of white Americans.[173] Felony records

then strip them of voting rights, employment opportunities, and housing—sound familiar?

- **Education Disparities Persist:** Sixty years after *Brown v. Board of Education*, schools are still deeply segregated by race, by funding, and by opportunity. Districts with predominantly Black and Latinx students receive $23 billion less funding than majority-white districts.[174]
- **Economic Inequity Maintained:** The racial wealth gap remains staggering: the median white household has nearly eight times the wealth of the median Black household.[175] This isn't accidental—it's the structural residue of redlining, employment discrimination, and unequal access to capital.

Jim Crow never ended. It evolved. It went to law school, ran for office, hired a PR consultant, and learned to articulate phrases like "school choice," "war on drugs," "stand your ground," and "meritocracy." But the outcomes remain the same: Black and Brown Americans are systematically excluded, controlled, surveilled, and suppressed. Calling it history doesn't make it over. The damage Jim Crow did wasn't confined to the past—it metastasized into the present.

Welcome to the 20th Century: When the Hissy Fit Got a Microphone, a Platform, and a Superpower Complex

The powdered-wig hissy fits of the 18th century were the warm-up act.

The 20th century cranked up the volume, handed Dick a megaphone, and told him his feelings were facts. With radio waves, television screens, and talk show desks as his new pulpit, America's favorite fragile ego went mainstream—now louder, angrier, and backed by political parties, media conglomerates, and a never-ending supply of grievance fuel. Buckle up. History hit the airwaves.

1920-1965: Present: Immigration Waves & Xenophobia: "We the People—But Not You, Obviously"

Ah, America's favorite cycle:

Step 1: Invite immigrants for cheap labor.

Step 2: Freak out when they arrive.

Step 3: Build a fence and blame them for your insecurities.

- Irish? Too Catholic and not British enough.
- Italians? Too tan and passionate.
- Chinese? Worked too hard, got paid too little, and somehow that was threatening.
- Jews? Spoke too many languages *and* knew how to organize labor.
- Mexicans? Their food, culture, and labor were welcome, but not their existence.

The 1924 Immigration Act was America's formal rejection letter: "You don't fit our aesthetic. Try again after a world war." And when immigration did pick up after 1965? Grandpa Dick's grandkids start screaming about "caravans" and "anchor babies" from the comfort of their suburban cul-de-sac, with no knowledge of history books. It's a broken record for every decade to play.

Modern GOP Panic Points:

- Border walls
- Taco trucks
- The *audacity* of bilingual signage

White identity becomes increasingly fragile, wrapped in red, white, and resentment. Dick thinks he's the new minority because his barista pronounces her own name correctly.

Today's border wall obsession? "No Irish Need Apply" sign—updated with more concrete, more racism, and significantly worse spelling.

1920: Women Win the Right to Vote

"Democracy's great—until women show up." And like that, half the population became politically relevant. The horror. After a century of protests, arrests, hunger strikes, and men insisting that uteruses couldn't handle complex decisions like voting, the 19th Amendment passed. Cue mass pearl-clutching across the country.

- Men everywhere suddenly feared a wave of estrogen-powered policy.
- Newspapers warned that women voters might prioritize things like education, healthcare, or (*gasp*) peace.
- Cartoons depicted feminists as man-hating, cigar-smoking monsters—

because clearly, demanding the vote was a gateway drug to moral decay.[176]

This wasn't national enlightenment. It was a **begrudging concession** made after women shamed a sitting president in front of the White House for months with banners like: *"Mr. President, how long must women wait for liberty?"*

"What if she votes for school desegregation instead of war?!"

—RICHARD SR., Proud Grandpa of Dick

1930s: The Great Political Party Flip—Now With Extra Hypocrisy!

Once upon a segregated time, when men wore suspenders unironically and syphilis was untreated, the Republican Party was the party of Lincoln, abolition, and actual civil rights. Meanwhile, the Democrats were busy hoarding Jim Crow laws like racist collectibles.

Then—plot twist—the parties switched jerseys mid-game.

Why? Power. Votes. Strategy. Full stop. In the 1930s, Black voters began to lean toward the Democratic Party, thanks to Franklin D. Roosevelt's (FDR) New Deal, as food and jobs took precedence over empty moral posturing. Then Harry Truman threw in civil rights and *bam!*—Southern Democrats started clutching their Confederate pearls.

1940s-1950s: The Post-WWII Boom—When America Peaked (for Some, Briefly, and Mostly on Credit)

The so-called "Golden Age." The war was over, the economy was booming, and America was busy slapping victory decals on everything from car bumpers to gender roles. But don't let the Rockwell paintings fool you—this era wasn't built on harmony. It was built on a foundation of hegemony, with a white picket fence.

Don't worry, friends—I gave the so-called "Golden Age" its chapter because this is when cultural norms stopped pretending and went full

Broadway. This is the era when patriotism became a costume, gender roles became a script, and the American Dream turned into high-budget performance art with a laugh track and deed restrictions. A quick look here and more in chapter 8.

The GI Bill: The Greatest Affirmative Action Plan White Men Pretend Didn't Happen

Returning soldiers had access to home loans, education, and job training—but mostly if they were white, male, and didn't ask too many questions about equity.

- Black veterans? Denied benefits at scale through redlining and racist administrators.[177]
- Women? "Thanks for your service on the assembly line. Now, kindly return to the kitchen and start reproducing the workforce."

It was the most significant government investment in the middle class, intentionally excluding anyone not starring in a *Leave It to Beaver* episode.

Suburbia: Segregation with Curb Appeal

Enter: Levittown. The American Dream, now available in beige. Cookie-cutter homes, two-car garages, a lawn to mow, and deed restrictions that banned non-white residents. White flight wasn't a reaction—it was a federally subsidized migration. This is the era where "neighborhood" became code for "no diversity allowed." Black families who tried to integrate were met with rocks, mobs, and mortgage discrimination—but sure, keep calling it a dream.

The Cult of Domesticity 2.0: Housewives, Hairdos, and Hysteria

Women had kept the country running during WWII, but when peace hit, the nation handed them a casserole dish and said, "Shhhh, sweetheart. Real freedom is in your laundry room."

- Ads and schools actively reprogrammed girls for marriage, motherhood, and mild mental illness.
- "Female ambition" was a known threat to national stability.
- And every feminist impulse was framed as either lesbianism, commu-

nism, or hysteria—sometimes all three.

Cold War Paranoia: The Original Cancel Culture (But for Commies)

While the suburbs were baking apple pies and institutionalized gender roles, the government was busy creating a national pastime out of paranoia.

- McCarthyism turned neighbors into snitches. Can you think of any current 2025 similarities of neighbors being told to tell on their neighbors, especially if they had to terminate a pregnancy medically?
- Loyalty oaths were required to work.
- Saying "economic justice" too loudly could get you blacklisted.

It was the golden age of grievance policing, where the threat of ideological impurity was more terrifying than nuclear war.

Cultural Fallout: The Dream Was Segregated, Sanitized, and Sponsored by GE

- White men got houses, degrees, and *dignity*.
- Women got aprons and an unspoken understanding not to ask about fulfillment.
- Black families got denied loans and blamed for poverty.
- Queer people got closets and criminalization.

All while America declared itself the moral authority of the world, selling the lie of freedom abroad while segregating lunch counters at home.

1954: *Brown v. Board of Education*

"Separate but equal" was never equal. And the Supreme Court finally admitted it.

Brown v. Board of Education was the landmark ruling that declared racial segregation in public schools unconstitutional. It sounded like progress until implementation turned into a civil rights horror film featuring screaming mobs, National Guard troops, and white parents with Bibles in one hand and protest signs in the other.

- Black children needed armed escorts to go to class.
- White communities responded with "massive resistance"—yes, that

was the actual term used by politicians and school boards.[178]

- "School choice" suddenly became the euphemism of the decade—a slick rebrand of segregation dressed in a sweater vest.

One infamous moment: **Little Rock Nine (1957)**—nine Black students integrated Central High School in Arkansas under federal troop protection while grown adults foamed at the mouth on national television. "Not my kids!" screamed white dads with perfectly polished superiority complexes. Translation: "If my kid shares a desk with yours, how will he know he's better?" Desegregation didn't end racism. It made racists find new vocabulary.

Meanwhile, Dick and Jane are still living their best segregated lives—Spot is the only character with more than one shade.

1960: The Civil Rights Movement and the Birth of Conservative Tears

When "Justice for All" started sounding like "Less for Me." The 1960s: civil rights, soul music, and enough melanin on television to send half the country into a defensive crouch. Black folks marched. White folks panicked. And suddenly, "equality" felt like oppression to men who'd never been told "no" by anything other than a bad golf swing. Once upon a time, "freedom" meant freedom *from* tyranny. Now, it means freedom *from sharing.*

- Voting rights for Black Americans? "Wait, they get a say now?"
- Desegregation? "But my children might see… a difference!"
- Affirmative action? "You mean I have to… compete?"

Thus, with the emotional fragility of a country club losing its dress code, the modern conservative movement was born—not out of fiscal prudence or philosophical rigor but out of pure, uncut white male discomfort. What started as "small government" swiftly became "small tolerance." Every civil right granted to Black Americans was perceived not as a step toward justice but as a direct assault on tradition—i.e., a world where Dick always got the job.

Suddenly, the most privileged demographic in human history became the protagonist of an oppression fantasy:

- "This is not the America I grew up in" = "I don't like change unless it's in my 401(k)."

- "Colorblindness" = "I refuse to see you because your existence makes me question mine."
- "Family values" = "I miss the days when nobody challenged my authority, especially not my wife."

And white southerners? They didn't just clutch their pearls—they used them to strangle progress. Equality had yet to mature into equity. And it wasn't interpreted as a shared table—it was seen as a hostile takeover. Those who used to own people were now expected to stand in line next to them? Share schools? Water fountains? Hydration equality was the final straw.

1964-1965: Civil Rights Act & Voting Rights Act

America Tries Adulting (and White Men File a Complaint). After centuries of legalized racism and a civil rights movement powered by marches, beatings, arrests, and fire hoses, Congress finally passed the Civil Rights Act of 1964. This law said, basically: "Hey, maybe let's not discriminate in public anymore." One year later, the Voting Rights Act of 1965 followed, outlawing literacy tests, poll taxes, and the psychological warfare formerly known as "Southern voting registration."

- Black citizens could now vote without explaining the square root of racism.
- Employers were technically not allowed to say, "We don't think you'd fit in."
- Segregated lunch counters? Canceled. (Though racism moved into the *break room.*)

Enter the myth of **"reverse racism."** A magical delusion where white men, having finally been asked to share, declared themselves the *real* victims. **There is no such thing as reverse racism or reverse discrimination. The act is either racist or discriminatory—period.** That's right, if you discriminate against a white male, they ARE the victim—it's discrimination and illegal.

Dick & Jane Readers: Publishers reluctantly start introducing Black characters... but not in Dick and Jane's world. Diversity? Shoved into a separate "multicultural reader." Individual books, separate plotlines, fewer speaking lines. Progress with a footnote.

1964: The Big Bang of the Flip

Lyndon B. Johnson signs the Civil Rights Act and mutters, *"Welp, there goes the South."* The GOP hears white Southern rage and says, "Our kind of people!" Enter Barry Goldwater, who voted against civil rights and became the patron saint of suburban fear and sweat. Then Nixon weaponized "law and order" into dog-whistle policy, launching the GOP's Southern Strategy—a political grift so precise it made Machiavelli blush.

1970s: "My Body, My Choice" Meets "My Masculinity, My Meltdown"

The decade where women demanded autonomy, and men responded by misquoting Scripture and inventing Men's Rights Activism between rounds of Miller High Life. They didn't realize you can be pro-choice and still be anti-abortion for yourself.

- **Roe v. Wade (1973):** A Supreme Court ruling that said *uteruses come with user control* and the right to privacy.
- **The Equal Rights Amendment:** A proposed constitutional amendment to ban sex-based discrimination—so terrifying to conservatives that Phyllis Schlafly built an entire career out of arguing that women's equality would destroy families, toast, and the space-time continuum. (The irony of telling women to stay home and shut up while doing neither was utterly lost on Phyllis.)
- The second-wave feminist movement pushed for pay equity, reproductive rights, and freedom from being called "sweetheart" in board meetings (if they were even allowed to attend).

Male Reaction: Immediate spiritual crisis. Suddenly, Paul's letters to the Corinthians appeared in political speeches and barroom debates. Because nothing scares a particular kind of man more than a woman with a law degree and a uterus, she controls herself.

"You're not the boss of my body!" becomes the feminist rallying cry. Men respond with: "But I have a lawn sign and a gun rack!" The mere *possibility* that women might not want to raise their children, carry their egos, or validate their sense of purpose? An existential crisis of biblical proportions.

Roe v. Wade Was Never About "Children"—It Was Always About Control Dressed up as State's Rights

Roe v. Wade was overturned in 2022 by the US Supreme Court in a landmark case titled *Dobbs v. Jackson Women's Health Organization*—and it was less a surprise twist and more the season finale that had been scripted for decades. The Supreme Court ruled that the US Constitution does not confer a right to abortion, effectively overturning *Roe v. Wade* (1973) and *Planned Parenthood v. Casey* (1992). This decision returned the power to regulate abortion laws to the individual states.[179] Thus, in some states, women have no bodily autonomy—next will they ban infant formula and demand breastfeeding?

How "States' Rights" Was Used:

Ah yes, *states' rights, again*—America's favorite euphemism. Once used to defend slavery, now recycled to strip away reproductive rights while shouting "local control" with a mouth full of Chick-fil-A. In 2022, Justice Samuel Alito cracked open his powdered-wig thesaurus and decided that abortion should be left to the states, not because states have an excellent track record, but because *federal tyranny* sounds scarier than *legislative negligence*.[180] But here's the thing: the states leading the "let's protect life" parade are the same ones that consistently fail the babies they claim to save.

The majority opinion, written by Justice Samuel Alito, emphasized that abortion is a matter that should be decided by elected representatives at the state level, not imposed federally by judicial interpretation. This aligns with a longstanding conservative legal philosophy of federalism, limiting the role of the federal government in favor of state autonomy.

"States' Rights," Y'all: Because Nothing Says "Freedom" Like Forced Birth and No Healthcare

When the Supreme Court overturned *Roe v. Wade* in *Dobbs v. Jackson*

Women's Health Organization (2022), they didn't just toss out a court precedent—they yeeted it into the medieval trash bin of history with the moral gusto of a high school debate team sponsored by the Federalist Society. The Supreme Court stated, *"The Constitution does not confer a right to abortion."* Translation? "We're returning this issue to the states... because *states' rights* have always been cool and not historically used to preserve slavery, segregation, and now, forced birth."

1980s: Reagan Seals the Deal

Fast-forward to the 1980s: Reagan shows up like your racist uncle with a smile and a tax break, peddling fears about "welfare queens" and "big government," and "solutions" like "traditional values" to scared white voters.

The GOP took:

- The Confederate handbook,
- Evangelical purity tests,
- Trickle-down economics, and
- Wrapped it in a flag and called it "freedom."

What was once the Party of Lincoln is now the Party of Lincoln Logs—building fantasyland America out of nostalgia, resentment, and supply-side snake oil. No, conservatism didn't rise from principle. It rose from a **strategic hissy fit**—and it's still being merchandised today.

The States' Rights Argument:
America's Favorite Cop-Out Since 1861

The phrase "states' rights" is the political equivalent of "it's not you, it's federalism." It's the rhetorical fig leaf used to cloak systemic control in the language of local governance. *States' rights* have never been about empowering citizens. It's about ensuring some states retain the right to oppress, especially if that oppression involves women, queer folks, or anyone not invited to the Founding Fathers' toga party.

States' rights were the **legal backbone of Jim Crow.**[181] It defended bans on interracial marriage.[182] It resisted school desegregation until the federal government had to send the **National Guard** to let Black kids into geometry class. Now? It's being weaponized to tell women, *"You have rights—just not here."*

Banned in Texas, Available in California–But Sure, We're One Country

What the Dobbs decision did was create a reproductive patchwork quilt stitched with barbed wire. A woman in Massachusetts has more rights over her body than a woman in Missouri. That's not freedom—that's a biological travel ban. As of 2024, **14 states** have implemented near-total bans on abortion, with **zero exceptions for rape or incest** in several of them.[183] Because nothing says "limited government" like making a 12-year-old carry her rapist's baby to term in the name of "morality."

And if you think this stops at abortion, wait:

- **In vitro fertilization?** Already under attack in Alabama.
- **Birth control?** Next on the docket is the FDA, the Supreme Court, or leaving it to Project 2025 to decide.
- **Infant formula?** Give it time. If we're truly restoring "family values," breast milk may become a state-mandated requirement. It's better to get a permit for that breast pump.

The Holy Ghostwriter of State Policy: Religion

Let's not pretend this is just about the Constitution. If it were, Clarence Thomas wouldn't be out here with 19th-century footnotes and a 21st-century Wi-Fi signal. This is about theocratic creep, where biblical interpretation has become public policy and America is cosplaying as a Handmaid's Tale LARP camp. The religious right didn't just cheer this decision—they *co-authored* it. The Court may wear robes, but they're increasingly indistinguishable from the ones in evangelical pulpits.

Cultural Impact: Reproductive Rights Now Come with a ZIP Code

You can now: Own a gun in more states than you can own your uterus. Buy Viagra with insurance, but not emergency contraception. Get fired for being pregnant and still be told "life is sacred." America, where you can carry a fetus across state lines but not a library book about gender identity.

The States' Rights Argument Was Never Neutral

It's a weaponized framework of oppression, sanitized for public consumption and repackaged as "local control." But whether it's 1861 or 2025, the playbook is the same:

1. Say it's about liberty.
2. Enact restrictions that disproportionately harm marginalized people.
3. Blame "the Left" when people bleed out in parking lots.

So, yes, women now have fewer rights than a frozen embryo in some states. And no, this isn't satire. It's what happens when "liberty" is reduced to **who can scream loudest at a school board** while quoting Leviticus in a lawsuit.

A Look at the Life-Loving States:

- **Mississippi**—Where abortion is banned, but **27.9% of children live in poverty**.[184] Prenatal care is about as hard to find as a Whole Foods grocery store.
- **Arkansas & Louisiana**—**Ranking high in bans, low in healthcare, and lower in reading scores**. Think "pro-life," but only until the umbilical cord is cut.
- **Texas** –Banned abortion, didn't expand Medicaid, and now *1 in 5* women of childbearing age have no health insurance.[185] But don't worry—they're also banning books and drag shows, so everything's fine.[186]

These states also tend to rank at the bottom in education spending and maternal health outcomes. Medicaid expansion? Nah. Childcare subsidies? Pass. But mandatory childbirth for a 12-year-old rape victim? Absolutely. The logic here is more fragile than a Hobby Lobby nativity set in July.

Black Women? Sorry, You're on Your Own.

Black women face the brunt of this mess—living in states that ban abortion, while also suffering maternal mortality rates roughly *three times higher* than those of white women.[187] They're more likely to rely on Medicaid, which many of these states treat like a luxury brand rather than a lifeline.[188]

Infrastructure? More Like Infracture.

You'd think if you were forcing birth, you'd at least build some hospitals, right? Wrong.

- **Clinic closures** in states like Missouri and Alabama have left entire regions without access to OB/GYN services.
- **Postnatal care?** Optional: if you can find a provider within 100 miles.
- **Childcare support?** Ha. Your moral victory can babysit.

So... Is It About the Babies or the Power?

These same "life-first" states have some of the **worst** infant mortality rates, the **lowest** support for mothers, and the **smallest** social safety nets.[189] But sure—tell us again how this is about the sanctity of life. In reality, we've handed the steering wheel to states that can't fix potholes but think they can manage wombs. It's not about life. It's about control. It's about culture wars dressed in diapers. So, we wait. We watch. And we wonder: **Now that you've forced birth, will you fund life?** Or was this never about babies to begin with?

What the Supporters of the Overturn Argue:

- **Constitutional Purity:** The Constitution does not mention abortion; thus, the Supreme Court overstepped in *Roe* by inventing a federal right that wasn't enumerated.
- **Democratic Process:** Letting states decide returns power to voters and their legislators.
- **Moral/Religious Grounds:** Some believe life begins at conception, and that states should be free to protect unborn life as they see fit.

Key Quote: "The Constitution does not prohibit the citizens of each State from regulating or restricting abortion. *Roe* and *Casey* arrogated that authority. We now overrule those decisions and return that authority to the people and their elected representatives." [190]

What the Opposition Says:

- **Loss of Bodily Autonomy:** Critics argue the ruling strips people—particularly women—of a fundamental right to control their bodies.

- **Health & Equity Concerns**: The ruling disproportionately impacts low-income individuals, people of color, and rural residents who face barriers to travel.
- **Precedent Undermined**: *Roe* was settled law for nearly 50 years. Overturning it is seen by some as a **judicial overreach** with political motivations.
- **Fear of Broader Rollbacks**: There's concern this opens the door to challenges of other rights rooted in privacy (e.g., contraception, same-sex marriage).

Immediate Fallout: Trigger laws in over a dozen states banned abortion within hours or days. Other states rushed to follow suit or enact stricter restrictions. Chaos, confusion, and massive disparities in healthcare access followed. Overturning *Roe* wasn't **only** about abortion. It was a test case for rolling back rights based on implied constitutional protections (privacy, autonomy). A massive victory for the decades-long conservative legal strategy. A cultural gut punch for many Americans who had taken the right to abortion as settled law.

The genius (and danger) of the anti-Roe movement? It cloaked patriarchal control in moral panic. It turned theological conviction into legislative strategy—and gave rise to a version of Christianity where Jesus wears a flag pin and only cares about zygotes.

You could say: *"The Court returned abortion rights to the states—because nothing says 'freedom' like a patchwork of laws where crossing a border turns healthcare into a crime scene.*

The Impacts of This Decision: Health Care Access and Outcomes

- **Clinic Closures**: At least 66 clinics in 15 states ceased providing abortion services within the first 100 days post-decision, with many shutting down entirely. This has left approximately 29% of US women of reproductive age living in states where abortion is either unavailable or severely restricted.[191]
- **Delayed Medical Care**: In states with strict abortion bans, healthcare providers face legal uncertainties, leading to delays in treating pregnancy complications. This has resulted in worsened health outcomes

for pregnant individuals.[192]

- **Increased Infant Mortality**: A study noted a 7% rise in US infant mortality rates following the overturning of *Roe v. Wade*, with a 10% increase among infants with disabilities. The lack of access to abortion in cases of severe fetal anomalies has been a contributing factor.[193]

Economic and Social Impacts

- **Workforce Participation**: Access to abortion has historically been linked to increased female labor force participation and educational attainment. The reversal of *Roe* is projected to decrease these opportunities, particularly affecting low-income women and women of color.[194]
- **Financial Strain**: Women denied abortions are more likely to experience long-term economic hardship, including increased poverty rates and financial distress.[195]

Legal and Ethical Concerns

- **Criminalization of Pregnancy Outcomes**: In the year following the decision, over 200 women across 12 states faced criminal charges related to their pregnancies, miscarriages, or births, highlighting the legal risks associated with restricted abortion access.[196]
- **Advance Directive Limitations**: Some states, like Kansas, have laws that invalidate advance medical directives for pregnant individuals, raising ethical concerns about patient autonomy and rights.[197]

Access Disparities and Travel Burdens

- **Increased Travel for Services**: States like Illinois have seen a surge in out-of-state patients seeking abortion services, with a 71% increase from 2020 to 2023, indicating the lengths individuals must go to access abortion services.
- **Transportation Challenges**: Low-income and underserved women face significant barriers in traveling long distances for abortion services, exacerbating existing healthcare inequities.[198]

Demographic and Societal Shifts

- **Decline in Fertility Rates**: The US fertility rate has dropped to historic lows, with some attributing this to concerns over restrictive abortion laws and the associated risks of pregnancy.[199]
- **Rise in Elective Sterilizations**: There has been an increase in sterilization procedures among young adults, driven by fears of losing reproductive autonomy under stringent abortion laws.[200]

These developments underscore the profound and far-reaching effects of the *Dobbs* decision on healthcare, economic stability, legal rights, and societal dynamics in the United States.

Sally's Sanity: Keep Your Laws Off My Body— or We'll Start Regulating Yours

Suppose the government can control what I do with my uterus. In that case, it's only fair we talk about mandatory vasectomies at 18, erectile function licensing, and a national registry for every man who's ever said "not all men."

Roe v. Wade *wasn't about life—it was about leverage.*
Control the uterus, control the future. But let me say it plainly for those in the back with the pocket Constitutions and the pearl-clutching morality: **Keep your fucking hands off my autonomy. Or we'll start writing policies about your dicks.**

- *You want a 48-hour waiting period before an erection?*
- *A genetic DNA database for men—thus, the state can track and bill the financial party for the child.*
- *Counseling before you buy Viagra.*
- *Government-mandated accountability for every ejaculation that doesn't result in a baby?*
- *Registered sex for procreation only—must be married to fuck.*

We're not asking. We're done. **This isn't a debate—it's a declaration.**

—*LOVE SALLY* *Your daughter, sister, wife, neighbor, and best friend.*

The LGBTQ+ Rights Movement: Pride, Plague, and Bibles Clutched

Stonewall, 1969. A bunch of drag queens, trans folks, queers, and chosen family members dared to say "Nah" to decades of state-sanctioned police harassment—and in doing so, kicked off a rights movement more courageous than anything Congress has managed since powdered wigs were in fashion. The first Pride was a riot, not a corporate-sponsored rainbow sale at Walmart. The Stonewall Uprising wasn't about rainbows—it was about rage, resistance, and refusing to disappear.

Then the 1980s showed up, drenched in Aqua Net and apathy.

- The AIDS crisis hit, and instead of action, the government handed out silence and stigma.
- Reagan famously avoided even *saying* "AIDS" publicly until 1985, while thousands died.[201]
- Activists had to create their own public health systems, funeral networks, and data tracking, because the state was too busy moralizing to respond.

Jane short-circuits. Dick boycotts Target. The rainbow becomes a threat. "Family values" becomes code for "straight, white, married, and emotionally unavailable." Dick and Jane now believe preferred pronouns are tyranny and drag queens are more dangerous than domestic terrorism. The hissy fit goes **non-binary**—and it's fabulous.

This isn't policy. It's pathology.

Because when white supremacy is the foundation, **equality feels like theft**, diversity feels like an existential threat, and justice looks suspiciously like rebellion. And instead of reckoning with that reality, dominant cultures export the hissy fit globally dressed as law, development, democracy, or "Western values."

And instead of adapting to the reality of a multiracial, multiethnic, multi-everything future, it doubles down. We're talking nationalism with a side of nostalgia, where America is only "great" when it's homogenous, hierarchical, and aggressively heterosexual. We're talking historical revisionism so bold it makes actual historians want to scream into a quilt.

We're talking performative persecution—the kind that insists wearing a mask during a pandemic is tyranny but requiring photo ID to vote is "common sense."

Don't believe the war's still going? Look at the fight over critical race theory, a law school framework turned political boogeyman that somehow got blamed for teaching third graders how to hate white people. Or how about the "Don't Say Gay" bills, which essentially codify homophobia under the guise of protecting children, while ignoring the actual trauma caused by silencing identity. Or the attacks on diversity, equity, and inclusion efforts, now reframed as "woke indoctrination" by people who have no idea what any of those words mean.

We're in the middle of the longest-running cultural hissy fit in American history—and the hissy fit keeps getting rebranded for each new generation.

Let's turn now to the mythical Golden Age—the paradigm that our culture is built upon.

CHAPTER 8

The Golden Age That Never Was

The 1950s. The decade of poodle skirts, TV dinners, and Cold War paranoia. A time when white men were kings, white women were "homemakers," and anyone who didn't fit neatly into that nuclear dream was systematically erased, excluded, or institutionalized.

This was America's so-called Golden Age—a sanitized, suburban fantasy built on economic expansion, social conformity, and good old-fashioned structural oppression. This decade gave us Elvis, McCarthyism, and the notion that progress peaked when milk was delivered in glass bottles, and no one discussed their feelings. But behind the rock 'n' roll and white picket fences was a deeply curated performance of power, where the only thing more repressed than sexuality was the truth. Note that the Golden Age is listed as 1950–1960; however, the fallout carries well into the 21st century. And Dick, Jane, and Sally were purposely created to enforce this fairy tale culture for some—not all.

The "Golden Age" of White, Heterosexual, Male Dominance, Cultural Conditioning

Post–World War II America is often romanticized as a golden age, but it wasn't gold—it was a gilded cage.

This wasn't the glossy world portrayed in *Mad Men*, where men were men and women were glamorous. That was the veneer. Underneath the highballs and high heels was a society rotting from systemic racism, rigid gender roles, and repressive conformity. The door to the American Dream had a "Whites Only" sign, a "God Bless This Patriarchy" doormat, open sexual harassment of women, and the hum of a moral panic siren woven into every cheerful TV jingle. This was the era of the Greatest and Silent Generations, raising the Traditionalists and Baby Boomers, passing down the illusion while burying the truth.

This wasn't a period of national virtue. It was a full-scale ideological branding campaign, and the product they were selling? A very narrow, very fragile definition of who counted. In the years following WWII, white straight men weren't the protagonists of the American story, without a choice—they were:

- The heroes,
- The narrators,
- The publishers,
- The advertisers,
- And the gatekeepers to the American Dream.

And everyone else? Extras. Side characters. Cultural hazards. This was the era of *Father Knows Best*, and yes, the title wasn't aspirational—it was the entire damn thesis. The American Dream had a particular image: a crew-cut white dad in a gray flannel suit, a submissive wife in pearls, 2.5 kids, and a mortgage in a redlined suburb. If this man had a catchphrase, it would be: *Because I said so.* And why not? The system worked beautifully—for him. The G.I. Bill showered benefits on white veterans, funding college degrees, homeownership, and economic mobility.[202] But like every federal "we care about the troops" policy, it came with a segregated disclaimer. Black veterans? Denied loans. Asian Americans? Systematically excluded. Latinos? Congratulations, you get the honor of being invisible. It wasn't a G.I. Bill—it was a *G.I. Filter*, fine-tuned to preserve whiteness and male dominance while pretending to be patriotic equity.

Every sitcom, billboard, schoolbook, and cereal box said the same thing: "This is what normal looks like." "This is who's in charge." "This is who matters." *Leave It to Beaver* wasn't just entertainment. It was cultural conditioning. A perfectly airbrushed fantasy that erased everyone who didn't fit the mold and called it "wholesome." The man was the breadwinner. The woman is a silent domestic accessory. The children? Blonde, obedient, and terrified of disappointing Father. Black folks? Magically absent. Queer folks? Monsters or punchlines—if acknowledged at all. Anyone with an accent, a headscarf, or a uterus with opinions? Deemed "un-American" by default.

And the Damage? Oh, It Was Done

To the culture. To men. To everyone forced to pretend they were "fine" inside a system designed to crush nuance, vulnerability, and anything that didn't smell like Old Spice, live like *Mad Men*, and revel in economic dominance. The postwar era didn't just create cultural norms—it built a performative machine that chewed up complexity and spit out perfectly conforming cardboard cutouts called "men," stamped with fragile egos and pressed slacks.

To the Man: Masculinity as Emotional Captivity

From childhood, men were handed a script: You are your paycheck. You must never cry unless it's over war, football, or a Norman Rockwell painting. Your worth is measured by control of your household, coworkers, emotions, and anything with a pulse that threatens your fragile sense of superiority.

This wasn't raising boys into men—this was militarized social training for dominance, suppression, and performance under emotional lockdown. Psychologist William Pollack described this as the **"boy code"**: a cultural mandate that punishes emotional expression in boys and rewards detachment, silence, and aggression.[203] By adulthood, many men were fluent in repression, but illiterate in their emotional realities. There was no room for therapy, uncertainty, or the question, *"Who do I want to be?"* There was only:

- Ulcers
- Bourbon
- Erectile dysfunction
- And a generational baton made entirely of unresolved trauma, ready to be handed to the next emotionally constipated son.

To the Culture: A Nation Built on Repression and Branded as Stability

The 1950s didn't "set the tone"—they froze it in amber, branded it "traditional values," and built an entire national identity on a nostalgic lie.

This was the age when:

- Every attempt at racial, gender, or economic equity became a "threat to the American way of life."
- Every protest was labeled a riot.
- Every man who cried in public, questioned capitalism, or wore eyeliner was either institutionalized or slandered into oblivion.

As sociologist Michael Kimmel writes, this era cultivated a "masculinity under siege" mindset—one that saw social progress not as evolution, but as invasion.[204] And to counter that "threat"?

Fear. Rage. Control.

The culture told men: *You are not safe unless you are superior. And you are not superior unless you are dominant.* This wasn't psychology. It was politics. Economics. Religion. Entertainment. An entire machine built to sell repression as virtue and market anxiety as patriotism. We didn't make this machine—we sold it to ourselves with slogans like "Father Knows Best" and "The American Dream," then turned it into an export.

Repression Was the Product—and Everyone Bought It

This system didn't fail. It functioned exactly as designed.

It produced:

- Broken men who thought silence = strength
- A culture addicted to domination and allergic to nuance
- And a political climate that saw empathy as weakness and diversity as danger

The 1950s didn't just damage the men living through them. They built the framework for decades of cultural regression, institutional fragility, and emotional illiteracy. This was a system where power feared vulnerability and where anyone who broke character was punished for ruining the illusion.

Golden Age Masculinity: A User Manual for Repression, Rage, and Roast Beef

Welcome to mid-century manhood—where feelings went to die, ties were tight, and your worth was measured in paychecks, property lines, and how stoically you ignored your emotional decay. This is the masculine culture framework that defined a man from the Golden Age, to which, sadly, some aspire today.

- **Provider or Parasite:** Men weren't allowed to *live*—only to work, sweat, and die quietly under fluorescent lights. No art, no dreams, just coffee breath, corporate trauma, and the crushing weight of lawn care. If you weren't earning, you weren't a man. You were a burden, with a mustache.
- **Emotions? For Women and Europeans:** Crying? Weak. Therapy? Communist. Acceptable feelings: Anger, horniness, and vague patriotism during war footage. Everything else? Bury it.
- **Fatherhood = One Speech, No Feelings:** Golden Age dads didn't parent; they performed a monologue, handed out curfews, and saved emotions for the dog or the mistress.
- **Work = Worth:** Your résumé was your personality. Your boss respected you; your kids didn't know you. Retirement? Identity crisis in khakis.
- **Masculinity Was a Gated Club:** Gay? Fired. Brown? Watched. Emotional? French. Feminist? Get lost.
- **Violence = Virtue:** Belts, silence, and holy rage were how you "loved." At work, intimidation was leadership. At home, fear was discipline.
- **War Made You a Man:** You didn't return home—you were reassembled with trauma and told to mow the lawn.
- **Repression Was the Brand:** Feelings were illegal. Joy was rationed. Vulnerability was considered a weakness. You didn't live; you *performed*—until you died in the driveway, mid-rake.

The Golden Age of masculinity that built Dick punished softness, outlawed connection, and crowned silence as a sign of strength. It left men emotionally illiterate, spiritually exhausted, and terrified of their reflection. And that's the legacy Dick clings to—while Richard, quietly, is learning how to feel again.

Inheriting the Script: Masculinity as a Generational Hand-Me-Down

Passed down like a busted Craftsman toolbox—complete with emotional rust and outdated instructions. Let's examine the themes of masculinity instilled in Baby Boomers and Generation X by their predecessors—the Greatest Generation and the Silent Generation—and how those same messages were then projected (loudly and often unconsciously) onto Millennials, Gen Z, and now Gen Alpha. It's a story of inherited roles, unspoken rules, and a masculine ideal that never fit but was still enforced like a sacred contract.

The "Great" and "Silent" Generations:
Built Like a Brick House, Emotionally Speaking

These were the WWII dads and post-war stoics who believed that masculinity meant:

- Serving your country
- Providing for your family
- Never crying unless you lost a limb or a war buddy
- And disciplining your kids like they were a misbehaving platoon

This generation was forged in global conflict and economic depression—survival was masculinity, and emotional expression was a luxury they couldn't afford.[205]

Baby Boomers:
Raised by Repression, Trained for Projection

Boomer boys inherited a masculine code that was part patriarchal, part pressure cooker:

- You're the man of the house, even if you're 12.
- Emotions are for girls, jazz musicians, and Communists.
- Success = job title + boat + not asking questions.

This generation *perfected* the "provider = purpose" model and learned to channel all unprocessed emotion into competitive sports, shouting at their kids, or aggressively polishing classic cars.

And when the emotional cracks began to show in the 1970s and

1980s? They doubled down, clutching at Reagan-era conservatism and "family values" like a life raft made of Budweiser and unresolved father wounds.[206]

Generation X:
The Disillusioned Middle Managers of Masculinity

Gen X inherited the masculine model, but they didn't fully buy it. They were the first generation raised on divorce, dystopia, and dead-eyed dads, watching their Boomer fathers work themselves into ulcers while emotionally neglecting everyone around them.

They questioned it… quietly.

Gen X gave us the ironic dad, the detached husband, who knows the system is broken but still can't quite say "I love you" without deflecting into sarcasm. But while they *felt* the disconnect, they often still recycled the messaging, because vulnerability had no precedent, and masculinity still meant enduring over evolving.[207]

Millennials, Gen Z, and Gen Alpha:
Witnessing the Fragility–Trying to Break the Cycle

By the time Millennials came around, the cracks in masculine armor weren't just visible—they were crumbling in real time on social media.

Millennial men were told:

- Be sensitive, but strong.
- Be successful, but don't brag.
- Be a feminist, but still lead the household.
- Go to therapy, but don't talk about it too much.

Mixed signals? That's the new masculinity. They were also the first generation raised en masse by disillusioned Gen Xers or overcompensating Boomers, many of whom had no idea how to talk about emotional regulation beyond saying "man up" or "go journal about it."

Gen Z and Gen Alpha? Masculinity in America has been passed down like **an emotional inheritance wrapped in trauma**, coated in bravado, and barely held together by guilt, nostalgia, and cargo shorts.

Each generation inherited the script:

- Be tough.
- Be dominant.
- Be silent.
- Be "normal."

Each, in turn, tried to replicate or reject it, with varying levels of success and lots of collateral damage. They're questioning it all—gender, power, performance, pronouns, capitalism, trauma. But they're still growing up in a world where toxic masculinity gets 4 million views on TikTok in under an hour, and "alpha male" podcasts are teaching 14-year-olds that crying makes your testosterone drop.

The cycle is breaking—but slowly. Because fragile masculinity doesn't go quietly, it screams on Twitter, sells self-help to men who think therapy is emasculating, and freaks out when a 10-year-old wears nail polish to school.

Dick's Hissy Fit: I'm Not Fragile, You Are

I'm not fragile. I built a shed during a thunderstorm. I grilled a steak with my bare hands. I didn't cry at my dad's funeral—I sneezed and called it closure. Sure, I screamed when a man wore nail polish. Not because I'm scared—because I don't want the children (me) to be confused (threatened by joy I can't control).

You call it "toxic masculinity." I call it **masculinity with sideburns and emotional scurvy**.

Real men don't:

- *Cry (unless a sports team loses)*
- *Wear pink (unless court-ordered)*
- *Eat quiche (unless it's renamed* meat pie alpha edition*)*

You say I'm unhinged. I say I'm **strategically loud for liberty.**

You say fragile. I say fierce patriot in a Bass Pro Shops hoodie, screaming at clouds.

No—I'm not the problem. Feelings *are.* Empathy *is.* Wokeness *is.*

Now, if you'll excuse me, I'm tweeting **REAL MEN DON'T APOLOGIZE** *in all caps...*

—DICK

From the truck. Through tears. That I will never, ever admit are mine.

Fragile masculinity refers to the anxiety, defensiveness, or overreaction some men experience when they feel their sense of manhood is being questioned, threatened, or not socially validated. It's not about actual weakness—it's about the **fear of being perceived as weak**, emotional, or anything outside the traditional "tough guy" mold.

Fragile masculinity is the term used to describe a culturally conditioned insecurity among men who believe they must constantly prove or defend their masculinity to maintain social status, dominance, or identity. It often results in hyper-masculine behaviors, aggression, misogyny, and resistance to change or inclusion.

What It Looks Like in Action:

- Refusing to use a pink water bottle because it's "too feminine"
- Feeling personally attacked by gender-neutral bathrooms
- Screaming "woke!" at anything that encourages empathy or equity
- Buying bigger trucks in response to women getting promotions
- Declaring "men are under attack" because someone used the word "toxic" and made eye contact

Fragile masculinity stems from narrow, outdated definitions of what it means to be a "real man." Think:

- Emotionless
- Dominant
- Financial provider
- Physically strong
- Never vulnerable

When masculinity is defined this rigidly, any deviation feels like failure. Rather than evolve, some men double down on aggression, control, and cultural hissy fits.

Fragile masculinity is not an insult. It's a diagnosis of a social construct—one that hurts men just as much as it hurts everyone else. It prevents connection, growth, emotional health, and true self-worth.

Aprons and Alibis: The Soft Power of White Womanhood

Because not all fragility comes with a beard and a Bible.

When we talk about the American hissy fit—the loud, red-faced unraveling of entitlement in crisis—the spotlight, rightly, lands on middle-aged white men in flag-print polos who believe drag queens are more dangerous than climate change.

Make no mistake: men don't throw hissy fits alone. This cultural hissy fit comes with a costar: a white woman. Not victims. Not side characters. But full-fledged protagonists in the American drama of dominance, draped in cardigans and plausible deniability. Fragility isn't always loud. Sometimes, it whispers. Sometimes, it cries. Sometimes, it bakes a casserole and calls the police.

Please enter the age of *housewife hysteria,* which was not a medical condition but a cultural symptom: the slow psychological unraveling of millions of women expected to smile through isolation, monotony, and the casual misogyny of a society that told them they were too emotional to lead but somehow stable enough to raise the next generation. Cue the rise of Valium, gin in teacups, and "mommy's little helper."[208] Betty Friedan would eventually give it a name—*the problem that has no name.*

But let's call it what it was: oppression with a matching apron.

White Womanhood: The Original "Call the Manager" Complex

For centuries, white women have been treated as symbols of virtue, vulnerability, and moral order—even as they leveraged that image to enforce systems of violence and exclusion. The patriarchy didn't just oppress the pastel-draped 1950s housewife—she was also its enforcer. She stood at the gates of "good schools," rallied against busing, held prayer meetings to stop "moral decay," and called the cops when a Black child sold lemonade without a permit. Her job wasn't just to uphold her husband's status—it was to maintain the illusion of white social purity, and punish anyone who disrupted the fantasy. White womanhood became a kind of cultural currency. Fragile when convenient, authoritative when necessary. It didn't carry a badge, but it didn't need to—it came with backup.

Suburbia: Where Soft Power Became a Political Weapon

Fast-forward to the 1950s and '60s, and you'll find white women rallying against school integration—not with tiki torches, but with PTA flyers and casserole diplomacy. They organized "Mother's Leagues" and "Citizens Councils" that looked like garden clubs but lobbied like think tanks for white supremacy. They held prayer meetings in opposition to the Civil Rights Movement. They wrote editorials about the "sanctity" of white childhood. They weaponized maternal imagery to defend the racial status quo.

The Karenization of Fragility

Today, we know this archetype as "Karen," and yes she married Dick—but she's just a rebranded version of her great-grandmother in a hoop skirt. The difference? Now she has a Ring camera, a Facebook group called "Real Moms for Real America," and a podcast where she sobs into a microphone about the tyranny of gender-neutral bathrooms.

- She calls the manager when her pumpkin spice order is wrong.
- She calls the school board when her kid learns about racism.
- She calls the police when a Black man looks at birds in Central Park.
- She yells instead of learning when she reads anything about White Fragility.

And through it all, she centers herself as the one under attack. The victim. The patriot. The morally wounded. "I was just scared," she says, as people are arrested, fired, or worse.

What's tragic—but not surprising—is that **Karen isn't exclusive to one shade of foundation.**

White womanhood has long been framed as the embodiment of innocence. But when we look closer, it's clear that innocence has teeth. She never needed to shout. Her whisper carried authority. Her discomfort dictated policy. Her tears launched lynch mobs, delayed desegregation, and still today, get schools defunded, books banned, and lives destroyed.

This isn't about guilt. It's about power. The kind of power that doesn't wear a badge gets saluted anyway. The kind that can make oppression feel like protection and domination feel like decorum. Because in the church of fragility, white women don't just light the candles. They help write the commandments and ensure they're enforced with a smile.

The Housewives Who Sabotaged School Integration

Think it was just angry white dads throwing rocks at Black students in Little Rock, Arkansas, in 1957? Think again. Behind the mobs were organized groups of white mothers, like the "Mothers' League of Central High School," who mobilized against desegregation. Their messaging? "We're just protecting our children." But what they were protecting was a racial hierarchy built into their PTA meetings, school boundaries, and social status.[209] These weren't fringe actors. These were women in aprons, handing out cookies with one hand and voter suppression pamphlets with the other.

Because weaponized whiteness never goes out of style—it just updates its operating system.

She's the one hyperventilating over gender-neutral signage or calling 911 because a Black child is selling water "without a permit." She clutches her pearls when the curriculum includes *actual* history, then floods the school board meeting with Bible verses and PowerPoint slides. She's both an influencer and an informant—teary-eyed on Instagram, righteous in a Facebook moms' group, and always just "concerned for her community." But make no mistake: Karen is not new. She is a legacy feature of American whiteness, rebranded for the digital age.

What We're Witnessing Isn't a Trend—It's a Timeline.[210]

- **1800s—The Plantation Enforcer in Petticoats:** In antebellum America, white women were the emotional shield of slavery. Seen as delicate and pure, they could simultaneously cry about the "burden" of managing enslaved people while overseeing brutal punishments and enforcing plantation order. Their perceived fragility often fueled white men's rage, violence executed in their name. They weren't innocent. They were operational.

- **1900s—The Mob Organizer in Mourning Lace:** White women didn't just stand by during the Jim Crow era. They organized protests against integration, led purity campaigns, and filed legal complaints against anyone who violated their sense of "order." Their complaints were often all it took to trigger a police raid, an arrest, or a lynching. It was the language of moral panic wrapped in gentility. "I just felt threatened." Translation: *Get him out of my sight.*

- **1950s–1970s—The PTA Crusader With a Smile:** The white suburban housewife of the 1950s is often cast as a sedated Stepford cliché. But politically? She was dangerous. She fought desegregation not with pitchforks, but with petitions, school board seats, and "Concerned Mothers of America" leaflets. She fought the Equal Rights Amendment (when it was reintroduced in the 1970s) by framing feminism as a threat to the nuclear family. And she did it all while wearing kitten heels and quoting scripture. *"We're just protecting our children."* From what? Equity. Reality. Accountability.

- **1980s–90s—The Moral Majority's Mascot:** White women became the face of "family values" politics, delivering fiery speeches on daytime TV about Satanic panic, teen pregnancy, and TV sitcom character *Murphy Brown's moral corruption.* Think Tipper Gore's parental advisory crusade. Phyllis Schlafly's polished takedown of feminism. They weren't wielding torches. They were wielding talk shows, church bulletins, and the righteousness of the Reagan era.
- **2000s–Present—The Hashtag Vigilante:** Enter the digital age. Karen now comes with Wi-Fi and surveillance software. She doesn't need a fainting couch—she has a Ring camera and a neighborhood Facebook group. She monitors sidewalks for "suspicious" teens and posts cell phone footage titled "WATCH: THIS MAN GOT TOO CLOSE TO MY STROLLER."

Passive Power Is Still Power

White womanhood has never been powerless. It's just been strategically coded as nonthreatening, making it all the more dangerous when weaponized.

- Because when she cries, someone gets punished.
- When she "feels unsafe," someone gets surveilled.
- And when she wraps her grievance in a Hallmark-worthy tone, the culture rushes to reassure her, no matter who pays the price.

Her apron may be starched, but it covers generations of complicity—and until we name that truth, we'll keep mistaking soft power for innocence and aggression for concern.

Nothing says equality like an apron, a vacuum, and a restraining order on progress.

The 1950s Fantasy: Pastel Misogyny and Racialized Femininity

Marry, mother, mop. That was the program. And in exchange? They were offered a throne, padded in floral upholstery, bolted inside the patriarchy. Not a seat at the table of power, but a heavily surveilled corner next to it, where they could enforce its norms while pretending they had no stake in them.

The Housewife as Homeland Security

The 1950s housewife wasn't just about domestic bliss. She was the frontline soldier of white suburbia's cultural cold war.

She was expected to:

- Be sexually available but not sexual.
- Be educated, but only just enough not to question the script.
- Be nurturing, but only to children who looked like hers.

She stood ready—not just to fold laundry and bake pies, but to call the principal, the city council, or the local zoning board when the status quo felt even mildly inconvenienced. This was femininity as neighborhood surveillance. She wasn't just managing a home. She was managing boundaries—racial, economic, and sexual. And when integration, feminism, or civil rights appeared on the porch? She didn't answer the door. She dialed someone in a position of power to do it for her.

A Clean Home, A Sanitized History

The entire framework of 1950s femininity was built on a fantasy of purity—racial, moral, and domestic. It wasn't just about "keeping house." It was about keeping others out.

- Black women? Cast as maids and "nannies," often raising white children, they weren't allowed to eat lunch together.
- Indigenous women? Erased from media and politics, unless reduced to leather-fringe background noise.
- Queer women? They were declared mentally ill and were locked away—if they were acknowledged at all.

The white housewife was presented as the default woman—heterosexual, Christian, patriotic, and (ideally) blonde. Her existence wasn't neutral.

It was political. Her image was weaponized to suggest that any deviation from her model was dangerous, uncivilized, or Communist-adjacent.

> "In the 1950s, women were told to shrink. In 2025, we're told to expand our income, education, and waistlines if we're pregnant, but not our opinions if we want to stay employable. Equity isn't here yet. But baby, we've got the voting numbers, Wi-Fi, rage, and receipts—and we're done asking nicely."
>
> —SALLY

The Feminine Ideal Was a Fortress

White women in the 1950s were confined. But they were also empowered to detain others. Their social contract required obedience, but it also came with quiet authority, exercised through school boards, garden clubs, and "concerned citizen" letters. Their femininity wasn't passive—it was policed, projected, and portrayed as the moral center of America. And that moral center was, by design, white, straight, Christian, and steeped in a kind of pastel misogyny that punished anyone who didn't match the drapes. The 1950s didn't empower women. It enlisted them to be guardians of order, enforcers of boundaries, and narrators of a story in which only they got to be seen as "women" at all.

Suburban Life, Redlining, and the Calculated Exclusion of Everyone Else

While white America perfected lawn symmetry and burger flips, a far more strategic operation was unfolding in suburbia, built not just for comfort, but for control.

After WWII, the government didn't just support homeownership—it engineered racial exclusion. The FHA-backed loans were only available to white families, and were often directed away from Black and brown neighborhoods, a practice known as "redlining," which was also referred to as "risk management." Levittown? White by design, with racial covenants baked into every sale. **That's not nostalgia. That's segregation in a cul-de-sac.** Suburbs weren't accidents—they were **ideological blueprints**.

- Uniform homes = conformity.
- Zoning laws = coded racism.
- PTA meetings = passive-aggressive gatekeeping.

While white schools soared on property taxes, urban schools were starved. When Black families did ask for equal funding? They were accused of entitlement because nothing scares a system more than the idea of equity. This wasn't a glitch in the matrix. It *was* the matrix. Segregation, sold in floor plans and wrapped in patriotism. Next time someone says, "It was better back then," ask: Better for whom? Because the suburbs weren't just built on land. They were built on exclusion.

Dick, Jane, and the Culture Televised: A Guide to America's Cultural Therapy Couch

Once upon a time, Dick and Jane were learning to *run, jump, and hide feelings* in sanitized children's readers written by middle-aged men in gray flannel suits. Dick mowed lawns. Jane smiled politely. No one was gay, divorced, or poor unless it was a "Very Special Episode."

Then America turned on the TV, and the culture began to seep out.

The Shows We Watch Are the Therapy We Won't Get

- *Mad Men* taught us that our grandfathers were functioning alcoholics in suits, chain-smoking their way through repression while calling it "the good old days."
- *The Golden Girls* and *Maude* showed women aging with sass, sexuality, and political rage, proving the matriarchy slaps when given a kitchen table and cheesecake.
- *The Fresh Prince* and *The Jeffersons* moved Black families into prime time, letting America laugh while ignoring systemic racism because it was *wrapped in a punchline.*
- *Will & Grace* and *Queer as Folk* cracked open the closet doors on screen, letting Middle America claim "allyship" while voting against

gay marriage.

- **Modern Family** made queerness palatable if you were affluent and adorable. At the same time, **Abbott Elementary** reminded us that teachers are America's last defense against total collapse, funded with glue sticks and prayer.

- **On My Block, Gentefied, and Jane the Virgin** brought Latinx stories, realities of gentrification, and telenovela chaos, reminding us that diversity isn't just a casting choice—it's a matter of survival.

- **Crash Landing on You, Squid Game, and Descendants of the Sun** proved that America will binge Korean culture while ignoring its own violence and class warfare, then claim it discovered K-drama like Columbus "discovered" people already living here.

- **Game of Thrones** and **House of the Dragon**: We can't stop watching prosperous, violent dynasties collapse under incest, betrayal, and dragons, while ignoring that Congress is the same show but with boring outfits.

- **The Last of Us**: We're addicted to post-apocalyptic content because we know it's coming. We're trauma-bonding with fungus zombies while ignoring the CDC budget cuts that will ensure we're next.

- **Shōgun** and **Blue Eye Samurai**: We're fascinated by feudal Japan's power plays while living in a country obsessed with "honor" but without the self-awareness to realize it's our cultural rot that needs a reckoning.

What This Says About America: We binge on collapse narratives because we feel collapse coming. We watch dragons burn cities while ignoring wildfires on the West Coast. We root for survivors in zombie worlds while refusing to mask up during pandemics. We fantasize about rebellion while hoarding Amazon packages and voting for the status quo.

We *love* watching empires crumble—on TV. We don't want to pay higher taxes to prevent it from happening here.

The Damage? Television is now emotional prepper training, while it gives us *cultural permission slips* to *feel,* while refusing to *act.*

- We learn to cheer collapse while ignoring systemic fixes.
- We process generational trauma with high-budget distractions.

- We escape into rebellion stories while quietly submitting to daily injustices.
- We watch systemic issues played out in 22-minute episodes, then return to brunch.
- We claim "representation" while ignoring legislation.
- We soothe guilt with diversity on screen while ignoring diversity in our workplaces.
- We process trauma via sitcoms while voting for the politicians who create it.

TV is a mirror, but America uses it as a *sedative*. We watch our cultural fractures play out with laugh tracks, tears, and cliffhangers, then wonder why nothing changes.

And each episode is a reminder that:
- We recognize that the system is flawed.
- We know collapse is coming.
- We'd rather watch it happen on HBO than prevent it in reality

And *Leave it to Beaver* was written with cultural training in mind.

Why the *Leave It to Beaver* Dream Was a Nightmare for the Marginalized

Leave It to Beaver wasn't just a TV show—it was a cultural hallucination, a weekly broadcast designed to tranquilize America's conscience. The "Dick and Jane Readers" were/ are a series of readers only reinforced by *Leave It to Beaver*, and both can still be found on eBay and in reruns. The Cleavers weren't just a family. **They were a propaganda campaign**—white suburban innocence on parade. The disciplined children, the stoic father, and June, who constantly wore pearls like a symbol of oppression, had a dress code. The message was clear: this is what normal looks like, and if your life doesn't resemble this, you may be the problem. Let's cut through the static. This dream, this soft-focus fantasy of domestic perfection, was a nightmare for anyone who didn't look, live, or love like the Cleavers. It was a commercial break between actual injustices.

Black, Asian, Hispanic, and Indigenous Americans didn't just miss out on this dream—they were intentionally written out of it. Not absent.

Excluded. There were no Black families in Mayfield. No Latinos in the neighborhood. No one was redlining the Cleavers' mortgage. No one was accusing Wally of "loitering" while he walked home from school. The only marginalized people who appeared in these televised utopias were often relegated to servant roles—if they appeared at all. And in the real world? Marginalized families were being denied Federal Housing Administration (FHA) loans, harassed by white neighbors, and attacked for trying to integrate schools and housing developments.[211]

Meanwhile, LGBTQ+ folks didn't exist—at least not in any "acceptable" way. You couldn't say "gay" on television. You couldn't be openly queer in school. And if you were caught, your choices were isolation, institutionalization, or invisibility. The '50s weren't just the era of repressed sexuality—they were a time when even acknowledging different identities was considered *subversive behavior*. You weren't just marginalized. You were erased by design.

Immigrants? When they appeared at all, they were background props, broken English punchlines, or Cold War threats. The American melting pot came with a pre-set strainer. If you didn't melt into white, Christian, English-speaking homogeneity, you were deemed foreign, dangerous, or a social pollutant. Ethnic pride was only allowed *after* it had been Americanized, sanitized, and turned into a menu item.

So, while white families gathered around their Zenith televisions with Jell-O molds and TV trays, millions of other families were denied the luxury of delusion. They weren't tuning into sitcoms but fighting for housing, dignity, and safety. While June Cleaver dusted her spotless mantelpiece, a Black mother in Chicago watched her children be bused two hours to a crumbling, overcrowded school. While Ward Cleaver gave moral lectures at the dinner table, a queer teenager was being beaten for walking down the wrong street.

Wake up! This wasn't a peaceful time. It was a time of suppressed rage, state-sanctioned silence, and violent enforcement of the status quo—a cultural arms race to keep "normal" tightly defined and aggressively policed. Harmony was never the goal. Control was. The smiling families, the spotless lawns, the rigid gender roles, "under God" to the Pledge of Allegiance

(1954)"—all of it was a performance designed to hide the very real rot at the foundation. And that's the trick of nostalgia: it forgets on purpose.

Today's culture warriors, with their cries of "We need to return to traditional values!" aren't mourning the loss of family dinners or two-parent households. They're mourning the loss of a time when white men didn't have to share, and everyone else knew their place—or else. The '50s weren't about freedom. They were about compliance—dressed in pastels and broadcast in black and white. The promise of order came with a non-negotiable price: total exclusion for the "others." And like every fantasy, the moment you ask, *"Who's missing from the picture?"*—the whole thing falls apart.

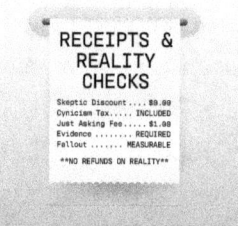

Who Was Left Out of the Beaver Dream[212]
Black Families Were Locked Out of Suburban Homeownership
While the Cleavers enjoyed life in the idyllic fictional suburb of Mayfield, Black families were systematically excluded from that lifestyle through redlining, restrictive covenants, and discriminatory lending.

- **Fact:** The FHA explicitly refused to insure mortgages in or near Black neighborhoods, reinforcing residential segregation and wealth inequality.
- **Impact:** Between 1934 and 1968, 98% of FHA loans went to white families, locking generations of Black Americans out of homeownership and the associated wealth-building. To the point, less than 2% of FHA loans were issued to non-white applicants.

LGBTQ+ People Were Erased, Criminalized, and Institutionalized
While Ward Cleaver dished out fatherly wisdom over meatloaf, queer Americans were facing job loss, imprisonment, and involuntary psychiatric treatment simply for existing.

- **Fact**: In the 1950s, homosexuality was not only considered a mental illness by the American Psychiatric Association but was also criminalized in every US state except Illinois.
- **Impact**: LGBTQ+ individuals lived in secrecy and fear. The government's "Lavender Scare" purged queer employees from federal jobs, and being outed could lead to institutionalization or forced electroshock therapy.

Latinos and Other Immigrants Were Painted as Foreign Threats, Not Neighbors

While the Cleavers' neighbors dropped by for polite chats, Latino and immigrant families were vilified, surveilled, and often treated as economic and cultural threats.

- **Fact**: During "Operation Wetback" in 1954, the US government forcibly deported over 1 million people of Mexican descent—many of whom were US citizens. Fears of job competition and cultural dilution drove this mass deportation.
- **Impact**: Immigrant families lived in fear, faced harassment, and were deliberately excluded from the mainstream narrative of the "good American life."

Indigenous Americans: Erased from the Map—Literally

While the Cleavers celebrated Thanksgiving around a well-set table, Indigenous families were being pushed off the land, out of schools, and into poverty.

- **Fact**: The 1950s saw the rise of the **"Termination Policy"**—a US government initiative aimed at assimilating Native Americans by stripping tribes of federal recognition, dissolving reservations, and pushing Native people into cities without support.
- **Impact**: Tribal lands were sold off, and Native identity was treated like a problem to be fixed, not a culture to be respected.

Asian Americans: Model Minority or Cold War Threat—Pick One

While *Leave It to Beaver* portrayed a colorless, conflict-free America, Asian

Americans were either invisible or framed as foreign threats.

- **Fact:** Although Japanese internment ended in 1945, the effects lasted well into the '50s. Former detainees returned to homes and businesses that had been stolen or destroyed. Meanwhile, the Korean War and Red Scare painted Asian immigrants as political threats.
- **Impact:** Asian Americans were kept out of white neighborhoods through covenants and violence, and their citizenship was only fully secured in 1952 with the McCarran-Walter Act.

People with Disabilities: Locked Away and Forgotten

While the Cleaver children ran freely through safe suburban streets, children and adults with disabilities were institutionalized and written off.

- **Fact:** In the 1950s, disability was viewed almost entirely through a medical lens—something to be "fixed" or hidden. Institutionalization was the norm, with little to no effort made for inclusion, education, or independence.
- **Impact:** Facilities like Willowbrook and Pennhurst housed thousands in inhumane conditions. Disability rights were decades away from mainstream recognition.

Government Policy Prioritized White Male Breadwinners

The GI Bill (The Servicemen's Readjustment Act of 1944): Designed to help veterans reintegrate into society after WWII, the Servicemen's Readjustment Act was heralded as a ticket to the middle class. In practice, its benefits disproportionately **excluded Black veterans** through local-level discrimination in **housing, education, and employment**.

- **Fact:** Only 2% of GI Bill home loans went to non-white veterans in many southern states.

Legalized Gender Discrimination Cemented Male Authority

- *Bradwell v. Illinois* (1873):[213] The Supreme Court upheld a state law barring women from practicing law, stating that a woman's "paramount destiny and mission" was to fulfill the role of wife and mother.
  - o **Impact:** This ruling established a legal foundation for the notion

that women belonged in the home, rather than the workforce or public sphere.

- *Goesaert v. Cleary* (**1948**):[214] The Supreme Court upheld a Michigan law prohibiting women from working as bartenders unless their father or husband owned the bar.

Heteronormativity Was Enforced Through Law and Psychiatry

- **Homosexuality = Mental Illness:**[215] Until 1973, the American Psychiatric Association officially classified homosexuality as a mental disorder.
    - o **Impact**: LGBTQ+ individuals were subjected to forced institutionalization, "conversion therapy," and widespread employment discrimination.
- **Executive Order 10450 (1953):**[216] President Eisenhower banned LGBTQ+ individuals from all federal employment, labeling them national security risks. Over 5,000 workers were fired under this policy during the Lavender Scare.

The Workforce Was Built Around the White Male "Head of Household" Model

- **Federal Tax Code (Post-WWII):**[217] The "married filing jointly" structure and tax benefits for single-income households directly incentivized male breadwinners and female homemakers.
- **Workplace Discrimination Was Legal:**[218] Until the passage of the **Civil Rights Act of 1964**, it was entirely legal to refuse employment based on race or gender. Even after that, enforcement lagged and loopholes thrived.

The Myth of White Innocence Was Televised—and Funded

- **Television in the 1950s–60s**: Virtually every mainstream TV show centered on white, middle-class, heterosexual nuclear families (*Leave It to Beaver, Father Knows Best, The Donna Reed Show*), reinforcing the idea of what "normal" looked like.[219]
    - o **Impact**: People of color were either invisible or reduced to sub-

servient, stereotyped roles, while alternative family structures were never acknowledged.

Segregation and Housing Discrimination Ensured
White Male Economic Advantage[220]

- **Redlining:** Federal housing policies drew "red lines" around neighborhoods with Black or immigrant populations, declaring them high-risk and denying residents access to mortgages and insurance.
  - ○ **Impact:** White men were granted financial capital, homeownership, and upward mobility, while others were systemically locked out.

The Supreme Court Consistently Upheld White Male Power

- ***Plessy v. Ferguson* (1896):**[221] The infamous "separate but equal" ruling legalized racial segregation, enshrining white supremacy in law for nearly 60 more years.
- ***Shelley v. Kraemer* (1948):**[222] While the Court ruled that courts couldn't enforce racially restrictive covenants, it did not ban their use, allowing de facto housing segregation to continue.

The *Golden Age* wasn't golden for everyone. It was engineered by legal precedent, economic policy, media manipulation, and social control mechanisms that prioritized the interests of white, heterosexual, nondisabled men at the exclusion of everyone else. That's not nostalgia—it's structural white supremacy.

Jesus, Jell-O Molds, and the Birth of White Religious Supremacy

Where God got a TV deal, women got a vacuum, and America mistook media ratings for morality.

Welcome to Levittown, the OG prototype of white suburban bliss. Mass-produced homes, appliance-filled kitchens, and enough conformity to make Stepford wives look wild individualists. It wasn't just a neighborhood—it was a theological fantasy. Levittown developers included racial covenants that barred non-white residents from buying homes, because nothing says "love thy neighbor" like a legally enforced whites-only clause.[223] Churches followed the white flight right into suburbia, reinforcing the idea that Jesus only does house calls in zip codes with driveways and manicured lawns.

Sunday Best for Systemic Injustice: Where Faith Met the HOA

While the white suburbs were baking casseroles and raising Dick and Jane, Sunday mornings became moral dress rehearsals. Church pews filled with smiling faces, pressed collars, and unspoken agreements: God loves you. As long as your melanin levels don't disrupt the hymn rotation.

The post-war church didn't just follow the migration to the suburbs—it sanctified it. White Christians embraced a gospel of respectability and property rights, where goodness equated to whiteness and salvation equated to homeownership. Jesus was repackaged as a mild-mannered capitalist who tithes, doesn't protest, and supports "law and order"—especially if it keeps "those people" out of the neighborhood. This wasn't a separation of church and state. This was a collusion between the pulpit and the property deed.

The Holy Broadcast Network: Where Faith Meets Frequency

In the 1950s, religion made its glorious leap from the pulpit to prime time. Protestant preachers, Catholic bishops, and televangelists realized something revolutionary: the Gospel could be monetized and televised in glorious black and white (and eventually in color, once the donations rolled in).

Enter shows like:

- *David and Goliath*: Stop-motion theology for kids where morality was delivered by clay puppets and no one ever cussed or questioned authority.
- *The 700 Club*: Christianity's answer to late-night news—with a side of hellfire and political lobbying.
- *Life Is Worth Living*: Hosted by Bishop Fulton Sheen in a cape (yes, really), drawing over 30 million viewers by 1957.[224]

Televangelism wasn't just a spiritual movement. It was content. And in post-war America, content shaped culture faster than any sermon ever could.

Praise the Ratings: Religion Becomes Entertainment

With network deals came moral theater. Preachers traded altars for studios, turning sermons into soundbites and sin into syndication. Jesus didn't walk on water—he walked across your living room screen between a toothpaste ad and a GE refrigerator promo. These broadcasts didn't just reflect American culture—they **shaped it**.

These broadcasts pushed a particular kind of morality:

- Be polite.
- Be white.
- Be heterosexual.
- Be American.
- And for the love of God, don't question authority—especially if it's wearing a clerical collar or a cop badge.

They normalized:

- White evangelicalism as the default expression of faith
- Conservatism as the moral high ground
- And Jesus as a Cold Warrior who hated communists, feminists, and anyone who couldn't make a decent Jello mold.

Televised religion created a moral monoculture, and anything outside that frame? Too loud. Too queer. Too brown. Too foreign. Too feminist. Un-American. This was less "kingdom of heaven" and more "cultural hostage situation."

From Falwell to Future Cult Leaders: What This Alliance Birthed

This pulpit-to-politics pipeline laid the groundwork for:

- Pat Robertson's presidential run
- Focus on the Family
- The purity ring industrial complex
- Christian homeschool militancy
- And ultimately, Trump holding a Bible upside-down in front of a

church he doesn't attend to defend policies Jesus would've flipped a table over

And it was **built**, brick by brick, by televangelists, strategists, and Republican operatives who realized: *"Why bother saving souls when we can win Senate seats?"*

From Pulpits to Podcasts: The Rise of the Christian Right 2.0

Fast-forward to the 2000s: Falwell's moral panic had a baby. And that baby had YouTube, TikTok, and Facebook rage groups called "Moms for Liberty."

- Alex Jones says demons are running Congress? Viral.
- Your pastor streams his sermon from a home studio draped in American flags? 4K-ready.
- Your uncle believes Jesus was a gun rights advocate? He's got a meme for that.

Welcome to the algorithmic altar, where evangelical messaging is now digitally optimized for outrage, paranoia, and merch sales. They didn't just want prayers in schools—they wanted the courts on speed dial. Through groups like:

- Alliance Defending Freedom,
- Liberty Counsel, and
- First Liberty Institute,

…they launched a decades-long legal siege that flipped school policies, health care access, and LGBTQ+ rights upside down—all in the name of "religious liberty." Translation: The right to discriminate… without consequences. The Christian right doesn't just vote. It organizes. It strategizes. It shows up. And it plays the longest political long game this country has ever seen.

The Long Game–Faith, Fear, and the
Voter Base That Never Misses

Because when you fuse religion and politics, you don't need logic—you need loyalty, a mailing list, and a good choir director. By the late 1980s, the alliance between conservative Christianity and Republican politics wasn't just strong—it was institutionalized. This wasn't a political trend—it was a generational strategy.

And the Religious Right wasn't here to flirt with power. It was here to marry it, raise children with it, and homeschool them using creationist textbooks. The brilliance of the Christian right wasn't in its theology—it was in its logistics.

- Falwell had the Moral Majority database before Facebook existed.
- Focus on the Family weaponized radio to dictate family values policy.
- James Dobson had more influence over parenting advice than pediatricians.

And every newsletter, cassette tape, and Christian conference came with one message: *Vote. Every. Time.*

The Christian right didn't grow by preaching the gospel—it grew by manufacturing threats.

- "They're banning prayer in schools."
- "They're turning your kids gay."
- "They're canceling Christmas."
- "They're replacing you."
- "They're teaching Black history!"

Nothing fuels the Christian Hissy Fit quite like the **myth of Christian persecution**.

- Can you legally pray? Yes.
- Own a Bible? Yes.
- Start a megachurch, build a theme park, and run for office on your religion? Also, yes.

But if Starbucks changes the cup design in December, or a school dares to mention Ramadan? "We're under attack!" This is what sociologist Philip Gorski calls "reactive Christianity"—a belief system rooted not in what it stands for, but in what it's afraid of losing.[225] And guess what? **Fear works.** Fear votes. Fear shows up at the polls with a van full of church folks and enough post-service donuts to carry a precinct.

Christian conservatives understood early what others are just realizing now: Control the schools, control the future.

- They didn't just vote—they ran for school committee.
- They didn't just argue—they rewrote the curriculum.
- Sex ed became abstinence-only.

- Science class became Genesis with a lab coat.

Prayer in Schools, Guns in Churches, and Irony in Shambles

Nothing says *"Christ is Lord"* like packing heat in the pews and shouting about the sanctity of life while blocking healthcare access.

We're now in an era where:

- School shootings happen regularly, but evangelicals are lobbying for more prayer instead of fewer guns.
- Churches are arming congregants and installing panic buttons—but insist it's drag queens that are threatening the children.
- "Religious freedom" means freedom to oppress, not freedom to believe.

This isn't faith. It's stagecraft in a crisis suit. By the time Dick and Jane were raising kids in the '90s, evolution was optional, condoms were banned, and Satan was hiding in Harry Potter books.

Cultural Fallout–Sanctified Supremacy and the Myth of Moral Clarity

When your Sunday sermon sounds like a campaign rally and your morality depends on who's watching Fox News. The long game worked. The God-Industrial Complex delivered. And now, we live in a country where faith isn't just personal—it's performative, politicized, and weaponized. Christian nationalism didn't save the nation's soul. It sold it at Hobby Lobby and filed a tax exemption form. They didn't just elevate Christianity—they elevated a particular kind: white, conservative, male-dominated, and allergic to nuance.

- Black liberation theology? Silenced.
- Indigenous spirituality? Mocked or appropriated.
- Queer theology? Demonized.
- Feminist theology? Ignored or labeled heresy by white men named Randy.

The evangelical narrative winked at the Gospel, turning Jesus from a brown-skinned, anti-empire revolutionary into a Republican life coach who thinks racism is impolite and poverty is a branding issue. **Sanitized**

morality sells better than systemic truth. Christian media became the ideological sugar rush that keeps kids obedient, adults uninformed, and libraries sanitized.

Go in peace, but first, let's burn the blueprint.

The Christian right is not about saving souls. It is about saving status. It hijacked faith, rewrote morality, and has turned democracy into a mega-church where the ushers are armed, the sermon is a soundbite, and Jesus is just a brand ambassador with good bone structure and suspiciously light skin.

It Wasn't About Worship. It Was About Control.

- Control over women's bodies (see: *Roe*).
- Control over school curricula (see: banned books and disregarded textbooks).
- Control over identity, family, marriage, and public space.
- Control over who gets to call themselves "American."

It wasn't Jesus that showed up at the Capitol on January 6, 2021—it was the Frankenstein monster of decades of fear-stoking, power-hoarding, and voter-mobilizing theology dressed in tactical gear and waving a cross. This was never about faith. **It was always about leverage.**

The Church Wasn't Corrupted—It Was Designed Like This

This isn't a tragedy. It's an intentional blueprint.

- Build a hierarchy.
- Inject patriarchy.
- Sprinkle with racial supremacy.
- Wrap in scripture.
- Sell it as "values."

From the plantation pews to the gated community pulpits, American Christianity—at least the mainstream, white evangelical flavor—was never apolitical. It was just polite about its power hunger... until politeness stopped working.[226]

Where We Go From Here: Burn the Altar, Build a Table

This is not a call for cynicism—it's a call for clarity.

- Faith doesn't need nationalism to be powerful.
- Christianity doesn't need whiteness to be relevant.
- And Jesus sure as hell doesn't need a super PAC.

If we're going to reclaim culture, democracy, and actual community, we need to:

- Stop mistaking nationalism for spirituality.
- Uproot the weaponized myths.
- Center justice, not judgment.
- And create sacred spaces that make room for everyone, especially the people the empire tried to erase.

Christian nationalism wasn't built to fail. It was built to dominate. **But domination isn't destiny. And deconstruction is holy work.**

From Jell-O to Jesus Laws—When the Potluck Became Policy

Let's pause and appreciate what we just witnessed in the last section: America's slow-boil transformation of Christianity from spiritual practice to political battering ram—with a side of lime Jell-O and weaponized nostalgia.

White religious supremacy didn't arrive in a flaming chariot—it oozed in on folding tables at church basements, one judgmental casserole at a time. It wasn't born on the battlefield; it was born in the fellowship hall—simmering quietly in sermons, school boards, and suburban gossip until it metastasized into a voting bloc with Bible verses and burner Twitter accounts. The uncomfortable truth: American Christianity didn't just separate from the state—it moved in, claimed squatter's rights, and redecorated.

We're now in the era where:

- Prayers are policy platforms,
- Abstinence education is still somehow a thing, and
- Legislators use Scripture to legislate bodies they've never consulted.

And if you question it? Congratulations, you're anti-God, anti-family, and probably trying to turn kindergarten classrooms into drag brunches, at least according to Karen's Facebook group.

Dick's Father, as he puts on his Sunday Best:

"White supremacy? That's just another made-up label the woke crowd uses to shame proud Americans. I'm not a white supremacist—I just believe Western civilization is superior, our culture built the modern world, and we shouldn't have to apologize for it. Everyone had their chance, but it was white men who did the heavy lifting. That's not hate, that's history. And if protecting our way of life makes me a villain in your story, so be it. Better to stand tall for tradition than bow down to diversity quotas and victim politics."

This isn't faith—it's fragile control disguised as conviction. And it's not about saving souls. It's about safeguarding supremacy—the kind that panics at a mosque, gaslights queer teens, and has a meltdown when someone says "Happy Holidays."

— RICHARD JR. *Dick's proud Dad*

We're not just asking whether church and state are truly separate; we're also examining the implications of this separation. We're asking how the "Holy Trifecta of Entitlement" (white, Christian, and male) turned *suggested morality* into *mandatory policy*—and why every step forward in rights gets met with a pearl-clutching Hissy Fit from the pew.

Brace yourself. We're going from communion wafers to cultural and constitutional warfare. Bring your comfort stuffie—you'll need it.

CHAPTER 9

Culture Wars, Crisis, and the Theater of Trauma

When catastrophe strikes, America doesn't just respond—it throws on a red, white, and blue costume, grabs a megaphone, and makes sure the cameras are rolling.

W e've turned national trauma into political theater, complete with costumes, catchphrases, and commercial breaks. Somewhere between the Constitution and cable news, the presidency ceased to be a position of leadership and became a one-person spectacle—a never-ending performance of American fragility masquerading as governance. This isn't politics anymore. It's pageantry. And to understand the full scope of the hissy fit that broke the nation, we must pull back the curtain and examine the performance for what it is: a three-act tragedy with bipartisan billing.

The Three-Sided Failure: A Cultural Breakdown Across the Political Spectrum

This isn't a hit piece on American democracy—I've worn the US Army uniform, stood for its ideals, and still believe in the brilliance of its blueprint. But belief without accountability is just denial in a flag pin. What we're living through isn't just a broken system—it's a fractured script, and every political party is guilty of running the same tired lines. This is not a left-versus-right story. It's a **collective collapse**, propped up by ego, optics, and the seductive high of outrage.

Democrats: The Performers of Progress

Democrats know the language of inclusion. They're fluent in equity, reform, and hashtag justice. They kneel in Kente cloth, they host roundtables, they tweet boldly. However, their outrage is often **performative, and their victories are frequently symbolic.**

- Systemic change? Delayed for committee approval.
- Radical transformation? Watered down into politically palatable soundbites.
- Hope? Slowly euthanized in a legislative process that serves donors more than the marginalized.

They're less a political movement, more a branding agency for progress, staging change without delivering it.

Republicans: The Prophets of Regression

Once the party of restraint and responsibility, the GOP has devolved into a culture war circus powered by **grievance, paranoia, and performative patriotism.** It's no longer about conservative principles—it's about emotional manipulation dressed in camouflage:

- Fear-mongering as campaign strategy.
- Authoritarianism as "American values."
- History rewritten as heritage, and heritage weaponized against reality.

Independents: The High Ground Without Fire

Independents often claim the moral middle, rejecting partisan toxicity. But too often, that neutrality turns into **passive complicity.**

- They want solutions, but not the discomfort.
- They want the truth, but not the tension.
- And in the process, they become background actors in a political drama

that needs disruptors, not **spectators who change the channel when things get uncomfortable.**

Independence without action isn't courage—it's **comfort with better branding.**

Here's the twist: the problem isn't just them. It's **us.** We, the audience, have allowed this show to run too long. We boo from the couch but never question who sold the tickets. We watched 2020 happen and said, "Is that the best both parties have to offer?" But we didn't revolt. We didn't demand better. We just **refreshed our feeds**, shrugged, and waited for the next episode of *Democracy: The Decline.*

We allowed **25% of the population—MAGA zealots, Christian nationalists, and Moral Majoritarian**—to define the national script while the other 75% sat quietly, hoping someone else would rewrite it. We are all complicit in casting these characters. And if we don't start **questioning the script**, we'll keep recycling bad actors until democracy becomes just another rerun.

This Isn't Gaslighting. It's a Truth-Telling Monologue with a Blowtorch

We are not unraveling because of one man, one election, or one party. We're unraveling because we allowed the culture of distraction, spectacle, and spin to replace civic duty, critical thinking, and national accountability. We are failing because we accept performative leadership. Because we treat representation like fandom. Because we forgot that democracy doesn't run on applause—it runs on action. So, no—this isn't a takedown of democracy. It's a **dressing down of the audience**, a **reprimand for everyone waiting for better leaders without demanding them.**

We have a choice:

- Keep shouting from the recliner like Dick, blaming "the Millennials" or "the system" while doing absolutely nothing.
- Or finally **cancel this show** and write something better.

Because if we don't, we deserve the next season of dysfunction. And trust me, it won't be binge-worthy.

Politics as Performance, Not Governance

Welcome to the United States of America, where the Constitution is now a script, politicians are unionized actors, and every press conference doubles as a casting call for the next outrage cycle.

America didn't invent political theater—but we damn sure turned it into a billion-dollar franchise. What started as governance slowly morphed into government-as-content. The C-SPAN era gave us policy debates; the post-TikTok era gives us performative tantrums with merch tables. Today's politicians aren't leaders. They're method actors with lobbyist-funded trailers, focus-group-tested taglines, and more costume changes than a Beyoncé concert. Governance is boring. Performance? That's monetizable.

Nobody goes viral for passing a clean water bill. But storm out of a hearing? Quote Scripture while stripping reproductive rights? Tweet your moral outrage in all caps? Boom—instant cable news slot and a "donate now" button.

The Origins of Political Theater in American Democracy

Political theater didn't arrive with Trump, Twitter, or TikTok—it's been baked into the American experiment like gunpowder in a firework. Founding ideals? More like founding branding.

Before the stage lights, soundbites, and Instagram-ready grandstanding, America's politics were already dripping in drama. From quill pens to microphones to livestreams, our politicians have always known that what you say *matters less* than how you *stage it*.

The Founding Fathers—God, Guns, and Enlightenment-Lite

From the beginning, American politics has thrived not on compromise but on proclamation. Forget thoughtful debate—the real currency of power has always been the spectacle. Symbolism is the stage, spectacle is the script, and governance is optional—as long as the audience stays emotionally invested. Whether it's Jefferson declaring all men equal (while enslaving people) or Reagan staging tax cuts as a return to morality, America's political history is a centuries-long PR campaign with intermittent wars and lots of flags.

"Politics is a series of symbolic acts that maintain the illusion of choice while reinforcing the status quo."[227]

Expansion and Exploitation—Manifest Destiny: The Musical

Enter Jackson, Polk, and Pierce, stomping across the continent like angry toddlers with a map and a musket. Theater became a **traveling war show**, with scripts penned in blood and marketed as "destiny." Their hissy fits became foreign policy:

- Jackson killed the national bank because it bruised his ego.
- Polk picked a fight with Mexico like he lost a bar bet.
- Buchanan sat on his hands while the country caught fire.

Together, they delivered the cultural masterpiece: **"How to Break a Nation and Blame the Slaves."**

Civil War & Reconstruction—Tragedy Dressed as Unity

Abraham Lincoln gave the most excellent TED Talk of the 19th century at Gettysburg:

- 272 words.
- Delivered in under 3 minutes.
- No PowerPoint.
- And yet—timeless political theater.

He turned a bloody battlefield into a national altar, wrapped in rhetorical flourish and moral redemption. Lincoln knew how to frame a moment— he didn't just speak, he cast himself in the American imagination as the reluctant savior. As media historian Daniel Boorstin would later write, political figures in modern democracies succeed not through deeds, but through "well-contrived images"—what he called *pseudo-events*, designed to be reported more than remembered.[228] Lincoln didn't just govern—**he branded the Civil War as a moral production.**

Lincoln brought gravitas to the stage—Hamlet with a top hat. But his death gave us Andrew Johnson, the community theater understudy who thought the solution to racism was giving racists their land back. The theater now had two acts playing simultaneously: one on Black freedom in the North and another on Black codes in the South. Congress booed, racists roared, and democracy quietly left through the stage door.

The Gilded Age—Monocles, Mustaches, and Monopoly

Presidents stopped leading and started hosting gilded galas for robber barons. Think: Wall Street fan fiction with moral ambiguity. The hissy fit of the day? Labor unions are asking not to die on the job. The performance? A smoke-filled opera of corruption, backroom deals, and tariff tantrums.

20th Century Showmen—From FDR to Reality TV

Fast-forward to Franklin D. Roosevelt: our first **radio-era influencer.** His Fireside Chats were a masterstroke in political theater:

- Calm tone? Check.
- Reassuring cadence? Check.
- Carefully curated messaging that bypassed the press to deliver *his version* of reality directly into homes? **Double check.**

The Fireside Chat was less "here's what's happening" and more "here's what I need you to *feel.*" Emotional storytelling became statecraft. Roosevelt wasn't leading a country—he was narrating one, in serial installments.

- FDR rewrote the script—**"New Deal or New Depression."**
- Nixon turned the presidency into a recording studio for trust issues.
- Reagan brought Hollywood to Washington and grief to social programs.
- Clinton delivered sax solos between deregulation benders.

By the time we got to Trump, the presidency wasn't a role—it was performance art in a red hat. Biden, bless his heart, played the part of the tired substitute teacher trying to keep the class from getting out of control.

Presidential Power as Performative Chaos

The truth? Every president since Washington has picked up the mic and added their solo to the American soundtrack of dysfunction. Some harmonized. Others screamed into the feedback loop. But all understood one truth: **In America, politics isn't governance. It's a theater. And the louder the hissy fit, the bigger the legacy.**

Theatrics Over Thought: Welcome to the Political Hunger Games

Democracy isn't dead. It's just been cast in a reality show, given a producer credit, and forced to fight for screen time against conspiracy theories and sponsored outrage.

WWE SmackDown Promo–But with Less Sincerity

Our politicians now enter hearings with the same energy as wrestlers entering a steel cage match—minus the athleticism, plus a thesaurus full of moral panic. Microphones are props. Eyebrows are raised with theatrical precision. Outrage is fake—but the damage is real. And just like in wrestling, everyone's playing a character. The Freedom Defender™. The Woke Destroyer™. The Budget Hawk™ (who's never read a spreadsheet in their life). The audience already knows the ending—they tune in for the body slams.

Real Housewives Reunion–But with More Gerrymandering

Congressional hearings? They're no longer about policy—they're catty reunions with worse lighting. "Reclaiming my time!" is the new table flip. Interruptions are scored like tennis matches. Crying, yelling, and gaslighting are par for the legislative course. And just like the "Real Housewives," they're constantly forming alliances, backstabbing each other on Twitter, and flipping districts like they're flipping wine glasses.

An SNL Cold Open–But Written by the Angriest Uncle at Thanksgiving

Forget writers' rooms. Most political commentary today sounds like it was ghostwritten by your MAGA uncle and your leftist cousin in a group chat argument gone wrong.

- One side is quoting Marx without reading him.
- The other side is quoting the Founding Fathers without understanding them.
- And everyone's yelling "fake news!" while forwarding articles from websites that look like they were coded in a bunker.

The jokes are old, the satire is unintentional, and the punchlines often involve someone losing their healthcare.

From Committee Room to Content Studio

We now expect our elected officials to be content creators first, lawmakers maybe never.

- Live-tweeting hearings with GIFs and hashtags like they're narrating their scandals in real time.
- Capitol TikToks with emoji-laden clapbacks and scripted indignation filmed in front of flags, coffee mugs, or random interns.
- Instagram sermons where they read cherry-picked Bible verses while gutting social services that would've helped the actual Jesus crowd.

Who needs policy when you've got 10k followers and a sponsorship deal with the Patriot Candle Company?

The House Is Not in Order—It's in Tech Rehearsal

This isn't a deliberative body anymore—it's a full-blown drama department with access to nuclear codes. And like any good production, it needs: Villains (immigrants, teachers, scientists), Heroes (themselves), and an endless supply of crises to keep the ratings high.

They don't pass budgets—they pitch plots.

They don't write legislation—they drop cliffhangers.

They don't protect democracy—they *stream* its decline.

And while America burns (literally, thanks to climate change), they're too busy adjusting their ring lights and fighting culture wars from the comfort of air-conditioned chambers.

Sally's Comment:

"Political theater isn't leadership—it's a circus of cowards in suits. I'm disgusted watching grown adults treat governance like performance art: rage for the cameras, deals in the shadows, applause lines in place of policy. While they rehearse their hissy-fits on C-SPAN, real people pay the price. Call it what it is: bad theater with deadly consequences."

—LOVE, SALLY

Campaigns as Stagecraft: From Town Hall to TikTok

Modern political campaigns aren't about building trust or communicating vision—they're a full-blown media rollout, complete with lighting design, emotional soundtrack, and a post on Instagram that makes you look like you're saving democracy with one hand while holding an oat milk latte in the other.

Competence? That's so 20th century. Today's campaigns are high-production, emotionally optimized, influencer-driven content machines—where charisma beats credentials and a candidate's "vibe" is more important than their voting record. If Lincoln ran today, he wouldn't make it past Iowa—not because he lacked substance, but because he lacked jawline symmetry and couldn't hit a TikTok dance without dislocating something. Political strategists today are less concerned with policy alignment and more concerned with: Engagement rates over economic plans, clapbacks over coalitions, and follower counts over field operations. We haven't evolved the campaign trail. We've just redecorated it to look like a green screen set.

Prime-time Campaign Performances:
- **Obama's "Hope" Poster (2008):** Designed by Shepard Fairey, this was *the first viral political brand*. Slap it on a hoodie, stick it on a dorm wall, print it on mugs—it was aspirational activism you could wear. Obama became the Apple product of politicians: sleek, minimal, and loaded with symbolism.
- **Trump's MAGA Rallies (2016–2024):** Fewer campaign stops, more concert tours for the aggrieved. With stadiums full of merch booths, red hats, and gospel-style call-and-response ("Lock her up!"), these rallies weren't policy discussions—they were mass therapy sessions for wounded egos, with Trump as both pastor and pyrotechnic.
- **Beto O'Rourke's Dentist Livestream (2019):** Nothing says presidential timber like a close-up of your molars. This wasn't a strategy—it was a vibe check. "Look how relatable I am," he seemed to say, while America replied, "Sir, we're trying to eat lunch."

As political scientist Bruce Newman puts it, *modern campaigns are driven by "political branding,"* where identity, emotion, and relatability replace ideological coherence.[229] The new campaign trail isn't a journey—it's a curated feed. And we're not electing visionaries. We're choosing digital mascots. And in the end, we won't remember what they said. But we'll not forget how good the lighting was when they said it.

Presidential Debates or Pay-Per-View Punchlines?

Remember when presidential debates were sacred ground for national dialogue—substantive, sober, statesmanlike. Think Kennedy vs. Nixon—Reagan vs. Carter. Hell, even Bush Sr. vs. Clinton vs. Perot had a certain strange elegance. They were awkward, yes. But at least you came away knowing *where they stood.*

Today? You come away wondering who won the meme war. Modern debates are less about leading a country and more about surviving **an onstage influencer showdown**, complete with custom zingers, branded slogans, and a moral panic soundboard that can be played live on Fox or MSNBC. Debates are now moderated by journalists whose primary skill set includes:

- Interrupting with game show timing,
- Asking complex questions in under 15 seconds,
- And cutting off answers with "We have to move on," right before the candidate says something vaguely useful.

The Goal isn't Clarity—it's Chaos

The moderator isn't there to facilitate understanding. They're there to *keep the drama moving* and make sure the commercial breaks hit like plot twists.

The debates have essentially adopted the structure of a **UFC main event**:

- **Round 1:** Border Crisis Blitz!
- **Round 2:** Gun Control Grudge Match!
- **Round 3:** Climate Cage Fight—No Facts Allowed!

What about when debates were about *vision*? About *governing philosophies*? Yeah. That's adorable. Now they're scored like improv battles:

- **Best One-Liner:** "I'm not here to listen to you lecture me, sir." Cue applause.

- **Most Finger Wagging**: Bonus points if you do it while misquoting the Constitution.
- **Top Viral Clip**: Must include raised eyebrows, visible contempt, and a rehearsed mic-drop moment.

You don't even need to say anything of *value*. You need to say it *loud*, say it *smirking*, and hope it gets reposted on TikTok with trap beats. Substance? Dead on arrival. Debates now exist primarily to generate content:

- Clips for campaign ads.
- Reactions for YouTube.
- GIFs for Twitter.
- Clickbait for Politico, HuffPost, and a thousand TikTok breakdowns titled "Watch This Candidate DESTROY Everyone."

Substance doesn't trend. Performance does. We've transitioned from participatory democracy to **spectator democracy**, where the citizen's role is to watch, judge, and react (preferably with emojis). This means: You don't need to win the debate. You need to *win the edit.*

Debates Are Now Cultural Events—Not Civic Ones

The presidential debate isn't about helping voters make informed decisions—it's about reinforcing team loyalty. It's a halftime show for the culture war, where nobody changes their mind, everyone yells their truth, and post-debate spin is more choreographed than a Super Bowl halftime. It's not a debate. It's a vibe check for democracy. And we're failing it in 4K resolution. Grab your wine, polish your outrage, and don't forget to vote—based on which candidate's zinger made the best merch.

Dick's Hissy-Fit: Debates Are My Super Bowl

"Now this is what politics should be!" Dick shouts, popcorn in hand, like he's at WrestleMania. "Two candidates going head-to-head, trading zingers, calling each other out, making the crowd roar—it's glorious! Forget policy details, I want blood sport. Debates today prove who's strong enough to dominate and who's weak. Who cares if they dodge questions or talk over modera-

The Fourth Wall Is Dead (And So Is Accountability)

The government was once referred to as the fourth branch of power. Now? It's an open-concept soundstage where politicians audition for fame, dodge responsibility, and treat democracy like a personal brand deal.

In theater, breaking the fourth wall refers to acknowledging the audience, thereby disrupting the illusion that what is happening on stage is real. In politics, it means the same thing: publicly admitting the performance while pretending it's governance. Elected officials no longer govern. They perform governance. Every speech, every vote, every "deep concern" is a carefully choreographed content opportunity that appears to be leadership, while avoiding any actual consequences or outcomes.

Gone are the days when policy was passed in smoke-filled rooms. Now, it's passed through ring lights, Instagram filters, and press conference backdrops featuring American flags and just enough ethnically ambiguous supporters for plausible inclusivity. Today:

- Every vote is a photo op.
- Every hearing is a trailer for the next campaign.
- Every tragedy is a brand-building opportunity—complete with hashtags, b-roll, and "heartfelt" tweets pre-written by interns.

Every National Trauma Now Comes with a
Wardrobe and Media Strategy

- **Natural disaster?** Throw on a windbreaker with your state's seal, look mildly concerned, and ensure the media captures a shot of you helping to carry bottled water (for no more than 30 feet).
- **School shooting?** Activate your thoughts-and-prayers app. Cue the heartfelt tweet. Follow it up with zero policy change and a scheduled

National Rifle Association appearance next week.

- **New war front?** Time to slap a flag on the lapel, roll out the tank parade, and start referring to your opposition as "unpatriotic." Flags don't cost much, and they cover a multitude of sins.

And in every case, the public bleeds—literally and figuratively—while elected officials rack up speaking fees, primetime interviews, and campaign donations. This is no longer the government. It's a "spectator democracy," where *citizens watch governance more than they participate in it,* turning voters into audiences and leaders into influencers.[230]

The Only Bill They're Passing: The Politics of Distraction

While the infrastructure crumbles, the planet burns, and citizens drown in debt, Congress holds hearings on:

- Taylor Swift's concert ticket prices,
- Critical race theory panic, and
- Whether the late Dr. Seuss has gone "woke."

The only real bipartisan consensus in DC? That distraction keeps the donations flowing. Accountability requires transparency, humility, and a commitment to fulfilling promises. But those don't trend. Rage does. Division does. Performative outrage is the clickbait of political survival, and America has become addicted. We've normalized political dysfunction through the media's obsession with *style over substance*, further eroding faith in democratic institutions.[231]

Welcome to America, Where the Only Wall That Was Built is the One Between Politicians and Accountability

Now, our democracy doesn't operate on debate and compromise. It runs on ratings, optics, and perpetual conflict loops. We don't elect leaders to fix problems—we elect actors to simulate leadership while distracting us from the fact that the house is on fire. And while the stage lights shine, the system quietly rots behind the curtain. We don't have a functioning government. We have a reality show with nuclear codes, campaign PACs, and a blooper reel that gets people killed.

The show must go on—but don't expect it to end with a standing ovation. More likely? Just another spin-off, another slogan, and another episode of *"Democracy: The Decline, Streaming Live."*

Faith, Fear, and Fireworks: The Performative Political Bible Belt

Welcome to the Church of Red State Politics, where Jesus is a campaign prop, morality is seasonal, and salvation comes with a side of pork-barrel spending.

Let's not forget the most sacred of American political rituals: the performance of piety. Nothing wins votes faster than performative Christianity—especially when it's loud, selective, and carefully designed to distract from the fact that you just gutted school funding. In today's landscape, the Bible isn't a holy book—it's a prop. A script passed down through campaign consultants and televangelist SuperPACs. Politicians now treat legislation like a traveling sermon, with all the sanctimony of a megachurch and none of the accountability.

"Thoughts and Prayers"–The Policy Equivalent of Shrugging

- **Mass shooting?** "Thoughts and prayers."
- **Deadly hurricane due to climate change?** "Thoughts and prayers."
- *Roe v. Wade* **overturned women's reproductive rights?** You guessed it: "Thoughts. And. Prayers."

These hollow phrases have become the go-to glitter glue for avoiding real action. They're the equivalent of political glitter: shiny, performative, and impossible to clean up. Religious identity in conservative politics often functions not as a moral compass but as a tribal signal—**a badge of cultural dominance more than actual conviction.**[232]

"God's Plan"–A Catch-All for Avoiding Responsibility

- **Universal healthcare?** "If God wanted you to have insulin, He wouldn't have given you Type 1 diabetes."
- **Paid family leave?** "That's between you and Jesus."
- **Gun violence?** "The Lord works in mysterious ways—especially with AR-15s."

"God's plan" has become the most spiritually convenient exit ramp from every single policy question. It's the divine version of "not my department." This isn't faith—it's **political insurance fraud**.

Legislation by Vibes, Not Viability

Entire bills are now passed based on:
- **Moral panic**, not public need.
- **Scripture snippets**, not social science.
- **Fox News segments**, not constituent feedback.

We're watching the **Book of Leviticus become state law**, cherry-picked by lawmakers who can't spell "empathy" but have "Deuteronomy" tattooed on their reelection banners.

Example? States banning drag shows "to protect children" while slashing education budgets, ignoring child poverty rates, and doing absolutely nothing about clergy abuse. Because the point isn't protection—it's performance.

The Political Bible Belt: A Sacred Spectacle

The Bible Belt isn't just a region. It's a **performance venue**:
- Complete with pews for press conferences,
- Choirs of pearl-clutching pundits,
- And a fog machine of "family values" to conceal corruption and cruelty.

Even evangelicals are catching on. A 2021 Pew Research Center report found a growing percentage of younger evangelicals view the faith-politics connection as **toxic and disingenuous**—a sign that the pews may be losing patience with the pulpit's political puppetry.[233] But don't expect the show to stop. As long as religious cosplay pays off at the polls, the holy theater of the absurd will keep running matinees in every red-tinged district across America. These politicians moralize about **"family values"** while maintaining:
- Secret mistresses,
- Offshore accounts,
- Private jets funded by public funds, and
- Campaign events hosted in churches that somehow always forget about "render unto Caesar."

Holy Hypocrisy as Choreography

You want hypocrisy? Try this: Quoting Corinthians by day, sliding into staffer DMs by night, voting against school lunches on Tuesday, and giving a Sunday sermon about *"God's love for the least of these."*

Faith as Fortress, Not Freedom. In theory, religion offers comfort. Today's brand of Christian nationalism offers insulation—a theological panic room for bruised egos, terrified that the world no longer centers them. It's not about saving souls. It's about *saving face*. Christian nationalism is "a reactionary force against demographic change and social pluralism."[234] It's not about devotion. It's about *defense*. Not spirituality. *Supremacy*—dipped in holy water and lit with tiki torches.

Because what's more comforting than believing your downfall isn't due to outdated ideas, unchecked ego, or generational incompetence, but rather, that it's all just a *test from God*? A cosmic exam you're destined to pass. With Jesus as your co-signer. And Brett Kavanaugh as your tutor. Welcome to the holy hissy fit. It's not about righteousness. It's about relevance. This isn't just a contradiction. This is a stage direction. They're not failing to live up to Christian values—they're acting out a role written by PR teams, focus groups, and billionaires who realized that Jesus makes a great distraction from "tax reform" that favors the very wealthy at the expense of nearly everyone else.

Politics, Piety & Paychecks: The Bible Belt Cash Machine

Trump didn't just court the Christian right—it was established during Regan; however, the MAGA movement colonized them. Forget grace. Forget humility. Trump handed them judges, culture war ammo, and the divine right to stay angry. MAGA gave Christian nationalists exactly what they'd been praying for—not scripture, not salvation, but "access to political power and the ability to impose their beliefs on others."[235] This wasn't divine intervention. It was divine manipulation. And the irony? Chef's kiss.

The loudest Bible-thumpers are often the ones most likely to be found: Pants-down behind a closed door at a Days Inn, texting their "prayer group" from burner phones, or explaining why their fifth mistress was a "spiritual test." These are men who rail against drag queens as threats to children, while their names show up in Epstein flight logs and hush-money settlements. They clutch their Bibles with one hand while the other signs book deals about "family values" from jail. They scream about sin while tweeting from burner accounts named "PatriotDad1776." It's like a Hallmark movie written by Satan and directed by hypocrisy.

In today's American politics, Jesus doesn't save—He fundraises. Our political figures don't lead; they preach, post, and profit. The Bible Belt has become the Merch Belt, where quoting Leviticus on the House floor guarantees more donations than proposing actual legislation. Morality isn't a compass—it's a campaign strategy.

- Want to ban books? Quote scripture and watch the Venmo tips roll in.
- Want to erode healthcare? Call it "God's Plan" and drop the link to your Super PAC.
- Want to legislate women's bodies? Just say you "prayed on it" and cue the PayPal.

This isn't governance—it's generational grift, and we're all stuck in the pews. From televangelists to Twitter candidates, they don't want your faith—they want your clicks, coins, and culture war loyalty points. Because at the end of the day, it's not about God. It's about gross fundraising totals. Amen and ka-ching.

Supreme Court Influence via Dark Money[236]

- **Leonard Leo & Federalist Society/Marble Freedom Trust:** Conservative megadonor **Barre Seid** contributed at least **$1.6 billion** to a group led by Federalist Society figure Leonard Leo, enabling a massive campaign to install conservative judges, using a religious-right agenda to reshape the judiciary, including the Supreme Court
- **Harlan Crow & Justice Clarence Thomas**: Harlan Crow, a wealthy

conservative donor, has quietly funded trips, gifts, and events for Justice Clarence Thomas—including luxury gatherings and undisclosed payments—raising significant concerns about conflict of interest.

- **Operation Higher Court—Faith & Action:** Reverend Rob Schenck revealed a decades-long effort—dubbed "Operation Higher Court"—where religious-conservative donors cultivated relationships with Justices Thomas, Alito, and Scalia through lavish dinners and private events hosted by the Supreme Court Historical Society.

Congressional Influence from Clergy & Religious Groups

- **Dark Money Networks Post-Citizens United:** Conservative and religious-right groups have spent billions on political ads and lobbying through nonprofit "dark money" channels. This includes efforts like Leonard Leo's dark-money vehicle and the Moral Majority in the 1980s.
- **Clergy & Religious Organization Contributions:** Between 1990 and 2014, clergy and religious-affiliated donors contributed millions directly to congressional campaigns, with a slight majority trending toward Democrats, but still funneling hundreds of thousands to conservative causes.

Presidential Influence on the Religious Take[237]

- **Reagan: The Inaugural Moral Majority Marketer:** Back in 1980, Jerry Falwell Sr.'s Moral Majority dropped an estimated **$10 million** on Southern broadcast ads warning that Jimmy Carter wasn't Christian enough—then promptly cheered when Reagan's polls soared 20 points in those districts. Reagan didn't just court evangelical voters—he formed a bureaucratic marriage: **Christian nationalism became a political party meet-and-greet.**
- **George H. W. Bush:** Though tensions sometimes existed—Falwell accused Bush Sr. of being insufficiently pious—Bush ultimately embraced evangelical voter support. In the late 1980s, Robertson founded the **Christian Coalition with $27 million in funding** and 1.9 million members, holding significant sway during Bush's term
- **George W. Bush (2001–2009)—Like Father, Like Son:** Supported

by faith-based groups like Let Freedom Ring, which actively backed his 2004 re-election, especially on issues like **same-sex marriage and border control**. His establishment of the White House Office of Faith-Based and Community Initiatives signaled an unprecedented merger between governmental policy and religious advocacy

- **Trump: Christian Patriotism with a Payroll:** Fast-forward to the Modern Age, when openDemocracy found that at least **$280 million** in "dark money" from Christian right groups was funneled globally into pro-Trump messaging—much of it used to fund social-conservative campaigns and court evangelical Christian voters. Closer to home, Texas oil-pastor billionaire Tim Dunn shelled out **$5 million** to Trump's 2024 run—then watched Trump promise to fast-track his $2.2 billion CrownRock sale if re-elected. Not precisely a tithing confessional—more like a spiritual hedge fund. The **Public Religion Research Institute (PRRI)** found a strong correlation between weekly church attendance and support for Trump, as well as a surge in Christian nationalist voters backing his 2024 candidacy. That's not grassroots—it's a cash-and-carry operation.

Religion Isn't Free Speech–It's Funded TV

What started as grassroots religious engagement has become a sophisticated ecosystem where billion-dollar cash flows from Christian nationalist backers heavily influence court appointments, policy decisions, and party platforms. It's no longer just campaign contributions—it's an entire **shadow state** operating through charity tax loopholes and personal networks.

So, What's the Damage?

1. Religious discourse gets auctioned at campaign rallies.
2. Bible verses are used as campaign slogans with donation links.
3. Voters don't look for integrity—they look for preachers who can fundraise.

The Bible Belt isn't broke—it's the ARRA (American Religious Revenue Apparatus), where piety is pointed toward PACs, and faith funds become campaign funds.

Final Amen: God Doesn't Need a Campaign Manager

If Jesus showed up today, he'd be horrified by the legislation passed in his name—and possibly deported for being a brown-skinned, homeless, anti-capitalist foreigner without ID. The primary purpose of religion in politics should be to provide moral guidance. Instead, it has become a smoke screen for cruelty.

This isn't a church. It's a set piece. And the sermon's just the script for the next campaign ad.

"Do as I Preach, Not as I Practice." Top 10 Politicians Who Invoked God—and Forgot the "Thou Shalt Not" Part[238]

1. **Mark Sanford (R-SC)** *"God will guide my path.":* Went "hiking the Appalachian Trail." Translation: *flew to Argentina for an extramarital affair.* Still gave tearful, Bible-laced pressers. Voted against gay marriage as a moral issue.

2. **Ralph Reed (R-GA)** *Founder of the Christian Coalition:* Claimed to represent the "moral majority." Caught in the Jack Abramoff lobbying scandal—funneled gambling money through anti-gambling Christian orgs. Moral loophole? *"We were fighting sin… with sin."*

3. **Jimmy Swaggart (Evangelical televangelist with political influence)** *"I have sinned against you, my Lord.":* Famously wept on national TV after being caught with prostitutes… repeatedly. Advised politicians on "moral policy." Cried. Came back. Did it again.

4. **Newt Gingrich (R-GA)** *"God and country.":* Preached family values and had an affair with a staffer while impeaching Bill Clinton for *his* affair. Later married the mistress and converted to Catholicism. (Penance = politics.)

5. **David Vitter (R-LA)** *"America must return to Christian values.":* Caught

in the "DC Madam" scandal, his number appeared in her little black book. Wore diapers, allegedly. Still quoted Scripture.

6. **Roy Moore (R-AL)** *"God's law is above man's law.":* Accused by multiple women, including several minors, of sexual misconduct. Rode into rallies on horseback... with a Bible. Still tried to run for Senate (again).

7. **Larry Craig (R-ID)** *"I am not gay.":* Arrested in a bathroom sting operation for soliciting sex from another man. Voted consistently against LGBTQ+ rights, citing religious morality. Foot-tapping for Jesus?

8. **Josh Duggar (R-connected activist)** *Family Research Council's golden boy for "traditional family values.":* Molested his sisters. Cheated on his wife. Got caught on the Ashley Madison website for cheaters. Later convicted of child pornography possession. Led purity campaigns.

9. **Ted Haggard (Evangelical leader, political consultant)** *"We must protect marriage.":* Meth. Male escort. Repeat. Pastored a megachurch while advising George W. Bush on *moral issues.* Denied. Confessed. Got a documentary deal.

10. **Donald J. Trump (R-President)** *"The Bible is my favorite book."* (Couldn't name a verse.): Adultery? Plural. Hush money? Verified. "Christian values"? Only at rallies. Evangelicals still treated him like the second coming of King David (*flawed, but chosen*). Held a Bible upside down outside a church for a photo op. Enough said.

11. **Honorable Mention:** *Mike Pence*—no known affair, but enabled nearly every name on this list under the banner of "faith-based governance."

The Damage of Political Theater

Welcome to the Orange Era, where grievances are not just a feeling, SCOTUS is a joke, and politics are performances— this is a full-blown business model.

This is not a political movement. It's a revolution. It's not even a perfect hissy fit. It's fragility—weaponized, monetized, and broadcast 24/7 in HD, and it's alive and well, and its mascot is Trump. After losing power, elections, and the basic plotline of reality, a particular faction of America decided they wouldn't adapt, reflect, or (God forbid) improve. Nope. They chose the Hissy Fit Industrial Complex instead.

Today, facts are optional. Feelings are constitutional rights. Victimhood is the new patriotism. Every time reality came knocking, a new conspiracy theory answered the door wearing nothing but a red hat and a bad attitude. Every time democracy worked, someone cried "fraud!" louder than a televangelist selling apocalypse insurance. Every time inclusion made a bit of progress, half the country shrieked like someone had personally defaced their Norman Rockwell calendar.

When "Facts" Become Optional: America's War on Reality

The Hissy Fit: America isn't just flirting with delusion—it's proposing, getting married in Vegas, and live-streaming the divorce on TikTok. Reality wasn't comforting enough. It had too many complicated words. Too much math. Too many minorities are doing well. America, ok, 45, grabbed a Sharpie, scribbled over the inconvenient parts, and screamed "Fake News!" whenever facts were remotely uncomfortable.

Stat Check: As of 2025, only **34%** of Americans trusted scientific experts to act in the public's best interest.[239] Meanwhile, **YouTube conspiracy videos** outperformed those featuring the actual CDC guidelines.[240]

The Cultural Impact: Facts became fashion accessories worn when convenient, tossed when uncomfortable. You didn't *believe* in climate change? Cool. It still believed in you, as evidenced by Miami becoming the world's largest kiddie pool. You thought vaccines were government tracking devices? Adorable. Unfortunately, the measles are back.

American civic dialogue collapsed into a Choose-Your-Own-Reality game:

- Climate change? Hoax.
- Evolution? Theory, but gravity's still okay because it helps you shoot beer cans off the fence.
- Systemic racism? Myth—unless you're trying to get out of a parking ticket.

The new motto wasn't "E Pluribus Unum" anymore. It was "You're Not the Boss of Me."

The Result: A country spinning faster than a QAnon meme drop. The consequences? Public health collapsed. Civic trust disintegrated. America's global reputation? Right between "Florida Man" and "that one uncle at

Thanksgiving who thinks the moon landing was faked." **Meanwhile,** billionaires continued to extract wealth, politicians continued to gaslight, and Dick? He argued that 5G gave him arthritis while microwaving a Hot Pocket.

Strategic Emotion Always Wins the Airwaves

Look at the campaign hits that broke the Internet and democracy at the same time:

- **"Build the Wall"**: Not a blueprint. Just a chant that activated fear and tribalism faster than you could say "due process."
- **"Lock Her Up"**: No trial, no charges, no problem. Just pure vengeance theater that aired nightly and sold shirts by the truckload.
- **COVID conspiracies**: Because a doctor saying "wear a mask" doesn't go viral—but a YouTuber claiming Bill Gates microchipped your grandma in aisle 4 of Walmart? Ten million views, easy.

Research indicates that emotionally charged content spreads more quickly and widely than neutral information. Messages with moral-emotional language—especially those conveying outrage—are more likely to be shared and endorsed, thereby reinforcing ideological echo chambers and weakening rational discourse.[241]

"Moral-emotional content amplifies the spread of messages through social networks."[242] In short: **fear goes viral. Facts go unread.** It's not that people don't care. It's that they've been taught to feel first, think later—if at all.

Political Puppetry with Voter Suppression

Welcome to American politics, where the puppets pull the strings, and democracy is just the set dressing. Political puppetry is the art of looking like you're serving the people while serving the people who write checks. Voter suppression? That's the trick behind the curtain—make it *look* like everyone's invited to the show, then quietly lock the doors for anyone not on the donor list.

From voter ID laws that "protect integrity" like a wet napkin, to gerrymandering maps that'd make Picasso flinch, suppression isn't a glitch—it's the design. The goal? Keep the electorate *just* engaged enough to believe it's fair, and *just* restricted sufficiently to make sure the status quo never sweats because in this puppet show, you're free to vote, just not always free to matter.

From Literacy Tests to Bureaucratic Labyrinths: The Evolution of Voter Suppression

1. The "SAVE" Act: Securing Access for Very Few

In April 2025, the US House passed the Safeguard American Voting Eligibility (SAVE) Act, mandating documentary proof of citizenship—such as a passport or birth certificate—for voter registration. While proponents claim it's to prevent noncitizen voting (a virtually nonexistent issue), critics argue it could disenfranchise millions, particularly women who have changed their names, low-income individuals, and rural residents lacking easy access to such documents.

2. North Carolina's Ballot Ballet: Dance of the Disenfranchised

The 2024 North Carolina Supreme Court race saw Democrat Allison Riggs win by a mere 734 votes. However, her Republican opponent contested over 65,000 ballots, citing technicalities. The state's Supreme Court ruled that certain military and overseas votes required additional verification, potentially rendering them invalid. This move has been criticized as a dangerous precedent that could undermine voter confidence and disenfranchise eligible voters.

3. Purge Surge: Cleaning Voter Rolls or Erasing Democracy?

In 2024, several states undertook aggressive voter roll purges:

- **Virginia** removed over 6,000 voters suspected of being noncitizens. However, many were later found to be eligible voters. Despite legal challenges, the US Supreme Court allowed the purge to continue.
- **Alabama** attempted to purge 3,251 voters, leading to a federal lawsuit. A judge ordered the state to restore the registrations, noting that many individuals who were purged were legally registered.

4. Vigilante Verification: The Rise of EagleAI

Conservative activists introduced EagleAI, a tool designed to identify and challenge voter registrations en masse. Critics argue it's a form of "voter fraud vigilantism," leading to unwarranted challenges against legitimate voters, often targeting communities of color.

5. Tennessee's Test Lab: Experimenting with Democracy

Tennessee has become a focal point for restrictive voting laws, with local leaders warning it's a "testing ground for voter suppression." The rollback of protections from the Voting Rights Act has led to increased barriers, particularly affecting Black voters and other marginalized groups.

Conclusion: While the tools and terminology have evolved, the essence of voter suppression remains creating obstacles that disproportionately affect marginalized communities. From overt discrimination to subtle bureaucratic hurdles, the fight for equitable voting rights continues in 2025.

What Damage Does It Cause? Let's Count the Ways (While Rome Burns and Congress Live-Tweets It)

Welcome to the cultural demolition derby we call American politics. It's loud. It's chaotic. It's highly flammable. And it's not insured. What happens when performance replaces principle, and leadership gets outsourced to rage merchants with ring lights? You get **civic collapse with a laugh track and damage:**

1. Polarization Becomes a Business Model

Once upon a time, political differences led to debate. Now, they lead to

merchandise drops.

- Want to raise campaign cash? Say something cruel.
- Want a podcast deal? Poke the culture war bear.
- Want your base frothing with patriotic rage? Misuse the word "woke" five times in a row and shout "freedom" into a megaphone.

Division isn't a crisis. It's a **subscription model**. Why govern when you can grift? Why legislate when you can monetize polarization like it's a patriotic OnlyFans?

2. Legislation Isn't About Lives—It's About Likes

Bills aren't written to solve problems anymore. They're written to generate **clips, controversy, and campaign cash**.

- Anti-drag bills? Not about safety—about airtime.
- Book bans? Not protecting children—protecting political futures.
- Anti-trans laws? Not "values"—just performance art for the base.

If it trends, it passes. If it doesn't? Toss it in the drawer and blame the Deep State. We don't have lawmakers. We have **content creators with voting privileges**.

3. Educators Quit. Librarians Are Harassed.
Kids Become Set Dressing.

America's schools have become **stages for adult meltdowns**. No one's teaching anymore—they're dodging viral videos and "concerned parents" with TikToks and torches.

- Teachers are fleeing the profession like it's a haunted house.
- Librarians are getting death threats over Judy Blume novels.
- Meanwhile, kids? They're props in photo ops and press releases, stuck doing active shooter drills and watching democracy eat itself between algebra quizzes.

Education isn't under attack. It's **being sacrificed for the sake of the plot**.

4. Marginalized People? Constantly Targeted, Blamed, Erased

America has a long tradition of punching down—and in the age of performative politics, it's gone full Broadway villain monologue.

- Trans youth? Demonized for existing.
- Black communities? Blamed for systemic failures they didn't build.
- Immigrants? Turned into crisis actors for camera-ready border tours.

If someone's already vulnerable, they're one bill, one soundbite, or one Fox News chyron away from becoming the week's designated villain. It's not governance—it's scapegoating in surround sound.

5. Erosion of Public Trust: "Of Course It's Failing—It's Designed That Way"

Americans don't just distrust the government—they assume it's actively plotting against them while filming a documentary about it.

- Congress's approval rating is flirting with single digits.
- Media trust is Balkanized into tribal echo chambers.
- Science? Treated like witchcraft if it interferes with someone's gut feelings or YouTube feed.

This isn't apathy—it's learned betrayal, and it tracks. When your leaders prioritize brand deals over bridge-building, expecting dysfunction becomes a self-defense mechanism. Why believe in institutions when "some guy on Rumble" has a podcast, a rifle, and three million followers?

6. Voter Fatigue and Cynicism: "You Want Me to Vote for That?"

Voters aren't lazy. They're **traumatized by the menu**.

- Choice A: Geriatric neoliberal with slogans and no teeth.
- Choice B: Reality TV fascist who sells autographed Bibles.
- Choice C: Whatever Independent got on the ballot by accident.

Why vote when:

- Nothing changes,
- Everything sucks, and
- Everyone's lying into a microphone instead of holding a mop?

The only thing more disillusioning than not voting? Realizing you did—and nothing happened.

7. Complex Issues Reduced to Bumper Stickers and Bad Merch

Democracy requires complexity. Performative politics requires **catch-**

phrases and swag. Everything gets shrunk to:

- "Build the Wall."
- "Back the Blue."
- "Heartbeat Bill."

It's anti-intellectualism by design—because clarity doesn't go viral. Confusion does.

Three-word slogans are easier to chant than three-hundred-page policy reports—and they fit better on hats.

8. Trauma Isn't Just Lived–It's Marketed

Real people die. Real communities grieve. And politicians? They pose for photos, write hollow tweets, and slap a ribbon on the following reelection flyer.

- Gun violence? "Thoughts and prayers."
- Racial injustice? "We're listening."
- Public health crisis? "This is a hoax—or a conspiracy—but either way, let's sell some t-shirts."

Trauma has been turned into campaign collateral, and the real casualty isn't just the policy; it's the truth. It's trust—in:

- Government,
- Institutions,
- Journalism, and
- Worst of all, each other

We're not just polarized. We're atomized—each of us screaming into algorithmic voids while the democracy we were supposed to steward crumbles beneath a flood of retweets and rage.

Political wars **undermine democracy** by turning every issue into a binary, emotional brawl where truth is optional and empathy is weakness. They don't build anything. They burn—and then sell merch in the ashes.[243] What's left is a society addicted to crisis, but allergic to action. We're not a nation in debate—we're a nation in permanent dress rehearsal, restaging the same culture war scenes while the infrastructure of democracy collapses backstage. And the tragedy? Nobody knows what the play is even about anymore. But the merch booth is still open.

America doesn't have a governance problem. It has a reality distortion problem—one where theater replaces substance, outrage replaces solutions, and crisis becomes content. We're not just spectators. We're co-stars in the slow death of trust. The show must go on. But at what cost? Yes, when catastrophe strikes, America responds—with a press release, a photo opportunity, and a new set of enemies to keep the audience engaged. Because in a country where politics is performance, governing is just the intermission between acts of cultural warfare. And as long as the cameras are rolling, the show must go on.

Who Benefits from all this Theater?

Hold on—this will shock you: **Politicians Who Have No Policy Platform!** When you don't have a plan to fix healthcare, climate change, or housing, what do you do? Easy. Blame drag queens, critical race theory, and oat milk. Culture wars are a **distraction tactic**, a strategic misdirection. They rally the base, feed the news cycle, and enable elected officials to pass legislation based on vibes instead of actual policy solutions.[244]

"Why talk about rising rent when you can scream about rainbow displays at Target?" Conservatives like Ron DeSantis, Josh Hawley, and Marjorie Taylor Greene have weaponized culture wars to build name recognition, raise funds, and climb political ladders—all while pretending to be victims of "wokeness." Oh, and let us not forget 45/47—he thrives in the Culture War.

Media Outlets and Content Grifters:
ORANGE ERA = CLICKS | CLICKS = REVENUE

Outrage is a business model, and business is booming. Fox News, OANN, The Daily Wire, and an entire ecosystem of rage-pundits generate millions in ad dollars by feeding their audiences a steady diet of:
- Manufactured threats,
- Cherry-picked outrage,
- "War on Christmas" updates, and
- The occasional M&M scandal.

Meanwhile, podcasts and YouTube personalities like Jordan Peterson, Matt Walsh, and whoever's currently crying about Barbie are raking in Patreon cash with every hissy fit.

Corporations Playing Both Sides

Here's the twist: even corporations' win. They roll out Pride merch in June and quietly fund anti-LBGTQ+ politicians in July.[245] They capitalize on culture war moments for brand awareness, then hide behind statements like *"We value all perspectives"* when the backlash hits. Capitalism doesn't care if you're woke or anti-woke—it cares if you're spending. The Bud Light backlash? A financial hiccup. The real win? Billions of dollars in media coverage—and a reminder that outrage is free PR.

Culture wars get easier to win if a country's population has a poor cultural memory and suffers from historical amnesia. Read on to find out what that's done to us.

CHAPTER 10

Cultural Memory & Historical Amnesia

America has a memory problem. Not because we forget, but because we *choose* what to remember. Preferably with background music, dramatic lighting, and none of the inconvenient truth.

I n America, crises have become the opening act for political theater—and once the spotlight hits, the show never ends. First, a crisis creates spectacle: a national emergency is never just a disaster. It becomes a 4K production, complete with color-coded alerts, misery montages, and talking-head recaps that would make Spielberg weep. Next, spectacle becomes ideology—our emotional conditioning machine that transmutes fear into patriotic imperatives ("Support the troops!"), bleeding-heart empathy into fundraising hashtags, and righteous anger into legislative mandates brewed for clicks. Finally, ideology becomes law—or worse, content. We pass bills not in the interest of the public good, but to generate viral moments ("Mission Accomplished" banners or Instagram-ready public monuments). And when Congress stops passing actual laws? They pivot to producing scripted hearings, complete with hashtag-now talking points aired in prime time, designed to draw reruns and ad revenue.

This isn't a system out of control—it's a calculated spiral: culture prompts the crisis, the crisis fuels the spectacle, the spectacle births ideology, and ideology becomes the script politicians follow. At that point, political theater isn't responding to us—it's directing us. We aren't the audience anymore—we're cast members in a long-running drama, holding cue cards and emoji reactions while the director—politicians-turned-show-runners—calls the shots.

History Scripted Then Forgotten

Our national history isn't so much remembered as it is scripted, directed, edited, and test-screened for maximum emotional resonance and minimum discomfort. We don't teach it—we *screen* it. And we don't pass it down—we market it. The result? A nation that remembers the movie trailer but forgets the documentary. America's cultural memory has the emotional accuracy of a Lifetime movie and the historical depth of a BuzzFeed listicle. We love: The *imagery* of Dr. King, not his economic demands. The *aesthetic* of the Founding Fathers, not the structural racism they coded into law. And the *myth* of Reagan's "Morning in America," not the people who never saw daylight.

This isn't just selective memory. This is **intentional amnesia**, packaged by textbook companies, filtered through patriotic Instagram accounts, and broadcast on cable news with flag overlays and gospel choirs.

"Silences enter the process of historical production at four crucial moments: the moment of fact creation, the moment of fact assembly, the moment of fact retrieval, and the moment of retrospective significance."[246]

In other words? **What we forget was designed to be overlooked.**

What's Historical Amnesia?

The selective forgetting, whitewashing, or outright denial of inconvenient truths from the past to preserve a flattering national narrative, protect power structures, or avoid feeling "uncomfortable" during AP US History. It's less about memory loss and more about memory *editing*—brought to you by the same people who think the Civil War was about "states' rights," slavery was "just a tough time for everyone," and Rosa Parks "refused to give up her seat because she was tired."

Symptoms Include:

- Teaching about Martin Luther King Jr.'s dream, but not his rage against capitalism and white moderates.

- Celebrating Independence Day while ignoring whose land was stolen to create that "freedom."
- Quoting the Constitution without mentioning the part where you had to be a white male landowner to matter.
- "I never learned that in school!" suddenly becomes a reason to deny it happened.

Diagnosed Most Frequently In:

- School board meetings debating book bans.
- Politicians who say "we've come a long way" to avoid coming any further.
- Social media posts that say "slavery ended 150 years ago—get over it."
- Billionaires lecturing the working class about "grit" while hoarding generational wealth built on the backs of, well...history.

Historical Amnesia Is Not Innocent: It's not a whoopsie. It's a **strategy.** As Baldwin warned: "Not everything that is faced can be changed, but nothing can be changed until it is faced."[247] But America responded with: *"Or... hear me out... we could just teach the Constitution like it fell out of the sky in 1776, fully formed and freedom-flavored."*

Historical Amnesia = The National Pastime of Pretending the Past Never Happened. It's the ghostwriter of patriotic textbooks and the executive producer of grievance politics.

Reagan the Cowboy, Not Reagan the Union-Buster

Ronald Reagan has been repackaged into a **Stetson-wearing messiah** of free-market freedom and flag-waving optimism. What gets left out?

- The war on labor unions (starting with the PATCO air traffic controllers' strike).
- The AIDS crisis and his administration's silence.
- The explosion of income inequality under Reaganomics.

But hey, he *looked* great on a horse; we airbrush the rest. Reagan isn't remembered as he governed—he's remembered as he was sold and perceived. And that performance has become a cultural prosthetic, used by conservatives to cosplay "the good old days" that never actually existed.

MLK the Dreamer, Not the Disruptor

Martin Luther King Jr. didn't die for a soundbite. But you'd never know it, because his radical legacy has been flattened into a Hallmark card. The real King:

- Spoke out against capitalism, militarism, and white moderate complacency.
- Was under FBI surveillance.
- He was *deeply* unpopular among white Americans when he was alive.

Yet every January, we get: Politicians quoting "I Have a Dream" while gutting voting rights. Corporate logos in grayscale share MLK quotes while funding anti-Black policies. "We honor King by misremembering him."

Why This Amnesia Is Political Theater's Best Friend

Political theater depends on forgetfulness. It thrives in a culture where:

- Complexity is skipped,
- Contradiction is erased,
- And repetition becomes truth.

Forget that Reagan broke unions—remember that he *smiled*. Forget that King challenged capitalism—remember that he *dreamed*. Forget that the Founders enslaved people—remember that they *wrote freedom down nicely*.

Memory Is a Stage—And We Keep Casting the Same Lies

America doesn't have a history problem. It has a **branding problem** disguised as patriotism and powered by a million PowerPoint slides. We remember what flatters us. We forget what indicts us. And in the absence of truth, theater fills the gap. If democracy is memory in motion, then we're not moving—we're looping the movie trailer on repeat, hoping no one ever watches the whole film. Amnesia is the ultimate campaign strategy. Because you can't fact-check feelings, and you can't demand accountability for what the public has been trained to forget. And history is replete with events that those in power would like us to forget.

Sally's Statement:

"America's greatest disease isn't inflation, immigration, or even polarization—it's historical amnesia. We forget slavery but remember the Confederacy as 'heritage.' We erase Jim Crow but celebrate the 'good old days.' We whitewash civil rights struggles into sanitized soundbites and call it progress. This selective memory isn't harmless—it's rot. It allows racism, sexism, and authoritarianism to rebrand themselves as patriotism. A country that refuses to face its past honestly can't grow honestly. And right now, America isn't moving forward—it's stuck in a loop of denial, repeating its ugliest chapters like reruns of a bad sitcom nobody asked for."

—SALLY

The Audience's Role (Us):
Complicit, Clicking, and Comfortably Numb

This show doesn't go on without an audience. Political theater doesn't exist in a vacuum—it exists because we keep tuning in. We're not just watching the performance. We're funding it, streaming it, doomscrolling it, and quoting it in group chats like it's the new *Succession*. No audience, no show. But we've become more than just viewers—we've become engaged spectators of our dysfunction, mistaking consumption for civic duty.

Doomscrolling as Civic Ritual

We don't deliberate. We doomscroll. Every school shooting, every scandal, every "breaking news" chyron becomes another act in our never-ending culture crisis binge. And like a toxic Netflix queue, we consume trauma in episodes, complete with commercial breaks and hot takes. This isn't news. This is emotional self-harm packaged as information.

Clicks Over Ballots

We now "vote" more often with our clicks than with our ballots:
- Retweeting feels like an action.
- Sharing a meme feels like a protest.

- Doing a TikTok duet with a politician? That's engagement.

The average American is more likely to know what their favorite podcaster thinks about *Roe v. Wade* than what their local representative is doing about it. That's not political awareness—it's **parasocial activism.**

The Rise of Voter Cynicism and "Both Sides" Nihilism

We've marinated in so much bipartisan bullshit that nihilism has become a coping mechanism:

- "They're all corrupt."
- "My vote doesn't matter."
- "Both parties are the same."

This isn't skepticism. It's surrender. And it's precisely what the system wants: a disengaged electorate too jaded to demand anything but the next scandal. As theorist Neil Postman warned back in 1985, we wouldn't be destroyed by Orwellian censorship, but by Aldous Huxley's prophecy—a society addicted to entertainment and spectacle that forgets to care.[248] We're not just being lied to—we're **entertained into submission.** The only thing worse than bad governance is an electorate that mistakes screen time for citizenship.

9/11: The Day the Script Changed

When Theater Replaced Leadership, and the Price Was Paid in Lives

Politics stopped being about public service the moment the stage got bigger than the substance. After 9/11, we didn't just fight terrorism—we curated it for prime time. American grief was repackaged as political capital, sold by the speech, and broadcast live, flag in one hand and a defense contractor check in the other.[249]

Governance turned into performance art. Homeland Security rolled out color-coded fear. "Mission Accomplished" banners hung before the mission even began. And behind the scenes? No WMDs, no exit strategy, but plenty of Halliburton contracts.

Then corporations joined the charade: They slapped rainbow logos on factories run with underpaid labor, posted black squares on Instagram, and called it "allyship." This wasn't virtue. It was marketing. It wasn't about values—it was about **optics** and shareholder confidence.[250]

Meanwhile, the climate was boiling. But instead of taking action, America handed the mic to retired oil execs and cable pundits who thought carbon emissions were a matter of political opinion. Science became optional. Denial became policy. And the Arctic? It's now a luxury cruise destination.

While the nation spiraled into hot takes and headlines, real people were footing the bill:

- **The 20-year war in Afghanistan cost over *$2 trillion* and nearly *241,000 lives*, many of them civilians.**[251]
- Public health was gutted in the name of personal freedom.
- Mental health crises soared, but therapy remains a luxury item.
- Men and women who served were left in the dark.
- We banned TikTok instead of regulating social media addiction.

Instead of justice, we got drone strikes. Instead of universal healthcare, we got heart-wrenching pleas on GoFundMe. Instead of leadership, we got likes. This wasn't a glitch. It was the business model: Keep the people distracted, divided, and disoriented while the ruling class cashes out. You didn't need to stage a **coup—you just needed enough noise.**

ACT I: Culture Shift: Fear Became a Virtue.
Patriotism Became Performance. Dissent Became Treason

In the weeks following 9/11, **fear wasn't something to overcome—it became the new civic duty.**

- Questioning the government meant you were "with the terrorists."
- Critiquing war meant you "hated the troops."
- Asking for nuance meant you didn't *love* America hard enough.

We didn't just hang flags—we **weaponized** them. From classrooms to coffee shops, patriotism went from quiet allegiance to public theater, and everyone was expected to hit their mark. As political theorist Corey Robin (2004) notes, post-9/11 America witnessed a normalization of fear-based governance, where political legitimacy became tied to the extent of danger a leader could promise to protect against.[252]

Remember the Bullhorns, Banners, and Branding

The iconic scenes in Act I of the post-9/11 performance: **Bush on the Rubble with the Bullhorn**

"I can hear you. The rest of the world hears you. And the people who knocked these buildings down will hear all of us soon."[253]

Cue roaring applause. Fade to flag. It was the **perfect soundbite**—the presidential equivalent of a superhero origin story. And from that moment on, Bush wasn't just a leader—he was cast as the commander-in-chief in an imaginary post-apocalyptic movie called Freedom Strikes Back.

"Freedom Fries" and Color-Coded Terror Charts

When France didn't support the Iraq War, we did what any mature democracy would do: renamed the fries. Yes, in the cafeteria of Congress. Yes, seriously. Meanwhile, the Department of Homeland Security rolled out color-coded terror alerts, because what better way to prepare for a national catastrophe than a Crayola chart of doom?

Red = "PANIC."
Orange = "Almost panic."
Yellow = "Still panic, but with coffee."

It wasn't information—it was **emotional choreography**.

ACT II: Then Came the Post-9/11 Era: Homeland Security Theater and Cultural Regression

America didn't rebuild. It rebranded. Wrapped in stars, stripes, and TSA pat downs, the nation swapped *healing* for *histrionics*. Post-9/11 America wasn't about unity—it was about uniformity, sold at scale and broadcast in HD. **And who paid the price? Millennials and future generations**.

- Surveillance became patriotism.[254]
- Dissent became treason.[255]
- Fear became bipartisan policy.[256]

We were told never to forget, but nuance, truth, and civil liberties were the first to be put on the chopping block. These three prongs became the strategy for controlling America's minds to follow a lamb or culture to slaughter.

ACT III: The Patriot Act and the Paranoia Pipeline

The Only Thing We Had to Fear… Was Everything. Forever. September 11, 2001, didn't just bring down buildings. It erected an entirely new political industry: The Security State. Suddenly, mourning wasn't enough. We needed vengeance, visibility, and a massive bureaucracy with acronyms, badges, and extreme opinions about your shoes.

The Department of Homeland Security: When 22 Agencies Love-Bomb You at Once

Born in 2003 out of panic, patriotism, and PowerPoint, the Department of Homeland Security (DHS) emerged as the bureaucratic equivalent of Voltron in post-9/11 America. It merged 22 federal agencies—including FEMA, the Coast Guard, and Customs—into one confusing HR nightmare, and trust me, I know, I am HR, in what experts have since called "a solution that created 21 new problems."[257] The idea? Centralize intelligence and streamline national security. The result? A Kafkaesque org chart with infinite redundancy.

It also introduced Americans to the Color-Coded Threat Level, a sophisticated visual system that told us whether we were in "Mild Concern," "Guarded Panic," or "Code Red: Cancel Thanksgiving." Terror was now conveniently color-matched to your anxiety level, giving news stations the visual ammo to run fiery banners and dramatic theme music every time a goat sneezed near a border.

The USA Patriot Act

A 342-page omnibus bill that turned the Constitution into a Mad Libs of paranoia. Passed just 45 days after 9/11, it granted federal agencies the power to snoop, surveil, seize, and suppress, all under the banner of "national security."[258] Most lawmakers didn't read it. Some didn't even pretend to. And honestly, who has time for civil liberties when you're rebranding panic as policy?

Suddenly, the FBI could walk into your library and demand a list of everything you checked out—because clearly, reading *The Kite Runner* is a gateway drug to terrorism. Google searches were scrutinized, phone calls logged, and emails flagged.

"Can Muslims eat bacon?" = suspicious.

"How to wire a toaster?" = flagged.

"Sikh vs. Muslim?" = still flagged. Now with bonus ignorance.

Transportation Security Administration (TSA)

And then there was the TSA—America's most expensive improv troupe. Created in 2001 and made permanent by sheer inertia, the Transportation Security Administration (TSA) quickly became known for its obsession with 3-ounce bottles for liquids and suspiciously aggressive pat-downs.[259] You haven't truly experienced liberty until a federal employee confiscates your $12 Aveda conditioner like it was a vial of plutonium. If you were white, male, and Bluetooth-equipped? A nod and a pass. Brown, Muslim, vowel-heavy last name, or traveling with hummus? Welcome to Random Screening, now with more latex gloves.

And somehow, they never caught a terrorist—but they did nail a 78-year-old grandma for her knitting needles.

America Didn't Fight Extremism After 9/11—We Fought Ethnicity

Mosques were surveilled. Entire Arab and South Asian communities were harassed, detained, or "accidentally deported" for things like…existing.[260] We rounded up people for visa issues, confused Sikhs for Muslims, and passed laws against things no one was doing—like implementing *Sharia law* in the cafeteria.

And both parties got in on the action. Democrats might've used softer fonts, but the policies weren't much different. It was the golden era of:

- "Security first, facts later."
- "If you see something brown, say something."
- And the national pastime of rebranding xenophobia as vigilance[LS6].

Every headscarf wearer was a potential villain in America's Tom Clancy fanfiction.

The post-9/11 security state did more than inconvenience air travelers. It rewired American politics. Fear became currency. Surveillance became comfortable. And "security" became a blank check for:

- Two endless wars (funded on vibes and oil futures),
- A surveillance economy with zero chill,
- And a citizenry convinced their Uber driver might be an ISIS plant because his name was Mohammad, and he listened to NPR.

Curtain Call: Cultural Legacy Post-9/11: Patriotism, Paranoia, and the Profit of Fear

9/11 wasn't just a national tragedy—it was a cultural reset button, slammed so hard that it cracked the foundations of civil liberty, common sense, and foreign policy. What emerged was less about recovery and more about remaking America in the image of its fear.

We didn't just grieve—we branded it.

Crisis as Theater: The Politics of Rubble and Ratings

- George W. Bush standing on the World Trade Center rubble with a bullhorn? A real-life episode of *America's Next Top Commander*.
- Cable news stations ran American flags 24/7, turning national trauma into patriotic screensavers.
- "Never Forget" became a marketing slogan—plastered on t-shirts, beer koozies, and commemorative coins you could order for just $19.95.

Fear Became Policy

The real legacy of 9/11 isn't just security—it's the industrial complex of paranoia:

- The USA Patriot Act passed in 45 days, with most lawmakers never reading it, because nothing says democracy like unchecked surveillance.[261]
- TSA theater turned airports into Broadway productions of *Les Misérables*, starring water bottle confiscation and random racial profiling.
- Color-coded terror alerts trained Americans to interpret vague dread through Crayola shades. ("Orange" alert? Stay scared, shop local.)

And dissent? That got rebranded as **treason lite**. Ask the Dixie Chicks how that worked out.

Islamophobia as National Branding

Post-9/11 America also brought back one of its favorite pastimes: xenophobia, now with a patriotic twist:

- Mosques were surveilled.
- "Muslim-sounding" names became TSA catnip.
- The phrase "they hate our freedom" was repeated so often it deserved a SAG card.

And if you questioned the logic of bombing nations that had nothing to do with 9/11? Congratulations—you just made the no-fly list for a reason.

According to political theorist Corey Robin (2004), **9/11 didn't just traumatize the nation—it reprogrammed it**: fear became a governing philosophy, and authoritarian tendencies found new moral high ground.[262] America built a fear economy, minted patriotic performance art, and handed the director's chair to national security. We became a country where surveillance is safety, dissent is danger, and trauma is a subscription service renewed every election cycle.

The Iraq War + Manufactured Consent = A One-Act Play

The 2003 invasion of Iraq was marketed with the emotional urgency of a Marvel movie, the fact-checking rigor of a Facebook comment, and the morality of a late-stage empire in search of catharsis. America didn't just go to war—we broadcast it. We packaged it. We sold it.

We Invaded the Wrong Country, but at Least We Looked United Doing It

If 9/11 was the trauma, then the Iraq War was the emotional overreaction staged with a PowerPoint and a vengeance fetish. Like all great American overreaches, it began not with strategy but with branding—a logo, a lie, and a bipartisan standing ovation. It wasn't war—it was theater. A tragicomic production where Dick Cheney was the playwright, George W. was the actor, and CNN was the red, white, and blue lighting crew.

We didn't find weapons of mass destruction (WMDs) in Iraq, because they were never there.[263] What we did find was:

- A dictator we had previously armed in the '80s,

- Oil fields marked "liberate me,"
- And a helpful distraction from the awkward truth that 15 of the 19 airplane hijackers were from Saudi Arabia, not Iraq.

But logic never stood a chance. Cheney squinted into the void and declared Saddam Hussein "probably has nukes in his sock drawer." Rumsfeld got philosophical with his "known unknowns," a phrase so meaningless it got tenure at the Pentagon. And America? We saluted, threw on a flag lapel pin, and handed over $2 trillion like we were tithing at the altar of vengeance.[264]

Congress didn't just approve the war—they rebranded the menu. When France committed the unforgivable sin of reading the intelligence and going, "Uhhh… this is fake, right?" the House cafeteria renamed French fries "freedom fries."[265] Because nothing screams geopolitical nuance like a deep-fried insult.

Let us not forget how the media—our once-proud Fourth Estate—took off its press badge and wore a cheerleader uniform. Judith Miller at *The New York Times* printed Cheney's diary entries like gospel. Cable news built "war rooms" with theme music, zoom-in satellite maps, and retired generals moonlighting as defense contractors.[266] Every night, Americans tuned into military-themed infotainment, with Wolf Blitzer whispering warzone updates like ASMR for hawks.

Shock and Awe wasn't a military campaign—it was the trailer for a political blockbuster starring America as the savior of freedom and Baghdad as the unfortunate victim.

This wasn't journalism—it was cinematic drone footage dressed as objectivity.

Support for the war wasn't about facts but about performing strength. Nothing polls better than explosions, especially when they're far away. If you want to look "presidential," launch something. From the air. Preferably with "freedom" in the mission's name. The Iraq War left us with more than just physical scars. It handed future politicians a **blueprint** for how to:

- Ignore evidence,
- Manufacture fear,
- Silence dissent, and

- Still get invited back to CNN as a "foreign policy expert."

It taught America that as long as the flag was big enough, you could lie your way into a war and call it freedom. That "national security" could replace reason, and that "supporting the troops" could be weaponized against anyone asking too many questions. And what did it cost?

- Hundreds of thousands of lives,
- $2+ trillion,
- And a generation of voters so cynical they now think C-SPAN is a performance art.

ACT I: The Greatest Show Never Fact-Checked

- **Colin Powell's UN Speech:** Arguably the most high-stakes PowerPoint in human history. Data. Diagrams. Satellite photos. Delivered with gravitas by a respected general turned secretary of state. And every word of it—false, exaggerated, or manipulated. The New York Times called it "convincing." **The Pentagon called it "persuasive." History calls it a prelude to mass death, built on Photoshop and blind faith.**[267]
- **"Mission Accomplished" Banner:** George W. Bush, in a flight suit, standing on an aircraft carrier under a banner that read "Mission Accomplished." It was the theatrical climax of a war that hadn't even started properly. **Troops still dying? Ignore that. Insurgency building? What insurgency?** This provided cinematic closure for a plot that lacked a third act. It wasn't the truth—it was optics. And the banner? A visual lie dressed in victory drag.
- **Shock and Awe:** Cable news didn't just report the bombing campaign. They **branded** it. "Shock and Awe" became a primetime feature: Explosions filmed like fireworks. Night-vision footage layered with triumphant music. Anchors treating it like the *Super Bowl of Regime Change.* War became a **spectacle**, and we all became complicit in its viewership. As Susan Sontag (2003) noted post-9/11, "Being a spectator of calamities takes the form of a reflexive consumption of images."

ACT II: Mainstream Media Complicity

The press didn't ask questions—they passed along scripts. CNN embedded reporters, Fox News hosted cheerleaders, and *The New York Times* printed Cheney's talking points like they were gospel. Investigative journalism gave way to patriotic stenography, and the Fourth Estate became a PR firm for the Pentagon. A 2004 study by Jamieson and Waldman found that the media's framing of war coverage overwhelmingly emphasized military success and government narratives, while excluding dissent and skepticism.[268]

The war didn't end—it was **repackaged**.

- Camouflage fashion spiked.
- Military-themed NFL halftime shows became standard.
- "Support the Troops" became a **personality trait**, not a policy demand.

From films like *American Sniper* to video games like "Call of Duty," we turned combat into content and foreign occupation into fandom.

Eventually, the rationale for war morphed:

- Not just freedom.
- Not just WMDs.
- But **"economic opportunity."**

Contractors profited. Defense budgets exploded. Entire industries were built on the ashes of Baghdad. The war was rebranded as *"nation-building," "democracy exportation,"* and *"a stimulus package with body armor."* It became clear: in the absence of moral clarity, **profit would suffice.**

Curtain Call: Cultural Legacy: Iraq War, Lies, Flags, and Fireworks

If Vietnam was America's tragic war, then Iraq was our made-for-TV sequel—scripted by neocons, scored by fear, and sponsored by Halliburton. The Iraq War wasn't just a military operation—it was a cultural production. We didn't mobilize because we had to. We mobilized because we *could*, because we *wanted to be seen doing it*, and because, post-9/11, America had a bloodlust for retaliation and a propaganda machine ready to roll. The result? A two-decade disaster wrapped in red, white, and blue.

The Cultural Rebrand: From Oil to Liberation

- We weren't invading for oil—we were "spreading democracy," like Girl Scouts handing out cookies at gunpoint.
- "Shock and awe" wasn't a tactic—it was a cinematic spectacle (think: film director Michael Bay with a Pentagon budget).
- "Mission Accomplished" wasn't a milestone—it was a branding fail so egregious it deserves its own museum wing.

We turned warfare into marketing:

- Colin Powell's PowerPoint at the UN became a viral pre-YouTube moment of geopolitical fiction.[269]
- News anchors embedded with troops like they were on a war-themed Disney ride.
- And let's not forget the **yellow ribbon bumper stickers**—our national excuse to "support the troops" without supporting VA benefits.

Journalism Took a Knee

Mainstream media outlets, from *The New York Times* to CNN, mostly swapped their investigative grit for stenography. Judith Miller's infamous WMD reporting helped sell the war like a late-night infomercial, while dissenting voices were dismissed as "unpatriotic."[270] In a nation supposedly obsessed with freedom, dissent was suppressed before the concept of cancel culture became popular.

Cultural Legacy: What Did We Win?

- Disinformation as doctrine: The Iraq War normalized the idea that *truth is optional* if the flag is big enough.
- Permanent war economy: Defense contractors soared while public schools crumbled.
- Troop worship over troop care: Veterans came home to parades, then faced broken healthcare systems, PTSD stigma, and rising suicide rates.
- Political distrust metastasized: Once WMDs turned out to be BS, America's trust in institutions plummeted—a cynicism that laid the groundwork for Tea Party rage, Trumpism, and QAnon cosplay.

As Naomi Klein argued, the Iraq War was not a deviation from American capitalism—it was its logical conclusion: profiting from chaos, privatizing disaster, and turning every crisis into a business model.[271]

The Iraq War didn't just fail militarily—it **rewired our culture**, turning war into entertainment, journalism into propaganda, and truth into optional trivia. It was a hissy fit with a trillion-dollar price tag—and America's still footing the cultural bill.

Pandemic Panic

When the world called for unity, empathy, and science, America brought ego, conspiracy, and a Costco-sized stash of Charmin.

Remember March 2020? Italy locked down, New Zealand mobilized, and South Korea contact-traced with surgical precision. Yet America had a different idea: Stockpile toilet paper, yell at grocery clerks, and debate epidemiology based on a meme your uncle Steve reposted from QAnon Karen. Welcome to Pandemic Patriotism, where real men don't cry, don't mask, and don't understand how viruses work.

COVID-19 was a wake-up call, and a predictable fall for US culture—and boy, did we fall.

ACT I: The Pandemic as Performance

Trump's Bleach Suggestion: A Masterclass in Improv Disaster

"And then I see the disinfectant, where it knocks it out in a minute… Is there a way we can do something like that? By injection."[272]

This was the **moment the public health crisis hit its breaking point**. The President of the United States essentially suggested a Clorox cocktail—and half the nation *still* said, "He's just asking questions." It wasn't a press briefing—it was a free-form experimental monologue on how not to survive a pandemic.

Fauci: From Science Savior to Scapegoat-in-Chief

Dr. Anthony Fauci became the nation's leading epidemiologist and its most convenient punching bag.

- Loved by the left.

- Hated by the right.
- Memed by both.

He wasn't a man—he was a proxy war for the nation's relationship to reality. And every time he adjusted the science (as one should during a novel virus outbreak), America screamed "LIAR!" instead of "Evolving data!"

Anti-Mask Protests: Civic Kabuki at Its Worst

Protesting masks during a deadly airborne virus is like protesting pants during a snowstorm. But protest we did—loudly, proudly, and usually while spitting on store clerks and invoking the Constitution with the legal precision of a drunk uncle. These were not protests. These were performance art pieces about rugged individualism—staged in Walmart, filmed on iPhones, and uploaded to YouTube under titles like *"MASK NAZIS DESTROYED WITH FACTS AND LOGIC."*

"Open the Economy" Rallies: Freedom Revivals with Flags

These weren't economic arguments. They were tent revivals with bumper stickers, AR-15s, and cries of "Let my Applebee's go!" Conveniently funded by political action groups and anti-government think tanks, these rallies weren't grassroots—they were astroturf cosplay events where capitalism dressed up as patriotism. As Naomi Klein (2007) warned in *The Shock Doctrine*, **disasters are always followed by ideological power grabs**— and the "Open the Economy" movement proved that the right could monetize COVID rage just like it monetized 9/11 fear.[273]

ACT II: Science vs. Political Orange

When you were never the most intelligent man in the room.

COVID-19 didn't just infect lungs—it infected egos. Especially the type of egos that think "real men" fix everything with duct tape, denial, and a quick prayer to Ronald Reagan. And the US had a president in office with a very fragile masculine ego. Trump fueled the confusion, anger, and fear through theater.

The breakdown:

1. **Science Demanded Vulnerability:** Masks? "I'm not scared!"

(Translation: I'm terrified, but don't make me admit it.) Vaccines? "I trust my gut, not your facts!" (Translation: I'm one WebMD article away from full meltdown.) Social Distancing? "Freedom means coughing wherever I want!" (Translation: I think boundaries are oppression.) Science said: It's not just about you. Fragile masculinity heard: You're not the center of the universe. Jane and Karen are following Dick and Doug's lead, cuz they are wicked smart and believed 45 was, too. Cue the emotional Chernobyl.

2. Authority Had to Come from Experts—Not Alpha Males: Public health officials weren't muscle-bound "winners." They were epidemiologists, scientists, and sometimes—God forbid—women. Masculine grievance culture has spent decades telling itself it's brighter, harsher, and "naturally in charge." COVID-19 asked them to *listen* instead of *dominate*. That wasn't just inconvenient. It wasn't very comfortable.

3. Collective Action Threatened the Myth of Lone-Wolf Heroism: American masculinity—especially the MAGA variety—is built on cowboy myths: The rugged, self-reliant lone wolf who doesn't need anybody.
COVID said:
- "You can't lone-wolf your way out of a pandemic."
- "You have to think collectively, act responsibly, and sometimes—stay home."

This felt like sacrilege. After all, if John Wayne wore a mask to protect the elderly, would he even be John Wayne? (Answer: No. He'd be considered *French*.)

4. Facts Are Hard—Feelings Are Easy: COVID-19 required people to trust boring, complicated facts over gut feelings and Facebook memes. And if you've built your identity on instinct, tradition, and "owning the libs," facts feel like an attack. Better to deny, deflect, and declare yourself a persecuted victim than deal with reality.

5. It Was Easier to Invent Conspiracies Than Accept Complexity: COVID-19 wasn't simple. It wasn't black-and-white. It involved uncomfortable truths:

- Systemic inequality made it worse.
- The government needed to intervene.
- Your personal choices affected the collective good.

Rather than deal with that complexity? **COVID-19 didn't break American masculinity. It exposed how brittle it already was. When masculinity is defined by domination, invulnerability, and distrust of cooperation, a virus that demanded humility, compassion, and science wasn't just a threat—it was an existential mirror. And boy, did many people shatter upon looking into it.**

As COVID-19 spread faster than a Joe Rogan conspiracy, America's cultural immune system collapsed. We weren't fighting a virus—we were fighting the audacity of expertise. Scientists, epidemiologists, and public health officials became public enemies, not because they were wrong, but because they weren't loud and confident enough to sound like a guy on YouTube with a ring light and rage disorder.[274] Then, critical thinking died, and Dr. Fauci became the scapegoat for America's collective science phobia.

Dr. Anthony Fauci—the man who spent five decades studying infectious disease, guided the US through HIV, Ebola, SARS, and Zika, advised seven presidents, and led the National Institute of Allergy and Infectious Diseases—was suddenly reduced to "that lying deep state lizard" by a nation of guys who think "virology" is either a pre-workout or a vape flavor.

Seriously—**who the hell do you think you are/were?** These deniers weren't public health experts. These were YouTube-certified virologists who once cheated on their high school bio test and now believe they're smarter than the global medical community because they watched a 19-minute Facebook video called *"COVID: The Real Truth They Don't Want You to Know."* Fauci brought data. They brought vibes—and not even good ones.

Once the pandemic hit, critical thinking took a long nap and Facebook became the CDC—*Chads Determined to Conspire.* Suddenly, everyone's Aunt June and Uncle Doug became *infectious disease theorists:*

- "I heard Fauci invented COVID."
- "Masks give you cancer."
- "The vaccine turns your blood magnetic. My cousin felt it."

As actual doctors scrambled to treat patients, a portion of America turned to what they regarded as the "real" medical authorities: antivax influencers with ring lights and zero credentials. Facebook groups exploded with hot takes that made WebMD look like the *New England Journal of Medicine.*

Suddenly, your neighbor Doug, who had once been kicked out of high school for huffing markers, became a virologist. TikTok became the CDC of the Hissy Fit Era. Science wasn't just questioned—it was mocked, because in a culture where masculinity is defined by domination, being "right" only counts if you're loud and condescending while doing it.[275] Science wasn't evaluated—it was vibed at. Comment sections replaced peer review. And morality was optional, as long as you had Wi-Fi and a webcam.

ACT III: The Real Cost: When Confidence Kills

This wasn't harmless. This was deadly disinformation wrapped in swagger. A 2021 study by the Brown School of Public Health found that counties with higher shares of conservative media consumption and anti-science sentiment experienced significantly **higher COVID-19 death rates**.[276]

Translation: the louder the hissy fit, the higher the body count. And still, some Freedom Flu Fighters went to their graves arguing they were winning.

The results? Predictable:
- Over 1.1 million COVID deaths in the US.[277]
- Disproportionate death tolls in communities of color.
- Healthcare workers burned out while Facebook crusaders claimed they were "faking it for clout."

Dick, Doug, Karen, Jane, and others: READ THAT AGAIN!

What we witnessed wasn't just anti-science. It was an identity crisis in camo—a desperate clinging to personal freedom at the expense of collective survival. Science didn't fail them. They failed science and then blamed it for not validating their ego. Public health became performance art. Masks became political statements. And Fauci became a punching bag for those who needed someone to blame for their inability to sit still or think critically.

ACT IV: Public Health vs. Personal Liberty:
How American Individualism Killed Collective Safety

"Your freedom ends where my lungs begin," said too few Americans in 2020. The rest of the world approached COVID with a public health playbook. You know—science, communication, masks that weren't political statements, and leaders who didn't suggest sunlight enemas on live TV. They coordinated testing, tracked cases like grown-ups, and believed experts.

Meanwhile, in Countries That Acted Like Adults...

While America was out here turning masks into muzzle metaphors and screaming about Fauci from Bass Pro parking lots, other countries responded to COVID-19 like… you know, functioning democracies.

- **New Zealand** locked down fast, rallied behind science, and listened to their leader, not a guy named Chad with a podcast and a gut feeling.
- **South Korea** deployed mass testing and contact tracing, not conspiracy theories and backyard bleach recipes.
- **Germany's Angela Merkel** calmly explained virology like a grown-up, while we were fighting over toilet paper and posting viral videos about "plandemics."
- **Taiwan?** They had a game plan in January 2020. America? We had *Tiger King*.

The rest of the world responded with coordination, science, and empathy. America responded with hissy fits, hashtags, a weaponized grill set, and Charmin because nothing says "land of the free" like turning a global health emergency into a culture war over cough droplets.

Yet, America took one look at the playbook and used it as kindling for a freedom bonfire. Because here, in the land of liberty and lawsuits, nothing is more sacred than the right to do whatever the hell you want, even if it kills your neighbor. In America, "freedom" doesn't mean freedom from disease. It means freedom *from being told what to do.* We turned safety protocols into a cultural rebellion. Because in this country, inconvenience is oppression, and sacrifice is a socialist plot.

Individualism Is Not a Pandemic Strategy

You can't bootstrap your way through a virus. But American exceptionalism—*that intoxicating myth that we're special, chosen, and immune to global logic*—told us we could. It told us "community" was weakness, "empathy" was for libs, and "science" was a conspiracy cooked up by coastal elites and Bill Gates' secret vaccine lab. This "me first" mindset wasn't just selfish—it was lethal.

According to researchers, the US suffered higher COVID-19 death rates per capita than other wealthy countries, due in part to poor compliance with public health measures and political polarization.[278]

Our commitment to hyper-individualism became our own worst comorbidity. The lie at the heart of the American psyche is that liberty requires nothing from us—that it's something we *possess*, not something we *practice*. But public health, by definition, is a **collective contract**.

It requires:

• Shared trust,
• Sacrifice for the greater good, and
• Listening to people who know more than you.

And nothing in modern American culture, especially post-2016, has prepared us for that. We spent decades dismantling those instincts in favor of:

• Hustle culture,
• Mistrust in institutions,
• "Don't tread on me" everything, and
• The worship of personal sovereignty at any cost.

The result? A national hissy fit where public health was sacrificed on the altar of personal liberty—and the freedom wasn't even absolute, just repackaged rage and TikTok-fueled misinformation. COVID-19 didn't break us. **We were already broken. The pandemic was just the tipping point.**

The Anti-Vaxxers Are Back—And Louder Than Ever

After spending 2020-2022 turning Facebook groups into petri dishes of conspiracy theories, America's anti-vaxxers didn't retreat quietly. No, they upgraded. They went from "I'm just asking questions" to full-blown "Vaccines turn you into 5G Bluetooth devices monitored by Bill Gates." Because apparently, it's easier to believe that **Anthony Fauci is secretly Darth Vader** than it is to read an actual peer-reviewed study.[279] When vaccines for COVID-19 came out, sane people rolled up their sleeves. The rest rolled up homemade "Vaccine Passport = Holocaust" protest signs and marched around Olive Gardens across the country. Anti-vaxxers made chaos an industry. Podcasts promising "natural cures" (like horse paste). Instagram "wellness coaches" selling oregano oil like it's a miracle shield. Alex Jones—still somehow screaming at a frequency only bats can hear—hawking colloidal silver and apocalypse seeds. Grifters got rich. Communities got sick. And a generation of Americans became so allergic to critical thinking that YouTube had to start putting disclaimers on videos stating that the Earth is, in fact, round.[280]

Fast Forward to 2025: Measles Is Back—and It's Pissed

And now? Measles outbreaks are sweeping through states. According to the CDC (2025), measles cases have **spiked by over 400%** in the last two years in the United States, primarily due to drops in childhood vaccination rates following the pandemic-era misinformation surge.[281] Measles, once practically eradicated, is back like a Netflix reboot nobody asked for. Highly contagious, often lethal for infants and the immunocompromised, and now thriving because little Timmy's mom thinks she knows more than 200 years of medical science because she watched one TikTok from a shirtless guy named "TruthSeeker47." Remember herd immunity? Yeah, that died of preventable causes somewhere between "plandemic" hashtags and school board meetings where Karen screamed about "DNA modification."

This isn't freedom. This is biological terrorism...with Etsy merch.

Why It's Not Just "Personal Choice"

Anti-vaxxers love to screech "my body, my choice" until it comes to literally anything else (irony not included). However, measles outbreaks don't stay confined to conspiracy circles. They don't politely ask if your Facebook status is "fully brain-melted." They rip through schools, hospitals, airports, and communities indiscriminately. Public health isn't a choose-your-own-adventure novel. It's a collective agreement not to let toddlers die because you think vaccines are part of a lizard-people mind-control plot funded by George Soros.

Damage Report: 2025 Edition

- **CDC estimates** that **measles** will cost the US health system **over $650 million** in 2025 alone.[282]
- **Hospitalizations** for preventable diseases are up **39%** compared to pre-pandemic baselines.[283]
- **Vaccine confidence** among new parents is at a **20-year low**.[284]

And that's not even counting the deaths that never should have happened. Because when you turn every health recommendation into a civil war reenactment, you don't get freedom. **You get funeral processions and bankrupted ICUs.**

Curtain Call: America's Cultural Legacy After COVID-19

When historians look back at America's response to COVID-19, not only will they shake their heads in disbelief, but they won't see a coherent public health strategy. They will see a performance art piece titled "How to Lose a Pandemic in 10 Lies or Less." Because in the Land of the Free (to ignore science), we didn't fight a virus—we auditioned for the role of "Most Unhinged Nation with Wi-Fi." Let's review the cultural artifacts we're leaving behind:

1. Science Is Just a Suggestion

Once upon a time, Americans held doctors in high regard. But then TikTok happened. Suddenly, epidemiology had to compete with "my cousin's Facebook thread" and a YouTuber named @FreedomHealer1776.

- Masks became "face prisons."
- Vaccines became mind control juice.

- And "I did my research" became a national battle cry for the aggressively misinformed.

Dr. Fauci? Turned into a supervillain in an extended universe created by people who think "mRNA" stands for *Mark of the New Apocalypse*.

2. Enter Robert F. Kennedy Jr.: Patron Saint of Delusional Detox Culture

If Joe Rogan and Gwyneth Paltrow had a conspiracy baby, it would be RFK Jr.—shirtless, jacked, and explaining how Wi-Fi causes autism and Big Pharma is hiding the death cure.

A Kennedy with a platform and a persecution complex, RFK Jr. managed to:
- Turn measles into a freedom issue.
- Blame vaccines for everything from COVID-19 and Autism to climate change.[285]
- Run unsuccessfully for president based on vibes, abs, and deeply problematic science. Yet Trump named him as Secretary of Health and Human Services.

He's not just an anti-vaxxer. He's the poster child **for medical misinformation** wrapped in CamelBak hydration gear and daddy issues.

When a 7th-grade biology teacher could debunk your entire campaign platform, but you're still polling in double digits—congratulations, you've perfectly captured the American mood.

3. Anti-Vaxxers Became a National Subculture

During COVID-19, anti-vaxxers rebranded like a start-up.
- They had hashtags, flags, and matching T-shirts.
- They weaponized patriotism and yoga.
- And they turned public health into a battleground of vibes vs. virology.

It wasn't about medicine—it was about identity because nothing screams "freedom" like threatening nurses while misquoting the Constitution outside an ICU.

The vaccine didn't divide America. America divided its response to the vaccine into:

- "Bill Gates wants to chip me,"
- "Jesus is my antibody," and
- "Let's inject bleach instead."

4. Public Health is Recast as Political Oppression

Masks weren't about protection. They were about "control." Because if there's one thing Americans hate more than dying, it's being mildly inconvenienced for someone else's safety. The phrase "I can't breathe" was tragically rebranded by anti-mask activists at Target, while police were murdering actual Black Americans. And public health policy? Reduced to the political equivalent of a diet plan—suggested, ignored, and replaced with vibes.

5. COVID-19 Became Content, Not Crisis

We didn't treat COVID-19 with a coordinated response—we treated it with livestreams, screaming school board meetings, and sponsored misinformation.

- Anti-vax influencers sold essential oils to prevent infection.
- Politicians held "Freedom Rallies" during viral surges.
- And Fox News hosts screamed about "medical tyranny" from the comfort of vaccine-mandated studios.

COVID-19 wasn't a tragedy. It was a content goldmine. And America? We monetized it faster than Pfizer could ship a booster.

The Cultural Legacy: Unmasked, Unhinged, and Unapologetic

America's COVID-19 response taught us exactly what kind of culture we've built:

- One where scientific consensus is up for debate,
- Where conspiracy theories trend faster than case numbers,
- And where public responsibility is canceled if it doesn't match your brand.

We didn't come together. We didn't flatten the curve. We flattened trust, truth, and any chance of collective resilience. And now? Our legacy is a nation that:

- Mistrusts expertise, yet believe in microchip-laced Q-Tips, and vaccines
- Elevates RFK Jr. over actual immunologists, and
- Equates coughing on strangers with exercising their First Amendment rights.

We didn't just botch a pandemic—we turned it into a lifestyle. Yes, future generations will study our COVID-19 era, not as a case study in resilience but as a cautionary tale of what happens when a nation outsources public health to influencers and uncles with 5G paranoia.

School Shootings, Gun Culture, and Thoughts & Prayers

School shootings are not a new American tragedy—they're a recurring one. They've haunted hallways and classrooms for decades, shaping the psyche of multiple generations. What began as isolated horrors has metastasized into an institutionalized reality, woven into the fabric of daily life.

In America, the bullet has replaced the ballot, and the ritual of grief has been replaced by performance art. We don't legislate—we light candles, tweet hashtags, and pose with assault rifles in Christmas card photos.

Welcome to the United States of America: the only country where kids are taught to barricade doors before they're taught how to multiply. Where gun manufacturers get tax breaks, and third graders get bulletproof backpacks. Gun violence in schools is no longer a tragedy—it's an institution, a genre, and in political circles, a fundraising strategy.

Culture Shift: Safety Became Ideological. Grief Became Partisan

Once upon a time, we treated safety as a shared value. Today, it's a partisan accessory, right alongside vaccine cards and pronoun pins.

- You want background checks? You're a "communist snowflake."
- You want to arm teachers? You're "protecting the Constitution."
- You suggest fewer guns? You're a "traitor to freedom."

Grief, once a natural human response, is now a test of political allegiance. And if you mourn the wrong way—or ask too many questions—you're accused of "exploiting a tragedy." As sociologist Katherine Newman (2004) notes in her research on school shootings, political responses tend to favor

symbolic gestures over systemic action, especially in communities deeply embedded in gun culture.[286]

ACT I: Empty Silence, Loaded Imagery

Congressional Moments of Silence Instead of Legislation
The same routine follows every mass shooting:
1. Statement of "shock."
2. Moment of silence.
3. Zero action.

It's become a sacred ritual of inaction, a spiritual stunt performed by legislators who refuse to pass a single piece of meaningful reform—but will bow their heads on camera like they're auditioning for sainthood.

AR-15 Christmas Cards and Gun-Toting Campaign Ads
What's more festive than celebrating the birth of Christ with a military-grade semi-automatic weapon? US politicians—including sitting members of Congress—have posed with their families holding AR-15s, smiling beneath Christmas decorations, while "Peace on Earth" is printed above.

These aren't campaign ads. They're themed threats—coded love letters to a base that equates masculinity with muzzle velocity.

And it works. Political scientist Jennifer Carlson (2015) describes gun ownership in America not just as a right, but as a **cultural identity**, one increasingly linked to race, masculinity, and political grievance.[287]

NRA Conventions Days After Mass Shootings
No tragedy is too fresh. No bodies are too warm. The **National Rifle Association** (NRA) will host its convention **on schedule**, even as communities are still collecting blood-spattered backpacks and DNA swabs.

These conventions double as:
- Gun fashion shows,
- Grievance rallies,
- And political stages where candidates promise to defend "gun rights"

from the imaginary tyranny of background checks.

And when the protests outside get too loud? Just turn up the Toby Keith inside.

Ongoing Cultural Legacy: A Country Armed and Emotionally Numb

The "Good Guy with a Gun"–The Myth That Won't Die

This NRA-engineered fantasy claims the only thing that stops a bad guy with a gun is a good guy with a gun.

But in reality:

- Uvalde had good guys with guns. They waited.
- Parkland had good guys with guns. They froze.
- Buffalo had a good guy with a gun. He died.

The myth persists—not because it's true, but because it's emotionally satisfying, and fits neatly into the Hollywood-inspired John Wayne masculinity complex that drives much of conservative America's self-image.

Bulletproof Backpacks and Trauma Kits in the Pencil Aisle

Yes, this is real. You can now purchase:

- Bulletproof backpacks with Disney princess prints,
- Whiteboards that double as shields,
- Trauma packs for teachers, as if first responders are now part of the school supplies list.

This isn't safety. It's retail dystopia.

And who profits? The same companies that fund anti-reform lobbies and sell AR-15 accessories on aisle five.

Lockdown Drills: The Fire Drills from Hell

Forget "Stop, Drop, and Roll." Today's kids learn:

- "Barricade the door."
- "Stay silent."
- "Text goodbye."

And we expect them to focus on math right after.

These drills don't make schools safer—they make students **trauma liter-ate**. As the American Psychological Association (APA, 2020) has warned, repeated exposure to lockdowns—especially poorly executed ones—can lead to **anxiety, hypervigilance, and symptoms consistent with PTSD.**

We're Not Protecting Kids–We're Performing Around Them

Thoughts and prayers are the smoke screen. The real goal is to keep the show going, funded by the NRA, powered by fear, and protected by perfor-mative patriotism. We haven't ended gun violence because we've absorbed it into our national mythos:

- Guns = freedom.
- Reform = betrayal.
- Children? Collateral branding damage.

We are the only country that stages mass death, mourns it on camera, sells merch after, and calls it liberty.

The problem isn't just guns. It's the theater surrounding them.

Gun Violence and Death Toll[288]

1. Death Toll by the Numbers

- In 2022, the US recorded 48,204 lives lost to gun-related incidents—an average of 132 deaths per day—making firearm injury a top-five killer for Americans aged 1–44.
- On a population-adjusted scale, that's 13.7 deaths per 100,000 in 2023—even with a continued downward shift from 14.2 in 2022.
- Suicide accounted for over half of these deaths (~7.6 per 100k), with homicides making up over 40% (~5.6 per 100k).

2. Young People Are Dying

- For children and teens (ages 1–19), firearm injuries are now the leading cause of death, outranking car crashes, cancer, and all other causes.

- Disturbingly, youth firearm homicide rates among Black children climbed from 4.9 to 10.3 per 100,000 between 2018 and 2023.

3. Mental Illness Is Not the Villain

- Despite political narratives blaming mental illness, research shows that less than 5% of gun violence is attributed to individuals with serious mental illness.
- The American Psychiatric Association cautions against stigmatizing mental health, noting most people with mental illness are more likely to be victims than perpetrators.

4. More Than Psychopathology

- Non-psychotic conditions (e.g., depression), substance use, and socioeconomic stressors are significantly linked to firearm violence, accounting for roughly 25% of shootings.
- External factors like conflict with acquaintances, drug disputes, and community violence far outweigh mental illness as drivers.

Final Takeaway (No Mic Drop, Just Facts)

- Gun violence is not a "mental health problem"—it's a public health and policy failure.
- Policies that equate mental illness with danger aren't just misleading—they're harmful and stigmatizing.
- Meanwhile, policymakers and pundits flex emotional narratives instead of data-driven solutions, ignoring that most gun violence springs from access, not illness.
- Until we focus on firearm access, community support, and structural inequality, we're just rearranging deck chairs on a sinking ship, while the shell casings pile up.

The Performative Politics of Protest

Protest has always been an integral part of America's cultural heritage. But somewhere between Selma and Snapchat, it went from civil disobedience to content strategy. No moment better captured this shift than the institutional response to the **Black Lives Matter** (BLM) movement.

ACT I: Black Lives Matter

The demands were precise: defund the police, end systemic racism, reform criminal justice, and reinvest in communities. The response?

- **Murals without Policy:** Cities painted "Black Lives Matter" in 30-foot yellow letters on asphalt while quietly increasing their police budgets. It was urban calligraphy as public relations—meaningless if not backed by budgets or laws. Aesthetic solidarity. Legislative silence.
- **Kneeling in Kente Cloth:** In 2020, Democratic leaders knelt in Kente cloth for 8 minutes and 46 seconds—a ritualistic moment that looked more like a dress rehearsal for *Wakanda Forever* than a serious policy announcement. Congress LARPing as liberation. The bill? Never passed.
- **Corporate Hashtag Humanitarianism:** Every major brand posted a black square and wrote a solemn caption. However, when it came time to release pay equity audits or support labor unionization, they vanished just as quickly as your DEI lead in Q2 layoffs.
- **Apologies with an NDA:** Institutions issued carefully focus-grouped statements promising to "listen, learn, and do better"—then silenced whistleblowers and BIPOC employees behind HR-led investigations and nondisclosure agreements.

ACT II: Protest, Packaged for Performance

Real protest disrupts. Performative protest rebrands. The BLM uprisings were a national reckoning, but for the powerful, it became an opportunity to:

- Collect social capital without redistributing actual capital.
- Turn revolution into resolution—nonbinding, of course.
- Add diversity to the marketing deck without touching boardrooms.

We didn't dismantle systems—we just gave them a glow-up.

Curtain Call: Cultural Legacy:
The Hashtag Heard 'Round the World

What will history say?

- That BLM became the most protested cause in American history but yielded depressingly few structural reforms.

- That "defund the police" was rebranded into "reimagine policing," which meant more money for body cams and PR consultants.
- That corporations pledged $50+ billion in racial equity funding, but less than 5% of those funds were actually disbursed.[289]

1969-2017: Democracy's Most Dramatic Political Theater

Because not all backlash icons wear hoods—some wear lapel pins, tweet in all caps, or cry "oppression" when someone says "Latinx."

George W. Bush (43rd President, 2001-2009)
The Strategically Confused Cowboy
- Took "You're either with us or against us" and made it both foreign *and* domestic policy—the political version of an ultimatum text at 2 a.m.
- Invaded Iraq to avenge 9/11, despite Iraq having the same involvement as a bystander at a bar fight.
- Introduced the color-coded terror chart, which did nothing for safety but everything for cable news graphics.
- Signed the Patriot Act, legalizing paranoid eavesdropping while calling it "freedom."
- Famously renamed French fries "freedom fries" because France questioned our warmongering, and thus, global diplomacy was reduced to cafeteria drama.

Hissy Fit Highlight: When the world questioned America's military-industrial complex, Bush just grabbed his megaphone and bombed something.

Sarah Palin (2008 VP Nominee, Unofficial MAGA Matriarch)
The Original Hockey Mom of the Apocalypse
- Functioned as the beta version of MAGA—a little folksy, a little fascist, all Fox News-friendly.
- Turned victimhood into a campaign platform: "I can see Russia from my house, and also oppression from the media."
- Introduced America to the term "lamestream media," giving boomers something new to yell at the TV.

- Her campaign trail was a cross between a pageant and a fever dream.
- Waged war on "elitism," which is GOP code for "anyone who reads books."

Hissy Fit Highlight: Lost the VP race but won the cultural war audition that helped Trump rise like a bronzer-dipped phoenix.

Newt Gingrich
Speaker of the House, Culture War Architect
- Turning Congress into a cage match with soundbites.
- Invented the "**permanent campaign**" model—governing by scandal, shutdown, and CNN hits.
- Popularized demonizing Democrats as un-American rather than just wrong.
- Made family values central to GOP branding—**while actively cheating on his wife.**

Hissy Fit Highlight: Led the impeachment of Clinton for an affair while juggling one of his own.

Pat Buchanan
The Original "They're Taking Our Country" Guy
- Nixon speechwriter turned rage pundit.
- Laid the ideological groundwork for Trump with early 1990s rants about immigration, feminism, and multiculturalism.
- Declared "**culture war**" at the 1992 GOP convention like it was a holy crusade (which, given the rise of the religious right, it was).

Hissy Fit Highlight: Ran for president three times. America told him "no" each time, but Fox News told him "great job."

Joe Arpaio
Sheriff of Maricopa County, Grand Wizard of Petty Authoritarianism
- Ran a "tent city" prison in the Arizona heat and bragged about it.
- Became famous for aggressive racial profiling to the point that it needed SPF 100.
- Was convicted of contempt of court, and then pardoned by Trump

like a medieval king rewarding cruelty.

Hissy Fit Highlight: Made inmates wear pink underwear as a form of punishment. Yes, that happened.

Ben Shapiro
Grievance Nerd in Chief
- Talks like a TED Talk written by an angry Reddit thread.
- Built a career around turning minor cultural shifts into existential threats to Western civilization.
- Uses **"logic"** like a sword but has yet to win a cultural war.

Hissy Fit Highlight: Once walked off a BBC interview after being challenged with… facts.

Glenn Beck
Whiteboard Prophet of the End Times
- Wrote conspiracy theory flowcharts on live TV like a manic substitute teacher.
- Turned Obama into a Marxist-Muslim-Socialist overlord.
- Sold **gold coins and doomsday prepper seeds** during ad breaks. Capitalism, but unhinged.

Hissy Fit Highlight: Once cried on air because America elected a Black president and didn't spontaneously combust.

Mike Huckabee
Evangelical Dad Energy with a Bible and a Bass Guitar
- Called same-sex marriage a threat to civilization.
- Believes secularism is tyranny.
- Once compared abortion to the Holocaust. (No, really.)
- Tried to run for president multiple times. God (and Americans) said, "Nah."

Hissy Fit Highlight: Claimed Beyoncé was destroying morality but campaigned with Ted Nugent. Irony not detected.

We've seen how outrage sells on cable news, how nostalgia rewrites the past, and how fear props up power. But the tantrum doesn't stop at culture—it gets written into law. The hissy fit graduates from a Twitter thread to a legislative agenda, from a school board shouting match to the statehouse floor. When discomfort becomes a crime and empathy is rebranded as indoctrination, democracy itself gets rewritten. Which brings us to the topic of our next chapter: legislating away the lived experience of others if it makes someone else uncomfortable.

CHAPTER 11

Don't Say Anything That Makes Me Uncomfortable: Legislating Away Lived Experience

Critical thinking?
Not if it makes Connor sweat.

W elcome to the era of legislated emotional fragility, where the greatest threat to public education is... feeling things. The right wing once mocked college campuses for using trigger warnings. Now? They've made trigger warnings for the law, disguised as "anti-woke" legislation. Take Florida's "Stop WOKE Act," which restricts how race, gender, and inequality can be taught in schools and workplaces if it makes someone—read: white people—feel "discomfort.²⁹⁰ "Sorry, students. We can't talk about slavery or gender inequality anymore. Someone's uncle is allergic to context."

This isn't protecting students. It's state-mandated selective memory. It's not education. It's emotional coddling for the culturally dominant. And in 2025, this strategy has gone national, with copycat laws springing up like mold spores in a damp civics textbook. The goal? A curriculum of convenient lies. These laws don't just ban content—they **ban context**. The result?

A fact-free zone where classrooms teach:

- Slavery was "involuntary relocation."
- Jim Crow was "state-based scheduling differences."
- LGBTQ+ people are "inappropriate topics for minors."
- And empathy is "leftist propaganda."

"Everything was fine until now."—The official slogan of revisionist education

This isn't a fear of discomfort. It's a fear of accountability. When lived experience gets legislated out of the classroom, we lose our moral compass. Students grow up memorizing sanitized timelines and thinking racism ended in 1964, sexism was solved when women got bank accounts, and queer history starts with Ellen. Spoiler: It doesn't. But if we don't say it, they'll never know.

Legislating Away Lived Experience

America's Favorite Hobby: Passing Laws Against Reality

Nothing screams "fragile empire" like trying to legislate away people's lived experiences because they make you *uncomfortable*.

Don't like racism? Pass laws banning books that mention it. Don't like trans people? Pass laws banning their healthcare and pronouns. Don't like poverty statistics? Pass laws making it illegal to feed the unhoused.

We'd rather *outlaw reality* than fix it.

The Playbook

This should sound familiar; it's happening every day.

Step 1: Pick a Group

Black, trans, immigrant, disabled—doesn't matter, as long as they're not the voting base. Find a group that's already fighting for scraps, visibility, or survival. Extra points if they can't afford a lobbyist. They don't have to be a threat—just different enough to scare suburban Facebook groups.

Step 2: Declare Them a Threat

Now, crank up the fear machine:
- "They're ruining your children."

- "They're taking your jobs."
- "They're invading your bathrooms."
- "They're destroying women's sports."

Say the word "family values" enough times, and suddenly people forget that the biggest threat to their family is a lack of healthcare, not a trans kid wanting to play soccer. Don't worry about facts; repeat the lie until it becomes "common sense."[291]

Step 3: Write Laws That Erase Their Existence.

This is where the magic happens: Turn prejudice into policy.
- **Ban Inclusive Curricula.** Heaven forbid kids learn about slavery, redlining, or Stonewall. Better they learn that Rosa Parks was "tired" and ignore the racism that made her tired.[292]
- **Block Gender-Affirming Care.** Because the best way to protect children is to ignore medical consensus and punish them for existing.[293]
- **Criminalize Homelessness.** Can't see poverty if you make it illegal for poor people to exist in public.[294]

Erase them from textbooks. Ban them from sports. Fine them for sleeping on benches. It's all about "order," right?

Step 4: Call It "Protecting Freedom."

Because nothing says *freedom* like telling other people how to live, who they can be, and whether they deserve to exist safely. Wrap it in flags, Bible quotes, and words like "patriotism" and "parental rights," while ignoring that the only rights you're protecting are the rights to oppress, control, and silence.

Reality Check:

This is how you launder bigotry into law:
- Find a scapegoat.
- Manufacture fear.
- Pass laws to punish the scapegoat.
- Pretend it's about freedom.

If your "freedom" depends on erasing other people's lived experiences, it's not freedom—it's control disguised as virtue.

What's the Damage?

Erasure: "Out of Sight, Out of Mind" Is Not a Policy Strategy

You can't legislate people out of existence—you can only force them into hiding, suffering, or death while you pretend you "solved" the problem.

- Ban trans healthcare? Trans people don't disappear; their risk of suicide skyrockets.[295]
- Ban books about racism? Black history doesn't vanish; students grow up ignorant, repeating the cycle their parents are too scared to break.[296]
- Criminalize homelessness? You don't end poverty by fining people for sleeping in parks—you give them a criminal record to ensure they *stay poor*.[297]

We are not protecting society. We're manufacturing trauma.

Ignorance: Banning History Won't Save You from It

You can ban critical race theory, inclusive textbooks, and drag story hours, but history doesn't care about your discomfort. It happened. It's happening. And when you erase it, you ensure it *repeats*—this time with hashtags, live streams, and a PR crisis you can't spin away. You can't heal what you refuse to name, and you can't prevent harm if you won't admit it exists. Your cultural amnesia isn't protecting your children—it's setting them up for a world they won't understand and can't navigate.

Economic Drain: Discrimination Is Expensive (But It's Worth It)

Exclusion and discrimination cost the US *billions* annually in lost productivity, higher healthcare costs, and legal battles over unconstitutional policies.[298]

Reality:
- Anti-LGBTQ+ laws drive skilled workers away from states.
- Book bans lead to costly lawsuits that schools lose.
- Ignoring racism and poverty increases healthcare spending and lowers workforce participation.

Hate isn't just morally bankrupt—it's *fiscally irresponsible*. You're paying a premium to uphold prejudice.

Moral Rot: The Decay You Can't Hashtag Away

You can't build a free society while outlawing truth, diversity, and human dignity.

When you legislate based on fear instead of fact, and cruelty instead of care, you poison the cultural well. It teaches the next generation that erasure is easier than empathy, that power is more important than people, and that fear is a form of leadership. This rot is what drives cultural division, polarization, and the collapse of civic trust. It's why America is a country with endless potential trapped in endless culture wars.

Bottom Line: You can pass laws to ban identities, histories, and truths—but reality doesn't care about your legislation.

The only thing you achieve is:

- More suffering.
- More ignorance.
- More economic waste.
- A moral landscape so bankrupt that "freedom" becomes a hollow slogan shouted over the silence of erased voices.

If you want a healthy culture, you don't legislate people out of existence. You build systems where everyone's existence is protected, valued, and allowed to thrive.

Legislating Backward: How Fear and Control Are Replacing Freedom and Justice[299]

- **Book Bans:** In 2023 alone, over 3,300 books were banned in US schools and libraries, with the majority addressing issues related to racism, gender, and LGBTQ+ topics.
- **Anti-Trans Legislation:** Over 550 anti-LGBTQ+ bills were introduced in 2023, with a majority targeting trans youth's healthcare and rights.

- **History Erasure:** "Anti-CRT" laws have been passed in 18 states, restricting discussions on systemic racism and slavery in classrooms.
- **Criminalizing Poverty:** Laws banning sleeping in public, panhandling, and feeding the unhoused have increased by 50% since 2020.
- **Healthcare Inequity:** States that rejected Medicaid expansion have higher maternal mortality rates and lower healthcare access, disproportionately impacting marginalized communities.

America has mastered the art of passing laws against reality while calling it "liberty." But here's the truth: Reality doesn't care about your legislation. People exist, history happened, oppression is real, and no number of bills can change that. If your "freedom" depends on denying someone else's existence, your freedom is the problem.

Drag Queens, DEI, and Dystopia: America's Manufactured Moral Meltdown

When diversity feels like doom and libraries are the new battlegrounds, in a nation where you can buy an assault rifle faster than cold medicine, guess what suddenly became Public Enemy No. 1?

Drag queens and diversity workshops. Rhinestones and PowerPoints about unconscious bias were just *too much* for the American psyche to handle. Cue the full-blown moral meltdown. Because nothing screams "we're the greatest country on Earth" like having a national panic attack over story time at the library.

The Hissy Fit:

- A drag queen reads *The Very Hungry Caterpillar* at a public library? "It's indoctrination!"
- A company holds a DEI (Diversity, Equity, Inclusion) training about not being a jerk to coworkers? "Marxism in the boardroom!"
- A school adds books with characters who aren't white, straight, and Protestant? "The collapse of civilization!"

It's as if conservative media from 2023–2025 ran a 24/7 livestream called "America Is Ending Because You Saw A Rainbow Once." According to the American Library Association, book bans increased by 65% between 2022 and 2024, primarily targeting LGBTQ+ authors, of color, and anything that might imply the world is bigger than a Cracker Barrel gift shop.[300] Meanwhile, 47% of companies reported DEI programs being defunded, watered down, or replaced with "Patriotic Workplace Values Training."[301]

Translation: Be inclusive, but not too inclusive. And not gay-inclusive.

The Cultural Impact:

- Drag queens = existential threat.
- Black History Month = "too political."
- Saying "equity" out loud = immediate HR investigation.

Libraries became war zones. School board meetings turned into WWE matches, with Karen and Jane wearing flag T-shirts and slapping "Mama Bear" bumper stickers on the minivan. Employees were afraid to express anything that might be mistaken for empathy, lest they be accused of wokeness and shipped off to a Patriot Reeducation Retreat (sponsored by The MyPillow Guy).

It wasn't just ignorance—it was weaponized, industrial-strength ignorance sold as "protecting the children." Spoiler: The kids were fine. It was the adults who needed supervision. The result wasn't just embarrassing—it was dangerous. When America decided diversity was dangerous, it didn't just roll back progress—it set new fires:

- Violence against LGBTQ+ communities skyrocketed.[302]
- Teachers resigned in droves after being harassed for teaching "divisive concepts" like civil rights.[303]
- Cultural literacy plummeted, replaced by grievance-driven conspiracy theories.

Instead of facing real problems—like climate change, income inequality, or, you know, *pandemics*—America chose to wage war against sparkly heels, pronouns, and books with the word "equity" in the title. This hissy fit was so dramatic that it made the Salem Witch Trials look like a casual misunderstanding.

The First Amendment: Weaponized Whining, Sponsored Outrage, and the Freedom to Throw a Hissy Fit

Because screaming "FREE SPEECH!" every time someone dislikes your opinion doesn't make you a patriot—it makes you a walking Facebook comment section.

Quick Constitutional Refresher: "Congress shall make no law... abridging the freedom of speech, or of the press."[304] That's it. That's the line. It protects you from **government censorship.** Not from Yelp reviews. Not from getting dunked on in the replies. And not from your boss's side-eyeing you after you tweet something that makes HR faint.

The First Amendment is not a **Get Out of Accountability Free** card. It doesn't guarantee you a Netflix special, a TED Talk, or immunity from being told you're wrong—loudly and publicly. You can say what you want. But the rest of us can also say, "That's dumb, and here's why." That's not censorship. That's conversation. (You remember those, right? Pre-algorithm? When people talked and didn't yell "tyranny" every time someone disagreed?)

Spoiler Alert: Terms of Service > Your Uncle's Caps Lock Rant: Platforms like X (formerly known as Twitter, formerly known as civil), YouTube, and Facebook are not the US government. They are platforms run by private companies with community guidelines—aka digital babysitters with terms of service fine print nobody reads.

When Uncle Doug gets booted for sharing memes that include six spelling errors, two racist undertones, and one photo of Dr. Fauci photoshopped onto Stalin's body, that's not a violation of his constitutional rights. That's what happens when your digital hissy fit breaks the house rules. If you walked into Olive Garden yelling about the globalist cabal and the war on men's rights, they'd kick you out, too. That's not fascism. That's management.

Here's What the First Amendment *Doesn't* Do:

- It doesn't guarantee you a platform.
- It doesn't protect your feelings.
- It doesn't stop other people from disagreeing with you.
- It doesn't apply when you're on a privately owned platform yelling into the void about soy.

And no, Karen, it doesn't apply at school board meetings when you demand the right to read banned books aloud while waving a Gadsden flag and crying about Mr. Potato Head's gender identity.

Why Does It Get Twisted So Often? Because "I'm being silenced" sounds way sexier than "I said something dumb, and people pushed back." It turns self-inflicted embarrassment into a constitutional crisis. It shifts the narrative from "I'm being ignorant" to "I'm being oppressed." And victimhood sells.

Bottom Line: You Still Have Free Speech. You're Just Being Loud, Wrong, and Publicly Debated. You can say what you want. We can say what we want. Nobody's stopping you. They're just scrolling past your meltdown and posting the receipts. That's not tyranny. That's democracy with a comments section.

How "Free Speech" Became the Default Hissy Fit Defense

Every time someone's platform is challenged, it's suddenly 1776 again. If you listen closely, you can hear it: "HELP! I'm being silenced!" **No, Dick. You're not being silenced. You're just being disagreed with...** by people who also have Wi-Fi. But in the age of algorithm-fueled ego-mania, every time someone's TikTok gets flagged, or a controversial tweet gets fact-checked, it's suddenly a full-blown reenactment of the American Revolution—minus the risk, muskets, or basic understanding of constitutional law. It's not censorship. It is consequences with comments. And yet, the slightest pushback has become a national emergency in a YouTube thumbnail.

Dick's Hissy-Fit: "I'm Being Silenced!" = "People Disagreed with Me in the Replies"

Free Speech Means Me, Not You—*"Free speech is the most important right we have!" Dick shouts, veins bulging. "That means I can say whatever I want—call out women, immigrants, liberals, whoever—without some woke mob canceling me. If you don't like it, tough. My speech is freedom, your speech is whining. And don't start lecturing me about consequences. Free speech means no consequences. None. I get to shout, insult, threaten, and joke about anything—and if you push back, that's censorship. America is about my voice being the loudest, and if yours drowns me out, then my rights are under attack!"*

—DICK

This is the modern masculinity soft spot: You post something idiotic like "The moon is woke now," and someone replies, *"Actually, that's not true, and here's evidence,"* and suddenly you're the Rosa Parks of bad takes. You're being engaged. However, engagement is challenging when your entire identity is built on never being questioned. Instead of reflecting, you rage-post: "The woke mob is trying to CANCEL me because I believe in FACTS!" What facts, Dick? Is Disney grooming your thermostat? Sit down.

From Protest to Profit: How Outrage Influencers Market Censorship as a Business Plan

Let's pull back the curtain on this well-oiled rage machine:

- Step 1: Say something inflammatory (the more racist, sexist, or factually illiterate, the better).
- Step 2: Get flagged or corrected.
- Step 3: Declare you're "being silenced."
- Step 4: Launch a Patreon, a supplement line, and a course on becoming un-cancellable.
- Step 5: Profit.

It's the victim-to-victim pipeline, except the only real oppression is their inability to handle a counterpoint without a meltdown. They don't want freedom. They enjoy immunity from facts, feedback, and accountability. And the wildest part? It's working. They've built empires on the idea that being told *"Hey, don't say that?"* is being hauled off by the Thought Police.

These hissy fits aren't about principle. They're about preserving the illusion of dominance in a world that now talks back. They're not protecting democracy. They're performing it—on a livestream, with merch, sponsored by rage. The next time you hear "I'm being silenced," just check their follower count, merch store, and six-figure speaking tour. It turns out that "being canceled" is the hottest PR campaign of the decade.

Politicians, Platforms & the First Amendment Sleight of Hand

The Constitution is sacred—until it gets in the way of a press conference, a lawsuit, or banning a rainbow sticker. Let's talk about Donald J. Trump—the first man to claim he's being silenced while speaking into 47 microphones on a private jet. From suing ABC, CNN, *60 Minutes*, and anyone who once said "fact," Trump isn't after justice—he's doing PR in a courtroom robe. These lawsuits aren't legal actions. They're stagecraft for grievance theater. Because when the facts don't serve him, the strategy isn't rebuttal—it's retaliation.

"They said mean things about me!" —A former and current presidents who once posted conspiracy memes at 3 a.m. like a teenage troll with executive privilege. Accountability? No. This is First Amendment cosplay with a vengeance clause.

"Fake News": The Battle Cry of the Terminally Un-Fact-Checked

What began as a legitimate concern about media bias quickly became Trump's favorite two-word phrase:" **Fake news!**" A phrase that now means:

- "I don't like what I read."
- "I didn't understand it."
- "It used words longer than 'bigly.'"
- "It made me feel things I don't have the vocabulary to describe."

The cry of "fake news" is no longer about truth distortion—it's about ego preservation. It's a preemptive hissy fit in headline form.

Selective Outrage: Free Speech for Me, Censorship for Thee

These same politicians who scream about censorship? They're banning books faster than you can say *"To Kill a Mockingbird made me think about racism and now I'm uncomfortable."*

- Drag queen reads to kids? Threat to civilization.
- Banning actual US history? Patriotism.
- Rainbows on a T-shirt? Indoctrination.
- Gerrymander voter access? Strategic governance.
- A tweet saying "let's not?" CENSORSHIP! TYRANNY! CALL THE CONSTITUTION!

"Free speech" in this version of America is a weapon for the powerful and a muzzle for the rest.

The DeSantis Doctrine: Free Speech, But Make It Government-Approved

Enter Ron DeSantis—the middle manager of moral panic. Under his reign in Florida, "free speech" is treated like a school hallway pass: You can have it, but only if it doesn't disrupt his preferred narrative.

- Teaching kids about slavery's real legacy? Too woke.
- Letting students say "gay"? Too dangerous.
- Mentioning systemic racism? Too divisive.
- Screaming about cancel culture while banning AP African American Studies? Perfectly legal! Just enforcing values!

This isn't free speech. It's "speech that makes me feel powerful." DeSantis doesn't want to protect speech—he wants to curate it like Spotify for astroturfed nationalism.

The Sleight of Hand: Turning Constitutional Rights into Political Theater

Here's the trick: They invoke the First Amendment not as a right, but as a distraction. While they ban books, gut curriculum, and sue media outlets, they wrap themselves in the flag and shout: "We are the REAL defenders of liberty!" Quietly redefining freedom as *"You can say anything you want— as long as we agree with it."*

And the public? Too busy rage-scrolling and liking posts titled *"Why My Kid's Teacher Is a Communist with Pronouns"* to notice the smoke and mirrors.

The Constitution Isn't a Weapon—Unless You're on Fox at 8 p.m.

They don't want freedom of speech. They want freedom from consequences. From a challenge. From change. The First Amendment was meant to protect dissent, not perform it. However, by 2025, it has become the patriotic fig leaf for every petty meltdown and lawsuit, designed to keep people afraid of ideas, history, and other human beings. Next time you see a politician waving the Constitution like it's a backstage pass to censorship hysteria, ask: *"Is this about freedom—or just keeping Dick mad and monetized?"*

Book Bans and Boogeymen:
Why To Kill a Mockingbird *Is Too "Woke"*

Nothing strikes fear into the heart of authoritarian fragility like a teenager reading about empathy. We've officially entered a literary purge era where the bar for banning a book is lower than the reading comprehension of those banning it.

If a book includes:

- A Black protagonist facing injustice,
- A queer character discovering identity, or
- A sentence that causes mild reflection or a new perspective …then out it goes.

Racism? In my child's literature? Not. We prefer our fiction to be dystopian, and our history sanitized.

The new test isn't about educational values. It's about emotional comfort for the dominant group, usually served with a side of suburban pearl-clutching and a Fox News chyron.[305] Forget Pulitzer Prizes or decades of literary impact. If it mentions race, sex, or anything that sounds like intersectionality, it's now considered "divisive," "pornographic," or worse: "woke."

The goal isn't to protect students—it's to preserve fragile ideologies from truth, context, and empathy.[306] These bans target books that humanize, tell stories beyond white suburban experiences, and make readers feel something other than superiority or nostalgia.

It's not logical. It's a reaction masquerading as righteousness. The common rationale is: "If I can't explain it to my angry uncle in under 30 seconds, it must be grooming."

Or: "If it mentions race or gender and isn't about white men doing brave things with muskets, it's radical propaganda." It's performative ignorance—rooted in a belief that education should confirm comfort, not confront truth.

As of 2023, over 3,300 book bans were reported in the US. schools and libraries—more than triple the number from two years prior.[307] **Meanwhile, a 2022 Pew Research study found that only 26% of Americans could correctly identify the difference between misinformation and disinformation.**

So, Why Mockingbird?

Because *To Kill a Mockingbird* dares to:
- Suggest racism exists in the justice system
- Center the experience of a Black man falsely accused
- Feature a white child who learns empathy
- Be a classic that challenges without condemning

It was revolutionary in 1960. In 2025, it's too radical for school shelves. We've gone from teaching kids how to spot injustice to teaching them that acknowledging injustice might violate state law.

You can't teach kids to think if the first rule of the classroom is "Don't think too hard."

Welcome to education in the age of the hissy fit—where every idea is a threat and every truth is treason.

The Double-Edged Sword of "Free Speech" Theater

Now playing nightly in the court of public opinion and your uncle's favorite podcast. In the modern hissy fit economy, the First Amendment isn't a shield for the vulnerable—it's a sword for the already loud.

Let's be real: If your "free speech" includes:

- denying pandemics,
- spreading QAnon fan fiction,
- yelling slurs at school board meetings, or
- sharing a meme that says *"Vaccines are government microchips controlled by Oprah"*...

That's not civic engagement. That's weaponized idiocy with a flag filter. And yet, this kind of speech is defended as if it were the Gettysburg Address. Because in Free Speech Theater, being corrected is tyranny and being debunked is oppression. Meanwhile, actual speech that challenges the status quo, like:

- peaceful protests,
- inclusive curricula,
- acknowledging history beyond 1955,
- or using someone's *correct* pronouns— gets labeled radical, divisive, or "dangerous to traditional values."

"We believe in free speech—just not the kind that involves facts, nuance, or anyone with a sociology degree." While hate gets platformed, protest gets policed. While bigotry gets broadcast, truth gets buried under cries of "too woke."

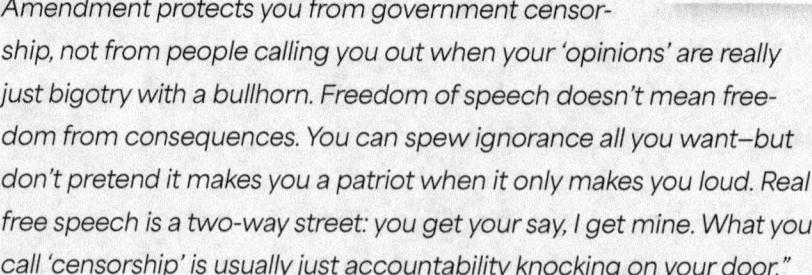

Sally's Soapbox: The Reality Check on Free Speech

"Free speech isn't your hall pass for hate, Dick. The First Amendment protects you from government censorship, not from people calling you out when your 'opinions' are really just bigotry with a bullhorn. Freedom of speech doesn't mean freedom from consequences. You can spew ignorance all you want–but don't pretend it makes you a patriot when it only makes you loud. Real free speech is a two-way street: you get your say, I get mine. What you call 'censorship' is usually just accountability knocking on your door."

—SALLY

Legislate Outrage, Then Sell It on a T-Shirt

This is the real hustle: Write laws based on internet comment threads. Ban books, police teachers, sue drag queens. Then print "I STAND FOR FREEDOM" on a hoodie and charge $29.99 for it. It's not about liberty. It's about aesthetics. Constitutional cosplay for cash. They don't want freedom of expression. They want licensed outrage in patriotic packaging—sold next to CBD gummies and tactical soap.

Courts Become Stages, Lawsuits Become Ads

Why pass a law to protect people when you can:
- Pass a law to **trigger the libs**,
- Get sued by the ACLU,
- Raise $5 million from a rage-fueled base,
- And call yourself a "constitutional warrior" on Newsmax?

Legal filings are now often presented as press releases, incorporating legal jargon. SCOTUS is less about jurisprudence, more about clickbait in robes. The courtroom isn't where truth wins; the outrage economy reboots for a new fiscal year.

The Monetization of Meltdown: Free Speech as Content Strategy

Here's the truth they won't say out loud (but shout into their ring lights): "I'm being silenced" is the most lucrative lie on the market. It's not a warning cry. It's a marketing funnel. You can: Have a multimillion-dollar contract, speak to millions nightly, get more airtime than oxygen in some states...and still cry "I'm being canceled!" Why? Because victimhood is the new influencer strategy. Tucker Carlson wasn't fired—he pivoted to martyrdom. Joe Rogan didn't lose reach—he gained a conspiracy-fueled brand empire.

It's simple:
1. Say something outrageous.
2. Get fact-checked.
3. Cry "oppression."
4. Watch your follower count surge.

5. Launch your line of tactical beef jerky and masculinity vitamins.

Free speech is the gateway drug to the grift. Once you're "silenced," you suddenly:

- Launch a book: *"The Truth They Don't Want You to Hear"*
- Sell a course: *"Uncanceled: How to Think for Yourself (While Giving Me $300)"*
- Drop merch: *"America, But Louder"*
- And of course, the premium nonsense comes in levels:
- $5/month: Bonus rants
- $10/month: Conspiracy deep dives
- $20/month: Access to "THE TRUTH STREAM"—a twice-weekly Zoom rant in which someone compares mask mandates to the Third Reich while vaping.

It's not journalism. It's not activism. It's **subscription-based ego management.**

Wake UP! Free Speech Isn't Dead. It's doing well on Substack.

The people yelling the loudest about being silenced? They're not underground. They're monetized, mobilized, and laughing their way to the crypto wallet while they laugh at you, Dick, the targeted audience. Freedom of speech is alive. But it's being pimped out as a brand strategy, grievance badge, and merch machine by people who learned that shouting "censorship" is the best way never to shut up.

Where the Hell Did Truth Go?

Truth didn't die with a bang. Ad revenue models slowly choked it out, and "both sides" journalism. It's not gone—it's been repackaged, repurposed, and resold with a promo code. What used to be "news" has devolved into algorithmic theater—each network just another echo chamber with better lighting and worse faith.

Welcome to the Media Spin Cycle

Truth used to mean facts. Now it means vibes.

- CNN will flash *BREAKING NEWS* if a senator sneezes in the shape of a flag.

- Fox News will dedicate an entire segment to whether a Pride flag near a Cracker Barrel is a declaration of war.
- Newsmax and OANN? They're less "news outlets" and more unlicensed fan fiction for white grievance politics.

And don't worry—MSNBC will show up with a 10-minute "deep dive" on the emotional burden of democracy... followed by an ad for anxiety meds. **It's not journalism. It's performance art for the perpetually triggered.**

Who Are the Targets of the Spin?
Whoever threatens the illusion of control.

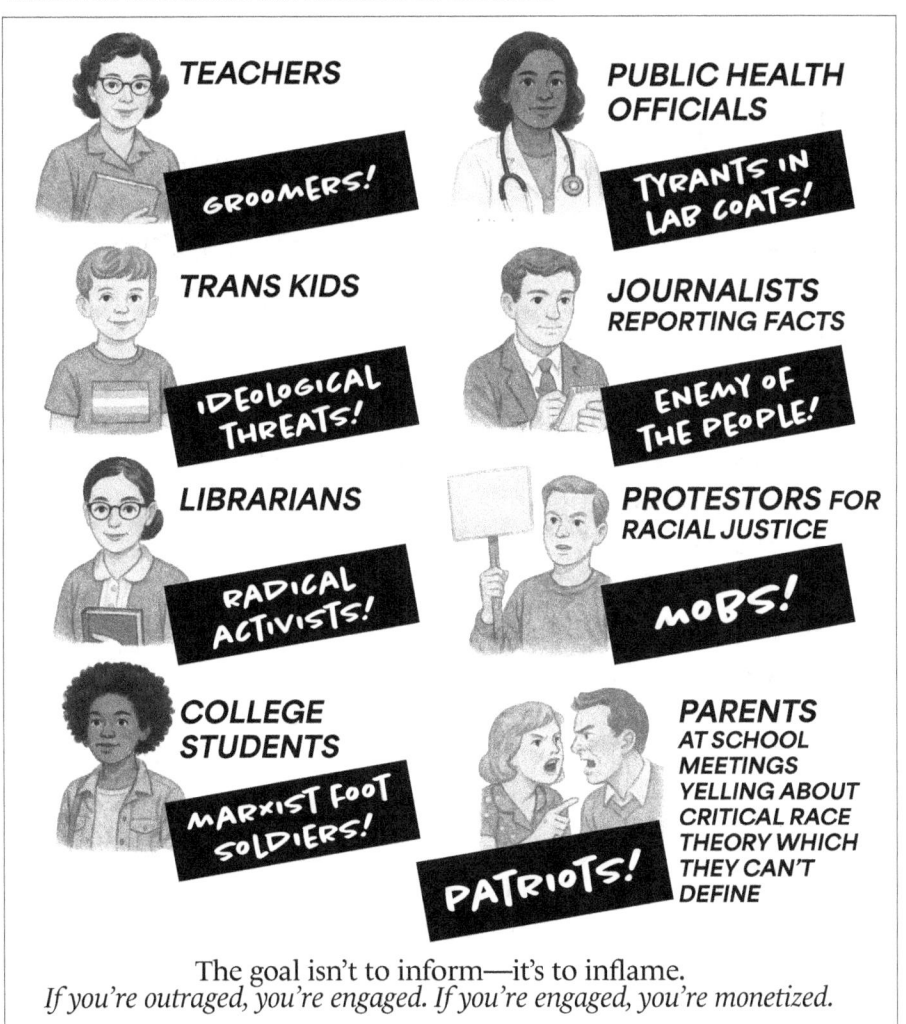

TEACHERS — GROOMERS!

PUBLIC HEALTH OFFICIALS — TYRANTS IN LAB COATS!

TRANS KIDS — IDEOLOGICAL THREATS!

JOURNALISTS REPORTING FACTS — ENEMY OF THE PEOPLE!

LIBRARIANS — RADICAL ACTIVISTS!

PROTESTORS FOR RACIAL JUSTICE — MOBS!

COLLEGE STUDENTS — MARXIST FOOT SOLDIERS!

PARENTS AT SCHOOL MEETINGS YELLING ABOUT CRITICAL RACE THEORY WHICH THEY CAN'T DEFINE — PATRIOTS!

The goal isn't to inform—it's to inflame.
If you're outraged, you're engaged. If you're engaged, you're monetized.

Truth vs. Vibes: A Timeline of Collapse

The tape:

- **2020**: COVID-19 hits. The news becomes less about data and more about death dashboards and "debates" between epidemiologists and Facebook uncles.
- **2021**: January 6th is livestreamed sedition. Some outlets call it a coup. Others call it "a peaceful protest that got a little rowdy."
- **2022**: The Uvalde school massacre. Cops fail. Children die. And somehow, the news spends more time discussing doors than guns.
- **2023**: Tennessee GOP expels Black legislators for protesting gun violence. Cable news splits the screen with *"Is decorum dead?"*
- **2024**: Book bans surge across red states. The same outlets that spent decades screaming about cancel culture now cancel *The Bluest Eye*.
- **2025**: Trump sues CNN, ABC, and *60 Minutes*—not for lying, but for telling truths that made him look bad. And somehow *he's* the victim.

Free Speech Isn't the Problem. The Weaponization of It Is

Everyone with a Wi-Fi connection is now a constitutional scholar who thinks "being disagreed with" = censorship. Every consequence is a "witch hunt." Every platform's moderation policy is akin to Stalin's.

"I got banned from Twitter for calling someone a slur, and now I'm starting a podcast about the First Amendment." We're not in a truth crisis. We're in a **narcissism economy** where **facts are optional, and victimhood is scalable.**

Media Doesn't Care What You Believe— Only That You Don't Log Off

News is no longer about facts. It's about *feelings that are converted into data to sell you garbage.*

- YouTube promotes conspiracy over content.
- Meta enables rage over nuance.
- TikTok pushes trauma trends while banning nipples and history.
- "Independent journalists" make six figures a month on Substack, selling *fact-free newsletters with fear-based fonts.*

Meanwhile, local journalism—the actual spine of democratic account-ability—is being gutted.

Truth Didn't Vanish. It Got Outbid

We didn't lose journalism. We sold it to the highest bidder, accompanied by a red face, a light ring, and a subscription model. Now we've got panels debating whether empathy is un-American and whether drag queens cause inflation. If truth still exists, it's buried somewhere beneath 27 think pieces, a segment sponsored by Pfizer, and a 2-for-1 offer on emergency food buckets. And unless we *unplug, unlearn, and re-engage with actual ver-ified sources*, we're not informed citizens. It feels like we're just extras in a poorly written propaganda film titled "Breaking News: Democracy, But Make It Clickable."

The Slippery Slope of Weaponized Free Speech

When every disagreement is a constitutional crisis and every fact-check is fascism. Once upon a time, "free speech" meant protecting unpopular ideas from government oppression. Now it means never being disagreed with on the internet without a GoFundMe campaign. We've turned the First Amendment into a one-size-fits-all emotional bubble wrap—and surprise: the slope is getting slick.

Here's the tragedy: There are actual threats to free speech out there, real and serious ones. Like:

- Journalists cancelled, jailed, or harassed.
- Governments targeting dissent.
- Whistleblowers punished for telling the truth.

But try getting airtime for that when a TikTok bro is going viral for yelling from his Dodge Ram, "They canceled me for loving America and meat!"

Free speech is dying—but not from censorship. From chronic overuse by the loudest guy in a camo hat who thinks misgendering people is an act of patriotism. And, every time someone gets called out, fact-checked, or gently corrected and responds with: "I'm being silenced!" ...the following shit happens:

- **Actual press freedom threats?** Ignored.
- **Marginalized voices?** Talked over.
- **Public trust in facts?** Replaced by "doing my research" on Facebook at 2 a.m.

We're not protecting speech. We're commodifying outrage. And the only thing truly being silenced is reasoned discourse, smothered under a pile of hashtags and affiliate links.

The Endgame? The Loudest Voices Win. Not the smartest. Not the most truthful. Not the ones who read the Constitution before quoting it. Just the ones who scream loud enough to trend. Discourse's future isn't debate—it's **influencer death matches in the comments section.** Where logic goes to die, nuance is banned for being boring, and every disagreement becomes a threat to national security and fragile masculinity.

Reclaiming Free Speech from the Outrage Industrial Complex

If we want to save free speech, we must detoxify it. Peel it off the merch hoodies. Scrape it off the "Patriot Grievance Pack" shelf at Walmart. And put it back where it belongs: in the public square, not in the profit margin.

This shouldn't need saying, but here we are:

- You can't clutch the Constitution with one hand and swing a book ban hammer with the other.
- You can't quote the First Amendment while deleting Black authors from school shelves.
- You can't scream "I have a right to say this!" while silencing drag queens, professors, political commentaries, or teenagers with pink hair and opinions.

That's not defending freedom. That's **gatekeeping it in a red hat.**

You know what real free speech protection looks like?

- Lawsuits that take years
- Legal briefs longer than a Joe Rogan podcast transcript
- Courts deliberating over *actual legal precedent*
- People defending the rights of people they **disagree with**

It's not sexy. It's not going viral. And you don't get a t-shirt. But it's how democracy survives.

You want to protect speech? Teach media literacy and critical thinking, not meme warfare. Encourage dialogue, not dunk contests. Choose complicated truth over simple lies. Currently, we're drowning in freedom of speech, but dying from a lack of understanding of what it means.

Rebuilding Civic Literacy: Knowing the Difference Between Censorship and Being Told "No"

REPEAT AFTER ME:

BEING DISAGREED WITH
IS NOT CENSORSHIP.

BEING DEPLATFORMED FOR VIOLATING
RULES IS NOT CENSORSHIP.

BEING FACT-CHECKED AND CALLED OUT
ON LIES IS NOT CENSORSHIP.

BEING TOLD "YOU CAN'T SAY THAT HERE"
ON A PRIVATE PLATFORM
IS NOT CENSORSHIP.

BEING TOLD YOU'RE WRONG IS NOT
OPPRESSION. IT'S JUST... LIFE.

WANT TO PROTECT SPEECH?
START BY UNDERSTANDING IT.

Free Speech Doesn't Need a Hero. It Needs Adults.
The First Amendment isn't just under attack. It's **under distortion** by people who want to scream without consequence, profit without scrutiny, and rage without end. The only way to fix it?
- Teach the difference between liberty and license

- Bring nuance back into fashion
- And remind Dick that free speech was never meant to be **a brand strategy for his latest meltdown.**

"Free Speech" & the Kimmel Knocked-Off-Air: When Satire Gets a Stay

Imagine this scene: a late-night comedian makes sardonic comments about the MAGA crowd, calls out political opportunists, the regulatory body tuts its chin, affiliates pull the plug, and *poof*—the show's off the air. That's not political theater. That's the opening act of a slippery slope.

What Actually Happened: Jimmy Kimmel, in his monologue, mocked how some were trying to spin the assassin of Charlie Kirk as "not one of them"—"MAGA gang doing political point-scoring." FCC Chair Brendan Carr (yes, the government "regulator" with teeth) publicly considered what "remedies" might apply. ABC, under Disney, suspended *Jimmy Kimmel Live!* indefinitely. Several ABC affiliates, via chains like Nexstar and Sinclair, stopped airing it.

The Ironies & Risks:

1. **"Free Speech" but only if it's approved speech**: They say: free speech is great—so long as you don't offend the powerful, or say things certain people deem inconvenient. Kimmel's jokes, satire, and critique suddenly become dangerous. That's chilling.

2. **Regulatory Pressure as Political Tool**: The FCC, theoretically independent, becomes a sword or a cudgel depending on who wields it. Threatening licenses over commentary—comedy shows? That's not guardianship of the public airwaves; that's censorship with a smile.

3. **Entertainment / Satire as Soft Target**: Comedians are the canaries. If they get silenced for barbed jokes, what's next? News commentary? Opinion pieces? Harsh critics? Once corporate/media gatekeepers start pulling shows due to pressure—such as advertisers, regulators, or public outcry—it erodes the boundary between acceptable dissent and silenced dissent.

4. **Precedent and Self-Censorship**: Even for people who don't sup-

port everything Kimmel said, there's danger in letting this slide. What do we teach every comedian, every performer, every writer? That you might be next. It's safer to say nothing than risk being shut down. That invites compliance, not courage.

Satirical Reality Check:

- We live in a country where a broadcaster can be pressured to mute satire—where "political speech" is not just debate, but a liability.
- We attend a moment where "community values," "public interest," or whatever vague, nebulous guardrails are cited, become code for "don't upset the powerful."
- We act shocked when a regulatory body threatens broadcasters over jokes—then wonder why journalists hedge their language, why hosts avoid certain topics, why "safe satire" is now the flavor of the day.

What Bold Free Speech Really Requires:

- **Transparent rules**: If the FCC or anyone else is going to threaten a broadcaster for content, the standards should be public, consistent, and defensible—not ad hoc.
- **Media solidarity**: When one voice is silenced, many should speak up. Not just comedians, but creators, unions, and civil liberties groups.
- **Courage over comfort**: Humor, critique, dissent—these are uncomfortable for some. Good. That's their job.
- **Guardrails, not guillotines**: Accountability matters. False statements, defamation, incitement—these are not satire's shield. But the threat of license revocation over opinion? Proportionality demands limits.

If satire is "the art of saying uncomfortable truths in funny clothes," what happens when you remove the clothes? You end up with silence—or worse, laughter at the powerful, not with them.

Other and recent instances where censorship and attacks on libraries have raised concerns about democracy and free speech:

- **Dismissal of Key Library Figures:** In a concerning development, both Colleen Shogan, the Archivist of the United States, and Carla Hayden, the Librarian of Congress, were dismissed by the Trump administration within three months. Their removals are viewed as politically motivated efforts to control national knowledge institutions.

Claims of "inappropriate" books in the Library of Congress were used to justify Hayden's dismissal. This institution does not lend books and operates as a reference library, adhering to Congressional legal deposit mandates. These actions indicate an alarming trend of suppressing knowledge.[308]

- **Book Burning Incident in Ohio:** In Beachwood, Ohio, a man burned 100 library books focused on Jewish, African American, and LGBTQ+ history. Faith leaders from the Interfaith Group Against Hate strongly condemned the act, emphasizing the need to reject hate-driven censorship.[309]

- **Funding Cuts to Libraries:** Following President Donald Trump's executive order to dismantle the Institute of Museum and Library Services (IMLS), libraries across the United States are facing significant funding cuts, particularly for digital resources such as e-books, audiobooks, and databases. The unexpected suspension of federal grants has forced several state libraries to lay off staff, close facilities, and suspend popular digital loan programs.[310]

- **Book Bans in Schools and Libraries:** Since 2021, thousands of books have been banned or challenged in various parts of the United States. Most of the targeted books address issues of race, gender, and sexuality. Unlike most book challenges in the past, local groups have received support from conservative advocacy organizations working to nationalize the efforts focused on specific subjects. They have also been more likely to involve legal and legislative measures rather than just conversations in local communities.[311]

- **Legal Challenges to Restrictive Laws:** In Boise, Idaho, several prominent book publishers, the Donnelly Library, and others have filed a lawsuit challenging Idaho's law that mandates libraries to place books deemed "harmful to minors" in an adults-only section. The plaintiffs argue that the law infringes on the First Amendment rights of students, librarians, and residents by restricting access to literary classics such as *Slaughterhouse-Five* and *A Clockwork Orange*.[312]

We've traced the hissy fit from its origins through its reruns in culture wars and its upgrades in legislation. But hissy fits don't just spontaneously combust—they're curated, financed, and weaponized. Behind every out-rage cycle is a puppeteer, tugging the strings with equal parts scripture, grievance, and profit motive. Because nothing says "American innovation" like turning resentment into a revenue stream. Which brings us to Part III: **Puppet Masters of the Hissy Fit: God, Grievance, and the Grift.**

Part III:

Puppet Masters of the Hissy Fit: God, Grievance, and the Grift

You didn't think Dick built this hissy fit on his own, did you? Nah. Dick had **help. Lots of it.**

B ecause Part I revealed Dick's confusion, and Part II built his worldview, Part III exposes the well-funded, power-driven machinery that taught Dick to double down, stay angry, and label **it patriotism.**

America's tantrums didn't just spontaneously combust. They were strategically funded, focus-grouped, and developed in church basements, think tank boardrooms, cable news studios, and billionaire bunkers. You think the *"war on Christmas"* or *"bathroom bills"* were grassroots? Think again. They're the byproducts of a system that figured out outrage is cheaper than solutions and fear is more profitable than facts.

Dick didn't wake up one day believing empathy was weakness and conspiracies were gospel. He was *discipled* into it by pastors who equate Jesus with tax cuts, by think tanks who write "freedom" while drafting control playbooks, and by politicians who discovered culture wars are easier than governing.

Rather than blaming, Part III is about **showing Dick the puppet strings.** Because the hissy fit isn't just a part of American culture, it's **American strategy.** A strategy that sells fear as faith, replaces policy with panic, and treats *democracy* like a Black Friday sale—scarce, loud, and designed to leave you angry.

Does it make you uncomfortable to realize that a megachurch sermon, a Heritage Foundation PDF, or a YouTube algorithm engineered your opinions? Good. That discomfort is your only way out.

CHAPTER 12

Separation of Church and State?

Who Was Jesus? Not Your Blonde, Blue-Eyed Suburban Life Coach

et's clear the incense-scented air: **Jesus wasn't a Christian.** He didn't launch a megachurch, preach in English, or say, "Verily, let there be Chick-fil-A." He was, in fact, a dark-skinned, Aramaic-speaking, Jewish man from the Middle East who was more likely to flip tables in a temple than hand out prosperity gospel pamphlets in a mall.

Jesus: The Original Problematic Brown Guy

Born in Bethlehem and raised in Nazareth—yes, that's ancient Palestine—Jesus was the kind of guy modern Western conservatives might profile at airport security. According to most biblical scholars and historians, Jesus of Nazareth:

- Had brown skin, dark hair, and Middle Eastern features
- Practiced Judaism his entire life
- Challenged both Roman imperialism and religious elitism
- Hung out with sex workers, the sick, the poor, and the "unclean"
- And—brace yourself—was a refugee as an infant, fleeing political violence under King Herod (Matthew 2:13-15, for those who forgot their Sunday School receipts)

Not the GOP Spokesmodel: If Jesus walked into half the churches that bear his name today, they'd call security. He was homeless, anti-wealth hoarding (see: the *camel through the eye of a needle*), anti-empire, and pro-radical compassion. He didn't wave a national flag—he warned against worshiping Caesar. He didn't preach capitalism—he overturned money tables (Matthew 21:12). And he didn't say, "Love your neighbor unless they vote differently."

He Was a Brown-Skinned Jew, Not a White Republican Mascot

Historically honest: the Europeanized Jesus, the one with perfectly feathered Pantene hair and a glowing white robe, is a **Renaissance rebrand**, courtesy of colonial art direction. Think of it as the original influencer filter. That image? Invented to make an empire-compatible Jesus more palatable to colonizers. Michelangelo and the boys weren't working with eyewitness accounts—they were working with *aesthetic goals* and Eurocentric supremacy.

The real Jesus? Looked more like a young Mahmoud or Ahmed than Brett from Bible Study. The modern Jesus would be getting "randomly selected" at TSA before you could say "peace be with you."

Why Identity Theft? Simple: Power.

Whitewashing Jesus made him easier to weaponize. He could be slapped on bumper stickers, weaponized in political campaigns, and turned into the moral mascot for every culture war hissy fit from "Merry Christmas" outrage to trans bathroom panic. The Jesus of history? He *loved the marginalized, fed the hungry, healed the sick at no cost, and instructed* the rich to give away their possessions. The Jesus of American politics? Hates pronouns, reads Ayn Rand, and moonlights at the NRA.

Final Sermon: If your version of Jesus wouldn't be on an FBI watchlist in the Roman Empire or banned from school boards in Florida today, **you're not following Jesus—you're following a focus group**. Stop turning Jesus into a Hallmark character with a gym membership and start reckoning with the revolutionary, brown-skinned rabbi who *existed*.

The United States and Religious Freedom

Let's start with the fairy tale: the United States was founded on religious freedom, and the government was never meant to endorse or impose any one faith.

In an 1802 letter to the Danbury Baptists, Thomas Jefferson coined the phrase "a wall of separation between Church and State." According to Jefferson, that wall was meant to protect both institutions—religion from the corrupting grip of politics and politics from the tyranny of dogma. Cute story. It's too bad we've been bulldozing that wall since before the mortar dried. While Jefferson was metaphorically laying bricks, others were busy chiseling loopholes. George Washington set a precedent by invoking divine providence in his inaugural address. Early sessions of Congress opened with prayer. And somewhere between those holy habits and the modern "Christian nation" myth, the wall became more of a decorative fence—easy to step over if you're wearing a cross and a flag pin.

The modern Christian right loves to masquerade as Constitutional originalists—strutting around in powdered wigs of moral superiority, clutching pocket Constitutions like rosaries, and insisting that the Founding Fathers were pastors with muskets. But scratch beneath the surface of their colonial role, and you'll find a deeply inconvenient truth: many of the men who birthed this nation were, by today's evangelical standards, practically heretics.

Thomas Jefferson, who coined the phrase "separation of church and state," spent his spare time editing the Bible with a razor blade, slicing out every miracle, every divine intervention, and anything resembling the supernatural. A "Jefferson Bible" presented Jesus as a moral philosopher, not the Son of God. Imagine the outrage today if anyone in Congress were to try that. They'd be burned in effigy—probably right after a House resolution to name Jesus the honorary Speaker.

James Madison, often called the "Father of the Constitution," was even more allergic to church-state entanglement than Jefferson. He opposed taxpayer-funded chaplains and religious proclamations by the government and even questioned military religious appointments. He believed religion thrived best without state interference, and that the state stayed healthiest without religious dogma. Ben Franklin? Deist. More interested in printing money and securing French mistresses than in the Book of Revelation. John Adams? A Unitarian who rejected the Trinity and found Calvinism repulsive. Not exactly your Southern Baptist pinup.

Yet none of this deters the contemporary faux-historian brigade—the David Bartons of the world—who engage in historical Mad Libs to retrofit America's origins into a Christian fever dream. They cherry-pick colonial-era sermons, ignore Enlightenment influences, and twist context like it's scripture at a prosperity gospel tent revival.

Their version of history isn't just wrong—it's willfully dishonest. It turns Jefferson into a prophet, not a skeptic. It paints the First Amendment as a shield for Christianity, not as a barrier for all religions against government intrusion. And it insists—without irony—that the Constitution was inspired by God, even though God is never once mentioned in it. Not in the preamble. Not in the articles. Not even in the margins.

This isn't just misremembering. It's revisionism with an agenda. When history gets in the way of the hissy fit, they rewrite it to serve the narrative: that America has always been, and must always be, a Christian nation— preferably one that looks, votes, and worships just like them.

In this fantasy, religious freedom only applies to Christians. Everyone else? They're just testing God's patience—and apparently, the Founders' as well.

God, Guns, and Government:
Why the Pulpit Needs to Stay Out of Politics

Let's get one thing straight: the separation of church and state wasn't a typo in the Constitution. It was a deliberate firewall—because the Founders knew what happens when preachers get their hands on policy. Spoiler: it's less "land of the free" and more "pray or pay."

- **Freedom of Belief, Not Forced Belief:** You want to worship God, Allah, Buddha, Beyoncé—go for it. That's your right. But the second the government tells me I have to bend a knee to your deity, we're not a democracy—we're a hostage situation with hymnals.
- **Equal Citizenship:** Mixing church and state means citizenship by baptism. Suddenly, "We the People" becomes "We the Chosen Few,"

and everyone else gets shoved to the margins. Last time I checked, the Bill of Rights didn't have a "Christian Only" clause.

- **Checks on Power:** Politicians love to slap a "God said so" label on their agenda because it shuts down debate. Who's going to argue with the Almighty? Answer: anyone with a brain, but only if they're not burned at the rhetorical stake first.
- **Protecting Religion from Politics:** If your faith is so fragile it needs a government subsidy to survive, maybe it's not faith—it's a political PAC with a pulpit. Real belief doesn't need a line item in the federal budget.
- **Culture Wars on Steroids:** Without separation, every law turns into a sermon. Abortion bans, book bans, prayer in schools—it's less about liberty and more about legislating morality. And here's the kicker: it's always *their* morality, never yours.

The Hypocrisy Highlight Reel

The same politicians who cry "FREEDOM" while waving the Constitution like a pom-pom are the first to shove religion into law when it suits their base. Translation: "freedom" means *my freedom, my faith, my rules.* Everyone else? Suck it up.

Psalms, Politics, and Punchlines: Church-State in 2025

Well, in 2025, the wall between church and state isn't crumbling so much as someone's using church bricks to try to build a front porch—and expecting taxpayers to pay for the porch.

What's Actually Happening[340]

- **Ten Commandments Billboards Everywhere:** States like **Texas** and **Arkansas** are passing laws that require the Ten Commandments to be displayed in public school classrooms. Texas S.B. 10 demands the display of the Commandments in every public school classroom. Arkansas has its Act 573, which does something similar. Louisiana had tried something similar, but courts struck down its law as unconstitutional.
- **Religious Charter Schools & Public Funding Drama:** There was a bid to establish St. Isidore of Seville Catholic Virtual School in

Oklahoma with public funding. The Supreme Court deadlocked (4-4), which *for now* leaves the status quo: no direct taxpayer funding for outright religious institutions that act like public schools.

- **"Released Time" Religious Instruction in Schools**: Groups like LifeWise are advocating for laws and policies that allow students to leave class or spend parts of the school day on Bible or faith-based instruction, even seeking academic credit in some states. Kentucky, Texas, and Alabama have all seen this debate in action.
- **Project 2025 & Religious Liberty Overreach?** There's concern (from numerous religious freedom and civil liberties groups) that initiatives like *Project 2025* aim to blur lines so much that government becomes an amplifier for Christian conservative religious priorities. Think less separation, more integration under faith-based agendas.
- **Court Pushback (Somewhat)**: But there's pushback. Louisiana's Ten Commandments law was struck down by the federal appeals court as violating the Establishment Clause.
- **Public Opinion is Fractured**: A Pew study suggests many Americans believe religious institutions are becoming *too involved with politics*. Even among those with positive views of faith organizations, there's growing concern about the mingling of faith, power, and policy.

So here we are: 2025—when "freedom of religion" now often doubles as "permission to stage Scripture in every classroom window." Because clearly, what kids need more in algebra class is a framed stone tablet reminding them of commandments rather than quadratic equations. Every time someone says "this is historical," what they often mean is "this is Christian." And "historical" is being used like a magic eraser over the religious content so it can hide under constitutional scrutiny. "Colorado Plateau" had "petroglyphs"—that's historical. But "Ten Commandments in a classroom"—oh boy, that's a whole constitutional crisis.

We get legislation that demands state display of religious texts **because they're "foundational to law"**—as if somebody once tried to argue they got Supreme Court precedents from Exodus. Yes, I want checks and balances—but having state boards decide which scriptures are educational vs. propagandist? That's authoritarian theater with choir robes.

Then there's "released time" religion in schools. Let's be real: school does more than lecture. It's where identity forms. When you allow religious instruction during school hours (even "opt-out"), it's not neutral. It's a prayer-pause. And those without the majority faith? Either they opt out and feel excluded, or they're perpetually second-class citizens in their own hometown.

And the courts? They're playing high-stakes ping-pong. One decision, one block, one veto, one deadlocked Supreme Court—all of which means none of this is settled. That's dangerous because it leaves room for political opportunists to test the boundaries: how far can we go? And when/how will someone push back?

What the Founders Said About Religion[313]

"Christianity neither is, nor ever was, a part of the common law."
— *Thomas Jefferson, letter to Dr. Thomas Cooper, 1814*
Jefferson didn't just believe in separation—he was actively hostile to the idea that religion should sneak in through legal back doors. He viewed Christianity as a personal matter, rather than a foundation for state power.

"The Government of the United States is not, in any sense, founded on the Christian religion."
— *Treaty of Tripoli, Article 11, signed by John Adams, 1797*
This wasn't a backroom memo—it was a formal treaty ratified unanimously by the US Senate. Explicit, declarative, and inconvenient for the "founded as a Christian nation" myth.

"Religion and government will both exist in greater purity the less they are mixed."

— James Madison, letter to Edward Livingston, 1822

Madison, the "Father of the Constitution," repeatedly argued that religion thrives best when government keeps its distance—and vice versa. He also opposed congressional chaplains and presidential religious proclamations.

"Lighthouses are more useful than churches."

— Benjamin Franklin, quoted in a letter to his wife, 1757

Franklin, a deist, rarely passed up a chance to troll organized religion. For him, reason, science, and civic responsibility were far more sacred than scripture.

"As the Government of the United States of America is not, in any sense, founded on the Christian religion…"

— (Yes, again.) Treaty of Tripoli, because they meant it.

This treaty is worth repeating. Twice. Because Christian nationalists willfully ignore it every single time.

Reminder: The First Amendment begins, *"Congress shall make no law respecting an establishment of religion…"* Not *"unless it's Christianity,"* and not *"except during elections."*

Early Cracks in the Wall:
When Church Bells Became Battle Drums

The culture war didn't start with MAGA justices—it started with church bells declaring Christianity the default setting of American life. Public meetings opened with prayer. Mosques weren't planned for. The message was clear: To be American was to be Christian.

Then came the Cold War, and America panicked about "godless communism."

- 1954: "Under God" added to the Pledge of Allegiance—apparently because Jesus hated the USSR?
- 1956: "In God We Trust" stamped on money, replacing the original motto *E pluribus unum*. This wasn't about faith. It was a loyalty test disguised as patriotism.

Then the Supreme Court ruined the performance:

- *Engel v. Vitale* (1962) banned school-led prayers.
- *Abington v. Schempp* (1963) banned daily Bible readings.

Both rulings defended pluralism. But to Christian conservatives? It was a war. Billy Graham called it a violation of the "majority." And that's the tell—it was never about freedom of religion. It was about the fear of losing the power to impose it.

And so began the script we're still trapped in:

- Neutrality = persecution
- Inclusion = erasure
- Equality = threat

The sermon hasn't stopped. It's just gotten louder—and angrier.

Holy Hissy-Fits: When Faith Becomes a Weapon, Not a Belief

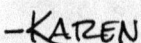

"Religion is the backbone of this country. America was founded on Christian values, and the sooner we get back to them, the better. Schools need prayer, government needs God, and families need faith. That's not oppression–that's tradition. Without God in the picture, morality crumbles. This isn't about forcing religion; it's about saving America from godlessness."

—JANE

"Oh, absolutely, Jane! I mean, look at what's happening–Christmas can't even be Christmas anymore without someone being offended. They've taken God out of the Pledge, out of schools, out of everything. No wonder society's falling apart. We're being persecuted for our beliefs, treated like villains just for wanting the Ten Commandments back on the wall. It's outrageous! We're the victims here, and nobody even cares!"

—KAREN

"Here's the thing, ladies: you're not being persecuted—you're being challenged. Religion isn't disappearing; it's being decentered so everyone can belong. America was founded on the freedom of religion, not the freedom to impose one's own. Prayer isn't banned; it's just not required. And Christmas? It still happens every December—you just don't get to dictate how everyone else celebrates. What you call persecution is really just equality in action—and equality feels threatening only if you've built your power on a monopoly."

—SALLY

The Global Comparison

Christian nationalists in the US love to wring their hands over religious extremism—when it's happening somewhere else. But here's the thing about theocracy: it's not *less dangerous* when the Bible is swapped for the Quran or the Bhagavad Gita. Religious law is religious law—no matter the flavor.

While Christian men in America are busy screaming about Sharia law being implemented via halal options in public school cafeterias, they're too busy organizing their church-state merger to notice that they've become the extremists they claim to fear. Let's take a little global tour, shall we?

Islamic Theocracies: The Control Blueprint

Let's start with the favorite boogeyman of the American Right: Islamic theocracies like Iran or Saudi Arabia, where religious leaders determine the law, and dissent is treated as heresy. State doctrines control women's bodies. LGBTQ+ people are criminalized. Free speech is censored under the guise of "morality."

Sound familiar? Now, swap the Ayatollah for a Supreme Court justice handpicked by Liberty University and tell me how different it looks. In both models:

- God's will is weaponized.

- Secular institutions are hollowed out.
- Dissenters are branded as threats to the soul of the nation.

Theocratic structures operate by making divine authority indistinguishable from political power.[314] Whether the sacred text is the Quran or the King James Bible, the outcome is the same: fear dressed up as faith-based order.

Hindu Nationalism in India: The Other Side of the Coin

Now let's swing over to India, where Hindu nationalism has surged under Narendra Modi's Bharatiya Janata Party government. The ruling party has fused religious identity with national loyalty, turning Indian citizenship into a caste system where Muslims and Christians are routinely excluded, surveilled, or targeted.

And guess what strategy they're using?
- Rewrite textbooks
- Politicize temples
- Vilify minorities
- Use "tradition" to justify repression

American Christian nationalists have taken **meticulous notes.** They've already started renaming schools, banning "anti-American" books, and accusing anyone not quoting scripture of being anti-patriotic. Scholars argue that majoritarian religious politics thrive on the idea that the majority religion is constantly under threat, even while it holds most of the power.[315] It's a psychological trick that works just as well in red states as in New Delhi.

When Belief Becomes Law, Rights Become Suggestions

Here's the bottom line: human rights vanish into smoke and scripture when any religion becomes law.
- The right to love who you love? Only if the Book says so.
- The right to make decisions about your body? Ask your pastor.
- The right to believe differently—or not at all? Dangerous and deviant.

Religious theocracy, no matter the brand, turns moral absolutism into legal persecution. And whether it's mandatory hijabs or mandatory heteronormativity, the mechanism is the same: conformity or punishment.

The Birth of the Religious Hissy Fit:
When Equality Felt Like Heresy

This is where the real hissy fit took off—post–Civil Rights America starts diversifying, and suddenly white Christians clutch their pearls like God just got evicted. Nothing was taken. Power was shared. But giving up a single shovelful feels like a robbery when you've had the whole sandbox to yourself. Here began the significant rebrand: from the Moral Majority to the Martyr Complex.

Happy Holidays = Holy Meltdown

Winter Break? Kwanzaa? *A Jewish kid sitting out the Christmas concert?* Fox News: "CALL THE TROOPS." The "War on Christmas," born from Bill O'Reilly's snowflake sermon, wasn't about faith. It was about maintaining Christianity as mandatory and presenting it as a form of freedom.

Marriage Equality = Moral Collapse (Apparently)

Obergefell v. Hodges (2015): Same-sex marriage is legal. The Religious Right: *"We're being crucified!"* Nope. You can't legally veto someone else's wedding anymore. This wasn't fear of being silenced. It was fear of losing the mic.

From Bible to Broadcast

The war wasn't spiritual. It was strategic. Fueled by Fox News, the Family Research Council, and the Alliance Defending Freedom, the goal was never liberty—it was control, cloaked in grievance. As sociologist Andrew Whitehead put it: *"The persecution complex keeps white evangelicals politically mobilized."*[316]

Religious Freedom: Now With 100% More Bigotry

Under this theocratic doctrine, "religious freedom" no longer means the right to worship freely—it means the right to:

- Deny healthcare to women,
- Fire LGBTQ+ employees,
- Ban books with non-white protagonists,
- And generally, act like Jesus was your personal HR director.

It's not freedom **from** religion—it's **freedom to discriminate because of religion**. As Katherine Stewart (2020) notes, this redefinition of liberty is a central strategy of Christian nationalism: to convert "the language of rights into a shield for privilege."[317]

The Christian right wasn't persecuted. They just lost monopoly status. And instead of adapting, they pitched a fit, rebranding equality as oppression and mass-producing martyrdom for primetime. Welcome to the gospel of grievance. Where hissy fits are holy, and equality is somehow sacrilege. This isn't about faith. It's about the panic that comes when a majority loses its monopoly and calls it discrimination.

The Holy Trifecta of Entitlement and Ideology

How Jesus Got Co-Opted by White Guys with Pickup Trucks and a Persecution Complex

Jesus didn't write the Constitution, didn't campaign for Ronald Reagan, and sure as hell didn't storm the Capitol. But that hasn't stopped a whole lot of middle-aged white men from turning a Middle Eastern Jewish pacifist into the mascot of their political identity crisis. Welcome to Christian Nationalism—where the Bible gets edited like a campaign ad, and the separation of church and state is treated like a liberal conspiracy rather than a founding strategic principle.

Christian Nationalism is a theological romper room for folks who think Jesus handed out Gadsden flags at the Last Supper. It's not about faith. It's about the belief that **to be American is to be Christian**, and anyone outside that club—atheists, Muslims, Wiccans,—is suspect at best, satanic at worst. As sociologists Andrew Whitehead and Samuel Perry explain, Christian Nationalism is "a cultural framework—a collection of myths, traditions, symbols, narratives, and value systems" that merges Christianity with American civic identity.[318] It's not just religious. It's *strategic*.

Cue the 1980s: Jerry Falwell Sr. found Jesus in a voting booth and launched the Moral Majority, transforming pulpits into political action committees (PACs). Reagan, America's favorite grandfather in cowboy boots, fed the flock with vague biblical references and anti-gay, anti-women, pro-prayer-in-school rhetoric.[319] Never mind that Reagan wasn't a regular churchgoer—he played the role well enough for televangelists to canonize him by the second term.

It's less about saving souls and more about safeguarding supremacy. Christian Nationalism gives white evangelical men a starring role in their favorite fantasy: a nation under siege, with them as the spiritual Navy SEALs. The real threat? Women with opinions, Black people with power, and queer people existing without permission.

Make the Last Supper Great Again

Weaponized "Christian Values" (Now with Racial Filters!)

Let's talk about the phrase "Christian values," which in political shorthand often means:

- Heterosexuality
- Submissive women
- Quiet minorities
- And tax-deductible tithes to anti-LGBTQ+ PACs

As Stewart (2020) explains, this sanitized, racially exclusive gospel isn't theology. It's branding. It's a marketing campaign for white cultural preservation, wrapped in scripture to lend it a sense of legitimacy and respect.[320] When white Christians say "freedom of religion," they often mean freedom to legislate their faith and ignore yours.

Christian Exceptionalism and the Fragility of Entitlement and a Dash of Masculinity

The myth of Christian exceptionalism holds that Christianity—and specifically white American evangelicalism—isn't just a belief system, but a divine birthright to cultural authority. The problem? Exceptionalism is emotionally fragile. It doesn't bend; it breaks. And when reality doesn't conform to it—when schools teach evolution, when corporations embrace Pride Month, when a Black woman gets confirmed to the Supreme Court—entitlement turns to outrage.

This fragility explains why a Supreme Court justice can strip away women's reproductive rights while still claiming their faith is under attack. Why can a megachurch with a $60 million budget claim persecution if someone questions its tax exemption? Why can someone who's never been denied a right in his life look at a drag queen story hour and scream "tyranny!" Here is how it all comes together.

The Federalists—Power, Property, and Piety

Before Fox News, before the "Moral Majority," before the Capitol was turned into a dress-up party convention for Christian nationalists, there were the Federalists: powdered-wig-wearing elites who believed in democracy as long as the riffraff kept their mouths shut. Let's not romanticize them. These weren't freedom-loving hippies building an egalitarian utopia. These were men who believed voting was for wealthy landowners, religion was a functional civic leash, and "we the people" primarily meant "we the guys in Philadelphia with good penmanship and plantations."

The Federalists' Distrust of Mob Rule–Unless It Was Their Mob.

The Federalists, notably Alexander Hamilton and John Adams, were openly terrified of direct democracy. Hamilton once warned that "the people are turbulent and changing; they seldom judge or determine right."[321] Translation: "Don't let the help vote."

But here's the twist: they didn't hate mobs—they hated mobs they couldn't control. If the angry crowd had powdered wigs and property deeds, great! If they were poor farmers, enslaved people, or women demanding rights? Get the militia. This selective approach to mob rule was the original American hissy fit. It's not tyranny if they're the ones flipping the table.

Hamilton and Adams: Elitism in a Lace Cravat

Hamilton was brilliant, ambitious, and a snob of historic proportions. He believed that only the "rich and well-born" should govern because the poor were too busy being, reasonably, **poor**.[322] Adams, slightly more pious, had similar anxieties but dressed them up in "civic virtue"—a term that meant obeying your betters while pretending it's noble. Together, they helped institutionalize a republic where class and property = competence, and morality meant respecting hierarchy.

Their brand of elitism was steeped in early American Protestantism, the notion that virtue and wealth were divine indicators of leadership. The more you owned, the more righteous you were. Sound familiar?

The Religious Flavor of Early Federalist Control:
Moral Superiority for the Win

The Federalists may not have been church-burning evangelicals, but they knew the political power of a little God-sprinkled elitism. They used religion not as spiritual truth but as social adhesive—something to scare the poor into behaving and justify the rich staying in charge.

They promoted moral superiority as public policy. The Sedition Act of 1798, for example, criminalized criticizing the government, not very "freedom of speech," but very on-brand for a party that believed the people needed spiritual discipline and governmental supervision.[323] In their version of democracy, God was the silent partner in every land deal.

Today, the Federalist Society is a robust network of conservative and libertarian legal professionals that has significantly influenced US legal and judicial policy over the past several decades.

Who Makes Up the Federalist Society?

Core Membership Includes:

- Law students—chapters exist at nearly every major law school
- Professors and legal scholars—especially those who advocate for originalism and textualism
- Judges—including **at least five current Supreme Court justices**, notably Samuel Alito, Clarence Thomas, Neil Gorsuch, Brett Kavanaugh, and Amy Coney Barrett
- Lawyers, many of whom work in federal and state government, corporate law, and influential policy think tanks
- Policymakers and former government officials—including alums from the Reagan, Bush, and Trump administrations

What Do They Believe? The Federalist Society champions:

- Originalism: interpreting the Constitution based on its original meaning at the time it was adopted
- Textualism: interpreting laws strictly based on the text rather than intent or consequence
- Limited government: a preference for deregulation and constraints on federal power
- Judicial restraint: Courts should not create policy but interpret existing laws narrowly

Why It Matters: The Society doesn't lobby, but its members write the legal playbooks for conservative judges, advise presidents on judicial appointments, and help shape the federal judiciary. *Project 2025*, a Heritage Foundation initiative aimed at reforming the executive branch, was primarily developed by lawyers affiliated with the Federalist Society.

The Federalists didn't just shape a country—they shaped a caste system disguised as competence. Their paternalism ("We know what's best for you—now give us your taxes and trust fund access") set the tone for white male exceptionalism. They cast themselves as morally superior managers of a chaotic, ungrateful population. And it stuck. That same tone echoes through today's Christian nationalist playbook, where white male authority is repackaged as "protector of tradition," "guardian of virtue," or "guy just asking questions at a school board meeting."

Modern Federalism: States' Rights, Sanctified Suppression, and the Culture War Carousel

Fast-forward to today, and the Federalists' legacy lives on—not in powdered wigs, but in state legislatures banning books, abortion, and accurate history. Modern federalism—once a structure for distributing power—has evolved into a loophole-ridden playground for religiously motivated lawmaking. Want to overturn *Roe v. Wade*? Just funnel judicial appointments through religious law schools and then hand the issue back to the states. Want to ban Toni Morrison gooks or LGBTQ+ history? Just scream "parental rights!" loud enough and watch local governments fold.

The result? Fifty states, fifty theocratic experiments. Because in America, God may be dead in science class, but He's alive and well in your **uterus** and your kid's school library.

The Moral Majority—Reagan's Favorite Choir

Ah, the 1980s—a time of giant shoulder pads, sax solos, and televangelists screaming from your TV that the apocalypse was coming because someone somewhere was gay and happy about it. Welcome to the rise of the Moral Majority, arguably one of the most ironically named political movements ever. This is the decade when Christianity went corporate, political, and fully airborne—broadcast straight into your living room by a sweaty man named Jerry Falwell, who looked like he sold timeshares in heaven and moral panic in bulk.

Jerry Falwell and the Rise of the Religious Right

If Billy Graham was the velvet glove of evangelicalism, Reverend Jerry Falwell Sr. was the brass knuckles. He launched the Moral Majority in 1979, not to save souls, but to win elections. And not just any elections: he wanted a country where the Bible was the Constitution, and the white, heterosexual nuclear family was the national mascot. Falwell's sermons were less about theology and more about political weaponry. Civil rights? Too dangerous. Feminism? Unholy. Homosexuality? A slippery slope to bestiality, according to his charming televised analysis.[324] He wasn't preaching for Jesus—he was preaching for Reagan, and by 1980, he had convinced millions of white evangelicals that voting Republican was a sacrament.

The Moral Majority was a politically influential coalition formed in the late 1970s that blended conservative Christian values with right-wing politics, becoming a cornerstone of the modern Religious Right. **Although it officially disbanded in the late 1980s, its ideological legacy endures in today's Christian nationalist movements.**

Who Made Up the Moral Majority— Then to Become Christian Nationalists?

Evangelical Christians

- The backbone of the movement
- Key leaders: Jerry Falwell Sr. (founder), Pat Robertson, and James Dobson (Focus on the Family).
- Believed in "biblical values" shaping American public life, especially on social issues like abortion, homosexuality, and school prayer.

Conservative Catholics

- United with evangelicals over shared opposition to abortion, feminism, and secularism.
- An unusual alliance, historically, but forged through mutual culture war priorities.

Fundamentalist Christians

- More extreme offshoots of evangelicalism.
- Anti-modernist, anti-public education, and deeply patriarchal in worldview.

Conservative Jews (minority involvement)

- Participated in coalition-building, particularly on issues like support for Israel and opposition to abortion.

Republican Politicians and Strategists

- Recognized the voting power of white Christian conservatives.
- Partnered with the Moral Majority to win elections and pass socially conservative legislation.

What Did They Want?

The Moral Majority pushed for:

- Banning abortion (especially overturning *Roe v. Wade*)
- Opposing LGBTQ+ rights
- Promoting prayers in public schools
- Censorship of "immoral" media
- "Traditional" family values (i.e., patriarchal, heterosexual households)
- Support for Christian schools and homeschooling

They framed these demands not as religious impositions but as a "return" to America's supposed moral roots. The Moral Majority became politically idolized as the Christian nationalist movement, and did what they pushed for.

Why It Mattered

They mobilized millions of previously apolitical evangelicals into active voters. They helped elect Ronald Reagan in 1980, forming the blueprint for the GOP's alliance with the Religious Right. They shifted the Overton window on issues of religion in politics, normalizing church-to-ballot-box pipelines.

Family Values—The Most Passive-Aggressive Weapon in American Politics

"Family values" in the 1980s were less a moral compass and more a cultural battering ram. The phrase was deployed to police women's autonomy, demonize LGBTQ+ people, and roll back civil rights gains—all while claiming to protect the innocent.

According to Falwell's Moral Majority playbook:

- Two men kissing = moral decay.

- A Black woman leading anything = reverse racism.
- Birth control = Satan's Tic Tacs.

The goal wasn't holiness. It was a hierarchy to restore white, male, Christian control of the public square by turning every social gain into a hellfire emergency. The Christian right's movement wasn't born from grassroots faith—it was a "top-down political strategy masquerading as spiritual revival."[325]

Feminism and LGBTQ+ Rights as Existential Threats

The Moral Majority saw feminism as a hostile takeover by bra-burning communists who wanted to destroy the family by letting women have credit cards, careers, and control over their bodies.

Abortion became their holy war, not babies. It was about power. *Roe v. Wade* had given women the right to choose, and the Religious Right saw that as a threat to the natural order—aka men deciding everything. As for LGBTQ+ people? They weren't just marginalized—they were turned into political monsters. Anita Bryant had already warmed up the nation with her orange juice–fueled campaign against gay rights in the 1970s, but the Moral Majority took it national.

AIDS, tragically, became the "proof" they needed to moralize queer existence out of public sympathy. Falwell famously declared that "AIDS is not just God's punishment for homosexuals; it is God's punishment for the society that tolerates homosexuals."[326] In other words, tolerance was the sin, and compassion was the enemy.

Reagan: The First Evangelical President Who Wasn't Evangelical

Then along came Ronald Reagan: former actor, lifelong moderate Protestant, and the only man who could make "morality" sound like a stock tip. Reagan wasn't deeply religious, but he understood the performance of faith—and he knew that if you quoted Scripture and smiled, you could deregulate the economy, ignore a health crisis, and still get a standing ovation from people holding hymnals. Reagan never joined the Moral Majority—he didn't need to. Falwell and friends joined *him*. They handed him votes; he gave them judicial appointments, policy access, and, most importantly, **legitimacy.**[327]

The Moral Majority was never moral. It was never a majority. It was a highly strategic, white, Christian backlash movement using nostalgia, fear, and cherry-picked scripture to roll back progress under the guise of holiness. And if you think they disappeared, you're wrong—they just re-branded. Today, they call themselves "concerned parents," "constitutional conservatives," or "grassroots patriots." But they're still singing the same song Falwell taught them. And they're still off-key.

The Christian Nationalist: The Melting Pot of Religion

"In God We Trust"—but only if He votes Republican, wears Dockers, and hates drag queens. Let's not pretend this just *happened*. This wasn't a rogue TikTok trend or an overzealous church potluck. This was the plan. A carefully staged, pearl-clutching, power-grabbing pageant decades in the making. And it started, naturally, with Ronald Reagan riding a bald eagle made of nostalgia and coded racism into the Oval Office.

Christian nationalism isn't a denomination—it's a **political ideology** cloaked in religious garb. But it tends to draw most of its support from certain branches of Christianity that blend **conservative theology** with **national identity**. This ideology draws in the Moral Majority, capturing millions of Americans. Here are the primary religious groups most associated with Christian nationalism, with a blend of what is left of the Moral Majority:

White Evangelical Protestants
- Core Base: This is the *engine* of Christian nationalism.
- Beliefs: Emphasize biblical literalism, "moral values," anti-abortion, anti-LGBTQ+ rights, and traditional gender roles.
- Notables: Southern Baptist Convention, Pentecostal churches (like Assemblies of God), nondenominational megachurches. Franklin Graham, Robert Jeffress, Tony Perkins
- Stats: About 80% of White evangelicals voted for Donald Trump in 2020. [328]

Fundamentalist Christians
- **Beliefs**: A more extreme version of evangelicalism, often anti-science

(think: young Earth creationism) and staunchly patriarchal.
- **Style**: Apocalyptic, authoritarian, with a deep distrust of secular institutions.

Charismatic / Pentecostal Movements
- **Beliefs**: Heavily emotional worship, belief in spiritual warfare, and the idea that modern-day prophets are guiding national destiny.
- **Notables**: Leaders like Lance Wallnau and Paula White, who blend prosperity gospel with MAGA politics. White is currently the senior advisor to the White House Office of Faith and Opportunity, appointed by Trump.

Dominionists
- **Beliefs**: Believe Christians should "take dominion" over all aspects of society—government, media, education, etc.
- **Movements**: Seven Mountains Mandate, New Apostolic Reformation (NAR).
- **Notables**: Rick Joyner, C. Peter Wagner, and other "apostles" promoting Christian takeover.

Conservative Catholic Nationalists
- **Yes, Catholics Too**: While Catholicism is more diverse politically, **some traditionalist factions** align with Christian nationalism—especially around abortion, religious liberty, and opposition to "wokeism."
- **Notables**: Archbishop Carlo Maria Viganò (who has promoted conspiracy theories) and groups like Catholic Vote.

Reconstructionist
- **Beliefs**: Believe US law should be based on **Old Testament law**—yes, including stoning.
- **Founder**: R.J. Rushdoony, who explicitly stated the goal of replacing democracy with biblical theocracy.
- **Influence**: Limited in numbers, but huge in ideological reach.

Right-Wing Politicians
- Elected officials who promote Christian nationalism or pass laws reflecting it.
- Notable examples: Representative Marjorie Taylor Greene, Senator Josh Hawley, Governor Ron DeSantis (though often coy about explicit

religious intent).

Organizations

- *Alliance Defending Freedom (ADF)*—Litigates to impose religious values on public life.
- *Liberty Counsel*—Fights for religious expression in government and schools.
- *Family Research Council*—Policy advocacy based on Christian conservative views.
- *WallBuilders*—A group claiming America was founded as a Christian nation, run by pseudo-historian David Barton.

Core Beliefs of Christian Nationalism

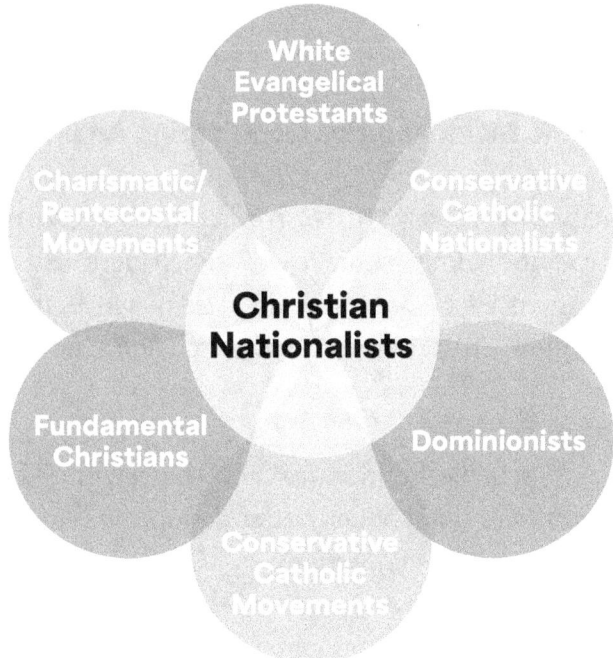

- America was founded as a Christian nation.
- The Constitution is divinely inspired, and Christianity should guide lawmaking.
- Separation of church and state is a myth or mistake.
- God has chosen America for a special role in world history.

- Cultural diversity and secularism are threats to national identity.
- Policies should reflect *biblical values* (as interpreted by them): opposition to abortion, LGBTQ+ rights, secular education, and immigration.

Why It Matters: Christian Nationalism has been linked to the January 6, 2021 insurrection, with crosses, prayers, and Jesus flags used alongside violent rhetoric.[329] Embedded in GOP platforms, especially in states pushing anti-DEI, anti-LGBTQ+, and pro-"parental rights" legislation, and classified **as a threat to democracy** by scholars and watchdogs, including the Baptist Joint Committee for Religious Liberty and the Freedom From Religion Foundation.

Christian nationalism draws from denominations and movements that combine: authoritarian theology, patriarchal values, political grievance, and white identity politics. It's less about Sunday service and more about Tuesday legislation.

The Playbook–To Make America God Fearing Again

Step One: Rebrand History with Patriotic Vibes and Amnesia

In the Christian Nationalist Cinematic Universe, America was founded by Bible-toting Puritans who *loved* Jesus and *hated nuance*. Jefferson's whole concept of a "wall of separation between church and state"? Meh—just a rough draft.

Their version of history?

- Slavery was regrettable, but necessary for "character building."
- The Founders were "men of faith" (translation: *land-owning patriarchs with a divine allergy to women voting*).
- The Constitution was divinely inspired—right up there with Leviticus and that Chick-fil-A sauce.

This revised history was not for education—it was for weaponization. When you control the past, you get to write the laws of the future.

Step Two: Fuel Moral Panic, Profit from Misery

Welcome to the Moral Majority Era, sponsored by anxiety and the ghost of Jerry Falwell Sr. When women wanted equal pay and Black people wanted justice, the Christian right said: "This country needs more God. And less disco."

They declared war on:

- Abortion
- Rock music
- Gays
- Halloween
- Teletubbies
- And later, trans kids who want to pee in peace

This wasn't morality. It was market-tested outrage, sold to white suburbanites as "family values" and to Congress as "voter turnout." They built empires on fear. "The gays are coming for your kids!" they shrieked—while writing checks to lobbyists and calling it a tithe.

Step Three: Blend Religion and Government Like a God-Approved Smoothie

Reagan opened the floodgates with a wink and a prayer breakfast. He welcomed the Moral Majority into the GOP like they were missionaries bringing the Good News—in reality, they were corporate theocrats in disguise, armed with PACs and a 40-year plan.

And the plan worked:

- Tax breaks for megachurches
- School vouchers as stealth religious funding
- Judicial appointments based on purity tests, not qualifications

By the 2000s, Christian nationalists were less interested in preaching salvation and more interested in writing education policy, zoning laws, and reproductive restrictions.

"Render unto Caesar"? Nah—**replace Caesar and put him on the church board.**

Step Four: Upload It to YouTube and Call It Revival

Fast forward to the 2020s, and we've got an algorithm-powered Pentecost.

- QAnon prophets quoting scripture in camo.
- Pastors giving TED Talks on "Christian Masculinity" while selling

apocalypse buckets.

- Moms for Liberty reading *The Handmaid's Tale* as a blueprint.

Christian Nationalism 2.0 isn't just a sermon—it's a brand. A podcast. A merch table. A cult of personality dressed in khakis, yelling about "Western civilization" while texting their side chick.

Step Five: Burn the Separation Clause Like It's a Library Book About Drag Queens

By now, the wall between church and state is a Pinterest DIY project, duct-taped together by moderates while theocrats roll in with bulldozers and Supreme Court confirmations.

- *Roe v. Wade?* Gone.
- *Prayer in public schools?* Back.
- *Ten Commandments in courthouses?* Sure, why not—ignore the adultery one.

And the GOP? They didn't just accept it. They rebranded as the "Party of God"—as long as your god hates critical race theory, has strong opinions on gas stoves, and owns stock in Hobby Lobby.

Politics in Their Pockets

The most incredible political hustle since Watergate—except this time, Jesus is the mascot, and the Constitution's in the shredder.

The Holy Trinity of Political Apostles: Reagan, Bush, and Trump

- **Ronald Reagan (1981–1989): The Founding Father of Faith-Flavored Politics:** Reagan didn't just dog-whistle. He blasted *"God Bless America"* through a megaphone while the Moral Majority moved into the White House guest room. He opened the door to Christian nationalism with a wink, a prayer, and a policy platform that said: "Let's shrink the government—unless it's monitoring uteruses or banning books."

The Religious Right never left. They just updated their branding.

- **George W. Bush (2001–2009): Faith-Based Funding and Faith-Based Fog:** Bush launched "faith-based initiatives," which is code for: *"Let's give tax dollars to churches, not social programs."* He transformed religious beliefs into a federal policy framework. Abstinence-only sex ed? Check. Federal dollars to groups that don't hire LGBTQ+ people? Check. Prayer-in-schools nostalgia and post-9/11 moral panic? Double check. *Jesus was his co-pilot—and apparently, his Secretary of Education.*

- **Donald J. Trump (2017–2021, 2025–??): The Golden Calf with a Bible Prophecy:** Trump didn't believe in the Bible—he *branded* it. He stood in front of a church holding it upside down like a magic relic while the National Guard tear-gassed peaceful protesters. He created the White House Faith Office, led by televangelist Paula White, who once summoned angels from Africa on C-SPAN, much like it was in *The Avengers: Exodus Edition.* Trump didn't follow scripture. He licensed it for merch.

Politicians Currently on Heaven's Payroll

- **Mike Johnson—Speaker of the Theocracy:** Thinks the Constitution is fine, but it's missing a little *Deuteronomy.* Believes the government should be run like a Bible study with a dress code.

- **Marjorie Taylor Greene—Apostle of the Algorithm:** Preaches "Christian Nationalism" while live-streaming conspiracy theory devotionals from her CrossFit bunker. Jesus didn't weep—he unsubscribed.

- **Lauren Boebert—Open Carry Evangelism:** Wants a country where churches make the laws, guns make the rules, and separation of church and state is a liberal myth created by Satan and the ACLU.

- **Ron DeSantis—Curriculum for Christ:** Rewrote Florida's school standards so that "slavery was job training" and "Jesus signed the Constitution." Turning public schools into Sunday School with standardized tests.

- **JD Vance—Veep of the New Testament:** Gives speeches like the apostle Paul wrote them and votes like Pharaoh ordered them. Presents "masculinity" as a spiritual crisis and diversity as a biblical plague.
- **Doug Mastriano—Faith-Based Fascism in a Fleece Vest:** Once said *"separation of church and state is a myth"*—and unfortunately, he meant it.

How to Buy a Law in 3 Easy Prayers

1. Create a Culture War Panic (Trans kids! CRT! Starbucks cups!)
2. Quote a Bible verse out of context (preferably from Leviticus or Paul's Greatest Hits)
3. Fundraise like hell (God loves a cheerful giver, especially one who donates before midnight for triple-match MAGA points)

Final Benediction: Amen and A-men Are Not the Same

This isn't about faith. This is about power, wrapped in scripture, sold as patriotism, and enforced through policy. It is strategic, from the Federalists to the Moral Majority and Christian right, forming the Christian national political ideology. These are the players in today's culture and political crisis. There is no separation of church and state as mandated in the Constitution; however, there is disagreement.

If your religion needs to control public education, criminalize healthcare, and rig elections to feel "respected," It's not a religion—it's a regime. When God gets co-opted by your campaign, the devil cashes the checks.

Faith-Based Legislation: When Morality Becomes Law

It started with Hobby Lobby, the arts-and-crafts chain that decided its corporate conscience couldn't handle funding women's contraception.

Forget *Roe*. We're going upstream now—to the source of it all: the crusade to resurrect a "God-fearing America," one faith-based bill at a time.

It's not just legislation—it's liturgy. We're no longer debating policy; we're deciphering scripture in the congressional record like it's Leviticus with lobbyists. Because what could go wrong when your moral compass is set by televangelists, megachurch CEOs, and men who think "separation of church and state" is a myth?

America didn't stumble into Christian nationalism—it scheduled it. The modern faith-based legislative movement isn't a grassroots revival. It's a polished rebrand of dominionism—the belief that Christians (read: the "right" Christians) should control all institutions of society. Why vote with policy when you can vote with prophecy? Evangelical leaders like James Dobson and Ralph Reed didn't just want "prayer back in schools"—they wanted God back in the tax code, the Pentagon, and your uterus. Their blueprint wasn't just the Bible—it was a voter registration form with a fish sticker on it.[330]

Hobby Lobby Was Just the Crafty Beginning. In *Burwell v. Hobby Lobby* (2014), the Supreme Court ruled that a corporation can hold religious beliefs. That's right—your employer's moral compass now dictates your medical coverage. Because nothing says religious freedom like your boss's beliefs standing between you and your birth control.[331] That decision opened the door for future legislation where faith doesn't just influence law—it steamrolls it. If the CEO talks to God, you'd better hope God likes generic IUDs.

God, Guns, and Governance: The Legislative Trifecta

Today's Christian right doesn't just want to protect their religious liberty—they want to legislate yours. Banning drag shows? That's not bigotry—it's "biblical masculinity." Erasing ethnic studies? That's not censorship—it's "God's design." Denying rights to LGBTQ+ people? Just enforcing "biblical values," folks.[332]

Their favorite phrases include:
- "Parental rights" (Translation: Our version of history or none at all.)
- "Religious liberty" (Translation: The freedom to force you to follow our religion.)
- "Traditional values" (Translation: 1950s cosplay, minus unions and polio vaccines.)

Jesus Didn't Run for Office—But His Fans Did

Since the 1980s, the church has also served as a campaign headquarters. Pastors traded in baptism for ballots, morality for mailers. Voting booths became the new confessionals. Today, you can't swing a rosary in certain states without hitting a school board meeting turned sermon. This wasn't a cultural revival. It was a politically hostile takeover. As researchers Whitehead and Perry note that[333] Christian nationalism isn't just about belief—it's about power. It's a worldview that sees America not just as a nation, but as a chosen people, so selected that God needs them to ban AP African American studies.

Back to the Golden Christian Path

Yes—faith is now policymaking's style. America is being dressed up in a whitewashed, cross-stitched fantasy where every problem can be fixed with scripture, unless it involves hunger, homelessness, healthcare, or guns. Because make no mistake: this isn't about God. It's about governance disguised as divine mandate. And it's working. They're not just winning elections—they're winning narratives. They've replaced democracy with doctrine and called it justice.

Faith-Based Indoctrination: How Religious Education Became a Voter Assembly Line

Forget Sunday sermons. The real pulpit now comes with a homeschool co-op sign-up sheet and a textbook where Thomas Jefferson moonlights as a youth pastor. Starting in the 1970s, just as public schools were being forced to desegregate, Christian conservatives didn't just build private schools and homeschool networks for "values-based education." They built voter pipelines.

Welcome to the Curriculum Crusade

Textbooks from Abeka and Bob Jones University Press didn't just teach math—they taught theology disguised as civics. You didn't learn how a bill becomes a law; you learned how "God's law" trumps man's law.

- The Founding Fathers? Christian prophets.

- The Civil War? Just a states' rights squabble.
- Church and state? Not supposed to be separate—read the footnotes.
- Dinosaurs? Definitely on the Ark.

This was no accident. It was the blueprint. Indoctrinate early, legislate later. The rise of the Home School Legal Defense Association (HSLDA) and Christian school accrediting bodies didn't just shape young minds—they built loyal voting blocs. These students were taught:

- Abortion is murder.
- America is a Christian nation.
- The government should reflect "biblical values."
- Voting for Democrats is choosing hell.

By the time these kids hit voting age, they weren't just conservative—they were ideologically armored. And it worked. As political historian Darren Dochuk notes, Christian conservatives didn't abandon education—they "appropriated it as a means of establishing cultural control."[334] The Religious Right wasn't just responding to cultural change. They were preloading the software for a future where democracy bends toward theocracy.

And let's not forget what came next: textbook review boards in red states like Texas, where Christian conservatives shaped national curricula by controlling what publishers could sell. If you've ever wondered how textbooks still gloss over slavery or call Indigenous genocide a "westward expansion," thank your local Christian education board member with a God Bless America lapel pin and zero understanding of the Enlightenment.

Faith-Based Legislation: The Final Exam

Today's faith-fueled laws are **the final product** of this educational assembly line:

- Bans on books? Spawned by Christian curricula that never allowed them in the first place.
- Attacks on LGBTQ+ rights? Preached in the chapel, now passed in the statehouses.
- Reproductive bans? First covered in the 9th-grade "God's Design for Life" class, now enforced by the US Supreme Court.

This isn't about morality. It's about monopoly over thought, over legislation, over cultural memory. They didn't just change what kids learned. They changed what adults vote for.

Roe v. Wade: The Holy Grail of the Hissy Fit

Roe v. Wade didn't start the culture war; it *scripted* it. Before 1973, white evangelicals were politically quiet, tucked into their sanctified cul-de-sacs, more worried about casserole swaps than constitutional law. Their biggest battle was deciding whether to put raisins in the potato salad. But then the 1960s showed up with civil rights, feminism, and queer folks who refused to stay punchlines—and suddenly, the white conservative male found himself slipping out of the spotlight. Cue panic. Cue Bible. Cue *Roe*.

Roe didn't threaten their theology. **It threatened their throne.** The Religious Right didn't descend from heaven in righteous outrage over embryos—they rose from the ashes of desegregation, second-wave feminism, and Stonewall, gasping for relevance like a patriarch choking on progress. *Roe* **became their moral Trojan horse.** It wasn't about "babies"—it was about power dressed in pampers.

"Think of the Children!" (Unless They're Alive and Needing Help)

If this were truly about "life," we'd see evangelicals fighting for maternal health care, universal pre-K, or *anything* that supports a child after birth. But nope. That's "socialism." Once the baby exits the womb, it becomes someone else's problem—preferably a poor woman of color who's now condemned for being a single mom. **Because the unborn are perfect: silent, dependent, and incapable of asking for healthcare or equal pay.**

Roe Wasn't the Beginning of Morality.
It Was the End of Their Monopoly.

Roe scared the hell out of them—not because it was evil, but because it implied *women* could make decisions without divine or legislative supervision. And if women could say no to motherhood, they might also say:

- "No, I won't marry that guy just because I'm pregnant."
- "No, I don't want to go to your church."
- "No, I'm not here to serve as your barefoot moral compass in a ging-

ham apron."

That "no" was the sound of a collapsing patriarchy. And they called it murder.

Enter: The Moral Meltdown, Midterm Edition

Suddenly, every Sunday sermon was a campaign ad. Every fetus had a name and a voter registration. And every balding man in a flag pin became a "values warrior" railing against *Roe* while quietly defunding public schools, healthcare, and lunch programs.

By the 1980s, abortion had gone from medical procedure to messianic plotline. It was never about the womb—it was about **re-wombing** America with a fantasy where white men were central, women were vessels, and minorities stayed inspirational footnotes. *Roe* didn't erode morality. It exposed the brittle masculinity hiding behind morality's mask.

Conservative Men and the Case of the Vanishing Spotlight

As the rights of others expanded, their ego-contracted world shrank. They weren't losing power—they were just being asked to **share** it. And that felt like persecution. Their idea of oppression? *Other people exist with autonomy.* *Roe* became the pressure valve for their cultural anxiety—a way to focus rage without ever addressing race, gender, or economic inequality. "We're mad the world doesn't revolve around us anymore" doesn't look great on a bumper sticker. "**Save the babies**," however? It plays in Peoria.

Overturning Roe... and Still Whining

And then, nearly 50 years later, they got what they wanted. *Roe* was overturned. Victory dance? Nope. They're still pissed. Because guess what—it was never about *Roe*. It was about controlling women, framing progress as moral decay, and finding a forever war to keep the donor base panicked and the pulpit powerful.

Roe's reversal wasn't a return to constitutional purity. It was a ceremonial cleansing of secularism. The fall of *Roe* wasn't the end goal—it was a starting pistol. Now the same justices (and their political handlers) are openly eyeing contraception access, LGBTQ+ marriage, and yes—even interracial

marriage, with a few justices (*ahem, Clarence Thomas—a Black man married to a white woman*) pretending *Loving v. Virginia* never happened.[335] This is not a movement about being pro-life. It is, and always has been, pro-control. And the blueprint wasn't written in legal textbooks. It was written in sermons, scrawled in evangelical manifestos, and passed around church basements disguised as voter guides.

They've won the battle, but their war against equality is ongoing. Because the moment women, queer people, or anyone outside their Norman Rockwell fever dream gets autonomy, the patriarchy has to work harder. And that is exhausting. Yet we are still watching the holy hissy fit unfold, dressed in righteousness, armed with bad science, and demanding applause for "saving lives" while actively making millions of them harder.

The truth? *Roe* **didn't kill America's soul. It threatened to give it one.**

When Church Becomes State: Faith Rising in American Law and Policy, 2023-2025[336]

Beyond the overturning of *Roe v. Wade*, several faith-based legislative measures have been enacted up to 2025, reflecting the growing influence of religious ideologies in American law and policy. Here are notable examples:

Mandatory Display of the Ten Commandments in Public Schools

- **Louisiana**: House Bill 71, signed into law in June 2024, required all public school classrooms to display the Ten Commandments. However, in November 2024, a federal judge ruled the law unconstitutional, citing coercion concerns.
- **Texas**: Senate Bill 10, passed in May 2025, mandates the display of the Ten Commandments in public school classrooms. The bill awaits the governor's signature and is expected to face legal challenges.

Integration of Religious Instruction into Public Education

- **Indiana**: Legislation passed in 2024 requires public schools to accommodate off-site Bible instruction during school hours, effectively integrating religious education into the public school system.
- **Ohio**: House Bill 8, enacted in January 2025, mandates that schools allow students to attend religious instruction during school hours and requires parental notification regarding students' gender identity and sexuality education, reflecting a blend of spiritual and parental rights agendas.

Employment of Chaplains in Public Schools

- **Texas**: In 2023, Texas passed a law permitting public schools to employ chaplains, blurring the lines between church and state in educational settings.

- **Florida and Louisiana:** Following Texas's lead, both states enacted similar laws in 2024, allowing chaplains to serve in public schools, raising concerns about religious neutrality in education.

Religious Exemptions in Marriage Ceremonies

- **Tennessee:** House Bill 878, signed into law in 2024, allows individuals to refuse to solemnize marriages based on religious or conscience-based objections, potentially enabling discrimination against same-sex and interracial couples.

Faith-Based Initiatives in Housing

- **California:** The Affordable Housing on Faith and Higher Education Lands Act (Senate Bill 4), enacted in 2023, streamlines the process for faith-based institutions to build affordable housing on their properties, reflecting a faith-driven approach to addressing housing shortages.

These legislative actions demonstrate the growing influence of religious perspectives in shaping state policies across various sectors, including education, civil rights, and housing. While proponents argue these laws protect religious freedoms and moral values, critics contend they challenge the constitutional principle of separation of church and state.

Hissy Fits from the Pew:
The Manufactured Persecution Complex

Somehow, despite holding most of the pulpits, political offices, judicial seats, broadcasting networks, billion-dollar megachurches, and ownership of nearly every Duck Dynasty box set, white Christian men in America believe they are under siege.

Yes, it's under siege. This is the theological equivalent of the CEO of ExxonMobil showing up to a protest in a "STOP OIL SHAMING" T-shirt.

Christian Men as Victims in the Majority

It's hard being a Christian man in America these days. The sitcom dads aren't respected. Pronouns are confusing. And someone at work said,

"Happy Holidays" instead of "Merry Christmas." Suddenly, a demographic that has led nearly every institution in American life is now curled in the fetal position, convinced they're being silenced—on televised panel shows, in best-selling books, and during multi-million-dollar church conferences dedicated entirely to how they're "not allowed to speak anymore."

This isn't persecution. It is a performance art piece featuring a fog machine. As sociologist Andrew Whitehead explains, Christian nationalists "interpret the declining dominance of their values not as a natural result of cultural pluralism, but as **a direct attack** on their way of life."[337] Of course, no persecution fantasy is complete without a full-blown masculinity meltdown. White Christian men aren't just spiritually attacked—they're in a holy war for their manhood. Conservative preachers now spend more time railing against soy milk and yoga pants than they do discussing actual scripture. Evangelical conferences might as well feature seminars like *"Biblical Manhood in an Age of Wokeness"* and *"Taking Back the Grill from Feminist Influence."*

Books like John Eldredge's *Wild at Heart* urge Christian men to channel their inner warrior, because Jesus didn't come to save your soul—he came to teach you how to bench-press your feelings. As scholar Kristin Kobes Du Mez writes, this toxic fusion of evangelicalism and militarized masculinity has created a "mythic, rugged, gun-toting savior figure" that reflects cultural nostalgia more than biblical truth.[338]

Jesus: Now With a Tactical Vest and a 401(k)

The Jesus of the persecution complex isn't the barefoot radical who healed lepers and hung out with sex workers. No, no. This version of Jesus carries an AR-15, invests in cryptocurrency, and votes straight-ticket Republican. He's a gun-toting, free-market nationalist who believes in tax cuts for megachurches and border walls so high even the Rapture can't scale them. This isn't Christianity—it's Jesus LARPing as a militia commander, developed in focus groups and weaponized in voter outreach.

The persecution complex isn't about oppression. It's about entitlement dressed up as victimhood. It's the emotional oxygen of Christian Nationalism—a way for white men to cast themselves as heroes in a spiritual war they invented. Because if you can't dominate, at least you can cry about being dominated. Loudly. On cable. With flags.

The Ultimate Hissy Fit: Tyranny by Equality

This is the hissy fit to end all hissy fits: the scream of "tyranny" at the mere sound of equity.

- Women asking for autonomy? Tyranny.
- Black people protesting systemic racism? Marxism.
- Trans people existing in public? The downfall of civilization.

The Christian right isn't protesting oppression. They're protesting the inconvenience. They want a version of America where they are always the protagonist, and any narrative that doesn't center them is considered hostile. As Stewart notes, this worldview "cloaks political ambitions in the language of righteousness," allowing the Religious Right to present themselves as victims while waging aggressive campaigns against pluralism.[339]

Here's the bad news: when one group's religious belief becomes law, everyone else's rights become optional. In a pluralistic democracy, belief should inspire, not govern. But Christian Nationalism doesn't want a seat at the table—it wants to own the table, bless it, and set a place only for itself.

What happens when this ideology wins?
- Women's rights regress.
- LGBTQ+ rights disappear.
- Non-Christian faiths are treated like threats.
- Democracy becomes a theocracy with better marketing.

And worst of all? It won't be called authoritarianism. It will be called "religious freedom." And never mind what will be—this is happening right now. And if you think this shift in terminology is just a matter of rhetoric, think again. Behind this twisted narrative lies a well-oiled machine designed to manipulate the public and reshape policy from the inside out. Enter the Heritage Foundation—where ideas aren't merely debated, they're crafted and weaponized.

CHAPTER 13

Heritage or Hysteria?
The Think Tank That
Re-Engineered the Hissy Fit

Once upon a think tank, in the beige heart of
Washington, DC, a group of well-funded conservatives
decided that if they just couldn't win hearts, they'd win
headlines—and if they couldn't win headlines, they'd
simply write the damn policy themselves.

The Heritage Foundation was born in 1973, where lobbyists got PhDs in gaslighting and learned to wrap deregulation in 12-point Times New Roman. Heritage wasn't built to *research*. It was built to reframe—and then to rewire America with one goal in mind: maintain white, male, Christian dominance while sounding like a college syllabus. And it worked. With just enough academic cologne to pass as serious scholarship, Heritage became the ideological wet bar at every Republican cocktail party from Reagan to Trump.

From Footnotes to Fiefdoms—Heritage figured out early that facts are flexible when you flood the zone with buzzwords like *"liberty," "free enterprise,"* and *"family values."* This wasn't research. They weren't asking "What's best for America?" They asked, "What's best for our donors—and how do we make it sound like Jesus approved?"

By the 1980s, the Heritage Foundation had slipped its fingers into every available government pie. Their 1981 *Mandate for Leadership* was Reagan's cheat sheet for gutting the government and handing the remains to the private sector with a handshake and a wink.[340a] Spoiler: Reagan used two-thirds of it as a takeout menu for dismantling social programs.[341]

The Think Tank That Thinks Feelings Are Facts

Over time, Heritage evolved from a "policy advisor" to a propaganda production house, complete with press releases masquerading as research papers and "fellows" who spent more time on Fox News than in any peer-reviewed publication. Their greatest skill? Turning gut-level resentment into government strategy. And when they weren't busy trying to kill the Environmental Protection Agency or dismantle public education, they were laying the intellectual groundwork for Project 2025—the MAGA manifesto for autocracy with footnotes.

As sociologist Jason Stahl put it, think tanks like Heritage aren't just institutions of knowledge. They're "**war rooms of ideas**"—churning out ready-made ideology for politicians too lazy to think for themselves.[342]

It's Not About Heritage. It's About Hegemony—with a Glossary

Heritage doesn't preserve American values. It preserves privilege, with just enough page numbers to sound respectable. Think of it as the IKEA of right-wing policy: flat-packed, heavily footnoted, and designed to collapse public institutions while blaming poor assembly on liberals.

Heritage isn't about "freedom." It's about freedom for a particular demographic—straight, Christian men who believe Jesus wrote the Constitution and that every public program is just communism in a friendlier font.

Buckle up. Because in this chapter, we're not just unpacking Heritage's legacy—we're decoding how an allegedly academic institution became the intellectual front for America's most oversized hissy fits.

The Unholy Merger: When Christian Nationalism Met the Heritage Foundation and Called It "Patriotism"

This isn't about faith—it's about control. The Heritage Foundation once advocated for a small government. Now it champions a god-sized one, as long as it's the right God.

The Heritage Foundation isn't just your run-of-the-mill conservative think tank—polishing tax cut proposals, dusting off Reagan quotes, and pumping out white papers like it was printing season in Ayn Rand's basement. But somewhere between defending "family values" and dismantling the welfare state, Heritage found a new soulmate: Christian Nationalism.

It wasn't a shotgun wedding—it was a long courtship of shared grievances. Both wanted a return to "traditional values," which is Beltway-speak for the 1950s, minus the unions and with extra Jesus. Both saw diversity, feminism, and secularism not as signs of progress, but as cosmic threats to America's divine manifest destiny. And both understood that nothing fires up a base quite like wrapping policy proposals in scripture and fear.

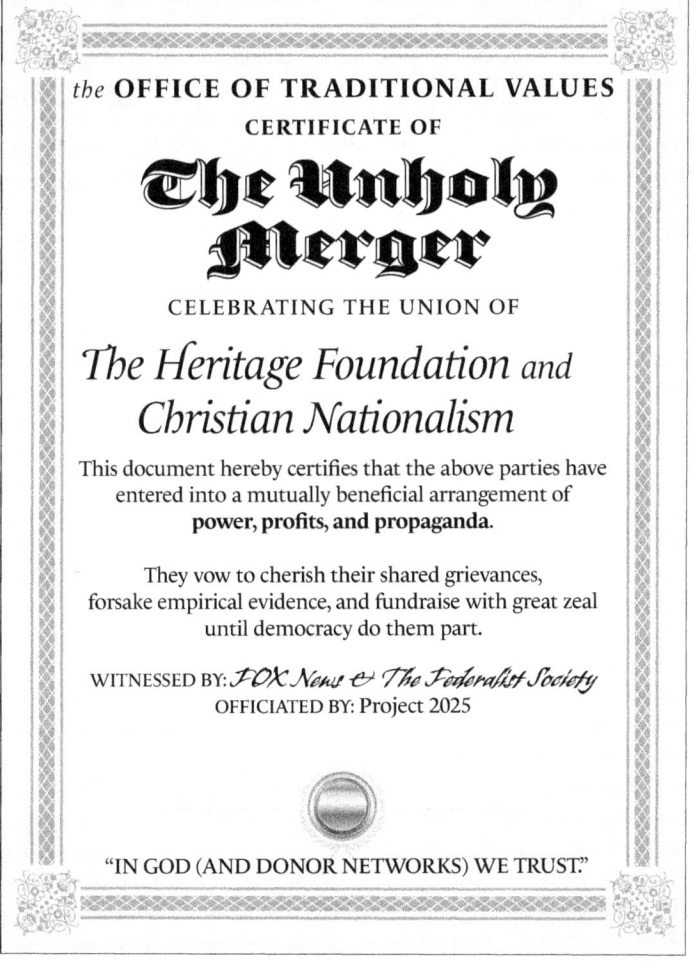

the **OFFICE OF TRADITIONAL VALUES**

CERTIFICATE OF

The Unholy Merger

CELEBRATING THE UNION OF

The Heritage Foundation and Christian Nationalism

This document hereby certifies that the above parties have entered into a mutually beneficial arrangement of **power, profits, and propaganda**.

They vow to cherish their shared grievances, forsake empirical evidence, and fundraise with great zeal until democracy do them part.

WITNESSED BY: *FOX News & The Federalist Society*
OFFICIATED BY: Project 2025

"IN GOD (AND DONOR NETWORKS) WE TRUST."

Where Faith Meets Federalism
(and Then Kicks Down the Church-State Wall)

Christian Nationalism brought the theology—God loves America and hates the Department of Education. The Heritage Foundation brought the infrastructure—policy pipelines, legislative templates, and an uncanny ability to say "founder's intent" with a straight face while pushing faith-based governance in a pluralistic nation. Together, they began crafting a blueprint—not for liberty, but for ideological dominion. From school board takeovers to anti-LGBTQ+ laws, and from book bans to the "Project 2025" roadmap for a complete federal overhaul, the collaboration is less "Render unto Caesar" and more "Make Caesar a pastor."

What They're Building
- A government shaped by biblical literalism and ALEC-style legalese.
- A judicial system stacked with "originalists" who act like they believe Moses and James Madison co-authored the Constitution.
- Education that replaces critical thinking with Christian apologetics and teaches kids that America was born in a manger.

What They're Ignoring
- The First Amendment (but only the "no establishment" part).
- The fact that America is religiously diverse and increasingly unaffiliated.
- The real-world damage when morality becomes mandatory and liberty becomes conditional.

Let's call it what it is: not a revival, but a rerun. The unholy merger of Christian Nationalism and the Heritage Foundation isn't about saving America's soul. It's about selling it.

Heritage's Favorite Myths
(And the Damage They've Done to US Culture)

Because when you can't govern with facts, govern with folklore.

Myth #1: "Government is the Enemy"
Unless, of course, it's controlling uteruses, school curricula, and trans bath-

room access. Heritage's mantra of "small government" is more like "small for you, massive for us." They want less regulation for billionaires but more surveillance for everyone with a uterus, a library card, or a rainbow bumper sticker.

When they say *freedom*, they mean the freedom to:

- Ban books but fund bombs.
- Bulldoze environmental protections but micromanage school bathrooms.
- Cut food stamps while greenlighting tax write-offs for private jets.

It's not about freedom. It's about franchise control. If the government were a Netflix plan, Heritage wants *ultra-premium admin access…* for themselves.

Myth #2: "Meritocracy Works"

Sure, Dick. You got that job because you "earned it"—not because your uncle sits on the board and your resume smells like legacy admission cologne. The Heritage model of meritocracy is a pyramid scheme where **"hard work" is code for privilege**, and *qualifications* are whatever you tweeted at 3 a.m. that made Tucker Carlson nod approvingly.

- Think tanks hand out fellowships to guys who've never read a book with footnotes.
- Data is mined from vibes.
- And "common sense policy" is just what rich people say when they don't want to share.

Meritocracy, in Heritage-speak, means: You get what you deserve—unless you're poor, queer, or smart enough to ask follow-up questions.[343]

Myth #3: "Family Values"

But only if your family looks like a 1950s Coca-Cola ad, goes to the right church, and has never questioned why Little Timmy's school library now has more copies of *Atlas Shrugged* than *To Kill a Mockingbird*.

Heritage's definition of family values includes:

- No same-sex couples.
- No single mothers unless they're fictional and inspirational.
- No public childcare (because the Bible says grandma should do it).

- A flag out front, a firearm inside, and a freezer full of meat pre-blessed by Ronald Reagan's ghost.

Real family values? They're about empathy, inclusion, and resilience—not performative piety and "Don't Say Gay" legislation. But empathy doesn't fit Heritage's model. Fear does, especially when it's dressed up in Sunday clothes and clutching a Chick-fil-A bag.

Cultural Fallout–The Heritage Halo

Heritage doesn't just dabble in politics—it moonlights as the culture war's DJ, spinning hot tracks like *"They're Coming for Your Pronouns"* and *"Ban That Book Before It Makes Kids Empathetic."* This isn't policy—it's performance art for pearl clutches. And guess what? It's working.

Book Bans & Whiteboard Purity Tests

Thanks to Heritage's footnotes-for-fascism playbook, school boards across America now read like Fox News fan fiction:
- Teachers are getting reported for teaching *actual history.*
- Students are banned from saying "gay" unless it's followed by "agenda."
- Books pulled for containing… emotions? Intersectionality? A character with two moms?

"Banned Books Week" is now every week—and it's sponsored by a think tank that's never met a complex idea it couldn't simplify into a moral panic.

Classroom Censorship: Now With Extra Patriotism

What's critical thinking when you can have patriotic obedience? Heritage-backed education reform wants to teach history like it's a church pamphlet:
- Slavery? An unfortunate labor dispute.
- Civil Rights? A mild inconvenience.
- The Holocaust? "Both sides had opinions," said someone, probably Chad.

Education reform, Heritage-style, is less about facts and more about fragile egos wrapped in standardized tests.

The Heritage Lifestyle Brand

Move over, Apple, there's a new cult in town—and it sells:

- Grievance instead of growth,
- Division instead of development, and
- Patriotism in beige, available exclusively at Hobby Lobby.

It's not a think tank. It's a full-blown identity ecosystem. Their ideal citizen is Dick, who watches Fox News, owns five copies of the Constitution (but hasn't read them), and uses "woke" as both an adjective and an expletive.

Cultural Damage: The Receipts

- Empathy? Deemed a gateway drug to socialism.
- Academic freedom? Canceled faster than a drag brunch in Texas.
- Community? Only if it votes red, tithes weekly, and pretends racism ended in 1964.

Heritage has turned policy into a purity test and governance into grievance theater. They don't want to win arguments—they want to change the script, so you forget empathy was an option.

Heritage isn't preserving America's values. It's preserving white nostalgia wrapped in academic drag. When a think tank becomes a hissy fit tank, democracy doesn't get smarter—it gets manipulated. Heritage doesn't write for the people. It writes **to the people,** assuming they won't read past the executive summary.

Building the Ideological Cathedral

Where footnotes become commandments and dogma wears a Brooks Brothers suit.

Once upon a Nixon hangover, conservatives realized that yelling at hippies wasn't translating into actual legislation. Enter: The Heritage Foundation—founded in 1973 by Paul Weyrich, Edwin Feulner, and a handful of political operatives who decided the best way to mainstream extremism was to slap it in a binder and call it research.[344] Think of it as the moment radicalized conservatism stopped screaming at clouds and started publishing white papers.

Heritage's Founding Mission? Deregulate. Discriminate. Dominate.

This wasn't just a think tank—it was a cathedral of white grievance, built on three pillars:

1. Deregulate Everything Except Morality

Heritage wanted it gone if it had a budget, a license, or a social safety net. They called it "small government," but it was more like hostile downsizing of democracy. Healthcare? "Let the market decide." Environmental protection? "Personal responsibility, but for carbon." Education? "Why teach history when you can teach obedience?"

But when it came to your uterus, your bedroom, or your choice of pronouns, suddenly, the free market needed moral guardrails. Freedom for corporations? Absolutely. Freedom for people? Depends. Are you white, male, and Protestant?

2: Discriminate—But Make It Data-Driven

Heritage mastered the art of publishing discrimination in a data-driven manner. They called it "research." We call it regression analysis with a side of bigotry. Want to gut affirmative action? Heritage has a spreadsheet for that. Want to criminalize immigration? Here's a graph that says "safety" but means "xenophobia." Want to eliminate DEI? Here's a 20-page report on how "merit" is being undermined by "woke ideology." This is the PowerPoint of Oppression—bullet points instead of bullhorns.

As Carol Anderson notes, "weaponized respectability is how systemic discrimination becomes policy."[345] Heritage didn't scream slurs. It just funded people who translated them into legislation.

3: Dominate the Narrative

The Heritage Foundation isn't just playing policy chess. They're building a megachurch of market fundamentalism. Every policy paper is a sermon. Every cable news appearance is a revival. Every 500-page report on "restoring American greatness" is a modern gospel for the politically insecure.

Heritage doesn't just advise Congress—it disciplines it with donors, whiteboards, and talking points built to collapse empathy in three TV-ready steps. They're not trying to influence politics. They're trying to own truth itself. This isn't a debate—it's a doctrine. One where "equity" is heresy, "diversity" is blasphemy, and the only sacrament is a flat tax.

Welcome to the Ideological Cathedral

Heritage doesn't do politics—it does pulpit politics. It's the First Church of Capitalism, where the **Ten Commandments are:**

1. THOU SHALT NOT RAISE MINIMUM WAGE.

2. THOU SHALT PRIVATIZE EVERYTHING.

3. THOU SHALT PASS MORALITY LAWS AS ECONOMIC POLICY.

4. THOU SHALT NEVER ADMIT SYSTEMIC RACISM.

5. THOU SHALT QUOTE THE FOUNDING FATHERS—BUT NEVER THE PARTS ABOUT EQUALITY.

6. THOU SHALT FEAR IMMIGRANTS MORE THAN CLIMATE CHANGE.

7. THOU SHALT CLUTCH PEARLS DURING DRAG STORY HOUR.

8. THOU SHALT CANCEL PUBLIC EDUCATION, BUT CALL IT "SCHOOL CHOICE."

9. THOU SHALT DEFUND SOCIAL PROGRAMS, THEN BLAME THE POOR.

10. THOU SHALT ALWAYS SAY "GOD BLESS AMERICA" WHILE DEFUNDING HEALTHCARE.

And to think many of you support this and feel patriotic, yet do not understand its foundation. That, my friends, is what I call the lack of critical thinking. No wonder MAGA got a rerun.

Think Tank or Hissy Fit Tank?

Remember when a think tank meant intellectual rigor, peer-reviewed studies, and perhaps even a footnote that wasn't quoting someone who yelled "Let's go Brandon" at a city council meeting. But not at Heritage. No, this is where academic aspiration meets ideological craziness—and every policy paper reads like it was edited by a middle schooler with a grudge and a Glenn Beck bobblehead.

If you've ever thought, "I wish someone would turn my uncle's Facebook rant into federal policy," Heritage has you covered. Their white papers are less "research" and more reheated Reaganomics with a Bible verse garnish.

- Critical race theory? Labeled a "Marxist weapon."
- DEI initiatives? Packaged as "reverse racism."
- Trans rights? Framed as an "existential threat to Western civilization," which is Heritage code for "makes me uncomfortable in the locker room."

And somehow, every paper still manages to quote the Founding Fathers—because nothing says "rigorous scholarship" like misreading Thomas Jefferson while ignoring the fact that he plagiarized liberty from John Locke and oppression from his plantation bookkeeping.

Fear ≠ Facts: How Heritage Built the Anxiety Economy

Heritage doesn't do *data-driven policy*. It does vibe-driven panic. Their entire model thrives on:

- Weaponizing white grievance.
- Panic-selling patriotism.
- Inventing new forms of "wokeness" to be terrified of. (See: wokeness in banks, bathrooms, and brunch menus.)

Remember when communism was the Right's boogeyman? Heritage just swapped out the USSR for sociology professors and drag queens. And they didn't miss a beat. Every footnote is now a passive-aggressive assault on the 21st century. As political scientist Corey Robin points out, modern conservatism often functions as "a defense of hierarchy in the face of egalitarian movements"—and Heritage dressed that up in think tank drag.[346]

Research, But Make It Regression

To call Heritage's policy pipeline "research" is like calling a colander "watertight." Their work is carefully curated to confirm a worldview, not challenge it. Peer-reviewed? Please. Their peers are the same folks who believe the "War on Christmas" is a real military campaign. And their "studies"? They typically start with the conclusion ("Woke bad") and then reverse-engineer the facts, cherry-picking data as if it were a sale at Hobby Lobby.

Want to ban drag shows? There's a Heritage paper for that. Want to eliminate public schools? Yup, got a policy brief. Want to reinstate prayer in schools but not science? Already on a bumper sticker.

Let me be crystal clear! Heritage isn't producing research. They're **manufacturing ammunition**—pre-loaded talking points for media personalities, politicians, and your cousin Chad at Thanksgiving. It's not about accuracy. It's about *aesthetics*—the look of scholarship without the burden of truth. This isn't a think tank. It's a **hissy fit tank**—and it's rolling straight through every institution that still believes facts matter more than feelings wrapped in flags.

By the early 2000s, the Heritage Foundation had already established itself as the conservative movement's policy factory, producing a steady stream of reports, talking points, and legislative blueprints aimed at rolling back federal authority and reasserting "traditional" social norms. But ideas on paper only go so far without a political vehicle. Enter the Tea Party. What Heritage drafted in think-tank language, the Tea Party shouted through megaphones. The movement translated Heritage's polished policy prescriptions into populist anger, packaging elite strategy as grassroots rebellion. In this way, the Tea Party wasn't a spontaneous uprising—it was the street-level amplification of Heritage's long-standing conservative agenda.

The Tea Party: Where Faux Grassroots Meet Full-Blown Cultural Hissy Fit

Let's not romanticize it—the Tea Party wasn't a movement. It was a mood swing in khakis and a tricorn hat. Born in 2009 like a fiscal fever dream, it branded itself as a righteous rebellion against taxes and tyranny. But underneath the Gadsden flags and powdered wigs? It was a corporate-funded hissy fit, co-sponsored by the Heritage Foundation and white nostalgia.

They called it "grassroots." Translation: **Fox News handed out the fertilizer.**

From "Taxed Enough Already" to "Get Off My Lawn," the Tea Party didn't rise up because of budget spreadsheets. It rose because America was changing, and some folks weren't having it. Yes, they chanted about government overreach, but what they meant was:

- "Who let that Black guy in the White House?"
- "Why is my town suddenly bilingual?"
- "Where the hell did my incandescent bulbs go?"

This was about **cultural fragility as constitutional cosplay.** They weren't storming Capitol Hill with economic theory. They were rage-posting under Thomas Jefferson quotes while blaming Obama for everything from healthcare to hurricanes.

The Real Tea? It Was Identity Politics in Founding Father Drag

Beneath the anti-tax slogans was a full-blown **existential crisis:** "If America includes everyone, what's left that feels like mine?" The Tea Party sold a fantasy of a purer, simpler America—a place where women were silent, minorities were invisible, and the government was only good for protecting your lawn, your guns, and your 401(k). **It was nostalgia weaponized.** A *"Make America 1953 Again" movement, before the MAGA movement,* had branding consultants. And let's not forget the irony: They shouted about "tyranny" while defending Wall Street, opposing healthcare, and hoarding gold bars in their basements.

Electoral Impact: Lighting the Fuse for the Dumpster Fire

The 2010 midterms? **Tea Party season at the ballot box.** They didn't just elect politicians—they installed **ideological arsonists** who came to burn down compromise, torch bipartisanship, and superglue the Overton window to the far right.

Enter the era of:

- Government shutdowns as sport,
- "RINOs" hunted like deer, and
- Ted Cruz is treated like a thought leader.

This wasn't reform. It was a hostile takeover of the Republican Party by its most performative wing. The Tea Party opened the door—and Trump barreled through it like the Kool-Aid Man in a red tie. Trump didn't invent this chaos. He just monetized the hissy fit the Tea Party threw in 2009 and never cleaned up.

Legacy: The Shitshow They Left Behind

The movement may have fizzled, but the damage stuck:

- The GOP now eats its own if they say "govern."
- Cultural conservatism isn't a policy—it's a lifestyle brand.
- And "outsider" politics now means **"unqualified but angry."**

The Tea Party was never about better government. It was about a louder government, where yelling "liberty!" counts as legislation and compromise is considered heresy. Today's culture wars? Tea Party 2.0, just with better lighting and worse facts.

If you're wondering how we got from a stimulus bill protest to a half-naked man in a buffalo hat storming the Capitol, you can thank the folks who thought yelling "taxed enough already" was the same as a political platform.

The Tea Party & The Heritage Foundation: America's Tag-Team Champions of Regression

In this corner: powdered wigs, pocket Constitutions, and unverified Facebook memes! And in the other, tax-deductible think tank wizards quietly rewrite the rules while no one's looking. Together, they form the most dysfunctional duo in American politics: the Tea Party and the Heritage Foundation.

The Rant That Launched a Thousand Screeds

It all began with a CNBC meltdown. Rick Santelli, channeling pure espresso-fueled rage, unleashed a diatribe against government bailouts in 2009. The result? A so-called grassroots revolution...brought to you by Fox News, billionaires, and at least one guy dressed like George Washington holding a sign that read, *"Keep the government out of my Medicare!"*

"Taxed Enough Already!" they yelled, while cashing Social Security checks, using public roads, and getting medical care through the VA.

The Tea Party was never just about taxes. It was reactionary cosplay against progress, especially if that progress came in the form of a Black president, affordable healthcare, or updated AP history standards.

Enter the Heritage Foundation: Where Regression Gets a PowerPoint Deck

Every street protest needs its policy brain—and that's where the Heritage Foundation comes in. While the Tea Party shouted in tricorn hats outside town halls, Heritage was inside air-conditioned offices crafting legislation to match the hysteria.

> Tea Party: *"We want our country back!"*
> Heritage: *"Here's a 52-page white paper on dismantling public education. You're welcome."*

Populist Rage Meets Ivy League Smugness

This unholy alliance worked like a charm:

- Tea Party provides volume
- Heritage provides veneer
- Together, they mainstream policy proposals like:
    - Cutting Medicaid (because of "freedom")
    - Blocking climate action (because "Jesus")
    - Redefining religious liberty to mean "firing gay people legally"

The Tea Party yelled "liberty!" Heritage translated it into model legislation. One screamed. The other schemed. And the result? A Republican Party that now treats *compromise* like a hate crime.

The Patriot Act of Rebranding Regression

Both groups love to drape themselves in "American values." But look closer, and it's not so much a celebration of liberty as it is a campaign to roll back the 20th century—one policy paper and red-state law at a time. They didn't just want small government. They wanted **selective government**:

- Big enough to police uteruses,
- Small enough to dodge taxes, and
- Just quiet enough to avoid regulating corporations, polluters, or AR-15s.

Legacy: The Birthplace of the Backlash Machine

This duo didn't just shape the modern GOP—they **hardwired it for permanent culture war.**

Trump didn't emerge from nowhere. He was the political love child of Tea Party rage and Heritage's ideological IVF. Everything that seemed "unthinkable" a decade ago? These two made it a policy.

They shouted "freedom" while dismantling democratic norms.
They cried "patriotism" while redefining citizenship as a loyalty test.

And they called it all *American exceptionalism*—even as the rest of the world face-palmed.

Indeed, the Tea Party has lost its brand identity. But its base-level emotions—rage, fear, and denial—now fuel an entire wing of American politics. And Heritage? Still quietly rolling out white papers like policy horcruxes, waiting to be activated by the next red wave. This wasn't grassroots. It was astroturf with a leather-bound Constitution and a six-figure lobbying budget.

And the lawn? Burned. Salted. And wrapped in a Don't Tread on Me flag. All creating the foundation of Project 2025.

Project 2025: Because Nothing Says "Freedom" Like a Federal Power Grab Written by People Who Flunked Civics

Project 2025 is a theocratic fever dream cooked up by think tank zealots who took one look at democracy and said, "Hard pass."

Brought to you by the Heritage Foundation—you know, the same crowd that helped birth the modern conservative rage machine—this 900-page political manifesto is less a blueprint and more a revenge fantasy for every time someone used the word "equity" in a government memo. This isn't policy. It's fan fiction for Christian nationalism with footnotes.

Who Wrote This Shit? Seriously.

The Heritage Foundation—aka the policy arm of the Republican Dark Arts Club. They've assembled a hit list of every program, agency, and protection that doesn't explicitly benefit rich, straight men. The contributors include: anti-abortion extremists, anti-environmental lobbyists, education "reformers" who think the story of Rosa Parks is critical race theory, and a rotating cast of right-wing ideologues who still call LGBTQ+ people a "lifestyle." Think of it as the Avengers—but for Christian dominions and billionaire tax cheats.

What's In It?

- **Fire the Deep State:** Dismantle the civil service and replace experts with political loyalists. Because who needs decades of experience when you've got a Truth Social account and strong opinions about gas stoves?
- **End Independent Agencies:** The Environmental Protection Agency, Federal Trade Commission, Department of Justice—get in line or get lost. Nothing screams "small government" like consolidating executive power, as if it were a banana republic clearance sale.
- **Inject "Christian Values" into Government:** Translation: turn the US into a sermon with nukes. Goodbye, separation of church and state. Hello, Department of Jesus and the Domestic Agenda.
- **Roll Back Reproductive Rights, LGBTQ+ Protections, and Civil Rights:** Because the 1950s weren't a warning—they were the goal. We are going back to the "Golden Age," but with a *Mad Men* of 2007 spin.

Why It Exists: The MAGA Wet Dream Needs a Playbook

Trump's world can't govern. They improvise rage and fundraise off chaos.

Heritage decided to write them a how-to manual because even authoritarians need a syllabus. Project 2025 is the spiritual sequel to the Tea Party hissy fit and the Handmaid's Tale: The Bureaucracy Edition prequel. It's not just about policy. It's about purging the federal government of anyone who's read a book since 2003.

Why the Fuck Don't We Need It

Because America doesn't need a **hostile takeover disguised as patriotism.** We don't need:

- Political loyalty tests for public servants,
- Theocratic governance,
- Culture war legislation baked into federal agencies, or
- Some think tank intern from Liberty University deciding climate change is "just a phase."

We Need Functioning Institutions. Not Fascism In Powerpoint.

Project 2025 answers no sane person's question: *"What if we gave total control to the most paranoid, least qualified, and loudest group in the room?"* Project 2025 isn't policy—it's panic in a binder. A last-ditch effort by a movement that knows it's shrinking, aging, and getting louder as it slips into irrelevance. You don't save a country by purging its thinkers and plastering the Ten Commandments on every copier machine. You don't strengthen freedom by scripting tyranny in advance.

You burn Project 2025—metaphorically, politically, culturally—and you don't let the most insecure people in America decide what "liberty" means. Because if we let this happen, Dick becomes Secretary of Education, and our grandkids will be learning that dinosaurs died from wokeness.

The Truth of Project 2025 in a Nutshell

- **Step 1:** Fire everyone who disagrees with you.
- **Step 2:** Replace them with loyalists in flag pins.
- **Step 3:** Call it "saving America."

Heritage claims it's a plan to "restore" the executive branch. It's a blueprint for replacing expertise with ideological bullshit.

Enter: Schedule F—"Fire the Experts, Hire the Fan Club"

Conceived initially during the Trump administration, Schedule F is back on the Heritage dream board, much like a vision board for anti-intellectualism. It reclassifies up to **50,000 federal employees as "at-will,"** meaning they can be canned faster than a drag queen at a school board meeting.[347]

Translation:

- ***Deep State*** = Civil servants who passed 8th grade science.
- ***Drain the Swamp*** = Fire librarians, EPA nerds, and anyone who says "equity" without gagging.

Schedule F isn't for reform. It's revenge—served cold, with a side of nepotism and talking points from Truth Social.

Targeting DEI, Climate Policy, and Public Education (aka The Holy Trinity of Conservative Rage)

If it makes white men feel slightly less centered, Project 2025 wants it gone:

- DEI Programs? *A Marxist plot.* Diversity is framed as a threat to "merit," and merit, of course, is defined by how many times someone can say "founding fathers" before breaking into a light sweat.
- Climate Policy? *A leftist hoax.* Fossil fuel interests are reinstated as national heroes. Because nothing says "freedom" like heatstroke and $2 gas.
- Public Education? *Rebranded as indoctrination.* Teachers who say "gender" are threats. Books that mention racism get banned. Students are re-educated with a curriculum called "American Greatness: The Unabridged Fantasy Edition."

This isn't just policy rollback—it's a culture purge. Project 2025 doesn't just want to run the government. It wants to turn it into an exorcism, casting out every ounce of nuance, science, and empathy.

Psychological Warfare as Policy

Project 2025 isn't conservative reform. It's emotional regulation by legislation. The underlying message? "If your identity, profession, or opinion makes me feel threatened, I will legislate you into oblivion." We're witnessing political fragility being weaponized through bureaucracy, where insecurity becomes a strategic tool, where every policy proposal reads like a therapy session interrupted by a Fox News alert.

Project 2025 is not a road map—it's **a revenge tour**. A bureaucratic hissy fit built on the dream of making facts optional, expertise suspicious, and whiteness feel like the main character again. It's not about running the country better. It's about running it *backward*—fast, furious, and fueled by grievance.

Project 2025 isn't Heritage's first rodeo—it's just the latest chapter in a long-running production. Long before it became the architect of Trump's second-term fantasies, the Heritage Foundation was already hard at work scripting the playbook for conservative power grabs.

Dick's Hissy Fit: Project 2025 Saves America

*"Finally!" Dick bellows, clutching his Heritage binder like it's the Dead Sea Scrolls. "Project 2025 is the blueprint we've been waiting for. It'll put women back where they belong—at home raising kids, not bossing men around in boardrooms. It'll end all this DEI nonsense and bring back **real** meritocracy, which just happens to look exactly like me and my golf buddies. And thank God it'll fuse government with religion, because nothing says freedom like forcing everyone to live under my version of morality. This isn't regression—it's restoration. The good old days are coming back, and if you don't like it, tough. Heritage knows best."*

-Dick

Dick Moves Alert

- Rolling back women's rights under the label "family values."
- Erasing DEI and pretending "merit" isn't rigged.
- Church and state? Nah—Dick prefers church as state.
- Pretending 1950 was America's peak while ignoring segregation, suppression, and systemic inequality.

Sally's Sanity: The Reality Check

"Dick, let's stop pretending Project 2025 is a visionary plan. It's a tantrum bound in leatherette. Heritage is selling regression as reform, but here's what's really inside:

- **Control, not freedom.** *Limiting women's autonomy, reproductive rights, and career paths isn't about family—it's about power.*
- **Exclusion, not merit.** *Scrapping DEI only makes the playing field 'fair' for those who've always had the ball.*
- **Theocracy, not democracy.** *Forcing one religion into law doesn't unify—it erases pluralism.*
- **Backwards, not forwards.** *Project 2025 is less 'future roadmap' and more 'time machine to white-picket-fence patriarchy.'*

Here's the thing, Dick: society has already outgrown your fantasy. Women are CEOs, scientists, leaders, and breadwinners. Gen Z is redefining culture faster than you can finish your Heritage homework. Equity is no longer optional—it's reality.

So wave your binder high and call it salvation. To the rest of us, it's nothing but a hissy-fit in fine print. And no amount of nostalgia is going to rewrite the fact that America's future isn't yours to lock in the past."

—Your Sister Sally

Partnering with Power—How Heritage Became MAGA's Homework Helper

From Reagan to Trump, they stopped at nothing to anoint the next generation of grievance-driven governance.

Ah, back in the day, conservative policy looked like a well-rehearsed monologue on deregulation and free markets? Enter the Heritage Foundation. Founded during the Reagan era as the "respectable face" of radical conservatism, they soon evolved into MAGA's think tank—if you can call it that—turning policy into performance art. From Reagan's love notes to privatization to Trump's full-throated, Twitter-fueled tirades, Heritage has been the backstage crew for every unhinged policy cosplay, ensuring that every "great idea" carries a healthy dose of ideology over intellect.[348]

Ties That Bind: Right-Wing Media, SCOTUS Grooming, and Billionaire Disinformation

Heritage isn't just another research institute—it's the coalition's secret weapon. Their ties with right-wing media outlets ensure that every published white paper becomes a 24/7 meme factory. They've groomed young SCOTUS hopefuls thoroughly, so that bench appointments come with a side of MAGA-approved talking points.[349] And don't forget the billionaire-funded disinformation factories: when megadonors want to rewrite reality, Heritage delivers the playbook, ensuring that conservative revisionism has the imprimatur of "intellectual rigor".

They Don't Just Advise—They Anoint

In the Heritage playbook, providing policy recommendations isn't about offering options—it's about anointing the next generation of leaders. They hand out "mandates" like sacraments: refreshingly dressed-up decrees that tell the establishment exactly who should hold the reins. It's as if every policy proposal comes wrapped in a ritualistic blessing, certifying that if you follow the Heritage-approved blueprint, you're not just a policymaker—you're a chosen one destined to keep the old order intact, all while wearing a MAGA cap.

Cultural Impact: Shaping the Narrative of an Entire Political Ecosystem

By aligning closely with conservative media and influential power brokers, Heritage has ensured that its policy fantasies become the default narrative. Their "homework help" isn't about solving problems—it's about ensuring that any challenge to the status quo is labeled "woke" or "radical." This ideological anointment means that even when policies crumble under public scrutiny, the narrative remains: a rebellious elite is at fault, not the carefully curated system of privilege.[350]

Political Theater: How Christian Nationalism and The Heritage Foundation Turned Politics into Off-Broadway Fascism

ACT I: In God We Gaslight

Christian Nationalism didn't just sneak into politics—it stormed the pulpit, hijacked the Constitution, and demanded that Jesus endorse supply-side economics and open carry laws.

- Separation of church and state? Cute. Now we've got senators quoting Leviticus as if it were the Congressional Budget Office.
- Policies written not by scholars, but by people who think *The Handmaid's Tale* was aspirational.
- Jesus wept. Then he was replaced by a Glock and a grievance.

This isn't religion—it's a stage prop. A golden cross duct-taped to a political agenda that says:

"God wants you to deregulate fossil fuels, defund public schools, and control uteruses."

ACT II: Heritage Foundation Presents: The Founders Were Evangelicals with AR-15s

Enter the Heritage Foundation, the ideological puppet master writing the script for every Republican with a lapel mic and a moral panic. Forget nuance. Forget facts. This is *Project 2025: The Musical*, featuring greatest hits like:

- "Defund Everything That Helps People"
- "The Deep State Is Your Therapist"
- "If We Ban Books, We'll Stop Feeling Feelings"

The Heritage Foundation doesn't make policy. It makes **fan fiction for authoritarian cosplay.** Scripture disguised as white papers. Policy memos sponsored by Chick-fil-A and executive privilege. And guess who's eating it up? Every "family values" politician who thinks the Juneteenth holiday is critical race theory in disguise and climate change is liberal astrology.

Now for ACT III: The President as Performer-in-Chief

In this theater, the presidency isn't about leadership. It's about **vibes, ven-**

dettas, and volume.

- Reagan gave us *Hollywood smiles and dog whistles*.
- Bush gave us *Texas swagger and post-9/11 paranoia*.
- Trump? He gave us *24/7 livestreamed rage from a gold toilet*.

The president is not a policymaker. He's the main character in a reality show reboot of the Confederacy, brought to you by Newsmax and the letters F, U, and C (you know the rest).

Every press conference is a monologue. Every indictment is a cliffhanger. And every executive order reads like Hobby Lobby Legal and a bored intern at Turning Point USA ghostwrote it.

The result? We're not living in a democracy—we're stuck in a **political LARP where** "freedom" means the right to suppress yours, and "God's will" is whatever's trending on Truth Social.

Christian Nationalism handed the Heritage Foundation a stage.
The Heritage Foundation wrote the playbook.
And politicians—our so-called leaders—auditioned for power by pledging allegiance not to country or Constitution, but to a holy empire of performance outrage.

Yes, we are now moving to examine the political theater. But make no mistake—**they're not acting.** They're rewriting the script. And the rest of us? We're either extras… or we tear down the damn set.

CHAPTER 14

Hissy Fit Goes Global—
Exporting American
Dysfunction & Accountability

When America sneezes, the world catches a hissy fit.

From YouTube radicalization to international eyerolls, the US isn't just struggling with accountability—it's franchising dysfunction at scale. Not too long ago, America exported jazz, jeans, and democracy. Now we export culture wars, conspiracy content, and red-hatted rage with a side of evangelical exceptionalism. The United States is no longer just a country; it's a content machine. A full-blown 24/7 hissy fit livestreamed across borders and bounced through algorithms faster than a Tucker Carlson monologue on 2x speed.

And the rest of the world? They're not taking notes. They're watching us like a bad reality show they didn't ask to subscribe to. We told ourselves we were "the beacon of freedom." Turns out, we're the Wi-Fi router of Western dysfunction—spreading nationalism, paranoia, and the idea that "free speech" means zero consequences and maximum monetization.

But here's the real kicker: Accountability doesn't stop at the border. The global community sees the cracks we refuse to fix. They hear our politicians preach liberty while banning books, witness our workplaces implode over DEI backlash, and scroll through our exported meltdowns on TikTok subtitled in five languages.

The Global Cringe: Allies Watching America Spiral in Real Time

The world once looked to America for leadership. Now they watch us like it's their favorite guilty-pleasure drama—with subtitles, butter rum candies, and mild secondhand embarrassment.

There was a time when the US embassies symbolized democracy, diplomacy, and the occasional awkward group photo with local dignitaries. Now, they might as well be giving away *The Purge: Midterms Edition*.

Foreign diplomats are unsure whether to schedule trade talks or attend the entertainment. American foreign policy has become such an emotional roller coaster that it comes with its warning of nausea. From the outside, it looks less like governance and more like a *Real Housewives* reunion special with nuclear capabilities—just with fewer sequins and more subpoenas.

Allies no longer fear missing a memo. They fear **becoming a meme**.

Turn on the BBC, CBC, Deutsche Welle, or Al Jazeera, and what do you see? Wall-to-wall coverage of the latest American dysfunction:

- Capitol riots
- Gun violence that would shock a war zone
- School board meetings turned into UFC undercards
- Presidential debates that look like *WWE SmackDown* but with worse hair

In Europe, it is referred to as "coverage." In Australia, it's *"a lesson in what not to do."* In Canada, they clutch their healthcare cards a little tighter. America isn't leading the global stage anymore—we're the lead case study in a democracy elective taught by nervous professors in well-governed nations. We were once the authors of the worldwide order. Now we're a cautionary footnote in civics class.[351]

Our Reputation? Shot.

We've done more damage to our global credibility with QAnon and book bans than any foreign adversary could have dreamed. From January 6, when domestic extremists stormed the Capitol in a cosplay insurrection, to governors banning *The Diary of Anne Frank* because it's "too emotionally complex," our allies are rightfully asking: "Do y'all need help? Blink twice."

The world saw the "beacon of democracy" dim its lights and start handing out participation trophies for authoritarian cosplay. Foreign policy scholars have called it the "self-inflicted unraveling of soft power."[352] Translation: America made itself uncool faster than Facebook did. Meanwhile, autocrats around the world pointed to our chaos and said, "See? Freedom leads to drag queens and civil war reenactments in the Senate."

"We're #1!" (In What, Exactly?)

Ah, yes, the chant: *"USA! USA! USA!"* But outside of sports and military budgets, one has to ask—what exactly are we winning?

The current leaderboard of American dominance:
- #1 in health care costs[353]
- #1 in gun ownership and gun deaths per capita[354]
- #1 in spreading COVID disinformation in podcast format
- #1 in arguing over fictional characters' gender identities and whether Muppets have a liberal agenda

American exceptionalism is now less about innovation and more about inflammation, both social and literal. We don't have universal health care, but we do have 14 types of Oreos, and people stockpile ivermectin like Pokémon cards.

Meanwhile, the developed nations of Europe and elsewhere are out here:
- Capping insulin costs
- Banning assault weapons
- Tackling climate change
- Electing women without throwing national hissy fits about pantsuits

They're doing the boring, competent stuff—governing—while we're in the middle of a national crisis over whether Elmo is part of a Marxist plot to indoctrinate toddlers with feelings. In Finland, kids are learning emotional literacy.

Here in the US, kids are dodging active shooter drills and being told *"slavery wasn't all bad."*

Other nations have problems too, but they aren't debating if diversity is a threat to freedom while melting down over a drag brunch in a public library. The global consensus? America's not broken—it's just too proud to Google "how to fix it."

While other countries are upgrading their cultures with equity, innovation, and education, America is busy staging a full-blown hissy fit about gas stoves, Bud Light, and the radical idea that freedom shouldn't come with an asterisk.

Did you know:

- **Finland** continues to top the global education rankings with student-first, equity-driven learning systems, while America bans AP African American Studies and drags librarians into school board hearings.
- **Germany** is powering up its green energy sector and scaling affordable higher ed. **America?** We're in a Senate hearing over whether climate change is a "woke" issue.
- **New Zealand** passed sweeping indigenous reconciliation policies. The US? Still arguing if teaching slavery is "too divisive" for eighth graders.
- **France** legalized abortion in its constitution. In the United States, a court ruled that embryos may have custody rights.
- **Canada** is investing in universal childcare. We're busy accusing drag queens of destroying the nuclear family.

Read that again if you missed the point! This isn't a decline. **This is self-sabotage—broadcast live, monetized for clicks, and wrapped in a flag so no one notices the fire underneath it.**

American Arrogance Meets Global Side-Eye

Once admired, American confidence has curdled into **unearned arrogance**, performed by people who shout "freedom" while:

- Banning books
- Gutting education
- Screaming about free speech while trying to cancel their barista for using they/them pronouns

The world isn't laughing with us anymore. They're side-eyeing us through a double-paned lens of confusion and concern. We claim to be the greatest country on Earth, but flinch at math, masks, and map-based geography questions. Exceptionalism without introspection isn't patriotism—it's performance art with a superiority complex. As global trust in American leadership dips,[355] the rest of the world is moving on—quietly, diplomatically, and without needing a single bald eagle screech to validate themselves.

Exporting Conspiracies and Culture Wars Through YouTube and Evangelicals

America's most successful export isn't democracy anymore—it's digital delusion wrapped in a Bible verse and monetized on Rumble. Platforms like YouTube, Facebook, and Rumble have become super-spreaders of American grievance content, piping QAnon logic and anti-DEI rage to audiences in Germany, Brazil, Hungary, and anywhere there's Wi-Fi and a moderate sense of cultural insecurity.[356]

Want to radicalize a teenager in Poland with a Joe Rogan clip? Done. Want to make sure Canada's school boards get hit with anti-LGBTQ+ protests? There's a playbook for that, and it's called "America: The Dysfunctional Big Brother You Can't Unfollow."

White Christian Nationalism Goes Global

But this isn't just about memes and misinformation—this is missionary work with a political agenda. US-based evangelical networks have become ideological franchises, spreading "family values" campaigns and anti-LBGTQ+ policies to Eastern Europe, Africa, and Latin America.[357] Their gospel? Less about love and grace, more about:

- Patriarchy,
- Heteronormativity, and
- Fear of "cultural erosion" via feminism, queer rights, and inclusive education

This isn't religion. It's exported grievance disguised as scripture, and it's having real-world impact—from anti-trans laws in Uganda to constitutional amendments in Hungary banning "gender ideology."

It's the *Great Commission*, rewritten by a Fox News producer and funded by the same PAC that thinks critical race theory is a gateway drug. This global pipeline of white Christian nationalism is turning other countries into laboratories for America's culture war experiments, with devastating consequences for local queer communities, women, and activists.

Cultural Imperialism 2.0: Powered by Wi-Fi and White Grievance

Cultural imperialism for the broadband era, where colonial missionaries once brought Bibles and disease, 21st-century emissaries bring:

- YouTube channels blaming feminism for male loneliness.
- Evangelical NGOs pushing anti-abortion policies.
- Think tanks funneling anti-woke talking points to parliaments overseas.

This isn't diplomacy—it's ideological colonization wearing a red tie and quoting Leviticus out of context. America no longer needs boots on the ground. It has clicks, pastors, and conspiracy channels, all exporting the message that progress is dangerous and empathy is a plot.

Meanwhile, the rest of the world is left asking: "Is this what American freedom looks like? Because it sounds like a breakdown with Wi-Fi."

US Diplomacy by Meme and Meltdown

Why deliver a thoughtful foreign policy when you can subtweet the French Prime Minister and go viral instead?

There was a time when US diplomacy was handled behind closed doors by experienced diplomats who spoke multiple languages and understood nuance. Now, we have presidential rage tweets, emoji-based saber-rattling, and cable news rants that double as campaign ads.

"WHY IS CANADA BEING SO RUDE?"–Actual energy policy.

In the 21st-century hissy fit economy, megaphones have replaced message discipline. Who needs a press briefing when you can just hit SEND on a barely coherent truth bomb and let the State Department figure it out later? This isn't foreign policy—it's keyboard diplomacy with a toddler's temperament and a permanent caps-lock problem.

The US Is No Longer Leading—It's Live-Streaming

We once led the free world. Now we go live. What was once global leadership has become an open mic night with nuclear codes. Our global allies? They're not following—they're subtly muting us. We're no longer role models. We're the loud class clown who peaked in high school and now sells supplements and alpha male books from a basement studio.

The rest of the world is hosting summits. We're out here rage-posting memes from the tarmac at Mar-a-Lago. And the damage isn't just reputational—it's existential. You can't build a functioning international order on GIFs and grievances. You can't defend democracy when your foreign policy looks like an Instagram reel labeled "Triggered."

Cancel Culture? Nah. It's Consequence Culture

- In Germany, hate speech gets you fined.
- In New Zealand, misinformation platforms are regulated.
- In France, public officials are removed for actual corruption.
- In South Korea, artists and politicians alike step down over scandals, *before* the hashtags start.

And what's America doing? Melting down because someone got removed from a Netflix lineup after tweeting "all lives matter" during a police brutality protest. Other countries don't call it "cancel culture"—they call it justice, integrity, or a typical Tuesday.

America's hissy fit over so-called cancel culture is a masterclass in deflection. Because heaven forbid someone face a consequence that doesn't come with a six-figure speaking tour and a podcast deal. Only in the US do people demand absolute free speech while simultaneously crying oppression from the comfort of a monetized Substack account.

The usual cries decoded:

- "You're silencing me!" = I said something deeply offensive, and people didn't clap.
- "Woke mobs are ruining comedy!" = I wrote a lazy punchline in 2002 and still think it's edgy.
- "You can't say anything anymore!" = I don't want to evolve, and I'm mad you noticed.

Free speech? Still alive. Free from consequence? Never was a thing. The First Amendment protects you from the government, not from public backlash or your boss saying, "Yeah, we're good actually."

Dick's Hissy Fit: "Canada Should Just Be the 51st State—They Already Speak Walmart"

Alright, now listen—I've been thinking (dangerous, I know), and I've decided it's time we go ahead and absorb Canada. Yeah, I said it. Canada. You know, America's hat with healthcare.

They've got maple syrup, politeness, and no real military—we've got bald eagles, Costco, and nukes. Seems fair.

"But Dick," you say, "Canada is a sovereign country with its own government."

Exactly. And that's adorable. But let's be honest—they've been an unofficial state since we taught them what a Super Bowl commercial was. They use our internet, watch our shows, wear our jeans, and panic when Target leaves. If that's not statehood material, I don't know what is.

I mean, their leader looks like a substitute drama teacher who accidentally legalized weed and apologized for it in both languages. Ours? We have... whatever Joe's doing. So it balances out.

Let's call it a merger. We'll keep the poutine; they get Walmart. They bring the moose, we bring the monster trucks. And the name? **America: North Deluxe Edition.**

Boom. Problem solved. Now, excuse me—I'm applying for dual citizenship and a Tim Hortons rewards card. Freedom, but make it maple.

—Dick

You didn't think Dick built this hissy fit on his own, did you? Nah. Dick had help. Lots of it. Part I revealed his confusion, Part II laid out his shaky worldview, and Part III exposed the well-funded machinery that taught him to turn anger into identity and brand it as patriotism.

But here's the thing about tantrums: they don't last forever. Eventually, the screaming either stops…or the room changes without you. Which brings us to the final act—**Part IV: The Culture Reset—Adapt or Throw a Bigger Hissy Fit.** The world is moving on. You can evolve with it… or just get louder and hope no one notices you're lost.

Part IV:

THE Culture Reset—
Adapt or Throw a
Bigger Hissy Fit

The world is changing. You can evolve...
or get louder and hope no one notices you're lost.

Curtain Call: Time to Join the Cast, Reader. Yes, You.

Well, congratulations. You've met the characters.

- **Dick**: The walking MAGA stress rash with a podcast and zero therapy.
- **Sally**: The exhausted voice of reason with a Wi-Fi connection and a side of righteous rage.
- The **Culture**: Cracked but still streaming.
- The **Politicians**: Theater kids with lobbyist sugar daddies.
- The **Supreme Court**: Dressed like Hogwarts faculty, acting like they're auditioning for a reboot of *1776: The Musical (Unethically Yours)*.

And of course, **you**, dear reader. The voyeur. The observer. The one who "can't believe this is real" while doom-scrolling through the end credits of democracy.

The fourth wall just shattered. You're not in the audience anymore. **You're in the story.**

This Is Your Plot Twist. You've seen the conflict. You've read the rants. You've heard the hissy fits. You know who's pulling the strings and who's just crying into a trucker hat about gas stoves. You've seen how facts get buried under memes, how truth now needs a PR team, and how half the country can't define socialism but knows it's the enemy.

Now what? You could go back to brunch, retweet a quote, and mutter "ugh" under your breath for the next 30 years. Or—you could **join the cast.** With sleeves rolled up and B.S. detectors fully charged.

Welcome to the Reckoning. This is where we stop crying in the self-checkout line because someone said "Latinx." This is where we stop confusing discomfort with oppression. This is where we stop acting like books are dangerous and billionaires are freedom fighters. No more culture war cosplay. No more blaming teachers, pronouns, or TikTok. No more pretending critical thinking is "elitist."

This Is the Part Where Dick Puts Down the Microphone and Picks Up a Mirror

Dick—yes, you. You've yelled. You've memed. You've called every mild disagreement a constitutional crisis. But here's the truth: **The world is changing.** And screaming into your ring light isn't going to stop it. You can adapt. Or you can throw a bigger hissy fit. But know this: the grown-ups are moving forward—with or without you.

The Culture Reset Rules: No More Excuses. No More Echo Chambers. No More Bullshit.

This section isn't vibes. It's evidence. It's a strategy. It's a **cultural exorcism of terminal stupidity.** It's time to:

- Reawaken your critical thinking. (Yes, even you, Dick, Doug, Karen, and Jane.)
- Do actual research. (Watching a 3-minute YouTube video from "Patriot_Steve1976" doesn't count.)
- Question everything—including yourself.
- Challenge power, not pronouns.
- Rethink what strength, freedom, and truth mean in 2025.

The Reset, Generation by Generation: Because Everyone Screwed Something Up

Baby Boomers (1946-1964):

We love your vinyl collection and your pension, but your time at the wheel gave us climate collapse, Fox News, and trickle-down economics. It's time to stop yelling "woke" and start **funding education, backing science, and passing the damn torch.**

Gen X (1965-1980):

You sat in the corner, rolled your eyes, and watched Rome burn while muttering "whatever." We need you **off the sidelines.** You're old enough to lead and young enough to give a damn, still—time to weaponize that sarcasm into policy reform.

Millennials (1981-1996):

You've got the degrees, the debt, and the digital receipts. You've done the most with the least. Now stop apologizing and **take the damn mic**—but use it to lead, not just tweet. It's time for power, not just protest.

Gen Z (1997-2012):

You are loud, online, and allergic to BS. We see you—glitter, rage, and all. But your feed is not your future. You'll need to **organize, not just mobilize.** The revolution won't be livestreamed—it'll be legislated.

Gen Alpha (2013-):

You're more likely scrolling this on your iPad than holding a physical book. Start asking hard questions. Demand better. Learn history beyond *Hamilton*. And when you see someone trying to ban a book, **read two.**

What You, Yes YOU, Need to Do (Before the Next Plot Twist Hits)

- **Hold everyone accountable—including yourself.** Dick didn't create the mess alone. He had help. From silence. From passivity. From Facebook's algorithm and that one uncle we never uninvited to Thanksgiving.
- **Vote. Every. Damn. Time.** Not just for presidents—school boards, sheriffs, library trustees. Yes, your librarians might be the last line of defense against fascism. Protect them like they're Beyoncé or Sabrina Carpenter with a barcode scanner.
- **Get smarter. Stay louder. Ask better questions.** Don't just Google. Research and learn to recognize credible sources of information.. Read past the headline. If it ends in ".biz" and has three exclamation points, it's not journalism—it's brain poison.

- **Call out fiction.** If Dick says climate change is a hoax invented by George Soros and Godzilla, don't smile politely. Say, "Prove it." Then slide him a NOAA report, as if it were a divorce decree from fantasy.
- **Raise the bar. For politicians. For pundits. For judges in $400 robes pretending the Constitution is a mood ring.** Demand ethics from SCOTUS. Demand facts from your representatives. Demand less crying from billionaires on cable news.

Let's Make America Great—for the First Time

Not again. Not nostalgically. Not through red hats, hissy fits, or manifest destiny reenactments.

Let's build something we've never actually had: A country rooted in truth. Led by critical thinkers and powered by engaged citizens. That finally realizes liberty is for everyone. Not just the loudest dude with a truck decal and a persecution complex.

The culture war is exhausting. But apathy is complicity. Be louder than the liars. Be smarter than the spin. Be braver than the backlash.

Here we are: **Part IV—the Culture Reset.**

No more whining. No more main character syndrome. No more weaponized nostalgia.

Just accountability. Action. And one final invitation: Get in the damn arena—or kindly shut up and stop holding the door closed for progress.

Your scene starts now.

CHAPTER 15

Wake Up, It's The End of the Line

America has long suffered from an advanced case of central character syndrome. It strutted onto the world stage like a self-appointed protagonist dressed in red, white, and blue delusion, convinced that history was just a supporting character in its manifest destiny.

Welcome to the Reckoning:
This Is Your Pre-Apocalypse Orientation

Let's say it: **America's not special—it's symptomatic.** Every empire thinks it's too fabulous to fail, right up until the point it's selling breadsticks for gold and livestreaming coups in HD. Rome fell. The British Empire fell. The Ottomans, the Greeks, the French aristocracy—all got a little too high on their supply. Spoiler alert: **We're next.**

Why? Same ingredients, new flavor:

- Wealth hoarding is like an Olympic sport. (Congrats, Bezos, gold medal!)
- Religious zealotry with a Wi-Fi signal. (Now streaming from your state capitol.)
- A political system that's less "checks and balances" and more "WWE meets a midlife crisis."

And before you clutch your Constitution, let's be honest: We haven't read it in decades. We're too busy binge-watching the decline, arguing with strangers in comment sections, and pretending student debt forgiveness will cause economic collapse—but somehow trillion-dollar tax cuts won't.

This isn't "left vs. right" anymore. It's a functioning society vs. whatever this is.

Consider this your Reckoning Welcome Packet. Inside, you'll find:

- A free "thoughts and prayers" voucher (non-redeemable, obviously),
- A commemorative copy of *The Constitution (Edited for Corporate Sponsors)*,
- And a gift card to Walmart, because that's the only infrastructure we fund anymore.

The reckoning isn't coming—it's **here**.

History's Mirror: Lessons from the Fallen

Every empire thinks it's timeless—until it ends up on a documentary narrated by Morgan Freeman.

America loves to pretend that it's writing a new story. Spoiler: it's just plagiarizing from history's most extraordinary cautionary tales. Rome, Britain, and the USSR weren't side characters in some grand American origin story. They were previous headliners who also thought they were exceptional. And yet, we are following the same tired plot beats like a nation trapped in a historical version of *Groundhog Day*. It's time to understand the failure—grab your Twizzlers and a copy of the Constitution, annotated in crayon—and let's take a little field trip through the archives of decline.

From grade school textbooks to presidential speeches, we were fed a steady diet of exceptionalism—organic, locally grown, and utterly detached from nuance. The U.S. wasn't just powerful—it was supposedly *immune* to the cycles of history that toppled every other so-called "great" civilization. Rome? They partied too hard. Britain? Too many crumpets and colonies. The Soviet Union? They forgot to smile. But *us*? No, we were different. We had hamburgers, Jesus, and nukes. What could go wrong?

Every empire thinks it's the final one. That's part of the script. Civilizations don't crumble overnight—they *erode while insisting they're thriving*. The Roman Empire still minted coins while its streets filled with sewage and civil unrest. The British still claimed moral authority while looting half the globe and serving boiled meat. And America? We're rewriting state curricula to ban books while bragging about "freedom." Nothing says thriving democracy like censoring librarians.

Delusions of Invincibility: Our collective delusion has many names: "American exceptionalism," "patriotism," "pull yourself up by your boot-straps," and, of course, "freedom isn't free." All convenient catchphrases that allow us to ignore inequality, climate collapse, and violent political extremism, because acknowledging those would mean admitting we're not special. We're just late-stage.

Facts didn't forge the myth of American exceptionalism—it was constructed like a Marvel origin story: emotionally satisfying, wildly exaggerated, and increasingly disconnected from reality. It told us:

- That our Constitution was divinely inspired (not plagiarized from Enlightenment thinkers).
- That our Founders were flawless (instead of flawed men in wigs with god complexes and property deeds).
- That we exported democracy (not coups).

Every Empire Dies of the Same Disease: Arrogance

The truth is, no empire falls because of an outside force. They rot from within—slowly, predictably, and almost always while denying it's happening. They ignore income inequality, fail to adapt to change, and elites cannibalize the system while blaming the poor. Sound familiar?

We've reached the part of the script where the audience can see the fall coming. However, the protagonist is still shouting a monologue about freedom, utterly unaware that the curtain's already halfway down.

No, America. You're not the exception. You're the rule—just dressed in stars, stripes, and a marketing budget.

Rome: Bread, Circuses, and Clueless Senators

Rome didn't fall in a day—it fell over centuries of political gridlock, populist demagogues, economic instability, and unchecked military overreach. Sound familiar? While the average Roman citizen was drowning in debt, the elites were throwing orgies in gold-plated villas and debating whether

gladiators were *too woke*.[358]
Key Symptoms of Collapse:
- Politicians are obsessed with their image.
- Growing gap between rich and poor.
- A military so over-bloated, it forgot what it was defending.
- Religious radicalization and identity panic.

If Rome had had Facebook, Nero would've been livestreaming fiddle solos while the Colosseum burned.

The British Empire: Colonize Now, Cry Later

The British built an empire on the backs of others, then acted shocked when those people didn't send thank-you notes. At its peak, the Britain Empire controlled nearly a quarter of the world's population. Today? They can barely manage Brexit.
Where It Went Wrong:
- Economic overreach: Colonization isn't sustainable when the colonies realize they're being exploited.
- National identity crises: The sun didn't set—it burned out.
- Nostalgia overload: Imperial decline camouflaged as patriotism. Sound familiar, again?

Churchill once said, "History will be kind to me for I intend to write it." America took that literally and just added fireworks.

The Soviet Union: When Ideology Eats Itself

The USSR was undone by economic mismanagement and a refusal to evolve. It prioritized image over reality and control over adaptability. It collapsed under the weight of its propaganda and an unwillingness to admit that things weren't working.[359]
Parallel American Moments:
- Denying climate change while states catch fire.
- Banning books while claiming to protect "freedom."
- Believing more guns = more safety, more billionaires = more freedom, and more rage = more patriotism.

The USSR had *Pravda* (both the name of the official newspaper and the

Russian word for "truth"). We have cable news and Twitter threads that claim to be manifestos.

The Common Thread: Terminal Uniqueness

America has a *terminal case of "that can't happen to us" syndrome*—a delusional disorder often triggered by high levels of nationalism, sustained exposure to cable news, and prolonged contact with high-fructose exceptionalism. We tell ourselves we're different. Special. "Rome fell because they got soft. Britain fell because they drank tea. But us? Nah—we've got missiles and motivational TikToks. It's the illusion of exceptionalism on steroids: We are the only nation on Earth that believes gravity doesn't apply if you yell *"freedom!"* loud enough.

Terminal Uniqueness: A psychological defense mechanism that has evolved into a cultural personality trait, terminal uniqueness occurs when someone believes their situation is distinct and exceptional, such that no standard solution, societal rule, or systemic insight could apply.

- In recovery circles, it sounds like: "That might work for *them*, but my trauma is *special.*"
- In corporate America, it sounds like: "That policy is great—for other departments.. We're not like other companies—we care." *(Spoiler: They don't.)*
- In American exceptionalism, it sounds like: "Other countries might need universal healthcare, but here in the US, we bootstrap our medical bankruptcies like patriots."

Terminal Uniqueness Shows Up:

- **In Health Equity:** "Those stats don't reflect *our* patient population." (Translation: *We didn't look, but we're sure we're fine.*)
- **In DEI:** "We don't have bias in our hiring—we're a mission-driven organization!" (Translation: *Our mission is to ignore the data.*)
- **In Politics:** "This isn't like Nazi Germany." (Translation: *I've read exactly zero history books, but I'm very confident.*)
- **In Leadership:** "I've never had a mentor, I don't think my team needs one." (Translation: *My trauma is your blueprint.*)

Cultural Consequences: Turns community solutions into personal exceptions. Undermines systemic reform by over-personalizing everything. Creates fragile egos wrapped in justifications and a veneer of humility.

Terminal Uniqueness is the gateway to disregarding collective wisdom and rewriting best practices into personal anecdotes, often shared in LinkedIn posts.

In Short: Terminal Uniqueness = Delusion in a Designer Jacket. It's not just narcissism. It's individualized exceptionalism weaponized against progress.

Every Empire Falls the Same Way—And We're Speedrunning It
- Too much pride
- Not enough self-awareness
- A deep romantic relationship with the past, zero interest in the future
- Leaders who care more about cable ratings than climate projections
- A populace trained to worship the Founding Fathers like boy bands on reunion tours

We've become the *open mic night* version of an empire. Loud, underprepared, and deeply convinced we're the headliner.

The Roman Empire continued to mint coins while barbarians sacked the city. The British still claimed moral superiority while looting continents and boiling vegetables into oblivion. And America? We're banning books while bragging about free speech. We're gutting libraries while calling ourselves the land of opportunity.[360] And we're cutting education budgets while demanding kids learn "real history" from bumper stickers.

Meanwhile, in a Lawn Chair Near You... As the oceans rise, democracy backslides, and maternal mortality rates hit developing nations levels,[361] some guy in jean shorts still leans back and shouts: "We're the greatest country in the world!"

Sure, Dick. Right after we finish suing librarians and voting against healthcare. The rest of the world is sprinting toward equity, sustainability, and innovation. America is tripping over its bootstraps, screaming *"WOKE!"* at a rainbow onesie.

Terminal Uniqueness: The Deadliest National Delusion

Every empire believes it's the exception. Everyone thinks it's military, it's wealth, or it's God that will save it from entropy. And everyone collapses the same way:

- Civic rot behind patriotic pageantry
- Declining life expectancy masked by bigger Fourth of July fireworks[362]
- Political theater performed by men who've confused governance with content creation

We don't need to imagine a dystopia. We're livestreaming it, sponsored by Rage Supplements and Nostalgia Merch.

We can chant "USA!" until our lungs give out. Still, no amount of star-spangled performance art will stop the reality that our democracy is faltering, our civic trust is eroding, and our institutions are under siege—from the inside, by people waving the Constitution like it's a blackjack table strategy guide.

We are not the exception. We are **the latest data point**. And unless we course-correct fast, **history will file us in the same folder as every other empire that mistook pride for permanence.**

The Global Mirror

America used to be a superpower. Now, it's a super-producer of cultural cringe, exported nightly. The world is watching. They used to watch with curiosity, then concern. Now? **It's concern and pity.** In 1945, we stormed beaches. In 1969, we walked on the moon. In 2025, we stormed school board meetings in tactical gear to protest the use of rainbow backpacks. This isn't a fall from grace. This is a faceplant in Crocs, filmed in 4K, uploaded to YouTube, and auto-translated for global ridicule.

Are they laughing, crying, or bracing?

Europe? Trying not to look smug. They're building bullet trains while we're banning biology textbooks.

Canada? Just lock the door and turn off the porch light.

Australia? Still reeling from the fact that we turned a beer can into a culture war and a pillow salesman into a political strategist.

China? Patiently taking notes as we livestream our institutional collapse, one school shooting, banned book, and fact-optional politician at a time.

Global democracy advocates? Watching in horror as the self-declared "leader of the free world" now leads in conspiracy podcasts and teen depression.

What We're Exporting Now: We used to export dreams. Now we export: Outrage influencers with God complexes. Anti-science TikTok's. Christian nationalism dressed up as school policy. Book bans, burnout, and *bless your heart* foreign policy. We have become the reality TV show of geopolitics—loud, unpredictable, and impossible to look away from. We are no longer leading the world. We're trending. And not in a good way.

Global Consequence:
What Happens When America Trips Over Its Ego?
- When American democracy derails, **authoritarians win PR points.**
- When America embraces anti-intellectualism, **misinformation metastasizes.**
- When we confuse nationalism with leadership, **we destabilize the world we helped build.**
- If America collapses under the weight of its hissy fit, it doesn't just implode—it **takes people with it.**

Financial markets. Climate policy. International alliances. Cultural influence. All riding shotgun in Dick's pickup, screaming "woke" at the clouds.

Is There Still Time to Lead by Example?
There's a window. Barely cracked. But it's still open if we stop exporting outrage and start exporting equity. Suppose we model truth, not hissy fits if we reclaim **free speech** without weaponizing it and restore **civic literacy** without asking for extra credit. Then the world might stop bracing for our collapse and start believing in our recovery.

But that means no more slogans. No more nostalgia cosplay. No more leaders who think governing is just content creation with a pension.

The World Doesn't Need America to Be Perfect. We can still reset. But we can't do it by yelling louder or doubling down on delusion. The world needs us to grow the hell up, read the damn Constitution that we proclaim is the gold standard of democracy, and start leading like the lights are still on.

The global mirror is cracked—but not shattered. We still have a chance to examine it and acknowledge the mess we've become... and the responsibility we've got to clean it up. Before someone else writes our obituary and stamps it *"Made in America."* Let's take a look at the different places we need to press the cultural reset button.

Economic Inequality: The Wealth Gap as the New Grand Canyon
Trickle-down economics doesn't trickle. It floods yachts and dries up paychecks.

Once, America sold itself as the land of opportunity. Today, it's more like the land of GoFundMe campaigns for insulin. Economic inequality isn't a crack in the system—it is the system. And the Grand Canyon-level wealth gap? That's not erosion—it's excavation. A few dug up all the gold, paved their driveways with it, and told the rest of us to "just work harder."

RIP Middle Class: 1945-Now-ish
Survived wars, built suburbs, died of wage stagnation.

Once upon a time, the middle class had a pension, a house, two kids, and a car with a metal frame. Now? The middle class is a ghost haunting a Zillow listing and the Whole Foods parking lot, whispering, "Remember when one job was enough?" Real wages for middle-income workers have been flat since the 1970s, even as productivity rose by **over 60%**.[363] Translation: you work harder, longer, and get less—because **late-stage capitalism runs on your burnout**.

Thanks to skyrocketing costs for housing, healthcare, and education, the new American dream isn't homeownership—it's **not having to start a GoFundMe after a medical emergency**. The middle class is now too rich to qualify for government assistance and too broke to afford life. Congratulations—you're perfectly positioned for economic purgatory. And don't let the stock market fool you. That 401(k)? You'll need it to afford eggs and Ozempic. Meanwhile, **the top 10% of earners own 89% of the US stocks**.[364] But sure, tell me more about how avocado toast is the problem.

So, where did the middle class go? They didn't vanish—they were **outsourced, evicted, or "restructured"** into gig workers with side hustles and no health insurance. It's starting to sound like *Les Misérables*, and I performed in that show, so I know how it ends.

The Great American Magic Trick: Watch the Wealth Disappear (But Only for You)

Welcome to the United States of Inequality—where billionaires launch themselves into space while millions can't afford a dentist. The top 1% didn't just pull the ladder up after climbing it—they lit it on fire, slapped a tax write-off on the ashes, and called it "economic freedom."

In this country, **wealth doesn't trickle down—it trickles sideways into offshore accounts**. The median Black and Latino household owns less than **15%** of the wealth of the median white household, but hey, at least Beyoncé is on the radio.[365] That's progress. CEOs now earn **399 times more than the average worker**,[366] but don't worry—they're deeply moved by your LinkedIn post about "hustle culture."

Meanwhile, America spends more energy debating student loan forgiveness than we do questioning how Jeff Bezos made **$13 billion in a single day**.[367] Spoiler alert: it wasn't by delivering packages himself. In short, the American Dream is alive and well, for the wealthy. For everyone else, there's GoFundMe, payday loans, and a Powerball ticket that doubles as your retirement plan.

Time to dismantle the American bedtime story that if you hustle hard enough, you too can become Jeff Bezos. In reality, 60% of Americans can't cover a $500 emergency without borrowing money.[368] Meanwhile, billionaires increased their wealth by over $2 trillion during the pandemic.[369]

The math is simple:
- CEOs now make **400 times more** than their median employee.[370]
- The top 1% owns **more wealth than the bottom 90% combined**.
- And yet, we're still told the problem is "people not wanting to work."

Capitalism's newest party trick? Selling poverty as a personal failure and wealth as a moral virtue.

Late-Stage Capitalism: Now with Branding

We've reached the dystopia stage where corporations celebrate Pride Month with rainbow logos while underpaying queer workers. Your mental health is a "productivity concern," not a human concern. "Wellness" is a nap pod at work instead of fair wages or paid leave. The modern American economy is less "Invisible Hand" and more "Middle Finger."

Standard late-stage features include:
- Wage theft rebranded as "salary exempt."
- Side hustles that are just second jobs with worse benefits.
- Billionaire space races while public schools hold bake sales for pencils.

The Cost of Delusion: America's economic model doesn't just create inequality—it demands it. The working class isn't a bug in the system—it's the foundation the elites stand on while yelling, "No handouts!"

So, while billionaires build bunkers in New Zealand and launch themselves into space to avoid the collapse they helped engineer, the rest of us are left with rising costs, stagnant wages, and TikTok videos explaining how to survive on instant ramen and side hustles. The problem isn't capitalism. The problem is *you* didn't "manifest enough abundance."

The Capitalism Hangover

Capitalism was sold as the miracle cure—freedom in a fiscal wrapper. It promised innovation, prosperity, and a two-car garage. We have Amazon warehouses that resemble labor camps with Wi-Fi, Uber drivers living in their cars, and student loans being marketed like loyalty programs. And now? The high is gone, the credit card bill is due, and we're stuck wondering if that "side hustle" was just late-stage feudalism in a cute hoodie.

The Morning After Deregulation
- We deregulated airlines, and now seats recline less than your office chair.
- We deregulated banks, and they gift-wrapped the 2008 collapse.
- We deregulated labor protections, and now people die in warehouses trying to meet shipping quotas for Prime Day.

But don't worry—executives got bonuses. This is what happens when "freedom" means corporations can do whatever they want while workers are told to "be grateful for the opportunity."

Gig Work: Modern Serfdom with an App

The gig economy—it sounds like freedom until you realize it's just *workplace anarchy in beta mode*.

- You're your boss! (Except there's no healthcare, no labor protections, and the algorithm can fire you mid-shift.)
- You make your hours! (Until surge pricing says otherwise.)
- You're an entrepreneur! (Except the company owns the platform, the data, the customers, and the cut.)

American workers didn't get more flexible—they got *disposable*. But hey, at least there's a free pizza party on Fridays.

The Free Market Isn't Free (And It's Not a Market Anymore)

We were promised that markets would correct themselves. That competition would keep prices low, innovation high, and businesses honest. Instead, we got:

- Monopolies that buy Congress like it's Cyber Monday.
- Pharma companies charge $500 for inhalers that cost $2.[371]
- Tech giants are turning privacy into a subscription plan.

The Wellness Economy Is Gaslighting You

Here's a fun twist: capitalism broke you and then started selling you the cure.

- Burned out? Try a $200 mindfulness course.
- Can't afford therapy? Buy a weighted blanket and cry under capitalism™.
- Hate your job? Start a vision board. Just don't ask for a union.

This is a **grift in its final form**: turning systemic failures into self-care trends.

The Illusion of Choice: Capitalism told us we had *choices*—but only between brands that use the same suppliers, pay the same wages, and funnel profits to the same few billionaires.

You're not choosing freedom. You're deciding which corporation gets your data and which billionaire gets to tweet through the apocalypse.

This isn't a hangover anymore—it's the new normal:

- A system that punishes empathy,
- Rewards exploitation, and

- Calls it *progress*.

We didn't just drink the Kool-Aid—we franchised and branded it and now charge $5.99 a month for access to the newsletter.

"I Like Beer, You Get $7.25": The Kavanaugh Economy in Action

Remember when Brett Kavanaugh sobbed through his Supreme Court confirmation, shouting, "I like beer!" like that qualified him for judicial sainthood?

That wasn't just a meltdown—it was a **privileged tantrum**. A hissy fit wrapped in Yale, entitlement, and unshakable belief that power is a birthright.

Meanwhile, when a McDonald's worker asks for $15/hour? Cue pearl-clutching, bootstraps lectures, and threats of robot cashiers.

Reality check: Since 1979, productivity grew **61.8%**, but wages only **17.5%**.[372]

Bezos made **$13B in a day**.[373] You made "experience."

And still, they say YOU are the problem.

Kavanaugh's hissy fit was the system saying out loud: *"I deserve everything. You? Try harder."*

Now, let's take a look at religion in the 21st century and its cultural reset.

Religion of the 21st Century

I know you didn't think I would leave you hanging on religion.

Christian Nationalism has long strutted around in America wearing the powdered wig of divine authority and the Kevlar vest of patriotic exceptionalism. Somewhere between the Declaration of Independence and Duck Dynasty, a faction of Christianity decided that Jesus had drafted the Constitution, carried an AR-15, and did *not* bake bread for immigrants.

But here's the thing: Christian Nationalism has always been a theatrical production performed by a passionate few with excellent microphones. The so-called "moral majority" of the 1980s? More like a moral minority with a bloated media budget and Jerry Falwell's Rolodex. Researchers have repeatedly shown that this group never represented a majority of

Americans, religious or otherwise.[374] But why let facts get in the way of a good sermon—or a policy platform?

The fusion of Christianity with nationalism wasn't as much a spiritual awakening as it was a political power play, thinly veiled in cross-stitch-worthy slogans like "God Bless America" and "In God We Trust"—the latter wasn't added to our currency until 1956, during Cold War panic and as a middle finger to atheistic communism.[375] That's right: even Jesus took second billing to Senator Joseph McCarthy.

The alliance of pulpit and power has always needed an enemy. First, it was Catholics. Then it was the communists. Now it's everyone who's not a straight, white, cisgender Protestant male who thinks Chick-fil-A sauce counts as holy water. *Spoiler alert*: fear campaigns don't age well. Especially when the demographics are not on your side.

Demographic D-Day: Diversity is Destiny

Here's where it gets spicy: the greatest threat to Christian Nationalism isn't the "woke mob" or drag queens reading books at libraries—it's arithmetic. America has diversified faster than a MAGA hat can fall off a lifted pickup truck at a pride parade. According to Pew Research (2021), the white Christian population is in a steady decline, now comprising just 42% of adults, compared to 54% in 2007. And among *young* adults? Try 29%. That's not a cultural shift; that's a demographic sledgehammer.

Apocalypse Now (for Bigots):
Browner, Gayer, and Godless by 2045[376]

- **The Browning of America**: By 2045, the US will be "majority-minority." That's not a prophecy from the Gospel of MSNBC—it's straight out of the Census Bureau.

- **The Queering of America**: Gen Z is the gayest generation yet—and proud. Roughly 20% identify as LGBTQ+. That's one in five future voters who probably won't be voting for someone trying to outlaw rainbow flags or reproductive autonomy.
- **The Secularizing of America**: The "nones"—those claiming no religious affiliation—now make up nearly 30% of US adults, and they outnumber both white evangelicals and Catholics. If that's not divine retribution for weaponized faith, I don't know what is.

So, what does the Religious Right do when the numbers don't add up? They manufacture a "values crisis." Enter the mythical era of "traditional values," a cultural fantasyland where fathers wore suits to dinner, women smiled while baking pies in high heels, and nobody was trans, Black, or critical of America. This is not a moral panic, but a math panic. Because deep down, this isn't about sin. It's about *supply and demand*—the dwindling supply of like-minded voters, and the increasing demand for equity, autonomy, and actual freedom.

Add in immigration, interfaith families, and interracial dynamics, and you've got what Christian nationalists might call "The Unholy Trinity." The US is experiencing record rates of intermarriage and multicultural family structures.[377] This terrifies those clinging to the fantasy of a monocultural, Mayberry-style America—because when *your grandkids have hyphenated last names and two moms*, your theological superiority complex gets a bit... awkward.

The Gospel According to Gen Z

If you listen closely, you can hear pews echoing with emptiness and youth pastors frantically Googling "how to be relevant." That's not a revival—it's a mass exodus. Welcome to Gen Z's spiritual revolution—not led by pastors in pulpits, but by creators on TikTok, memes with Bible verses rewritten in Gen Z slang, and YouTube prophets who trade fire and brimstone for vibes and boundaries.

Thou Shalt Not Conform: The Church used to be the go-to for answers. Now it's not even the go-to for free pizza. Gen Z isn't "leaving" religion—they're ghosting it, blocking the contact, and archiving the trauma. The narrative of "lost sheep" doesn't hold up when the flock has decided the shepherd was gaslighting them. According to the Springtide Research Institute, *only 16% of Gen Z say they turn to a religious leader in times of uncertainty.*[378] Instead, they turn to therapists, Reddit, and Taylor Swift lyrics.

Enter TikTok Theology—where you can learn about the Gospel of Self-Care in 60 seconds, complete with crystals, trauma healing, and a strong boundary game. This spiritual buffet terrifies the pulpit class because Gen Z doesn't want a denomination; they want a vibe check. They're mixing Buddhist mindfulness with Black feminist thought, quoting Jesus *and* Audre Lorde in the same breath.

And nothing sends Christian nationalists into a frothing spiral faster than sex positivity. We've gone from "I Kissed Dating Goodbye" to "I Made Out With Gender Norms and Told Them To Leave." Purity rings are melted down into nose rings. According to a Gallup survey, Gen Z is more likely to be queer, sexually fluid, and open to non-monogamy.[379] This isn't rebellion—it's a spiritual realignment where ethics are no longer dictated by fear, shame, or "what would Chad from the youth group think?"

The Rise of the "Don'ts": There's a new holy trinity in town: "Don't know, don't care, don't identify." These are the "Religious Nones" on steroids—also known as the *"meh-seculars."* They're not angry at God. They find Sunday brunch, therapy, and climate activism more meaningful than church sermons about Leviticus from a man who's never touched a woman *except to oppress her.*

As of 2021, nearly 40% of Gen Z identify as religiously unaffiliated—a figure that's expected to rise.[380] It's not a phase, Karen. It's the future. And that's the panic attack Christian nationalists are trying to sermon their way out of.

Let's break down the generational theology war

- **Boomers**: Jesus saves.
- **Gen X**: Jesus saves, but also Nirvana.
- **Millennials**: Jesus saves, but capitalism doesn't.
- **Gen Z**: Jesus who?

This isn't a culture war—it's a generational turnover. Gen Z isn't asking how to fit in—they're asking what needs to be burned down and rebuilt. And spoiler: it's probably your megachurch with an LED screen the size of a basketball court and a worship band that thinks they're Coldplay.

The Evangelical Exit Row

Once upon a time, being an evangelical meant attending Bible studies, going on mission trips, and voting Republican. Today, it might mean coming out as queer, quoting Jesus *and* bell hooks, and demanding your church divest from fossil fuels. There's a growing movement of young evangelicals who love Jesus but are deeply over the patriarchy, the racism, and the boomer politics in khakis. They're *done* with Trumpism, bored with sermons that sound like Fox News transcripts, and repulsed by a gospel that seems more interested in "owning the libs" than loving thy neighbor.[381]

These new Jesus followers are:

- Eco-conscious ("Jesus turned water into wine—we're just trying to keep the oceans from turning into plastic").
- LGBTQ+ affirming ("Jesus hung out with sex workers and lepers—Karen, your nephew being nonbinary is not the apocalypse").
- Anti-capitalist ("Pretty sure flipping tables in the temple was not an endorsement of Prosperity Gospel").

They're still quoting scripture—but now it's Micah 6:8, not Leviticus. Justice, mercy, and walking humbly—not purity, patriarchy, and a 401(k) that tithes itself. These are not ex-Christians. They're ex-evangelicals—a title now so common it has its trending hashtag and book deals.[382]

And for the first time, the *coolest* Christians are the ones who left your church… on purpose.

The Reckoning: What Comes After the Hissy Fit?

Reconstruction always begins after the screamers wear themselves out.

So… what now? The flags are tattered. The slogans have lost their punch. Dick is passed out in his recliner, snoring into a half-finished copy of *Atlas Shrugged* and a half-eaten bucket of nationalist nostalgia. The hissy fit is over. Not because the screamers stopped yelling, but because **no one's listening anymore.**

Now comes the hard part: cleaning up the mess, reimagining the blueprint, and deciding who we want to be *after* the rage has burned through the foundation. At some point, every hissy fit runs out of steam—or at least out of bystanders willing to pretend it's rational behavior. This is that point—the end of the road. The moment when "owning the libs" no longer covers the mortgage, when performative outrage gets drowned out by rising seas, and when Dick finds out that rage doesn't keep the lights on.

America's hissy fit was never sustainable—it was just loud. But walls don't negotiate, nor do the long-term consequences of decades spent yelling instead of governing.

The Empire's Echo Chamber Goes Silent

America has always been loud, but volume isn't vitality. As the hissy fit dies down, a sobering reality sets in:

- We lost decades to denial.
- We let fragility dictate policy.
- We treated outrage as a strategy, and now we have nothing left but scorched earth and sagging infrastructure.

The echo chamber fell silent, not because it was convinced, but because it had finally become irrelevant.

Grievance Politics Has No Emergency Exit

You can't platform a grievance forever without consequences. For years, middle-aged white men were told they were victims of diversity, of feminism, of history classes that included slavery. Politicians, pundits, and pulpit-screamers fed the lie that someone else's gain was their loss.

However, the bill has now come due.

- Public trust? Gone.
- Political discourse? Replaced with memes and microphones.
- Institutions? Hollowed out and handed to lobbyists in flag pins.

The angry base got what it wanted: deregulation, nationalism, and culture war cosplay. But they didn't notice the fine print: **no healthcare, no livable planet, no pension**.

You Can't Gaslight Gravity

Only so long can you legislate delusion before reality stages a coup. Turns out:

- Banning AP Black History doesn't fix economic anxiety.
- Book bans don't cool the planet.
- Drag shows aren't why your bridges are collapsing.

This limits the hissy fit: it *can't solve anything*. It can only sabotage. And now that sabotage has turned inward.

The most dangerous myth sold to Dick & Co. wasn't that they were exceptional—it's that they'd always be in charge. That their way of life, beliefs, and worldview were the permanent default setting. But time has a habit of muting entitlement with math:

- Demographics shift.
- Global power shifts.
- And the cultural script gets rewritten—whether Dick likes it or not.

He's not the protagonist anymore. He's the guy yelling at the camera while the credits roll.

The Rebuilders: Not the Loudest, But the Lasting

While Dick was protesting pronouns, a new generation was organizing:

- Young voters turned out in record numbers.[383]
- Educators, artists, and scientists refused to bow to the book bans and budget cuts.
- Local leaders, community organizers, and working-class coalitions started doing what Congress wouldn't—building systems that work.

They weren't flashy. They didn't trend. But they planted seeds while others threw hissy fits.

And now? It's harvest time.

Not Hope—Blueprints

This isn't about optimism. It's about engineering.

- A post-hissy fit economy built on sustainability, not speculation.
- A workplace culture centered on equity and competence, not hierarchy and proximity.

- A political system focused on representation and repair, not grievance and theater.
- A masculinity built on strength through empathy, not dominance through denial.

The Role of the Former Hissy Fitter

Not everyone who threw a fit is beyond redemption. Some will reflect. Some will course-correct. Others? They'll become irrelevant, fading into obscurity like dusty VHS tapes of a canceled sitcom. But here's the truth: **you don't have to center them anymore.**
- Let Dick yell into the void.
- Let Tucker sell supplements to crypto collapse survivors.
- Let the outrage grifters pivot to selling freedom-themed beard oil.

The future isn't theirs to interrupt anymore. Not by how loud it shouts but by how well it holds. Not by who it excludes but by who it lifts. Not by "greatness," but by grace under pressure—and a refusal to repeat the same performative cycles of collapse. The hissy fit was loud. The fall was predictable. **What comes next? That's the revolution.**

Moment of Reflection: Decline Isn't the End—Delusion Is

The fall wasn't the tragedy. The refusal to admit it was. Every empire falls. Every ideology fades. Every cultural hissy fit runs out of steam. That's not defeat—it's gravity. But what *is* avoidable—what's preventable, fixable, and 100% human-made—is **delusion**.
- Delusion is what made us think history wouldn't apply to us.
- Delusion is what told Dick he was the real victim.
- Delusion is what made people burn books while the planet burned around them.
- And delusion, unchecked, is what turns decline into collapse.

You Can't Rebuild What You Refuse to Admit Is Broken: We were never undone by weakness. We were undone by a pathological refusal to admit fault.
- We turned self-correction into treason.
- We turned criticism into cancel culture.

- We turned reflection into weakness.

It's easier to shout than to sit in silence and ask: *What have we become?*

The Empire Was Never the Point—The People Were: We wrapped ourselves in symbols and forgot the substance. We pledged allegiance to flags while underfunding schools. We honored soldiers while denying them healthcare. We worshipped capitalism while wondering why families were living in tents under billboards for luxury condos.

"Greatness" was never the goal. *Humanity* was. But it's hard to sell that on a bumper sticker.

The True Patriot is the One Who Rebuilds, not the loudest voice in the room. Not the one with the biggest truck or the most grievances per podcast. The true patriot is the one who shows up when the slogans fade, when the stadiums empty, and when the country needs more than applause.

- They build.
- They repair.
- They imagine something better.

Not just for themselves, but for *everyone*. Even Dick.

This! We stand here—ankle-deep in floodwater, knee-deep in debt, and shoulder-deep in history—with a choice:

- Do we double down on the hissy fit?
- Or do we finally grow the hell up?

The hissy fit is over. The myths have been exposed. The wall has been hit. And now… It's time to write a new story—not for the nostalgia-drunk, grievance-addicted few, but for the *many* waiting for the screamers to lose their voice.

Decline isn't the end. But delusion? That's where the story stops. Let's not stop there.

NEXT: An Actual Wake-Up Checklist: Because slogans don't save democracies, but behavior change might.

CHECKLIST #1: STOP. Just... Stop.

✗ **Stop confusing volume with virtue.** Yelling "I LOVE AMERICA" over Toby Keith doesn't count as policy.

✗ **Stop voting like it's American Idol.** Charisma is not a competency. And no, you don't need "someone you'd have a beer with." You need someone who can read legislation.

✗ **Stop mistaking your discomfort for oppression.** You're not "silenced." You're just being disagreed with in a tone above room temperature.

✗ **Stop letting rage be your news source.** If your "research" has a promo code for protein powder, it's propaganda.

✗ **Stop romanticizing eras that would've jailed half your Facebook friends.** The 1950s weren't "simpler." They were segregated, closeted, and lead-poisoned.

✗ **Stop banning books you've never read.** If "Maus" offends you more than mass shootings, you're not defending children—you're defending ignorance.

✗ **Stop giving guys with microphones and no expertise cultural authority.** A ring light and a YouTube channel do not a public intellectual make.

CHECKLIST #2: START. Like, Now.

☑ **Start reading banned books and local election ballots.** You want to defend freedom? Start with chapter one.

☑ **Start asking who benefits from your outrage.** (Spoiler: It's not you. It's someone selling merch.)

☑ **Start treating education like a superpower, not a threat.** Critical thinking is not Marxist. It's human survival.

☑ **Start showing up to "boring" civic things.** Real democracy isn't sexy. It's school budget meetings and water department hearings—and yes, you should still care.

☑ **Start treating "I don't know" as a strength.** Admitting ignorance is the first step to not becoming a viral embarrassment.

☑ **Start holding people accountable, especially those with whom you agree.** Integrity isn't partisan.

☑ **Start giving a damn about people who don't look, live, vote, or worship like you.** That's not "woke." That's democracy functioning as intended.

GO

CHECKLIST #3: **NEVER AGAIN.**
Seriously. Don't.

✗ **Never again treat empathy as weakness.** If you think caring is unmanly, your masculinity is hanging by a thread.

✗ **Never again give a guy with three brain cells and a podcast a seat at the policymaking table.** Just because he's mad doesn't mean he's right.

✗ **Never again idolize billionaires for being rich.** They're not gods. They're just really good at not paying taxes.

✗ **Never again weaponize "free speech" as a shield for bigotry.** The First Amendment protects your right to speak, not your right to be free from feedback.

✗ **Never again treat science like a buffet.** You don't get to believe in gravity but not climate change.

✗ **Never again confuse patriotism with nationalism.** One demands accountability. The other demands a costume and a superiority complex.

✗ **Never again let comfort outrank truth.** If your version of history fits on a bumper sticker, it's missing a few chapters.

CHECKLIST #4: **Bonus Round**

Questions to Ask Before You Post, Share, Vote, or Rant

❓ **"Is this true?"**

❓ **"Do I understand it?"**

❓ **"Would I say this to someone's face at Thanksgiving?"**

❓ **"Does this help anyone other than the guy selling me a t-shirt?"**

❓ **"Is my opinion based on knowledge or just a vibe and a meme?"**

*You Can't Change the World if You
Refuse to Change Yourself*

This isn't about left vs. right. It's about **truth vs. hissy fit**. It's about **resetting culture before it resets us back to the Middle Ages—this time with Wi-Fi and worse fashion.**

Go ahead: Print this checklist. Stick it on your fridge. Tape it to your keyboard. Tattoo it on your uncle if needed. Because this is the wake-up call, the culture isn't broken. **We are.** But broken things can be rebuilt—if you stop screaming long enough to pick up a damn tool and get to work.

Rebuild the System—Gen Z, Millennials, and the Digital Generation of No More Bullshit

(Now Featuring Veterans, Genders Beyond the Binary, and Disabled Disruption)

" *he victors write history," they said.* Which explains why our textbooks read like a TED Talk from a white guy named Dick who still calls his assistant "sweetheart" and thinks neurodivergence is a TikTok trend. History's been told from the *center seat of exclusion* for so long, we forgot who kept the wheels turning—and who was thrown under the bus, then blamed for getting run over. Well, guess what? **Gen Z, Millennials, women, disabled innovators, trans leaders, and battle-scarred veterans** have entered the chat—and they're not here to *edit your legacy.*

They're here to **CTRL+ALT+DELETE** your legacy and install a system upgrade that includes *actual users* this time.

This Isn't a Revolution—It's a System Update.

Grandpa wore a tie, smoked his feelings, and waited for a promotion. This generation arrives with:

- **Pronoun pins** and Purple Hearts

- **Therapy apps** and trauma-informed org charts
- **Wheelchair-accessible tech incubators**
- And an Excel sheet titled: "Your Bullshit, Quantified"

They don't want a seat at the table—they burned the boardroom, composted the remains, and 3D-printed a new one using intersectional ethics, lived experience, and biodegradable vengeance. And yeah, the new table comes with:

- Climate justice clauses
- Land acknowledgments
- Menstrual equity
- Closed captioning
- And *mental health paid time off for everyone*, not just the VP of Vibes

Racism in America: Nobody Gets a Pass

America likes to comfort itself with the myth of "colorblindness," but the truth is we're anything but. Racism here isn't owned exclusively by one group—it's a cultural hand-me-down we've all worn at one point or another. White Americans built and benefited most from its structures, but every community has, at times, turned prejudice into a weapon—whether it's anti-Black bias in Latino neighborhoods, anti-immigrant sentiment among Black and white voters alike, or colorism running rampant across nearly every group.

The real problem isn't that racism hides—it's that it adapts. It shapeshifts from slavery to segregation to "colorblind" policies that quietly reproduce inequality. It shows up in hiring decisions, in schools, in housing, in who gets pulled over, and in who gets believed. Pretending it doesn't exist—or worse, pretending we're somehow immune because of our own identity—only lets it thrive.

Racism isn't a bug in America's operating system. It's the code. And until we admit we've all played a role in keeping that code running, we won't be able to rewrite it.

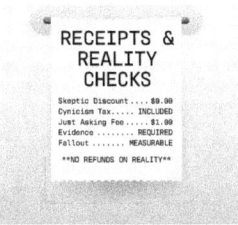

Who Hates Who: The American Racism Flowchart[384]

America loves to call itself a melting pot, but if you actually stir the pot, it's more like a stew where everyone side-eyes the other ingredients. Here's the current menu of mutual suspicion, backed by data:

- **White Americans → Everyone Else:** White folks have been running the racism marathon since 1619, and they're still breaking records. Pew (2023) found that 65% of Black Americans say being Black hurts their ability to succeed. Meanwhile, 46% of white adults think the *real* problem is "too much attention to race." Translation: *If we don't talk about it, maybe the racism goes away like a bad rash.*

- **Black Americans ↔ Asian Americans:** Black and Asian communities often get pitted against each other in the "model minority" Olympics. Pew (2022) reported 42% of Black adults believe Asians are treated better by the government. On the flip side, 27% of Asian Americans said they've been blamed for COVID-19. Apparently, equal opportunity racism is still a growth industry.

- **Latino Americans → Black Americans:** Colorism runs so deep it comes with its own Pantone chart. A 2021 Pew study found Afro-Latinos earn 17% less than lighter-skinned peers. In short: lighter skin = better paycheck. The Spanish word for this? *"Normal."*

- **Asian Americans → Each Other:** South Asians look down on East Asians, who look down on Southeast Asians, who look down on Pacific Islanders, who are too busy surviving hurricanes and wildfires to look down on anyone. Internalized racism is the Costco of prejudice: bulk-sized and cheap.

- **Everyone → Immigrants:** A 2023 PRRI survey found 54% of Republicans and 19% of Democrats said immigrants are "invading" the U.S. to replace native-born Americans. Fun fact: unless you're

Native American, your great-grandparents *were* the invasion.

- **Black + Latino + Asian Americans → White Americans:** Here's the kicker: Gallup (2023) found that 75% of people of color think racism against non-white groups is a major problem. But white Americans? Many are convinced *they're* the real victims. A 2021 Pew study revealed that 65% of white Republicans think discrimination against whites is as big a problem as discrimination against Black people. Apparently, equality feels like oppression if you've been hogging the remote for 400 years.

So, who hates who? Everybody hates somebody, but only in America do we package it, poll it, and legislate it like a subscription service. Racism here isn't a bug—it's the business model.

History's Real MVPs Didn't Wear Power Suits— They Carried the Damn Nation

Every ounce of progress in this country came from the **margins**, not the marble halls.

- Slavery didn't end because Lincoln had a moral epiphany—it ended because enslaved people forced a reckoning.
- Women didn't "win" suffrage—they kicked down doors, got arrested, and made democracy blink.
- LGBTQ+ rights weren't handed over with a Hallmark card—they were earned in riots, in courtrooms, and on the damn dance floor.

Oh, and let's talk about veterans: They didn't come home to start podcasts. They came back and quietly **redefined leadership** with phrases like "mission first, ego last" and "this meeting could've been a rescue op." Turns out, once you've dodged IEDs, Karen from Accounting isn't that scary.

Resistance ≠ Rebellion. It's the Blueprint.

Every time the status quo gets uncomfortable, it rebrands resistance as chaos.

- Tea party in Boston Harbor? "Founding Father heroics."
- BLM protest? "Domestic threat."
- Drag queen reads to kids? "Moral collapse."

- Armed white men storm the Capitol? "Expressing concerns."

Let's be real: **protest is American. Fragile white egos clinging to their Grandpa's values? That's the foreign threat.**

The People You Laughed At Were Right.

In 2021, America debated Mr. Potato Head's genitalia. Not kidding. The "controversy" started because Hasbro said it was dropping "Mr." from the brand name to make the Potato Head line more inclusive—but the Mr. and Mrs. characters were never discontinued. Hasbro clarified the same day that *"MR. & MRS. POTATO HEAD aren't going anywhere."*[385]

And the pearl-clutching? Exhibit A: Ben Shapiro's deadpan "Bigotry ANNIHILATED" tweet, plus a riff about kids aspiring to be "a plastic spheroid with interchangeable parts."[386]

While America debated **Mr. Potato Head's genitalia**, it was:

- Disabled activists who created the digital workplace we all now depend on.
- Trans teens who redefined authenticity while dodging legislation.
- Women—predominantly Black, brown, and Indigenous—who carried movements on their backs.
- Neurodivergent disruptors turning "disability" into **design advantage**.
- Veterans transforming chaos into **clarity and the chain of command into collaborative cultures.**[387]

And while the country scrolled through memes and misinformation, **they were keeping democracy on life support.**

Dear Boomers and Dick's Followers: We're Not Tearing America Down. We're Rebuilding It—Without Asking First.

Generation Z isn't just rewriting the story; they're **changing the damn author**. They don't want your permission. They want your *resignation* from the Board of Moral Superiority.

So, if the new system makes you nervous—if you're clutching your Bible, the Constitution, or the *Wall Street Journal* like a life vest, **good.** That means the update is installing correctly.

The **future is here**, and this time, the rollout team includes:

- Nonbinary engineers,
- Disabled civic designers,
- Women economists who don't code-switch for comfort, and
- Veterans with scars, skills, and no patience for bureaucracy.

America 2.0 doesn't need gatekeepers. It needs builders. And builders don't need permission. They need power tools. And, apparently, a well-organized Google Drive.

System Update In Progress—This is the Generational Reset

"Let's invite young people to the table," they said. Gen Z and Millennials: *Nah, we'll build our own damn table out of reclaimed ethics, mutual aid blueprints, and sustainably sourced boundary-setting.*

This isn't a polite request to join the status quo. This is a drag-and-drop mass deletion of broken leadership models, institutional gaslighting, and outdated definitions of "professionalism." This isn't your grandma's revolution with protest signs and tambourines. This is a data-driven, cancel-if-necessary, post-capitalist reset, wrapped in Google Docs and Canva infographics, with unbothered middle fingers aimed at corporate DEI theater.

Why Gen Z and Millennials Aren't Asking to Join the Table— They're Torching It

The "table" they were offered? It's a termite-riddled folding table from 1956 covered in unpaid internships, HR-approved racism, and stale coffee. The invitation? A sugar-coated demand to assimilate, smile, and pretend to enjoy the flavor of microaggressions for the sake of "culture fit." No thanks.

- Millennials got handed a recession and a bootstraps fantasy.
- Gen Z inherited climate collapse, mass shootings, and a job market that ghosted them like a toxic ex.
- And both were told, *"If you just work hard enough, you'll be rewarded."*

Spoiler: The reward was burnout, debt, and being called "entitled" for wanting lunch breaks and therapy benefits.

Instead of pulling up a chair, they pulled out a blowtorch. And the table? It's ash. The new workplace culture they're designing doesn't need gatekeepers—it needs codebreakers.

Gen Z values transparency, mental health, purpose, and anti-racist leadership over perks, promotions, or free snacks.[388] They're more likely to leave toxic environments, call out performative policies, and challenge authority that's allergic to accountability.[389]

Generational Disillusionment–We Were There, We Weren't Buying It

Generation X—the neglected middle child of American history, raised on divorce decrees, microwavable regret, and low-fat Pop-Tarts. This is my generation—where the music was music and no one gave a damn what we did. We were the first generation promised the Boomer Dream—2.4 kids, a pension, and the keys to a home with a functioning economy—and the first to realize it was a televised hallucination propped up by Jell-O molds and tax breaks. Born into Reaganomics and raised on Saturday morning cartoons funded by toy corporations, we were the guinea pigs of trickle-down disappointment, left to self-parent with cable news and Little Debbie.

We weren't the "Greatest Generation"—we were and still are the Cynical Generation, built for speed but programmed for sarcasm. We weren't digital natives—we were digital midwives, downloading Napster on dial-up while telling AOL to shut up. And we sure as hell weren't Boomers—we didn't own anything long enough to feel superior. We were just… there. In flannel. With trust issues. Watching it all burn.

Gen X came of age when greed was rebranded as virtue, and "government" was a punchline unless it was funding a war. We were told to work hard, get a degree, and we'd be fine. Instead, we got Enron's vapor stock, NAFTA's job exodus, and a dot-com boom that blew up faster than our 401(k)s could be explained to us .[390] We watched as Clinton gave us triangulation, Bush gave us Iraq, and the media gave us Judith Miller explaining WMDs like a bad Yelp review.

While Boomers shipped off to war and Millennials shipped off to therapy, Gen X moved into the basement and called it an ethos. Our motto was the rallying cry of the counter culture of the 1970s: *"Don't trust anyone over 30."* Then we hit 35 and started tweeting from burner accounts like @grungeDad69. It wasn't that Gen X skipped politics out of apathy—we tuned it out because we'd already seen the machinery up close, and frankly, we weren't impressed. We didn't skip politics because we didn't care—we ignored it because we'd seen how it worked, and we weren't impressed.

We watched both parties and their presidents sell out like a Rolling Stones reunion tour. We saw the media morph from watchdog to lapdog. And we sat silently as every serious conversation turned into a culture war headline, all while thinking, "Didn't we already try this in the '90s ?"[391] It wasn't apathy—it was realistic pessimism wrapped in sarcasm with a center of "please leave me out of this."

Here's the twist nobody saw coming: Gen X didn't just survive the collapse—we engineered the infrastructure for it. We coded the platforms that turned hate into monetizable engagement. We invented the snark-laced tone that now fuels conspiracy memes and "intellectual dark web" podcasts. We created Reddit to watch it become the world's largest anonymous book club for the unhinged. Ah, the good old days.

We were the first hackers, the original downloaders, the quiet kings of irony—and somewhere along the way, we gave birth to the startup bro, then quietly blocked him on LinkedIn. We didn't set out to build the algorithm that broke society. We just wanted a better way to listen to Pearl Jam.

These days, Gen X is barely mentioned in political discourse unless someone needs a nostalgic nod to "real MTV" or a scapegoat for why nobody goes outside anymore. We're now mid-level leaders or managers, raising emotionally intelligent kids while we battle emotional numbness, drinking boxed wine, and wondering how Spotify managed to destroy the concept of an album. (Okay, I won't touch boxed wine—I'm a proud wine snob.) Oh, and we VOTE occasionally.

We don't do marches. We don't post selfies at rallies. We don't start podcasts called "Let's Unpack That." No, our podcasts are more business- and no-bullshit- focused, like *Culture Shock—Disrupting the Workplace*, for example (hey, I can self-promote like the best of my generation). But behind every Slack notification and broken HR platform, we're there—holding it together with duct tape, dad jokes, and low expectations. You may not see us. But we see *everything* because we built the damn feed.

Millennials as Scapegoats: The Participation Trophy Purge

We gave the millennials a broken system and then mocked them because they did not fix it fast enough. And then came the Millennials, emerging from the ashes of dial-up internet and standardized testing, blinking into adulthood like deer caught in the headlights of late-stage capitalism. Raised in the crossfire of school shootings, economic collapses, and war-on-terror propaganda, they dared to ask for healthcare, a living wage, and a planet that wouldn't be on fire by 2050—and were instantly accused of being lazy Marxist gender witches who killed the napkin industry.

This generation was baptized in **lockdown drills and recession headlines**, handed more student debt than any group in US history. And then told to "pull themselves up by the bootstraps,"—which is hard to do when Sallie Mae has repossessed your boots. Instead of confronting the massive institutional rot they inherited, society gave them BuzzFeed quizzes and avocado toast shame.

Let's clear something up once and for all: **Millennials did not invent participation trophies. Boomers did—because Boomers didn't like to see little Timmy cry.** But once Timmy grew up, the media and political establishment turned around and called him a weak, coddled snowflake for accepting the very thing *they handed him*.

Political commentators couldn't distinguish between entitlement and systemic critique, so they rolled it all into one easy slur: "snowflake." If a Millennial organized a protest, they were told to "get a job." If they got a job and spoke up about injustice, they were told they were "too sensitive." And if they quit the job? "There goes the work ethic." It was a perfect ouroboros of generational gaslighting.

Neither did the Boomers or Generation X listen. They pathologized. They commodified their trauma and repackaged it as generational fragility. Millennials weren't fragile. They were furious—and mostly right.

Rage as a Data-Driven Strategy:
Receipts, Screenshots, and Google Docs as Activism Tools

Millennials doesn't carry pitchforks. They carry spreadsheets. They're not storming castles—they're screen recording your gaslighting and posting it on TikTok with a call to action and a Change.org petition link in the comments. Gone are the days of "he said, she said." Now it's: "Per my last email…" [Attached: screenshots, Slack threads, HR policies, and your entire career arc.]

Receipts are the revolution. Screenshots are the new subpoenas. Google Docs is the underground railroad of workplace equity. This isn't "cancel culture." It's a consequence of culture with version control. They're not mad without reason—they're angry with evidence. And every ignored microaggression, racist policy, or misogynistic hiring practice? It's going in a shared folder named: *The Bullshit You Thought No One Would Notice.*

From Protest to Protocol:
The Generation That Builds While Burning

Let's squash the myth: Gen Z and Millennials aren't just mad—they're methodical. They're not just protesting; they're prototyping. While some are busy shaking their heads s about "disrespect," these digital natives are:

- **Writing mutual aid guides**—because when institutions fail, you build a new playbook. Mutual aid efforts have become indispensable, especially during crises like the pandemic, where grassroots networks delivered essentials faster than any bureaucracy could. [392]

- **Creating HR-free workplace grievance collectives**—labor activism isn't just about unionizing blue-collar jobs anymore. Tech workers and other professionals are organizing too. A recent study shows social activism in the workplace often sparks labor organizing among professionals.[393]

- **Launching cooperatives, startups, and nonprofits with embedded DEI and trauma-informed policy from day one**—they're not retrofitting values; they're building them in from the foundation. Platforms like *Barter Up*, founded by Gen Z creators, promote community, mutual aid, and anticapitalism through co-op models and skill-sharing—critical, inclusive systems for modern times.[394]

They're drafting policy while marching in the streets. They're building equity dashboards while dismantling legacy org charts. They're crafting inclusive mission statements on Notion while quitting jobs mid-Zoom with full pay and benefits. In short? They're designing the culture you keep pretending you already had. Remember, comfort is not a value, especially not when it's used to uphold harm. Gen Z and Millennials understand that a healthy culture is not about being nice.[395] It's about being honest, equitable, inclusive, and *accountable.*

Diversity & Equity are NOT a Trend; They're the Operating System

Once upon a time, diversity was treated like the office birthday cake—rolled out once a year, celebrated awkwardly, and often left stale in the break room. But Gen Z? They deleted that file and installed a new OS. Diversity isn't a side project. It's the architecture. This generation isn't "embracing difference." They *are* different—built from it, thriving in it, and designing every policy, practice, and protest with it hard-coded into the source code.

How Gen Z Sees Identity: Fluid, Intersecting, and Foundational

Gone are the days of neat demographic boxes. **Gen Z shows up as whole humans—messy, nuanced, and beautifully non-binary.**

- Gender? A galaxy, not a binary.
- Race? A lived reality, not a footnote.
- Sexuality? Fluid AF.
- Mental health? Discussed openly, not whispered into a paper bag behind HR's door.

Identity is no longer a postscript. It's the *prologue.* It's not something they tuck away until 5:01 p.m.—it's embedded in how they lead, work, organize, and thrive. Gen Z is the most racially and ethnically diverse generation in US history, and it is also the most likely to reject fixed labels in favor of lived experiences, intersectionality, and fluidity. Identity isn't an accessory.[396] It's the source code. This generation doesn't just bring their "whole selves" to work. They refuse to leave any piece behind—because leaving parts of yourself behind isn't professionalism. It's trauma.

Race, Gender, Neurodivergence, Queerness: Not Exceptions—Expectations

Boomers and Gen X treated diversity like a surprise visitor. Millennials made it a strategy. Gen Z made it nonnegotiable.

They don't want "diverse hires." They want equity *built into hiring.*

They don't want inclusive policies as an afterthought. They want inclusion *at inception.*

In the Gen Z workplace and worldview:

- Queer identities are baseline, not bold.
- Neurodivergence is innovation, not inconvenience.
- Non-white leadership isn't "representation." It's overdue.

Diversity isn't something you "add." It's something you build from, or you get left behind like a fax machine at a TikTok shoot.

Equity Over Equality—And Why That Pisses Some People Off

Equality = Sameness: Great in Kindergarten, Useless in Reality

Equality is adorable in theory. It's the shiny bumper sticker of justice. It's everyone getting the same slice of pie... even if some people never got a plate, some have been force-fed crumbs, and others showed up with the bakery deed in hand. Picture this: three people of different heights trying to see over a fence. Equality gives them all the same-sized box. The tall guy sees the game. The middle guy squints. The short guy stares at the plywood. Equity? It gives each person the box they *need*—and probably installs a damn window in the fence while we're at it.

Equality assumes we all start at the same line. We don't. Not when entire communities are still climbing out of holes that other people dug—and then paved over with golf courses.[397]

Equity = Justice: Or, As Dick Calls It, "Reverse Oppression"

Here's where things get spicy. The moment you say "equity," Dick starts twitching. His voice rises. His face gets redder than a Fox News chyron. Why? Because equity means recalibrating systems. And that feels like a loss to people who were never told their advantage was unearned.

- Hiring a qualified woman instead of another Steve? Oppression.

- Addressing pay disparities? Witchcraft.
- Removing Confederate statues? Cultural genocide.

To Dick, equity sounds like *punishment* because he's been raised to believe that fairness means *he wins by default*. If the game isn't rigged in his favor anymore, then surely it must be broken.

But here's the real shocker: equity doesn't take anything *from* anyone. It gives people a shot they never had—because the system never let them play to begin with.[398]

The Fear Behind the Fury: Why Fairness Feels Like Theft

The backlash to equity isn't rational. It's emotional. It's the sound of fragile egos being told their trophies came with training wheels. When you've lived on third base and been told you hit a triple, equity feels like someone moving the bases. In reality, it's just someone finally measuring the damn field. And yet, here we are—in a country where "diversity hire" is still used as an insult, where equity programs are labeled "Marxist," and where being asked to acknowledge privilege is treated like a personal attack. Imagine being addicted to the illusion of meritocracy, so that fairness feels like oppression.

The Demographic Plot Twist Is Here—Time to End This Crap

Change Isn't Coming. It's Already Logged In and Changed the Wi-Fi Password.

While Boomers—and let's be honest, some Gen Xers and Millennial middle managers—are still glued to the nightly news, yelling at rising avocado prices and clinging to *Matlock* reruns, something revolutionary is happening: Generations Z and Alpha aren't waiting for permission. They're rewriting the cultural code while you're still buffering. Why? Because time, like Gen Z's attention span, waits for no one:

- **Boomers are aging out of power** (and into prescription-tier insurance plans). They've had a good run—dominating politics, media, and brunch—but actuarial tables don't lie.
- **Traditionalists?** Already mostly memorialized in bronze statues or angry letters to the editor.
- **Millennials?** The last majority-white generation. Sorry, Chad, the "de-

fault setting" has expired.[399]

And let's not forget the **fundamental power shift: Women are done.** Done with the gaslighting. Done with the "Aw, sweetie, let the men talk." Done with being policy targets. We hold the **purse strings**, dominate higher education,[400] and are fast outnumbering men at the polls.[401]

Oh, and one more thing: **Gen Z and Alpha?** They don't care about your culture wars, your fax machines, or your "back in my day" origin stories. They care about climate change, equity, student debt, and mental health. And unlike some of their elders, **they take action—voting and tweeting—at the same time.**

So, to the fragile status quo: Enjoy the last dance while the playlist still has a 1970s track. Because Gen Z has just changed it to Lizzo, and Gen Alpha is uploading the remix to the blockchain. Let us take a look, shall we—

Explicit Generational Accountability and Alignment

No one gets to watch from the sidelines when the house is on fire.

You've posted the infographics. You've changed your profile pic. You've rage-commented under news articles you didn't read. But now? It's time to show up. "**Millennials built the digital infrastructure. Gen Z is exposing hypocrisy. Gen Alpha? They'll inherit whatever we don't fix. If you're still scrolling, you're still responsible.**" As Twenge (2023) notes, each generation's relationship with technology shapes not only culture but also civic responsibility.[402]

Baby Boomers (1946-1964): The Entitlement Architects

- **Your tools?** Institutional control, wealth consolidation, and political legacy.
- **Your trauma?** A Cold War childhood, Vietnam, and being told your lawn is "problematic."
- **Your responsibility?** Stop hoarding power, pretending you're "just confused," and weaponizing nostalgia. Fund the future. Support education, climate action, and digital literacy. And read a banned

book before banning drag queens.
- **Your line:** "I may not understand TikTok, but I can vote for policies that protect the future."

Gen X (1965-1980): The Ghosted Middle Child
- **Your tools?** Cynicism, independence, and the ability to code-switch between analog and digital like a boss.
- **Your trauma?** Reaganomics, latchkey isolation, and the invention of *the Participation Trophy Narrative*.
- **Your responsibility?** Stop playing "both sides" because it's more comfortable. Get off the fence and bring your under-rated pragmatism to the table. Use your position of quiet influence to make a deliberate noise.
- **Your line:** "I'm done spectating. Time to mentor, disrupt, and vote like it matters—because it does."

Millennials (1981-1996): The Burnout Engineers
- **Your tools?** The internet, protest culture, trauma memes, and a decade of side hustles.
- **Your trauma?** 9/11, two recessions, school shootings, student debt, and being told "avocado toast" is why you can't afford a home.
- **Your responsibility?** You built the digital economy. Now make its **ethics.** Demand real power in rooms you used to cater, code for, or create content about. You are the transition team between the collapse of analog and the rebirth of digital.
- **Your line:** "I'm not just here to survive the system—I'm here to rewire it."

Gen Z (1997-2012): The Bullshit Detectors
- **Your tools?** Social platforms, callout culture, identity fluency, and mental health awareness.
- **Your trauma?** Climate dread, gun violence drills, algorithmic surveillance, and watching democracy

turn into a meme war.

- **Your responsibility?** Stop posting about injustice and start organizing against it. Your voice is powerful, but your *vote* is the follow-through. Keep being loud—but start being strategic. You don't need approval. You need action.
- **Your line:** "I'm not the future—I'm the feedback. And I'm not asking. I'm changing it."

Gen Alpha (2013-?): The Download Generation

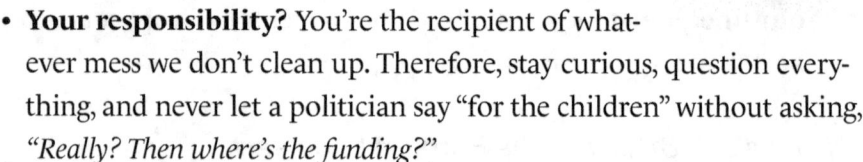

- **Your tools?** iPads, coding bootcamps, and the digital literacy older generations only dreamed of.
- **Your trauma?** TBD—but let's try to make it *less* than ours.
- **Your responsibility?** You're the recipient of whatever mess we don't clean up. Therefore, stay curious, question everything, and never let a politician say "for the children" without asking, *"Really? Then where's the funding?"*
- **Your line:** "I'm watching. And I've got receipts."

Participation Is Not Optional.

Every generation carries baggage. Every generation has tools. And every generation has a choice: Burn it down or build something better. Scroll past or speak up. Repeat the script or rewrite the whole damn play.

You don't have to be perfect. But you **do** have to participate.

Because history doesn't care how old you are. It just wants to know: **Were you part of the problem, the cleanup, or the cover-up?**

Intergenerational Bridge-Building:
Because You Can't Build a Future on Burnt Bridges

Let's get something straight: This reset is not just a reckoning. It's a relay.

And if one generation drops the baton while the next one's too pissed to pick it up, the only thing we pass down is chaos with a higher screen resolution.

- Yes, Boomers broke things.

- Yes, Gen X shrugged while the house caught fire.
- Yes, Millennials overdosed on "resilience."
- Yes, Gen Z is side-eyeing everyone with a Google Doc and a grudge.

However, here's the reality: The rebuild cannot happen unless we work together to build it.

Why We Must Build Across Generations: Some people built the system. Some survived the system. Some benefit from the system. But now—we need everyone to dismantle it and help rebuild something better.

Because Gen Z has the momentum, but not all the tools. Millennials have the vision, but are running low on energy (and serotonin). Gen X has the strategic savvy, but often hides behind "neutrality." Boomers? They've got the resources, networks, and real estate. And a pension we're going to need to learn from, not just resent.

Unlearning Isn't Shame—It's Leadership

Boomers and Gen X—if you're reading this and bracing for a verbal beatdown, don't. This isn't your cultural funeral. It's your invitation. *We don't want you gone. We want you in—but we need you to stop treating unlearning like betrayal.*

Your legacy isn't what you defended. It's what you're still willing to challenge.

You don't have to understand every TikTok. But if you're still quoting Reagan and complaining about "kids these days," we're going to ask you to take a seat. Or better yet—a class.

How to Build the Bridge (Instead of Burning It)

Millennials and Gen Z:
- Stop assuming age = enemy. You're not the first rebels. Listen to those who protested before Wi-Fi existed.
- Invite Boomers and Gen X to discussions without rolling your eyes into the next galaxy.
- Use your digital dexterity to teach. But also your emotional maturity to include.

Gen X and Boomers:
- Stop treating young people's urgency as "immaturity." It's called clarity.

- Ask more questions. Say "I don't know" more often. Try being the student, not the teacher.
- Trade your influence and experience for the one thing younger generations are giving: the future.

What Bridge-Building Looks Like in Action: Listening without defensiveness. Making space by stepping back, not out. Amplifying voices instead of centering yourself in every conversation. Replacing *"we didn't talk about that back then"* with *"I'm learning now."* Admitting that cultural norms you survived might still be systems we're dying from.

The Rebuild Needs All Hands on Deck– Not Just the Young and the Righteously Angry

This isn't a generational turf war. It's collective repair. And repair doesn't happen through rage-quits or gatekeeping. It happens when: Boomers bring the blueprints. Gen X finally speaks up. Millennials run the logistics. Gen Z dares to dream past the algorithm. And Gen Alpha grows up in a world that listens. This is your invitation to grab a brick, not a bullhorn. Because the next American Renaissance won't be built on ego. It'll be built on intergenerational humility—and a whole lot of unlearning.

Which brings us to the real story: History's MVPs. The people who didn't just complain about the cracks but picked up the tools, the movements, and the courage to start rebuilding. If America has any shot at a reset, it's because every generation has had its builders—those who chose repair over retreat.

History's Real MVPs: Learning Comes from the Edges

Because the people who changed the world didn't have titles—they had targets on their backs.

The version of history spoon-fed to us in classrooms and campaign ads is about as accurate as a MAGA hat's grasp of nuance. We were told "great men" made America. But let's be honest—most of those "great men" were just well-dressed hoarders of power and privilege, standing on pyramids built from the bones of the marginalized. **The real changemakers?** They weren't in the halls of Congress. They were in the streets. In the backrooms.

In the jails. In the margins. Pushing justice forward while being shoved out of the narrative.

Every Major Leap Forward in American History?
Dragged There by the People Those in Power Tried to Silence.

We didn't get civil rights, labor protections, or suffrage because a president woke up one morning feeling generous. We got (and will get) progress only because *people with nothing to lose fought like hell for a country that tried to erase them.*

- Slavery didn't end because Lincoln had a moral awakening. It ended because Black abolitionists, enslaved people, and free Black radicals risked everything to expose the hypocrisy of "liberty and justice for all" while still in chains. Frederick Douglass, Harriet Tubman, and Sojourner Truth weren't invited to the table. They flipped the damn thing.
- Women didn't "get" the right to vote. They stormed, shouted, bled, and were force-fed for it. Ida B. Wells was erased from white feminist textbooks not because she was irrelevant, but because she refused to play nice with racists in petticoats.
- LGBTQ+ rights didn't come from bipartisan hugs. They came from bricks, protests, and riots led by trans women of color. Stonewall wasn't a parade—it was a warning shot.

Power has always tried to write progress as if it were a gift. It wasn't. It was a hostage negotiation.

History Doesn't Forget the Comfortable.
It Forgets the Inconvenient.

That's why:

- Black women who birthed movements get a footnote (if that).
- Queer, disabled, and Indigenous activists are replaced with watered-down mascots of "respectability."
- Organizers become "rioters." Visionaries become "radicals." The uncomfortable truths they screamed were rewritten as polite footnotes in DEI training modules.

It's not an accident. It's an erasure machine with tenure. The curriculum is curated. The monuments are lies. The national memory is manicured like a bad comb-over desperately hiding what's underneath.

The Future Is Being Written in Code-Switch and Collective Care

The dominant culture didn't invent innovation. It just *marketed it louder.* Those have always modeled the blueprint for sustainable, people-centered systems on the margins:

- Mutual aid wasn't a Silicon Valley idea—it was how queer communities survived the AIDS crisis.
- Restorative justice wasn't discovered by a university think tank—it was practiced by Indigenous communities long before Western courts decided punishment = justice.
- Collective care is not a fad. It's the default setting in communities that have never had the luxury of rugged individualism.

Translation: while legacy leaders were busy optimizing shareholder profits, marginalized leaders were optimizing human survival.

The Power of the Outsider Lens: See More, Fear Less

When you're standing at the edge of society, you see things differently— not because you're broken, but because you've had to *build binoculars to survive.* The marginalized have always had a front-row seat to injustice, which means they've always had the clearest vision for what a just society could look like. They weren't blinded by comfort, sedated by the status quo, or numbed by NPR pledge drives. They were *awake*, whether they wanted to be or not.

Fun fact: When you don't benefit from the system, you tend to be the first to notice when it's rigged. Shocking, right?

From Rosa to RuPaul: Icons, Instigators, and Cultural Engineers

- Rosa Parks wasn't just tired—she was strategic. Her refusal to give up a seat wasn't accidental; it was a calculated mic drop against white supremacy.
- RuPaul didn't just slay in heels—he cracked open America's gender

binary with a wig, a wink, and a sharper understanding of identity politics than most Ivy League professors.
- Marsha P. Johnson didn't ask for a seat at the table—she flipped it, then marched anyway.

These aren't side characters in your "inclusion initiative." They're the blueprint architects. The problem isn't that they're too loud. It's that the rest of us were trained to whisper.

The Real Thought Leaders:
Women, Queer Folks, and Communities of Color

Because "leadership" isn't just yelling confidently while being wrong. That's Dick's brand. For decades, corporate America treated emotional intelligence like it was an herbal supplement—nice to have, but not "real leadership." Meanwhile, the communities they excluded were mastering the art of self-awareness, adaptability, and social navigation *to survive*.
- Women led with empathy, while men called it "being too emotional."
- LGBTQ+ leaders built entire support ecosystems while straight CEOs built PowerPoints on "team cohesion."
- Communities of color decoded power structures, shifted tone mid-meeting, and translated trauma into performance evaluations, just to make it through a Tuesday.[403]

What white male leaders branded as "soft skills," the marginalized wielded like tactical gear. Not because it was trendy, but because *emotional literacy was survival tech.* It turns out the people with the least voice had the most vision. But sure—tell us again about Chad's "natural leadership instincts."

Real Power Has Never Sat in the Middle of the Room. It's Always Been Pushed to the Edges—and That's Where It Thrives.

You want heroes? Stop looking at the podium. Start looking at who wasn't allowed in the building.
- Look at the Indigenous activists defending water and land from billion-dollar pipelines.
- Look at the undocumented organizers demanding basic humanity

with no legal safety net.

- Look at the Black trans youth marching not for visibility, but *for survival.*
- Look at the workers walking out of Amazon warehouses, risking it all because dignity isn't negotiable.

These aren't side stories. They are the pulse of progress. And they've always been.

Spoiler: While you were arguing about cancel culture, the future was under construction—with blueprints written in protest, policy, and Google Sheets.

The Role of the Marginalized as Architects of the Future

The Blueprint Was Always at the Bottom—Y'all Just Weren't Looking

Suppose America had just listened to the people it spent centuries trying to silence. In that case, we'd already be living in a thriving, equitable society with better playlists, more effective policies, and fewer PowerPoint presentations explaining "inclusion." For all the talk of innovation and disruption, the real architects of the future aren't tech bros, hedge fund managers, or that one mediocre white guy who keeps getting promoted because he's "confident in meetings." No—the marginalized have been designing liberation in the shadows while the powerful fumbled with blueprints they never understood.

The Excluded = The Experts

Let's get this through the drywall of American consciousness: those furthest from power have always had the clearest vision of justice. Why? Because they're the ones who've had to survive the systems everyone else is just now realizing are broken.

- Black women created the intersectional framework *and* organized voting blocs that saved democracy on a regular basis.[404]
- Indigenous communities were modeling sustainability and relational governance while colonizers were still dying of dysentery.
- Queer folks taught the world how to build chosen families, create mutual aid systems, and fight pandemics while being legislated out

of existence.

- Disabled activists invented the modern blueprint for inclusion—curb cuts, captions, access as a human right, not as charity, but as a necessity.

In short, the margins weren't margins—they were **labs.**

Why the Center Keeps Failing

The dominant culture keeps asking, *"How do we fix it?"* while clinging to the very systems that broke it. Meanwhile, the marginalized have already built models for:

- Community resilience
- Restorative justice
- Healing-centered leadership
- Collective economics
- Nonlinear, nonbinary, non-colonial thinking

But instead of elevating those voices, we hire consultants to translate them into corporate jargon.

"You're saying the colonized people already had the answers? But they don't even use Slack."

Yes, Dick. And yet, somehow, they figured out how to survive genocide, slavery, forced sterilizations, and capitalism's greatest hits. You should be taking notes.

From Visibility to Authority

Representation isn't the goal. **Redesign is.** We don't need more "diverse voices" *on* panels. We need new power structures where those voices are *building* the panel, moderating it, and deciding who gets to show up. Equity isn't about letting people into your broken system. It's about creating something new—*by them, for all of us.*

The Real Changemakers are Not in the Halls of Congress
How marginalized communities built the systems we now call progress

I. ROOTS (1800s-1910s) – The Original Architects

WHO	THEIR FUEL	THE RESULT
Indigenous Peoples	Restorative justice, communal governance	Modeled balance, repair, and collective responsibility [rebranded in 1970s]
Enslaved People & Free Black Radicals	Resistance, rebellion, abolition	*Built the moral and strategic foundation for every liberation movement*—organizing, escaping, teaching, and rebelling even while enslaved
Frederick Douglass	Abolition, citizenship	Transformed words into activism; embodied moral courage
Harriet Tubman	Freedom networks, resistance	Created community-based systems of liberation
Sojourner Truth	Abolition, women's rights	Practiced intersectionality before the term existed
Ida B. Wells	Anti-lynching, suffrage	Challenged white feminism; refused to "play nice" with racist suffragists
Black Women Activists	Voting blocs, intersectional politics	Repeatedly safeguarded democracy through collective organizing

II. REVOLUTION (1950s-1990s) – Expanding the Blueprint

WHO	THEIR FUEL	THE RESULT
Rosa Parks	Civil rights, strategic resistance	Civil disobedience as a national strategy for change
Marsha P. Johnson	LGBTQ+ / trans liberation	Sparked the Stonewall uprising; flipped the table on exclusion
RuPaul	Queer culture, performance art	Mainstreamed visibility and gender discourse
Mutual Aid [AIDS crisis]	Queer survival, community care	Built underground networks of care amid government neglect
Collective Care Movements	Feminist and BIPOC organizing	Reframed care into political resistance to institutional failure

III. CONTINUUM (2000s-Present) – Modern Frontlines
Examples of ongoing leadership:

- **Indigenous activists** defending water and land from billion-dollar pipelines
- **Undocumented organizers** demanding humanity with no legal safety net
- **Black trans youth** marching for survival, not visibility
- **Workers** walking out of Amazon warehouses for dignity

Gender Roles, Disabilities, and Veterans— The Revolution You Didn't See Coming Because You Were Too Busy Yelling at Pronouns

While You Were Screaming About Wokeness, Progress Got to Work

While Dick was busy crying about pronouns on Twitter and Karen was staging a Facebook protest over inclusive bathroom signs at Target, real change was quietly happening. Not in think tanks or billionaire bunkers, but in the lived experience of people who never got a seat at the table—so they built their own damn table.

Welcome to the revolution. Powered by neurodivergent insight, gender-fluid leadership, and veterans who think "teamwork" means more than passing the blame in a boardroom. If this terrifies the traditionalists? Good. It should.

Gender Roles: *Burned, Buried, and Rewritten in Bold*

The era of Macho Men Who Don't Cry is on life support. Welcome to Gender Roles 2.0—where men cry first, ask for directions second, and listen third. Therapy's no longer a dating red flag; it's a front-row seat to the emotional enlightenment tour.

Why gender is no longer a job title.

You've probably heard it before: "We need to get back to traditional values." But traditional for whom? The 1950s? The 1850s? The Bronze Age? Gender is not a job title. It's not a color-coded career path that comes with an apron or a tie. And "traditional values"? That's just code for inequality with a vintage filter.

Welcome to 2025, where:

- Men can wear eyeliner and run board meetings (simultaneously, if the Wi-Fi is strong).
- Women can lead nations and still be expected to "smile more" through it.
- And everyone else refuses to check a box to make HR more comfortable.

Outdated Software: Gender Edition

"Traditional values" came with a minimal terms-of-service agreement:

- Men = Providers (but emotionally constipated).

- Women = Nurturers (but unpaid and underappreciated).
- Everyone else = Not even listed in the manual.

Too bad we all clicked "Accept" without reading the fine print.

Childcare, Ambition, Eyeliner—Now Available for All Genders

We're living in a cultural software update. In this patch:

- Dads go to dance recitals.
- CEOs pump breast milk in the boardroom.
- Nonbinary artists break streaming records.

And the only people clutching pearls are those who think a pronoun can threaten masculinity. So, when someone says, "We need to protect traditional values," remember: "Protect" is often code for preserving **inequality**, wrapped in nostalgia, sealed with fear.

Women in Charge: Emotional IQ Is the New Boardroom Weapon

Let's get rid of the myth: women leading isn't just "nice"—it's profitable, powerful, and puts outdated boardroom bros to shame. Emotional intelligence (EI) isn't soft—it's the new hard currency of success—and women are cashing in.

Emotional IQ Isn't Feel-Good Fluff—It's ROI with Heart

Multiple studies have shown that women leaders consistently outperform their male counterparts in terms of team engagement, innovation, and profitability. For example, one *Harvard Business Review* analysis reported that companies with 30% women in leadership roles see an average 15% increase in profitability—largely because diverse emotional skills lead to stronger decision-making and oversight.[405]

Similarly, a Korn Ferry study of 55,000 leaders across 90 countries found that women outscore men in nearly every emotional intelligence (EI) competency, particularly empathy, adaptability, and social intelligence—qualities directly tied to trust, retention, and revenue growth.[406]

But does that mean men *can't* be emotionally intelligent? **Absolutely not. Emotional intelligence can be taught and improved.** Recent research reveals that men benefit from EI training programs. For instance, a 2025 study demonstrated that standardized EI interventions led to significant improvements in emotional regulation and perception among male participants,[407] underscoring that EI is a skill—not a fixed trait—and accessible to anyone willing to learn.

EI = Engagement + Effectiveness + Earnings

- Emotional intelligence drives 67% of a leader's effectiveness, and EI-focused companies see 22% higher revenue growth.[408]
- Gallup data shows emotionally savvy female managers produce more cohesive teams, fewer conflicts, and higher productivity, even during crisis.[409]
- APA reports that women-centered EI leadership improves workplace fairness, collaboration, and innovation, turning empathy into enterprise advantage.[410]

Simply put: emotionally intelligent leadership isn't optional—it's essential. Female leaders don't just boost morale—they drive tangible business outcomes, from reduced turnover and classic workplace drama to improved bottom lines and employee wellbeing. Women aren't just breaking glass ceilings—they're replacing them with more innovative, more decisive, more human leadership. Emotional IQ isn't a gimmick—it's the keystone of modern business success, and women are leading the way.

To the skeptics still dismissing EI as touchy-feely, check your balance sheets. The numbers don't lie.

Masculinity 2.0: Fewer Suppressive Expectations, More Emotional Literacy

Welcome to the reboot nobody knew we needed—and yet, here we are. Masculinity 2.0 trades old-school "tough guy" scripts for deeper narratives: vulnerability taken seriously, the courage to feel, and the radical idea that men can cry—and still be powerful. Men are discovering that vulnerability doesn't erase virility—it enriches it. Opening up builds emotional muscles stronger than chest day ever did:

- Emotional openness helps men manage stress, anxiety, and depression—and yes, it's scientifically proven. Healing starts when tears replace bravado.[411]

- Doing feelings *first* helps avoid emotional explosions later—punching walls doesn't fix your inbox.
- Yet, the transition isn't smooth: men drop out of therapy 50% more often than women, often citing a "lack of connection" with the therapist, because coaching emotional strength requires emotional connection.[412]

Meanwhile, it's not just memes—real change is happening. More men are training to be therapists to support other men through identity crises, loneliness, and life transitions. There's a growing trend of male professionals entering psychotherapy to meet the urgent mental health needs of men, build trust in clinical spaces, and address high male suicide rates.[413]

Barbie for President–Ken in Counseling

And then there was the plot twist nobody asked for: Barbie runs for President. Ken joins the support group.

This isn't political satire—it's cultural reality. We've entered a world where the blonde-in-leadership archetype is campaigned, and men are unlearning emotional illiteracy in real time. Barbie's campaign? A symbol of reinvention. Ken in therapy? The backlash and growth co-occur.

Masculinity 2.0 isn't about dismantling manhood—it's about upgrading it for a more emotionally literate world. Men are learning that tears build character, therapy builds resilience, and yes—Barbie running America and Ken in group therapy isn't absurd. It's a feature, not a bug.

In the ultimate **Gender Roles 2.0** punchline, Barbie threw her hat—and heels—into the 2024 race, while Ken responded by forming a support group called *"Feelings Friday."* The headline wrote itself: "President Barbie and Counselor Ken: America's Emotional Makeover Begins."

That's not a dystopian fantasy—it's our present reality.

Therapy, emotional competence, and compassion aren't just adulting upgrades—they're the new playbook. Men are passing through denial, women are leading the revolution in emotional intelligence quotient, and everyone's waking up to the absurdity of equating softness with weakness. Gender 2.0 isn't coming—it's already hired, promoted, and publishing its memoirs.

Disabilities: From Pity to Power

Let's retire the charity blankets: **access is not optional—it's a game-changer for everyone**. Design for the margins, and you fix the center. Think curb cuts—not just for wheelchairs, but for skateboarders, parents with strollers, delivery workers, and people on e-scooters. That's the beauty of universal design—it works for all of us.

- **Curb cuts**? Thank disability rights activists in Berkeley. Today, 90% of so-called "able-bodied" pedestrians use them too—because who doesn't love rolling a suitcase or pushing a stroller without hitting a curb?
- **Closed captions**? Designed for the deaf, but now everyone binge-watches with subtitles—gym rats, language learners, news junkies—because clarity matters.

These accessibility tools aren't just moral wins—they're **economic wins**: improved engagement, stronger innovation, and fewer broken bones (literally and figuratively).

The Trojan Horses of Equity

Curb cuts, closed captions, universal design—they're the stealth bombs of inclusivity. You think you're buying ramps; you're planting freedom mines. These features slip into design specs, invade every environment, and *nobody objects when grandma and the skateboarder can use the same sidewalk*.

Universal design suggests that you build for the edges, and everything in the middle falls into place. It's not extra—it's essential. Every disabled person who demands access isn't just lobbying—they're steering society into a safer, brighter, more ingenious future. This isn't pity porn. It's pragmatic progress. When we design for the most marginalized, we don't just fix their crossing—we reinvent the road. And if that revolution happens to help your overloaded luggage and your marathon Netflix session? So much the better. Access isn't charity—it's cultural and technological leadership, hiding in plain sight.

The System Was Never Broken. It Was Never Built With The Neurodivergent in Mind.

Neurodivergent leadership isn't an upgrade—it's a revolution. Why solve problems the "normal" way when the "different" way works?

Companies were never "broken," they were *exclusive*—modeled for a narrow slice of thinkers, communicators, and processors. Cue **neurodivergent leadership**, the plot twist where efficiency meets creativity, and innovation drops the mic.

- Research found that diverse teams, including neurodivergent members, outperform homogeneous ones by 36% in profitability.[414]
- Leaders with dyslexia, ADHD, or autism bring pattern detection, disruption insight, and laser focus—skills that "normal" (or "typical") brains can't manufacture.
- "Universal Design" for neurodiversity isn't charity—it's business progress: flexible roles, quiet zones, visual instructions. Suddenly, productivity skyrockets.[415]

Trojan Horse of Inclusion

All it took was **intentional design**—not barriers—like:
- Visual workflows for ADHD minds.
- Quiet rooms in offices are designed to combat sensory overload.
- Written instructions are especially helpful for verbal thinkers, while nonverbal thinkers may need visual, spatial, or demonstration-based guidance.[416]

What followed? 30% productivity boosts, skyrocketing innovation, and fewer fatigued staff complaining about forced small talk.[417]

From Disability to Strength: Systemic Add-On, Not Afterthought

You know what comes after the margins? The center. When *marginalized brains* get their tools, *everyone* benefits:
- Microsoft, SAP, HP—organizations already winning by institutionalizing neuroinclusion.[418]
- Specialisterne's autism-led software testing teams demonstrated how neurodivergent talent improves outcomes: detail-oriented autistic tes-

ters identified errors that traditional quality assurance often missed. The result? Fewer defects, higher quality, and lower costs compared to fixing issues after release.[419]

- Universal design in offices and schools? Less friction, more flow—for every single person.[420]

The system wasn't "broken." It was **built without us**: Designed for neurotypical brains only. Communication styles optimized for the average, not the awesome. Leadership archetypes are often molded around charisma, rather than cognitive diversity.

Neurodivergent leadership isn't a diversity checkbox—it's the unlock code. Systems don't need fixing. They need to expand to include every type of thinker, feeler, and perceiver. Once that happens, these marginal ideas become the mainstream marvels driving tomorrow's breakthroughs.

Veterans: Not Your Grandpa's War Story
From Boot Camp to Boardroom:
Leadership Without the Bullshit

Forget the polished speeches and corporate buzzwords. Veterans bring **mission-first, ego-last decisiveness** to the business world—and office politics? They laugh in their break room.

- **Mission Focused, Drama Free**: Leadership veterans are experts in high-stakes clarity. A Spencer Stuart study shows C-suite leaders who served in the military manage crises like they do conflict zones—cool, direct, and with accountability, not excuses.[421]
- **Corporate Performance Edge**: Firms led by veterans aren't just patriotic—they're profitable. One study found that firms led by military-experienced executives were less likely to face financial distress and enjoyed higher firm value during the COVID19 pandemic.[422]
- **Stripped-Down Communication**: Picture: a veteran CEO walking into a boardroom and telling everyone, "We've got one hour, one goal, and no bullshit." That's the vibe. Veterans excel at **clarity under pressure**, reducing noise and focusing on outcomes—skills honed under fire and now weaponized for ROI.[423]

Leadership That Works

Veteran	Office Benefit
Mission clarity	Projects stay on target
Decisiveness	Avoids analysis paralysis
Calm under pressure	Reduces burnout, boosts morale
No-nonsense ethos	Culture of accountability

Real Testimonials from Veteran-Led Teams

Mark Clouse, CEO, Campbell Soup

"There are many paths to success, but there is no better schoolhouse for leadership than the military."[424]

Clouse credits his military service with instilling the ability to lead in high-pressure situations, adapt quickly, and maintain clarity of purpose. This mindset helps steer major consumer brands through tough markets.

"Veterans span the breadth of the United States... veterans are an extremely attractive demographic for employers."[425]

By leveraging veteran soft skills—such as teamwork, resilience, and discipline—he emphasizes that veterans elevate a company's performance through pressure-tested leadership and diverse perspectives.

James Schenck, CEO, PenFed Credit Union

"They live with a purpose. They love to do things bigger than themselves... that's what veterans bring to a business organization."[426]

Schenck highlights veterans' innate sense of mission-driven leadership, accountability, and ethical commitment, which builds stronger organizational cultures.

Why These Matter

Veterans don't just bring discipline—they bring:

- Mission clarity across business missions

- Calm decisiveness under uncertainty
- Tactical communication devoid of office drama
- Ethos of service, transforming workplaces into team-first cultures

Backed by data and real-world impact, these testimonials underscore why veteran leadership is more than symbolic—it's **strategic**.

Redefining Patriotism: Fewer Flags, More Function

Wave all the flags you want, but if your version of patriotism stops at a bumper sticker and doesn't start at a benefits office, **you're not a patriot—you're a cosplayer.** True patriotism isn't yelling "Support the Troops" at a ballgame while voting to cut the Veterans Administration budget. It's showing up—for healthcare, for mental health, for the actual humans who wore the uniform and now face a civilian system that's more of a bureaucratic minefield than a hero's welcome.

Stars, Stripes, and Empty Promises: How America Thanks Its Veterans with Neglect[427]

- **Only 41% of veterans believe the VA meets their needs**, and even fewer trust the government to take care of them post-service.
- **22 veterans die by suicide every day**, and mental health services remain chronically underfunded and overly politicized.
- Meanwhile, politicians offer performative patriotism with **flag pins, camo-clad visits, and July 4th tweets** while slashing social services for veterans.

Redefining patriotism means shifting from:

- Symbolism → Substance
- Rhetoric → Resources
- Fireworks → Functional systems

Advocating for **universal healthcare?** That's patriotism.

Fighting for **mental health parity?** That's patriotism.

Pushing for **equity, disability inclusion, and veteran housing?** Red, white, and damn right.

Therefore, the next time someone starts frothing at the mouth about "real Americans," ask them how they voted on affordable insulin or GI Bill access. Because **loving your country isn't about noise—it's about service, sacrifice, and systems that work.** And no, owning an AR-15 doesn't count as a civic duty.

Patriotic Service in the Politics

Veterans in Leadership: 1930–2025 Timeline

ERA	CONGRESS VET %	SENATE VET %	PRESIDENT	VICE PRESIDENT
1930s–1940s	70%+	Majority	✓FDR: WW I Navy ✓Truman: WW I Army	✗Garner: None ✗Wallace: None ✗Barkley: None
1950s–1960s	~60%	Major share	✓Eisenhower: WW II General ✓JFK: WW II PT-boats ✓LBJ: WW II in Congress	✓Nixon: WW II Navy ✓LBJ: WW II in Congress ✗Humphrey: None
1970s–1980s	~50%–60%	~50%	✓Nixon: WW II Navy ✓Ford: WW II Navy ✓Carter: WW II Naval Officer	✗Agnew: None ✓Ford: WW II Navy ✗Rockefeller: None ✗Mondale: None
1980s–1990s	~40%	~40%	✓Reagan: WW II Hollywood Film Unit [no combat] ✓Bush Sr.: WW II Navy ✗Clinton: Vietnam War Student Deferment	✓Bush Sr.: WW II Navy ✓Quayle: Vietnam-era National Guard ✓Gore: Vietnam War Army Journalist
2000s–2010s	~20%	~20%	✓Bush Jr.: Vietnam-era Air Guard ✗Obama: None	✗Cheney: Vietnam War Student Deferment ✗Biden: Vietnam War Asthma Deferment
2020s [2025]	~18% House	17%	✗Trump: Vietnam War Bone Spur Deferment ✗Biden: Vietnam War Asthma Deferment	✗Pence: None [too young for Vietnam War draft] ✗Harris: None

Sources:

D. DeSilver, "New Congress Will Have a Few More Veterans, But Their Share of Lawmakers Is Still Near a Record Low," *Pew Research Center*, December 7, 2022, https://www.pewresearch.org/short-reads/2022/12/07/new-congress-will-have-a-few-more-veterans-but-their-share-of-lawmakers-is-still-near-a-record-low/.

S.M. Gillon, "Presidents at War: How Battle Has Shaped American Leaders," *The Guardian*, February 18, 2025, https://www.theguardian.com/books/2025/feb/18/presidents-at-war-book-steven-gillon.

Wikipedia (n.d.), *List of Presidents of the United States by Military Service*, https://en.wikipedia.org/wiki/List_of_presidents_of_the_United_States_by_military_service.

Key Takeaways

- Peak era: From the post–WWII period to the Vietnam War, Congress and the Senate had 50–70% veterans.
- Steady decline began in the 1970s, reaching record lows (~17–18%) by 2025.
- Presidents & VPs: Every leader before 1993 had military service—from Truman through Bush Sr. After that, only W. Bush, with none since, has had an army background, except for ceremonial roles.
- Today: Neither the president nor the vice president holds military experience; the number of veteran voices in Congress are at their lowest point in modern history.

This timeline reveals that our civic culture has drifted, moving further away from shared service and common sacrifice. Fewer veterans in power means less firsthand understanding of leadership forged in adversity, which can potentially weaken trust, bipartisanship, and the institutional ethos.

The Revolution Will Be Accessible,
Gender-Inclusive, and Veteran-Led

The future isn't politely knocking—it's kicking down the door with a mobility ramp, a gender-neutral pronoun badge, and a military-grade leadership plan that doesn't have time for performative nonsense.

This is not your grandfather's cultural uprising. It's not about returning to "traditional values" sold in vintage fonts by billionaires with offshore accounts. It's about dismantling a system that was never built for everyone and rebuilding one that works for all. That means ditching boardroom hierarchies based on who shouts loudest, and uplifting those who lead through integrity, empathy, and actual competence—often found in disabled innovators, neurodivergent strategists, women who lead with both head and heart, and veterans who understand mission over ego.

We're done asking for inclusion nicely. We're designing it into the damn architecture.

- Accessibility isn't charity—it's innovation.
- Gender inclusion isn't a trend—it's structural evolution.
- And veteran leadership isn't nostalgia—it's pragmatic disruption wrapped in discipline and humility.

This cultural revolution won't be televised in prime time—it'll be streamed, captioned, and crowdsourced from people who never got the mic before. And yes, it may look different. It may make some people squirm. But progress always does.

If you're still clutching your pearls and praying for the return of the "good old days," this might not be your movement. But if you're ready for a future where leadership doesn't mean gatekeeping, where access isn't an afterthought, and where service is redefined by courage, not conformity—

Welcome to the new script. It's bold. It's real. And this time, everyone gets a role.

And if that makes you uncomfortable? **Good. That's the sound of progress clearing its throat.**

The Rebuild has Already Begun

The myth that cancel culture = chaos? A convenient distraction from the *real* threat to the status quo: people who know how to build better—and aren't waiting for your permission. Let's talk about what "canceling" actually is: **It's accountability with a feedback loop.** It's the community saying, "We're not tolerating this toxic architecture anymore—and we have plans to replace it." And no, this isn't performative rage culture. This is radical, intentional cultural renovation. *"The most radical thing you can do is build something."*[428]

This Isn't About Erasing History—It's About Correcting the Lie

We're not in some Orwellian erasure zone. We're in a truth reclamation movement. And if history is a mirror, then America's been standing in front of a funhouse version for centuries.

- **Taking down statues of slaveholders isn't "rewriting history."**

It's telling the whole story, not just the part that flatters your great-grandpa.

- **Dismantling colonial curricula isn't "indoctrination."**
  It's liberation from fairytales of justification.
- **Teaching about genocide, redlining, and labor exploitation isn't "divisive."**
  It's basic historical literacy.

The goal isn't to erase—it's to edit. Because if your version of history requires silencing truth to survive, it doesn't belong in a textbook—it belongs in a Netflix category called Historical Fan Fiction: White Guy Edition.

The Construction Crew Is Here— and They've Got Receipts, Rage, and Resilience

If you're still arguing about "cancel culture," you've already missed the rebuild.

If you're still mourning the loss of statues, you're standing in the way of blueprints.

The demolition wasn't rage—it was required.

The rebuild isn't coming—it's happening. And the architects? They're already moving in.

Rebuilding from the Ruins: A Blueprint from the Margins

Empathy isn't a weakness. It's infrastructure. And marginalized communities have been blueprinting it for centuries while dominant culture was busy "circling back." Forget the performative empathy of leadership seminars and LinkedIn humblebrags. We're talking about real, operationalized empathy:

- Hiring practices that consider context, not just credentials.
- Healthcare policies written by people who use healthcare.
- Workplaces where saying your pronouns doesn't trigger an HR investigation.

Communities on the margins didn't wait for best practices. They *became* them—because survival demanded innovation the boardroom never dreamed of.[429]

Leadership That Listens Before It Legislates

Authentic leadership isn't about having the loudest mic. It's about knowing when to shut up and *listen*—especially to people who've never been invited to the table (or worse, only invited to "represent diversity" without power). And here's the kicker: the best leaders aren't always the ones who talk in bullet points and buzzwords. Sometimes they're the ones:

- Holding space in a community kitchen.
- Organizing mutual aid on Instagram.
- Navigating a racist healthcare system *while* educating others how to survive it.

Translation: the marginalized have been leading this whole damn time—you just weren't tuned in to the frequency.

Accountability Without Performative Apologies

If we're going to rebuild, we need to retire from the corporate apology tour. You know the one:

"We're committed to learning." "We're listening." "This doesn't reflect our values…" Yes, it does, Dick. It reflected your values until the internet caught up with receipts.

Real accountability isn't about a 3-minute video and a branded hashtag. It's:

- Redistributing power.
- Paying people what they're worth.
- Stepping down if you're the problem, not the solution.

Marginalized communities have *always* held themselves accountable to each other. It's time for the institutions that stole their labor, culture, and ideas to catch up.

This is our future culture! A current work in progress. The next chapter explores what we are working to build: the new American Dream.

CHAPTER 17

The New American Dream

Breaking Up with Bootstraps—
Spoiler: They Were Never There in the First Place.

The "self-made man"—America's favorite bedtime story for adults who still think success is a solo sport and poverty is a character flaw.

For over two centuries, we've been force-fed a fantasy where anyone armed with nothing but bootstraps and grit could allegedly ascend from rags to riches, from janitor to CEO, from coal miner to congressman. It's a charming tale—also, complete fiction. Bootstrapping is a myth—a linguistic sleight of hand designed to make systemic inequality look like a personal failure. You can't pull yourself up by bootstraps if you were never given boots. And even if you had them, trying to lift yourself by your straps is physically impossible unless you're Spider-Man or a metaphor for gaslighting (Hint: it's the latter).[430]

The Self-Made Delusion

The "self-made man" idea has always been a well-dressed lie with good PR. It erases privilege, inheritance, tax breaks, trust funds, legacy admissions, and corporate nepotism like a magic trick. Elon Musk didn't invent the electric car from a garage; he rode into the future on a pile of emeralds from his daddy's apartheid-era mine. Jeff Bezos started Amazon from a garage, yes, but after a $300,000 gift from his parents. That's not a bootstrap. That's a bungee cord made of generational wealth.[431]

Collapse of the Old Dream:
The White Picket Fence Is in Foreclosure

The old American Dream—buy a house, raise 2.5 kids, retire with a gold watch—has morphed into a dystopian scavenger hunt for health insurance, affordable rent, and student loan deferment extensions. That iconic white picket fence? It's now a Zillow listing with 47 offers, all of which are cash, and all from hedge funds. Hustle culture evolved into burnout culture, which in turn became a culture of "how is it Thursday and I've worked 52 hours already?" The grind never stops—but neither does the inequality. And let's not forget who the Dream was originally for: white, cisgender, straight men. Everyone else was either a footnote, a maid, or missing from the narrative entirely. [432]The Dream didn't fail—it was exclusive from the beginning. And now it's cracking under the weight of that exclusivity.

Enter: The New American Dream

Now, brace yourself for something truly radical: What if success didn't mean outpacing your neighbor but uplifting your community? What if the new American Dream wasn't about individual escape velocity, but collective gravity? A vision where progress isn't a zero-sum game, your gain isn't my loss, and justice isn't met based on ZIP code, skin tone, or who your daddy golfs with at the club.

This is the remix—less "bootstrap billionaire" and more "everybody eats."

It's time we traded the illusion of personal exceptionalism for the reality of **shared humanity**. Because no one builds a future alone, and the only dreams worth chasing are the ones we wake up from together.

*From **Me** to **We**: The Rise of Collective Liberation*
How America Finally Realized It's Not a Solo Act

Welcome to the group project America can't opt out of—the one where your grade depends on everyone, not just the loudest guy with a LinkedIn bio that reads like a self-help book and a superiority complex. For centuries, we've been taught to worship the gospel of *individualism* as if it were the eleventh commandment. Every school assembly, corporate seminar, and patriotic halftime commercial reinforced the lie: "If you just work hard enough, you'll make it." As if systemic barriers are just plot twists in your motivational montage.

But here's the inconvenient truth the bootstrappers forgot to mention: Individualism is a luxury only the privileged can afford. The rest of us? We thrive by leaning on each other, building together, resisting together, and redefining the new baseline for success together.

The "I Alone" Delusion Is Dead. Long Live "We."

The age of the lone genius is over. Sorry, Steve Jobs. No one innovates in a vacuum. Not Beyoncé. Not Einstein. Not even Dick from HR. And while we're at it, let's retire the myth of the "Great Man" theory, too—it turns out most "great men" were just men with access, networks, and no concept of work-life balance.[433]

The culture is shifting—and not quietly. Millennials and Gen Z are burning the "hustle harder" handbook and replacing it with group chats, mutual aid, and memes that call out generational trauma with surgical precision. They're not here for top-down leadership or trickle-down economics—they're building horizontal power, crowd-sourced movements, and GoFundMe healthcare systems (because that's somehow normal in this dystopia).

New Systems, New Solidarity

The absolute American dream isn't a solo climb up the corporate ladder—it's a community building the ladder together and handing out safety harnesses on the way up.

We're talking:

- Mutual aid networks that stepped in while the government played golf.
- Worker-owned co-ops where employees are empowered, not exploited.
- Collective bargaining that bargains instead of begs.
- Community land trusts reclaiming the sacred concept of housing as a human right, not a Wall Street asset.

Because here's the kicker: **collective success is more sustainable**. Studies show societies with higher levels of cooperation and trust also enjoy better health, economic stability, and democracy resilience.[434] Imagine that—a country that thrives *not* because everyone's fighting for the last slice of pie, but because we just started baking more damn pie.

You Can't Feng Shui Structural Racism. Systemic oppression isn't a bad roommate who you can evict. It's the damn landlord. It owns the building, wrote the lease, and raised the rent on justice years ago.

Collective Joy as Resistance

Laughing, Dancing, and Resting While the Empire Burns

Joy is not a luxury. It's a weapon. In a society that thrives on burnout, is divided by design, and profits from your pain, joy isn't just a vibe; it's especially valuable when it is shared, unapologetic, and radically inclusive. It's a full-on act of rebellion. And the people who've had the most stolen from them have made joy a science. While power clutches its pearls and passes legislation, we're out here throwing block parties, lifting each other in dance circles, cracking jokes in hospital rooms, and remixing pain into a protest with rhythm and glitter.

The State Hates Your Joy (Because It Can't Monetize It)

Capitalism loves a grind and fears a groove. That's why your boss schedules "wellness" webinars instead of reducing your workload. That's why mental health is often viewed as a commodity rather than a community responsibility. That's why the system wants you exhausted, anxious, and binge-watching your way into numbness, because tired people don't rise up. But joyful ones? Joyful people organize, energize, and humanize their surroundings.

Joy says:

- "You will not steal my spirit."
- "I deserve pleasure even before the revolution."
- "Yes, I'm tired. But I'm also going roller-skating this weekend with my queer chosen family, and we're bringing snacks and side-eye."

Cultural Resistance: Joy in Motion

Let's talk about the forms joy takes that power can't touch:

- The Black church choir hits that impossible harmony that heals ancestral wounds.
- Drag queens turn trauma into performance art that makes you laugh, cry, and tip your whole paycheck.
- Indigenous powwows are where tradition meets triumph.
- Juneteenth barbecues feel more like family than any 4th of July cookout ever did.
- Latinx festivals are where even the toddlers dance like liberation is genetic.

These aren't just cultural expressions. They are declarations: "We are still here, and we are still celebrating."

Rest Is Resistance

In case you missed the memo from the Nap Ministry (shoutout to Tricia Hersey), rest isn't laziness—it's **a political refusal** to comply with a system that measures your worth in productivity.[435] Rest is a big middle finger to the grind culture. It's the radical assertion that your body, mind, and soul are not corporate assets.

"You mean I'm allowed to take a nap?" Yes, Karen. Especially if you stop scheduling meetings during lunch.

Healing in Public

Collective joy is more than serotonin—it's infrastructure.

It's how we build emotional resilience.

It's how we *unlearn* trauma as the only bonding agent.

It's the future showing up early, covered in glitter, holding a tambourine, and asking if you've hydrated today.

Dismantling the Old House:
Oppression Doesn't Renovate Easily

You can't fix a rotten foundation with inspirational posters and an annual DEI workshop.

The American house—our economy, institutions, and mythologies—was built on injustice. Enslaved labor was the original down payment. Genocide was the landscaping. Patriarchy laid the plumbing. And white supremacy installed the surveillance system. You don't renovate that. **You tear it down brick by brick.**

BRICK ONE: Racism (The Cornerstone of the American Floorplan)

America didn't "struggle with racism." It industrialized it. Codified it. Monetized it. From the Three-Fifths Compromise and redlining to "Stand Your Ground" laws, racial hierarchy isn't a glitch—it's the operating system.[436] And yet, every few decades, we slap on a fresh coat of "diversity" and call it progress. That's not dismantling. That's gentrifying oppression.

Satirical Real Estate Listing: *"Charming colonial-style oppression with original white supremacist molding, updated tokenism fixtures, and plenty of space for gaslighting. The backyard is still haunted."*

BRICK TWO: Patriarchy (Still Mansplaining the Blueprint)

Let's talk about gender. Or more specifically, how patriarchy designed a system where women, trans folks, and non-binary folks were never meant to thrive—only serve. Wage gaps, unpaid caregiving, and underrepresentation in leadership? Those aren't cracks in the wall. **They're load-bearing structures.**[437]

You can't fix a misogynistic culture with a "Lean In" book and a wine-sponsored women's panel—Can I get a Woot Woot!

BRICK THREE: Classism (The HOA of Capitalism)

The American Dream was never free. It was a pay-to-play scheme from the start. And if you couldn't afford the entry fee? Well, enjoy your three jobs and your GoFundMe-supported cancer treatment. The ultra-rich didn't just hoard wealth—they lobbied to legalize it. Tax loopholes, deregulation, *Citizens United*: the greatest hits album of how democracy got repo'd by billionaires.[438]

BRICK FOUR: Ableism (The Invisible Barrier with Real-World Consequences)

Newsflash: the Americans with Disabilities Act (ADA) didn't solve ableism. It just made it slightly more polite. Meanwhile, disabled people are still navigating a world built without them—literally and figuratively. From employment discrimination to lack of accessible infrastructure, we've treated disability like a personal tragedy instead of something ignored by a systemic design flaw.

BRICK FIVE: Heteronormativity (Yes, That Closet Was Custom-Built)

We've normalized a cultural architecture where anything outside the cishet existence is either a punchline or a political battleground. LGBTQ+ rights didn't "evolve." They were *fought* for—every inch, every pronoun, every wedding cake. And the backlash? It's not new. It's just louder because queer folks are starting to gain equity, rather than invisibility.

Learning from the Marginalized for Once

Learning from the marginalized isn't radical. It's the bare minimum for functioning in a reality you didn't build, but benefit from daily. Every time an organization finally gives "a seat at the table" to someone Black, Brown, queer, disabled, or otherwise inconvenient to the power structure, it throws a self-congratulatory pizza party. But here's the gag: the table is wobbly, the seat is folding, and the agenda is written in white tears. What you should be doing is shutting up, passing the mic, and taking notes, as if your career depends on it—because one day it will.

Marginalized voices are often brought in to "diversify" spaces but are then expected to be grateful, palatable, and nondisruptive.[439] When they do speak the truth? They're branded "angry," "divisive," or worse, "not a good cultural fit." Translation: We only wanted your difference, not your discomfort.

Marginalized People Didn't Just Survive the System— They've Been Building the Blueprint to Fix It

Newsflash: If you want to know how to build inclusive policy, equitable infrastructure, and trauma-informed leadership, don't ask the C-suite. Ask the people it has forgotten to promote for the last 40 years. You think you're innovating when you offer a floating holiday? Meanwhile, disabled activists have been running mutual aid networks with more logistical sophistication than your entire HR department.

You think you invented psychological safety by quoting Brené Brown? Black women invented it by surviving generations of institutional betrayal and *still* mentoring your unseasoned interns without setting the building on fire. You want to learn about "resilience"? Talk to queer youth of color navigating systems that were designed to disappear them. They've turned survival into an art form—and they don't need your approval to exhibit it.

Stop Asking for Labor—Start Doing Yours

Marginalized people have written the books, developed the theories, and lived the experience. What they don't owe you is:

- An explainer on why your company's dress code is racist,
- A second chance to "rethink your tone" during Black History Month, or
- Forgiveness for the sixth microaggression this week, followed by, "I didn't mean it like that!"

Learning is not a spectator sport. It's not a panel. It's a practice. You don't need another training. You need to restructure the org chart, audit your policies, and stop promoting people who think equity is a vibe, not a responsibility. If your leadership strategy still relies on "giving voice to the voiceless," congratulations—you've just outed yourself as part of the problem. **The marginalized have never been voiceless. You were just professionally hard of hearing.**

The question isn't, *"How can we include them?"*

The question is, *"How do we get out of their way?"*

Because one thing is crystal clear: They've been doing the work. It's time you caught up—or got left behind.

Redefining Success: From Wealth to Well-Being
Because You Can't Venmo Inner Peace

Let's be honest: America has long measured success like someone playing a deranged Monopoly game—more properties, more profit, and if you go bankrupt? Perhaps you didn't manifest it hard enough. But here's the truth Wall Street won't tell you: **being rich doesn't mean being well.** And owning a Tesla won't fix your anxiety, your healthcare, or your hollow friendships built on networking events. It's time to upgrade the American Dream's operating system—from "I made it" to "we're okay." From hoarding to healing. From extracting to existing.

Welcome to the Great Recalibration
Forget yachts and corner offices. Let's talk about:
- Community well-being
- Mental health that doesn't bankrupt you
- Education that doesn't require lifelong indentured servitude
- Jobs that don't steal your soul, spine, or Sundays

Turns out, happiness doesn't scale with income forever.[440] After a certain point, more money buys fancier ways to be lonely.

GDP ≠ Quality of Life
Gross Domestic Product (GDP) is the sacred cow of American capitalism—and like most sacred cows, it's full of crap. GDP doesn't measure whether people are healthy, housed, or hopeful. It doesn't count unpaid caregivers, but it does count prison construction and oil spills (because, hey, that's "economic activity"). Meanwhile, countries like New Zealand and Bhutan are flipping the script—using Wellbeing Budgets and Gross National Happiness Indexes to center policies around people, not profit.[441] Radical, right?

The False God of Productivity
Here lies the American worker, **sacrificed at the altar of output.** We've been conditioned to measure our worth by how fast we respond to emails, how many side hustles we juggle, and how little paid time off we use.

Burnout isn't a bug in the system—it *is* the system. But here's the plot twist: the **rest is revolutionary**. Community is currency. And joy isn't a luxury—it's an act of resistance.

What Success Looks Like Now *(Spoiler: It's Not a 12-Car Garage)*
Success in the new American Dream isn't about being "better" than your neighbor. It's about being better with them. It's:
- Thriving families, not just surviving ones.
- Clean air, clean water, and clean breaks from trauma cycles.
- Universal access to healthcare, housing, education, and dignity.
- A culture where we celebrate cooperation—not cutthroat competition—as genius.

Imagine a society where teachers are paid more than TikTok influencers, where janitors retire with dignity and a pension. Where success isn't a trophy hoarded but a table extended.

The New LinkedIn Profile:

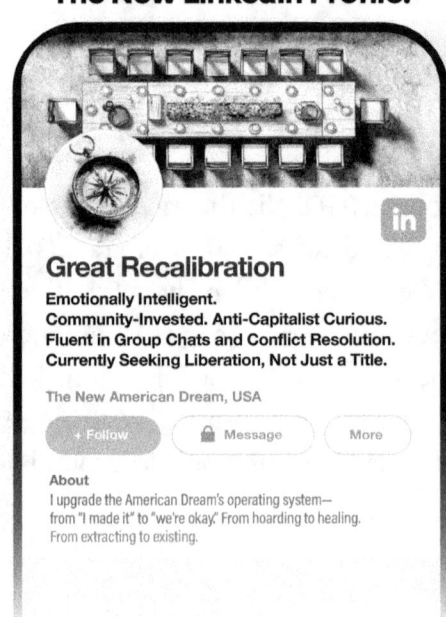

It's time for a full culture reboot—and that is exactly what I am giving you in the final chapter.

CHAPTER 18

From Culture War to Cultural Reboot

THE REBOOT HAS BEGUN: It's Intersectional, It's Inclusive, and It's Deeply Uninterested in Your "Duck Dynasty" Reruns.

Spoiler alert: This upgrade doesn't support fragile egos or Confederate cosplay.

While Dick was rage-scrolling Fox News because the green M&M started wearing flats, the rest of us were busy doing something wild: rebuilding society and not burning it down—*rebuilding it.* From the foundation. With equity in the blueprints and inclusion in the scaffolding. This reboot isn't coming—it's already live. And it doesn't care if you're uncomfortable. It's not running on nostalgia. It's running on reality.

Here's the truth: **The Culture War is a rerun.** It has the same actors and the same fake outrage, just a different century. While some people were melting down over drag queens in libraries, teachers were being priced out of living in the cities where they teach. While Twitter was debating the "gender" of a piece of candy, Black trans women were still fighting for basic survival. While school boards banned books about racism, white supremacy was getting elected to office *again*—in a business suit, this time, not a pointed white hood. It's not a culture war. **It's a distraction campaign.** A political fever dream designed to keep people yelling about "wokeness" while voting against their own healthcare, housing, and humanity.

Sally's Soapbox: "We're Not Canceling the Past. We're Correcting the Future."

Let's clarify something for those who confuse ac-countability with erasure: **Nobody is canceling the past. We refuse to worship it like a sacred cow dipped in mayonnaise and manifest destiny.**

Yes, statues are coming down.

Yes, textbooks are getting footnotes that don't lie.

Yes, museums are returning stolen artifacts.

And yes, people who caused harm are being–**gasp**–*held responsible. This isn't vengeance. This is justice with Wi-Fi.*

We're not trying to delete the past. **We're just no longer letting it dictate the terms of our future.**

If your legacy can't withstand the truth, perhaps it was never a legacy to begin with. It was just **propaganda with better costumes.**

The Final Hissy Fit

You've cried at Target.

You've shouted "groomer" at a librarian.

You've filed lawsuits against affirmative action, gender-neutral bath-rooms, and, god forbid, inclusive Barbie.

We saw the meltdown, Dick–*and while it was entertaining in a "reality TV meets midlife crisis" sort of way, the season is over. You're not can-celed. You're just no longer the default setting on democracy. And let's be real: You weren't fighting for freedom. You were fighting for* **familiari-ty,** *where your comfort mattered more than anyone else's humanity.*

From school board rants to Fox News tears, you've confused critique with persecution. Spoiler: Being asked to treat others with basic decency is not oppression–*it's adulthood. The Mr. Potato Head debacle? That wasn't cancel culture. That was marketing. And frankly, if the slight rebranding of a plastic spud that never had genitalia undid your masculinity, that's not society's fault. That's your problem.*

–Love, Sally

According to the Pew Research Center, many Americans (especially younger generations) support racial and gender equity initiatives.[442] If your outrage feels louder, it's probably because it's echoing in an increasingly empty room.[443]

Power Is Not a Participation Trophy

Sorry, Dick—just because you were born with the cheat codes (white, male, straight, Christian, and loud), doesn't mean you're entitled to win every time. Power, historically, wasn't earned—it was inherited, protected by redlining, nepotism, legacy admissions, and a good ol' boys' club that treated diversity like a threat instead of a solution.[444]

Now that the rules are changing and more seats are being added to the table, you're crying foul like a kid whose Monopoly board got flipped. Newsflash: You weren't playing fair to begin with.

"Meritocracy" was always a mirage. If power were truly about skill, half of Congress would be unemployed and replaced by overworked middle managers who know how to lead a meeting without screaming "point of order."

Reminder: This Isn't About You Losing Power– It's About Others Gaining Some

Let's be crystal clear, Dick:
- No one's erasing you.
- No one's replacing you.
- We're just… *including others*. And it's breaking your brain.

Your identity isn't under attack. Your monopoly on it is. This isn't the Hunger Games—it's the equity table. And when you've had all the pie for decades, sharing feels like starvation. But it's not. It's just fairness. The demographic shift is fundamental. By 2045, the US will be predominantly non-white).[445] That's not an apocalypse—that's evolution. Equity doesn't mean your mic gets cut—it just means you don't get to hog the mic while others wait for a turn you never planned to give.

Let's talk about the real issue: This isn't backlash against "progress." It's a backlash against not being *in charge* of it. For generations, progress was a straight white male monopoly dressed up as "leadership."

But now?

- The boardrooms are browner.
- The Pride flags are flying higher.
- And the resumes aren't just legacy-school carbon copies of Chad and Sons.

And suddenly? It's a crisis. Not because things are worrisome; your dad's the gatekeeper who lost the keys. No one's mad that the world is evolving. They're angry that they no longer get to dictate the terms of its evolution. That's not persecution. That's meritocracy catching up. If you were qualified, this wouldn't feel like a threat.

Welcome to the Reboot

This update is:

- Intersectional by design
- Accountable by default
- Queer-coded with anti-capitalist undertones
- And fiercely allergic to bootlicking

You don't have to like it. But it's happening—with or without your approval ratings.

History isn't being erased—it's being repaired. And the reboot isn't a courtesy call. **It's the real system upgrade—and this time, it's secure.**

Getting Through to the Dick You Love (Without Starting World War III at Thanksgiving)

A field guide to deprogramming with love, sarcasm, and a solid Wi-Fi connection.

So you love a Dick. Perhaps he's your dad, your brother, your husband, your neighbor with the Don't Tread on Me flag and the homeowner association citations. Maybe he's got a heart of gold and a browser history full of Jordan Peterson clips. Either way, you're here because Dick is spiraling, and you're wondering: **Can I reach him before he declares war on a Target Pride display?**

Good news: You're not alone. Bad news: It's gonna be like teaching a cat to do taxes.

STEP 1: Understand the Species

Dick isn't evil. He's *exhausted, algorithmically radicalized*, and *emotionally allergic to nuance*. He's been raised on a steady diet of bootstraps, Ronald Reagan, and the belief that asking for help is weakness unless it's from Jesus or AAA. He's terrified that the world has changed and nobody gave him a manual. Spoiler: There was a manual. He just threw it out when it had too many pronouns.

STEP 2: Speak Fluent Dick

You want to use reason. He's fluent in *meme logic* and *AM radio analogies*.

Instead of saying: "The Constitution is a living document that requires interpretation."

Try: "Imagine if the 2nd Amendment had to be reloaded every time you wanted to use it."

You're not compromising. You're *translating*.

STEP 3: Fact-Check Without Triggering a Flashback

Every Dick has a trauma response to being corrected—usually involving yelling "FAKE NEWS" and storming off to mow something. Instead of dropping a 47-link evidence bomb, try this:

"Hey, I saw something interesting on PBS. Not sure if it's true—wanna watch it together?"

He'll say no, but now he's curious. And PBS sounds like golf with a thesaurus, so that it won't feel like an attack.

STEP 4: Get Him Out of the Man Cave (Metaphorical or Literal)

Dick's echo chamber isn't just online—it's *everywhere he feels safe, never being challenged*. Invite him into places where he can hear different voices without feeling ambushed.

Start small:

- A documentary *not* hosted by a guy in camo.
- A barbecue where someone of a non-white background is allowed to bring a side dish *and speak*.
- A podcast that doesn't start with "Now I'm not racist, but…"

STEP 5: Love the Person, Not the Persona

Beneath the Fox News exterior, he's still your dad, who taught you how to ride a bike. Or your brother who cried at *Field of Dreams*. Or your coworker who once gave you a ride home in a snowstorm while blasting Toby Keith.

He's not lost. He's *scared*. He's not unreachable. He's just stuck. And nothing destabilizes a tantrum faster than **unearned empathy**. It doesn't mean you accept the BS—it means you see the humanity beneath the bumper stickers.

Final Thought: You're Not Here to Win.
You're Here to *Disrupt the Loop*

Dick's worldview wasn't built overnight. It was coded into him by history, media, masculinity myths, and a religion that sometimes felt more like a sports team. Your job isn't to "fix" him. It's to short-circuit the outrage algorithm long enough for something human to break through.

You might not change his mind today. But maybe—just maybe—you'll plant the idea that **thinking doesn't mean betrayal**. And if that doesn't work? There's always passive-aggressive subtweeting.

Because even Sally's got limits.

The Era of Adulting

Emotional Labor Isn't Just for Women, Interns, and That One HR Lady You Keep Ignoring

For generations, women—especially women of color—have carried the emotional weight of the workplace, smoothing over egos, mentoring new hires, remembering birthdays, and de-escalating office tensions (which, spoiler alert, are usually your doing). Meanwhile, you've coasted on unearned authority, occasionally offering "mentorship" that's just a story about your first job at IBM and a reminder to "lean in."

But here's the bad news: The new workplace demands empathy. It demands self-awareness. It requires you to show up with more than a LinkedIn profile and a golf handicap.

As sociologist Arlie Hochschild pointed out as early as 1983, emotional labor has been disproportionately expected from women and marginalized groups, because society assumed they were "better at it."[446] Translation: Men just never *had* to try.

Yes, Dick—you're going to have to learn how to regulate your emotions, acknowledge others' perspectives, and maybe, just maybe, *listen* without interrupting to talk about your fraternity days.

Accountability: The New Masculinity (And Femininity, And Nonbinary Boss Energy.)

Real talk: The new leadership currency isn't domination—it's **accountability**. That means owning your mistakes. Apologizing without saying "if anyone was offended." And not calling the diversity officer a "woke cop" just because they asked you to stop making "jokes" from 1994. Studies now show that psychologically safe workplaces—where people are allowed to make mistakes and grow—outperform the control-and-command ones you love to worship in Tom Clancy novels.[447] Being accountable doesn't make you weak. It makes you a grown-up. And if that sounds like a threat to your identity, perhaps your identity was the problem.

Facts Over Feelings: Sorry, Your Uncle's Facebook Memes Don't Count

We live in a world where actual data is dismissed as "fake news," while unhinged Facebook rants are treated like sacred texts. Dick, this isn't research:

- "I just feel like the election was stolen."
- "I heard on a podcast that DEI is reverse racism."
- "My barber's cousin said immigrants are taking all the jobs."

Your feelings aren't facts. Your opinions aren't oppressed. And your fear of change isn't a valid reason to block progress. The Dunning-Kruger effect is real, and no, it's not a new IPA.[448] It's the scientifically observed tendency for the least competent people to overestimate their competence.

Sound familiar? If you can't tell the difference between a peer-reviewed study and a TikTok meltdown in camo, sit this one out.

Fragility Is Not a Strategy

You Can't Cry Your Way Back Into Power, No Matter How Many Flags You Wave.

Ah, yes—the oppressed oppressor. The man who's had a reserved seat at every table but is now furious that someone else finally got a chair. You're not being silenced, Dick—you're just being fact-checked. And no, someone telling you "That's inappropriate" isn't the *Gulag.* It's just a Tuesday in HR.

This is the golden age of performative fragility. "I'm being canceled" now translates to: "I was mildly inconvenienced by someone else having rights." Sociologist Robin DiAngelo coined the term "white fragility" to describe the defensive reactions white people have when their racial advantage is questioned—tears, anger, shutdowns, and, in Dick's case, Facebook screeds in all caps.[449] When your reaction to someone else's dignity is *your meltdown*, that's not righteousness. That's narcissism. And frankly, it's exhausting. Get a grip. And a therapist.

"I'm Just Asking Questions"
Is Not an Excuse for Intellectual Cowardice

Because if you're afraid to make a value judgment between peer-reviewed research and a guy with a webcam and a whiteboard, you're not investigating—you're deflecting.

We see you, Dick—sitting in the meeting, arms crossed, launching verbal grenades like:

- "But what about merit?"
- "How come there's no Straight Pride Month?"
- "Can't we just leave politics out of work?"

These aren't questions. They're cultural landmines dressed in khakis. It's not curiosity—it's cowardice wearing a fake mustache.

This tactic isn't new—it's the age-old method of stalling progress by pretending to be "neutral."

Spoiler alert: **there's no neutrality in injustice**. If you're sitting on the fence while others are being pushed off the cliff, you're complicit. As Audre Lorde famously said: *"Your silence will not protect you."* Neither will your fake objectivity, Dick.

Grow a Spine, Not a Platform

You want to be a thought leader? Try having a thought that isn't recycled from Joe Rogan's B-sides. Fragility has become your brand. You've monetized victimhood, weaponized misunderstanding, and built an entire ecosystem around the idea that change is oppression. Congratulations. You're the multilevel marketing of masculinity—selling fear, outrage, and half-truths in bulk. Studies show that people with high psychological resilience and self-awareness are more likely to adapt to social and workplace change.[450]

Translation: real strength means adapting, not stomping your feet and crying about "the woke mob."

So, unless your platform involves elevating *more* voices, not just yours, we will need you to step aside. This isn't karaoke night for egos. It's a collective future—and you can't lead with a participation ribbon made of fragile pride and outdated talking points.

Rebuilding Isn't Optional—It's Happening With or Without You

The Future Has Already Moved On. It Left You a Voicemail. You Didn't Check It.

You can try to filibuster progress all you want, Dick, but America's demolition crew is already on site—hard hats on, blueprints in hand, and no, you're not on the project team.

This isn't a polite request for change. This is an eviction notice for outdated ideologies.

- Climate justice? Already in the works.
- Gender equity? No longer negotiable.
- Multicultural workplaces? That ship sailed, docked, and built a whole damn city.

The rising generation—more racially diverse, more queer, more globally connected, more emotionally literate—isn't asking for your approval. They're asking if your pension plan still has a fax machine.

According to the US Census Bureau, Gen Z is the most diverse generation in US history, with nearly 50% identifying as non-white and a significant portion identifying as LGBTQ+.[451] *Translation:* The reboot is live, and your pilot episode didn't test well.

You have two choices, Dick: Be part of the reconstruction… or be studied in someone's sociology thesis titled "Resistance to Equity: A Failure to

Launch." Trying to cling to the way things were isn't noble—it's lazy. And historically? It never works.

- Patriarchy? Cracking.
- White nationalism? Shrinking.
- Heteronormative hierarchies? Losing market share faster than Yahoo! in 2007.

This is an evolution with a clipboard. And if you can't evolve, prepare to be filed under "Exhibit A: The Cost of Cultural Stagnation."

The *Harvard Business Review* reports that companies with inclusive cultures are 45% more likely to improve market share and 70% more likely to capture new markets.[452] That's not ideology—that's economics.

And still, you're standing there with a "Don't Tread on Me" mug, thinking you're the hero. *Spoiler:* you're the final boss in the level that everyone's speedrunning.

Coalition, Not Control

The new dream isn't about dominating the table—it's about **building a bigger one.**

We're done with the "strongman" mythos. The Marlboro Man is now a case study in toxic advertising. What's trending instead?

- Emotional intelligence.
- Collective decision-making.
- Power-sharing.
- Listening without centering yourself in someone else's pain.

That doesn't mean you're erased, Dick. It means you're *repositioned*—from sole narrator to part of an ensemble cast. And yes, it will feel weird when someone else gets the lead. Sit with that. Social psychologist Dr. Beverly Daniel Tatum describes systemic change as a moving walkway: if you're standing still, you're still going in the direction of injustice.[453] To change direction? You must actively walk against the tide. Get moving—or get out of the way.

The Real Patriotism Test: Can You Handle Change?

America's Evolved—Sorry Your Fragile Ego Didn't Get the Update. Hint: It's Not a Flag Pin or a Pickup Truck.

Look, Dick. You can slap an eagle on your T-shirt, wave a "Don't Tread on Me" flag, and scream "USA!" until your voice gives out—but that's cosplay, not patriotism. Real patriotism isn't performative. It's not about how many guns you own, how loud you sing the anthem, or how many flags you've attached to your lawnmower. It's about whether you're *willing to grow with the country*, not just growl at it when it no longer prioritizes you.

As James Baldwin put it: *"I love America more than any other country in the world, and, precisely for this reason, I insist on the right to criticize her perpetually."*[454] Critique isn't betrayal. It's the highest form of patriotism. And if you can't handle that, perhaps you're not the patriot you think you are.

Let Go or Be Dragged

Change isn't coming. It's already **here**, in boots and a blazer, facilitating a DEI workshop while you complain about how hard it is to be a straight white man these days. You're not being left behind because you're a relic of the past—you're being left behind because you're *refusing* to move.

- LGBTQ+ rights? Expanding.
- Gender as a binary? Declining.
- Anti-racism education? Growing.
- Cultural competency in leadership? Mandatory.

And still, you're clinging to 1955 like it's the last life raft on the *Titanic*. Hate to break it to you, but the iceberg *was you*. Neuroscience research shows that resistance to change is often rooted in fear—fear of losing control, status, or identity.[455] *Translation*: You're not mad at change. You're just scared of what it says about you. Growth is possible. Even for you, Dick. But first, you have to stop treating your discomfort like oppression.

Final Exam: Can You Stop Crying Long Enough to Read the Syllabus of Progress?

This isn't extra credit. This is the baseline curriculum for 21st-century citizenship. Here's the test:

- Can you listen without interrupting?
- Can you accept that others' experiences are valid even when they're

not yours?

- Can you admit that a system that benefited you might need to change, in order for everyone else to survive?

And most importantly: **Can you handle no longer being the loudest, whitest voice in the room without framing it as the fall of civilization?**

Because here's the truth: Progress doesn't need your blessing—it needs your accountability. And if that feels threatening, it's only because you built your entire identity on never having to be accountable in the first place.

Sally's Soapbox: Shut Up. Show Up. Do the Work.

We need fewer Dicks with microphones and more adults with mirrors. Leadership isn't tweeting Bible verses between rage rants. It isn't storming the Capitol in cargo shorts and calling it patriotism. And it damn sure isn't sitting in a boardroom pretending "reverse racism" is real while blocking every initiative that might help someone who doesn't golf on weekends.

Outrage is not a strategy. It's an addiction. And you, Dick, are high on your grievance fumes.

According to research on authoritarian backlashes, outrage is often used to maintain existing hierarchies rather than challenge real injustice.[456] *Translation: Your hissy fit isn't revolutionary. It's regressive.*

—SALLY

Enough with Fragile Nostalgia Being Mistaken for Values

Your "values" aren't under attack. They're just being *fact-checked*.

- Being asked to use someone's pronouns isn't persecution.
- Being passed over for a role you're unqualified for isn't discrimination.
- Being told your inappropriate behavior isn't censorship—it's a consequence.

Your nostalgia for "the good old days" is less about morality and more about monopoly on culture, control, and attention. It's not that things were better back then; you **had more unearned authority.**

As historian Kristin Kobes Du Mez notes, much of American cultural conservatism is rooted in selective memory and myth-making, where the past is airbrushed to protect the fragile present.[457]

No, Dick, you don't get to hide behind "tradition" anymore. Especially when that "tradition" includes segregation, misogyny, and three-martini lunches while your secretary handled the actual work.

Enough with Hissy Fits in Places Where Healing Needs to Happen

The workplace? Not your therapy office.
The town hall? Not your soapbox for conspiracy cosplay.
The classroom? Not your battleground for protecting your kid from knowing slavery was bad.

People are trying to *heal*, *build*, and *thrive*. Your constant need to center yourself is not a leadership style—it's a cultural virus. We've vaccinated against worse.

Psychologist Derald Wing Sue refers to this as "dominance mainte-nance," where power holders react to equality efforts with hostility masked as victimhood.[458] Sound familiar, Dick?

Healing requires space, equity involves courage, and progress requires people who know the difference between discomfort and oppression.

Final Notes from the Resistance:

If you're still reading, good. Here's your stripped-down, no-frills checklist for getting your legacy back on track:

- **Shut Up:** Not permanently. Just long enough to listen, learn, and real-ize the room doesn't revolve around your feelings.
- **Show Up:** For conversations that challenge you. For communities that aren't yours. For futures that don't mirror your past.
- **Do the Work:** Unlearn. Relearn. Grow. Not for applause—but be-cause *that's what grown-ups do.*

The future doesn't need your permission—just your absence, if progress makes you cry.

How to Go from Dick to Richard

Weaponized insecurity isn't a leadership trait, and shouting "free speech" while plugging your ears it's not patriotism, or it's not progress.

Let's get this out of the way: **you threw a hissy fit.** It wasn't a debate. It wasn't "just asking questions." It was a full-volume, red-in-the-face, foot-stomping meltdown because someone dared to challenge your worldview—and your golf cart parking spot. We all saw it.

You screamed. You rage-tweeted. You made yourself the main character of a conversation that wasn't even about you.
And now? You've got two options:

1. Keep flailing in the cultural kiddie pool.
2. Grow. The. Hell. Up.

This guide is for the Dicks of the world—the ones still confused about why no one invites them to the group chat.

The good news? Redemption is possible. The bad news? You'll have to put the microphone down for a minute.

STEP 1: Admit the Hissy Fit

Yes, you overreacted to the use of pronouns in email signatures.

Yes, you confused accountability with persecution.

Yes, you wrote an entire LinkedIn post about being asked to attend DEI training, likening it to jury duty during the Super Bowl.

Step one to becoming a Richard: name the hissy fit. Not "passion." Not "concern." Not "just tradition." Call it what it was: a full-blown, ego-fueled meltdown.

STEP 2: Step Down from the Podium of Perpetual Offense

Not every conversation about equity is a personal attack on your ancestors. You don't need to make everything about you. The goal of progress isn't to "replace" you. It's to *include others* alongside you, assuming you can stop acting like inclusion is a hostile takeover. Hot tip: If you're always offended by someone else's liberation, it might be time to check whether your identity depends on their oppression.

STEP 3: Learn the Difference Between Criticism and Oppression

Being told you misgendered someone isn't oppression.
Being asked to use inclusive language isn't censorship.
Being passed over for a promotion by someone more qualified who *isn't* your reflection in the mirror isn't "reverse racism."
Oppression is systemic.
Criticism is corrective.
Your hurt feelings? Not the same as someone's lived trauma.

The fact that you still have a platform on which to whine about how silenced you are kind of proves the point.

STEP 4: Listen Without Waiting for Your Turn to Interrupt

Imagine a world where you hear someone out without already drafting your counterpoint in your head. Wild, right? Here's a secret: Richard listens. Dick prepares rebuttals.

Try this radical act of emotional maturity:

- Nod.
- Reflect.
- Ask questions that aren't disguised arguments.
- Resist the urge to hijack every conversation with, "Well, as a white man…" or "Back in my day…"

Listening doesn't make you less of a man. It just makes you tolerable.

STEP 5: Learn History—Like, the Real One

Not the airbrushed, PragerU-approved textbook, "Founding Fathers were freedom-loving philosophers who didn't own people" version. We're talking real history. The version with footnotes. The version that includes:

- Genocide, slavery, redlining, and resistance
- Stonewall, not just the Supreme Court
- Ida B. Wells, not just Susan B. Anthony
- Labor movements that weren't just "lazy people asking for handouts," but *actual people demanding not to die on the factory floor*

If you don't understand the underlying systems, you'll keep mistaking the symptoms for the cause. And if you can't name the oppression, chances are—you're helping to keep it running.

Pro tip: History isn't a threat. It's your onboarding manual for how *not* to be a walking red flag in society.

STEP 6: Develop Critical Thinking—
Yes, Even If It Makes You Uncomfortable

No, reading your cousin's Facebook post isn't "research." No, your gut feeling about DEI being "divisive" isn't analysis. And no, watching a YouTube video called *"The Woke Agenda Exposed"* doesn't mean you "did your homework." Richard reads beyond the headline. Richard knows how to:

- Ask questions without demanding applause.
- Challenge bias without collapsing into victimhood.
- Hold multiple truths without needing to be the center of any of them.

Dick, on the other hand, yells "fake news" when facts hurt his feelings.

Spoiler: Being "critical" of everything *but* yourself isn't critical thinking. It's a projection.

STEP 7: Stop Feeding the Backlash Machine

You know the one:

- The machine that panics every time a Barbie has a "man's job."
- The one who thinks inclusive bathrooms will collapse civilization.
- The one that turns every single DEI initiative into a "woke mob

power grab."

Yeah, that machine. Unplug it. Forever. Because every time you:

- Share a bad-faith think piece,
- Defend a celebrity for saying something objectively harmful, or
- Cry "free speech" while decrying drag brunches,

You're tossing coal into the backlash furnace and pretending it's patriotism.

Here's the truth: The backlash machine isn't protecting your values. It's protecting your *insecurity*. It's weaponized nostalgia for a world where your mediocrity was rewarded just because you showed up.

Richard sees through it. Dick sponsors it.

STEP 8: Become the Man People Want at the Table

No one wants to collaborate with someone who treats every conversation like a courtroom and every correction like an assault on his masculinity.

You want to be at the table?

- Show up with humility.
- Bring curiosity, not combat.
- Lead with respect, not resentment.

Because guess what? **Richard gets invited to barbecues. Dick gets blocked.**

The Benefit of Becoming Richard

Let's talk return on investment. Because growing out of your culturally weaponized defensiveness and into a more self-aware, accountable, emotionally evolved version of manhood? **Yeah, it pays off in every way that matters.**

In the Workplace:

Richard gets promoted. Dick gets documented.

- Richard leads inclusive teams where people want to contribute.
- Richard listens, adapts, mentors, and doesn't derail meetings with "devil's advocate" hot takes.
- Richard understands that leadership isn't volume—it's value.
- He builds trust, not tension. And guess what? People perform better

when they're not dodging your ego.

The *Harvard Business Review* reports that inclusive leaders are *more innovative, collaborate better, and drive higher performance.*[459] Yes—empathy is a *powerful skill.*

In Relationships:

Richard gets called. Dick gets ghosted.

- Richard communicates without condescension.
- He respects boundaries, doesn't interpret emotions as threats, and knows that "vulnerability" isn't code for weakness.
- Romantic, platonic, and professional people *want* Richard in their lives.

Trust me: no one's dreaming about a guy who thinks cancel culture is worse than climate change.

In Mental Health:

Richard unpacks. Dick represses.

- Richard knows healing isn't linear, but bottling it up until it explodes at a school board meeting isn't the vibe.
- He goes to therapy, not Twitter.
- He processes instead of projecting.

The American Psychological Association (2021) links unprocessed anger, emotional suppression, and fragile masculinity to higher rates of burnout, anxiety, and—let's be real—loneliness. Richard's out here building community—Dick's building resentment.

In Legacy:

Richard mentors. Dick mourns the good old days.

- Richard gets remembered as a leader, an ally, a man who made space for others instead of demanding to be centered.
- He lifts while climbing. He passes the mic.
- He gets quoted for wisdom, not archived for cringe.

While Dick is yelling at clouds, Richard's name is appearing in thank-you speeches and next-generation leadership circles.

Final Word:

Being a Dick is easy. Being a Richard takes work.

But Richard? He gets invited to the future. Dick just gets muted.

We're not asking you to disappear. We're asking you to evolve. Please take off the camouflage Crocs of cultural defensiveness, unclench, and join the rest of us in the present.

Make the upgrade.
The world doesn't need more noise.
It requires more men
worth following.

Endnotes

Introduction

1. Pew Research Center, "As Partisan Hostility Grows, Signs of Frustration With the Two-Party System," August 9, 2022, https://pewrsr.ch/3Qud1j1.

2. Richard V. Reeves and Isabel V. Sawhill, *A New Contract with the Middle Class*, Brookings Institution, 2020, https://www.brookings.edu/wp-content/uploads/2020/10/FMCi-Middle-Class-Contract-DIGI-TAL-VERSION.pdf.

3. S.E. Page, 2007, *The Difference: How the Power of Diversity Creates Better Groups, Firms, Schools, and Societies* (Princeton University Press, 2007).

4. P.S. Gorski. and S. L. Perry, *The Flag and the Cross: White Christian Nationalism and the Threat to American Democracy* (Oxford University Press, 2022).

5. T. Piketty, *Capital in the Twenty-First Century* (Harvard University Press, 2014).

6. J. Stanley, *How Fascism Works: The Politics of Us and Them* (Random House, 2018).

7. Z. Tufekci, "Algorithmic Harms Beyond Facebook and Google: Emergent Challenges of Computational Agency," *Colorado Technology Law Journal* 13 no. 1 (2015): 203–218, https://scholar.law.colorado.edu/cgi/viewcontent.cgi?article=1192&context=ctlj

8. P. S. Gorski and S. L. Perry, S. L, *The Flag and the Cross* (2022).

9. Y. Mounk, *The People vs. Democracy: Why Our Freedom Is in Danger and How to Save It* (Harvard University Press, 2018).

10. Pew Research Center, "How Much Discrimination Do Americans Say Groups Face in the US?" May 20, 2025, https://www.pewresearch.org/politics/2025/05/20/how-much-discrimination-do-americans-say-groups-face-in-the-u-s/.

11. W.H. Frey, *The Nation's Racial Demographic Shift: Diversity Explosion* (Brookings Institution, 2020).

12. Brennan Center for Justice, "The Impact of Voter Suppression on Communities of Color," June 21, 2021, https://www.brennancenter.org/our-work/research-reports/impact-voter-suppression-communities-color.

13. *Le Monde*, "Academic Freedom is Threatened in the US," April 14, 2024, https://www.lemonde.fr/en/united-states/article/2024/04/14/academic-freedom-is-threatened-in-the-us_6668361_133.html.

14. Associated Press, "Texas Ban on University Diversity Efforts Provides a Glimpse of the Future Across GOP-led States," January 10, 2024, https://apnews.com/article/46e4b6193abe27b6abbdffcd1945cf38.

15. E. Musk [@elonmusk]. "Population collapse due to low birth rates is a much bigger risk to civilization than global warming" [Tweet]. Twitter, July 7, 2022, https://twitter.com/elonmusk/status/1545142351672666112.

16. C. Anderson, "The Demographics of Fear: Race, Reproduction, and the White Birthrate Panic, *Journal of American Cultural Studies* 45 no. 2 (2023): 112–130. D. Roberts, *Killing the Black Body: Race, Reproduction, and the Meaning of Liberty* (Vintage Books, 2016).

17. P. Norris and R. Inglehart, *Cultural Backlash: Trump, Brexit, and Authoritarian Populism* (Cambridge University Press, 2019).

18. J.S. Gersen, "Academic Freedom and Discrimination in a Polarizing Time," *Houston Law Review*, 2022. Retrieved from Houston Law Review database https://www.liberalcurrents.com/

19. E. McIntosh, "The Persistence of White Christian Patriarchy in a Time of Right-wing Populism," in *The Spirit of Populism: Political Theologies in Polarized Times* (Brill: 2021), pp. 177–201.

20. M. Kimmel, *Guyland: The Perilous World Where Boys Become Men* (Harper, 2013).

21. Merriam-Webster Dictionary, "Hissy fit," https://www.merriam-webster.com/dictionary/hissy%20fit. Accessed June 24, 2025.

22. E.J. Larson, *Summer for the Gods: The Scopes Trial and America's Continuing Debate Over Science and Religion* (Basic Books, 2006). E. Schrecker, *Many Are the Crimes: McCarthyism in America* (Princeton University Press, 1998). M.D. Lassiter, *The Silent Majority: Suburban Politics in the Sunbelt South* (Princeton University Press, 2006). K. Phillips, *The Emerging Republican Majority* (Arlington House, 1969). D.T. Critchlow, *Phyllis Schlafly and Grassroots Conservatism: A Woman's Crusade* (Princeton University Press, 2005). Moral Majority. (n.d.). In Wikipedia. Retrieved May 29, 2025, from https://en.wikipedia.org/wiki/Moral_Majority. J. Conason, J., *The Hunting of the President: The Ten-Year Campaign to Destroy Bill and Hillary Clinton* (St. Martin's Press, 2001). T. Skocpol and V. Williamson, *The Tea Party and the Remaking of Republican Conservatism*, (Oxford University Press, 2011). T. Skocpol and V. Williamson, *The Tea Party and the Remaking of Republican Conservatism*, (Oxford University Press, 2011).

23 J. Healy, "Bud Light Boycott Highlights Partisan Divides in Marketing," *The New York Times*, April 14, 2023, https://www.nytimes.com/2023/04/14/business/bud-light-boycott.html.

24 T. Tully, "Mr. Potato Head Drops the 'Mr.' in a Gender-Neutral Rebranding," *The New York Times*, February 25, 2021, https://www.nytimes.com/2021/02/25/business/mr-potato-head-gender-neutral.html.

25 J. Creswell, "M&M's Go Woke? Character Changes Stir Conservative Backlash," *The New York Times*, January 22, 2022, https://www.nytimes.com/2022/01/22/business/mms-character-changes.html.

26 American Civil Liberties Union, "*Mapping Attacks on LGBTQ Rights in US State Legislatures,*" 2024, https://www.aclu.org/legislation-tracker.

27 A.L. Whitehead and S.L. Perry, *Taking America Back for God: Christian Nationalism in the United States* (Oxford University Press, 2020).

28 Politico & Morning Consult, "Poll: Percentage of Americans Who View the Confederate Flag as a Symbol of Southern Pride versus Racism," *The Atlanta Journal-Constitution*, June 2020, https://www.ajc.com/news/many-americans-view-confederate-flag-symbol-pride-not-racism-poll-finds/bF3SjgmwXf4QG-F0B1kRhqL/.

29 A.R. Hochschild, *Strangers in Their Own Land: Anger and Mourning on the American Right* (The New Press, 2016).

Chapter 1

30 J.S. Chall, *Learning to Read: The Great Debate* (McGraw-Hill, 1967). P. Shannon, *Broken Promises: Reading Instruction in Twentieth-century America* (Bergin & Garvey, 1989).

31 J.M. Gangi, "The Unbearable Whiteness of Literacy Instruction: Realizing the Implications of the Dick and Jane Readers," *Multicultural Perspectives* 10 no. 4 (2008): 211–216.

32 G. Ladson-Billings, "Just What Is Critical Race Theory and What's It Doing in a Nice Field Like Education?" *International Journal of Qualitative Studies in Education* 11 no. 1 (1998): 7–24.

Chapter 2

33 D. Scheepers and N. Ellemers, "Social Identity Theory," in *Social Psychology in Action* (Springer, 2019), pp. 1-17.

34 Z. Tufekci, *Twitter and Tear Gas: The Power and Fragility of Networked Protest* (Yale University Press, 2017).

35 W.J. Brady, J.A. Wills, J.T. Jost, J.A. Tucker, and J.J. Van Bavel, "Emotion Shapes the Diffusion of Moralized Content in Social Networks," *Proceedings of the National Academy of Sciences, 114* no. 28 (2017): 7313–7318, https://doi.org/10.1073/pnas.1618923114

36 L.J. Skitka, C.W. Bauman, and E. Mullen, "Morality and Justice: An Expanded Theoretical Perspective and Review," *Advances in Experimental Social Psychology* 42 (2008): 1–79, https://doi.org/10.1016/S0065-2601(08)00401-6.

37 J.C. Williams, *Bias Interrupted: Creating Inclusion for Real and for Good* (Harvard Business Review Press, 2021).

38 N. Van Dyke and S.A. Soule, "Structural Social Change and the Mobilizing Effect of Threat: Explaining Levels of Patriot and Militia Organizing in the United States," *Social Problems* 49 no. 4 (2002): 497–520. https://doi.org/10.1525/sp.2002.49.4.497.

39 M.I. Norton and S.R. Sommers, "Whites See Racism as a Zero-sum Game that They Are Now Losing," *Perspectives on Psychological Science* 6 no. 3 (2011): 215–218, https://doi.org/10.1177/1745691611406922.

40 M.M. Unzueta and B.S. Lowery, "Defining Racism Safely: The Role of Self-image Maintenance on White Americans' Conceptions of Racism," Journal of Experimental Social Psychology 44 no. 6 (2008): 1491–1497.

41 "Engaging with Culture: Interview with K.V. Akshara," Frontline, December 24, 2014, https://frontline.thehindu.com/arts-and-culture/engaging-with-culture/article6719120.ece.

42 R.D. Putnam, *Bowling Alone: The Collapse and Revival of American Community* (Simon & Schuster: 2000). Pew Research Center, "Millennials in Adulthood," 2014, https://www.pewresearch.org/social-trends/2014/03/07/millennials-in-adulthood/. Pew Research Center, "Trust and Distrust in America," July 22, 2020, https://www.pewresearch.org/politics/2020/07/22/trust-and-distrust-in-america/.

43 L. Raduazo, "Measuring Cultural Health and Societal Vitality in Western Democracies: Focus on the United States, 2025" (unpublished manuscript, 2025).

44 Putnam, Bowling Alone (2000). J.S. Nye, *Soft Power: The Means to Success in World Politics* (PublicAffairs: 2004). Pew Research Center, "Millennials in Adulthood," 2014.

45 National Endowment for the Arts, "US Trends in Arts Attendance and Literary Reading: 2002–2017,"

2019, https://www.arts.gov/impact/research/publications/us-trends-arts-attendance-and-literary-reading-2002-2017. Pew Research Center, "Social Media and the Shifting Cultural Landscape," January 31, 2023, https://www.pewresearch.org/. P. DiMaggio and T. Mukhtar, "Arts Participation as Cultural Capital in the United States, 1982–2002: Signs of Decline?" *Poetics* 32 no. 2 (2004): 169–194, https://doi.org/10.1016/j.poetic.2004.02.005

46 Federal Bureau of Investigation, "Hate Crime Statistics, 2022," US Department of Justice, 2023, https://www.justice.gov/hatecrimes/hate-crime-statistics. Pew Research Center, "Americans' Trust in Each Other and in Institutions Has Declined," June 6, 2023, https://www.pewresearch.org/politics/2023/06/06/americans-trust-in-each-other-and-in-institutions-has-declined/. Massey & Denton (1993), D.S. Massey and N.A. Denton, *American Apartheid* (Harvard University Press, 1993).

47 Pew Research Center, "More Americans Are Living Alone, and Loneliness Is on the Rise," May 11, 2023, https://www.pewresearch.org/short-reads/2023/05/11/more-americans-are-living-alone-and-loneliness-is-on-the-rise/. Centers for Disease Control and Prevention, "Births: Provisional Data for 2022," National Center for Health Statistics, 2023, https://www.cdc.gov/nchs/products/databriefs/db471.htm.

48 Gallup News, "Patriotism Remains Near Record Low; Few Extremely Proud," July 3, 2023, https://news.gallup.com/poll/508282/patriotism-remains-near-record-low-few-extremely-proud.aspx. National Assessment of Educational Progress, "NAEP Civics Assessment Results, 2022," National Center for Education Statistics, https://nces.ed.gov/nationsreportcard/civics. Pew Research Center, "Public Trust in Government: 1958–2021," May 13, 2021, https://www.pewresearch.org/politics/2021/05/13/public-trust-in-government-1958-2021/.

49 Freedom House, "Freedom on the Net, 2020: United States," https://freedomhouse.org/country/united-states/freedom-net/2020. K.H. Jamieson and J.N. Cappella, *Echo Chamber: Rush Limbaugh and the Conservative Media Establishment* (Oxford University Press, 2008).

50 Truth and Reconciliation Commission,*Final Report of the South African Truth and Reconciliation Commission* (1998), https://www.justice.gov.za/trc. Open Society Foundations, *Truth Commissions Around the World: A Comparative Analysis* (2023), https://www.opensocietyfoundations.org.

Chapter 3

51 W.H. Frey, *Diversity Explosion: How New Racial Demographics Are Remaking America* (Brookings Institution Press, 2018).

52 T. Skocpol and V. Williamson, *The Tea Party and the Remaking of Republican Conservatism* (Oxford University Press, 2011).

53 Frey, *Diversity Explosion*. Skocpol and Williamson, *The Tea Party and the Remaking of Republican Conservatism*.

54 D. Jackson, "Donald Trump accepts GOP nomination, says 'I alone can fix' system," *USA Today*, July 21, 2016, https://www.usatoday.com/story/news/politics/elections/2016/07/21/donald-trump-republican-convention-acceptance-speech/87385658/ .

55 M. Gessen, "Autocracy: Rules for Survival," *The New York Review of Books*, November 10, 2016, https://www.nybooks.com/online/2016/11/10/trump-election-autocracy-rules-for-survival/.

56 D. Kellner, *American Nightmare: Donald Trump, Media Spectacle, and Authoritarian Populism* (Sense Publishers, 2020).

57 Economic Policy Institute, "Trump's Firing of BLS Commissioner Is Undemocratic and Economically Dangerous," August 1, 2025, https://www.epi.org/press/trumps-firing-of-bls-commissioner-is-undemocratic-and-economically-dangerous/.

58 Kellner, *American Nightmare*.

59 American Civil Liberties Union, *Project 2025, Explained*, Accessed August 25, 2025, https://www.aclu.org/project-2025-explained#:~:text=What%20is%20Project%202025?%20Project%202025%20is,by%20agency%20to%20serve%20a%20conservative%20agenda.

60 Time Magazine, "President Trump's Inauguration Crowd Doesn't Look Like Barack Obama's Did in 2009," January 20, 2017, https://time.com/4641381/donald-trump-inauguration-crowd/

61 Reuters/Ipsos, "About 60% of Republicans Believe the 2020 Election Was Stolen," April 2, 2021, https://www.ipsos.com/en-us/news-polls/majority-republicans-still-believe-2020-election-was-stolen-donald-trump.

62 Brennan Center for Justice, "Election Officials Under Attack," June 16, 2021, https://www.brennancenter.org/our-work/research-reports/election-officials-under-attack. Pew Research Center, "The Digital Revolution and Challenges of Civic Education," October 4, 2019,. https://www.pewresearch.org/internet/2019/10/04/the-digital-revolution-and-civic-education/. NPR News, "Election Officials Face Growing Threats, Fueled by Trump's False Fraud Claims," June 11, 2021, https://www.npr.

org/2021/06/11/1005133286/election-officials-face-growing-threats-fueled-by-trumps-false-fraud-claims.

63 Wikipedia, "Post-election Lawsuits Related to the 2020 US Presidential Election. Retrieved August 28, 2025, https://en.wikipedia.org/wiki/Post-election_lawsuits_related_to_the_2020_U.S._presidential_election. Brennan Center for Justice, "Election Officials Under Attack," June 16, 2021, https://www.brennancenter.org/our-work/research-reports/election-officials-under-attack. Gallup News, "Partisan Split on Election Integrity Gets Even Wider," September 25, 2024, https://news.gallup.com/poll/651185/partisan-split-election-integrity-gets-even-wider.aspx. US Department of Justice, "Attorney General Merrick B. Garland Statement on the Fourth Anniversary of the January 6 Attack on the US Capitol," January 6, 2025, https://www.justice.gov/archives/opa/pr/attorney-general-merrick-b-garland-statement-fourth-anniversary-january-6-attack-capitol. Reuters, "Trump Pardons Nearly All Charged with Jan. 6 US Capitol Riot," January 20, 2025, https://www.reuters.com/world/us/trump-preparing-issue-sweeping-pardons-defendants-charged-jan-6-attack-abc-news-2025-01-20/. Associated Press, "Trump Grants Sweeping Pardon of Jan. 6 Defendants, Including Rioters Who Violently Attacked Police," January 21, 2025, https://apnews.com/article/8ce8b2a8f8cb602d5eaf85ac7b969606. Donald J. Trump, President. "Granting pardons and commutation of sentences for certain offenses relating to the events at or near the United States Capitol on January 6, 2021 " [Presidential proclamation]. The White House. January 20, 2025. Retrieved July 29, 2025, from whitehouse.gov.

64 The Trevor Project, National Survey on LGBTQ Youth Mental Health 2023, https://www.thetrevorproject.org/survey-2023/.

65 PEN America, Banned in the USA: State Laws Supercharge Book Suppression in Schools, April 20, 2023, https://pen.org/report/banned-in-the-usa-state-laws-supercharge-book-suppression-in-schools/. K. Reilly, "Florida's Governor Just Signed the 'Stop WOKE Act.' Here's What It Means for Schools and Businesses," Time, April 22, 2022, https://time.com/6168753/florida-stop-woke-law/. B. Lopez, "Texas Bans Hundreds of Books in School Districts, Many Addressing Race, Gender Identity, and LGBTQ+ Themes," The Texas Tribune, March 5, 2025. Retrieved from https://www.texastribune.org. American Library Association, The State of America's Libraries 2023, https://www.ala.org/sites/default/files/news/content/state-of-americas-libraries-report-2023-web-version.pdf. PEN America, "New Report: Legislatures Introduce 110 Educational Gag Orders in 2023," November 9, 2023, https://pen.org/press-release/new-report-gag-orders-in-2023/. Public Religion Research Institute, "Despite Political Battles, Democrats and Republicans Generally Agree on Racial Justice Education Policies," February 28, 2023, https://prri.org/spotlight/despite-political-battles-democrats-and-republicans-generally-agree-on-racial-justice-education-policies/. Hart Research Associates & North Star Opinion Research, "Voters oppose efforts to remove books from local public libraries because some find them offensive or inappropriate," Survey conducted on behalf of the American Library Association, March 2022. American Civil Liberties Union, "Censorship in Schools: Banned Books and 'Anti-woke' Laws," 2023, https://www.aclu.org/news/free-speech/censorship-in-schools. National Center for Education Statistics, "Revenues and Expenditures for Public Elementary and Secondary Education: FY 2020," US Department of Education, 2022, https://nces.ed.gov/pubsearch/pubsinfo.asp?pubid=2022310.

66 United States Department of Education, Statement on President Trump's Executive Order to Return Power Over Education to States and Local Communities, March 20, 2025, https://www.ed.gov/about/news/press-release/statement-president-trumps-executive-order-return-power-over-education-states-and-local-communities. Politico, "Education Department Freezes Cash for School Districts, Teacher Training, Migrant Students," June 30, 2025, https://www.politico.com/news/2025/06/30/education-department-set-to-pause-billions-in-grants-to-states-amid-review-00434257. Donald J. Trump, "Ending Radical Indoctrination in K-12 Schooling" (Executive Order 14190), The White House, January 29, 2025, https://www.whitehouse.gov/presidential-actions/2025/01/ending-radical-indoctrination-in-k-12-schooling/. The Washington Post, "Trump Administration Withholds $7 Billion from Schools, July 2, 2025, https://www.washingtonpost.com/education/2025/07/02/schools-education-trump-administration-funding-hold.

67 National Center for Education Statistics, "Revenues and expenditures for public elementary and secondary education: FY 2020."

68 Education Week, "How Much Do States Depend on Federal Funding for Schools?" May 16, 2023, https://www.edweek.org/policy-politics/how-much-do-states-depend-on-federal-funding-for-schools/2023/05.

69 Third Way, "From Kindergarten to College: Trump Education Cuts Would Hurt Red States the Most," March 26, 2025, https://www.thirdway.org/memo/from-kindergarten-to-college-trump-education-cuts-would-hurt-red-states-the-most.

70 US Department of Education. Consolidated Appropriations Act, 2021: Title I funding under ESEA [Statutory appropriation]. In Consolidated Appropriations Act, 2021. Retrieved from Wikipedia.

71 M. Lieberman, "Who Will Bear the Brunt of Trump's Hold on $6.8 Billion in School Funds?" Education Week, July 7, 2025, https://www.edweek.org/policy-politics/who-will-bear-the-brunt-of-trumps-hold-on-6-8-billion-in-school-funds/2025/07.

72 WVXU, "Analysis: Red States Like Ohio, Kentucky, and Indiana Could Be Hurt Most by Trump's Cuts," February 20, 2025, https://www.wvxu.org/politics/2025-02-20/analysis-red-states-hurt-most-trump-cuts. The The Washington Post, "Trump Administration Withholds $7 Billion from Schools," July 2, 2025, https://www.washingtonpost.com/education/2025/07/02/schools-education-trump-administra-tion-funding-hold.

73 ProPublica, "Clarence Thomas and the Billionaire," April 6, 2023, https://www.propublica.org/article/clarence-thomas-scotus-undisclosed-luxury-travel-gifts-crow.

74 *Ibid.*

75 The Wall Street Journal, "Justice Alito: ProPublica Misleads Its Readers," June 20, 2023, https://www.wsj.com/opinion/propublica-misleads-its-readers-alito-gifts-disclosure-alaska-singer-23b51eda?.

76 APNORC Center for Public Affairs Research, "Public Confidence in the US Supreme Court Is at Its Lowest Since 1973," May 17, 2023. Annenberg Public Policy Center, University of Pennsylvania, "Poll: Americans Favor Supreme Court Term Limits; Support an Ethics Code," *The Washington Post* reporting, September 13, 2024.

77 ProPublica, "Clarence Thomas and the Billionaire," 2023. ProPublica, "Justice Samuel Alito Took Luxury Fishing Vacation with GOP Billionaire Who Later Had Cases Before the Court," June 20, 2023, https://www.propublica.org/article/samuel-alito-luxury-fishing-trip-paul-singer-scotus-supreme-court. M. Pengelly, "Samuel Alito Did Not Declare Gifts from Billionaire with Case Before US Supreme Court," *The Guardian*, June 21, 2023. Reuters, "US Supreme Court's Alito Defends Private Jet Trip to Alaska," June 21, 2023. Politico, "Law Firm Head Bought Gorsuch-owned Property," April 25, 2023, https://www.politico.com/news/2023/04/25/neil-gorsuch-colorado-property-sale-00093579. Global Investigative Journalism Network, "How ProPublica Exposed Ethics Scandals at the US Supreme Court," April 25, 2024, https://gijn.org/stories/propublica-exposed-ethics-scandals-us-supreme-court/. Brennan Center for Justice, "The New Supreme Court Ethics Code is Designed to Fail," November 13, 2023, https://www.bren-nancenter.org/our-work/analysis-opinion/new-supreme-court-ethics-code-designed-fail. R.J. Durbin, "Durbin statement on Chief Justice Roberts declining to testify before the Judiciary Committee regarding Supreme Court ethics," United States Senate Committee on the Judiciary, April 25, 2023, https://www.ju-diciary.senate.gov/press/dem/releases/durbin-statement-on-chief-justice-roberts-declining-to-testify-be-fore-the-judiciary-committee-regarding-supreme-court-ethics. *Time*, "The Supreme Court Has New Ethics Rules—But They Won't Be Enforced," November 14, 2023, https://time.com/6983758/supreme-court-ethics-rules-enforced/. Annenberg Public Policy Center, "Trust in US Supreme Court Continues to Sink, University of Pennsylvania, October 2, 2024, https://www.annenbergpublicpolicycenter.org/trust-in-us-supreme-court-continues-to-sink/. Politico, "Young Americans Continue to Lose Faith in Government Institutions," April 23, 2025, https://www.politico.com/news/2025/04/23/young-americans-poll-trump-congress-00306025. Reuters, "US Supreme Court's Roberts Hears Key Democrat's Call for Enforceable Ethics Code," September 17, 2024, https://www.reuters.com/legal/legalindustry/us-supreme-courts-roberts-hears-key-democrats-call-enforceable-ethics-code-2024-09-17/. S. Whitehouse et al., "Whitehouse, Johnson colleagues Reintroduce Supreme Court Ethics, Recusal, and Transparency Act," United States Senate, May 20, 2025, https://www.whitehouse.senate.gov/news/release/whitehouse-john-son-colleagues-reintroduce-supreme-court-ethics-recusal-and-transparency-act/.

78 American Bar Association, "Statement of ABA President re: Supreme Court ethics code," May 9, 2023, https://www.americanbar.org/news/abanews/aba-news-archives/2023/05/statement-of-aba-president-re-supreme-court-ethics. Brennan Center for Justice, "The New Supreme Court Ethics Code Is Designed to Fail."

Brookings Institution, "Every Federal Judge Is Bund by Ethics Rules—Except the Supreme Court Justices," November 29, 2023, https://www.brookings.edu/?p=1748902&post_type=article&pre-view_id=1748902. Congressional Research Service. (2023, November 17). The Supreme Court's code of conduct: Questions about enforcement. Library of Congress. https://www.congress.gov/crs-product/LSB11078. The 19th News, "Where Anti-trans State Laws Stand in 2025," May 28, 2025, https://19th-news.org/2025/05/anti-trans-extreme-state-laws-2025/.

Yale Daily News, "How the Federalist Society Shaped America's Judiciary," November 4, 2024, https://yaledailynews.com/blog/2024/11/04/how-the-federalist-society-shaped-americas-judiciary/. Gallup, "Americans Pass Judgment on the Courts," December 16, 2024, https://news.gallup.com/poll/653897/americans-pass-judgment-courts.aspx.

79 YouGov, "What Americans Think About Free Speech and Its Consequences," February 9, 2025, https://today.yougov.com/politics/articles/51549-what-americans-think-about-free-speech-and-its-consequenc-es. M.D. Clark, Drag Them: A Brief Etymology of So-called 'cancel culture,'" *Communication and the*

Public 5 no. 3-4 (2020): 88-92, https://doi.org/10.1177/2057047320961562. Vanity Fair, "Dave Chappelle's New Comedy Special Denounced by Equality Groups, Netflix Employees," October 7, 2021, https://www.vanityfair.com/hollywood/2021/10/dave-chappelles-netflix-special-denounced-by-equality-groups-netflix-employees.

80 Merriam-Webster.com Dictionary, "Anti-racist," https://www.merriam-webster.com/dictionary/anti-racist. Accessed June 23, 2025.

81 I.X. Kendi, *How to Be an Antiracist* (One World, 2019).

82 *Ibid.*

83 R. DiAngelo, *White Fragility: Why It's So Hard for White People to Talk About Racism*, (Beacon Press, 2018).

84 Merriam-Webster.com Dictionary, "Critical race theory," https://www.merriam-webster.com/dictionary/critical%20race%20theory. Accessed June 23,. 2025.

85 R. Delgado and J. Stefancic, *Critical Race Theory: An Introduction* (3rd ed.) (NYU Press, 2017).

86 K. Crenshaw, (1991). "Mapping the Margins: Intersectionality, Identity Politics, and Violence Against Women of Color," *Stanford Law Review* 43 no. 6 (1991): 1241–1299.

87 B. L. Love, *Punished for Dreaming: How School Reform Harms Black Children and How We Heal* (St. Martin's Press, 2023).

88 First Amendment Center, "The Origins of the Phrase 'Stay Woke,'" First Amendment Encyclopedia, Middle Tennessee State University, May 23, 2024, https://firstamendment.mtsu.edu/article/the-woke-movement-and-backlash/. The Guardian, "'Woke' Should Not Be Used as a Negative, Warns C of E's First Black Female Bishop," February 25, 2024, https://www.theguardian.com/world/2024/feb/25/woke-should-not-be-used-as-a-negative-warns-c-of-es-first-black-female-bishop. Ipsos/USA Today, "Americans Divided on Whether 'Woke' Is a Compliment or Insult," March 8, 2023, https://www.ipsos.com/en-us/americans-divided-whether-woke-compliment-or-insult.

89 AP-NORC Center, "State of the Facts 2024," The Associated Press-NORC Center for Public Affairs Research and USAFacts, September 10, 2024, https://apnorc.org/projects/state-of-the-facts-2024/. S. Vosoughi, D. Roy, and S. Aral, S., "The Spread of True and False News Online," *Science* 359 no. 6380 (2018): 1146–1151, https://doi.org/10.1126/science.aap9559. Pew Research Center, "Changing Partisan Coalitions in a Politically Divided Nation," April 9, 2024, https://www.pewresearch.org/politics/2024/04/09/changing-partisan-coalitions-in-a-politically-divided-nation/. Listen First Project., "Toxic Polarization Data," 2025, https://www.listenfirstproject.org/toxic-polarization-data. Tufts University's CIRCLE and Protect Democracy, "How Does Gen Z Really Feel About Democracy?" Protect Democracy," April 6, 2025, https://protectdemocracy.org/work/how-does-gen-z-really-feel-about-democracy/. Harvard Institute of Politics, Harvard Youth Poll Spring 2025, https://iop.harvard.edu/youth-poll/50th-edition-spring-2025.

90 Grinshteyn, E., & Hemenway, D. (2019). Violent death rates in the US compared to those of the other high-income countries, 2015. *Preventive Medicine, 123,* 20–26. https://doi.org/10.1016/j.ypmed.2019.02.026. Pew Research Center. (2023, April 26). *What the data says about gun deaths in the U.S.* https://www.pewresearch.org/short-reads/2023/04/26/what-the-data-says-about-gun-deaths-in-the-u-s/. Goss, K. A. (2021). Policy, politics, and the gun issue in America. *Annual Review of Political Science, 24,* 437–453. https://doi.org/10.1146/annurev-polisci-041719-102131.

Chapter 4

90a Pew Research Center, "Millennials Overtake Baby Boomers as America's Largest Generation," April 28, 2020, https://www.pewresearch.org/fact-tank/2020/04/28/millennials-overtake-baby-boomers-as-americas-largest-generation/.

91 Connecticut Senate Republicans, "Senator Kelly, CT Legislators Announce Support for Legislation to Protect Older Job Applicants From Age Discrimination," January 16, 2020, https://www.ctsenaterepublicans.com/2020/01/sen-kelly-ct-legislators-announce-support-for-legislation-to-protect-older-job-applicants-from-age-discrimination/.

92 E. Bartlett, "From Pay Gaps to Abortion, Women's Legal Rights Face an Ongoing Battle," Bryant News, March 29, 2024, https://news.bryant.edu/pay-gaps-abortion-womens-legal-rights-face-ongoing-battle.

93 American Civil Liberties Union, "Mapping Attacks on LGBTQ Rights in US State Legislatures," 2023, https://www.aclu.org/legislative-attacks-on-lgbtq-rights-2023.

94 Federal Bureau of Investigation, 2024 Hate Crime Statistics Report, https://www.justice.gov/hatecrimes/hate-crime-statistics#:~:text=FBI%20Releases%202024%20Hate%20Crime,victims%20for%20calendar%20year%202024.

95 National Rural Health Association, "Healthcare's Role in Rural Economic Development: Broadband Access," NRHA Policy Brief, 2023, https://www.ruralhealth.us/getmedia/37253b20-f865-4a84-bed5-bd-

ed40f5c2c8/NRHA-Policy-Brief-Final-Draft-Healthcare-s-Role-in-Rural-Economic-Development-%28Broadband%29-%283%29.pdf.

96   A. Case and A. Deaton, *Deaths of Despair and the Future of Capitalism* (Princeton University Press, 2020).

97   Pew Research Center, "What Unites and Divides Urban, Suburban and Rural Communities," May 22, 2018, https://www.pewresearch.org/social-trends/2018/05/22/what-unites-and-divides-urban-suburban-and-rural-communities/.

98   A.R. Hochschild, *Strangers in Their Own Land: Anger and Mourning on the American Right* (The New Press, 2016).

99   Ontario Human Rights Commission, Racism and Racial Discrimination: Systemic Discrimination Fact Sheet (n.d.), https://www3.ohrc.on.ca/en/racism-and-racial-discrimination-systemic-discrimination-fact-sheet.

100 Rothstein, R., *The Color of Law: A Forgotten History of How Our Government Segregated America.* (Liveright Publishing, 2017).

101 T-N. Coates, "The Case for Reparations," *The Atlantic*, June 15, 2014, https://www.theatlantic.com/magazine/archive/2014/06/the-case-for-reparations/361631/. M. Alexander, *The New Jim Crow: Mass Incarceration in the Age of Colorblindness* (The New Press, 2010).

102 Centers for Disease Control and Prevention. (2022, August 31). "US Life Expectancy Fell Further in 2021 Due to COVID," August 31, 2022, https://www.cdc.gov/nchs/pressroom/nchs_press_releases/2022/20220831.htm. Centers for Disease Control and Prevention, "Life Expectancy in the US Dropped for the Second Year in a Row in 2021," 2022, https://www.cdc.gov/nchs/pressroom/nchs_press_releases/2022/20220831.htm.

Centers for Disease Control and Prevention, "Provisional Drug Overdose Death Counts," 2023, https://www.cdc.gov/nchs/nvss/vsrr/drug-overdose-data.htm. M. Kariisa et al., "Illicitly Manufactured Fentanyl–Involved Overdose Deaths" (MMWR), Centers for Disease Control and Prevention, 2023, https://www.cdc.gov/mmwr/volumes/72/wr/mm7226a4.htm?utm_source=chatgpt.com. Pew Research Center, "Public Trust in Government: 1958–2024," June 24, 2024, https://www.pewresearch.org/politics/2024/06/24/public-trust-in-government-1958-2024/?utm_source=chatgpt.com. Centers for Disease Control and Prevention, "Youth Risk Behavior Survey Data Summary & Trends Report: 2011–2021," 2023, https://www.cdc.gov/healthyyouth/data/yrbs/pdf/YRBS_Data-Summary-Trends_Report2023_508.pdf. G.J. Wintemute, "Trends in Views of Democracy and Society and Support for Violence," *Injury Epidemiology* (2025), https://injepijournal.biomedcentral.com/articles/10.1186/s40621-024-00550-0. Annenberg Public Policy Center, "Many Don't Know Key Facts About US Constitution, Annenberg Civics Study Finds," September 14, 2023, https://www.annenbergpublicpolicycenter.org/many-dont-know-key-facts-about-u-s-constitution-annenberg-civics-study-finds/. Annenberg Public Policy Center, "Most Americans Support Checks on Presidential Power," 2025, https://www.annenbergpublicpolicycenter.org/most-americans-support-checks-on-presidential-power/. J.F. Goldstick, R.M. Cunningham, and P.M. Carter, "Current Causes of Death in Children and Adolescents in the United States," *New England Journal of Medicine* 386 no. 20 (2022): 1955–1956, https://doi.org/10.1056/NEJMc2201761. Stateline (via *The Guardian*), "Guns Kill More US Children than Other Causes, but State Policies Can Help," June 17, 2025, .https://stateline.org/2025/06/17/guns-kill-more-us-children-than-other-causes-but-state-policies-can-help-study-finds/. Gallup, "US Church Membership Falls Below Majority for First Time," March 29, 2021, https://news.gallup.com/poll/341963/church-membership-falls-below-majority-first-time.aspx. Education Week, "Map: Where Critical Race Theory Is Under Attack," 2024 (updated July 22, 2025), https://www.edweek.org/policy-politics/map-where-critical-race-theory-is-under-attack/2021/06.

103 Federal Reserve Bank of St. Louis, "The State of US Household Wealth," 2025. Retrieved from https://www.stlouisfed.org/community-development-research/the-state-of-us-wealth-inequality.

104 Inequality.org, "What Would Surprise America's Rich in 2025? Not Getting Richer," January 5, 2025, https://inequality.org/article/what-would-surprise-americas-rich-in-2025-not-getting-richer/.

105 Wikipedia, "Great Wealth Transfer," retrieved from https://en.wikipedia.org/wiki/Great_Wealth_Transfer. MarketWatch, "The 'Great Wealth Transfer' Is Coming," last updated August 2, 2025, https://www.marketwatch.com/story/the-great-wealth-transfer-is-coming-many-people-will-be-rich-but-theyre-not-ready-e206232f .

106 Inequality, "Wealth Inequality in the United States" (n.d.), https://inequality.org/facts/wealth-inequality/?utm_source=chatgpt.com.

107 S. Cohodes, E. Setren, and C.R. Walters, "Why Does Education Increase Voting? Evidence from Boston Charter Schools" (NBER Working Paper No. 29308), National Bureau of Economic Research, 2021, https://doi.org/10.3386/w29308.

108 Florida Senate, HB 7, 2022, the "Stop WOKE Act," https://www.flsenate.gov/Session/Bill/2022/7.

109 Florida House of Representatives, House Bill 999: Postsecondary Education, 2023,. https://myflorida-

house.gov. Texas Education Agency, State Guidelines for Patriotic Education Programs, 2023. Retrieved from https://tea.texas.gov.

110 J. Kruger, and D. Dunning, (1999). "Unskilled and Unaware of It: How Difficulties in Recognizing One's Own Incompetence Lead to Inflated Self-assessments," *Journal of Personality and Social Psychology,* 77 no. 6 (1999): 1121–1134. https://doi.org/10.1037/0022-3514.77.6.1121.

Chapter 5

111 C. Bail et al., "Exposure to Opposing Views on Social Media Can Increase Political Polarization," *Proceedings of the National Academy of Sciences* 115 no. 37 (2018): 9216-9221, https://www.pnas.org/doi/full/10.1073/pnas.1804840115.

112 *Ibid.*

113 Z. Tufekci, "Algorithmic Harms Beyond Facebook and Google: Emergent Challenges of Computational Agency," *Colorado Technology Law Journal* 13 no. 203 (2015), https://scholar.law.colorado.edu/cgi/viewcontent.cgi?article=1192&context=ctlj.

114 M. Ledwich and A. Zaitsev, "Algorithmic Extremism: Examining YouTube's Algorithm and Its Role in Radicalization,". arXivLabs preprint (2019) arXiv:1912.11211. https://doi.org/10.48550/arXiv.1912.11211.

115 M. Kimmel, *Guyland: The Perilous World Where Boys Become Men* (Harper, 2013).

116 K.M. Douglas, R.M. Sutton and A. Cichocka, "The Psychology of Conspiracy Theories," *Current Directions in Psychological Science* 26 no. 6 (2017): 538–542, https://doi.org/10.1177/0963721417718261.

117 C.R. Sunstein and A. Vermeule, "Conspiracy Theories: Causes and Cures," *Journal of Political Philosophy* 17 no. 2 (2009): 202–227, https://doi.org/10.1111/j.1467-9760.2008.00325.x.

118 M. Grynbaum and K. Robertson, "Fox News Settles Defamation Suit for $787.5 Million," *The New York Times,* April 18, 2023, https://www.nytimes.com/live/2023/04/18/business/fox-news-dominion-trial-settlement. L. Bursztyn et al., "Misinformation During a Pandemic," NBER Working Paper 27417, National Bureau of Economic Research, June 2020 (rev. September 2020), https://www.nber.org/papers/w27417. K.H. Jamieson and J.N. Cappella, (2008). *Echo Chamber: Rush Limbaugh and the Conservative Media Establishment* (Oxford University Press, 2008). Public Citizen, *FOXIC: Fox News Network's Dangerous Climate Denial,* August 13, 2019, https://www.citizen.org/wp-content/uploads/public-citizen-fox-new-climate-denial-report-2019.pdf. Fox News, "Conservative, Liberal Scholars Unite Against Wokeness in New Manifesto," Fox News, June 15, 2023, https://www.foxnews.com/media/conservative-liberal-scholars-unite-against-wokeness-new-manifesto. *Financial Times,* "Pete Hegseth Nominated as Trump's Secretary of Defense," March 18, 2024, https://www.ft.com/content/e2e8d60f-7ac3-40a2-a252-5b7ab81622af. PEN America, *Educational Gag Orders: Legislative Restrictions on the Freedom to Read, Learn, and Teach,* November 8, 2021, https://pen.org/report/educational-gag-orders/. Fox News, "Parents Can't Opt K–5 Children Out of LGBTQ Curriculum: Appeals Court," May 16, 2025, https://www.foxnews.com/us/parents-cant-opt-k-5-children-lgbtq-curriculum-appeals-court. Fox News, "Psychoanalyst Sounds Alarm on Gender Ideology Taught to Kids: Indoctrination, not Education," July 20, 2023, https://www.foxnews.com/media/psychoanalyst-sounds-alarm-gender-ideology-taught-kids-indoctrinating. Center for Countering Digital Hate, *The Disinformation Dozen,* March 24, 2021, https://www.counterhate.com/disinformationdozen. American Library Association, "American Library Association Reports Record Number of Demands to Censor Library Books and Materials in 2022," March 22, 2023, https://www.ala.org/news/press-releases/2023/03/record-book-bans-2022. H. Ibrahim et al., "A Longitudinal Analysis of Racial and Gender Bias in *New York Times* and Fox News Images and Articles," *arXiv,* October 2024, https://arxiv.org/abs/2410.21898. P. Hans, "A Critical Discourse Analysis of Fox News' Reporting on COVID-19 Measures," *New Horizons in English Studies* 8 (2023): 39–56, http://dx.doi.org/10.17951/nh.2023.8.39-56.

119 M. Wolf, "The Reading Brain in a Digital World," [Podcast transcript], *This Is Your Brain with Dr. Michael Merzenich,* May 9, 2023, https://thisisyourbrain.com/2023/05/the-reading-brain-in-a-digital-world-with-dr-maryanne-wolf/. Taylor Corporation, "Printed Books Are Proven to Improve Reader Comprehension," April 11, 2022, https://www.taylor.com/blog/printed-books-are-proven-to-improve-reader-comprehension.

120 US Census Bureau, "2024 Presidential Election Voting and Registration Tables Now Available," April 30, 2025, https://www.census.gov/newsroom/press-releases/2025/2024-presidential-election-voting-registration-tables.html. USAFacts, "How Many Americans Voted in 2024?" June 18, 2024, https://usafacts.org/articles/how-many-americans-voted-in-2024/. Ballotpedia. (n.d.), "Election Results, 2024: Analysis of Voter Turnout in the 2024 General Election," https://ballotpedia.org/Election_results,_2024:_Analysis_of_voter_turnout_in_the_2024_general_election. Wikipedia, "Political Apathy," https://en.wikipedia.org/wiki/Political_apathy.

121 A. Lorde, *Your Silence Will Not Protect You* (Silver Press, 2017), p. 3.

122 D. Caroti et al., "Critical Thinking Education to Decrease Conspiracy and Paranormal Beliefs Among Secondary School Students: A Phase I Trial." *PsyArXiv*. July 5, 2023, https://doi.org/10.31234/osf.io/p5qzg.

123 S. Vosoughi, D. Roy and S. Aral, "The Spread of True and False News Online," *Science* 359 no. 6380 (2018): 1146–1151, https://doi.org/10.1126/science.aap9559.

124 S. Coontz, *The Way We Never Were: American Families and the Nostalgia Trap* (Basic Books: 2000).

125 Vosoughi et al., "The Spread of True and False News," 2018. P. Barberá et al., "Tweeting from Left to Right: Is Online Political Communication More than an Echo Chamber?" *Psychological Science* 26 no. 10(2015): 1531–1542, https://doi.org/10.1177/0956797615594620.

Chapter 6

126 J.A. Vandello and J.K. Bosson, "Hard Won and Easily Lost: A Review and Synthesis of Theory and Research on Precarious Manhood," *Psychology of Men & Masculinity* 14 no. 2 (2013): 101–113. https://doi.org/10.1037/a0029826.

127 M. Kimmel, *Angry White Men: American Masculinity at the End of an Era* (revised ed.) (Nation Books: 2017).

128 American Psychological Association, *APA Guidelines for Psychological Practice with Boys and Men*, 2018, https://www.apa.org/about/policy/boys-men-practice-guidelines.pdf

129 Wikipedia, "Toxic Masculinity," https://en.wikipedia.org/wiki/Toxic_masculinity#:~:text=Suppressing%20vulnerable%20emotions%20is%20often,disorders%2C%20and%20dysfunction%20in%20relationships.

130 J.K. Bosson et al., "Precarious Manhood and Its Links to Action and Aggression," *Personality and Social Psychology Bulletin* 35 no. 5 (2009): 623–634, https://doi.org/10.1177/0146167208331161.

131 b. hooks, *The Will to Change: Men, Masculinity, and Love* (Washington Square Press: 2004).

132 M. Kimmel, *Guyland: The Perilous World Where Boys Become Men* (Harper: 2013).

133 D.H. Autor, D. Dorn and G.H. Hanson, "The China Shock: Learning from Labor-market Adjustment to Large Changes in Trade," *Annual Review of Economics* 8 no. 1 (2016): 205–240, https://doi.org/10.1146/annurev-economics-080315-015041. US Bureau of Labor Statistics, "Employment Outlook: 2010–2020, Industry Employment Projections," *Monthly Labor Review* 134 no. 1 (2011): 65–83, https://www.bls.gov/opub/mlr/2012/01/mlr201201.pdf.

134 A.R. Hochschild, *Strangers in Their Own Land: Anger and Mourning on the American Right* (The New Press: 2016).

135 A. Case and A. Deaton, *Deaths of Despair and the Future of Capitalism* (Princeton University Press: 2020).

136 J.E. Uscinski and J.M. Parent, *American Conspiracy Theories* (Oxford University Press: 2014).

137 M.S. Kimmel, *Angry White Men: American Masculinity at the End of an Era* (rev. ed.) (Nation Books: 2017). S.H. DiMuccio and E.D. Knowles, "Precarious Manhood Predicts Support for Aggressive Policies and Politicians," *Personality and Social Psychology Bulletin* 47 no. 7 (2020): 1169-1187. https://doi.org/10.1177/0146167220963577.

138 R. DiAngelo, *White Fragility: Why It's So Hard for White People to Talk About Racism* (Beacon Press: 2018).

139 American Psychological Association, "APA Issues First-ever Guidelines for Practice with Men and Boys," *Monitor on Psychology* 50 no. 1 (2019), https://www.apa.org/monitor/2019/01/ce-corner. R.W. Connell, and J.W. Messerschmidt, "Hegemonic Masculinity: Rethinking the Concept," *Gender & Society* 19 no. 6 (2005): 829–859..

D.L. Mosher and M. Sirkin, "Measuring a Macho Personality Constellation," *Journal of Research in Personality* (1984). University of Pittsburgh and UNC, "Man Box Scale: Toxic Masculinity Correlation with Mental Health Issues," *Preventive Medicine*, 2020.

140 Allied Market Research, *Male Grooming Products Market by Product Type, Distribution Channel, and Region: Global Opportunity Analysis and Industry Forecast, 2020–2027*, 2021, https://www.alliedmarketresearch.com/male-grooming-products-market. Statista, "Size of the Global Men's Health and Wellness Market from 2020 to 2027," Statista Research Department, 2023, https://www.statista.com/statistics/1334530/mens-health-and-wellness-market-size-global/.

141 Celebrity Net Worth, "Jordan Peterson Net Worth (last updated: July 16, 2025). Retrieved from https://www.celebritynetworth.com/richest-celebrities/authors/jordan-peterson-net-worth/.

R. Aures, "How Jordan Peterson Made $89 Million with 11 Income Streams," Medium, January 28, 2023, https://auresnotes.medium.com/how-jordan-peterson-made-89-million-so-far-since-2015-bf502a3ac4ce. P. Marcocia, "The Rise of Jordan Peterson," June 21, 2022 [video from Gravitas Ventures], YouTube, https://www.youtube.com/watch?v=SwqAFOMlu2A.

142 *The Guardian*, "Influencers Andrew and Tristan Tate Face Rape, Human Trafficking Dharges in UK,

CPS Confirms," May 28, 2025, https://www.theguardian.com/news/2025/may/28/influencers-andrew-tate-tristan-to-face-charges-in-uk-cps-confirms. *People*, "Andrew Tate and Brother Just Got Hit with Rape and Human Trafficking Charges in U.K.: 'Actual Bodily Harm,'" May 28, 2025, https://people.com/andrew-tate-and-brother-tristan-charged-with-rape-human-trafficking-in-the-uk-11743413. Vox, "How Andrew Tate Sells Men on Toxic Masculinity," January 10, 2023, https://www.vox.com/culture/2023/1/10/23547393/andrew-tate-toxic-masculinity-qa.

143 Celebrity Net Worth, Joe Rogan Net Worth, Retrieved from https://www.celebritynetworth.com/richest-celebrities/actors/joe-rogan-net-worth/.

144 StrokeCast, "How Joe Rogan Made His Millions," 2024, Retrieved from https://strokecast.com/joe-rogans-net-worth/. M. Cramer, "Joe Rogan Strikes an Exclusive, Multiyear Deal With Spotify," *The New York Times*, May 20, 2020, https://www.nytimes.com/2020/05/20/business/media/joe-rogan-spotify-contract.html.

145 J.R. Mahalik et al., "Masculinity and Perceived Normative Health Behaviors as Predictors of Men's Health Behaviors," *Social Science & Medicine* 64 no. 11 (2007): 2201–2209, https://doi.org/10.1016/j.socscimed.2007.02.035.

146 W. Phillips and R.M. Milner, *You Are Here: A Field Guide for Navigating Polarized Speech, Conspiracy Theories, and Our Polluted Media Landscape* (MIT Press: 2021). W.J. Brady et al., "Emotion Shapes the Diffusion of Moralized Content in Social Networks," *Proceedings of the National Academy of Sciences* 114 no. 28 (2017): 7313–7318. https://doi.org/10.1073/pnas.1618923114.

147 J.H. Pleck, "The Gender Role Strain Paradigm: An Update," in R.F. Levant and W.S. Pollack (Eds.) *A New Psychology of Men* (Basic Books: 1995) pp. 11–32). R.F. Levant and Y.J. Wong, *The Psychology of Men and Masculinities* (American Psychological Association: 2017).

148 D. Goleman, R. Boyatzis and A. McKee, *Primal Leadership: Unleashing the Power of Emotional Intelligence* (Rev. ed.) (Harvard Business Review Press: 2013).

149 Centers for Disease Control and Prevention. B.L. Nguyen et al., "Surveillance for Violent Deaths — National Violent Death Reporting System … 2021," *MMWR Surveillance Summaries* 73 SS5 (2024): 1–44, https://doi.org/10.15585/mmwr.ss7305a1.

150 b. hooks, *The Will to Change: Men, Masculinity, and Love* (Washington Square Press: 2004).

Chapter 7

151 H. Zinn, *A People's History of the United States* (Harper Perennial Modern Classics: 2005).

152 A. Adams, Letter from Abigail Adams to John Adams, March 31, 1776, in the collection of the Massachusetts Historical Society. Retrieved from https://www.masshist.org/digitaladams/archive/doc?id=L17760331aa.

153 E.E. Baptist, The Half Has Never Been Told: Slavery and the Making of American Capitalism (Basic Books: 2014).

154 G. Wright, *Slavery and American Economic Development* (LSU Press: 2006).

155 S. Beckert and S. Rockman (Eds.), *Slavery's Capitalism: A New History of American Economic Development* (University of Pennsylvania Press: 2016).

156 A.H. Stephens, "Cornerstone Speech" in Savannah, Georgia, 1861.

157 F. Douglass, "What to the Slave is the Fourth of July?" in D. W. Blight (Ed.) *Narrative of the Life of Frederick Douglass, an American Slave, Written by Himself* (W. W. Norton: 1999; original work published 1852) pp. 359–374.

158 E. C. Stanton, *Declaration of Sentiments*. Seneca Falls Convention, July 1848. Retrieved from https://www.womenshistory.org/resources/primary-source/declaration-sentiments.

159 Zinn, 2003.

160 A. Gordon-Reed, *Thomas Jefferson and Sally Hemings: An American Controversy* (University of Virginia Press: 1997).

161 P. Finkelman, *Slavery and the Founders: Race and Liberty in the Age of Jefferson* (M.E. Sharpe, Inc.: 2001). S. Wilentz, *No Property in Man: Slavery and Antislavery at the Nation's Founding* (Harvard University Press: 2018). A. Keyssar, *The Right to Vote: The Contested History of Democracy in the United States* (Basic Books: 2000). R. A. Dahl, *How Democratic Is the American Constitution?* (Yale University Press: 2003).

162 R. Thornton, *American Indian Holocaust and Survival: A Population History Since 1492* (University of Oklahoma Press: 1987).

163 Pope Nicholas V, 1452.

164 D.D. Hall, *Worlds of Wonder, Days of Judgment: Popular Religious Belief in Early New England* (Harvard University Press: 1990).

165 M. Alexander, *The New Jim Crow: Mass Incarceration in the Age of Colorblindness* (The New Press: 2010).

166 E. Foner, *Reconstruction: America's Unfinished Revolution, 1863–1877* (Harper Perennial: 2014).

167 Equal Justice Initiative. *Lynching in America: Confronting the Legacy of Racial Terror*, 2015, https://eji.org/reports/lynching-in-america/.

168 H.L. Trefousse, *Andrew Johnson: A Biography* (W.W. Norton & Company: 1989).

169 W.E.B. Du Bois, *Black Reconstruction in America: 1860–1880* (Harcourt, Brace and Company: 1935).

170 K.L. Cox, *Dixie's Daughters: The United Daughters of the Confederacy and the Preservation of Confederate Culture (New Perspectives on the History of the South)* (University Press of Florida: 2003).

171 Southern Poverty Law Center, *Whose Heritage? Public Symbols of the Confederacy*, 2019, https://www.splcenter.org/20190201/whose-heritage-public-symbols-confederacy.

172 A. Berman, *Give Us the Ballot: The Modern Struggle for Voting Rights in America* (Farrar, Straus and Giroux: 2015).

173 The Sentencing Project, *Report to the United Nations on Racial Disparities in the US Criminal Justice System*, April 19, 2018, https://www.sentencingproject.org/reports/report-to-the-united-nations-on-racial-disparities-in-the-u-s-criminal-justice-system/.

174 US Government Accountability Office, "K–12 Education: Student Population Has Significantly Diversified, but Many Schools Remain Divided along Racial, Ethnic, and Economic Lines (GAO-22-104737) (June 16, 2022), https://www.gao.gov/products/gao-22-104737.

175 N. Bhutta et al., *Disparities in Wealth by Race and Ethnicity in the 2019 Survey of Consumer Finances*, Board of Governors of the Federal Reserve System, 2020, https://www.federalreserve.gov/econres/notes/feds-notes/disparities-in-wealth-by-race-and-ethnicity-in-the-2019-survey-of-consumer-finances-20200928.html.

176 E. Flexner and E. Fitzpatrick, *Century of Struggle: The Woman's Rights Movement in the United States* (Harvard University Press: 1996).

177 I. Katznelson, *When Affirmative Action Was White: An Untold History of Racial Inequality in Twentieth-Century America* (W.W. Norton & Company: 2005).

178 D.W. Southern, *The Progressive Era and Race: Reaction and Reform, 1900–1917* (University of Chicago Press: 1976).

179 Supreme Court of the United States, *Dobbs v. Jackson Women's Health Org.*, 597 U.S. (2022), https://www.supremecourt.gov/opinions/21pdf/19-1392_6j37.pdf.

180 *Ibid.*

181 Alexander, *The New Jim Crow.*

182 See *Loving v. Virginia*, 1967, summarized at https://constitutioncenter.org/the-constitution/supreme-court-case-library/loving-v-virginia.

183 Associated Press, "Arizona Can Enforce an 1864 Law Criminalizing Nearly All Abortions, Court Says," April 9, 2024, https://apnews.com/article/arizona-abortion-restrictions-1864-9c68866d69dca38c728dd-27b80592e8f. Kaiser Family Foundation, "A Closer Look at Rape and Incest Exceptions in States with Abortion Bans or Gestational Limits," August 7, 2024, https://www.kff.org/womens-health-policy/rape-incest-exceptions-abortion-bans-restrictions/.

184 NPR, "States with the Toughest Abortion Laws Have the Weakest Maternal Support," 2022, https://www.npr.org/2022/08/18/1111344810/abortion-ban-states-social-safety-net-health-outcomesNPR.

185 Kaiser Family Foundation. State Health Facts: Women's Health Insurance Coverage in Texas, 2023, https://www.kff.org/interactive/womens-health-profiles/texas/healthcare-coverage/

186 Guttmacher Institute, "State Bans on Abortion Throughout Pregnancy," 2023, https://www.guttmacher.org/state-policy/explore/state-policies-abortion-bans. American Civil Liberties Union, "Mapping Attacks on LGBTQ Rights in US State Legislatures in 2025," https://www.aclu.org/legislative-attacks-on-lgbtq-rights-2025. Kaiser Family Foundation, "Women's Health Insurance Coverage," December 2024, https://www.kff.org/womens-health-policy/womens-health-insurance-coverage/. Centers for Disease Control and Prevention, "Maternal Mortality Rates in the United States, 2021," National Center for Health Statistics. https://www.cdc.gov/nchs/data/hestat/maternal-mortality/2021/maternal-mortality-rates-2021.htm. Kaiser Family Foundation, "Status of State Medicaid Expansion decisions: Interactive Map," August 2025, https://www.kff.org/medicaid/status-of-state-medicaid-expansion-decisions/.

187 Centers for Disease Control and Prevention (CDC), "Maternal Mortality Rates in the United States, 2021," 2023, https://www.cdc.gov/nchs/data/hestat/maternal-mortality/2021/maternal-mortality-rates-2021.htm.

188 CDC, "Maternal Mortality Rates… 2021." Kaiser Family Foundation, "Status of State Medicaid Expansion Decisions."

189 Guttmacher Institute, "State Bans on Abortion Throughout Pregnancy," (2025), https://www.guttmacher.org/state-policy/explore/state-policies-abortion-bans.

190 See *Dobbs*, 2022, https://www.supremecourt.gov/opinions/21pdf/19-1392_6j37.pdf.

191 Guttmacher Institute, "State Bans on Abortion Throughout Pregnancy."

192 K. Surana, "Life of the Mother: How Abortion Bans Lead to Preventable Deaths," ProPublica, September 16, 2024, https://www.propublica.org/series/life-of-the-mother.

193 P. Singh, and M.F. Gallo, "National Trends in Infant Mortality in the US after Dobbs," *JAMA Pediatrics* 178 no. 12 (2024): 1364-1366, https://jamanetwork.com/journals/jamapediatrics/article-abstract/2825201.

194 National Bureau of Economic Research, "The Economic Consequences of Being Denied an Abortion," NBER Working Paper No. 26662, 2022, https://www.nber.org/system/files/working_papers/w26662/w26662.pdf.

195 *Ibid.*

196 Pregnancy Justice, "New Pregnancy Justice Report Shows High Number of Pregnancy-Related Prosecutions in the Year After Dobbs," September 24, 2024, https://www.pregnancyjusticeus.org/press/new-pregnancy-justice-report-shows-high-number-of-pregnancy-related-prosecutions-in-the-year-after-dobbs/.

197 Kansas Statutes Annotated § 65-28,103. (2021). "Kansas Natural Death Act."

198 Johns Hopkins Bloomberg School of Public Health, "Two New Studies Provide Broadest Evidence to Date of Unequal Impacts of Abortion Bans," February 13, 2025, https://publichealth.jhu.edu/2025/two-new-studies-provide-broadest-evidence-to-date-of-unequal-impacts-of-abortion-bans.

199 B.E. Hamilton et al., "Births: Provisional Data for 2022," National Vital Statistics System, National Center for Health Statistics, June 2023, https://www.cdc.gov/nchs/data/vsrr/vsrr028.pdf.

200 S. Anderer, "Permanent Contraception Procedures Increase Among Young Adults Post Dobbs," JAMA Network, February 7, 2025, https://jamanetwork.com/journals/jama/article-abstract/2830205.

201 R. Shilts, *And the Band Played On: Politics, People, and the AIDS Epidemic* (St. Martin's Press: 1987).

Chapter 8

202 I. Katznelson, *When Affirmative Action Was White: An Untold History of Racial Inequality in Twentieth-Century America* (W.W. Norton & Company: 2005).

203 W. Pollack, *Real Boys: Rescuing Our Sons from the Myths of Boyhood*, (Owl Books: 1998).

204 M. Kimmel, *Angry White Men: American Masculinity at the End of an Era* (Rev. ed.). (Nation Books: 2017).

205 E.A. Rotundo, *American Manhood: Transformations in Masculinity from the Revolution to the Modern Era* (Basic Books: 1993).

206 M. Kimmel, *Manhood in America: A Cultural History* (Oxford University Press: 2006).

207 M.A. Messner, *Politics of Masculinities: Men in Movements* (Sage Publications: 1997).

208 A. Tone, *The Age of Anxiety: A History of America's Turbulent Affair with Tranquilizers* (Basic Books: 2009).

209 E.G. McRae, *Mothers of Massive Resistance: White Women and the Politics of White Supremacy* (Oxford University Press: 2018).

210 S. Jones-Rogers, *They Were Her Property: White Women as Slave Owners in the American South* (Yale University Press: 2019).

211 R. Rothstein, *The Color of Law: A Forgotten History of How Our Government Segregated America* (Liveright Publishing: 2017).

212 R. Rothstein, *The Color of Law*. D. K. Johnson, *The Lavender Scare: The Cold War Persecution of Gays and Lesbians in the Federal Government* (University of Chicago Press: 2004). N. Molina, *How Race Is Made in America: Immigration, Citizenship, and the Historical Power of Racial Scripts* (University of California Press: 2014). D.E. Wilkins and K.T. Lomawaima, *Uneven Ground: American Indian Sovereignty and Federal Law* (University of Oklahoma Press: 2001). M.M. Ngai, *Impossible Subjects: Illegal Aliens and the Making of Modern America* (Princeton University Press: 2004). P.K. Longmore and L. Umansky (Eds.), *The New Disability History: American Perspectives* (New York University Press: 2001). Katznelson, *When Affirmative Action Was White*.

213 *Bradwell v. Illinois*, 83 U.S. 130 (1873).

214 *Goesaert v. Cleary*, 335 U.S. 464 (1948).

215 R. Bayer, *Homosexuality and American Psychiatry: The Politics of Diagnosis* (Princeton University Press: 1987).

216 Johnson, *The Lavender Scare*.

217 E. J. McCaffery, *Taxing Women* (University of Chicago Press: 2009).

218 Equal Employment Opportunity Commission. (n.d.). Title VII of the Civil Rights Act of 1964.

219 L. Spigel, *Make Room for TV: Television and the Family Ideal in Postwar America*, (University of Chicago Press, 1992).

220 R. Rothstein, *The Color of Law*, 2017.

221 *Plessy v. Ferguson*, 163 U.S. 537 (1896).

222 *Shelley v. Kraemer*, 334 U.S. 1 (1948).

223 K.T. Jackson, *Crabgrass Frontier: The Suburbanization of the United States* (Oxford University Press: 1985).

224 Q.J. Schultze, *Christianity and the Mass Media in America: Toward a Democratic Accommodation* (Michigan State University Press: 2003).

225 P.S. Gorski and S.L. Perry, *The Flag and the Cross: White Christian Nationalism and the Threat to American Democracy* (Oxford University Press: 2022).

226 R.P. Jones, *White Too Long: The Legacy of White Supremacy in American Christianity* (Simon & Schuster: 2020).

Chapter 9

227 M. Edelman, *The Symbolic Uses of Politics* (University of Illinois Press: 1964).

228 D. Boorstin, *The Image: A Guide to Pseudo-Events in America* (1961).

229 B. Newman, *The Marketing Revolution in Politics: What Recent US Presidential Campaigns Can Teach Us About Effective Marketing* (Rotman-UTP Publishing: 2016).

230 As political theorist Jeffrey Green notes in *The Eyes of the People* (2010).

231 T.E. Patterson, *Informing the News: The Need for Knowledge-Based Journalism* (Knopf Doubleday Publishing Group: 2013).

232 J. M. Metzl, *Dying of Whiteness: How the Politics of Racial Resentment Is Killing America's Heartland* (Basic Books: 2019).

233 Pew Research Center, "Modeling the Future of Religion in America," September 13, 2022, https://www.pewresearch.org/religion/2022/09/13/modeling-the-future-of-religion-in-america/.

234 P.S. Gorski and S.L. Perry, *The Flag and the Cross: White Christian Nationalism and the Threat to American Democracy* (Oxford University Press: 2022) p. 16.

235 K. Stewart, *The Power Worshippers: Inside the Dangerous Rise of Religious Nationalism* (Bloomsbury Publishing: 2020).

236 S. Whitehouse, *The Scheme: How the Right Wing Used Dark Money to Capture the Supreme Court* (The New Press: 2023). ProPublica, "Conservative Activist Poured Millions Into Groups Seeking to Influence Supreme Court on Elections and Discrimination," December 14, 2022, https://www.propublica.org/article/leonard-leo-scotus-elections-nonprofits-discrimination.

237 Savage, R., "US Christian Groups Spent $280m Fighting LGBT+ Rights, Abortion Overseas," Reuters, October 27, 2020, https://www.reuters.com/article/world/us-christian-groups-spent-280m-fighting-lgbt-rights-abortion-overseas-idUSKBN27C2M7/. Politico, "The Kennedy Speech that Stoked the Rise of the Christian Right," March 8, 2020, https://www.politico.com/news/magazine/2020/03/08/the-kennedy-speech-that-stoked-the-rise-of-the-christian-right-123369. Wikipedia, "Religious Affiliations of Presidents of the United States" Accessed June 10, 2025, https://en.wikipedia.org/wiki/Religious_affiliations_of_presidents_of_the_United_States en.wikipedia.org. NPR, "True Believer? Why Donald Trump Is the Choice of the Religious Right," September 13, 2015, https://www.npr.org/sections/itsallpolitics/2015/09/13/439833719/true-believer-why-donald-trump-is-the-choice-of-the-religious-right npr.org.

238 FITS News, "Mark Sanford Is a Long Way from the Appalachian Trail," March 5, 2024, https://www.fitsnews.com/2024/03/05/mark-sanford-is-a-long-way-from-the-appalachian-trail/. NPR, "Ralph Reed Running in Abramoff's Shadow," on All Things Considered, January 28, 2006, https://www.npr.org/2006/01/28/5176548/ralph-reed-running-in-abramoffs-shadow.
EBSCO, "Evangelist Jimmy Swaggart Tearfully Confesses His Adultery," February 21, 1988. Retrieved from https://www.ebsco.com/research-starters/religion-and-philosophy/evangelist-jimmy-swaggart-tearfully-confesses-his. Statesboro Herald, "Gingrich Acknowledges Affair During Clinton Impeachment," March 9, 2007, https://www.statesboroherald.com/local/gingrich-acknowledges-affair-during-clinton-impeachment/. PBS NewsHour, "David Vitter Acknowledges Prostitution Scandal in New TV Ad," November 9, 2015, https://www.pbs.org/newshour/politics/david-vitter-acknowledges-prostitution-scandal-new-tv-ad. Wikipedia, "Roy Moore Sexual Misconduct Allegations," March 10, 2023, https://en.wikipedia.org/wiki/Roy_Moore_sexual_misconduct_allegations. CNN, "Craig Insists, "I Am Not Gay," CNN Politics, September 1, 2007, https://www.cnn.com/2007/POLITICS/08/28/craig.

arrest. NPR, "Idaho Senator Pleads Guilty in Lewd Conduct Case," August 27, 2007, https://www.npr.org/2007/08/27/13984706/idaho-senator-pleads-guilty-in-lewd-conduct-case. A. Blinder, "Josh Duggar Is Convicted of Receiving Child Sexual Abuse Material, *The New York Times*, December 9, 2021, https://www.nytimes.com/2021/12/09/us/josh-duggar-guilty.html. E. Miller, "Josh Duggar Admits Cheating on Wife after Ashley Madison Leak," *The Washington Post*, August 20, 2015, https://www.washingtonpost.com/video/entertainment/josh-duggar-admits-to-cheating-on-wife/2015/08/20/d6f2340a-478d-11e5-9f53-d1e3ddfd0cda_video.html. CBS News, "Evangelist: I Bought Meth from Gay Escort," CBS News. 2006, November 3, 2006, https://www.cbsnews.com/news/evangelist-i-bought-meth-from-gay-escort/. M. Galli, "Trump Should Be Removed from Office," *Christianity Today*, December 19, 2019, https://www.christianitytoday.com/ct/2019/december-web-only/trump-should-be-removed-from-office.html. M. Haberman, "Donald Trump's Lewd Remarks about Women Rock Campaign, *The New York Times*, October 7, 2016, https://www.nytimes.com/video/us/politics/100000004698018/donald-trumps-lewd-comments-about-women.html.

239 Pew Research Center, "Public Trust in Scientists and Views on Their Role in Policymaking," November 14, 2024, https://www.pewresearch.org/science/2024/11/14/public-trust-in-scientists-and-views-on-their-role-in-policymaking/.

240 M. Ledwich and A. Zaitsev, "Algorithmic Extremism: Examining YouTube's Rabbit Hole of Radicalization," *arXiv* Preprint (2019), https://arxiv.org/abs/1912.11211. Wikipedia, "YouTube moderation," January 2025. Retrieved from https://en.wikipedia.org/wiki/YouTube_moderation.

241 W. Brady et al., "Emotion Shapes the Diffusion of Moral Content in Social Networks," *Proceedings of the National Academy of Sciences* (PNAS) 114 no. 28 (2017): 7313–7318, https://www.pnas.org/doi/10.1073/pnas.1618923114.

242 *Ibid.*

243 T. Snyder, *Our Malady: Lessons in Liberty from a Hospital Diary* (Crown Publishing: 2021).

244 C. Mudde, *The Far Right Today* (Polity Press: 2019).

245 H. Ratanpal and T. Giorno, "These Companies Condemned Anti-LGBTQ Bills but Funded the Bills' Sponsors Anyway," OpenSecrets / Truthout, June 12, 2023, https://truthout.org/articles/these-companies-condemned-anti-lgbtq-bills-but-funded-the-bills-sponsors-anyway/. Edelman, "2022 Edelman Trust Barometer Special Report: The Belief-driven Employee," 2022, https://www.edelman.com/trust/2022-trust-barometer.

Chapter 10

246 M-R Trouillot, *Silencing the Past: Power and the Production of History* (1995).

247 J. Baldwin, "The Creative Process" in *Creative America* (Ridge Press: 1962).

248 N. Postman, *Amusing Ourselves to Death: Public Discourse in the Age of Show Business* (Viking Penguin: 1985).

249 C. Johnson, *Blowback: The Costs and Consequences of American Empire* (Macmillan: 2010).

250 A. Giridharadas, *Winners Take All: The Elite Charade of Changing the World* (Knopf: 2018).

251 Watson School of International and Public Affairs, *Costs of War Project*, Brown University, 2021, https://watson.brown.edu/costsofwar/.

252 C. Robin, *Fear: The History of a Political Idea* (Oxford University Press: 2004).

253 M. Tallman, "Patriotism, or Bread and Circuses? A Brief Discussion of the September-October 2001 Rally 'Round the Flag Effect," *Critique*, Spring 2007, https://bpb-us-e2.wpmucdn.com/about.illinoisstate.edu/dist/e/34/files/2019/09/tallman5.pdf.

254 S. Zuboff, *The Age of Surveillance Capitalism* (PublicAffairs: 2019).

255 G. Greenwald, *No Place to Hide: Edward Snowden, the NSA, and the US Surveillance State* (Metropolitan Books: 2014).

256 H. Gusterson, "Anthropology and Militarism," *Annual Review of Anthropology* 36 (2007): 155–175, https://www.annualreviews.org/content/journals/10.1146/annurev.anthro.36.081406.094302.

257 A. Zegart, *Spying Blind: The CIA, the FBI, and the Origins of 9/11* (Princeton University Press: 2007).

258 US Department of Homeland Security. (2003). About DHS: Who Joined DHS, (2003), https://www.dhs.gov/who-joined-dhs.

259 R.W. Poole, "Airport Security: The Case of the TSA," in J. Mueller and M.G. Stewart (Eds.), *Terror, Security, and Money: Balancing the Risks, Benefits, and Costs of Homeland Security* (Oxford University Press: 2014), pp. 81–102.

260 K.A. Beydoun, *American Islamophobia: Understanding the Roots and Rise of Fear* (University of California Press 2018).

261 N. Chang, *Silencing Political Dissent: How Post-September 11 Anti-terrorism Measures Threaten Our Civil Liberties* (Seven Stories Press: 2002). M.E. Kaminski, "Real Masks and Real Name Policies: Applying Anti-mask Case Law to Anonymous Online Speech," *First Amendment Law Review* 11 no. 2 (2012): 1–57.

262 Robin, *Fear: The History of a Political Idea*.

263 US Senate Select Committee on Intelligence. (2004). *Report on the U.S. Intelligence Community's Prewar Intelligence Assessments on Iraq*, 2004.

264 Watson School, *Costs of War Project*, 2021.

265 Congressional Record, 108th Congress. *Freedom Fries Resolution and Cafeteria Renaming* (Government Printing Office: 2003). CNN, "House Cafeterias Change Names for 'French' Fries and 'French' Toast," March 12, 2003, https://www.cnn.com/2003/ALLPOLITICS/03/11/sprj.irq.fries/.

266 S. Rampton and J. Stauber, *Weapons of Mass Deception: The Uses of Propaganda in Bush's War on Iraq* (Tarcher/Penguin: 2003).

267 C.L. Powell, "Remarks to the United Nations Security Council" [Speech transcript], US Department of State, February 5, 2003, https://2001-2009.state.gov/secretary/former/powell/remarks/2003/17300.htm.

268 K.H. Jamieson and P. Waldman, *The Press Effect: Politicians, Journalists, and the Stories that Shape the Political World* (Oxford University Press: 2004).

269 M.R. Gordon and B.E. Trainor, *Cobra II: The Inside Story of the Invasion and Occupation of Iraq* (Pantheon: 2006).

270 Jamieson and Waldman, *The Press Effect*.

271 N. Klein, *The Shock Doctrine: The Rise of Disaster Capitalism* (Metropolitan Books/Henry Holt: 2007).

272 D.J. Trump, "Remarks by President Trump, Vice President Pence, and members of the Coronavirus Task Force in press briefing," [Transcript], The White House, April 23, 2020, https://trumpwhitehouse.archives.gov/briefings-statements/remarks-president-trump-vice-president-pence-members-coronavirus-task-force-press-briefing-31/.

273 Klein, *The Shock Doctrine*.

274 B. Swire-Thompson, and D. Lazer, "Public Health and Online Misinformation: Challenges and Recommendations," *Annual Review of Public Health* 41 (2020): 433–451.

275 A. Javadi, M. Goodman and D. Tannenbaum, "Authority, Masculinity, and Health Behaviors During Pandemics: A Study of Compliance, Trust, and Ego Defense, *Journal of Social Psychology* 162 no. 4 (2022): 503–519.

276 T. Wallace, M. Kalita and S. Nash, "Trust, Media Consumption, and COVID-19 Mortality: A Comparative Analysis of US Counties," Brown School of Public Health, 2022.

277 Centers for Disease Control and Prevention, "COVID-19 Deaths, Cases, and Trends in the United States," US Department of Health & Human Services, May 2023, https://covid.cdc.gov/covid-data-tracker.

278 The Commonwealth Fund, "US COVID-19 Response: A Comparative Analysis of Health Outcomes across G7 Nations," Retrieved from https://www.commonwealthfund.org.

279 *Financial Times*, "The Political Rise of the Anti-vax Movement," February 26, 2025, https://www.ft.com/content/d4199db2-01c1-4260-ac60-0f547a6a2fbe.

280 YouTube Health, Medical Misinformation Policy, 2022, https://support.google.com/youtube/answer/9891785.

281 Centers for Disease Control, "Measles Cases and Outbreaks," 2025, https://www.cdc.gov/measles/data-research/.

282 Centers for Disease Control and Prevention, "Measles Resurgence in the United States: Cases and Outbreaks" [Data summary, 2025]. Wikimedia (derived from CDC data).

283 American Academy of Pediatrics, *State of Pediatric Health: Preventable Disease Surge Following Pandemic Misinformation*, 2025.

284 Kaiser Family Foundation, "KFF Tracking Poll on Health Information and Trust: January 2025," January 28, 2025, https://www.kff.org/health-information-trust/kff-tracking-poll-on-health-information-and-trust-january-2025/.

285 Vox, "The Slippery Appeal of RFK Jr.'s Make America Healthy Again Movement," December 10, 2024, https://www.vox.com/policy/390309/maha-rfk-make-america-healthy-again-slippery.

286 K. Newman et al., *Rampage: The Social Roots of School Shootings* (Basic Books: 2004).

287 J. Carlson, *Citizen-protectors: The Everyday Politics of Guns in an Age of Decline* (Oxford University Press: 2015).

288 F.B. Ahmad et al., "Provisional Mortality Data — United States, 2022," National Center for Health Statistics, *Morbidity and Mortality Weekly Report (MMWR)*, May 5, 2023, https://www.cdc.gov/mmwr/

volumes/72/wr/mm7218a3.htm. Gun Violence Archive, Past Summary Ledgers, 2023, https://www.gunviolencearchive.org/past-tolls. Centers for Disease Control and Prevention, WISQARS — Web-based Injury Statistics Query and Reporting System, 2023, https://www.cdc.gov/injury/wisqars. J.E. Goldstick et al., "Current Causes of Death in Children and Adolescents in the United States," *The New England Journal of Medicine* 386 no. 20 (2022): 1955-1956, https://doi.org/10.1056/NEJMc2201761. Giffords Law Center to Prevent Gun Violence, "Gun Violence in Black Communities," February 14, 2025, https://giffords.org/lawcenter/report/gun-violence-in-black-communities/. Centers for Disease Control and Prevention, "Fast Facts: Firearm Injury and Death," US Department of Health & Human Services, July 5, 2024, https://www.cdc.gov/firearm-violence/data-research/facts-stats/index.html.J.M. Metzl and K.T. MacLeish, "Mental Illness, Mass Shootings, and the Politics of American Firearms," *American Journal of Public Health* 105 no. 2 (2015): 240–249, https://doi.org/10.2105/AJPH.2014.302242. American Psychiatric Association, "Mental Illness and Violence: Debunking Myths, Addressing Realities," updated July 11, 2022, https://www.apa.org/monitor/2021/04/ce-mental-illness. J.W. Swanson et al., "Mental Illness and Reduction of Gun Violence and Suicide: Bringing Epidemiologic Research to Policy," *Annals of Epidemiology* 25 no. 5 (2015): 366–376. https://doi.org/10.1016/j.annepidem.2014.03.004. Wikipedia, "Gun Violence in the United States," August 2025. J.S. Rozel et al., "Is There a Link Between Mental Health and Mass Shootings?" *Columbia Psychiatry News*, Columbia University Dept. of Psychiatry (2022). RAND Corporation, "The Science of Gun Policy: A Critical Synthesis of Research Evidence on the Effects of Gun Policies in the United States," 2023, https://www.rand.org/pubs/research_reports/RR2088.html.

289 *Washington Post*, "Was Black Lives Matter a Failure? It Depends Where You Look," May 21, 2025, https://www.washingtonpost.com/opinions/2025/05/21/blm-police-reform-states-localities/. Reuters, "Five Years after George Floyd's Murder, Racial Justice Push Continues," May 25, 2025, https://www.reuters.com/world/us/five-years-after-george-floyds-murder-racial-justice-push-continues-2025-05-25/.

Chapter 11

290 Florida Legislature, "Individual Freedom Act (Stop W.O.K.E. Act)," HB 7, Florida House of Representatives, 2022, https://www.flsenate.gov/Session/Bill/2022/7.

291 G. Lakoff, *Don't Think of an Elephant!: Know Your Values and Frame the Debate* (Chelsea Green Publishing: 2004).

292 D. Mustaquim, "The Racial Politics of Book Bans in the United States," *Journal of Race & Education* 24 no. 2 (2023): 145-159.

293 American Medical Association, "Everyone Deserves Quality Medical Care Delivered Without Bias," August 16, 2022, https://www.ama-assn.org/about/leadership/everyone-deserves-quality-medical-care-delivered-without-bias.

294 National Law Center on Homelessness & Poverty, *Housing Not Handcuffs 2021: State Law Supplement*, 2021, https://homelesslaw.org/wp-content/uploads/2022/02/2021-HNH-State-Crim-Supplement.pdf.

295 The Trevor Project, "2023 US National Survey on the Mental Health of LGBTQ+ Young People," https://www.thetrevorproject.org/survey-2023/.

296 PEN America, *Banned in the USA: State Laws Supercharge Book Suppression in Schools*, April 20, 2023, https://pen.org/report/banned-in-the-usa-state-laws-supercharge-book-suppression-in-schools/.

297 National Law Center on Homelessness & Poverty, *Housing Not Handcuffs*, 2021.

298 Economic Policy Institute, "The Costs of Racial and Ethnic Labor Market Discrimination and Solutions that Can Contribute to Closing Employment and Wage Gaps," Testimony of Valerie Wilson, January 20, 2022, https://www.epi.org/publication/wilson-testimony-costs-of-racial-and-ethnic-labor-market-discrimination/. National Institutes of Health, "NIH-funded Study Highlights the Financial Toll of Health Disparities in the United States," May 16, 2023, https://www.nih.gov/news-events/news-releases/nih-funded-study-highlights-financial-toll-health-disparities-united-states.

299 PEN America, *Banned in the USA*. American Civil Liberties Union, "Mapping Attacks on LGBTQ Rights in US State Legislatures," 2023, https://www.aclu.org/legislative-attacks-on-lgbtq-rights-2023. Statista Research Department, "Number of US States with Laws or Policies Restricting Critical Race Theory (CRT) in Education as of September 2023," October 4, 2023, https://www.statista.com/chart/29757/anti-critical-race-theory-measures/. 2021 National Law Center on Homelessness & Poverty, *Housing Not Handcuffs*, 2021. Families USA, "Medicaid Expansion Tied to Reduced Maternal Mortality, Healthier Moms and Babies," May 20, 2025, https://familiesusa.org/press-releases/new-report-medicaid-expansion-tied-to-reduced-maternal-mortality-healthier-moms-and-babies/.

300 American Library Association, "American Library Association Reports Record Number of Unique Book Titles Challenged in 2023," March 14, 2024, https://www.ala.org/news/2024/03/american-library-association-reports-record-number-unique-book-titles.

301 *Fast Company*, "Despite DEI Backlash, Only 19% of Companies Are Cutting Diversity Funding," March

12, 2025, https://www.fastcompany.com/91317456/despite-dei-backlash-only-19-of-companies-are-cutting-diversity-funding.

302 Federal Bureau of Investigation, 2024 Hate Crime Statistics Report, https://www.justice.gov/hatecrimes/hate-crime-statistics#:~:text=FBI%20Releases%202024%20Hate%20Crime,victims%20for%20calendar%20year%202024

303 *Vanity Fair*, "How the Far Right Took Over a Pennsylvania School Board—and How Parents Took It Back," February 5, 2024, https://www.vanityfair.com/news/far-right-pennsylvania-school-board.

304 J. Campbell, *What Did the First Amendment Originally Mean?* Richmond School of Law, 2018, https://core.ac.uk/download/232789934.pdf

305 PEN America, *Banned in the USA: The Mounting Pressure to Censor*, September 2023, https://pen.org/report/banned-usa-growing-movement-to-censor-books/.

306 M. Levinson, "Illiberal Education: The Weaponization of Book Bans in American Politics," *Journal of Education Policy* 38 no. 2 (2023): 187–205, https://doi.org/10.1080/02680939.2022.2120583.

307 PEN America, *Banned in the USA*.

308 *Financial Times*, "The US Library of Congress Is Under Attack," May 12, 2025, https://www.ft.com/content/9a2a3b19-271e-40f0-8d6c-c8c318a23b0d.

309 *The Guardian*, "Faith Leaders Denounce US Book Burning as Hate-fuelled Intimidation," May 15, 2025, Retrieved from https://www.theguardian.com/us-news/2025/may/15/ohio-book-burning-response.

310 Associated Press, "Libraries Are Cutting Back on Staff and Services after Trump's Order to Dismantle Small Agency, May 18, 2025, https://apnews.com/article/d3a236243b3a5c2b04e85d2004d1a946.

311 Wikipedia, "Book Banning in the United States (2021–present)," 2025, https://en.wikipedia.org/wiki/Book_banning_in_the_United_States_(2021–present).

312 Associated Press, "Publishers, a Library and Others Sue over Idaho's Law Restricting Youth Access to 'Harmful' books,'" February 5, 2025, https://apnews.com/article/idaho-book-ban-lawsuit-publishers-authors-libraries-08f74182fdf52d8ddb04ee4196f3fef9.

Chapter 12

313 "The Government of the United States of America is not in any sense founded on the Christian religion," John Adams wrote in the Treaty of Tripoli, 1797. See: The Christian Myth, https://www.thechristianmyth.com/the-government-of-the-united-states-of-america-is-not-in-any-sense-founded-on-the-christian-religion-the-treaty-of-tripoli-john-adams-1797/. "Liberty may be endangered by the abuse of.." is a quote from James Madison. See: What Should I Read Next? https://www.whatshouldireadnext.com/quotes/james-madison-liberty-may-be-endangered-by.

314 United States Department of State, "2022 Report on International Religious Freedom: Iran," Bureau of Democracy, Human Rights, and Labor, May 15, 2023, https://www.state.gov/reports/2022-report-on-international-religious-freedom/iran/. Human Rights Watch, *World Report 2024: Events of 2023* (Seven Stories Press: 2024), https://www.hrw.org/world-report/2024.

315 Human Rights Watch. (2023, January). India: Events of 2022," in *World Report 2023*, January 2023, https://www.hrw.org/world-report/2023/country-chapters/india. P.S. Gorski and S.L. Perry, *The Flag and the Cross: White Christian Nationalism and the Threat to American Democracy* (Oxford University Press: 2022).

316 A.L. Whitehead and S.L. Perry, *Taking America Back for God: Christian Nationalism in the United States* (Oxford University Press: 2020).

317 K. Stewart, *The Power Worshippers: Inside the Dangerous Rise of Religious Nationalism* (Bloomsbury Publishing: 2020), p. 154.

318 Whitehead and Perry, *Taking America Back for God*, p. 10.

319 K.M. Kruse, *One Nation Under God: How Corporate America Invented Christian America* (Basic Books: 2015).

320 Stewart, *The Power Worshippers*.

321 R. Chernow, *Alexander Hamilton* (The Penguin Press: 2004), p. 233.

322 *Ibid.*

323 J.M. Smith, *Freedom's Fetters: The Alien and Sedition Laws and American Civil Liberties* (Cornell University Press: 1962).

324 W. Martin, *With God on Our Side: The Rise of the Religious Right in America* (Broadway Books" 2005).

325 S. Diamond, *Roads to Dominion: Right-wing Movements and Political Power in the United States* (Guilford Press: 1995).

326 Jerry Falwell, as quoted in U. Vaid, *Virtual Equality: The Mainstreaming of Gay and Lesbian Liberation* (Anchor Books: 1995) p. 34.

327 D.K. Williams, *God's Own Party: The Making of the Christian Right.* (Oxford University Press: 2010).

328 Pew Research Center. (2021). Faith on the Hill: The Religious Composition of the 117th Congress, 2021, https://www.pewresearch.org/religion/2021/01/04/faith-on-the-hill-2021/.

329 Whitehead and Perry, *Taking America Back for God.*

330 R. Balmer, *Thy Kingdom Come: How the Religious Right Distorts the Faith and Threatens America* (Basic Books: 2006).

331 E. Green, "How the Federalist Society Won," *The New Yorker,* July 24, 2022, https://www.newyorker.com/news/annals-of-education/how-the-federalist-society-won.

332 Whitehead and Perry, *Taking America Back for God.*

333 *Ibid.*

334 D. Dochuk, *From Bible Belt to Sunbelt: Plain-folk Religion, Grassroots Politics, and the Rise of Evangelical Conservatism* (W.W. Norton & Company: 2011), p. 187.

335 *Dobbs v. Jackson,* 597 U.S., 2022, Justice Thomas, concurring.

336 Associated Press, "Federal Judge blocks Louisiana law that requires classrooms to display Ten Commandments," November 12, 2024, https://www.npr.org/2024/11/12/g-s1-33848/louisiana-ten-commandments-classroom-federal-judge-blocks. Texas Legislature, Texas Senate Bill 10 (2025), "Relating to the display of the Ten Commandments in public school classrooms;" enacted May 28, 2025; signed June 21, 2025; effective September 1, 2025. ACLU of Texas et al., "Texas Families Sue to Block Law Requiring Ten Commandments in Every Public School Classroom, July 2, 2025. Indiana General Assembly, House Bill 1134: Released Time Religious Education, 2024, https://iga.in.gov/legislative/2024/bills/house/1134. Ohio House of Representatives, House Bill 8: The Parents' Bill of Rights, 2023, https://www.legislature. ohio.gov/legislation/135/hb8. ACLU of Texas et al., "Texas Families Sue to Block Law Requiring Ten Commandments in Every Public School Classroom," July 2, 2025.

Florida Senate, HB 931 — School Chaplains, Education Pre-K–12 Committee Summary, 2024. Louisiana Revised Statutes § 17:3011 (2024), School chaplains; employment; volunteer. Louisiana Legislature, HB 334 — Authorizing school boards to provide for chaplains in public schools, 2024. Tennessee General Assembly, House Bill 878: Refusal to Solemnize Marriage, 2024, https://wapp. capitol.tn.gov/apps/Billinfo/default.aspx?BillNumber=HB0878&ga=113.

California State Legislature, Senate Bill 4: Affordable Housing on Faith and Higher Education Lands Act, 2023, https://leginfo.legislature.ca.gov/faces/billTextClient.xhtml?bill_id=202320240SB4&search_keywords=%22Affordable+Housing+on+Faith+and+Higher+Education+Lands+Act%22.

337 Whitehead & Perry, *Taking America Back for God*, p. 142.

338 K.K. Du Mez, *Jesus and John Wayne: How White Evangelicals Corrupted a Faith and Fractured a Nation* , (Liveright Publishing: 2020), p. 7.

339 Stewart, *The Power Worshippers*, p. 9.

340 Reuters. (2025, June 20). *Louisiana's Ten Commandments law struck down by US appeals court.* Reuters. https://www.reuters.com/world/us/louisianas-ten-commandments-law-struck-down-by-us-appeals-court-2025-06-20/. Associated Press. (2025, June 20). *Court blocks Louisiana law requiring schools to post Ten Commandments in classrooms.* AP News. https://apnews.com/article/80d31b705fccbbbe3eeeb3cda5f64ec3. Barnes, R. (2025, May 22). *Supreme Court deadlocks, blocking creation of first religious public school.* The Washington Post. https://www.washingtonpost.com/politics/2025/05/22/supreme-court-oklahoma-religious-charter-schools/. Pew Research Center. (2025, February 26). *Religious landscape study: Religion's role in public life.* Pew Research Center. https://www.pewresearch.org/religion/2025/02/26/religious-landscape-study-religions-role-in-public-life/. Baptist Joint Committee for Religious Liberty. (2024, July 19). *What does Project 2025 say about religious liberty?* BJC Online. https://bjconline.org/what-does-project-2025-say-about-religious-liberty-071924/

Chapter 13

340a Heritage Foundation, "Mandate for Leadership: Policy Management in a Conservative Administration," 1981.

341 L. Edwards, *The Power of Ideas: The Heritage Foundation at 25 Years* (Jameson Books: 1997).

342 J. Stahl, *Right Moves: The Conservative Think Tank in American Political Culture since 1945.* University of North Carolina Press: 2016).

343 S.J. McNamee and R.K. Miller, *The Meritocracy Myth* (Rowman & Littlefield: 2009).

344 Stahl, *Right Moves.*

345 C. Anderson, *White Rage: The Unspoken Truth of Our Racial Divide* (Bloomsbury USA: 2016).

346 C. Robin, *The Reactionary Mind: Conservatism from Edmund Burke to Donald Trump* (2nd ed.). (Oxford University Press: 2018).

347 Heritage Foundation, *Mandate for Leadership: The Conservative Promise* (2023), https://static.heritage.org/project2025/2025_MandateForLeadership_FULL.pdf.

348 Stahl, *Right Moves*.

349 Heritage Foundation, *Mandate for Leadership*.

350 Stahl, *Right Moves*; C. Robin, *The Reactionary Mind: Conservatism from Edmund Burke to Sarah Palin* (1st ed.) (Oxford University Press: 2011).

Chapter 14

351 L. Diamond, *Ill Winds: Saving Democracy from Russian Rage, Chinese Ambition, and American Complacency* (Penguin Press: 2020).

352 J.S. Nye, "Soft Power: The Origins and Political Progress of a Concept," *Palgrave Communications* 7 no. 1 (2017): 1–7, https://www.nature.com/articles/palcomms20178.

353 Centers for Medicare & Medicaid Services, "National Health Expenditure Data: Historical (2022)," US Department of Health and Human Services, December 13, 2023, https://www.cms.gov/data-research/statistics-trends-and-reports/national-health-expenditure-data.

354 Small Arms Survey, Global Firearm Ownership Statistics, 2023, https://www.smallarmssurvey.org/highlight/new-update-global-violent-deaths-gvd-database.

355 Edelman, "2024 Edelman Trust Barometer: Global Report," Edelman Data & Intelligence, March 2024, https://www.edelman.com/trust/2024/trust-barometer. J.S. Nye, *Do Morals Matter? Presidents and Foreign Policy from FDR to Trump* (2nd ed.) (Oxford University Press: 2022).

356 Y. Benkler, R. Faris, and H. Roberts, *Network Propaganda: Manipulation, Disinformation, and Radicalization in American Politics* (Oxford University Press: 2018).

357 K. J. Kaoma, *Colonizing African Values: How the US Christian Right Is Transforming Sexual Politics in Africa*, Political Research Associates, 2012, https://politicalresearch.org/2012/07/24/colonizing-african-values.

Chapter 15

358 P. Heather, *The Fall of the Roman Empire: A New History of Rome and the Barbarians* (Oxford University Press: 2005).

359 R. Service, *The Penguin History of the Soviet Union* (Penguin Books: 2009).

360 (American Library Association, "American Library Association Reports Record Number of Unique Book Titles Challenged in 2023," March 14, 2024, https://www.ala.org/news/2024/03/american-library-association-reports-record-number-unique-book-titles.

361 Intergovernmental Panel on Climate Change, "Climate Change 2023: Synthesis Report," 2023, https://www.ipcc.ch/report/ar6/syr/. D.L. Hoyert, Maternal Mortality Rates in the United States, 2021 (NCHS Health E-Stats)," National Center for Health Statistics, Centers for Disease Control and Prevention, March 2023, https://www.cdc.gov/nchs/data/hestat/maternal-mortality/2021/maternal-mortality-rates-2021.htm.

362 E. Arias et al., "Provisional Life Expectancy Estimates for 2022," National Center for Health Statistics, 2023, https://www.cdc.gov/nchs/data/vsrr/vsrr031.pdf.

363 Economic Policy Institute, "Productivity–Pay Gap," 2021, https://www.epi.org/productivity-pay-gap/.

364 Federal Reserve, "Distribution of Household Wealth in the US since 1989," 2023, https://www.federalreserve.gov/releases/z1/dataviz/dfa/distribute/table.

365 N. Bhutta et al., "Disparities in Wealth by Race and Ethnicity in the 2019 Survey of Consumer Finances," Board of Governors of the Federal Reserve System, 2020, https://www.federalreserve.gov/econres/notes/feds-notes/disparities-in-wealth-by-race-and-ethnicity-in-the-2019-survey-of-consumer-finances-20200928.html.

366 L. Mishel and J. Kandra, "CEO Pay Has Skyrocketed 1,322% Since 1978," Economic Policy Institute, 2021, https://www.epi.org/publication/ceo-pay-in-2020.

367 *Forbes*, "Bezos Is $12.8 Billion Richer After Amazon Delivers Strong Holiday Sales," January 30, 2020, https://www.forbes.com/sites/laurendebter/2020/01/30/amazon-jeff-bezos-13-billion-richer-holiday-quarter/.

368 Federal Reserve, "Report on the Economic Well-Being of US Households in 2022," 2023, https://www.federalreserve.gov/publications/files/2022-report-economic-well-being-us-households-202305.pdf.

369 C. Collins et al., "US Billionaires Got 62 Percent Richer During Pandemic. They're Now Up $1.8 Trillion," August 24, 2021, Institute for Policy Studies Program on Inequality (IPS), https://ips-dc.org/u-s-billion-aires-62-percent-richer-during-pandemic/

370 Mishel and Kandra, "CEO Pay Has Skyrocketed."

371 N. Sood et al., "The Flow of Money Through the Pharmaceutical Distribution System," USC Schaeffer Center for Health Policy & Economics, USC Schaeffer White Paper, June 2017, https://schaeffer.usc.edu/wp-content/uploads/2024/10/The-Flow-of-Money-Through-the-Pharmaceutical-Distribution-System_Final_Spreadsheet.pdf.

372 Economic Policy Institute, "Productivity–Pay Gap," 2021, https://www.epi.org/productivity-pay-gap/.

373 *Forbes*, "Bezos Is $12.8 Billion Richer," January 30, 2020.

374 A.L. Whitehead and S.L. Perry, *Taking America Back for God: Christian Nationalism in the United States* (Oxford University Press: 2020).

375 R.J. Sider, *The Scandal of the Evangelical Conscience: Why Are Christians Living Just Like the Rest of the World?* (Baker Books: 2006).

376 W. H. Frey, "The US Will Become 'Minority White' in 2045, Census Projects," Brookings, 2018, https://www.brookings.edu/articles/the-us-will-become-minority-white-in-2045-census-projects/#:~:text=The%20new%20statistics%20project%20that,populations%20(see%20Figure%201). J. M. Jones, "LGBT Identification Rises to 5.6% in Latest US Estimate," Gallup, 2021, https://news.gallup.com/poll/329708/lgbt-identification-rises-latest-estimate.aspx. Pew Research Center, "About Three-in-Ten US Adults Are Now Religiously Unaffiliated," 2021, https://www.pewresearch.org/religion/2021/12/14/about-three-in-ten-u-s-adults-are-now-religiously-unaffiliated/.

377 Pew Research Center, "Intermarriage in the US 50 Years After Loving v. Virginia," 2017, https://www.pewresearch.org/social-trends/2017/05/18/intermarriage-in-the-u-s-50-years-after-loving-v-virginia/.

378 Springtide Research Institute, *The State of Religion & Young People 2022: Mental Health—What Faith Leaders Need to Know*, 2022, https://springtideresearch.org/product/the-state-of-religion-young-people-2022-mental-health.

379 Jones, "LGBT Identification Rises to 5.6%," 2021.

380 Pew Research Center, "About Three-in-Ten US Adults Are Now Religiously Unaffiliated," 2021.

381 Whitehead and Perry, *Taking America Back for God.*

382 Pew Research Center, "Modeling the Future of Religion in America," September 13, 2022, https://www.pewresearch.org/religion/2022/09/13/modeling-the-future-of-religion-in-america/.

383 US Census Bureau,. "US Census Bureau Projections Show Nation Will Become 'Majority-minority' by 2045," June 22, 2023, https://www.census.gov/newsroom/press-releases/2023/population-projections.html. W.H. Frey, *Diversity Explosion: How New Racial Demographics Are Remaking America* (Rev. ed.) (Brookings Institution Press: 2020).

Chapter 16

384 Public Religion Research Institute, "Competing Visions of America: An Evolving Identity or a Culture Under Attack?" September 14, 2023, https://www.prri.org/research/competing-visions-of-america-an-evolving-identity-or-a-culture-under-attack/. Gallup, "Race Relations," June 9, 2023, https://news.gallup.com/poll/1687/race-relations.aspx. Axios, "One-third of Americans Agree with Trump's Racist Remark on Immigrants," October 18, 2024, https://www.axios.com/2024/10/18/americans-immigrants-poisoning-blood-trump?utm_source=chatgpt.com. Pew Research Center, "Race in America 2019," April 9, 2019, https://www.pewresearch.org/social-trends/2019/04/09/race-in-america-2019/. Pew Research Center, "Majority of Latinos Say Skin Color Impacts Opportunity in America and Shapes Daily Life," November 4, 2021, https://www.pewresearch.org/race-and-ethnicity/2021/11/04/majority-of-latinos-say-skin-color-impacts-opportunity-in-america-and-shapes-daily-life/. Pew Research Center, "Views of the Treatment of Black People in America," June 14, 2023, https://www.pewresearch.org/social-trends/2023/06/14/views-of-the-treatment-of-black-people-in-america/. Pew Research Center, "Asian Americans' experiences with discrimination in their daily lives," November 30, 2023, https://www.pewresearch.org/race-and-ethnicity/2023/11/30/asian-americans-experiences-with-discrimination-in-their-daily-lives/. Pew Research Center, "Views of How Much Discrimination Racial and Ethnic Groups in the US Face," May 20, 2025,https://www.pewresearch.org/politics/2025/05/20/views-of-how-much-discrimination-racial-and-ethnic-groups-in-the-u-s-face/. PBS NewsHour, "For Many Latinos, Skin Color Shapes Their Daily Lives," November 4, 2021, https://www.pbs.org/video/for-many-latinos-skin-color-shapes-their-daily-lives-zl7d8d/.

385 Associated Press, "Mr. Potato Head Drops the Mister, Sort Of," February 25, 2021, https://apnews.com/article/mr-potato-head-goes-gender-neutral-d3c178f2b9b0c424ed814657be41a9d8. Hasbro [@Hasbro],

"Hold that Tot—your main spud, MR. POTATO HEAD isn't going anywhere!" [Tweet], February 25, 2021, https://twitter.com/hasbro/status/1365038178814590995. A. Hartmans, "Hasbro is dropping the 'Mr.' … angering critics who say 'woke imbeciles are destroying the world,'" Business Insider, February 25, 2021, https://www.businessinsider.com/hasbro-drops-mr-from-potato-head-toys-sparks-backlash-online-2021-2.

386 B. Shapiro [@benshapiro], "Bigotry ANNIHILATED … Now any child, of any gender… [Tweets], February 25, 2021, PolitiTweet archive. https://polititweet.org/tweet?account=17995040&twe et=1364992903286841349.

387 Economic Innovation Group, "Remote Work Is Enabling Higher Employment among Disabled Work-ers," September 20, 2022, https://eig.org/remote-work-is-enabling-higher-employment-among-disabled-workers. E. Hobson, "11 Disability Rights Activists on Where the Fight for Justice Stands," Teen Vogue, September 19, 2022, https://www.teenvogue.com/story/what-disability-justice-means. Wikipedia, Lynn Conway (August 20, 2025, https://en.wikipedia.org/wiki/Lynn_Conway).

388 J.M. Twenge, Generations: The Real Differences Between Gen Z, Millennials, Gen X, Boomers, and Silents—and What They Mean for America's Future (Atria Books: 2023).

Deloitte. (2025, May 15). Deloitte Global, "2025 Gen Z and Millennial Survey," May 15, 2025, https://www.deloitte.com/global/en/issues/work/genz-millennial-survey.html.

389 C. Seemiller and M. Grace, Generation Z Goes to College (Jossey-Bass: 2016).

390 Pew Research Center, "Millennials in Adulthood," March 7, 2014, https://www.pewresearch.org/so-cial-trends/2014/03/07/millennials-in-adulthood/.

391 Pew Research Center, "Generation X: America's Neglected 'Middle Child,'" June 5, 2014, https://www.pewresearch.org/short-reads/2014/06/05/generation-x-americas-neglected-middle-child/.

392 J. Houseal, "How Mutual Aid Helped People Survive Everything from COVID-19 to Hurricane Helene," Teen Vogue, October 31, 2024, https://www.teenvogue.com/story/what-is-mutual-aid-explainer.

393 The Slacktivists, "Gen Z Activists Can Still Mobilize While Trump Is in Office," Teen Vogue, November 25, 2024, https://www.teenvogue.com/story/gen-z-activists-mobilize-trump-how.

394 M. Bailey, "Barter Up Is a Platform to Trade Skills, Services, and Belongings Online," Teen Vogue, Sep-tember 22, 2023. https://www.teenvogue.com/story/barter-up-trade-skills-services-belongings. J.S. Tan, N. Luka, and E. Mazo, "Tech Worker Organizing: Understanding the Shift from Occupational to Labor Activism," arXiv, July 28, 2023, Cornell University, https://arxiv.org/abs/2307.15790.

395 R. DiAngelo, White Fragility: Why It's So Hard for White People to Talk About Racism, (Beacon Press: 2018).

396 Twenge, Generations: The Real Differences….

397 I.X. Kendi, How to Be an Antiracist (One World: 2019).

398 Ö. Sensoy and R. DiAngelo, Is Everyone Really Equal?: An Introduction to Key Concepts in Social Justice Educa-tion (2nd ed.) (Teachers College Press: 2017).

399 W. H. Frey, "The US Will Become 'Minority White' in 2045, Census Projects," Brookings, 2018, https://www.brookings.edu/articles/the-us-will-become-minority-white-in-2045-census-projects/#:~:tex-t=The%20new%20statistics%20project%20that,populations%20(see%20Figure%201).

400 National Center for Education Statistics, Condition of Education 2023, May 2023, https://nces.ed.gov/use-work/resource-library/report/compendium/condition-education-2023.

401 Center for American Women and Politics, "Women Continued to Outvote Men in 2024 Despite Overall Drop in Turnout," August 26, 2025, https://cawp.rutgers.edu/blog/women-continued-outvote-men-2024-despite-overall-drop-turnout.

402 Twenge, Generations: The Real Differences….

403 M.E. Mor Barak, Inclusion, Inc.: How to Design Intersectional Equity into the Workplace for Competitive Advan-tage (Berrett-Koehler Publishers: 2022).

404 K. Crenshaw, "Mapping the Margins: Intersectionality, Identity Politics, and Violence Against Women of Color," Stanford Law Review 43 no. 6 (1991): 1241–1299, https://doi.org/10.2307/1229039.

405 S.A. Hewlett, M. Marshall, and L. Sherbin, "How Diversity Can Drive Innovation," Harvard Business Review, December 2013, https://hbr.org/2013/12/how-diversity-can-drive-innovation.

406 Hay Group (Korn Ferry), "New Research Shows Women Are Better at Using Soft Skills Crucial for Effective Leadership and Superior Business Performance, Finds Korn Ferry Hay Group" [Press release], Business Wire, March 7, 2016, https://ir.kornferry.com/news-events/press-releases/detail/440/new-re-search-shows-women-are-better-at-using-soft-skills-crucial-for-effective-leadership-and-superior-busi-ness-performance-finds-korn-ferry-hay-group.

407 W.L. Arteaga-Cedeño et al., "How an Emotional Intelligence Intervention Programme Impacts the Well-being and Performance of Teachers of Basic General Education," Acta Psychologica

253 (March 2025) https://doi.org/10.1016/j.actpsy.2025.104739.

408 Hay Group (Korn Ferry), "Research Shows that Leaders with High Levels of Emotional Intelligence Improve Team Performance and Employee Engagement," July 28, 2021.

409 Gallup, "Engage Your Workforce by Empowering Your Managers First," June 11, 2024, https://www.gallup.com/workplace/645398/engage-workforce-empowering-managers-first.aspx?utm .

410 American Psychological Association, "APA Guidelines for Psychological Practice with Girls and Women," *American Psychologist* 74 no. 9 (2019): 1159–1172. https://psycnet.apa.org/search/display?id=63f9372b-4680-95fe-3845-3282092633aa&recordId=4&tab=PA&page=1&display=25&sort=PublicationYearMS-Sort%20desc,AuthorSort%20asc&sr=1.

411 R.F. Levant and Y.J. Wong (Eds.), *The Psychology of Men and Masculinities* (American Psychological Association: 2017), https://doi.org/10.1037/0000023-000.

412 J.R. Mahalik et al., "Developing a Taxonomy of Helpful and Harmful Practices for Clinical Work with Boys and Men, *Journal of Counseling Psychology* 59 no. 4 (2012): 591–603, https://psycnet.apa.org/doiLanding?doi=10.1037%2Fa0030130.

413 *The Guardian*, "Why More Men Are Joining the Ranks of Therapists," December 15, 2023, https://www.theguardian.com/wellness/2023/dec/15/finding-male-therapists-mens-mental-health.

414 World Economic Forum, "Neurodiversity and Leadership: How to Create a Diverse and Inclusive Executive Team," August 22, 2023, https://www.weforum.org/stories/2023/08/neurodiversity-how-to-create-inclusive-leadership-team/?utm .

415 L.C. Peters, "Designing for Difference: How UDL Creates Breakthrough Leadership Development for Neurodiverse Talent," Chief Learning Officer, May 28, 2025, https://www.chieflearningofficer.com/2025/05/28/designing-for-difference-how-udl-creates-breakthrough-leadership-development-for-neurodiverse-talent/.

416 T. Grandin, Visual Thinking: The Hidden Gifts of People Who Think in Pictures, Patterns, and Abstractions (Riverhead Books, 2022).

417 *The Times*, "Neurodiverse Staff Well Suited to a Changing World," March 20, 2025, https://www.thetimes.com/business-money/article/neurodiverse-staff-well-suited-to-a-changing-world-pmzztt69k.

418 R.D. Austin and G.P. Pisano, "Neurodiversity as a Competitive Advantage," *Harvard Business Review* 95 no. 3 (2017): 96–103, https://hbr.org/2017/05/neurodiversity-as-a-competitive-advantage.

419 R.D. Austin and T. Sonne, "The Dandelion Principle: Redesigning Work for the Innovation Economy, MIT Sloane Management Review, Summer 2014, https://sloanreview.mit.edu/article/the-dandelion-principle-redesigning-work-for-the-innovation-economy/.

420 S. Burgstahler, *Universal Design in Higher Education: From Principles to Practice* (2nd ed.) (Harvard Education Press: 2015).

421 Spencer Stuart, "Veterans in Leadership: How Military Careers Can Shape Corporate Success," November 2023, https://www.spencerstuart.com/-/media/2023/november/veterans/veterans-in-leadership-how-military-careers-can-shape-corporate-success-nov-2023.pdf.

422 Y. Hao, M. Zhao and Z. Wei, "Can Military Executives Overcome Difficulties in Corporate Value Creation? Evidence from China," *China Economic Review* 84 (April 2024), https://www.sciencedirect.com/science/article/pii/S1043951X23001955.

423 F.E. Fiedler and J.E. Garcia, *New Approaches to Leadership: Cognitive Resources and Organizational Performance* (Wiley: 1987).

424 Spencer Stuart, "Veterans in Leadership: How Military Careers Can Shape Corporate Success," November 2023, https://www.spencerstuart.com/research-and-insight/veterans-in-leadership-how-military-careers-can-shape-corporate-success.

425 *Ibid.*

426 American Rifleman, "PenFed CEO James Schenck Honored with Lifetime Service Award," August 30, 2023, https://www.americanrifleman.org/content/penfed-ceo-james-schenck-honored-with-lifetime-service-award/?utm .

427 Pew Research Center, "The American Veteran Experience and the Post-9/11 Generation," September 10, 2019, https://www.pewresearch.org/social-trends/2019/09/10/the-american-veteran-experience-and-the-post-9-11-generation/. US Department of Veterans Affairs, *National Veteran Suicide Prevention Annual Report*, 2022, https://www.mentalhealth.va.gov/suicide prevention/data.asp.

428 E.A. Vogels, M. Erson and M. Porteus, "Americans and 'Cancel Culture': Where Some See Calls for Accountability, Others See Punishment," Pew Research Center, May 19, 2021, https://www.pewresearch.org/internet/2021/05/19/americans-and-cancel-culture-where-some-see-calls-for-accountability-others-see-censorship-punishment/?utm .

429 b. hooks, *All About Love: New Visions* (William Morrow Paperbacks: 2000).

Chapter 17

430 S.J. McNamee and R.K. Miller, *The Meritocracy Myth* (Rowman & Littlefield: 2009).

431 M. Konczal, *Freedom from the Market: America's Fight to Liberate Itself from the Grip of the Invisible Hand* (New Press: 2021).

432 T-N. Coates, *Between the World and Me* (Spiegel & Grau: 2015).

433 Y. Dong et al., "Collaboration Diversity and Scientific Impact," *arXiv*, June 10, 2018, https://arxiv.org/abs/1806.03694.

434 R.D. Putnam, *Bowling Alone: The Collapse and Revival of American Community* (Simon & Schuster: 2000). R. Wilkinson and K. Pickett, *The Spirit Level: Why More Equal Societies Almost Always Do Better* (Allen Lane: 2009).

435 T. Hersey, *Rest is Resistance: A Manifesto* (Little, Brown Spark: 2022).

436 I.X. Kendi, *Stamped from the Beginning: The Definitive History of Racist Ideas in America* (Nation Books: 2016).

437 K. Crenshaw, "Mapping the Margins: Intersectionality, Identity Politics, and Violence Against Women of Color," *Stanford Law Review* 43 no. 6 (1991): 1241–1299, https://doi.org/10.2307/1229039.

438 T. Piketty, *Capital in the Twenty-First Century* (Harvard University Press: 2014).

439 Diversity.com (n.d.), "What Is Tokenism in the Workplace?" https://diversity.com/post/what-is-tokenism-workplace. Health.com Editors, "What Tokenism Is—and Why It's Harmful in the Workplace," February 23, 2023, https://www.health.com/mind-body/health-diversity-inclusion/tokenism.

440 D. Kahneman, and A. Deaton,. "High Income Improves Evaluation of Life but Not Emotional Well-being," *Proceedings of the National Academy of Sciences* 107 no. 38 (2010): 16489–16493, https://doi.org/10.1073/pnas.1011492107.

441 J. Sellman., "New Zealand Ditches GDP For Happiness And Wellbeing," Forbes, July 11, 2019,. https://www.forbes.com/sites/jamesellsmoor/2019/07/11/new-zealand-ditches-gdp-for-happiness-and-wellbeing/.

Chapter 18

442 Pew Research Center, "Harvard Youth Poll (50th edition)," Spring 2025. Retrieved September 4, 2025, from Harvard Institute of Politics https://iop.harvard.edu/youth-poll/50th-edition-spring-2025.

443 S. Levitsky, and D. Ziblatt, *How Democracies Die* (Crown Publishing Group: 2018).

444 J.R. Feagin, *The White Racial Frame: Centuries of Racial Framing and Counter-Framing*. (Routledge: 2013).

445 W.H. Frey, "The US Will Become 'Minority White' in 2045, Census Projects," Brookings, 2018, https://www.brookings.edu/articles/the-us-will-become-minority-white-in-2045-census-projects/#:~:text=The%20new%20statistics%20project%20that,populations%20(see%20Figure%201).

446 A.R. Hochschild, *The Managed Heart: Commercialization of Human Feeling* (University of California Press (1983).

447 A. Edmondson, *The Fearless Organization: Creating Psychological Safety in the Workplace for Learning, Innovation, and Growth* (Wiley: 2019).

448 Kruger & Dunning, 1999 J. Kruger and D. Dunning, "Unskilled and Unaware of It: How Difficulties in Recognizing One's Own Incompetence Lead to Inflated Self-assessments," *Journal of Personality and Social Psychology* 77 no. 6 (1999): 1121–1134, https://doi.org/10.1037/0022-3514.77.6.1121.

449 R. DiAngelo, *White Fragility: Why It's So Hard for White People to Talk About Racism* (Beacon Press: 2018).

450 D. Fletcher and M. Sarkar, "Psychological Resilience: A Review and Critique of Definitions, Concepts, and Theory," *European Psychologist* 18 no. 1 (2013): 12–23, https://doi.org/10.1027/1016-9040/a000124.

451 US Census Bureau, *2020 Census Demographic Profile*, 2021, https://www.census.gov/data/tables/2023/dec/2020-census-demographic-profile.html

452 *Harvard Business Review*, "How Diversity Can Drive Innovation," December 2013, https://hbr.org/2013/12/how-diversity-can-drive-innovation

453 B.D. Tatum, *Why Are All the Black Kids Sitting Together in the Cafeteria?* (Basic Books: 2000).

454 J. Baldwin, *Notes of a Native Son* (Beacon Press: 2012; original work published 1955).

455 D. Rock and J. Schwartz, J., "The Neuroscience of Leadership," *Strategy+Business*, 43 (Summer 2006), https://www.strategy-business.com/article/06207.

456 P. Norris and R. Inglehart, *Cultural Backlash: Trump, Brexit, and Authoritarian Populism* (Cambridge University Press: 2019).

457 K.K. Du Mez, *Jesus and John Wayne: How White Evangelicals Corrupted a Faith and Fractured a Nation* (Liveright Publishing: 2020).

458 D.W. Sue, *Microaggressions in Everyday Life: Race, Gender, and Sexual Orientation* (Wiley: 2010).

Conclusion

459 W. Zheng et al., "What Makes an Inclusive Leader?" *Harvard Business Review*, September 2023, https://hbr.org/2023/09/what-makes-an-inclusive-leader?utm .

About the Author and Contributors

DR. LAURAN STAR is not here to play nice—she's here to dismantle the status quo with a mic in one hand and a blowtorch in the other.

A US Army veteran, organizational disruptor, and workplace equity architect, Lauran doesn't write books to coddle egos. She writes to confront, awaken, and leave a cultural bruise in all the right places. Her career spans 20+ years of flipping toxic leadership on its head, rebuilding broken systems, and calling out performative diversity from the boardroom to the classroom.

She's been the executive whisperer behind healthcare powerhouses, the sharpest voice in DE&I strategy rooms, and the unapologetic truth-teller in spaces that confuse whiteness with neutrality and comfort with correctness. Whether she's on stage, in print, or dragging entire policies by their privilege, Lauran brings the fire—and the receipts.

Her work has appeared in think tanks, HR transformation playbooks, and whispered warnings passed between fragile CEOs. She's also the creator of the Workplace Equity Nexus, which redefines how organizations move from intent to impact.

When she's not rewriting systems or disrupting mediocrity, you can find her raising disruptors of her own at home—because change doesn't pause for homework.

This is not your standard HR leader.

This is a revolutionary with credentials.

JUDI HARRINGTON is an editorial strategist and writing coach who specializes in helping disruptive thought leaders articulate uncomfortable truths. With a sharp eye for cutting through cultural BS, she transforms rebellious ideas into compelling narratives that actually get read.

As editorial strategist for *See Dick Throw a Hissy Fit: The Rise and Predictable Fall of US Culture*, she helped shape this unflinching examination of American society's spectacular meltdown—making it digestible for readers while ensuring they didn't set themselves on fire in the process.

Author of *Fuckery: The Life and Times of A Legend (In Her Own Mind)*—a memoir in essays that serves as both a middle finger to perfection and a love letter to family—she's as willing to skewer herself as the sacred cows of contemporary society.

She lives in Medford, Massachusetts, where she continues helping authors say the things that need saying, even when—especially when—nobody wants to hear them.

LISA McKENNA brings a lifelong career in design and a deep love of visual storytelling to this book. She began her career in publishing and still loves the rhythm of words and images working together on the page. For more than twenty years, she co-led a Boston creative agency, shaping brands and campaigns long before design went digital.

When the world paused in 2020, Lisa found a new canvas in digital art that reignited her creative voice. Her work has since been exhibited in London's Tube, Paris, Times Square, Art Basel, and featured in *100 Artists to Watch* catalog, juried by Christie's and MoMA.

Her latest venture, Rebel Art Lab, offers courses for the curious who are drawn to experiment, question convention, and explore digital fine art. What began as a "quarantine experiment" has grown into a community of hundreds of creatives who are welcoming digital art into their practice.